THE MANAGED HEALTHCARE INDUSTRY

A MARKET FAILURE

A wise man asked six blind people to settle on what an elephant looked like. As they felt different parts of the huge animal's body, they began to argue. Every one of them insisted they were right. The wise man agreed.

JACK CHARLES SCHOENHOLTZ, MD

Copyright © 2011 by Jack Charles Schoenholtz MD
Second Edition © 2012 All rights reserved.

ISBN: 1439280614
ISBN-13: 9781439280614
Library of Congress Control Number: 2011925188
CreateSpace, North Charleston, South Carolina

Table of Contents

FOREWORD

Dr. Schoenholtz and I first met in 1995 during my national campaign for the presidency of the American Psychiatric Association. Following a candidates debate before the psychiatric society of Westchester County, New York, one of the seventy-six district branches of the APA, Dr. Schoenholtz, then president of the Westchester District Branch, offered to drive me back to my hotel. During that ride, I learned that we shared values and had many experiences in common.

He had been an early researcher into the use of lithium for bipolar illness and I, early in my career, had done research on the blood-brain barrier and biochemical aspects of schizophrenia. Both of us had written about the dangers of the new "managed care," which we experienced first-hand in the 1980s in its early forms, and we both had testified before local, state, and federal regulatory bodies as to the hazards it posed to quality healthcare. As our perspectives differed from many within government, the medical profession, and among the public, we were frequently interviewed on these issues by newspaper, radio, and TV reporters. I found him the most articulate, well-informed colleague I had met. His grasp of the complex issues, which he abundantly elucidates in this book, surpassed mine, and I came to value him as an important teacher and consultant. Following my victory as president-elect and then president of our national association, we worked on committees, councils, and grassroots organizations, reaching out to the public—to patients and professionals alike—to help clarify for them the "what" and "how" of the developing catastrophe.

Government involvement in the economic and social history of healthcare activity in the United States grew dramatically during the last third of the past century, radically transforming government and corporate business relations. In the 1960s and '70s, explosive growth occurred in other social welfare legislation, as well as regulation focusing on workplace safety, environmental preservation, consumer protection, and their related goals. Government regulation of prices and legal conditions of service, first applying to transportation and public utilities, was extended to healthcare and to other sectors, first by the Nixon-era Congress and then by the Reagan administration, and taxpayers' money was legislatively funneled into corporate coffers when prices and costs were mimicked by insurance companies. It was wrong to do so. I recall debating one of the medical directors of a managed care firm who argued that it did not matter how much he, the other directors, and the managed care companies made, if they saved on costs and provided quality care. Of course, they did neither, as Dr. Schoenholtz points out: the managed segment of the commercial healthcare system devitalized how the sick were cared for.

The expansion of government regulation making quasi-utilities out of Wall Street ventures did not proceed without conflict. As the managed-care monolith swept through healthcare—choosing with particular discrimination the mentally ill and those within the field of psychiatry as its first victims—most of the country and its medical professions, gradually, but powerlessly, became convinced we were correct. Some critics argued that many of the regulatory programs produced negative net benefits, while defenders of what was considered necessary regulation pointed to the soundness and potential economic and social gains from many of the same programs.

This book informs the ongoing debate surrounding choices available to regulatory healthcare policy by making the author's significant and relevant research accessible to scholars, decision-makers, and to the deeply frustrated healthcare-hungry public. It presents new insights into the history of healthcare insurance coverage failures and corporate attempts to profit from the social welfare programs as they arose, and it explores the important economic, political, and administrative aspects of the regulatory process that cut across these boundaries.

The chapters are notable for the exceptionally high quality of research and analysis and for the book's concern with matters of vital importance for public policy. Clearly, here, the whole becomes greater than the sum of its parts. By the skillful illumination of different aspects of the political economics of regulation, a reader is offered new insights about the economic history of the contemporary managed healthcare insurance industry as it manipulates the delivery of healthcare and the regulatory process. This second, expanded edition, brings an up-to-date awareness of the strengths and weaknesses of traditional methods of analyzing that regulatory process and offers hope for healthcare's future under the Affordable Care Act.

Harold I. Eist, MD
Past President, American Psychiatric Association
Bethesda, Maryland

PREFACE

The U.S. outspends all other industrial countries on health-care, and yet we do not enjoy better health. Quite the opposite: an American baby born in 2006 can expect to live to 78—two years less than a baby born across the Canadian border. Of the 30 major industrial countries, the U.S. ranks 28th in infant mortality.

—*Scientific American* (October 2010)

Of the 33 countries that the International Monetary Fund describes as "advanced economies," the United States now has the highest infant mortality rate according to the data from the World Bank. It took us decades to arrive at this dubious distinction. In 1960, we were 15th. In 1980, we were 13th. And in 2000, we were 2nd.

—Charles Blow, *The New York Times* (February 2011)

Managed healthcare insurance is a market failure. After twenty years of exponential growth, economic losses for groups serving the "managed" segment of the commercial healthcare system devitalized the manner in which the sick were traditionally cared for and the healthy kept healthy as independent managed-care organizations were acquired and brought into the business of healthcare insurance. This started the post-Millennium healthcare privatization tide. It largely transformed the conventional insurance "indemnity" risk into a business, or speculative risk, propped up by the false presumption that it could manage the illnesses for which it was solely to provide payment.

Before enactment of President Obama's health reform law—the 2010 Patient Protection and Affordable Care Act (ACA)—risk management by managed care insurance companies had also cultivated an increase in the number of working uninsured rising to over fifty million maintained as a larder of potential patients "cherry-picked" for coverage by deselecting those with preexisting conditions. In fact, the healthcare economy had been subjected to waste, fraud, and abuse of public and private dollars by managed-care insurance companies on a scale vastly above the abuses allegedly caused by healthcare providers.

The commercial health-insurance industry burgeoned after the Nixon administration ran interference for it in 1972 by enacting changes in Medicare and Medicaid reimbursement to providers from an "actual cost" to a "reasonable cost" basis that could be mimicked commercially. In 1973, President Nixon signed what was originally a not-for-profit Health Maintenance Organization Act. In 1974, the Employee Retirement Income Security Act (ERISA) was signed into law by President Gerald R. Ford. It superseded state pension laws and added "self-insured" health and welfare benefit plans it preempted from state insurance regulation and state court review, "deeming" them not in the "business of insurance." The 1980s Reagan-era Congress refined the commercial "copycat" price potential by establishing Medicare prices-per-disease: Diagnosis-Related Groupings (DRGs). In 1997, the 104th Congress passed Medicare + Choice (M+C) or Medicare Part C as part of the Balanced Budget Act, which gave Medicare beneficiaries and Medicaid recipients the option of enrolling in a variety of private plans. It included payment to for-profit health maintenance organizations (HMOs), preferred provider organizations, provider-sponsored organizations, and fee-for-service plans, and it urged members to start Medical Savings Accounts (MSAs) coupled with high deductible commercial managed-care insurance.

In *Closing the Health Gap,* published in the October 2010 issue of *Scientific American*, Christine Gorman, pointed out that in the nineteenth century "primary care used to be the only game in town," where a family would rely on the same caregiver for most care. In the twentieth century, especially after World War II, specialists became associated with "medical progress," and the term "primary care" was "invented during the 1960s, in an effort by pediatricians and generalists to resist the pull toward specialists." It became "critical" for primary care doctors to coordinate patient care after discharge from hospital because of the multiple providers frequently involved, as the regular clinician "attended the whole person, not just the body part." Gorman gave the following caution:

"This coordination task is very different from the managed care trend of the 1990s that, under the guise of care coordination, turned many providers of primary care into gatekeepers who, in fact, mostly denied care."

Although in 1992, more than 50 percent of the privately insured were still being treated by fee-for-service medicine, by 1995, that number dropped by half while those entering managed-care "preferred provider organizations" almost doubled. Managed-care organizations and managed-care insurance companies embedded themselves in the American healthcare system; their prodigious and protean growth, led by government cost-containment programs they mimicked, was in direct proportion to public and media antipathy to the changes that took place. Ironically, a June 1998 *The Wall Street Journal*/NBC News poll reported the startling statistic that over 80 percent of those who had seen a doctor in the past three years had no insurance at all, either choosing to pay privately (or not at all) or using hospital emergency departments. As we shall see later on, the use of "hospitalists" to treat patients in hospital was no match for the independent family doctor of the past. They could perhaps be used, after the patient's discharge, as conflict-laden gatekeepers to circulate patients in and out of specialty care offered by Medicare "Accountable Care Organizations"(ACO) proposed by the 2010 health reform law. However, according to the ACA, in order to participate, an ACO must, among other protective features, have a sufficient number of primary care professionals for the number of assigned beneficiaries (to be 5,000 beneficiaries at a minimum); similar to President Clinton's Health Security Act of 1993, which required that employers with over 5,000 employees could opt out of the Act's coverage requirements if they paid a one percent payroll tax.

Following the Republican takeover of the House and Senate in the 1994 midterm elections, and the Republican "revolution" called the "Contract with America," more than one hundred thousand people each month began joining the ranks of the over 45 million uninsured, a number that increased despite the greater employment figures of the Clinton years. A Roper study showed that from that point until 1999, while pharmaceuticals, laboratory, biotechnology and supply firms had made substantial economic gains, there were disquieting losses for hospitals (26.6 percent); medical practice management (28.9 percent); diagnostics (45.1 percent); and surgical devices (56.5 percent). With almost 90 percent of the managed-care industry showing financial losses in 1997 over the previous year and as much as 49 percent in negative cash flow, portentous increases in healthcare insurance premiums raised doubts that managed care had successfully met any of its avowed social and economic goals.

By 2000, M+C enrollment declined from 27 percent to 11 percent of the Medicare population and was projected by the Congressional Budget Office to shrink to 8 percent by 2010. After that dismal experience, the post-Millennium Congress and George W. Bush (Bush II) administration vigorously entered the path of privatization of government insurance programs, establishing Medicare Advantage (MA) or Medicare Part D, pursuant to the Medicare Prescription Drug, Improvement, and Modernization Act of 2003 (MMA), slated to become effective January 1, 2006. The new law included payment for prescription drugs, offering huge discounts to large insurers' formularies while shifting higher prices to all non-members. This was the tipping point of where the commercial managed-care health insurance industry established its hegemony over the American healthcare system.

After the Millennium, WellPoint, a for-profit healthcare insurer incorporated in 1992, began to acquire the operation of Blue Cross plans across the country, many of them becoming for-profit in turn, effectively creating wholly owned, for-profit subsidiaries out of what were formerly high-risk, front-end, nonprofit insurance companies. By 2008, WellPoint's thirty-six million customers moved the company into second place behind UnitedHealth Group Inc. (UHG), which was providing coverage mostly in the small-group and individual markets. In 2010, WellPoint's proposed 39 percent increase in California's individual premium market occurred at the same time as the Obama administration's health reform bill was enacted. The proposed price increases were swiftly withdrawn after much protest from the state and national governments, and the ACA included surveillance of "Medical Loss Ratios" (MLRs)—the proportion of premium dollars health insurers spend on patient care compared to administrative expenses. However, by March 2011, WellPoint's Anthem subsidiary was back, raising New Hampshire's Blue Cross and Blue Shield smaller groups' increases of 40 percent to 60 percent or more.

Americans never liked HMOs and commercially managed care but had no choice about them. They also were not aware of the subtle switch from the nonprofit "federally qualified" HMOs to control by the giant managed-care health insurers. At the turn of the Millennium, the AMA, the Missouri Medical Society, the New York State Medical Society, and others brought a class-action lawsuit against UnitedHealthcare (UHC), by sales the largest healthcare insurer in the country. The suit alleged that UHC's subsidiary, Ingenix, developed a database to determine the "usual, customary and reasonable charges" (UCRs) that were derived from unreliable and insufficient data. The data were also shared with UHC's competitors. The case challenged UHC and American Airlines' reimbursements for out-of-network health medical services and procedures; the insurers used the faulty data to lower the rates they paid to doctors, which had shifted costs to patients and clients from March 1994 through the date of the final court approval of the settlement. By January 2009, a settlement agreement for $350 million was reached between the new parent of UHC, United Health Group (UHG), and its various affiliates and subsidiaries and the plaintiffs on behalf of the health plan members, health plan providers, the AMA, and various state medical societies and associations.

Six months later, UHG agreed to acquire Health Net Inc.'s Northeast licensed subsidiaries for up to $570 million, at the same time as Health Net, which manages mental health benefits, settled a class action against it for $249 million. The U.S. Department of Defense then delivered a stunning blow to Health Net Inc. and awarded the company's $2.8 billion annual TRICARE military healthcare contract to Aetna Inc. On December 4, Bloomberg News announced the U.S. District Court judge's tentative authorization, finalizing a settlement that recognized that UnitedHealth's payment scheme resulted in significant damages to physicians who provided out-of-network care to patients enrolled with UnitedHealth. By late 2010, like a phoenix rising from the ashes, UHC was actively advertising its wares on television, newspapers, and the Internet, its slogan revealing boundless aspiration: "Health in Numbers." However, UHC's audacious numerical proclamation that its seventy thousand insurance company employees participate in the "care" of its seventy million members revealed nearly the same ratio per thousand of its subscribers as primary care physicians per thousand treated Americans; a peek into why healthcare costs are so high: managed-care's "one doctor for the price of two."

My two monographs, *Managed Care or Managed Costs?*, in 1988, and in 1997, *Aspects of Antitrust Behavior in the Managed Care Industry*, were followed by a two-volume work, *Collusive Behavior in the Managed Healthcare Industry*, written in collaboration with its principal author, Kenneth C. Anderson, a former section chief at the Antitrust Division of the U.S. Department of Justice (DOJ). In late 1996, Ken Anderson and I made a presentation to the Department of Labor (DOL) outlining the need for regulatory changes under ERISA. This included a comprehensive analysis of ERISA, its regulations, and proposals for specific regulatory changes for the protection of beneficiaries. The 1988 and 1997 monographs and the two-volume work were distributed to leaders of the medical and legal communities and to government officials who at the time were concerned with the effects of managed care on the government-based and private healthcare systems.

This book, largely completed by 2000, was set aside when the Bush II administration began methodological deconstruction of what remained of the Clinton administration's healthcare reform efforts. Although the people-centered Social Security fund continued to be safeguarded by its beneficiaries' fierce resistance to privatization, the Bush II administration allowed Medicare and Medicaid to enter a transformation controlled by the commercial insurance industry. That change portended a shift from the nonprofit, 3 percent administrative cost center of government healthcare programs to a for-profit one ranging from 15 to 40 percent, permitting costs to soar out of proportion to population growth and secular inflation trends.

During the Bush II years, the uncritically accepted social value of the "efficiencies" that managed care introduced seemed to have insulated insurance companies from renewed challenges to their anticompetitive-behavior in the past. However, after fifty years of state regulation to prevent insurance companies from exploiting their promises to indemnify risk, the insurance industry had directly entered the medical treatment arena as a putative provider of the healthcare services it had promised solely to insure. The price of healthcare became "at list"—similar to "manufacturer suggested retail pricing" or "MSRP"—where profit margins were so much greater than when based on a natural market that they were subject to discounting to out-rival competition.

The managed-healthcare industry can survive for a time because in a managed-care environment, compared with the indemnity era, the revenue to the insurers is no longer encumbered by a state-regulated indemnity risk and statutory reserves. By basing its entire revenue income on artificial list prices of healthcare obligated by its enormous administrative costs, the insurance industry-supported managed-care system exposes itself as a market failure, where the price of its services do not reflect its true costs and are not allocated effectively or efficiently. It has served largely to redirect our country's huge healthcare-earmarked revenue stream out of a provider system and into the market-manipulated cash-flow coffers of the private investment community.

I have chosen to add graphic visual aids to this edition to demonstrate further the dynamics of the healthcare system in the U.S., and offers diagrams depicting socio-economic cost and relative high-or-low stability equilibriums. The graphs show U.S. healthcare before managed care, during the managed-care era, and presumably the effect of the Affordable Care Act. Because the dynamics of the US healthcare system before managed care rested on the movement of individuals, i.e., "cooperating members," in-and-out of coverage of one type or another, or "free-riding," the graphs demonstrate that the most stable equilibrium point offers the lowest socio-economic cost based on the social compact. The "metastable" equilibrium point is a state where output or significant change is unpredictable. The peak of each graph is the tipping point effecting a change to either increased stability and lower socio-economic cost or the reverse. In the healthcare system, the changes are effected by injecting either personal money or subsidies through legislative action. For example, *See* Plates 6, 7 and 17, each of which will be explained in more detail throughout the book.

There is a fundamental difference in the way the two major political parties promote healthcare reform both in their election platforms, and during their corresponding administrations. Much of the modern debate over healthcare coverage problems began with the Democratic administrations of Presidents Kennedy and Johnson. There was only a four-year Democratic Carter administration wedged in between the Nixon-Ford Republican seven years and the Reagan-George H.W. Bush twelve Republican years, before the eight Democratic years of President Clinton (whose final two years were with a Republican Congress) to make evident the distinction. The following excerpts from the national Republican platforms—1980 through 2008—serve as support for the proposition that the American health insurance industry provides the scaffold for the national Republican positions on healthcare reform since 1980.

- 1980: "Republicans unequivocally oppose socialized medicine, in whatever guise it is presented by the Democratic Party. . . What ails American medicine is government meddling and the strait-jacket of federal programs. The prescription for good health care is deregulation and an emphasis upon consumer rights and patient choice."
- 1984: "Many health problems arise within the family and should be dealt with there. We affirm the right and responsibility of parents to participate in decisions about the treatment of children. We will not tolerate the use of federal funds, taxed away from parents, to abrogate their role in family health

care. . . Government must not impose cumbersome health planning that causes major delays, increases construction costs, and stifles competition. It should not unduly delay the approval of new medicines, nor adhere to outdated safety standards hindering rapidly advancing technology."

- 1988: "Yesterday's science fiction regularly becomes today's medical routine. The American people almost lost all that in the 1960s and 1970s, when political demagogues offered quack cures for the ills of our health care system. They tried to impose here the nationalized medicine that was disastrous in other countries. . . Republicans believe in reduced government control of health care while maintaining an unequivocal commitment to quality health care."

- 2000: "Every Medicare beneficiary should have a choice of health care options. We want them to have access to the health plan that best fits their medical needs. In short: no more governmental one-size-fits-all. George W. Bush says, 'We will not nationalize our health care system. We will promote individual choice. We will rely on private insurance.'

- A major reason why health insurance is so expensive is that many state legislatures now require all insurance policies to provide benefits and treatments, which many families do not want and do not need. It is as if automakers were required by law to sell only fully equipped cars, even to buyers who didn't want or need all the extras. These mandates, extending far beyond minimum standards, increase costs for everyone, price low-income families out of the insurance market, and advance the interests of specific providers. They have no place in a health care system based on consumer rights and patient choice.

- In a Republican administration, the first order of business at the Department of Health and Human Services will be to eliminate regulations that are stymieing the effectiveness of S-CHIP program and to stop imposing unwarranted mandates, so states can make sure children who need health care can get it."

- 2004: "We reject any notion of government-run universal health care because we have seen evidence from around the world that government-run health care leads to inefficiencies, long waiting periods, and often substandard health care."
- 2008: "The American people rejected Democrats' attempted government takeover of health care in 1993, and they remain skeptical of politicians who would send us down that road. Republicans support the private practice of medicine and oppose socialized medicine in the form of a government-run universal health care system. . . Radical restructuring of health care would be unwise. We will continue to advocate for simplification of the system and the empowerment of patients. This is in stark contrast to the other party's insistence on putting Washington in charge of patient care, which has blocked any progress on meeting these goals."

In 2010, a large observational study of heart failure treatment in hospitals over the period of 1993 to 2006—correlated with the development of managed care—demonstrated that the reduction in hospital length of stay reduced the risk of hospital-associated adverse events but increased adverse events in both post-hospital readmission and mortality risk in the post-discharge period. Because the early days in hospital are the most costly, the shorter "managed" hospital stays are inversely proportional to the revenue generated and directly proportional to increased chances of readmission for more serious illnesses.

In this present work, the focus is on the failure of the managed-care insurance marketspace to satisfy the need for better allocation of healthcare resources to improve the healthcare of the populace by "selling" healthcare to subscribers at losses to providers and their patients. It crossed the threshold of a market failure that has produced enormous deadweight losses for our economy. With the carefully paced implementation of the Obama administration's ACA, it will still take several years to find out whether the managed-care insurance industry will succeed in its attempt to apply managed-care "cost-saving" techniques to the ACA's "Exchange" groups and stimulate a dialogue on whether a form of national health insurance will be required to replace it. Although the new health-reform law initiates a sea change in America's healthcare system, ERISA-based self-insured coverage will not be as comprehensively regulated as state-regulated, conventional insured plans, and equilibrium must await the congressional reconciliation process. This book explores and develops the answers to these questions, giving readers an opportunity to broaden their knowledge of this vital subject. The history of the managed-healthcare economy, with its mantle of the public-health policy doctrine of cost containment, is scrutinized. Managed care is portrayed as an industry unproductively related to healthcare, one that stifles innovation and penetrates the traditional doctor-patient relationship at the patients' peril while perverting the federal government's constitutional role to promote the general welfare.

The Managed Healthcare Industry - A Market Failure examines the legislative and economic changes of the past thirty-five years that have resulted in today's increasing number of uninsured Americans. Bringing together in one book the elements of such a complex socioeconomic phenomenon as the perversion of the system and structure of modern healthcare insurance requires it to be written in a manner that would reach readers with differing background and training. Thus, some readers may find it advisable to skim through some of the subsections as they link together technical economic and legal theories to explain the market failure. However, skimming through such parts should not seriously interfere with following the remaining parts.

Part I of the book sheds light on the onset of the healthcare "cost-containment" era, from the insurance-company friendly HMO Act to the advent of the managed-care industry. Parts II and III tackle the implications of federal antitrust law, particularly in terms of the power of federal "preemption" fashioned by the 1974 enactment of ERISA, the "Employee Retirement Income Security Act." Part IV attempts to illuminate the contributing factors that lead to companies created to "manage" the delivery of healthcare externally and how so many failed to survive. This section addresses whether or not insurers were legitimately cutting costs or actually coercively lowering prices in a predatory manner to eliminate rivals and assesses the healthcare "monopsony," wherein patients have become reluctant participants in their compromised offerings, and why this sets up a paradigm of market failure. Parts V and VI demystify the business of insurance companies, revealing when their former insurance" policies became "noninsurance," which exploits alike employers and their employees' benefit plans. Parts VII, VIII, and IX consider managed healthcare as a market failure, where the social and economic costs of delivering healthcare services are maximized and result in a waste of resources. After the Part X "Summary Judgment," the book weighs the ethics of physician participation in managed care, and the possibility of state and federal governmental "managing" managed care by way of the Obama administration's Affordable Care Act of 2010.

This work provides a chronicle of managed care's overlobbied, toxic effluent into government programs and its takeover of the indemnity health-insurance industry. My hope is that it will be useful to not only legislators, policy planners, antitrust and other government regulators, and advocates who have more than a passing acquaintance with healthcare issues, but also to educators, and to healthcare professionals and their patients whose interests are centered solely on offering and receiving incorruptible healthcare.

As the post-Millennium fracturing of the healthcare system was continued by the Bush II administration, allowing the resurgence of the insurance cartelization of the 1930s and 1940s, this work restarted. This historical canvass of the multidisciplinary political economics of healthcare presents a fact-based inquiry that may generate conclusions as being what the author sought; however, the objective was to be analytic and factual—endorsement is left to the reader, perhaps to answer the question of whether managed healthcare insurance is worth having at all.

Jack Charles Schoenholtz, MD
Rye, New York

I. INTRODUCTION

"Daniel V. Jones, 40, who was apparently distraught over
what he believed was inadequate care from health maintenance organizations, set himself and his dog on fire in front
of television cameras and, minutes later, still smoldering,
propped a shotgun under his chin and pulled the trigger. He
tumbled onto the freeway carpool lane where he had parked
his pickup truck and died next to a banner he had unfurled
that read, "HMOs are in it for the money. Live free, love safe
or die."

—*The New York Times* (May 1, 1998)

"The purpose of the [Sherman] Act is not to protect businesses from the workings of the market; it is to protect the
public from the failure of the market. The law directs itself
not against conduct which is competitive, even severely so,
but against conduct which unfairly tends to destroy competition itself."

—*Spectrum Sports, Inc. v. McQuillan* (1993)

June 6, 1944 was an auspicious day. Elderly Americans who regularly read *The New York Times* might say that they remember the italicized, banner headlines: ***"ALLIED ARMIES LAND IN FRANCE . . .
GREAT INVASION IS UNDERWAY."*** Few would remember that on
the same day, on the same front page and in plain sight above the fold,
was a much smaller headline: **"FEDERAL LAW HELD RULING**

1

INSURANCE–Supreme Court, 4–3, Decides Business Is Inter-state and Subject to Trust Act" *See* Plate 1.

WASHINGTON June 5 – The Supreme Court, by a four-to-three decision today held that the insurance companies of the country, with assets of $37,000,000,000 and annual premium collections in excess of $6,000,000,000 are inter-state commerce and thus subject to the Sherman Anti-Trust Law . . . The suit was based on a charge that the South-Eastern Underwriters Association, representing nearly 200 private capital stock fire insurance companies in six South-ern States, had conspired to fix premiums and monopolize trade . . . Justice Black wrote [for the majority] that Con-gress has the power under the Constitution, to govern trans-actions which "affect the peoples of more States than one . . . That power, as held by this court from the beginning, is vested in the Congress, available to be exercised for the national welfare as Congress shall deem necessary. No commercial enterprise of any kind which conducts its activities across State lines has been held to be wholly beyond the regulatory power of Congress under the Commerce Clause. We cannot make an exception of the business of insurance." *See* Plate 2.

Associate Justice Black's was citing from Chief Justice Marshall's seminal decision in *Gibbons v. Ogden* (1824): "Commerce, undoubt-edly, is traffic, but it is something more: it is intercourse. It describes the commercial intercourse between nations, and parts of nations, in all its branches. . . ." Commerce is interstate, [Marshall] said, when it "concerns more States than one." Black went on to quote the *Federal-ist Papers* saying, "The power confined to Congress by the Commerce Clause is declared in The Federalist to be for the purpose of securing the 'maintenance of harmony and proper intercourse among the States.'"

The historic 1944 decision in *United States v. South-Eastern Under-writers* brushed aside more than seventy-five years of contrary decisions of the High Court, including repeated precedents, since the enactment in 1890 of the Sherman Antitrust Act. The following year, Congress saw fit to protect regulation of the now-beleaguered "business of insurance" industry by enacting the McCarran-Ferguson Act in 1945. In his January 1945 State of the Union message delivered when he was too sick to go to Congress, President Franklin D. Roosevelt proposed a "Second Bill of Rights," which included the following: "The right to adequate medical care and the opportunity to achieve and enjoy good health; and the right to adequate protection from the economic fears of old age, sickness, accident, and unemployment." On March 9, in signing the McCarran-Ferguson Act, which left partial regulation of insurance to the states, President Roosevelt explained the nexus between state regulation of insurance and the federal antitrust laws: "Congress did not intend to permit private rate-fixing, which the antitrust act forbids, but was willing to permit actual regulation of rates by affirmative action of the states."

What was to be the "affirmative action by the states?" One hundred and seventy years earlier, Adam Smith said in his *Wealth of Nations*, "People of the same trade seldom meet together, even for merriment and diversion, but the conversation ends in a conspiracy against the public, or in some contrivance to raise prices." Such collusive behavior was not limited to "trades." After Associate Justice Black said in *South-Eastern Underwriters*, "No commercial enterprise of any kind which conducts its activities across State lines has been held to be wholly beyond the regulatory power of Congress under the Commerce Clause," courts also began to find that "learned professions," too, could be involved in anticompetitive activity. Indeed, the Federal Trade Commission (FTC) and the Antitrust Division of the Justice Department have since 1982 concerned themselves more with antitrust violations by members of the professional healthcare community than with insurer-based organizations. However, considerable evidence has emerged to show that provider joint actions were more indicative of patient-protective rejoinders by the professions to the painstakingly unregulated insurance-industry constraints on them.

Despite the 1966 introduction of Medicare and Medicaid, the U.S. Department of Health, Education and Welfare—now the Department of Health and Human Services (DHHS)—estimated that the

22 million having no health insurance had risen to over forty million by 1977, the same eleven percent taking population growth into account. From the mid-1980s forward, the interdependence of regulation and private conduct in healthcare insurance, self-insured healthcare coverage and healthcare delivery by providers intensified. As many of the insurance plans did not pay for increasing "catastrophic" expenses among the aging, there was proportionately less coverage by 1995 under managed-care imposed limits per unit of healthcare delivery. There was slippage in coverage. Whereas by 1978, around 90 percent of the 222 million Americans had health insurance, by 1996, only 84 percent of the country's 265 million were protected by some form of coverage. The twenty-one million not covered by some form of insurance in 1976, and 40.6 million not covered in 1995, was a proportionate increase of 100 percent in the not-covered yet growing population, a paradox suggesting that a significant number of non-covered might be beneficial to the industry.

This increased lack of coverage occurred notwithstanding a 100 percent mushrooming of HMOs and a 10 percent decrease in the number of hospitals. It was associated directly with a 50 percent decrease in days of hospital care per one thousand persons, a 24 percent decrease in surgical procedures, yet an increase of more than 50 percent in total annual patient visits to physicians in the same period. According to the Commerce Department's Statistical Abstract of the United States, though the national death rate from all causes had been steadily dropping from 9.5 per one thousand Americans in 1960 to a low of 8.6 in 1990, it rose to 8.8 percent by 1995 during the rapid growth of managed care. The death rate dropped once more to 8.5 percent in 2002 and 8.1 percent in 2006 with the development of new prevention programs, medical technology, and pharmaco-therapeutics. However, the Statistical Abstract's "deaths from all causes" included both good and bad news. The good news was the decrease in heart disease, cancer, accidents, homicide and surgical failures. The bad news was double-digit increases in complications from diabetes, septicemia, and pulmonary diseases, illnesses that have been found to accompany premature, shortened-stay discharges from hospital. They are directly proportionate with absence of 24-hour hospital care and the "management" of patient care introduced by the insurance industry.

Such data offer an epidemiological inference: Since the early 1980s, there was an absolute increase in chronic disease and HIV/AIDS and its maintenance during the growth of the new system of managed care, piloted by the government healthcare-reimbursement scheme with its "Prospective Payment" methodology of DRGs and cost-limits to hospital stays. Septicemia and pneumonia are diseases that when occurring at home, post-hospital, could have been prevented if their care had not also been constrained by Medicare's "utilization review" methods, DRG fixed-price fiats, and commercial managed care. These shortened stays extinguished opportunities to prevent the common new or co-morbid illnesses from occurring when hospitalized patients were sent home prematurely—some saying "quicker-and-sicker." Moreover, the 1973 HMO Act and the 1974 ERISA stimulated growth in HMOs and the ERISA's self-insured health and welfare benefit plans between 1980 and 1985. ERISA also limited both federal and state oversight of those health plans' costs as well as state judicial remedies previously available to indemnity insurance subscribers. By 1982, the increase in illnesses coincided with otherwise unexplained major rises in deaths from pneumonia, chronic lower respiratory diseases, and diabetes mellitus—excluding even those who died from HIV/AIDS—and continued until 2000.

These were no statistical aberrations; rather, they represented the beginning of a healthcare market failure, an accessory to soaring growth in the managed-care industry, whose cash flow-based profit margins began narrowing, demanding more aggressive efforts to cut the costs of providers' care. Even taking into account the tens of millions of entrants into Medicare and Medicaid since 1965, nothing has more spectacularly affected our healthcare system than the shift of potential patients to managed-care surrogacy of indemnity insurance. The conventional indemnity health insurance market share dropped from 71 percent in 1988 to 18 percent in 1997 with the growth of ERISA health plans. A 1997 KPMG Peat Marwick survey of firms with 200 or more workers indicated that 81 percent of enrollments in employer-sponsored health plans were already in the gatekeeper-based, managed care of HMOs (33%), preferred-provider organizations (PPOs) (31%), and point-of-service (POS) plans (17%). The survey indicated that the share-accorded preferred provider organizations continued to grow while the share of POS plans stabilized. The market imperfections, which resulted from the private insurance sector's conferring upon itself a public-policy halo in the arena of remedial healthcare legislation, introduced a basis for periodic albeit weak scrutiny of commercial behavior in the healthcare field by state and federal antitrust agencies. Commercial insurers lobbied for legislation that enhanced manipulation of healthcare providers' prices. They then mimicked governmental programs through administratively expensive, remote "managing" of medical care. This permitted raising premium prices to cover those costs; especially the costs for mental health and substance abuse treatments, which were more heavily managed as patients were churned through shortened periods of treatment whether as outpatients or inpatients. *See* Plates 8 and 9 (which will be discussed thoroughly later on).

State governments began to set up "managed care" departments often for Medicaid purposes, as the term "managed care" insinuated itself into the federal and state lexicons. Start-up managed-care companies (MCOs), at first independent of indemnity insurers, began to be formally acquired by some indemnity insurance companies or subcontracted to larger managed-care organizations. When challenged regarding the proximity of their cost-cutting role to the indemnity promise in insurance policies, they proclaimed that they were supporters of legislation that might obtain government acceptance of their methods. Charges questioning their apparent anticompetitive behavior such as price-fixing and coercion were met with statements that they were simply pursuing the accepted public policy of cost-containment in the spirit of the "Noerr-Pennington Doctrine." The doctor-patient relationship was near an end. *See* Plate 5.

The Noerr-Pennington Doctrine was based on two 1960s Supreme Court decisions: *United Mine Workers v. Pennington* and *Eastern Railroad Presidents Conference v. Noerr Motor Freight, Inc.* In those cases, private entities were found to be immune from liability under the antitrust laws for attempts to influence the passage or enforcement of laws even if the laws they advocate for would have anticompetitive effects—that is, except if their behavior was found to be a "sham." In healthcare, the Noerr Doctrine had been particularly effective in lobbying for managed-care growth, namely that the erstwhile insurers and managed care organizations (MCOs) pursuit of the public policy of cost-containment is both legal and socially redeeming even if, as a result, competitors attempting to enter the system may be damaged.

The *Noerr* Court emphasized that it was irrelevant whether the motive behind the petitioning was to harm competitors: "The right of the people to inform their representatives in government of their desires with respect to the passage or enforcement of laws cannot properly be made to depend upon their intent in doing so." Antitrust investigators were stymied, in part, because *Noerr* appeared to be a civil-rights issue. Managed care insurance companies developed trade associations, such as America's Health Insurance Plans (AHIP) and the National Committee for Quality Assurance, which spend much time attempting to influence government and accrediting competing MCOs by standards-setting for medical treatment. *See* Plate 5. The Supreme Court in *Noerr-Pennington* concluded that the challenged activity—coordination among competitors in a standard-setting organization—even though designed to urge government action was not the type of conduct that the antitrust laws traditionally scrutinized.

In healthcare, there were few commercial cases brought to court, since the Noerr Doctrine was seen largely as being in the arena of free speech. However, it remained that if misrepresentations and conduct otherwise violative of antitrust law were found—such as price-fixing, control of market prices, a pattern of abuse of administrative process, or baseless claims covering the true motivation to injure a competitor—the "sham" would be exposed. In the managed healthcare situation, the MCOs' "products" revealed to many that they were largely a counterfeit set of promises to pay for healthcare coverage. In 1970, Yale Law School Professor Arthur A. Leff, a noted expert on consumer protection, explored how consumer contracts have become "products."

Others, notably professors Oren Bar-Gill and Elizabeth Warren, in 2008, posited that if a contract is a product, then it can be unsafe in the same way other products can be unsafe. Thus, the 1982 Supreme Court decided in *American Medical Association v. Federal Trade Commission* that the FTC has jurisdiction where such trade organizations are "organized to carry on business for its own profit or that of its members." During the Clinton administration, as healthcare controversies burgeoned, new guidelines were developed by the FTC and the Department of Justice, which appeared to be shifting the emphasis on provider indiscretions to those of the managed-care industry. An example of the Clinton administration's efforts in a related arena, pursuant to the federal False Claims Act, was a series of fraud probes by the office of the Inspector General of the DHHS, which investigated whether "Medigap" insurance or managed Medicare health plans would weed out unhealthy seniors and scrimp on medically necessary services to improve their profitability. As the managed-care glitter began to show more tarnish than patina, the investor community, too, lost some of its enthusiasm, making it clearer that the problem was not a parochial one of providers versus payers but one of payers versus patients.

Because of the complexity of a situation that presents as a market failure, possible antitrust activity involving vertical and horizontal restraints, boycott, coercion, predatory behavior, and price and non-price predation must be considered. Indeed, "sham" practices have been found in situations where predation might work if the predator could find some method that inflicts costs on rivals at no cost to itself. An example is if at a trivial lobbying cost the predator can convince a government to ban, tax, or regulate the rival's product. Such a situation was found by the 1988 Supreme Court in *Allied Tube & Conduit Corp. v. Indian Head, Inc.,* where employees of steel conduit manufacturers packed a meeting of the National Fire Protection Association and voted against approving plastic conduit. The NFPA is a private organization that includes members representing industry, labor, academia, insurers, organized medicine, firefighters, and government and sets and publishes product standards and codes related to fire protection. Its National Electrical Code, which establishes requirements for the design and installation of electrical wiring systems, is routinely adopted into law by a substantial number of state and local governments, and is widely adopted as setting acceptable standards by private product-certification laboratories, insurance underwriters, and electrical inspectors, contractors, and distributors.

Where the economic impact of certain practices are not readily apparent, especially those under color of public-policy assertions, a historical canvass must illustrate the events leading up to the present condition of the failed managed healthcare delivery system and which of its illegitimate aspects could survive the 2010 ACA obligations or require further remedial legislation.

II. BACKGROUND:
The Dominant Changes In Healthcare Law and Policy during the Past Thirty Years

Someone should be studying the whole system, however crudely that has to be done, because no gluing together of partial studies of a complex nonlinear system can give a good idea of the behavior of the whole.

—Murray Gell-Mann, Nobel Laureate in Physics

A. Phase One: The Healthcare "Cost-Containment" Era Begins

In 1965, President Johnson's Great Society measures, Medicare and Medicaid, amended the Social Security Act of 1935 to assure healthcare coverage for significant numbers of elderly and poor. Prior to that time, although "home relief" left over from the Great Depression and federal and state aid for the indigent was available, resources for healthcare were meager. There was no national uniformity of healthcare allocation by the states, and the commercial insurance industry was apparently not interested, many MCOs concluding publicly that those actuarial groups were impossible risks to assume.

Actuarial analysis of healthcare is the application of probability and statistical methods performed by professional statisticians working for government or an insurance company to calculate, from prevalence and incidence data, the possible occurrence of events such as illness, the need for hospitalization, or the chances of disability or death for members of a given population. A common use of actuarial analysis is the calculation of risk-insurance premiums and, for the insurer or government healthcare-coverage regulator, the necessary reserves in anticipation of the predicted risk. "Risk management" is different. It is used by business organizations to identify and reduce the impact of safety issues, accidents, credit, and operational and market risks on their businesses and customers. Its use has no place in indemnity insurance when used by the insurer, because it seeks to avoid a risk secondary to the insurance purpose. The primary purpose of indemnity insurance is the assumption actuaries implement into a model for underwriters to price a specific insurance policy. A secondary purpose, risk management, hedges on the chance that the actuaries' assumptions may turn out wrong or somewhat inaccurate. The function of actuarial analysis is to help underwriters form the basis for a premium paid by an insured for the coverage as stated in a policy; it is not to protect insurers from the risk of ineffectual actuaries. When such a secondary rationale as risk management is merged with indemnity insurance, it turns its insurance risk into a business or speculative risk and reduces the value to the purchaser of a premium based originally on indemnifying, or promising to reimburse for a predicted loss.

In the 1980s, the increasing power of the insurers together with the Pentagon began a dialogue with what were considered the weakest of healthcare lobbying groups in the country: the two "APAs," the American Psychological Association and the American Psychiatric Association. There were two reasons for their economic fragility. They were competitive for similar patients, and their patients were socially stigmatized, therefore, inherently weak as protestors. Essentially, the APA's were told that if they didn't cooperate and join in peer reviewing their own members' therapy styles, the insurers would do it for them, so all local branches set up Peer Review Committees. At the same time, insurance-company Peer Review was being challenged in the Supreme Court by a chiropractor. Essentially, the High Court said it was not the business of insurance to perform peer review. This complicated the mental-health organizations' efforts when they found that what they were doing for federal grant demonstration project money and the insurance companies could not be legally done anymore, even if by the insurers themselves. After too many protests from patients, providers and the legal advocacy community, the two APA's programs ended and the insurers had MCOs and HMO gatekeepers perform direct denials of care.

The Supreme Court in 1982 declared in *Union Labor Life Insurance Co. v. A. Alexander Pireno* that the insurance risk is "completely" transferred to the insurer at the time the policy is sold, not when the claim is made. The Court held that

"the use of [the insurer's peer-review company] as an aid in
its decision-making process is a matter of indifference to the
policyholder, whose only concern is *whether* his claim is paid,
not *why* it is paid." (Emphasis made by the Court.)

An insured is thus said to be "indemnified" against the loss covered in the policy. Therefore, when from the outset, managed healthcare companies were hired by indemnity insurers attempting to manage their risks to reduce the chance that their actuaries were wrong, they were devaluing the premium charged the purchaser and their social value as indemnity insurers as well.

Before managed-care involvement, indemnity insurers had to estimate their risk more closely, because they were state regulated and forbidden to influence it further than the policy language permitted. Moreover, they could not sustain their competition with each other by withholding payments. In the 1980s, the indemnity insurers still had to keep the managed-care companies at a distance—"outside" the business of insurance, so to speak. Formerly, medical directors employed by the insurers had to assess questionable "losses." However, competition between indemnity insurers began to be significantly affected when they found that the start-up managed healthcare companies some contracted with could control payouts by denying the medical necessity of quantities of care rendered and by "suggesting" that the insurers should withhold payment for medical and hospital services such third-party "experts" deemed not medically necessary. However, with the growing number of pension-based, "self-insured" plans of larger companies, that ceased to be a problem. ERISA had declared that though healthcare coverage for employees in pension plans was clearly in interstate commerce, it was not insurance covered by the McCarran-Ferguson Act and regulated by the states. The young MCOs and one-time indemnity insurers had only to offer "administrative services only" to the employers' plan and state to the patients, by letter or by terms of the plan document: "The availability of medical coverage is determined by the terms of your plan. All we do is verify the medical necessity of the services rendered." That seemed all that was necessary to enable employers and plan fiduciaries to deny payment to the providers.

The Great Society's Medicare and Medicaid programs were legislation to provide remedies where none previously existed. In the original 1965 act, the definition of reimbursement by the government for services rendered was one of vague "efficiency" and based on federal regulations:

"The reasonable cost of any services shall be the cost actually incurred, excluding therefrom any part of the cost found to be unnecessary in the efficient delivery of needed health services, and shall be determined in accordance with regulations establishing the methods to be used, and the items to be included, in determining such costs for various types or classes of institutions, agencies, and services."

In 1972, toward the end of the Nixon presidency, the language become more restrictive and defined the reasonable costs of services— formerly considered as those that were "actually incurred" in the efficient delivery of needed services—by adding a still-vague footnote:

"The regulations may provide for the establishment of limits on the direct or indirect overall incurred costs or incurred costs of specific items or services or groups of items of services to be recognized as reasonable based on the estimates of the costs necessary in the efficient delivery of needed services."

Because both programs were federal, with Medicare payments coming from Social Security funds and Medicaid from general revenue, the government could set limits on healthcare providers' income and could base reimbursement on "limits" or "indirect" costs incurred instead of on the "prices" charged patients by the healthcare providers. The latter occurs today with private payers and companies in the indemnity insurance market, but it is mitigated by techniques such as contractually fixed copayments, deductibles, and participation in PPOs.

Over time, the nonprofit and for-profit healthcare insurers began to change their payment language, too, inserting limits mimicking Medicare, such as "usual, customary and reasonable charges" or using "regional" rates charged by providers, although the non-profits, such as the Blue Cross and Blue Shield Plans (the "Blues") still had to justify those changes for state insurance departments. Before the 2010 ACA, in almost all states, although insurance companies were allowed to increase premiums without prior approval, they were usually required to file them with their relevant state departments.

As a result of the lowered Medicare pricing methods, price-shifting by the government to the private insurance companies was reflected in the higher premiums paid by policy holders even though the insurance actuaries were relieved that the elderly population was largely removed from the risk pool. The Medicare premium, for example, was inexpensive compared to small group and individual policies, because the government-operated plan did not cover all providers' treatments and fixed costs. As a result, supplemental, "Medigap" coverage could be offered by the commercial and Blue Cross plans with major discounts for "elder" organizations such as the American Association of Retired Persons (AARP). Medigap policies bought from non-governmental insurance companies added to the total cost of the expanded coverage for the elderly to save the government's costs; meanwhile, premiums for the nonelderly did not fall. Medicare had a large base, and the administrative costs were (and still are) around 3 percent of all expenditures.

In later years, notwithstanding the elderly buying additional insurance policies to cover deductibles and copayments, the administrations of Ronald Reagan, George H. W. Bush (Bush I), and Bush II administrations inserted provisions into the Medicare regulations that further narrowed the participating providers' incomes by limiting the total

15

amount of copayments and "balance billing" providers were allowed to charge. Balance billing had been practiced by providers and hospitals to regain privately what supplemental insurance policies did not pay for. This was soon further co-opted by the managed-care insurers who devised the exclusionary terms "in-network providers" (IN) and "out-of-network providers" (OON), which effectively passed the increased aggregate healthcare costs on to patients, its devaluation of the premium could pay towards "management" costs, and at the same time could eliminate rivals among doctor or hospital groups.

Under Medicare, funds were directly paid on beneficiaries' behalf out of the Medicare Trust to providers as assigned to them. For the poor, funds to the states for medical assistance were made available on the basis of a "federal medical assistance percentage" provided states that had a Medicaid state plan approved by the Secretary of Health and Human Services. In August 1971, President Nixon ordered a ninety-day freeze on prices, wages, salaries and rents, and created a Cost of Living Council to administer the freeze and to advise on further economic stabilization policies. Three months later, Phase II of the Economic Stabilization Program (ESP) began. The ESP goal was to reduce the rate of inflation to about one-half that of the pre-freeze rate. In December 1971, specific mandatory Phase II rules were promulgated for the healthcare industry, which were to continue only for healthcare when Phase III, the "voluntary" control program, began in January 1973. Phase IV, modified controls, were imposed on the healthcare industry in June and ended in April 1974 after President Nixon resigned and President Gerald Ford took office. The 1972 amendments to the Social Security Act significantly expanded Medicare and Medicaid coverage for the last time until the 1997 Clinton-era Balanced Budget Act (BBA), which enacted a section for "utilization review" to strengthen the "necessary cost" provisions of the law. The newly covered consisted of workers under age 65 made eligible for disability benefits as well as Medicare; a group made up of "aged, blind, and disabled" poor who would receive "Supplemental Security Income," provided in part with federal funds through state plans; and medical assistance for poor children under 21 suffering from "nervous or mental disease" when treated in psychiatric hospitals. Coverage for "nervous and mental diseases" was from the beginning not on par with coverage for other illnesses and remained so until the Mental Health Parity Acts began to take effect after the end of the Bush II administration. *See* Plates 10, 11 and 12.

In 1976, the Committee on Ways and Means of the House of Representatives found that on an annualized basis, all consumer prices, less medical care, had risen by 9.3 percent for the post-control period ending in September 1975, while medical care prices had risen 12.6 percent, leaving a 3.3 percent spread between them. Capital projects and purchases for depreciated equipment or new technology, necessary to hospitals and physicians, had been seriously limited or delayed under the mandatory price controls; this greater rate of post-Phase IV medical-care price increases in part reflected catch-up by medical providers for the years of mandatory controls faced by the healthcare industry.

In 1996, a weak form of Mental Health Parity Act was passed, which generally required parity of mental health but not substance abuse or chemical dependency benefits, with medical/surgical benefits with respect to the application of aggregate lifetime and annual dollar limits under group health plans already offering mental health coverage. The 1996 Parity Act provided that employers could retain discretion regarding the extent and scope of mental health benefits offered to workers and their families, including cost sharing, limits on numbers of visits or days of coverage, and requirements relating to medical necessity, and also did not include substance use disorders. Because its adoption was under unsupervised managed-care policies, it was largely ineffective. This remained so until the Mental Health Parity and Addiction Equity Act of 2008, which provided to participants who already had mental health and substance use disorders coverage parity with benefits limitations under their medical/surgical coverage, which was to start in 2010 but became fully effective on January 1, 2011 as part of the Affordable Care Act. *See* Plates 10, 11 and 12.

Federal mental health parity does not require ERISA plan sponsors to cover mental health or substance abuse benefits. However, if a plan sponsor chooses to offer mental health or substance abuse benefits, the law prohibits imposing more restrictive financial requirements (such as co-pays or deductibles) or treatment limitations (including quantitative treatment limitations, such as day or visit limits, and non-quantitative treatment limitations) on mental health or substance abuse benefits than those applied to medical or surgical benefits. Moreover federal parity does not dictate how parity should be achieved. For example, the law does not say that parity should be achieved through reducing medical benefits or by increasing mental health benefits. The law only requires "parity" however the health plan chooses to structure the benefits. Ironically, because government plans are not considered "insurance" plans by the federal Centers for Medicare and Medicaid (CMS), the new law apparently did not extend parity to Medicare or Medicaid patients. Although it does cover "managed Medicaid" when run by commercial insurance companies, it does not apply to commercially based Medicare Advantage. Part of the reason appears to be that despite the 1997 HIPAA Parity Act, Medicare lifetime limits for mental hospitalization have not changed and are still limited to 190 days, except if psychiatric treatment is given in general hospitals; there the law does not count them as "psychiatric days." Another reason may have been political, because leaving parity out of MA might have helped with getting the AHIP to join in pushing for the ACA, and with those of its members not having to offer what the insurance industry long considered loss leaders mental and substance-use disorders. Medicaid, too, covers such illnesses occurring in persons of all ages when in general hospitals, while in state-operated or freestanding psychiatric hospitals, Medicaid covers only patients under the age of 21 and over 65. As a stimulus to commercial insurers to get into the Act, "managed Medicaid" had been "carved out" from regular medical assistance and covers patients of all ages in all hospitals.

Federal Mental Health Parity does not require ERISA-plan sponsors to cover mental health or substance abuse benefits. However, if a plan sponsor chooses to offer mental health or substance abuse benefits, the law prohibits imposing more restrictive financial requirements (such as co-pays or deductibles) or treatment limitations (including quantitative treatment limitations, such as day or visit limits, and non-quantitative treatment limitations to be described later on) on mental health or substance abuse benefits than those applied to medical or surgical benefits.

In 1972, the Senate Finance Committee

"believ[ing] that the potential social and economic benefit of extending Medicaid inpatient mental hospital coverage to mentally ill persons between the ages of 21 and 65 deserves to be evaluated . . . [has] authorized demonstration projects for this purpose."

This language, allowing similar demonstration projects, reappeared twenty-eight years later in the ACA.

Starting in 1972, the original Great Society intent of extending access to healthcare was simultaneously pared thin through take-back amendments that had the effect of converting the Medicare trusts into a fungible feeding trough to be used for other governmental purposes—including the financing of wars through IOUs written against the Social Security Trust—while setting in place a paradigm for mimicry by private insurance policies. The utilization review sections and the cost-reporting sections of the 1972 law helped all this. The first section, allowed the Secretary of DHHS to

"utilize the procedures [used by states under Medicaid] if such procedures were determined to be superior in their effectiveness . . . , [and encouraged the Secretary to contract with] 'utilization and quality control peer review organizations . . . in order to promote the effective, efficient, and economical delivery of healthcare services of proper quality for which payment may be made.'"

The review section and the one that followed it, the Professional Standards Review Organizations (PSROs), were eventually repealed and replaced by sections of the Tax Equity and Fiscal Responsibility Act of 1982, which established the present "Prospective Payment System" and the DRGs. After ten years of operation, the PSROs were apparently unable to satisfy the "efficiency" and "economical" requirements of the government take-back expectations, because they ended their legislated existence with a net loss of $125 million. More money was spent on scrutinizing the effectiveness and quality of care than was recovered from finding ineffectiveness and poor quality. The PSROs were replaced by Peer Review Organizations, which have been able to perform somewhat more efficiently in prospective and retrospective denials of reimbursement to hospitals and practitioners for patient care, but their minimal cost-cutting "efficiency" paled in comparison with the healthcare denials by managed care organizations as they appeared after the Millennium.

Congress had also changed the "reasonable cost" section referred to earlier by adding a provision defining such costs. The original section included a non-cost-shifting clause that has been the subject of much litigation over the years:

"[T]he necessary costs of efficiently delivering covered services to individuals covered by the insurance programs established [under Medicare] will not be borne by individuals not so covered, and the costs with respect to individuals not so covered will not be borne by such insurance programs."

The perplexing assurance of setting "limits" on costs the Secretary of DHHS deems "unnecessary" in the "efficient delivery" of healthcare in effect promised the opposite: other government programs, private payers and private sector insurance, would in fact have to bear the costs of the Medicare program. Of course, by so doing, government was cueing the managed-care industry to mimic its care denials. Apparently, the negative effect of cost shifting to small-group and individual plan members in the form of higher deductibles and copayments continue to be ignored by all in government, but not by the insurers who simply raise their premiums to maintain the cash flow level. Despite much subsequent judicial review of challenges to this obvious cost-shifting to the private sector by government, the die was now cast for healthcare costs to increase proportionately for the non-governmental indemnity insurance programs as well as for those individuals who continued to pay privately. Illness has always presented an inelastic demand for care; however, managed care presented a cross-elasticity of demand between the healthcare product and "alternatives" or substitutes for it. When a government entity could ration the care for it for a sustainable amount of time, the prevalence of illness increased but veiled by a "subacute" condition created by the inadequate level of care rendered. Governmental "cost cutting" seemed only to stimulate the rise in overall healthcare costs, and the chronic ineffectiveness of its historical methods demonstrated the fundamental inelasticity of illness care. As the losses to doctors and hospitals were routinely passed through to the commercial insurance sector, the prices of individual and group premiums began to soar from the mid-1970s through the late 1980s, giving rise to the fiction that doctors and hospitals were the beneficiaries of such profits when it was only the insurers' profitability that was being subsidized.

Looking back, by far the most significant aspect of the Nixonian 1972 amendments to the Social Security Act was that it marked the end of much of the social remediation of healthcare as envisioned first by President Kennedy and then by the Johnsonian Great Society. It was in fact President Nixon who started the government on a path of regulatory micromanagement of healthcare sections of the Social Security Act, and not until the Parity Acts for coverage of mental and substance use disorders of 1997 and 2008, and the Obama administration's ACA, that a framework was erected for universal coverage for all ages and conditions. As part of the planned deconstruction and privatization of Medicare, George W. Bush signed into law the Medicare Prescription Drug Improvement and Modernization Act of 2003 to provide Medicare Advantage if M+C would falter.

The direct entry of government into protecting the big insurers' hegemony can be seen in footnotes to a section of the law:

"Construction: Pub. L. 108–173 . . . provided that: 'Nothing in Part C of Title XVIII [of Medicare] shall be construed as preventing an MSA [Medical Savings Account] plan or MA private fee-for-service plan from having a service area that covers one or more MA regions or the entire nation.'"

Because of that unusually expansive construction, the Bush administration began making contracts with private insurance companies to act as commercial Medicare fiscal intermediaries, who would, among other things, act as Quality Improvement Organizations (QIOs). Originally known as Peer Review Organizations, their name was officially changed to QIOs, per the Federal Register on May 24, 2002, in large part to reflect the Bush II administration's emphasis on "quality improvement." Aside from verifying hospital and other institutional cost reports, they were to have the ability to deny payment for care rendered, at times extending to denying payment for an entire admission to hospital. The irrational aspect of the financing mechanism was revealed by the fact that a hospital could have its reimbursement denied while the doctor taking care of the patient in the hospital would still receive payment for seeing the patient during that admission.

Ironically, the same congressional "construction" of the 2003 law cited earlier allowing the insurance industry to spread its services to the "entire nation," also laid the basis for future federal control of commercial companies participating in MA, because it formally allowed them to participate in interstate commerce without protection by the McCarran-Ferguson Act. In the plan to lower the cost of Medicare by the 2010 ACA, President Obama called for eliminating "waste, fraud and abuse" in the Medicare program. However, the forty-one QIO contractors, which cover all fifty states plus Washington DC, Puerto Rico, and the Virgin Islands, also appeared to present just as much waste, if not more, when the president noted in early 2009,

> "This is the first year that CMS has shared its annual QIO Report to Congress with the public as part of its pledge to be more open and transparent about the operations and the impact of the QIO Program."

The following exposition of the QIO program was part of the report delivered to the new president by Michael O. Leavitt, outgoing Secretary of Health and Human Services, for fiscal year 2006:

> "The QIO Program spent $400 million in FY 2006, performing activities such as:

Protecting the Medicare Trust Fund. In FY 2006, QIOs reviewed 41,000 medical records under the Hospital Payment Monitoring Program and identified $14.5 million in overpayments and $2.0 million in underpayments.

Protecting Medicare beneficiaries. In FY 2006, QIOs reviewed 90,646 medical records and 3,717 beneficiary complaints.QIOs also reviewed 22,464 medical records relating to beneficiary appeals of terminations of services provided in a number of care settings."

Note that the private sector QIOs got $400 million dollars for their review work and recaptured only $12.5 million for the government! Such a venture would easily fail any cost-effectiveness test. While the report conceded that 25 percent of beneficiary appeals were for "terminations of services," no mention was made of the number of appeals of "terminations" that had been reversed by administrative law judges of the CMS on appeal, or the amount of money the denials required to be returned to the beneficiary or provider. According to an official at Region II of the DHHS, hospitals across the country had been complaining about payment denials made by the QIOs and the new laborious and expensive administrative appeals process established by the remaining Bush II CMS regulations. According to federal regulations, a QIO cannot be a healthcare facility, healthcare facility association, a healthcare facility affiliate, or in most cases a payer organization. However, under the Bush II administration CMS, it was decided that the statutes provide that

"in the event CMS determines no otherwise qualified nonpayor organization is available to undertake a given QIO contract, CMS may select a payor organization which otherwise meets certain requirements to be eligible to conduct Utilization and Quality Control Peer Review. . ."

Based on that interpretation, in 2008, National Government Services (NGS), a wholly owned subsidiary of the giant managed-care insurer WellPoint, was awarded a three-year contract as a QIO. One hospital reviewed in 2009 by NGS had 100 percent of its appeals of QIO denials reversed on behalf of the beneficiaries by three separate Administrative Law Judges' decisions. That QIO also functions as an approved "fiscal intermediary." After the first denial, a "redetermination" was also denied. The cases were then submitted for a "second-level" appeal to an "independent" contractor, Maximus Federal Services, which upheld NGS's denials. Each case was then appealed to the DHHS Office of Medicare Hearings and Appeals' Administrative Law Judge service, and each case was reversed against the QIO and found "fully favorable" for the beneficiary. The process took a full year, increased the legal costs for the hospital on behalf of the beneficiary, and benefitted no one except WellPoint.

In many states, indemnity insurance with a claims expense below 65 percent cannot be sold as "insurance," because the financial risk to the insurer is so low that their premium prices would amount to a sham. Insurers claim nonetheless that selling individual policies is an even greater "loss leader" than losses sustained from group policies because of the greater cost to administer, yet the extreme profitability of individual policies is obvious. Because of its very low medical loss ratios (MLRs), it barely constitutes enough of a risk to be called insurance. According to House of Representatives Ways and Means Committee's 1974 data collection, the "operating expenses" of the nonprofit "Blues" plans were 5.4 percent of premium income and their MLR was 96.1 percent, while commercial individual plans listed operating expenses as 47 percent of premium income and had an average 46.3 percent MLR. Ironically, this was the same year that ERISA was passed. Most types of health insurance showed annual underwriting losses while only individual plans had net underwriting gains of 6.7 percent. Of course, the insurance companies did not have to go out of the insurance business notwithstanding their published high-loss MLRs, because their profits shown on consolidated corporate income statements were from investment elsewhere.

As part of the Democratic congressional thrust for passing the 2010 healthcare insurance reform, the Senate Committee on Commerce, Science, and Transportation, chaired by Senator Jay Rockefeller, published a Majority Staff report on MLRs. The report discussed the new minimum MLRs that eventually became law as part of the legislation President Obama signed on March 23, 2010. In August 2009, the Committee had opened its investigation by sending letters to the fifteen largest health insurers asking for information on how the companies spent their premium dollars and to provide "medical loss ratio information broken down by state, and by individual, small-group, and large-group market segments."

The insurers as a group, were "reluctant to share" such information in the form that the Committee asked, so the Committee had to collect this information from state forms filed with the National Association of Insurance Commissioners (NAIC). In its answer to the government's Request for Comments, the AARP noted:

"As the data already provided to the National Association of Insurance Commissioners demonstrate, current state MLR standards vary significantly. It is noteworthy that there are significant differences between the [Affordable Care Act] MLR requirements and the NAIC guidelines."

Nonetheless, the analysis found that the largest for-profit health insurers spend a lower percentage of their customers' premium dollars on patient care than other health insurers. The analysis also found that in the individual and small-group markets, health insurers spend a significantly smaller portion of each premium dollar on medical care than they do in the large group market:

"For example, UnitedHealth told its investors that the company's overall 2008 medical loss ratio was 82%. But the NAIC Accident and Health Experience filings revealed that the company's medical loss ratio was 71% in the individual market, 79% in the small group market, and 84% in the large group market."

Of incidental interest, too, was a significant finding that among the six largest public insurers, while five of them had individual plan MLRs below 80 percent and large group plans' MLRs of over 80 percent, only CIGNA reversed the insurer "loss-leader strategy." CIGNA's individual plans' MLRs were 86.9 percent, while their large-groups' MLRs averaged 37.5 percent! For that to have happened successfully, they had eliminated doing any "small employer policy business" in 2008; in effect they were "cherry picking" patient groups at a mass level. However, this strategy seemed to fail in the roiling merger and acquisition years, since they re-entered the small employer market in 2009 where their MLR turned out to be a whopping 92 percent; robust proof that healthcare insurance offers nothing more to society than being a cash-flow business.

Under the new health reform law, MLRs will have to become balanced at 80 percent. Companies that have MLRs below 80 percent in the individual and small-group markets, and below 85 percent in the large-group market, will be under pressure to perform "MLR shifts," rebates that will bring their ratios closer to the newly mandated federal minimums. The following example illustrates how this rebate process will work under the new law:

> If an insurer collected $100 million in premiums from business owners for small group coverage, but only spent 78 percent of these premiums on medical care, the law requires the insurer to rebate 2 percent of the premiums collected ($2 million) to the policyholders on a pro rata basis.

Rebates like this were unheard of in the insurance industry, and the Republican leadership promised a repeal fight in the House after their 2010 midterm election victory in the House of Representatives. The promised vote for repeal was held in the House, 285-189, in February, but the Senate voted forty-seven for repeal and fifty-one against in a party-line decision.

It is interesting to note one way insurance companies plan to make the MLR shifts profitable in the mental health insurance areas: The Obama administration's attempt to enforce the 2008 Wellstone-Dominici Parity law, which abolished discriminatory insurance coverage for the treatment of mental health and substance abuse, met with furious resistance by lobbyists for the insurers. Apparently, this was because the new administration had introduced an interpretation of managed care called "nonquantitative treatment limits." *See* Plate 12. Insurers used these techniques in selecting in-network providers and the rates by which they were paid "prior authorizations," which included submission of treatment plans for mental health services—where none were required for comparable medical-surgical services—along with different deductibles for IN and OON providers. It was a good start in the business of regulating the discriminatory practice; however, simply by requiring "parity," as long as an insurer uses managed-care techniques such as capitation and marginal-cost pricing, which we will describe later, providers' prices can still be fixed to provide profits to the insurers.

In addition, as insurance companies made an effort to reach the required minimum loss ratios of 80 percent by 2014, they endeavored to figuratively double-down and shift some of their managed-care expenses into the MLRs. In a September 2009 half-page ad in *The New York Times*, WellPoint, with an embodiment of moral rectitude, arrogantly proclaimed that the private insurance companies' "administrative costs" and "insurer profits" were 9 percent of "The Health Insurance Dollar," but they didn't reveal that they were three times Medicare's administrative costs. And, although Medicare's administrative costs have traditionally been 3 to 4 percent of its total expenditures, the commercial insurance industry was shown in a 2008 Commonwealth Fund issue brief to range from 13 to 18 percent!

The issue brief based examination on sources of administrative costs and described how a national insurance exchange would largely replace the present individual and small-group markets and substantially lower such costs:

> "In three variations on that approach, estimated administrative costs would fall from 12.7 percent of claims to an average of 9.4 percent. Savings—as much as $265 billion over 2010-2020—would be realized through less marketing and underwriting, reduced costs of claims administration, less time spent negotiating provider payment rates, and fewer or standardized commissions to insurance brokers."

The 1972 legislative "reasonable costs" amendments to Medicare also set in place a congressional and administrative ethos of cost containment as public health policy that the private insurance industry eagerly adopted and exaggerated for years, adding layer upon layer of commercial administrative costs, benefiting cash flow, and reducing their premium-based risk.

B. Phase Two: Broadening the Actuarial Base of Healthcare

1. The HMO Act as Amended—More "Take-Back"

> "Don't worry, it'll play in Peoria."
> —John Ehrlichman, Assistant for
> Domestic Affairs to President Nixon

As part of enacting constraints on government funding for healthcare, Congress passed the 1973 Health Maintenance Organization Act. It was one of the last pieces of legislation signed by President Nixon and has been considered his healthcare legacy. This legislation transformed a healthcare system previously suffering what the health-insurance industry liked to call a "moral hazard" into a potentially much wider scheme, and it substituted the "care of illness" with a socially redeemable-sounding objective of "maintaining health." Although ostensibly originating as applied to fire-damage risk, "moral hazard" has been used by legislators and insurance industry lobbyists alike to explain part of the high costs of healthcare insurance. As defined in Black's Law Dictionary, it is

> "the risk that an insured will destroy property or allow it to be destroyed (usually by burning) in order to collect the insurance proceeds" and, "as measured by the character and interest of the insured . . . his habits as a prudent and careful man or the reverse, his known integrity or his bad reputation, and the amount of gain he would make by collecting the insurance."

In short, according to insurance companies, the "moral" hazard rested with the immoral: their customers.

The HMO legislation optimistically contained a powerful stimulus to its public acceptance, because it required every employer with more than twenty-five employees that had a health benefits plan to offer a "dual option," so that the employees would be free to choose from one of the kinds of HMO available or hold on to the coverage already offered. Under the dual option, no employer or employee would be required to pay more in premiums for HMO benefits than for their previously held indemnity policies with comparable benefits. Of course, there was no "managed care" at the time, as we know it, so the choice was between two types of indemnification: one with HMO treatment by "efficiently minded" salaried or group practice doctors, the rest by independent fee-for-service physicians or by an "individual practice association."

The statute contained extensive requirements, previously associated with high-option indemnity plans, for an organization to become federally "qualified" and thereby entitled to start-up grants, government contracts, and loan guarantees for public and nonprofit group HMOs. Private sector market entry was encouraged by the 1976 Amendments to the HMO Act during the Carter administration. The "basic health service" to be provided by a qualifying HMO included physician services, inpatient and outpatient hospital services, emergency services, short-term outpatient evaluative and crisis intervention services (not to exceed twenty visits), medical treatment and referral services for the abuse of or addiction to drugs and alcohol, diagnostic laboratory and therapeutic radiology services, home health services; and preventive services. "Supplemental health services" included services of facilities for intermediate and long-term care, vision care not included as a basic health service, dental services not included as a basic health service, mental health services not included as a basic service, long-term physical medicine and rehabilitative services including physical therapy, and prescription drugs prescribed in the course of basic service treatment.

The well-intentioned preventive services included immunizations, well-child care from birth, periodic health evaluations for adults, voluntary family-planning services, infertility services, and children's eye and ear examinations conducted to determine the need for vision and hearing correction. These were to be provided at "full financial risk," which had to be "available and accessible twenty-four hours a day and seven days a week" for enrollees who were to be "broadly representative of the various ages, social, and income groups within the area it serves," which meant lower-cost "community rating" rather than "experience" rating based on local costs. Federally qualifying HMOs originally could "not expel or refuse to re-enroll any member because of his health status . . . at least one-third of the policymaking body [of the HMO] will be members . . . and there must be . . . equitable representation on such body of members from medically underserved populations served by the organization."

It is impossible to imagine today's giant HMOs, UHG, Aetna/U.S. Healthcare, or others of their ilk having such "equitable" representation on their corporate "policy-making" bodies, but then again, these insurers lost the incentive to be federally "qualified" long ago. They knew that even by exposing that their business was in interstate commerce, they did not need to worry about state regulation, and the federal administrative climate was reasonably friendly, because they were ostensibly "keeping healthcare costs low." Indeed, the Reagan administration's amendments to the HMO Act of 1988 made being federally qualified unnecessary as it removed the previously required employer contribution. By 1995, only 4 percent of all HMOs were federally qualified, although they accounted for 68 percent of total enrollment. The shameless repeal of the well-intentioned Carter administration's regulatory requirements by the Reagan and Bush I administrations gutted the original congressional intent for community input and allowed employers and HMOs—what was noted in the 1980s legislative history—the "additional flexibility they need in the ever-changing healthcare market place." According to a Senate Report to the 1987–89 100th Congress, the changes that were made to the HMO Act in 1988 effectively allowed an HMO to set up a

"non-federally qualified health benefit plan without undergoing the time and expense of establishing a separate corporation. . . [and allowed the entity to] engage in an activity outside the scope of the Act, such as offering fewer than the required level of benefits."

Further erosion took place as the 100th Congress allowed the breakdown of the low-cost advantages of community rating. It established a system of rating risk by age and sex, including such rate-manipulative factors as a "premium to be set for a specific group such as teachers in a school district" called "community rating by class," all of which would transform risk-spread costs into "list prices." This is the historical point where the original intent in building a meaningful extension of federal standards of healthcare to "maintain" the health of the community vaporized during the Reagan-Bush administrations and changed the HMO Act into a Wall Street feeding trough for the next twenty years.

In a 1979 federal Seventh Circuit Court of Appeals case, *St. John's Hickey Memorial Hospital, Inc. v. Califano*, the DHHS Secretary's authority under the Medicare Act was found by the Circuit Court to be significantly more circumscribed than the authority delegated in Social Security benefit cases. The appeals court found, nonetheless, that the regulations promulgated under the Medicare Act "must take into account both direct and indirect costs and must avoid the result of shifting costs to non-Medicare patients." In 1985, the same Seventh Circuit Court in *St. James Hospital v. Heckler*, quoted the lower court and affirmed this view:

> "When as here, the chosen method neither assures that Medicare costs will not be borne by non-Medicare patients nor that hospitals will be reimbursed the reasonable costs for their services . . . the regulation does not carry out the mandate of the Medicare statute and is invalid."

This dichotomy, Congress's explicit language prohibiting cost shifting to the private sector, contrasted with the reality of Medicare's costs inevitably shifted to nongovernmental payers by the government's cost-finding and reimbursement methodologies, would also accelerate and intensify the putative "soaring" costs of healthcare during the late 1980s and provide a socially accepted incentive for insurers to switch to managed-care models.

As expected, there was a small shift of healthier young people out of the indemnity insurance arena, which caused the premiums of those who remained in the insured pool to rise further. There was little growth of the HMO industry over the first fifteen years of the HMO Act, because few new HMOs could satisfy these extended-services, high-option requirements to qualify and remain solvent. The older HMOs, such as the Group Health Cooperative of Puget Sound, Kaiser-Permanente, the Harvard Community Health Plan and HIP of New York, seemed to have passed their solvency-test periods well before the cost-containment era began. Even that did not insulate Group Health and its five hundred thousand enrollees from managed-care's early market failure, and it was absorbed into Kaiser. After optimistically freezing premiums for the two years prior, the company had to raise premiums more than expected and stretch the nurse work force at the two hospitals it owned, switch some care to lower-paid workers, shorten hospital stays, and tighten pharmaceutical costs. *The Wall Street Journal* presciently reported in August 1998, "A rate war among health insurers has put a strain on Group Health's finances. It posted a $10.4 million loss last year on revenues of $1 billion, and it expects to be in the red this year, too." About a 1 percent loss on a billion dollars of cash flow does not seem to be too bad for a company that seeks only to fail and then be acquired for significant cash!

There is little evidence that the commercial business of healthcare insurance was ever really threatened by the HMO Act. In fact, the Act provided for commercial "stop-loss" insurance for losses over $5,000 in any year or for the cost of providing services rendered its members who could not use the HMO's facilities for some reason. It is also interesting to note that the HMO Act appears to be the first statute to coin the term "medical necessity," so diligently used today to support managed-care reviewers' decisions denying payment for care. In the original altruistic HMO language, this term was not used at all. On the contrary, a similar term "medically necessary" was used only in the context of payment in connection with emergency admissions, "when medically necessary twenty-four hours a day when services were obtained elsewhere before they could be provided by the organization, and for unforeseen illness, injury, or condition."

2. ERISA and Federal Preemption

Within one year after cost containment went from being a constraint on public health policy to becoming public health policy itself, and being eager to resolve the problems created by the multistate, motley variety of public and private pension and benefit plans left in the wake of the McCarran- Ferguson Act passed thirty years earlier, Congress passed the Employee Retirement Income Security Act or ERISA. Section 2 of the Act, "Congressional findings and declaration of policy," described the purpose of the Act. For our purposes, note that the words "employer" or "for help to employers" appear nowhere in the declaration of policy:

"Despite the enormous growth in such plans many employees with long years of employment are losing anticipated retirement benefits . . . owing to the inadequacy of current minimum standards, the soundness and stability of plans with respect to adequate funds to pay promised benefits may be endangered; that owing to the termination of plans before requisite funds have been accumulated, employees and their beneficiaries have been deprived of anticipated benefits; . . . that it is therefore desirable in the interests of the employees and their beneficiaries, for the protection of the revenue of the United States, and to provide for the free flow of commerce, that minimum standards be provided assuring the equitable character of such plans and their financial soundness [and] by establishing standards of conduct, responsibility, and obligation for fiduciaries of employee benefit plans, and by providing for appropriate remedies, sanctions, and ready access to the federal courts."

In fact, the act was so beneficiary-specific that any considerations for employers or sponsors in the statute are used in adjuring fiduciaries to act with prudence and diligence and in a section admonishing the "inurement" to an employer of any assets of the plans. The term "inure" is defined by several federal Circuit Courts of Appeals as meaning broadly to "become of advantage to the employer."

"Preemption" is a term that extends by "federal supremacy" the reach of the federal government to supersede state laws, a right given the federal government over the states by the Tenth Amendment to the Constitution. However, the Tenth Amendment protects states, too: "The powers not delegated to the United States by the Constitution, nor prohibited by it to the states, are reserved to the states respectively, or to the people," exempting church and state employees from the Act. ERISA is a statute that has both preemptive sections as well as sections that "save" for the states the right to maintain by state action laws and regulations of activities by their citizens that do not conflict with federal supremacy in that area.

Actions of the state itself are not subject to the Sherman Act, but the 1975 Supreme Court indicated in *Goldfarb v. Virginia State Bar* that state regulatory agencies, by virtue of their status alone, are not immune from the antitrust laws. State regulatory agencies, including licensing boards, may be exempt from antitrust laws by fulfilling the requirements of the "state action immunity doctrine," a doctrine created by the Supreme Court, which exempts from prosecution under the antitrust laws certain activities undertaken in specific areas where the state has decided to regulate. There, the state, rather than allow the marketplace to discipline economic actors, can consciously displace competition. For the state action doctrine to apply to competitors in cases where providers or citizens in the market for healthcare services sue corporations or licensing and regulatory boards on antitrust grounds, the state must not only have relevant, clearly articulated laws but must actively supervise those laws. The doctrine therefore creates a balance between states rights and national policies favoring competition.

To strengthen the ERISA mandate, Congress enacted a supersedure section that worked its way around McCarran-Ferguson's state-permitted regulation, federally preempting "all State laws insofar as they may now or hereafter relate to any employee benefit plan . . ." The federal Sixth Circuit Court of Appeals in *Thiokol Corporation, Morton International, Inc. v. Robert*, citing from a 1988 Supreme Court decision in *Fort Halifax*

Packing Company v. P. Daniel Coyne, Bureau of Labor Standards of Maine, et al., later construed this section in 1999 as follows:

> "Interpreting 'relates to' as being concerned with state laws' significant effect on covered plans serves Congress's purpose in enacting ERISA, *viz.* to avoid encouraging 'employers with existing plans to reduce benefits, [or] those without such plans to refrain from adopting them.'"

The decision left untouched the church and state employees' exemptions from ERISA. To preempt while not disturb "state laws' significant effect on covered plans" that regulated the "business of insurance," Congress "deemed" health and welfare benefit plans "noninsurance." Federal preemption has its good sides. In fact, in a 2009 article "Trends in Congressional Preemption" in *The Book of the States*, Joseph Zimmerman, professor of political science at Rockefeller College of the State University of New York at Albany, finds that George W. Bush signed 123 preemption bills into law from 2001 to 2008. Many of them related to "antiterrorism" needs, but others related to banking, commerce, energy, and finance, three acts relating to the jurisdiction of courts, thirty-seven to environmental protection, health, and safety ("partial-birth abortion"), and many other areas. He notes:

> "A partial preemption statute assumes one of five forms:
>
> States may lose their regulatory authority only in part of the field.
>
> A statute may include a savings clause stipulating a state law is not preempted 'unless there is a direct and positive conflict' between it and the concerned federal law.
>
> A statute may establish minimum regulatory standards and/or authorize a national department or agency to promulgate minimum standards.
>
> A statute may establish maximum regulatory standards in a specified field that may not be exceeded by states.
>
> Allowing a state to establish procedures [for example] to conduct background checks for drivers hauling hazardous materials that are more stringent than the federal procedures,

as long as there is a state appeals process similar to the federal one."

He concludes:

"Congress should give serious consideration to innovative preemption statutes preserving state powers to an extent while generally achieving harmonious regulations throughout the nation . . . In sum, changes in the global economy, inventions and technological innovations, as well as lobbying by business, civil rights, environmental, telecommunications and other interest groups will result in Congress continuously preempting completely or partially the regulatory powers of state and local governments unless state legislatures initiate additional actions to harmonize their regulatory laws and implementing administrative rules and regulations."

C. Phase Three: The Advent of the Managed-Care Industry—The Move from Indemnity to "list prices"

> "Price and competition are so intimately entwined that any discussion of theory must treat them as one. It is inconceivable that price could be controlled without power over competition or vice versa.
> — *United States v. E.I. du Pont de Nemours & Co* (1976)

As indemnity healthcare premiums began to rise during the inflationary mid-1970s, employers were sold "new products" by insurers. Among them were "experienced-rated contracts"—for those who were attempting to take their chances on the apparent good health of their employees—or "minimum-premium" policies, where employers paid only for administrative costs and actual claims made rather than those anticipated and which were to be covered by stop-loss insurance paid for by the employer or insurance company. It was self-insurance "lite." Health-insurance brokers also contacted small- to medium-sized businesses that had paid or partially paid for employees' health insurance and offered to find them lower-cost healthcare coverage, which would be "helped" by the offer of "managed care" endorsements. Medium-sized to large employers had to change their pension plans to ERISA-based pension and health and welfare benefit plans for their employees after the new law preempted state oversight. The benefit plans would have to be "self-insured" for ERISA to "deem" them "noninsurance"; however, that change made their cost-risk greater as it was being spread only over the individual company with price help from the "administrative services only" insurer's actuaries. In effect, employers were exchanging the potential premium price from a lower one based on widespread indemnity risk groups to one based on a narrowed-risk list price. The former insurers who were now providing Administrative Services Only (ASO) also arranged for them stop-loss insurance that further increased the costs (or partly reduced potential losses). At the same time, start-up managed-care organizations—some capitalized on public stock offerings—offered to significantly lower the potentially increased costs of self-insured plans by the use of "managed care," which promised to both "lower costs" and to "improve the quality of care."

After the enactment of ERISA, almost a decade passed before there was another significant change in the system of healthcare coverage. Until 1983, old and new HMO growth had made a very poor showing, and the development of employee health and welfare benefit plans was desultory. An important reason for this appears to have been the general economic climate. Soon after ERISA was enacted, the country entered a five-year period of inflation accompanied by interest rates exceeding 15 percent and high unemployment. Those in the insurance industry, long invested in real estate and other relatively stable funding vehicles, saw no reason to jeopardize cash flow in major untried ventures. The early years of the Reagan presidency were beset by two recessions. There was also a precipitous drop in interest rates, which made large real estate investment less attractive to cash flow needs. (They have a strong inverse relationship; it was uncertain for a real estate investment how much money would need to be currently invested, at a given rate of return, to yield the cash-flow needs of the future.) Meanwhile, the cost-shifting threat to the private insurance indemnity sector from the new Medicare Prospective Payment System threatened the profitability of the health insurance industry, because the DRGs portended paying "prices-per-illness." However, some in the industry saw the positive potential of being able to safely lower their payments to providers as long as they were doing their work under the aegis of a public policy of cost containment, mentioned earlier as the *Noerr* defense.

Incidental to this sea change was the major hysteria encountered in the early 1980s by the life and health insurance industry generated by news of a possible AIDS pandemic. Moreover, capital improvements were inevitably limited by the recession-caused diminution of contributions and endowments made to the largely nonprofit hospital industry, even though labor-intensive illness care remained stable. It is this capital- and labor-intensive stability of the healthcare sector, which makes its costs and prices seem to rise inappropriately out of proportion to the rest of the economy that politicians and pundits use to publicize the need to stop the "soaring cost of healthcare." While other more recession-volatile industries such as transportation and utilities are subject to major domestic and international pressures, healthcare as a stable sector of the economy has the appearance of inflating when compared to others as a percentage of the Gross Domestic Product (GDP). That is, if "transportation" as a percentage of the GDP is reduced, "healthcare" automatically rises, albeit with no change in actually incurred healthcare costs.

Knowing that the federal government was about to launch the new payment system for Medicare patients, health indemnity insurers had acted in lock step between 1983 and 1986 and, in concert, lowered their premiums, appearing to fit the recession competitively. During that same period, the insurance industry seized the moment presented by growing government cost-containment initiatives and joined the call to put an end to what they self-servingly called "soaring" healthcare costs. Because health insurance premium percentage increases were greater than benefit increases even before the federal Prospective Payment System (PPS) became effective, the only way for the claimed "soaring" healthcare costs of insurers to require higher premiums successfully after PPS started was for the insurers to lower premiums in those three years. Thus, both increases in benefits and the Consumer Price Index would appear as exceeding premium increases. That is exactly what happened, as shown by a Hay-Huggins report for the Healthcare Financing Administration. By 1986, reflecting shrinking insurance company portfolios that could not support selling risk-type indemnity insurance, all of the major health insurers raised indemnity premiums dramatically. By 1987, the insurance industry made up for their three years of "losses." Ironically, however, contemporaneous out-of-pocket costs of healthcare for consumers remained relatively flat until the insurance company premium data were combined with the slowly and subtly shifted increase in deductibles and copayments that rose starting in 2001.

The 1984 PPS did not "gear up" until 1986, whereupon the insurers acted boldly again, and private premiums began to soar. This was timed with the introduction of the "new system of managed care," the DRG, in hoped-for mimicry of the federal government's stabilizing prices-per-illness. Since health insurance benefits and the Consumer Price Index had remained essentially flat throughout the pre-PPS period, there appeared to be no reason for the enormous increases in 1987 other than to mimic the style and exceed government-established prices even though the DRGs were for treatment of the elderly and sicker, rather than the healthier, younger people in commercial plans. As we shall see, monopsonistic behavior typically controls output or sells below marginal cost to drive small competitors out of the system—then eventually prices rise. In this case, the commercial insurers were satisfied to act in concert to "support" the government's cost-containment efforts.

1. "Quality review": Myths and Truths—Mergers and the Use of Uniform Standards to Stabilize Prices

"We firmly believe that the quality of healthcare must not be reduced along with costs. Last year we saved our clients over $600 million through our medical cost containment programs. And that's in a year when national health spending *increased* dramatically. . . Our case management approach, for example, not only reduces costs, but can actually *improve* the quality of care."

—CIGNA advertisement: "Is This Next?"

"People used to feel that having private health insurance was necessary to ward off the dangerous costs of illness. Today, it's more likely that the danger comes from the costs of managed health insurance."

—Jack C. Schoenholtz

Managed-care review procedures of today are precisely the type of controls, which through private policy rules and regulations, were condemned by congressional proponents of the McCarran-Ferguson Act in 1945. Because of the ambiguous nature of ERISA preemption of any state laws that would "relate to" benefit plans—ERISA's deeming of benefit plans to be "noninsurance"—the courts were slow to develop the common law necessary to reify the new system, as was predicted by the Supreme Court in the *Pilot Life* and *Firestone* cases discussed in Chapter III. Because the insurance industry has much more success lobbying individual states, managed healthcare remained poorly and inconsistently state regulated until the privatization era intensified.

Psychiatric managed-care arrangements before the 2008 Parity Act were able to be somewhat different from general medical management because the typical benefit-plan contract with the patient for psychiatric services provided for "carved out" coverage tied to external monitoring of that care. This was performed by managed-care company doctors, nurses and social workers who were held out as "peers" and depicted as parties professionally equipped to evaluate psychotherapeutic care of other doctors' patients. However, the only clinical evidence for peer reviewers came from portions of medical records and telephone conversations with the patients' doctors. For hospitalized psychiatric patients, initial evaluations were almost exclusively performed by telephone by nurses or social workers taking up expensive clinical time from the patients' doctors. Managed care peer reviewers have no access to the most pertinent origin of the data—the patients, whom they cannot hear, see, examine, or observe. Moreover, few of the allied "peer" disciplines had appropriate psychiatric training to treat patients in psychiatric hospitals, and while each one has a specific scope of practice and training, licensed under individual state laws, none of the state-licensed training relates to "managing" care by telephone, and virtually all of it occurs across state lines.

Thus, it was managed care that blurred the distinctions of these disciplines, effectively pitting them against each other to compete for patients. What they did was, "de-skill" each of them, changing them from clinicians into reviewers in order to stabilize and ultimately lower costs for their employer/insurers and client employers' bottom line, at the patients' expense. By letter or telephone call, the MCO typically denies that it is involved in making decisions about payment for care. It is merely "verifying" the nature and medically necessary extent of treatment on behalf of the payer, whom they usually define as the employer or benefit plan, telling the treating doctors that they nonetheless remain responsible for patient care. The fact that the benefit is supposed to be for the beneficiary or plan participant and not the payer apparently got lost somewhere.

In 1983, Preferred Healthcare (PHC) of Wilton, Connecticut was one of the first new-era managed-care "carve out" companies in the country designed for the specific purpose of "managing" the delivery of mental healthcare. It was a good place to start, because providers of mental healthcare are by nature fine advocates for their patents but poor economic advocates for themselves. A PHC advertisement in a Health Opportunities section of *The New York Times* in 1990 sought "mental-health professionals (PhD, MSW, RN)," asking seductively: "Burned out? Frustrated? Need to use your clinical skills in a new setting? Do concurrent clinical reviews with primary therapists." The 1983 prospectus for PHC's initial public stock offering promised: "The Services to be rendered by the Company will not relate to direct patient care."

Because PHC's major cash flow came from a contract providing administrative services for a private psychiatric hospital, most of whose board members shared ownership in both companies, its peremptory telephone pressure for discharge of competitor hospitals' patients for lack of "medical necessity" seemed to them to make business sense. However, PHC had from its inception direct, day-to-day involvement in psychiatric treatment of its competitor hospitals' patients. Its president, Robert K. Lifton, was quoted in *Barron's*: "The Company actually has been able to save customers at least 30 percent of their healthcare costs, and it splits those savings with the employers." A corporate vice president of APM enthusiastically characterized the managed-care review process in 1988 as "it's like shooting ducks [sic] in a barrel. There's very little risk involved."

Note that "splitting those savings with the employers" amounted to a *de facto* wage cut for insured hospitalized patients. Because employees' indemnity insurance premiums they negotiated with their employers were supposed to make the insurance company assume the entire insurance risk, outsiders' interference with their doctors' treatment constituted a devaluation of the indemnification promise. Moreover, if the healthcare plan was one pursuant to ERISA protection, such inurement of the "self-insurance" or "minimum premium" money to the employer was expressly forbidden by law but nonetheless used and supported by fiduciary discretion.

The following example demonstrates the methodology of managed-care companies to fleece their own clients as well as the patient. In 1988, GTE Corporation revealed the statistics from the first year's operation of its managed-care program that covered fifteen thousand employees in the Los Angeles area. Using PHC as its "carve-out" company for mental health benefits, GTE published data demonstrating that while the reputed $3.6 million in savings was 26 percent below cost reductions "expected' for the period, and notwithstanding that "admissions" were up 15 percent and total "claimants" were up by 44 percent, "cost reductions were achieved." PHC's success was attributed by GTE's benefits manager to have resulted in

1. A 75 percent reduction in inpatient days.

2. A 30 percent reduction in cost per inpatient case.

3. A 41 percent reduction in average length of stay.

Such inpatient data reveals nothing other than the churning of patients through premature discharges and re-admissions. More "admissions" than before were approved by PHC care managers for hospitalization ("admissions up 15 percent"), and the employees' incidence of mental illness ("claimants up 44 percent") increased by GTE's decision to hire PHC to manage its mental healthcare benefits program. Both assumptions contradict what managed mental healthcare presumed to offer, yet aside from the inherent dishonesty of the system, it is also economically foolish. From a purely financial standpoint, because the first few days in hospital have the highest cost, the shorter hospital stay produces the greater cost per day both for the individual and for the aggregate, ultimately raising costs for all. However, managed-care companies did not need to tell that to their corporate clients, because they would both benefit from the short-term cash flow they "split" with each other. In any event, impressed by PHC's cost-reduction style, GTE eagerly signed PHC to cover its Tampa, Florida operation.

Another example of managed-care's aggressive style of "improving" the quality of care came from Empire Blue Cross/Blue Shield of New York in an August 22, 1992 letter and an enclosure to New York subscribers that stated:

"Empire Blue Cross and Blue Shield is committed to enhancing the quality of your healthcare and helping you avoid the risks of unnecessary surgical procedures . . . Empire Expert Review will apply the collective medical knowledge of leading physicians—and the expertise these doctors would use if they

were consulting with you and your physician about your case.
[For procedures] subject to Empire Expert Review . . . you will
be referred to a specially trained nurse reviewer."

The collective medical knowledge of leading physicians" as used by
a "specially trained nurse" indicated that only textbook learning and
computer-based algorithms were being used, not clinical practice. The
enclosure's small print, however, exposed the coercive and intimidating
reviewer-appeals process: "Failure to call Managed Benefits will result
in a reduction of benefits, as indicated in your contract, even if upon
later review the procedure is deemed appropriate."

The following is a short list of how managed-care firms and their
board members meandered dizzyingly into the business of health insurance companies and the hospital industry, incurring losses along the
way.

After several years of operation, PHC was acquired during the mid-
1980s by its largest competitor, American PsychManagement (APM)
and then acquired by Value Behavioral Health, Inc. and its parent,
Value Health, Inc., owned by the hospital chain, Columbia/HCA, Inc.
Among the five members of the board of directors of subsidiary Value
Health, Inc. were Walter J. McNerney (who until 1981 was president
and chief executive officer of the Blue Cross and Blue Shield Associations, and known as a promoter of ending the exclusions by commercial
insurers of pre-existing illnesses), and Rodman W. Moorhead, III, who
was at the same time also a director of Coventry Healthcare Inc., a
competitor of its parent Columbia/HCA, Inc. The other three directors
were a vice chairman of the venture capital firm, Warburg Pincus, LLP,
a director and legal counsel of one of Washington D.C.'s largest lobbying firms, and the former chairman and CEO of Avon Products, Inc.

In 1998, Coventry merged with PHC and moved its headquarters
to Bethesda, Maryland, from Nashville, Tennessee, the home of HCA.
PHC then made several mergers and was itself acquired by First American Group for $4.3 million cash in 1998. First American Group was
the holding company for a number of managed care ventures including
American Healthcare Providers, Inc., DBA American HMO, one of the

longest-serving HMOs in Illinois. PHC of Florida Inc. was then sold to Blue Cross Blue Shield of Florida, Inc. for $95 million in cash. In addition, in December 1998, Coventry acquired Healthcare America Plans, Inc., which then merged with the operations of PHC of Kansas City, Inc. For the year, Coventry had generated more than $2.1 billion in revenues though netting an income loss of $11.7 million.

By 1997, Columbia/HCA had become the world's largest health-care provider with more than 340 hospitals, 130 surgery centers, and 550 home health locations in thirty-eight states and two foreign countries. In August 2010, *Bloomberg BusinessWeek* reported that since 1997 Value Health, Inc. had been a subsidiary of Columbia/HCA, Inc. By 2010, notwithstanding such enormous cash flow, bonds of HCA and Tenet Healthcare, among many others of their ilk, were rated as junk. Despite the rating, zealous Wall Street bulls' juices began to flow once more as Community Health Systems announced on December 9 a $3.3 billion unsolicited offer for its smaller rival, Tenet Healthcare, "hoping to seize upon the Obama administration's overhaul of healthcare to create a new hospital giant," as reported by *The New York Times*. Such a combination would allow Community Health Systems' 176 hospitals to overtake the 150 privately held by HCA. Community Health Systems had struck seventeen such deals since 2006.

Following the lead of PHC's originating style in commendably elegant fashion, the now much larger managed-care progeny, Value Behavioral Health, Inc., could "manage" the length of stay and cash flow generated by a patient's hospital stay for its parent to the disadvantage of its rivals' patients. Recall that the length of a "managed" hospital stay is inversely proportional to the revenue it generates, the reason for readmission, and its cost. In 2001, the DOJ settled with HCA the largest fraud case in U.S. history, netting a record total of $1.7 billion for fourteen felonies committed by the company. Richard L. Scott, whose tenure as CEO of HCA spanned the years of the DOJ's felony investigation, resigned in 1997 nine days after the FBI raided thirty-three Columbia/HCA hospitals and offices in six states. Between 2005 and 2006, Scott provided the initial round of funding of $3 million to Alijor.com, which offered hospitals, physicians, and other healthcare providers the opportunity to post information about their prices, hours, locations, types of insurance accepted, and personal backgrounds online, and it was sold in 2008 to Health Grades, Inc. In February 2011, the *Orlando Sentinel* reported that "Rick" Scott ran on the Republican Party and won as governor of Florida after he spent $85 million to get elected, including more than $73 million of his own family's money. By March 13, *The Palm Beach Post* reported that, in January, the new governor had transferred all stock he owned in thirty-two urgent care clinics, worth $62 million, to his wife, in the "Frances Annette Scott Revocable Trust."

This did not put an end to the media's interest in the new governor. Two weeks later, *The Palm Beach Post* reported that Mr. Scott issued an executive order for "mandatory drug testing for all prospective hires, and random drug testing of current employees in agencies whose directors he appoints." In 2004, the random drug testing was found to be unconstitutional in Florida by federal U.S. District Judge Robert Hinkle. In that case, a Florida employee refused to comply, claiming it violated his civil rights, and the state ended up paying the employee $150,000. In the same announcement for all "new hires," he praised the Florida Legislature for its "plans to require all welfare applicants to undergo drug testing as well." Apparently, "the legislature tried a North Florida pilot program in 1998, which found that fewer than 4 percent of the 8,797 welfare applicants who were drug tested came back positive. The program cost the state $2.7 million, which worked out to about $90 per test." The governor's clinics at the time charged only $35 per test. As they are Medicaid applicants, those seeking help will have to pay out of pocket wherever they go for their testing. In any event, according to the newspaper report, the governor's clinics do not take Medicaid patients unless they are in a "private Medicaid HMO" program.

According to the March 29 edition of *The Palm Beach Post*, Governor Scott was reported to be promoting legislation to reverse a drug-monitoring database that was authorized by Florida law in 2009, having said that the database was an intrusion on privacy and should be "squashed before it begins working." The next day, the paper reported that proposals in the state's House and Senate would "put most of the state's 2.9 million Medicaid patients into managed care [divide] the state into regions and allow managed care plans to operate each region." In addition, *The New York Times* of April 2011, reported that Governor Scott promoted a state Senate bill that would require "almost all of Florida's Medicaid recipients into state authorized, for-profit HMOs or networks run by hospitals or doctors [which would then shift the elderly] away from nursing homes and leading to an expansion of in-home care." By October 2011, it was reported that almost 1,600 people applying for welfare benefits in Florida declined to undergo drug testing, which is required by the new state law. According to state officials, less than one percent of the 7,028 welfare applicants who underwent screening tested positive for drugs since the law went into effect in July The American Civil Liberties Union filed a lawsuit to challenge the new law. The lawsuit asserts the law's drug-testing requirement represents an unconstitutional search and seizure. Although Florida is one of a growing number of states requiring drug testing for recipients of welfare, food stamps, unemployment and other benefits. Legislators in three dozen states have proposed drug testing laws for people who receive welfare benefits.

Many states have hybrid Medicaid systems that mix capitated HMOs, primary care case management and prepaid plans that cover certain health services, such as hospital or mental health care. About 70% of Medicaid enrollees in 2008 received at least some services through managed care plans, according to a February 2010 report by the Kaiser Family Foundation. While many state governors applaud the move to privatize Medicaid, it became clear that there is "no free lunch" and that shifting around some budget items often ends up more costly.

Illinois is implementing a managed care expansion that was signed into law in January. It requires the state to expand a capitated-care coordination program to more than 50% of its Medicaid enrollees by 2015. As reported in the June 6 2011 *American Medical News*, though the state estimates that the move will account for the bulk of more than $600 million in projected savings over five years, the Illinois State Medical

Society opposed the legislation in part because it will allow some of the state's limited Medicaid resources to be diverted to private-plan profits and administrative costs. Some of the privatizing appears to have been made by insurers and MCOs in anticipation of the Affordable Care Act: The legislation will take effect before physicians and hospitals can form accountable care organizations that might compete with private HMOs in order to provide Medicaid care coordination.

The National Committee for Quality Assurance (NCQA) and America's Health Insurance Plans (AHIP) are trade associations undertaking to help reduce the prices of healthcare providers on behalf of their clients in the ERISA-based self-insured insurance industry. Indemnity insurance companies were previously concerned only with paying the subscriber's debt to a healthcare provider based on "proof of loss." However, along with help from government and media enthusiasm, insurers have converted the meaning of that phrase into "lowering the costs of patient care." Though most of the NCQA and AHIP members aver that they do not serve patients directly but only "manage" those that do, they behave as if they are the providers of that care. Furthermore, conflicts of interest distinguish them from regulatory agencies, organizations like the Joint Commission on Accreditation of Hospitals and state licensing departments. The NCQA and AHIP boards of directors' interests are driven primarily by the profit motives of nonpatient purchasers of care, the employer/sponsors and sponsor-supported fiduciaries of employee benefit plans.

Have aggregate costs of providing healthcare been cut by managed care? Has the advent of managed care even slowed the growth of healthcare costs relative to technological expansion and the population? A comparison between national healthcare expenditures as a percentage of the GDP in relation to population growth reveals that nothing of the sort has occurred. From 1960 to 1990, there was a significant rise in the total cost of healthcare, which did not differ from the proportionate increase in the population. From 1990 to 1996, the relative cost of healthcare, coinciding with the accelerating expansion of managed care, leveled off in virtually the same proportion as population growth. Nevertheless, an examination of the average annual out-of-pocket expenditures by consumer units for healthcare from 1980 to 1995 reveals that while total expenditures by consumers increased 137 percent from $730 to $1,732, the amount spent for health-insurance premiums rose four-fold in the same period!

As individuals grow older, their costs for healthcare increase as a percent of their total living expenditures. Between 1985 and 1995, costs for the sixty-five to seventy-four age group increased from 9.1 to a 10.3 percent, an average increase of 13 percent; and in the seventy-five-and-over group, the average costs went from 12.2 to 14.4 percent of their total expenditures, an increase of 18 percent. However, the same over-sixty-five population grouping, if expanded to include those over age eighty-five, grew from 28,536 million in 1985 to 33,544 million by 1995, an increase of just under 18 percent, although another indication that it was not their costs that had risen, only the expended aggregate dollars of coverage.

The aggregate healthcare costs rose, forced upward by insurance companies that mimicked the Medicare Prospective Payment System's cost-containment scheme, but the cost containment measures only lower providers' fees-per-patient unit, not the income to the insurance industry or total costs to society. In addition, insurance is a cash-flow business with premiums paid in advance, so any net cost reduction remains in the insurers' coffers as profit. Healthcare insurance companies do not routinely return the "unused" part of a premium or even use its possible presence to lower the next year's rates. Moreover, insurance policy services are incidence- and prevalence-based anticipation prices; that is, actuaries cannot legitimately predict the effect of cost-containment efforts on premiums, only on policy limits. The market failure of managed care once again reveals itself, as the premium prices charged do not reasonably reflect the premium costs or the promised benefits of consuming the service offered. The managed-care structure assures only that, barring epidemics, the premium price will exceed the cost. The reason the 2010 ACA sets up MLRs—the ratio of total losses paid out in claims and adjustment expenses divided by the total "earned" (collected) premiums—is that insurance companies spend a more-than-substantial portion of consumers' premium dollars on the managed-care share of administrative costs.

From their own data, the insurance industry administrative expenses and profits went from 18 percent in 1980 to 22 percent in 1994 (in dollars, from $10.7 billion to $23 billion). This reveals only the money directly attributable to earned premiums. It does not include any income earned from investment of the premium money elsewhere, the real currency of the insurance industry. Recall that most healthcare indemnity insurers' profitability is a function of its investment portfolio, not from actuarial accuracy or sharp underwriting. Because premiums are collected before claims are made, only the risk portion unprotected by retention, such as deductibles and copayments, which includes the cost of reinsurance, encumbers their investment. The cash flow provided from that "float" period is the amount of money at hand at any given moment that an insurer has collected in premiums but has not paid out in claims or occurrences.

This "exposure" is where the greatest profitability lies with indemnity insurers, but with managed care, large portions of the float can be taken out of the healthcare system as profits, being insulated by the take-back of premium-promised benefits. With managed care's entrance into the insurance industry, there was no longer an incentive to contain healthcare costs based on occurrences, only to reduce the price per occurrence. The increased rate of occurrences, the readmissions for care, and the growing subacute population, characterize the market failure of the managed-care insurance industry. Simply put—more occurrences, more cash flow.

The newly expanding service-industry economy, triggered by the two Reagan recessions of 1982 to 1984, overtook the size of the manufacturing sector, and the small businesses and service industries that subsequently hired those unemployed had no or little coverage to offer, leaving a growing number of uninsured to enter the insurance industry larder for all or parts of the year. By 1998, notwithstanding twelve million new jobs created in the Clinton era, the uninsured or partly insured population reached over forty million, which resulted in keeping coverage scarcity intact and narrowed-risk premium prices artificially high. By 2011, there were 50 million uninsured.

2. More Myths and Truths of Healthcare Costs—The Catastrophic Coverage Act and FASB 106

Although in July 1998 the National Center on Health Statistics reported an all-time high in life expectancy of 76.1 years, it cautioned that those in poverty and having less education continued to die sooner and suffer more often from virtually every health problem. In fact, the average life expectancy for black men and women over age sixty-five in 2001 was equal to white men and women over age sixty-five in 1979 to 1981, a twenty-year lag. If managed care was to have had a positive effect on America's healthcare, its goal of "improving quality while lowering costs" did not have that effect on the country's largest economically disadvantaged population.

During the 1980s, there was an outpouring of concern over the apparent holes in the misallocated system of healthcare. Underserved areas, a growing uninsured population, and the need for coverage for catastrophic illnesses became evident. By 1987, with the elderly lobby led by the AARP pressing for remedial legislation, Congress was ready to pass a "catastrophic coverage" act. Where the money was to come from was hurriedly and briefly discussed in committee testimony, but because a presidential election year loomed, the bipartisan consensus had to be done right away. Effective July 1, 1988, the Medicare Catastrophic Coverage Act was put in place.

As if in anticipation of the downside of its new actuarial dimensions, Medicare premiums in January 1988 rose 38.5 percent. Unfortunately, in January 1989, the new act imposed higher annual premiums and deductibles only on those eligible for the coverage instead of on all who paid into Social Security. In effect, this placed a surtax solely on the beneficiaries, the direct opposite of risk spreading, crafting a benighted marriage with the "moral hazard." The approach unnerved those who had lobbied for it, as it was diametrically opposed to the methodology maintained by the parent Social Security trust fund, which planned for future generations. Not surprisingly, that same year the nonprofit Blue Cross/Blue Shield (BCBS) was able to halve its $2 billion deficit as the

Catastrophic Coverage Act relieved it of much of its previous actuarial burden, and in the fourth quarter of 1989, the major commercial insurers reported their highest earnings in memory. These profits were due to copycat Medicare premium increases of 10 to 35 percent in 1988 and 20 to 35 percent in the first quarter of 1989.

Now that the elderly were protected by low-cost government coverage formerly provided by "major medical" carriers, the commercial companies could reap the advantage gained by the lower costs of the younger, healthier risk population. Nevertheless, *American Hospital Association News* reported that the companies offered an incomprehensible excuse that the increases were merely an attempt to cover the loss of premium income from the government-structured shift of the elderly insured away from commercial coverage. Even though the shift of the elderly to Medicare catastrophic coverage left behind a younger and healthier insured population that reduced insurer risk, their boosting of premiums confirmed that indemnity risk insurance needed a wide base if premiums were to be competitive. Considering that the elderly group cost unpredictably much more per commercial subscriber, it had to be that more cash flow and not "cost" was the reason for the increases.

At that point, the insurance price increases outpaced medical inflation, which had not exceeded 7 percent in each of the prior four years. Nonetheless, the increases led to the corporate exploitation of managed care's ability to save on "costs" to generate greater income at the expense of both the government and the insured. Sadly, the Catastrophic Coverage Act (CCA)—which gave greatly expanded coverage to disabled and elderly Social Security beneficiaries, after gliding through congressional hearings and signed by President Reagan in time to stimulate George H. W. Bush's 1988 election—was repealed a year later after even fewer hearings on the subject. It was no surprise to some when reported that the Catastrophic Coverage Act had to be repealed in response to protests by the vocal elderly lobby, disappointed that they had been asked to shoulder the entire burden of financing it.

A major contribution to this twisting of our already troubled healthcare system, after more than a decade of deliberations, was the 1990 Rule 106 of the nongovernmental Financial Accounting Standards Board (FASB). FAS Rule 106—Employers' Accounting for Postretirement Benefits Other Than Pensions—required employers to accrue the cost of retiree health and other postretirement benefits. The professed purpose of the rule was to bring companies to their truer valuations starting in 1993 and was to continue for the next twenty years by requiring companies to accrue on their balance sheet healthcare obligations to retirees that had accumulated since 1965 when Medicare began. Anticipation of FAS Rule 106, designed to account for those obligations of coverage to retired workers in their benefit plans, spurred the need for charges against corporate income, offering consequent potential tax write-downs in the hundreds of billions of dollars. In prior years, corporations had generally not recorded a liability for these anticipated benefit payments, with most large-group employers using a tax-deductible, pay-as-you-go structure, expensing the costs on the income statement rather than accruing the amount attributable to benefits paid each year. To have accrued it, an actuarial estimate would have to have been made of the liability over the expected lives of the retirees.

The A. Foster Higgins consulting firm published a Retiree Healthcare Survey in 1991 relative to Rule 106, with nearly half of the Fortune 500 companies participating, as well as forty-eight state governments, and made the following helpful suggestion to related employers:

"Case Study: Managing FAS 106 Liability. . .

PROBLEM: Under pay-as-you-go accounting, the utility's annual retiree medical expense—$10 million—was affordable, equal to approximately 3 percent of payroll. Under FAS 106, however, it increased seven times—to $70 million for 1993.

RESULTS: With the new design, management met most of its objectives: Tax-deductible funding: Initially, the funding plan will allow for tax-deductible contributions of about 65 percent of combined FAS 106 and FAS 87 [Employers' Accounting For Pensions] expense; ultimately, the entire expense should be deductible. Implementing these changes led to other gains. Although developed in response to FAS 106, the managed care programs for retirees under age 65 will be provided to active employees as well, resulting in additional savings of $5 million per year."

It is ironic that while A. Foster Higgins apparently knew the cost-saving value of including the entire universe of beneficiaries in any accrual for future benefits, Congress did not appear to consider that spreading the risk of the CCA costs by charging all taxpayers proportionately less for it would have helped to maintain a viable catastrophic coverage system. The bipartisan nature of the repeal vote, plus being signed by President Reagan, virtually guaranteed the election of George H.W. Bush.

FAS 106 recognized that some companies had more retirees than active workers and some male retirees were marrying younger women and increasing the size of families that would have to be covered by the plans. Indeed, aggressively unleashing FAS 106 might pose a threat to companies' stock prices, earnings per share and bond ratings. Banks were concerned at first; they had been lending money to companies based on their now-seen-as-overstated valuations and would have to try to renegotiate the loans. The fact that these charges against corporate income could amount to corporate devaluations, revealing that the companies that had not accrued the liability were overvalued, caused anxiety among some corporate board members. However, since retiree costs are independent of current operations, sophisticated lenders realized that production decisions ought not to be affected by such costs.

Retiree healthcare costs—like pension costs—affect profit "margins," not profit rates. Profit margin is a ratio of profitability calculated as net income divided by revenues or net profits divided by sales. In 1991, a *Study Project on Healthcare Reform and American Competitiveness*, by the Wharton School of the University of Pennsylvania, indicated that "very few instances have been found other than where retiree health costs would not be expected to fall entirely on capital." The FASB had found, however, that because of the unpredictability of self-insured healthcare costs, there may also be an effect on profit rates, especially since most corporations did not break out retiree healthcare costs from those of active employees. Thus, the burgeoning commercial managed care became more attractive; it offset the effect on current operations of unconstrained, active employees' potential healthcare costs rather than keep the earlier high-cost, experience-rated indemnity contracts.

The Wharton study indicated:

"If retiree costs take the form of defined future contributions, the equity market will quickly respond by adjusting stock prices until expected profit rates return to the market level. Thus, shareholders take a one-time loss, but there is no continuing impact on firm operations. If, on the other hand, retiree healthcare costs take the form of defined benefits, a similar effect occurs as soon as the market recognizes the magnitude of future liabilities. In either case, profit levels decline but profit rates are unaffected."

The threat of less corporate profit meant less government revenue, so if Congress and the Reagan administration in election year 1988 could respond to the persistent clamor of the powerful Medicare lobby, give the retired elderly expanded benefits paid for by themselves and at the same time relieve corporate America and the commercial insurance industry of potentially trillions of dollars in healthcare liabilities, what elegant political parsimony that would be. Even though the act originally required employers' "maintenance of effort," that is, adding new benefits to employees' plans, neither the DOL nor Treasury could envision policing such a phenomenon. Thus, a combination of the Catastrophic Coverage Act and FAS Rule 106 heralded that corporations would not have to be revalued downward, that there would be no rocking of the stock market, however temporary, and that a legitimate social objective would appear to have been achieved all around. Certainly, in the upcoming election, a Democratic Congress and a Republican president could both expect clear sailing.

Barely noticed by the press and most shareholders, several large corporations began quietly phasing in the new rule in 1989, significantly in advance of its mandatory date. However, with the repeal of the Catastrophic Coverage Act, the pressure on employers to fund their retirees' healthcare coverage increased again, and some employers terminated their benefit plans entirely. Taking advantage of the Bush I era recession of 1991, more major corporations began taking Rule 106 charges against income. General Electric, for example, took a $1.8 billion charge against income for retirees' benefits that year and set a projected annual reserve accrual of $279 million. IBM took a $2.25 billion one-time charge and set its actuarially based accrual at just under $400 million a year. Smaller firms ordinarily do not have the flexibility to revalue themselves by major funding charges, so by late 1991, only 41 percent of nongovernment employers had determined their Rule 106 liability, with 57 percent saying they would await 1993. As of 1991, 90 percent of employers still did not prefund retiree benefits and continued to use a pay-as-you-go plan.

The Wharton School study exposed more myths:

"The effect of rising health benefit costs on total compensation, and thus on prices and trade flows, is positive and significant but quite small in magnitude. For example, U.S. import volume during the 1980s increased by 125 percent, but only 0.14 percent could be explained by health benefit cost growth. Likewise, during this period, U.S. export volume increased by 75 percent, although health benefit cost exerted a negative influence of 0.16 percent. It is therefore not clear from this research that employer-paid health benefit costs, by themselves, have materially harmed the competitiveness of U.S. industry in aggregate."

Such write-offs reduce government revenue by the amount of taxes that these corporations would otherwise have had to pay to offset the revenue loss, as with the sale of assets in the half-trillion-dollar savings and loan crisis in the late 1980s, so the money to make up for the hit on the Treasury would have to come either from a greater reduction in government spending or an increase in taxes. What actually happened and partially saved the economy was an *increase* in government spending accompanied by an *increase* in taxes. *The New York Times* reported in July 1996, "The General Accounting Office today released the costs of the savings and loan bailout as being $500 billion, including more than

$130 billion from taxpayers." That the vast majority of American businesses did not prefund their employees' healthcare in plans containing postretirement benefits illustrated that such benefits were not employer largesse but benefits fought for and won by employees in negotiations over many years. Eroding benefits further or forcing increased deductibles and co-payments on beneficiaries' amounts only to *de facto* wage decreases, as they narrow the coverage risk, defeats the insurance value and sullies the concept of fiduciary trust and contractual responsibility.

Providing healthcare to under-served groups and areas of the country had long been a problem for health planners. Before the Bush II administration, Medicare and Medicaid had done much to fill gaps in allocation of healthcare primarily directed at supporting the doctor-patient relationship. By attempting to keep the managed care groups at arm's length, that is, outside the "business of insurance," such price-stabilizing arrangements were expected to insulate the insurance companies from federal antitrust scrutiny. In the first eight post-Millennium years managed care was enabled to interpose itself between the patient's illness and the doctor with "capitation," insurance-companies' acquiring MCOs, and the Medicare and Medicaid programs moving in a privatizing direction, along with M+C, MA, and Managed Medicaid.

The healthcare insurance companies used complex financial relationships with multiple intermediaries, from general managed-care entities to psychiatric and substance abuse disorder "carve-out" organizations. From an economic standpoint, it is a myth that patchwork reduction of healthcare costs offers a social good or enhances competition, as some pundits would offer to explain the "efficiencies" of managed care. Such corporate-reduced healthcare costs are passed on to consumers and providers solely as healthcare debt, creating a circular process. Since debt always has a chilling effect on consumer spending, saving on society's healthcare costs does not produce significant price reductions, nor does it have a net positive effect on competition. What reductions in healthcare spending do accomplish is solely a return to corporations of income formerly earmarked for employees' fringe benefits based on health need, which proportionately reduces the amount of healthcare, thus damaging the health of the nation.

Managed care is also a market failure because it has not demonstrated any redeeming clinical advantages for the patient population over the fee-for-service or group-physician system, because ultimately, all patient illnesses receive treatment from physicians one doctor at a time, notwithstanding how many managers, consultants, or ancillary personnel are involved. The managed-care telephone-reviewer phantoms and the costly reviewers-from-a-distance are furnishing more evidence that they are the most significant part of the "waste, fraud, and abuse" so often blamed on the medical profession in past years. Because the core business of providing public and private healthcare is disrupted by the externalities of insurance companies who joined the governmental monopsony of market-power price fixing, along with the emboldened post-Millennium addition of managed-care activities to control output of Medicare and Medicaid, the healthcare market failure intensified.

III. The Availability
of Federal Antitrust Law

A. The Supreme Court's *Pilot Life, Firestone,* and *Travelers* Cases

For our purposes, the major significance of the 1989 Supreme Court case, *Firestone Tire & Rubber Co. v. Bruch,* was that it gave the employer, as a plan fiduciary, the discretion to decide not to pay for treatment if a claim is deemed by an MCO or insurer-turned-administrator to not be covered by the ERISA plan document. In *New York State Conference of Blue Cross/Blue Shield Plans v. Travelers Insurance Co.,* Associate Justice David Hackett Souter, writing for a unanimous 1995 Supreme Court, held that "the historic police powers of the states were not to be superseded by the federal act unless that was the clear and manifest purpose of Congress." *Travelers* also noted, however, that the Supreme Court has repeatedly held that ERISA *does* preempt "state laws that mandate employee benefit structures or their administration." However, as the 1996 Fifth Circuit Court of Appeals said, in *CIGNA Health Plan of Louisiana, Inc.; Connecticut General Life Insurance Co. v. State of Louisiana*:

"ERISA preemption is not without limits. The Supreme Court has cautioned that 'Some state actions may affect employee benefit plans in too tenuous, remote, or peripheral a manner to warrant a finding that the law 'relates to' the plan. [The unanimous Supreme Court] held in this regard that ERISA does not preempt state laws that have 'only an indirect economic effect on the relative costs of various health insurance packages' available to ERISA-qualified plans. ERISA itself contains provisions

61

which limit the scope of preemption . . . it is relevant that under [the savings clause] of ERISA, preemption stops short of 'any law of any State which regulates insurance.'"

In *Firestone Tire & Rubber Co. v. Bruch*, the Supreme Court cited from a 1987 case *Pilot Life Ins. Co. v. Dedeaux*:
"ERISA abounds with the language and terminology of trust law . . . Given [the statutory definitions and legislative language and] history, we have held that courts are to develop a 'federal common law of rights and obligations under ERISA-regulated plans.'"

The admonishment for the courts to do so has barely surfaced. The High Court determined that a plan administrator could reduce benefits virtually at will as long as it assumed discretionary responsibility and its act were found to be neither arbitrary nor capricious. The *Firestone* Court, finding no evidence under the Firestone company termination pay plan that the "administrator has the power to construe uncertain terms," only decided that a *de novo*, not deferential standard of review, should be used.

ERISA was found to have an unclear methodology for a civil action challenge to denial of benefits, so the High Court was left with the role of construing the relevant section as lower courts had begun to adopt the "arbitrary and capricious" standard of the 1947 Labor Management Relations Act (LMRA). Just three years earlier than *Pilot Life*, in *Chevron U.S.A. v. Natural Resources Defense Council*, the Court had explored the deferential standard in a case unrelated to a healthcare plan fiduciary:
"In these cases the Administrator's interpretation represents a reasonable accommodation of manifestly competing interests and is entitled to deference . . . the regulatory scheme is technical and complex, the agency considered the matter in a detailed and reasoned fashion, and the decision involves reconciling conflicting policies."

Firestone temporized, "In light of ERISA's failure to provide an appropriate standard of review for that section [the LMRA standard] should not be imported into ERISA on a wholesale basis." Nonetheless, the Court therefore effectively accorded a civilian, a commercial health plan administrator, with the same power of judicial scrutiny a governmental agency official receives simply because the plan administrator accepted discretionary responsibility. For one thing, the *Chevron* Court was quite clear that an administrative agency has to determine conflicting issues within the context of adjudicating "technical and complex" governmental schemes, but granting such deference to for-profit corporate ERISA-plan administrators is quite another. In 2008, in *Metropolitan Life Insurance Co. v. Glenn*, Associate Supreme Court Justice Breyer, attempting to reach consensus for a majority in which Chief Justice Roberts found himself, parsed the standards more moderately regarding "the lion's share of ERISA plan claims denials" being made by administrators that both evaluate and pay claims:

". . . a reviewing court should consider that conflict as a factor in determining whether the plan administrator has abused its discretion in denying benefits; and that the significance of the factor will depend upon the circumstances of the particular case. . . . The conflict of interest at issue here, for example, should prove more important (perhaps of great importance) where circumstances suggest a higher likelihood that it affected the benefits decision, including, but not limited to, cases where an insurance company administrator has a history of biased claims administration."

Based on this statement, it was therefore important that a standard of "intermediate" or "heightened" judicial scrutiny be considered for such disputes, not simply assuming that the plan administrator's decision was entitled to deference for the "good of the plan" unless found to be arbitrary and capricious. After all, Congress had made a plenary decision for the states to strictly regulate the business of insurance more than fifty years earlier in McCarran-Ferguson. Although Medicare is now considered to not be an insurance program, the eligible participants still are beneficiaries in the true sense, because they paid into the program by payroll deductions put into a government-run trust, and the program furthers an important governmental interest as well. ERISA plans are not employer largesse, and employee participants are self-paid-in beneficiaries. This is especially so, because they will still have Medicare as a secondary payer of their corporate plan after retirement.

Nonetheless, in 2008, the *Chevron* and *Firestone* administrative review processes were similarly rewoven by the High Court. The Bush II administration used them to make contracts with giant commercial insurers like WellPoint to review Medicare claims, instituting lengthy, self-serving appeals procedures that had to be navigated before an aggrieved beneficiary or provider could reach the bench of an administrative law judge. Some courts have held Medicare's appeals processes distinctly separate from other types of claims' actions because Congress built in an appeals process for Medicare such as the Provider Reimbursement Review Board. The fact that many employees and their families have both ERISA coverage at work and Medicare as a secondary payer should remind us that the original purpose of ERISA was to end the variegated multistate pension and welfare laws; albeit a necessary part of any legislation, it was not to increase the complexity of an appeals process.

For years, an issue remained problematic for the courts: is a plan administrator who incorrectly interprets a plan document still entitled to an abuse of discretion standard of review when courts review the administrator's actions? The activist judicial style, if not callous indifference, to employees' rights under ERISA by the conservatives on the post-Millennium High Court, was confirmed in April 2010 in *Conkright v. Frommert*. Chief Justice Roberts, this time writing for a conservative majority, took advantage of Justice Breyer's consensus view of "where circumstances suggest a higher likelihood that [the administrator's conflict of interest] affected the benefits decision," and pushed back at employees' rights even further. He said:

"People make mistakes. Even administrators of ERISA plans . . . The question here is whether a single honest mistake in plan interpretation justifies stripping the administrator of that deference for subsequent related interpretations of the plan. We hold that it does not."

Writing for the minority, Associate Justice Breyer replied,

"I agree with the Court that 'people make mistakes,' but I do not share its view of the law applicable to those mistakes. To explain my view, I shall describe the three significant mistakes involved in this case."

Justice Breyer did, at some length. He opined that the Chief Justice's loose language about allowing "one honest mistake" to a plan administrator reached a new height for deference to the boss's agent, because ERISA admonishes even mistakes of fact if they result in "inurement of plan assets" to the employer. When Congress federalized the patchwork quilt of state pension and welfare benefit laws with ERISA, it was not written primarily for the good of plans and certainly not for corporate plan administrators but for the good of plan participants and beneficiaries. As we noted earlier, the "Congressional findings and declaration of policy" in section 2 of ERISA makes it clear that employers' rights were not considered by Congress. Thus, it is wrong when benefits are reduced or copayments and deductibles are inappropriately raised, unless they are conceded to be *de facto* wage decreases for the participants, change the value of plan benefits, and inure employees' plan assets to the employer. That such negative revisions in congressional intent by the courts as have appeared during the investiture of managed care do not seem to have been specifically contemplated by Congress, or embraced by the judiciary as a by-product of ERISA's enactment, is rarely explicated or construed in judicial decisions or pundit or media analyses. Nonetheless, issues concerning the "quality" of such benefits have increasingly become actionable under state common law and not deemed preempted by ERISA, ironically creating a two-class system for similarly situated people whose benefits are also covered under state insurance law.

In the famous 1992 "tobacco" case, *Cipollone v. Liggett Group, Inc.,* the majority opinion of the High Court expressed two presumptions about the nature of preemption when it analyzed the distinction between specific preemption language in section 5(b) of the 1965 Federal Cigarette Labeling and Advertising Act. The first was that Congress does not cavalierly preempt state law causes of action, and the intent of Congress is the ultimate touchstone in every preemption case. The second was that there is no general, inherent conflict between federal preemption of state warning requirements and the continued vitality of common law damages actions.

"Moreover, those fraudulent misrepresentation claims that do arise with respect to advertising and promotions are not predicated on a duty 'based on smoking and health' but rather on a more general obligation—the duty not to deceive."

According to *Firestone*, when a plan administrator expressly assumes discretion in the benefit plan, he or she is accorded deference by the courts to construe the plan's benefits absent a clear finding of arbitrary and capricious behavior, a standard requiring finding only *any* reasonable basis for the court's deferential adjudication of the administrator's act. In other words, there would have to be no rational connection between the facts found and the choice made for deference to be discarded. Only when discretion is not assumed by the administrator is a *de novo* analysis required, that is, one that doesn't presume to accord deference to the administrator. This contorted type of common-law analysis creates two geometrically distinct classes of citizens—each protected by different governments—one federal, one state—and differently supervised healthcare coverages, both creating similar contractual and fiduciary expectations, and both relying on nationally recognized healthcare standards of providers. Under the 2010 Obama administration's health reform act, the federal government appears to be leaning on the side of equilibrating these issues by entering into the supervision of parity and other pricing arrangements of insurers who participate in the state healthcare-pool "Exchanges."

As *Firestone* found in 1989, "we have held that courts are to develop a 'federal common law of rights and obligations under ERISA-regulated plans.'" However, the ERISA/state law double standard has not been dealt with by the courts, although the section that was withdrawn from the 2010 House of Representative's health reform bill at markup did require repeal of the McCarran-Ferguson Act's deference to state law. As we will see, the *Pilot Life's* "federal common law of rights and obligations under ERISA" did not truly need to be kept within the discriminatory ambit of "preemption." Because the years since the Nixon administration have seen a public health policy evolve from a constraint on healthcare costs to become a Reagan administration public health policy of cost containment, the pre-ACA attitude toward healthcare limits its value in terms only of its instant cost, not its future costs. In reality, such a policy sees only the price paid for providing healthcare but ignores the social and individual cost that results from not providing it appropriately. Based on the nature of the ACA, providing healthcare appropriately appears to be the evolving public health policy of the Obama administration, especially as it requires as a "teachable moment," the phasing in of insurance coverage for all by 2014.

B. ERISA's Core Problems—A Nexus with Antitrust Law

1. Contract versus Trust law

On the cusp of the indemnity/self-insured/managed-care era, in *FTC v. Indiana Federation of Dentists*, the 1986 Supreme Court appeared to balance the equities:

> "Insurers deciding what level of care to pay for are not themselves the recipients of those services, but it is by no means clear that they lack the incentives to consider the welfare of the patient as well as the minimization of costs. They are themselves in competition for the patronage of the patients— or, in most cases, the unions or businesses that contract on their behalf for group insurance coverage—and must satisfy their potential customers not only that they will provide coverage at a reasonable cost, but also that coverage will be adequate to meet their customers' dental needs."

The rather strained and inapposite "by no means clear that they lack incentives" suggestion in this case introduced a presumption that from an antitrust standpoint, insurers could have any reason at all to consider the patient's welfare other than that of pricing lower than their competitors. Competing insurers need be concerned only with the patient's choice in purchase of coverage based on a clear explanation of the benefits, usually made by brokers. The fact that a unanimous court correctly found that the dentists acted in restraint of trade by a "horizontal agreement," in the face of insurers' request for x-rays, did not require a conclusion that insurers might have a positive social motive to be in the business of health insurance. However, such a conclusion moved the courts closer to later judicial and legislative decision-making in favor of insurers when ascribing social motives to managed-care actions. By conceding that the managers "deciding what level of care to pay for are not themselves the recipients of those services," the High Court moved other courts closer to acceptance of the external management of care by imputing motives to insurers and employers that are irrelevant to the antitrust laws and to the business of insurance. This thinking affected later judicial decisions concerning the federal preemption in the ERISA statute, and a distinction of sorts developed between the "quantity" and "quality" of health benefits. Because of federal preemption, the "quality" of benefits offered by fiduciaries of self-insurance plans, by employers, could remain in a federal common-law safe harbor, while the "quantity" of insurance benefits for similarly situated citizens in insurance plans remained saved for state regulation.

There are two complementary categories of antitrust analysis. The first includes agreements whose nature and necessary effect are so plainly anticompetitive that no complex study is needed by the courts to establish that they are illegal; they are illegal *per se*. The second category concerns a "rule of reason" methodology used by the courts after the 1918 Supreme Court's *Board of Trade of the City of Chicago v. United States*, where the agreements alleged were found to be evaluated only by analyzing the facts peculiar to the business, the history of the restraint, and the reasons it was imposed. Although the antitrust laws were enacted to prevent anticompetitive behavior and were developed in an atmosphere of realizing the social good of competition, seeing them as "procompetition" laws is a distraction offered by market-power monopolists as an excuse for avoiding the laws' diluting effect on them. The two categories of antitrust analysis of cases and controversies were designed to punish violators, not *ipso facto* to stimulate competitive behavior.

From an antitrust standpoint, it is not a matter of whether competitors do well but only whether competition is not impeded by anticompetitive behavior and when at least some of the competitors remain in the arena after the competitive battle. It is a matter of preserving competition by removing predators that would destroy it, not of saving competitors' ventures. If applied to healthcare, one could say the antitrust laws are not designed to ensure that a public health policy of cost containment is maintained either but only that anticompetitive restraints among the actors when found are eliminated, notwithstanding the reason for the restraint. No law prevents an MCO from providing greater access to care if it maintains responsibility for affecting the course of the treatment process it purports to "improve" by so doing, but MCOs refuse such responsibility at the same time that they influence the treatment process to limit it. It begs analysis to read the disclaimers by the MCOs that they are only "verifying medical necessity, but the responsibility for the care rests with the provider" and to expect a provider to continue to treat a patient with the only remuneration coming from the Hippocratic Oath. Thus, with healthcare, whether by *per se* analysis or rule of reason, an antitrust analysis must form a judgment about the competitive significance of the economic restraints and how they apply.

In *National Soc. of Professional Engineers v. U.S.*, the 1977 Supreme Court said "it is not to decide whether a policy favoring competition is in the public interest or in the interest of the members of an industry" and that such a decision should be addressed to Congress, not to the courts. No law prevents an MCO from offering a smoother system of doctor-patient contact than a competitor does. However, by merger and often quasi public utility capture of marketspace, MCOs prevent rivals from entering and participating in the healthcare community. By their profit-oriented algorithmic methods for establishing minimums for medical necessity, they reduce the impetus for medical innovation and quality improvement by those trained to produce it.

2. The Fiduciary Double Standard and the Health Insurance Benefit Plan Dichotomy

The unanimous 1997 Supreme Court in *Inter-Modal Rail Employees Assn. v. Atchison, Topeka and Santa Fe Railway Company, et al.*, citing from its unanimous 1990 decision in *Ingersoll-Rand Co. v. McClendon*, held that

> "By its terms, section 510 protects plan participants from termination motivated by an employer's desire to prevent a pension from vesting. Congress viewed this section as a crucial part of ERISA because, without it, employers would be able to circumvent the provision of promised benefits."

Note again that the High Court required that the benefits were to the beneficiaries, not to the plans themselves. A parallel exists between *Firestone* and *Indiana Federation* in that the employer, trade union or insurer—whether or not for ERISA plans—are presumed motivated to have a healthy work force and be a healthy insurance purchaser, because both require insurance coverage. That would hold for both employees' desire for healthcare and health, and doctors and dentists' desires that as patients, too, they should be healthy. Managed-care insurers' assertions that doctors have an incentive to keep patients in a chronically re-examined, unhealthy state in order to reap income is internally contradictory, because the same insurers insist that doctors perform too many tests because they don't want to be sued for missing diagnoses. The healthcare provider admittedly derives income from attempting to treat illness, while the healthcare insurer concedes profit margins increase by reducing premium costs—that is, decreasing its MLRs. Thus, the managed-care insurer has an incentive to keep patients in a chronically examined state in order to maximize income.

Remembering the history of dentists' pressure to have mass fluoridation of reservoirs to protect people's teeth should put to rest the self-serving, managed-care rhetoric against the basic integrity of that learned profession. Although the employer formerly offered indemnity insurance coverage, this should hardly serve as an affirmative defense for it in an ERISA case, where there is a contractual triad—the self-insured employer, the insurer-turned-administrator, and a managed-care company—and where all three are adversarial to the expenses generated by beneficiaries' illnesses and by their control of doctor-patient relationships. If anything is to be learned from *Inter-Modal*, it is that there is a right way and a wrong way to deny benefits. America's healthcare paradox is that state-regulated insurance adjudication is based on common-law, which requires decisions to be looked at in a light less favorable to the policy writer. ERISA trust law, on the other hand, accords deference to a conflict-based plan administrator or other fiduciary, looking first in the light least favorable to the plan participant, requiring a showing of arbitrary and capricious behavior by means of internal appeals, and going to federal court to redress the grievance.

There are two problems encountered in the healthcare benefits domain that occur only rarely in the pension setting. One problem is the assumption that individuals' benefits—the promise to pay for care of illness described on ERISA-backed paper such as the plan's benefits booklet—are somehow distinguishable from the specific performance expected of an indemnity insurance policy. The second problem arises from the lack of internal consistency in ERISA, which appears to have separated the protection of healthcare benefits from that of pensions, setting up a double standard for fiduciary behavior in handling both types of plans. The Internal Revenue Code and its abundant regulations shape the pension portions, while the health and welfare benefit plans are put together largely by the rules of prudent behavior and the DOL's relatively small number of healthcare regulations.

In the first case, by not reading ERISA preemption as consolidating the positive features of former state regulation, which benefitted both health and welfare plans and pension plans for their citizens and, instead, tying daily needed health and welfare benefits to the future-based, postretirement pension benefits, the courts seem to have missed the parallelism that Congress intended. There is a critical distinction in ERISA that distinguishes the behavior of a fiduciary of a pension plan from a fiduciary of a health and welfare benefits plan: the pension fiduciary directly causes cash or securities to be distributed to the pensioner, while the benefit plan fiduciary distributes money only to a third party—that is, to an insurance company or a provider on behalf of a sick beneficiary. However, the Supreme Court in *Inter-Modal* found that "vesting" of healthcare benefits was to be protected the same as for pensions, but it did not go so far as to say that the healthcare benefits should be accorded the same protection as state-supervised indemnity insurance benefits, which have the same social goal on behalf of similarly situated beneficiaries. In fact, the *Firestone* Court said that the definition of a participant "must be naturally read to [have] a colorable claim to vested benefits." Even so, according to *Firestone*, and two years earlier in *Pilot Life Insurance Co. v. Dedeaux*, a fiduciary could change healthcare benefits language "midstream" between contract negotiations. *Pilot Life* held that ERISA's "right of action" provision did not constitute just *a* remedy but the *exclusive* remedy for challenges to benefit administration and effectively sealed the judicial end of a benefit plan employee's day in state court.

The *Pilot Life* Court held that ERISA's remedial provision "preempted" all state remedies otherwise available to ERISA beneficiaries. Thus, if beneficiaries suffered serious injuries as a result of wrongful denial of benefits, they would be precluded by federal preemption from bringing state law damages actions against their ERISA plan to recover for the harm suffered, even when the plan was found to have negligently denied medical coverage. Associate Justice O'Connor—accorded the honor to deliver the majority opinions in *Ingersoll-Rand*, *Inter-Modal*, *Pilot Life,* and *Firestone*—held that ERISA participants and beneficiaries would have to receive the same treatment by the courts when fiduciaries that modify pension promises to active employees are compared with those that make changes to promises in the midst of employees' receiving their healthcare benefits. If that were to be otherwise, it would have made a dead letter out of ERISA's original purpose, which was to provide national uniformity of protection for beneficiaries. However, such a harmonizing analysis ignored that it left millions of employees without the healthcare protection they enjoyed previously under state law.

In August 1974, Congressman Jacob K. Javits (R-NY) explained to the Senate Committee on Labor and Public Welfare his observation that the ERISA conference committee had chosen broad preemption language to mitigate "the possibility of endless litigation over the validity of state action that might impinge on federal regulation." However, to the extent there was much litigation, it was compounded expensively and unnecessarily by the dichotomy created by the preemption and fiduciary structure of the insurance/noninsurance parts of the law. *Pilot Life* and *Firestone* cases confirmed the irony of establishing an ERISA that sold out individuals' health insurance under the state antitrust exemption afforded by the McCarran-Ferguson Act by unweaving the crazy quilt of state pension legislation. At the same time, it allowed the "business of [the same] health insurance companies" to have a seamless safe harbor from state litigation by providing "administrative services only" and stop-loss insurance to preempted health and welfare benefit plans. Providing ASO for benefit plans necessarily include the same actuarial and underwriting activities as performed for indemnity insurers; the only difference is that with ERISA self-insured plans, the employer is stuck with the higher cost of the narrowed risk, which also contributes to the so-called "soaring costs of medical care."

In the private-sector ERISA context, the judicial extension of *Chevron* "deference" has nonetheless been to bootstrap what the *Travelers* Court called ERISA's "unhelpful text" onto both a *Chevron* and a trust law defense:

> "We simply must go beyond the unhelpful [ERISA] text and the frustrating difficulty of defining its key term, and look instead to the objectives of the ERISA statute as a guide to the scope of the state law that Congress understood would survive."

There was no doubt that the country's healthcare system was misallocated and needed remediation, yet there is little evidence after thirty-five years of managed care that ERISA benefit plans have even helped extend appropriate medical care to citizens in areas that were poorly served previously. The facts were demonstrating otherwise: the same managed-care companies that provided ASO to ERISA plans fled in mass retreat from its unprofitable Medicaid population, and HMOs started cutting out services to unfavorable Medicare and Medicaid regions of the country. By shifting the responsibility back to the government, this had the effect of creating more scarcity of coverage for the poor and elderly, and thus higher prices for the ERISA plans. In 1998, an article in *The New York Times*, "Largest HMOs Cutting the Poor and the Elderly," reported:

> "Managed care organizations like Aetna U.S. Healthcare, PacifiCare, Oxford Health Plans, Kaiser Permanente and Blue Cross and Blue Shield Associations have shut down some of their Medicaid services in at least 12 states, including New York, New Jersey, Florida, Massachusetts, and Connecticut."

In 2002, *The New York Times* reported in "Many HMOs for the Elderly Cut or Abolish Drug Coverage":

> "The nation's largest health insurers, which recruited elderly people to Medicare H.M.O.'s by dangling offers of free prescriptions, are eliminating drug coverage or demanding sharply higher payments for drugs and treatments from some of their sickest members."

Characteristically unaware of contemporary secular issues in the country around it, the Supreme Court continued to allow the reduction of current benefits in the healthcare sector and made possible the contrivances of a managed-care, pseudo-insurance market that was doomed to embark on its market failure. Little social or economic redemption can be expected for a maverick, managed-care insurance industry that profits from reducing both healthcare output and the payment to providers for each unit of that output. The paradox is that no rational healthcare system, even one that rations, can reward doctors and hospitals for denying care and survive. In June 2010, the Commonwealth Fund said that

> "Despite having the most expensive healthcare system, the United States ranks last overall compared to six other industrialized countries—Australia, Canada, Germany, the Netherlands, New Zealand, and the United Kingdom—on measures of health system performance in five areas: quality, efficiency,

access to care, equity and the ability to lead long, healthy, productive lives."

Indeed, along with South Africa, the effective administration and
distribution of the healthcare system in the United States remains far
behind the major industrialized nations. Worse still, according to the
2010 *World Fact Book* (published by the Central Intelligence Agency),
the United States was found to rank first in healthcare costs and forty-
ninth in life expectancy when compared with all other nations. The
remedial legislative purpose of ERISA benefit plans has turned out to
be something quite short of a forward-looking attempt to fix the complex social problem of even-handedly protecting healthcare benefits for
citizens.

All insurance policies are essentially "contracts of adhesion," that
is, they adhere to the insurer that wrote or controlled the language, and
a court will generally see to it that any controversy over ambiguities in
such a contract is looked upon in the light least favorable to the profferor. Such contracts are historically based on the common-law contract
principle of *contra proferentem*, which provides that ambiguities in insurance contracts be construed against the insurer, because it is the insurer
that wrote it. The 1970 Supreme Court in *United States v. Seckinger* said,
notwithstanding that the Constitution's contract clause cannot allow
the federal government to recover for its own negligence, that even in a
contract with the government

> "an ambiguous provision [should be] construed most
> strongly against the person who selected the language. This
> principle is appropriately accorded considerable emphasis in
> this case because of the Government's vast economic resources
> and stronger bargaining position in contract negotiations."

It is the opposite in managed-care disputes, where the courts tend
to look deferentially or more favorably on the fiduciaries, who control
the language of the benefit plan contract, because the managed-care
companies are not seen by the courts as functioning within the "business of insurance." In those cases where the MCO, the ASO-providing

insurance company, or the managed-care insurer sees a lost case on the judicial horizon, frequent, swiftly sealed monetary settlements with the aggrieved traditionally have wiped off potential precedent. The courts do not consider the ERISA benefit-plan relationship contractual even though virtually all corporate-based healthcare promises originated in contracts of indemnity insurance written and sold by the same ASO company, because the statutorily deemed noninsurance nature of the ERISA benefit plan allows the sponsor to appoint trustees and administrators and confer upon them discretion to construe the plan document.

The *Firestone* Court noted that under trust law,

"Where discretion is conferred upon the trustee with respect to the exercise of a power, its exercise is not subject to control by the court, except to prevent an abuse by the trustee of his discretion . . . Of course, if a benefit plan gives discretion to an administrator or fiduciary who is operating under a conflict of interest, that conflict must be weighed as a 'factor in determining whether there is an abuse of discretion.'"

However, the fact that the *Firestone* and *Pilot Life* Courts said, "ERISA abounds in trust law," and that courts are to develop a "federal common law of rights and obligations under ERISA-regulated plans," does not mean that only trust law may be applied to cases that arise under ERISA. As the declaration of policy establishing ERISA noted,

"minimum standards [must] be provided assuring the equitable character of such plans and their financial soundness . . . [and] standards of conduct, responsibility, and obligation for fiduciaries of employee benefit plans, . ."

ERISA does not say, however, that its 'equitable' dimensions were its only functions.

The word "abounds" has multiple meanings ranging from "predominates" to "teems" to "prevails." Had Congress demanded equitable exclusivity for settlements under ERISA—saving contractual issues for state-regulated indemnity insurance only—it would have explicitly distinguished ERISA healthcare coverage benefits from healthcare coverage benefits under indemnity insurance. Instead, ERISA distinguished only the quantity of coverage, not the quality of healthcare benefits, which in any case are expected to be identical whether delivered by a hospital or doctor to an ERISA beneficiary or to an indemnity-insured person. However, Congress's "deeming" benefit plans to be noninsurance was to continue both the McCarran-Ferguson construct of state exemption from antitrust scrutiny, and to avoid a conflict with states' rights and allow the insurers, through the "savings clause" to have more discretion as "administrators." This double standard for fiduciaries responsible for the pensions and healthcare payments for persons obviously similarly situated reveals still another reason for managed-care's ineluctable market failure.

In an interesting 1991 Eleventh Circuit Court of Appeals case, *Brown v. Blue Cross and Blue Shield of Alabama*, the Court invoked a standard of deference that balanced the conflicting interest of the fiduciary at the expense of the affected beneficiary counterpart. It was later called a "presumptively void test" that allowed the fiduciary to "justif[y] the interpretation on the ground of its benefit to the class of all participants and beneficiaries." Five years later, the Tenth Circuit Court of Appeals in *Chambers v. Family Health Plan Corp.* differed with *Brown v. Blue Cross*, which had required a "substantial" conflict of interest, and established a lower standard for a conflict of interest termed a "sliding scale approach," identifying with its interpretation of the instruction in *Firestone*, to treat a conflict of interest as a "factor in determining whether there is a conflict of interest." The 2008 Supreme Court in *Metropolitan Life Insurance Co. v. Glenn* affirmed a similar interpretation of conflict of interest scrutiny.

A number of judicial decisions have adopted an administrator-favored concept denying plan benefits for the beneficiary for the "good of the plan," that is, subrogation rights of the fiduciary. However, nothing in ERISA has been found by the Supreme Court that allows for balancing the good of the plan that disfavors a beneficiary or participant except if the beneficiary has also recovered for its injuries from a third party, as found in a rare situation by the Supreme Court in *Sereboff v. Mid Atlantic Medical Services, Inc.* in 2006. ERISA's "prudent man standard of care" requires only that a

"fiduciary shall discharge his duties with respect to a plan solely in the interest of the participants and beneficiaries and . . . for the exclusive purpose of providing benefits to participants and their beneficiaries."

In other words, if a beneficiary has a rightful claim—because only upon making a colorable claim does an employee become a beneficiary—that claim should be paid and should not be balanced with the "needs of the plan" as if to give the plan the same rights as the beneficiary. In fact, ERISA's civil enforcement section allows a participant or beneficiary or the Secretary of Labor to bring an action to "recover benefits due to him under the terms of his plan, or to clarify his rights to future benefits . . . or to enjoin any act or practice which violates any provision of [ERISA] or the terms of the plan" but confers no such standing to the plan itself.

By 2004, the NAIC, the organization of the state insurance commissioners of all fifty states, approved a model rule that prohibited discretionary clauses from the language of any policy issued in a state and proposed adoption by all such commissioners. As of 2009, when a beneficiary made a claim for disability income and treatment, only sixteen states had prohibited the discretionary clause in ERISA policies, while thirty-four states left their citizens under what was thought of as a federally preempted part of ERISA. Nevertheless, on May 17, 2010, the Supreme Court in *Standard Insurance Co. v. Lindeen* denied *certiorari* to an insurer challenge of a unanimous judgment of the Ninth Circuit Court of Appeals, which held that the commissioner's practice of disapproving any insurance contract containing a discretionary clause is not preempted by ERISA's "savings clause."

As mentioned earlier, the trust/fiduciary basis of healthcare promises under ERISA and the contractual basis of indemnity insurance have split in two the federal and state benefits-covered healthcare population and, thus, the healthcare of the population. The patient's relationship to the ERISA trust is nonetheless burdened under a plethora of relations between the trustees of the plan and their managed-care contractors, with contracts debatably made inverse to the purposes of ERISA to act "exclusively in the interests of the participants and beneficiaries." So burdened, it would seem that for courts to find such ERISA relationships are only equitable in nature is fundamentally unfair and a fit subject for constitutional claims of disparate impact on similarly situated individuals both within and across state lines—one sounding in equity and one sounding in contract—with no opportunity for punitive damages as in the case of a breach of fiduciary duty in pension plans. In equity, one is simply owed consideration. In contract, one party owes specific performance of a duty to another.

Even more interesting is that when the Supreme Court cited its 1993 decision in *Mertens v. Hewitt Associates*, "Equitable relief must mean something less than all relief," it brought the conservative members head to head with the liberal members, who insisted on keeping ERISA as an "equitable" law. *Mertens* is a case of alleged medical malpractice that, by preemption, effectively denied any remedy for employees who are harmed by medical malpractice or other bad acts of their health plan if they receive their healthcare from their employer. It was decided by a mixed majority of liberals and conservatives and dissented in by a mixed minority of liberals and conservatives. For the Supreme Court to articulate healthcare benefits or malpractice remedies, as in *Mertens*, that "equitable relief must mean something less than all relief," meant simply that it's all right for patients to get less than necessary and proper healthcare when they are under the care promised by a fiduciary in an ERISA plan.

However, in 1987, a federal Second Circuit district court for the Southern District of New York, in *Schoenholtz v. Doniger,* found that the employees' ERISA stock ownership plan should be made whole in law, not in equity, because of the willful and intentional behavior of the fiduciary defendants. Avoiding the issue of an award for punitive damages, the Court awarded compensatory damages in the amount of $460,000 with prejudgment interest and costs and attorneys' fees in the amount of $405,000. In addition, the defendants were held jointly and severally liable to the other fiduciaries (individually) for attorneys' fees of $34,762.50. The Court added that the award was

"in view of the fact that the Court had previously denounced without reservation the callous and cruel disregard by each defendant of the pension rights of the employees and their families, so that they suffered the stigma of highly critical judicial appraisal of their misconduct, and in view of the heavy awards of compensatory damages and attorney fees."

However, the Third Circuit in 1993, citing a 1992 Second Circuit case, *Diduck v. Kaszycki & Sons Contractors, Inc.*, formally disagreed with the *Schoenholtz* holding, stating:

"Trustees generally are not subject to punitive damages at common law for a breach of fiduciary duty. The exception permitting recovery of punitive damages in cases of fraud or extreme disloyalty is just that—an exception—occasionally awarded in a few states."

What the *Diduck* Court did not mention was that in *Schoenholtz*, five years earlier, the "trustees," "custodians," and "investment managers" were all the same individuals, as so often occurs in small-business ERISA plans. Their disloyalties as fiduciaries were no different from the potential breaches of such duty created by the conflict of interests of employers, sponsors, and managed-care insurers of large ERISA benefit plans versus the non-conflicted interests of the beneficiaries.

The federal courts' mitigating metronome swayed back and forth to favor first the employer/fiduciaries then to favor the plaintiff employees. In 1996, in *DeFelice v. American International Life Assurance Co. of NY*, the Second Circuit Court of Appeals found ERISA cases to be "inherently equitable in nature, not contractual, and that no right to a jury trial attaches to such claims," as is otherwise held in insurance-conflict cases. Moreover, the Second Circuit, in a disagreement with the Eleventh Circuit in *Brown v. Blue Cross,* decided that on conflict of interest issues

"a shifting of the burden of proof to the defendants is contrary to the traditional burden of proof in a civil case [and that]
the burden of proving that the conflict of interest affected the
administrator's decision rests with the plaintiff."

In a 1996 federal Second Circuit case, *Sullivan v. LTV Aerospace and
Defense Co.*, the Court of Appeals decided that jury trials were not available to plan participants and beneficiaries under ERISA. These decisions began to crumble in 2001 when the five conservative members of
the 2002 Supreme Court decided against the petitioners, in *Great-West
Life & Annuity Insurance Co. et al. v. Knudson, et al.*, that under ERISA,
money damages sound not in equity but in contract law. The Court
pointed to ERISA's section on civil actions (502(a)(3):

"[The section] authorizes a civil action: by a participant,
beneficiary, or fiduciary (A) to enjoin any act or practice which
violates . . . the terms of the plan, or (B) to obtain other appropriate equitable relief (i) to redress such violations or (ii) to
enforce any provisions of . . . the terms of the plan."

Justice Ginsberg, writing for the dissent disagreed with the
majority's decision

"to treat as dispositive an ancient classification unrelated to the
substance of the relief sought; and to obstruct the general goals of
ERISA by relegating to state court (or to no court at all) an array
of suits involving the interpretation of employee health plan provisions. Because it is plain that Congress made no such "choice,"
I dissent. . . [and citing the 1993 *Mertens* v. *Hewitt Associates*, the
meaning of 'equitable relief' in the ERISA section] must be determined based on 'the state of the law when ERISA was enacted'."

Moreover, Justice Stevens' dissent, supported Justice Ginsberg
saying that

"it is fanciful to assume that in 1974 Congress intended
to revive the obsolete distinctions between law and equity as a
basis for defining the remedies available in federal court for vio-

lations of the terms of a plan under the Employee Retirement Income Security Act of 1974 (ERISA). . . I am persuaded that Congress intended the word 'enjoin,' as used in [the section], to authorize any appropriate order that prohibits or terminates a violation of an ERISA plan, regardless of whether a precedent for such an order can be found in English Chancery cases."

Finally, on May 16, 2011, Supreme Court Associate Justice Breyer delivered the opinion for the Court, which ended the more than 35 years of judicial wavering and managed-care injustice under ERISA, in *CIGNA Corporation v. Janice C. Amara*. The 8-0 decision, vacated and remanded the case to the District Court "consistent with this opinion," in which Chief Justice Roberts, and Associate Justices Kennedy, Ginsburg, Alito and Kagan joined; Scalia, filed an opinion concurring in the judgment, in which Thomas, joined. Justice Sotomayor, took no part in the consideration or decision of the case. The Court decided that ERISA fiduciaries who have breached their fiduciary duty are subject to the make-whole remedy of surcharge and other equitable monetary awards under ERISA section 502(a)(3).

". . . insofar as an award of make-whole relief is concerned, the fact that the defendant in this case, unlike the defendant in *Mertens,* is analogous to a trustee makes a critical difference. . . In sum, contrary to the District Court's fears, the types of remedies the court entered here fall within the scope of the term 'appropriate equitable relief' in §502(a)(3). . . We are asked about the standard of prejudice. And we conclude that the standard of prejudice must be borrowed from equitable principles, as modified by the obligations and injuries identified by ERISA itself. Information-related circumstances, violations, and injuries are potentially too various in nature to insist that harm must always meet that more vigorous "detrimental harm" standard when equity imposed no such strict requirement."

That interpretation of the ERISA statute, reversing the 1993 *Mertens,* "make-whole" concept that "equitable relief must mean something less than all relief," may also provide a remedy that has significant implications for the rights of employees whose long-term disability insurance benefits have in the past been held to the former very strict guidelines of ERISA. Moreover, on June 13, 2011, the DOL, the primary regulatory and enforcement agency of ERISA, filed an Amicus Brief, in the U.S. Court of Appeals for the Seventh Circuit, in the case of *Deborah Kenseth v. Dean Health Plans, Inc.*, in support of the patient for "make-whole remedies as a result of the alleged fiduciary breach in erroneously pre-authorizing the $77,000 gastric bypass surgery."

> "Although Dean pre-authorized Ms. Kenseth's surgery to correct the ill effects of a prior gastric bypass, it denied her claim for benefits after she had the surgery, citing a plan provision that excludes surgery for morbid obesity and complications resulting from such surgery."

Kenseth claims that Dean violated its duties as an ERISA fiduciary when it erroneously pre-authorized her surgery and left her liable for over $77,000 in medical bills, mostly owed to providers employed by or affiliated with Dean Health Systems, the parent company of Dean. The 2010 ACA adopted federal law ERISA claim regulation in its entirety as the minimum ACA internal claims standards, for disbursement of reimbursement checks and claimant status for all claims and appeals. Kenseth filed the suit under ERISA section 502(a)(3) for "appropriate equitable relief" to remedy this. *Kenseth* was brought as a violation of the ACA regulation regarding the definition of a "claimant." ACA Claims and Appeals Regulations define a healthcare provider with valid designation of authorized representative as a claimant regardless of network participation status:

> "(iii) Claimant. Claimant means an individual who makes a claim under this section. For purposes of this section, references to claimant include a claimant's authorized representative."

Successful state-court challenges to HMOs had earlier become increasingly common and were found in favor of the plaintiff based on theories of insurance bad faith, breach of warranty, agency, and ostensible agency, among others. In a San Diego, California 1998 Superior Court case, *Self v. Associated Medical Group*, a doctor who said he was fired because he refused to compromise his quality of care in order to save money was awarded $1.75 million by a jury. *The National Law Journal* reported that the director of the Santa Monica, California-based Consumers for Quality Care said:

> "This is the first national verdict where a doctor beat a medical company for blackballing them for providing high-quality care. It sends a message that healthcare organizations, which interfere with doctor-patient relationships, will pay a price."

In Phoenix, in the same year, a bemused jury awarded a woman $3 million from CIGNA HealthCare of Arizona. It took four months to determine that a bacterial infection was destroying sections of her spinal cord and assigned 75 percent of the responsibility for her problems to CIGNA, 10 percent to the orthopedic surgeon who operated on her back, and 15 percent to the plaintiff for not being persistent in demanding care!

In *Crocco v. Xerox, Nazemetz and American PsychManagement*, the 1997 federal Eastern District Court in Connecticut said that the primary responsibility of the MCO benefit-plan relationship was supposed to be to satisfy the client/employer's desire to cut costs. However, the court added, "While it may be true that the fee arrangement between APM and Xerox did not encourage the denial of coverage, [its] desire to satisfy Xerox's expectations certainly did." The "certification" APM was to be giving was based solely on medical record information for the company plan administrator to determine whether to pay for the promised benefits. Recall the ERISA standard for fiduciary responsibility as one who "exercises any authority or control concerning the management and disposition of plan assets." Why would deference be given the plan administrator to override the only information she had as to medical necessity, and on what basis could she do other than support the MCO? If she could override such information on no other input, why spend the money on the managed-care company in the first place? Certainly, one cannot confer deference in medical decisionmaking to a medically unqualified administrator. As the appellate court noted and "assumed" but did not decide, it was the managed-care company that denied the benefits.

The Court of Appeals agreed: "In due course, Nazemetz affirmed APM's partial denial of benefits. In a letter to Crocco's attorney, Administrator Nazemetz explained her decision this way:

"Please note that treatment which is not certified by [APM] is not eligible for reimbursement under the Plan. Since APM determined that the level of acute care provided to [the patient] was inappropriate for reimbursement after March 3, 1990, such treatment was not certified and therefore, is ineligible for reimbursement under the Plan."

After conducting a thorough analysis of the administrative record and hearing the testimony of Nazemetz, the district court found that, even under this highly deferential standard, Nazemetz had failed to conduct the statutorily prescribed "full and fair review." Accordingly, the court remanded the case so that the administrator could carry out a review of the denial of benefits that complied with the requirements of ERISA. The decision was appealed by Xerox to the Second Circuit and the decision of the district court was affirmed, holding that the plan administrator's decision ratifying the denial of benefits by the case management company was arbitrary and capricious. However, the Circuit Court—disagreeing with the 1992 decision of the First Circuit in *Rosen v. TRW, Inc.* and the 1991 Eleventh Circuit decision in *Law v. Ernst and Young* holding employers responsible as *de facto* administrators—reversed the fact-finding district court's holding that the employer, too, could be liable for failure to pay benefits as a *de facto* co-administrator or as a plan fiduciary, and it severed Xerox in a contorted decision, denying jurisdiction:

"Although we reverse the district court's determination that Xerox is a proper party to the suit, the remedy Crocco seeks—the award of benefits—is available solely against the Plan, the administrator, and the trustees, and hence is undiminished by the dismissal of Xerox."

By the mid-1990s, all federal circuit courts of appeals had adopted that practice of "hypothetical" jurisdiction used by the Second Circuit, despite the fact that it violated fundamental tenets of judicial power. The Second Circuit *Crocco* Court relied on the jurisdiction doctrine and said that the lower court's formulation favoring the beneficiary against the appellant had the same effect as finding no jurisdiction at all, thus avoiding difficult jurisdictional issues and split-Circuit decisions and, in addition,

> "decline[d] to consider, as unnecessary to our disposition of the case, any questions concerning possible conflicts of interest on the part of [the MCO (APM)] or inadequacy of [the MCO's] notice to Crocco."

The Circuit Court had assumed jurisdiction and upheld the lower court, yet removed Xerox as a defendant. That practice, where a lower court would "assume without deciding" the existence of jurisdiction and could thus dismiss a case on easier grounds than the merits, was ended by the Supreme Court in 1998—about two weeks after the Second Circuit *Crocco* decision—in *Steel Co. v. Citizens For a Better Environment*. Like many expensive and complex cases, notwithstanding receiving full attorney's fees, Crocco's attorney decided not to continue with his client's case, because the district court ordered a remand to the Xerox-employed administrator, Nazemetz, to whom Crocco had already appealed twice. Crocco and her attorney had so far recovered quite well, but the hospital and treating doctor were never fully paid for their efforts.

It was of signal importance; however, that the partial affirmance of the district court's decision in *Crocco* left less room for plan administrators, at least within the Second Circuit, to rubberstamp the denials of benefits by a company-paid contractor/reviewer. Ironically, the district court had refused "both sides" their day to argue in court because, pursuant to *Firestone*, it simply read the pleadings, heard no witnesses other than the company-paid administrator and, on the arbitrary and capricious basis, found for the plaintiff *Crocco*. In contrast with the 1997 *Crocco* district court, the 1993 Third Circuit Court of Appeals held in *Heasley v. Belden & Blake Corporation* that where the ERISA group plan language was ambiguous as to the administrator's maintaining discretion to interpret eligibility for benefits or to construe terms of the plan, the rule of *contra proferentem*—the standard used for insurance policies—would require that discretion should *not* be granted the administrator and, distinguishing *Firestone*, ordered the lower court to use a *de novo* standard of review. The court cited several other courts that have required a "clear statement of discretion" before granting deference to an administrator, adding:

> "Yet in construing a Plan to determine whether it grants discretion, Firestone directs us to consider 'the provisions of the [plan] as interpreted in the light of all the circumstances and such other evidence of the [plan's creator] with respect to the [plan] as is not inadmissible' [noting that] other Courts of Appeals have resolved ambiguities in plan exclusions through application of the rule of 'contra proferentem.'" (Brackets in the original.)

That deferential "clear statement of discretion" gave even greater power to a plan administrator than the U.S. government received from the Supreme Court in the 1970 case, *United States v. Seckinger*:

> "Finally, our interpretation adheres to the principle that, as between two reasonable and practical constructions of an ambiguous contractual provision, such as the two proffered by the Government, the provision should be construed less favorably to that party which selected the contractual language. This principle is appropriately accorded considerable emphasis in this case because of the Government's vast economic resources and stronger bargaining position in contract negotiations."

Thus, by "named" fiduciaries who "accept discretion" for ERISA plan document language, the ambiguity that would be resolved by courts in contracts of adhesion—that is, to be decided in the light least favorable to the one that wrote it—would now be decided in the light most favorable to the fiduciaries that wrote it. Even though what was being disputed was a plan for employee healthcare benefits, it would not be so here because as *Firestone* noted, ERISA "abounds in trust law." It begs the question of "whom" to trust.

What are the "ambiguities" that could be disputed in benefit plan language, and where would the dispute originate? Should an employer/ sponsor or insurer fiduciary merely by accepting "discretion" be given greater preference than the now-luckless employee's need for benefits for which ERISA was written? An apparent answer came from a government research grant twenty years after *Firestone*. In 2003, DHHS issued a special report, "Medical Necessity in Private Health Plans," prepared by the Center for Health Services Research and Policy at the Department of Health Policy of the George Washington University School of Public Health and Health Services, summing up the critical nature of language that is determinative of plan document discretion:

"Despite the limited number of definitions available directly from the industry, those available suggest that insurers and insuring organizations use a definition of medical necessity far more complex than whether the prescribed treatment is consistent with accepted practice in the field."

The Second Circuit Court of Appeals' *Crocco* case confirmed that it was the managed-care company determination the plan administrator used to deny payment. It was the managed-care company *ipso facto* that denied the benefits but was still not considered a fiduciary under ERISA. Because the case never proceeded further, only the bare bones left by judicial review on the desert of Congress's 1974 "comprehensive and reticulated scheme" protect the employee—controlled by ERISA's commercial "noninsurance" industry. All these issues would be resolvable if the McCarran-Ferguson Act were repealed, as proposed by the House of Representatives' initial health reform bill in 2010.

The Supreme Court's 2010 denial of *certiorari* in *Lindeen*, mentioned earlier, opened the way not only for state-court *de novo* review of the *Firestone*-preempted discretionary clause claims by aggrieved benefit plan members but potentially set in motion the reversal of the ERISA-preempted, "trust law" style of discrimination. The country moved toward more equitable healthcare insurance coverage tendered by the 2010 ACA.

C. Managed Care after Travelers—the ERISA Compromise with States Rights

The Supreme Court reached the preemption issue somewhat diffidently in the unanimous *Travelers* decision, steering clear of the "elephant in the room" of the employer-favored ERISA distinction between federally defined "noninsurance" and state-based insurance coverage for all. "The basic thrust of the preemption clause, then, was to avoid a multiplicity of regulation in order to permit the national uniform administration of employee benefit plans." Because ERISA was designed to promote national uniformity of promised benefits, its path of removing most employer-based health insurance from the reach of state-based common law by placing it squarely under trust law could only minimally offer abridged fiduciary duties for those establishing such trusts, in effect, presuming that all that had to be done was "trust" trustees. Thus, government implemented relatively few regulations for health and welfare benefit plans.

ERISA section 403 is entitled "Establishment of trust." However, that the benefit plan assets are to be "held in trust" by "trustees" who are named in the trust instrument is no indication that the *Pilot Life, Firestone,* and *Travelers'* dicta that ERISA "abounds in trust" law meant "exclusively." In fact, the same section has an inurement *exception* when the assets of a plan "which consist of insurance contracts or policies [are] issued by an insurance company qualified to do business in a state." This exception was apparently put in the law to be consistent with the McCarran-Ferguson Act and save insurance companies, McCarran-regulated by the states, from federal antitrust regulation. It is one more area where the purposes of ERISA have been made to conform to "states-rights" statutory construction at the expense of the law's original congressional purpose to make nationally uniform benefits out of the former patchwork quilt of state insurance-supervised employee healthcare benefits. The beneficiary and the plan administrator, in fact, do not make a plan document "contract." The employee does not negotiate with the plan to obtain healthcare coverage, nor is the plan offered out of corporate largesse; it is either part of the negotiations for fringe benefits or advertised to induce future employment to enhance the corporation's competition with rival companies. Moreover, benefit plans are only part of the ERISA scheme, as it includes pensions, too.

It would hardly have been acceptable to employees' negotiators if told that the healthcare coverage they asked for and expected was going to be "noninsurance," with no recourse to equivalents comparable to their former state insurance protection, however different from state to state. Congressional rationale in producing "uniformity" was misplaced as far as healthcare benefits, because the latter had the endpoint of receiving medical care from doctors, not pension money, which concededly required either National Board of Examiners qualification or National Board Specialty certification, and that medical care was similar in all states both before and after ERISA. The ERISA section requiring the holding of plan assets as "trusts" contains an important admonishment that prohibits inurement to the employer of plan assets, expressly requiring that "the assets of a plan shall never inure to the benefit of any employer and shall be held for the 'exclusive' purposes of providing benefits to participants in the plan and their beneficiaries."

Mindful of the constitutional rights of states and the broad regulatory oversight and control of insurance conferred on them by the McCarran- Ferguson Act, ERISA interposed federal supremacy and "deemed" such plans to be noninsurance and, thus, involved in interstate commerce. In a noninsurance cash-flow market such as managed care, where the risk and resource use can be "managed," profit is not generated simply by selling prepaid benefits to more people than the actuaries found could be expected to use them, as with conventional insurance (*See* Plate 4), but by "managing" the care to provide less use of the prepaid expected benefit. It should go without saying that a managed-care company would have no function at all if it generally allowed "what the doctor ordered" let alone suggested *more*. Thus, its only role is to manage that less care be provided based on the actuarially prevalued benefits. "Indemnification risk"—the risk associated with insurers that accept a risk to be transferred to them upon payment of a premium—differs significantly from ERISA plans' "business" or "speculative risk." Insurance indemnification requires a contractual promise to pay under certain conditions. It is a guarantee of payment upon showing "proof of loss," while business or speculative risk implies ordinary risks incident to engaging in business with no guarantee of return if income loss occurs unless such loss is covered additionally by further, stop-loss insurance.

Managed care plus ERISA preemption allows any employer or plan sponsor the opportunity to avoid state insurance regulation of its benefit plans while handily "saving" for the states the continued regulation of "insurance, banking, or securities." In the post-Millennium United States, nearly 70 percent of healthcare coverage is for employees in benefit plans subject to ERISA. As a practical matter, if their health benefits or services are denied, the claimants are limited to the appeals and grievance procedures in the plan document. The employee cannot sue in state court for such common-law remedies as breach of contract, breach of the implied covenant of good faith, fair dealing or bad faith, or infliction of emotional distress or fraud. In fact, after extensive appeals to the employee's plan administrator, the only legal remedy is to ask a federal court to review the claim denial decision to see if there is an abuse of discretion. ERISA "uniformity" therefore robbed millions of workers of their previous healthcare coverage expectations and charged them for it at list prices to boot.

The Medicaid poor and the Medicare elderly and disabled, whose health and economic conditions generally constitute risks for society as a whole, were lumped together with the same population that paid for its risk coverage through indemnity insurance companies by illnesses that knew no such legalities. The ERISA group consisted largely of healthy, active employees of medium to large corporations whose coverage, now preempted, lost the protection previously afforded by state regulation of insurance benefits. No more insurance policies, no more contributions by the insurers to state risk pools (until the 2010 ACA), and no more premium taxes had to be paid by the insurer when the employer "self-funds" the coverage contributions to an ERISA-qualified benefit plan. In fact, because the costs to the employer were fully deductible, the social coffers were the worse off. Although some employers found it more cost effective to carve out certain segments of their health plan such as mental health benefits or prescription drugs, by so doing, the carved-out segments may indirectly become regulated by the state in which the benefit was available. "Stop-loss" insurance, such as with *Great-West Life & Annuity*, when used, brings only the insurance contract under state regulation, not the benefit plan.

As they were unburdened by the risk being shifted to the employees' plans, thus to employers' profits and to society at large, the insurers-turned-administrators could provide relatively risk-free administrative services to the plans and leave the "care managing" to the growing lot of start-up MCOs. ERISA provided that benefit plans could purchase coverage from state-regulated insurance companies. However, such purchases would leave the benefit plans with the same high "experienced-rated" premiums the companies had purchased previously, because the actuarial group would be small. If a plan were set up directly through an insurance contract, the contract would not even need to be held in trust and controlled by corporate fiduciaries, showing that the ERISA law attempted to provide something for everyone. In an experience-rated contract, the premium costs were affected by, among other things, the number and size of claims. The premiums were apt to rise with unexpected events, as the purchaser was "betting against himself" with a small group on which to base the risk. When the benefit plans could purchase managed-care-influenced coverage that promised sharply lower costs, the outcome was inevitable that a general shift to managed care would occur rapidly. Because of the federal preemption, which separated millions of Americans similarly situated by their illnesses, ERISA assured that the managed-care insurance industry would be born and sold as lawfully protected, damaged goods until the advent of the ACA.

ERISA's preemption effectively created the regulatory void referred to earlier and gave rise to the present for-profit system of various forms of managed care, of which HMOs became a major part. From the time President Carter left office in 1981, through the Bush II administration, and the time the ACA went into effect, the departments of Labor and Treasury promulgated few regulations for health and welfare benefit plans to implement the congressionally declared need for "standards of conduct for fiduciaries" of medical benefit plans required by the statute's declaration of purpose. Finally, in late June 2010, the Treasury, DHHS, and the DOL moved quickly and promulgated regulations entitled "Requirements for Group Health Plans and Health Insurance Issuers Under the Patient Protection and Affordable Care Act Relating to Preexisting Condition Exclusions, Lifetime and Annual Limits, Rescissions, and Patient Protections." This, in significant part, removed the "grandfathering" status if insurance companies were changed. "Thus, an insured plan can maintain its status as a grandfathered health plan only by renewing its contract with the same health insurance issuer." The new restrictions on lifetime and annual limits, waiting periods, and pre-existing condition limitations were to apply to both self-insured and fully insured plans, as do the new requirements expanding coverage for adult dependent children, and the compliance effective dates for employer health plans do not vary based on whether the plan is insured or self-insured.

The *Pilot Life* and *Firestone* decisions presumed that a body of federal common law would develop, ignoring that any such development of a body of federal common law would be significantly constrained, because ERISA contemplated no awards for exemplary or punitive damages, which could stimulate the interest of attorneys. ERISA provided only remedies that require an expensive, protracted and often intimidating process of federal litigation that would discourage most aggrieved parties, offering no significant awards for supportive contingency-fee arrangements as in state-regulated insurance cases. Indeed, after *Pilot Life* and *Firestone*, most federal courts that decided such cases ruled that the ERISA fiduciary that assumed discretion would get deference in determining the appropriate level of benefits, setting in place poor soil for enrichment of public healthcare needs. Indeed, the dearth of regulations defining the ambit of fiduciary discretion in benefit plans compounded the problem. Because plaintiffs' successes in tort actions for personal injury have traditionally depended largely on contingency fee arrangements, and because the courts held that ERISA affirmatively provided only for medical payments and attorney fees, there was little incentive on anyone's part for other than pretrial settlements, the sealed-documents insurer sanctuary for egregious managed-care denials of care. As a result, without the courtroom testing of legal theories, the development of that hoped-for body of federal common law was seriously handicapped, and the promised "ready access" to the courts was largely empty and incompatible with the express language of the ERISA declaration of policy.

The economics of the manufacturing model, so often relied on by pundits as a model for defining healthcare "efficiency," necessitates having a synthesis of physical materials; it is hoped that the outcome will become commodities—goods made or created for sale—in contrast with having "products," the insurance term for what that industry sells. Healthcare involves the opposite. As a service, it requires analysis, not synthesis. Analysis entails the investigation of a situation including examination, deduction, review, diagnosis, judgment, reporting, direct knowledge-based treatment and, sometimes, trial-and-error treatment by an appropriately trained professional. In the modern healthcare industry, there is a tension between the traditional service delivery of the individual doctor-patient relationship, the overlay of micromanaged, healthcare reimbursement methodologies of government-regulated programs, and the largely unregulated and unlicensed managed-care-constrained treatment.

Understanding this distinction in healthcare is particularly important for market failure analysis, because Congress has seen fit to create a contradictory relationship between discretionary healthcare-coverage benefits under ERISA and healthcare contract-based insurance governed by the McCarran Act exemption from federal antitrust laws favoring state action. Another type of "conflict preemption" between state and federal law occurs in a family where a working wife may have managed-care coverage under ERISA from a benefit plan that covers her spouse and her husband may have a family indemnity policy that covers his wife. State-regulated "coordination of benefits" laws (splitting the cost between insurers of the same person) would come into conflict with the federal law and cannot apply to ERISA plans. Because that presumption would be under ERISA supersedure, the purpose of state-regulated coordination of such benefits would be frustrated.

This type of conflict was highlighted in 2004. The Supreme Court in *Aetna Health Inc. v. Davila*, consolidated two hospital and medical care cases, giving an early hint of the role a future federal health reform law might play:

"Pilot Life's reasoning applies here with full force. Allowing respondents to proceed with their state-law suits would 'pose an obstacle to the purposes and objectives of Congress.' . . . As this Court has recognized in both Rush Prudential and Pilot Life, [the ERISA section] must be interpreted in light of the congressional intent to create an *exclusive* federal remedy. Under ordinary principles of conflict preemption, then, even a state law that can arguably be characterized as 'regulating insurance' will be pre-empted if it provides a separate vehicle to assert a claim for benefits outside of, or in addition to, ERISA's remedial scheme."

The earlier "exclusionary" decision arrived, ignoring how in 1989 Associate Justice Souter, writing for the Court in *Travelers,* and two years after *Pilot Life's* deconstruction of ERISA progress, elegantly distinguished the entire arena of ERISA preemption and states' rights in healthcare regulation. The great significance of the unanimous *Travelers* decision that "cost uniformity" is *not* within the ERISA domain, is that it occurred notwithstanding that the federal government had already created a Medicare public policy of cost uniformity many years earlier, the DRGs' price per illness. As a result of *Travelers'* clarification, ERISA's seeming regulation-free "safe harbor" for MCOs lost some of its former appeal, making the provision of care to citizens the priority, state-based or not.

Travelers said:

"In sum, cost-uniformity was almost certainly not an object of preemption . . . It remains only to speak further on a point already raised, that any conclusion other than the one we draw would bar any state regulation of hospital costs. The basic [Medicare] DRG system (even without any surcharge), like any other interference with the hospital services market, would fall on a theory that all laws with indirect economic effects on ERISA plans are preempted under [those sections]. This would be an unsettling result and all the more startling because several States, including New York, regulated hospital charges to one degree or another at the time ERISA was passed . . . And yet there is not so much as a hint in ERISA's legislative history or anywhere else [*sic*] that Congress intended to squelch these state efforts." (Parentheses made by the Court.)

The earlier statement was only partially accurate. When ERISA became law, its purpose was precisely to "squelch" the "crazy quilt" of state laws regulating pensions that contained retirement healthcare benefits for ordinary employees. Unfortunately, church-plan members and federal and state employees' plans were exempted from ERISA, leaving fiduciary protections unavailable to those workers whose plans could then be subject to changes in state politics or the control of organized religions. This was seen in 2011 when Wisconsin's Governor Scott Walker conceded under oath before Congress that his campaign to reduce state workers' pension rights did nothing to improve the state's budget situation, and when Governors' Christie of New Jersey and Cuomo of New York also proposed to increase copayments and decrease benefits of state workers

ERISA's frailty in creating national "uniformity" of pension and benefit plan rights for employees and the Constitution's Tenth Amendment protecting state's rights was most dramatically witnessed in February 2011, when Wisconsin's governor used state power to "balance the budget" by curbing what he termed as union excesses. Because there was no federal supersedure by ERISA for state employees, the newly elected Republican governor was able to propose cutting pension contributions and require copayments for healthcare formerly made on behalf of politically selected state employees unions. At the same time, he bootstrapped an attempt to eliminate most collective bargaining by state employees unions, a move apparently wholly unrelated to balancing the budget, as media analysts pointed out. Texas had eliminated collective bargaining by public employees in 1993, yet faced a much bigger deficit than Wisconsin, which had a similar deficit to Massachusetts, a state sympathetic to collective bargaining. Massachusetts' budget deficit was $1.8 billion in one current estimate and trailed well behind states such as California ($25.4 billion), Texas ($13.4 billion), New Jersey ($10.4 billion), and New York ($9 billion), demonstrating that the issue of union collective bargaining was irrelevant to budget balancing but politically relevant to anti-union sentiments. On Election Day in November 2011, Ohioans overturned by referendum a divisive anti-union law that restricted collective bargaining rights.

The 1965 Medicaid Act provided federal money to states under "cooperative federalism," where "categorically needy" indigent and disabled patients would also have uniformity of care. It is interesting that by assurances made by states to the secretary of Health and Human Services, states would receive federal assistance percentages based on uniform payments to providers in Standard Metropolitan Statistical Areas, many of which crossed state lines. The 1980 "Boren Amendment" to Medicaid required a state plan to provide "reasonable and adequate" rates for nursing home and hospital services.

> "through the use of rates determined in accordance with methods and standards developed by the state which, in the case of hospitals, took into account the situation of hospitals that served a disproportionate number of low income patients with special needs; rates that are reasonable and adequate to meet the costs incurred by efficiently and economically operated facilities."

The repeal of the Boren Amendment in the 1997 Balanced Budget Act strengthened the Republican-led congressional scheme that states should decide for themselves the cost of caring for their poor citizens, albeit with a continuing federal contribution. However, nursing home and hospital providers warned that Medicaid reimbursement levels were already too low and that further reductions would adversely affect quality of care. In response to a 1998 General Accounting Office (GAO) report identifying quality of care deficiencies in California nursing homes, the U.S. Senate Special Committee on Aging held critical hearings on nursing homes and their regulators, and President Clinton unveiled tougher federal enforcement standards.

In 2003, in response to the statutorily required report to Congress, "Impact of Repeal of the Boren Amendment," Tommy G. Thompson, Secretary of Health and Human Services under George W. Bush, said, "The substantive requirements of the Boren Amendment were replaced by a new [section], requiring only that each state's Medicaid rate-setting process be open to participation by the public." The report continued:

> "the effect of the repeal of the Boren Amendment on the financial status of hospitals, Medicaid beneficiaries' access to inpatient care, and the quality of the care provided was limited. . . Many hospitals are in financial difficulty but there is no evidence that any decline in their financial status is due to the repeal of Boren. Hospitals with heavy Medicaid loads are generally worse off, but they were generally worse off prior to repeal as well."

However, by 2010, Medicaid rates for some hospitals lagged far behind those based on Medicare PPS rates, in some cases, up to $300 per day less. After the Bush II free-falling economy, the pressure was on states to balance their budgets with even further cuts. Though the federally regulated Medicare DRGs allowed for regional actuarial influences, when controlled by states through Medicaid, all bets were off for meaningful uniformity for healthcare payments to providers caring for the poor.

D. Cutting "Costs" or Coercively Lowering Prices?

1. The "Treating Physician Rule"—Can Your Doctor Be Trusted?

> "Requiring acquiescence by co-practitioners has no rational connection with a patient's needs and unduly infringes on the physician's right to practice."
>
> —*Doe v. Bolton* (1973)

The Supreme Court in pre-ERISA 1973 acknowledged both a tension and a nexus between the payment for delivery of healthcare services and possible mechanisms for nonpayment of such services already delivered. The 1973 Supreme Court decision in *Doe v. Bolton*, a companion case to *Roe v. Wade* decided on the same day, regarded a Georgia law permitting abortion only in cases of rape, severe fetal deformity, or the possibility of severe or fatal injury to the mother. The High Court found that the "right to receive medical care in accordance with [the patient's] licensed physician's best judgment and the physician's right to administer it is substantially limited by this statutorily imposed overview." The Court stated further:

> "We conclude that the interposition of the [approval committee's standards] is unduly restrictive of the patient's rights and needs that, at this point, have already been delineated and substantiated by her personal physician . . . Requiring acquiescence by co-practitioners has no rational connection with a patient's needs and unduly infringes on the physician's right to practice."

A "treating physician rule" was found appropriate in certain circumstances but not in others. In 1984, the Fifth Circuit in *Babineaux v. Heckler*, along with most other Circuit Courts, recognized the use of the treating physician rule in cases involving termination of Social Security benefits. In 1991, the Second Circuit in *Jones v. Sullivan* required that deference be given to a treating physician's testimony unless substantial evidence contradicted the testimony. In *Richardson v. Perales*, the 1971 Supreme Court said, "'Substantial' evidence is defined as 'more than a mere scintilla. It means such relevant evidence as a reasonable mind might accept as adequate to support a conclusion.'" Other appellate courts such as the Fifth Circuit have also applied the treating physician rule in suits brought under the Federal Tort Claims Act.

However, in 1992, in *Salley v. DuPont de Nemours & Co.*, notwithstanding its support of the treating physician rule in decisions in Social Security disability cases, the Fifth Circuit doubted holding the rule applicable in ERISA cases. Its virtually incomprehensible ruling has been cited in more than 100 cases since by counsel wishing to either invoke or prevent application of the rule to ERISA determinations. The Court reasoned that:

> "We have considerable doubt about holding the rule applicable in ERISA cases. Under it, the treating physician would stand to profit greatly if the court were to find benefits should not be terminated. There is a clear and strong conflict of interest, and we are doubtful that a court should defer automatically to his or her testimony."

Clearly, the distinguishing factor in disability versus ERISA cases is that when government money is to be spent, determination of "disability" requires a five-step inquiry, while ERISA requires only discretionary "prudence." The relevant issues here are these: (1) whether the plaintiff suffers from a severe impairment and (2) whether the impairment prevents the plaintiff from continuing past relevant work, because that involves actual treatment decisions having been made. Torturously avoiding making a decision on the rule in ERISA cases, the Fifth Circuit Court of Appeals found that the district court had erred in applying the "treating physician rule" but, calling it "harmless error," accepted the treating physician's testimony anyway, because a "court nevertheless may properly assess each case's individual circumstances and evaluate the witnesses' credibility." Ironically, the Circuit Court found that the lower court's error in *Salley* on using the rule was the same justification supporting a treating physician's testimony that

Justice Blackmun used twenty years earlier in *Doe v. Bolton*, a nondisability case. The district court said, "Of all the witnesses heard, the one most interested in the welfare of this patient, and not in the insurer's pocketbook, was the treating physician."

The use of the treating physician rule in disability cases militating against the Fifth Circuit's reasoning in *Salley* has evolved. Prior to 1991, the rule, as applied to disability cases by the Second Circuit among others, was as established in *Jones v. Sullivan*, where the opinions of treating physicians were "binding on the fact-finder unless contradicted by substantial evidence."

In 1991, the Bush I secretary of DHHS promulgated new regulations limiting the weight accorded such opinions. The prior rule was changed from being "binding" on the courts to giving the treating physician's opinions a lesser standard, that of "controlling weight," and then only if they are "well-supported by medically acceptable clinical and laboratory diagnostic techniques and [are] not inconsistent with the other substantial evidence in the case record." Where the treating physician's opinions are not to be given "binding" or "controlling weight," an administrative law judge (ALJ) under the old scheme would merely give "some extra weight" to the opinions. An even more restrictive section of the regulations closed the door, adding that the ALJ would also consider "all evidence from non-examining physicians and psychologists to be opinion evidence." Under the new regulations, the ALJ would need to consider the following factors in order to determine the proper weight to accord such opinions:

"(i) the frequency of examinations and the length, nature and extent of the treatment relationship; (ii) the evidence in support of the opinion, i.e., 'the more a medical source presents relevant evidence to support an opinion, particularly medical signs and laboratory findings, the more weight' that the opinion is given; (iii) the opinion's consistency with the record as a whole; (iv) whether the opinion is from a specialist; if it is, it will be accorded greater weight; and (v) other relevant but unspecified factors."

Clearly, the need for considering a nonexamining physician's opinion evidence was to establish an "expert" basis for denying benefits when a person would be found either not to have a viable claim or to no longer be disabled. However, the overwhelming consideration given to the treating physician remained embodied in the spirit of the regulation where "we give more weight to the opinion of a source who has examined you than to the opinion of a source who has not examined you."

In the 1993 class-action suit, *Shisler v. Bowen,* the Second Circuit Court of Appeals reviewed the new regulations for applying the treating physician rule in disability cases. It decided that (1) the secretary of DHHS had the authority to promulgate regulations concerning weight to be given opinions of treating physicians; (2) the new regulations were neither arbitrary, capricious, nor contrary to statute, and thus were valid, even though they departed from the Circuit's prior version of the rule; (3) found that the regulations were binding on the courts and not merely on administrative proceedings; and (4) defined the courts' role as permissibly "establishing rules governing agency proceedings in areas where there are no comprehensive regulations than where such regulations exist."

By 2003, the treating physician rule had been elaborated, and it further minimized the role of the doctor-patient relationship in favor of employers' benefit plans. The Supreme Court relied on "deference" for administrators of healthcare benefit plans in *Firestone* and *Pilot Life* but would not grant deference to the employee-patient's treating physician. In *Black & Decker Disability Plan v. Nord,* a unanimous 2003 Supreme Court held:

> "ERISA does not require plan administrators to accord special deference to the opinions of treating physicians. . . Nothing in ERISA or the Secretary of Labor's ERISA regulations, however, suggests that plan administrators must accord special deference to the opinions of treating physicians, or imposes a heightened burden of explanation on administrators when they reject a treating physician's opinion. . . But the Secretary has not chosen that course [therefore] courts have no warrant to require administrators automatically to accord special weight

to the opinions of a claimant's physician; nor may courts impose on administrators a discrete burden of explanation when they credit reliable evidence that conflicts with a treating physician's evaluation."

The treating physician rule in disability cases still remains in stark contrast to the insurance industry's managed-care concept of external, nonexamining decision making on the "verifiability of medically necessary" patient care and provides a model that should be used in claims of any type. To argue that a person is disabled in a way that does not or has not needed some treatment is absurd. The parameters used by ALJs and courts demonstrate how evaluations will be made to determine disability, which in all cases is based on the chronic or acute need for medical treatment, nothing more. According to Social Security Employee Benefits regulations:

"Medical opinions are statements from physicians and psychologists or other acceptable medical sources that reflect judgments about the nature and severity of your impairment(s), including your symptoms, diagnosis and prognosis, what you can still do despite impairment(s) and your physical or mental restrictions. . . We will evaluate every medical opinion we receive . . . we give more weight to the opinion of a source who has examined you than to the opinion of a source who has not examined you, since these sources are likely to be the medical professionals most able to provide a detailed, longitudinal picture of your medical impairment(s) and may bring a unique perspective to the medical evidence that cannot be obtained from the objective medical findings alone or from the reports of individual examinations, such as consultative examinations or brief hospitalizations.

"If we find that a treating source's opinion on the issue(s) of the nature and severity of your impairment(s) is well-supported by medically acceptable clinical and laboratory diagnostic techniques and is not inconsistent with the other substantial evidence in your case record, we will give it controlling weight."

Moreover, the regulations say,

"Generally, the longer a treating source has treated you and the more times you have been seen by a treating source, the more weight we will give to the source's medical opinion. When the treating source has seen you a number of times and long enough to have obtained a longitudinal picture of your impairment, we will give the source's opinion more weight than we would give it if it were from a nontreating source. . . . When the treating source has reasonable knowledge of your impairment(s), we will give it more weight than we would give it if it were from a non-treating source."

The section on opinions of nonexamining "medical and psychological consultants and other nonexamining physicians and psychologists" says further:

"We consider all evidence from non-examining physicians and psychologists to be opinion evidence. When we consider the opinions of non-examining sources on the nature and severity of your impairments, we apply the rules set forth in paragraphs (a) through (e) of this section."

This level of evidence standard goes far beyond that of the "substantial evidence standard of what a reasonable mind might accept," as decided by the 1971 Supreme Court in *Richardson v. Perales*. The World Health Organization considers the term "disability" to reflect the consequences of impairment, because not all disabilities require regular treatment, as some have been the result of long-standing impairments. Only in cases where the condition produces a state of being not amenable to medical treatment or rehabilitation is disability not subject to some form of treatment. If treatment is rendered, and the people still cannot work because of their condition, they are disabled to that extent. There are pertinent federal regulations concerned with "evaluating medical opinions about your impairment(s) or disability(s)." The definition, for purposes of enabling Social Security Act disability, is that "which has lasted or can be expected to last for a continuous period of not less than twelve months."

The Fifth Circuit *Salley* decision as used in disability cases always involves a treating physician who is aware that the patient is applying for further disability claims. Of course, it appears to present the same potential conflict as with ERISA plan patients that "the treating physician would stand to profit greatly if the court were to find benefits should not be terminated." However, in ERISA cases, the opposite is true: the treating physician has no conflict at all, because there would be no claim of disability of long-standing by the treating physician but only the need for active treatment, as in the *Crocco* case cited earlier. The treating physician rule is, by definition, not attached by law solely to Social Security disability determinations, nor is there any indication in statute, regulation, or case law that the treating physician rule cannot be applied legally to the determination of illness for purposes of adjudication outside of the determination of specific disabilities pursuant to the SSA.

The fact that the *Black & Decker* Supreme Court required ERISA to explicitly embrace the treating physician rule in order to be acceptable makes no sense and, by its overwrought narrowness, forswears its own 1958 views in *Trop v. Dulles*, requiring "the evolving standards of decency that mark the progress of a maturing society." The "treatment" of illness is what the treating physician rule is concerned with, and all people with conditions that require medical treatment are similarly situated to that extent. If the rule were to be limited only to diagnosis, rather than being indicia of the need for treatment itself, such limit would have been embodied in the regulations; *viz.*:

"Medical opinions are statements from physicians and psychologists or other acceptable medical sources that reflect judgments about the nature and severity of your inpairment(s), including your symptoms, diagnosis and prognosis, what you can still do despite impairment(s), and your physical or mental restrictions."

These regulations contain references to evidence of treatment and of a course of treatment of a claimed disability and are not solely limited to the diagnosis of a disability to which they extend. They also require "length of the treatment relationship and the frequency of examination" and "nature and extent of the treatment relationship." In fact, the

1983 Second Circuit Court of Appeals in *McBrayer v. Sec. of DHHS* held that an ALJ "cannot arbitrarily substitute his own judgment for competent medical evidence." In 1997, in *Pietrunti v. Director, Office of Workers' Compensation Programs*, the Court found an ALJ is not free to substitute his or her own lay opinion for opinions from treating sources. It is therefore self-evident that an MCO's analysis of the validity or medical necessity of patient care by telephone calls, examining a chart, or using an algorithm to evaluate a patient's condition should fail to convince a court of the need to be bound by such judgments. However, because of preemption and the seeming exclusion of ERISA plan administrators from *contra proferentem*-based adjudications, the unambiguous public policy of giving greater, if not controlling, weight to the treating physician's decisions about medical necessity has been disregarded for ERISA cases, favoring employers and managed-care insurers.

For benefit-plan beneficiaries who have been declared disabled and in need of treatment by a treating physician to then have the treating physician rule ignored by commercial adjudication is a gaming of constitutional law as influenced by the managed-care insurance industry, which has failed the entire system of healthcare treatment of disabilities *qua* disabilities. In *Ardary v. Aetna Health Plans of California,* the 1997 Ninth Circuit Court of Appeals stated, "Without clear guidance from the Supreme Court or Congress on these facts, we must begin with the strong assumption that Congress does not intend to preempt state law causes of action with a federal statute," and the Supreme Court denied *certiorari*. However, if in 1997, *Ardary* sought "clear guidance from the Supreme Court," it did not receive it from the unanimous 2003 *Black & Decker v. Nord* decision of the High Court, which took the challenge and, by remanding the case but supplying dismal illumination, vacated the Ninth Circuit's opinion on adopting the treating physician rule for disability determinations by ERISA plans. In its remand, the Supreme Court stated that it was not holding that plan administrators may arbitrarily refuse to credit reliable evidence from a treating physician. It was merely holding that courts may not *require* administrators to give that evidence special consideration or to specify why they are crediting reliable opinion evidence that conflicts with the opinion of the treating physician.

Again, tortuous, if not scandalous, managed-care-favored logic was used by the unanimous Supreme Court to distinguish a treatment relationship from that of consultancy:

"But the assumption that the opinions of a treating physician warrant greater credit than the opinions of plan consultants may make scant sense when, for example, the relationship between the claimant and the treating physician has been of short duration, or when a specialist engaged by the plan has expertise the treating physician lacks."

What could be of "shorter duration" than the relationship of a consultant compared with that of a treating physician? It was plainly lacking in helpful "guidance" for the *Black & Decker* Court to ride roughshod over what had long been considered

1. "Substantial evidence" from the treating physician versus conflict-laden relationships by the employer;

2. "Disability" laws meant to increase government support of medical needs, which were historically so egregiously violated by state-supervised pension and welfare benefit plans "pre-ERISA," by distinguishing with different terms the Americans with Disabilities Act "disabilities" and Social Security Act-based disability determinations; and

3. Setting up an artificial distinction without a difference between federal preemptive laws, such as Social Security, which created a nationwide benefits program funded by Federal Insurance Contributions Act payments; and in ERISA' declaration of purpose, among other things, "to provide for the general welfare and the free flow of commerce . . . in the interest of the employees and their beneficiaries."

As Associate Justice Souter in *Travelers* described ERISA as having an "unhelpful text," so too "clear guidance" on the issues surrounding state insurance laws versus federally preemptive ERISA benefits is still not at hand, in such part even from the 2010 ACA.

2. Interstate Commerce in the "Chain of vents" of Managed-Care Insurance Management

In a singularly prescient statement, contemplating the potential for concealment in cartel-based contractual relations made almost sixty years earlier, the Supreme Court reasoned in the seminal antitrust insurance case that led to the McCarran-Ferguson Act, *United States v. South-Eastern Underwriters Assn.*:

> "It does not follow from this that the Court is powerless to examine the entire transaction of which that contract is but a part, in order to determine whether there may be a chain of events which becomes interstate commerce."

Indeed, in 1993 Associate Justice Antonin Scalia may have struck on the edges of the concerted manner in which managed-care insurers function when writing the opinion of the High Court in Part 1 of *Hartford Fire Insurance Co., et al., Petitioners v. California et al.,* an insurance case alleging coercion, when he said:

> "It is not a 'boycott' but rather a concerted agreement to terms (a 'cartelization') where parties refuse to engage in a particular transaction until the terms of that transaction are agreeable." (Justice Scalia's parenthetical.)

The "chain of events" in healthcare delivery today links the patient, as purchaser or beneficiary of managed-healthcare coverage whose physician is in direct privity with the patient, and an outsider managed-care company, "verifying the medical necessity of coverage," working for a multistate insurance company or "contract administrator," representing fiduciaries, ostensibly guaranteeing such coverage. Even accepting the congressional distinctions of the "business of [indemnity] insurance" in the 1945 McCarran- Ferguson Act, from the "business of insurance companies," a Supreme Court of today must find that ERISA (self-insured) "noninsurance" aided by insurance companies' "administrative services only" to be interstate activity within the business of insurance companies. *See* Plates 2, 4. As we shall see later, several new "managing partners" have entered the scene to grab pieces of the rich healthcare pie. The patient is clearly the one damaged by anti-trust behavior in the chain of contractual events connecting the parties involved in delivering treatment today, as may be seen in the Supreme Court's 1977 holding in *Illinois Brick Company v. Illinois. Illinois Brick* was a case that denied "pass-on" treble damages pursuant to section 4 of the Clayton Antitrust Act to other parties found in the chain of events:

> "We decline to abandon the construction given [Clayton] 4 . . . that the overcharged direct purchaser, and not others in the chain of manufacture or distribution is the party 'injured in his business or property' within the meaning of the section, in the absence of a convincing demonstration that the Court was wrong [in a 1972 case, *Hawaii v. Standard Oil Co*] to think that the effectiveness of the antitrust treble-damages action would be substantially reduced by adopting a rule that any party in the chain may sue to recover the fraction of the overcharge allegedly absorbed by it."

The Court also held that "whatever rule is to be adopted regarding pass-on in antitrust damages actions, it must apply equally to plaintiffs and defendants." In *Illinois Brick,* the damages resulted from the over-charges allegedly absorbed by plaintiffs that were indirect purchasers of concrete block from petitioners.

The deadweight losses and damages from the direct and indirect effects, such as from managed-care insurance's "interference with the hospital services market" conceded for state action in *Travelers*, occur in a number of ways:

1. To the patient after having paid or contributed on his or her behalf, what amount to actuarially inflated prices to the MCO for attenuated care.

This results from direct, "capitated gatekeepers'" or fee-for-service doctors in groups woven together by withholds, overcharges by the HMO to the beneficiary or to the benefit plan, or from the MCOs fraudulently charging by issuing denials, for engaging in time-consuming concurrent review or by billing the government or indemnity insurers for services incompletely tendered by a falsely assumed premium. Many occult overcharges have resulted even from coding inappropriately for the attenuated services. Originating with HMOs as incentives, "withholds" or those concealed as "bonuses," were contractual arrangements that placed physicians at financial risk for services delivered. The Federal government issued rules in 1996 mandating that Medicare, HMO and other health plans disclose physician payment methods to patients who request this information. *See* Plate 5.

2. To the physician or hospital, from restraint of trade through boycott, coercion or actuarial distortions by capitation or other cost-shifting mechanisms, which inevitably cause the reduction of unit output to the patient while maintaining the price for providing full coverage.

A summary in 1990, of the then-current literature concerning inappropriate medical services that questioned whether a significant proportion (up to 20 percent) of medical care is necessary, found that only 2 percent of the claims reviewed by the Medicare Peer Review Organizations (PROs) were found unnecessary;

3. To society, arising from false actuarially based advertising that "quality of care is improved" while "costs are saved," which result in methodical under-treatment of entire populations.

Such damages are generally buried within statistics demonstrating increased chronic illnesses and absenteeism-reduced productivity;

4. To society, resulting from state attempts to shore up economically unstable HMOs that reduce output or use marginal-cost pricing to minimize losses, and by subsidizing or allowing unstable premium increases to deter rivals while using tax dollars to provide profits for them.

These types of subsidy of for-profit companies are in no way like subsidizing farmers with price supports for their costs of raising produce, because managed care "produces" nothing. The idea of an insurer being "too big to fail" was a major issue in 2010 when the giant insurer American International Group (AIG) required mega-billions to survive because of economic practices during the Bush II economic recession. As it is inappropriate for a company to pay dividends when it is in negative cash flow, there is without doubt no demonstrable social good from public support of an unprofitable commercial health insurance company's profitability without an examination of its sustainability;

5. To the entire population now that Social Security funds and general revenues from the federal and state governments have been allowed to flow directly to the managed-care industry in the form of various governmental plans such as M+C, MA, and Managed Medicaid.

The Balanced Budget Act of 1997 also created a "Medical Savings Account" demonstration project scheduled to begin in October 1998. They were called "Health Savings Accounts" (HSAs) in 2003, in the MMA. Consumers or their employers, or the government in the case of Medicare, paid for relatively inexpensive tax-deferred, high-deductible medical insurance through a qualified trustee that covered them fully against very expensive illness or injury, which if used for other than medical purposes could be taxed. The Act was seen in an October 2004 *Duke Law & Technology Review* article as providing elusive benefits for seniors and merely creating a windfall for the pharmaceutical and insurance industries. In other words, unlike Flexible Spending Account ("Flex Plan") forfeitures set up through employer cafeteria plans, unused money in the HSA wasn't to be forfeited. Nonmedical withdrawals from a health savings account were simply taxable income, and this type of medical insurance paid nothing for as much as the first $2,250 in annual medical expenses for individuals or $4,500 for families. As a conservative solution replacing the demise of the Clinton universal health insurance plans, these proposed accounts were believed by the Clinton Administration to destroy a cost-saving risk pool and amounted ultimately to little more than providing a cash conduit paid with pretax dollars for corporate managed care. They were too few in number and too disparately spread for any significant actuarial conclusions to be drawn. Moreover, as reported in *The New York Times*, October 13, 2004, they were said to be a drawback for employers, because workers could take their accounts with them when they changed jobs—undermining the employee loyalty and retention that companies sought to cultivate by providing health coverage in the first place.

Capitation—a fixed amount of money per patient (actuarially priced-based on expected unit of time spent on care) paid prospectively to a physician for the delivery of health-care services to individuals—became a major consideration to MCOs losing money on contracts to pay for healthcare's "passed-on" damages, similar to those contemplated by the Supreme Court's *Illinois Brick* and *Hawaii* cases. In deciding whether indirect or direct purchasers should share in treble damages, capitation, which pays in advance of the actuarially predicted act of treatment, introduces the opportunity of courts to not mechanically apply the *Illinois Brick* doctrine and thereby exclude anyone who is not a direct purchaser from the original seller. Capitation also turns the provider into a midlevel insurer. Indeed, in the Supreme Court's 1982 *Blue Shield of Virginia v. McCready*, in which the plaintiff had already paid her psychologist's bills and Blue Shield refused to reimburse her, the Court found that compared to *Illinois Brick* and *Hawaii* there was not

> "the slightest possibility of a duplicative exaction . . . and whatever the adverse effects of Blue Shield's actions on *McCready's* employer, who purchased the plan, it is not the employer as purchaser, but his employees as subscribers, who are out of pocket as a consequence of the plans failure to pay benefits."

Consequently, it would seem possible that the Supreme Court would ignore any claims by parties along the delivery path other than

113

patients who claim direct damages from possible antitrust activity. To the extent that rivals are prevented by monopolists' predatory practices in their attempt to create competitive managed-care delivery systems, ordinarily the antitrust laws address the classical parameters unrelated to patient care as a cause of action. However, from a public policy standpoint, the antitrust equation should encompass the conspiratorial aspect related to the purpose behind the predatory practice. This would include the nature of the managed-care methodologies to create artificial scarcity and limit productivity by coercive "efficiencies" that merely increase cash flow to the industry as a whole, with competitors alike. Advertising by the big HMOs today represents little more than an iridescence of competition, because they all irrationally price below marginal cost, as we shall see later.

The importance to healthcare planners as well as to insurers and managed-care companies of "actuarial distortion" cannot be overstated. An actuary describes a risk by assessing the "incidence" of illness, that is, the portion of illness prevalent in a community-at-large that could be expected to come to treatment. Since managed-care, companies have only one proven economic claim to their social role—that of reducing insurers' costs—they leave us today with the still-unproven, claimed "improvement in the quality of care." Managed care produces distorted actuarial data of incidence and prevalence of illness by making illness less evident, either because doctors see it less or treat it less intensively per unit of care.

Health "incidence" data gathering gets quite complicated, similar to unemployment figures, where some receive financial aid, some run out of aid, some stop looking for work, some enter the labor market for the first time, and some die. With healthcare, some get "well," some have coverage limits, some simply delay seeing a doctor and get sicker per unit time, some get lesser amounts of treatment with each visit and develop "subacute" (smoldering) illnesses, and some die from inadequate treatment, distorting death rates from "natural" causes. Although death by illness is not recorded when coming from natural causes, death or co-morbid illnesses from new drug-drug-food interactions—having become increasingly common—can produce cardiac arrest, which would also not be detected if medications were taken in prescribed but possibly dangerous, negatively interactive, amounts.

Actuarial distortion may occur by other means. Obviously, the one with the most far-reaching implications would be faulty assumptions by the actuary. There is little probability that managed-care actuaries, when assessing the prevalence of particular illnesses, could or would take into account the number of denials of care for that illness, because these data end up untracked in gross revenues. Interposing a "reviewer" from outside of the actual treatment situation should require that such information held by managed-care companies be identified. Widespread shortening of hospital stays and denials of care rendered by reviewing MCO physicians physically unrelated to the treatment setting demands that actuarial assumptions include tracking their relationship to the consequent increased incidence and prevalence of that illness in a given population. It appeared that the Clinton administration health initiative began creating manifold ways of dealing with these subterranean phenomena, because the Republican 1984 Contract with America formally ended that effort with the Republican-piloted 1997 Balanced Budget Act.

In 1998, the Healthcare Financing Administration (HCFA) Inspector General assessed how HCFA was responding to the need for effective oversight of the growing number of managed care plans that have Medicare contracts. The findings were startling:

"The HCFA's primary oversight approach—a site visit that relies on a rigid monitoring protocol—has fundamental limitations as a way of overseeing managed care plans' performance.

The monitoring review is not structured to keep pace with the rapidly evolving managed care market. It does not address delegation of administrative and clinical functions, or mergers between health plans.

The review protocol has limited flexibility to focus the monitoring visit.

The 2-year interval between monitoring reviews provides only an intermittent snapshot of a plan's operations.

The HCFA is making only limited use of the information it gathers in these reviews for national program management. The agency does not aggregate the results of the reviews to continuously monitor plan performance, national trends, or variations among regions.

Many regional offices do not routinely track beneficiary inquiries and complaints as a means to identify problematic situations in managed care plans.

The HCFA does not routinely analyze its own data, such as disenrollment rates or number of appeals, to identify trends that raise questions about plan performance.

The HCFA is not requiring plans to submit basic operational data, such as grievance and appeals data that could be used to assess the delivery of services to Medicare beneficiaries.

The HCFA does not have a formal system in place for receiving input about managed care concerns from the beneficiary advocacy community. The HCFA provides funding for Insurance Counseling and Assistance programs, but does not require these organizations to report routinely on managed care issues.

The HCFA's oversight processes should pay greater attention to capturing information that reflects plans' performance in the constantly evolving managed care market.

The HCFA's oversight processes should provide greater flexibility to target reviews on the specific characteristics of individual plans. We recommend that HCFA take better advantage of data that are currently available to the agency as a way of monitoring plan performance on an ongoing basis.

Toward that end, we believe that the agency should:

-immediately establish and implement a centralized information system that aggregates the results of plan monitoring reports in electronic format.

-immediately establish and use a system to track beneficiary inquiries and complaints that the agency receives regarding managed care.

-provide monthly reports to regional offices on enrollment, disenrollment, and rapid disenrollment.

-require that the Insurance Counseling and Assistance programs report routinely to central office and to regional offices on managed care issues.

-take full advantage of new data that it is collecting, such as the HEDIS measures and consumer surveys, for oversight purposes.

-require health plans to routinely submit data on appeals and grievances."

By 2001, the DHHS Office of Inspector General (OIG) examined the HMO audits conducted by the NCQA. In a typical commercially self-serving structure, NCQA is the insurance company trade group that also audits managed-care insurers' use of its Healthcare Effectiveness Data and Information Set (HEDIS), a tool developed by the NCQA and used by health plans to measure their own performance including enrollment, disenrollment, and denial appeals data acceptable to the managed-care industry. The HCFA OIG concluded:

"With close to 100 million individuals enrolled in these organizations and hundreds of thousands of physicians and dentists associated with them, fewer than 1,000 adverse action reports over nearly a decade serve for all practical purposes as'nonreporting.'"

The Bush II DHHS OIG paradoxically found that while some

"managed care organizations devote considerable attention to the quality of care being provided to their enrollees. . . we learned that in a healthcare marketplace that has been changing rapidly, many managed care organizations devote little attention to clinical oversight [*sic*]. . . Managed care officials emphasized to us that they rely upon these entities to protect patients from poor performers. They explained that these entities are more directly concerned with the delivery of care and therefore in a better position to take actions that would call for reporting. They added that as an ongoing check on the competency of practitioners, they rely heavily on the staff privileging functions of hospitals."

So much for the self-policing. The managed healthcare insurance industry declares as its main goal the improving of quality of care and saving on costs, but if they "devote little attention to clinical oversight," what is the purpose of the algorithms and monitoring telephone calls? When the Bush II administration took over in 2001, the NCQA was anointed by the new HCFA (now CMS) to establish quality assurance for the MCOs through the self-developed HEDIS system, and the DHHS OIG appeared to have receded from its legally required role. The publication *Healthcare Financing Review*, the official journal of HCFA put a gloss on the 1998 and 2001 OIG Reports and reported in July 2002:

"According to Maxwell et al. [1998 *Health Affairs*], many public employers and State agencies today consider themselves value-based purchasers of healthcare services by way of managed care health service delivery systems. Several years ago the U.S. Department of Health and Human Services Office of Inspector General and the U.S. General Accounting Office produced reports critical of CMS's Medicare managed care performance assessment efforts. We believe that this reporting framework for HEDIS process and outcomes measurement could have a positive impact on MCOs' ability to evaluate their own performance."

With only a short-term profit motive to guide it, however, such data, if impartially collected at all, would only see the light of day if the MCOs' contribution were scientifically supportable. After another decade of managed care, nothing of the sort had surfaced. In the short term, actuarial distortion of cost is essential to an unregulated cash-flow industry. Because managed care promotes more undetectable cash to flow through the system and out of healthcare, it simultaneously fashions its own demise and manages its own chronic market failure as it causes the aggregate costs to payers to rise from increased demands for treating chronic illnesses.

On April 21, 1998, a complaint was filed by the Maryland Hospital Association with the state's Insurance Administration charging that the two largest private insurers, Blue Cross/Blue Shield of Maryland and Mid Atlantic Medical Services, LLC (MAMSI, now a subsidiary of UHG) were illegally denying payment to hospitals for necessary care. The hospital association was reported as saying that the Blues' plans denied twice as many claims in 1997 as in 1996 and failed to pay for one of every eight days of inpatient treatment. The controversy revolved around guidelines published by Milliman & Robertson (M&R), the actuarial and consulting firm.

M&R was a closely held actuarial firm at the time with twenty-six offices throughout the country. Its U.S. revenues in 1995 exceeded $165 million. It later became a worldwide operation with fifty-six offices and reported revenues of $610 million in 2009. *The Wall Street Journal* reported in June 1998 that M&R

"has become a strategy shop for the managed-care industry, offering money-saving ideas that [competitor] clients put to work . . . [and publishes] adult-care guidelines for everything from sore throats to heart surgery."

By 2010, its website showed that it maintained a professional staff of 2,400, including 1,100 qualified actuaries and consultants, and was owned and managed by three hundred principals. A central feature of its consulting services is the M&R Healthcare Management Guidelines, which the company described as having been developed by its actuarial and medical consultants through the "integration of actuarial sciences with the practice of medicine."

In testimony before the 1997 Joint Venture Project of the FTC in collaboration with the Department of Justice, Dr. Thomas Reardon, chair of the American Medical Association (AMA) Board of Trustees said:

"Sometimes the risk of error is increased by inappropriate use of guidelines. For example, an actuarial firm, Milliman & Robertson, has used actuarial data to develop guidelines for hospital stays. These guidelines are based on stays achieved by the least costly cases. It is reported that the guidelines are based on the 90th percentile with the 100th percentile being the least costly cases. In other words, in the data base used by Milliman & Robertson, 90 percent of the actual cases had hospital stays greater than the stays called for by the guidelines."

This present-day, managed-care-enabled activity by insurance companies, when subscribed to and applied by competing insurance companies across state lines, was the type of concern evidenced by Congress in enacting the 1945 McCarran-Ferguson Act as a reaction to the cartel-busting 1944 Supreme Court finding in *United States v. South-Eastern Underwriters Assn.* Within two weeks of that bill's introduction, and without holding any hearings on the new measure that would require state regulation and sent it to the House of Representatives and on to President Roosevelt for signing. While McCarran-Ferguson protects insurers from price fixing and data dissemination as *per se* antitrust behavior, it does not save them from federal antitrust offenses such as boycott, intimidation, or coercion, the latter two *sine qua non* of managed-care techniques.

In its introduction to the Guidelines, M&R describes healthcare management as "the process of managing the delivery of healthcare services." It then draws a glaring distinction between two models of healthcare management systems. First, a "loosely managed system," described as

> "one where the provider is reimbursed by traditional fee-for-service coverage sold through a commercial carrier or Blue Cross/Blue Shield plan, or administered by a Third Party Administrator. The services provided under this type of delivery system, by definition, include some medically unnecessary services. Typically, a loosely managed system does not utilize a provider network or incorporate comprehensive utilization management techniques."

Second, a "well-managed system" is described as

> "one where medically unnecessary services have been significantly minimized. The characteristics of practice patterns inherent to this type of delivery system are consistent with the best observed performance levels observed in various client projects."

Obviously, "some" unnecessary medical services "sold through a commercial carrier" to be "significantly minimized" could not be a one-time act; they would have to be the result of an ongoing treatment oversight process. The "system" is not analogous to significantly taking the mechanical "bugs" out of a car or a computer program. Finding allegedly unnecessary care is something that must be evaluated individually with each medical intervention *ad infinitum*. It requires a double set of health professionals: one to treat a patient (the provider doctor or hospital) and one to oversee and/or criticize—in other words, one to directly sell healthcare (the provider doctor or hospital) and one to skim from the sale.

M&R Guidelines ostensively defines "managed care" as

> "the outcome or output of applying healthcare management principles. The degree of healthcare management determines the effectiveness of the managed care organization or provider group. The greater the degree of healthcare management, the greater the amount of managed care generated. The greater the degree of healthcare management, the lower the consumption level and the cost of services provided by the managed care organization. This concept helps our clients understand and interpret the results achieved by various types of managed care organizations."

Nothing could indicate more clearly the deadweight loss to society of managed care, to wit, "a greater degree of managed healthcare generates reduced consumption of healthcare." In a July 1998 letter to the editor of *The Wall Street Journal* titled "Healthcare 'Factory' Isn't Our Intention," the president of M&R, disclaiming that its guidelines are to be used for denying payment for treatment received or denying authorization for treatment without proper "consideration of the unique characteristics of each patient," stated that the guidelines were simply

> "optimal clinical practice benchmarks for treating common conditions for patients who have no complications, based on actual practice of physicians throughout the U.S. They are not intended to produce 'factory-like efficiency' in healthcare. They are designed to be flexible and must be adapted to fit local [*sic*] needs. . . They are designed solely to support the efficient delivery of quality healthcare. They are not based on financial objectives or volume targets."

If the "unique characteristics of each patient" are to be considered, one wonders what "adapted to fit local needs" means. Could it be that each HMO use its own doctors to modify M&R algorithms for cases that "have no complications" and produce from them treatment protocols for finding cases *with* complications? Either the latter would represent the major need for reducing the costs of complicated care or the guidelines would merely reinvent already-expensive medical school and residency training. When M&R says, "They are not based on financial objectives or volume targets," what do the MCOs mean when they refuse to reveal publicly their protocols, claiming they are "proprietary" data? One would reasonably assume that medical care guidelines are scientifically in the public domain.

In its measures of "optimal clinical practice benchmarks for treating common conditions for patients who have no complications," M&R has also established a global "Efficiency Index" (ostensibly not "factory-like") covering all illnesses, with complications obviously included, as its "Index" has professed that more than half of all Medicare inpatient hospital stays are potentially unnecessary. In a miracle of inductive reasoning, M&R's 1996 length-of-stay, efficiency, and admission-appropriateness indices—determining hospital efficiency relative to length of stay and estimating the percentage of admissions that might have been denied—found that 58 percent of admissions did not reach "optimal efficiency," and thus as much as 36.7 percent of admissions might have been avoidable. The annual profit to client managed-care insurers, resulting from numbers of patients denied admission or discharged from the hospital, as M&R's Efficiency Index suggests, would be in the hundreds of millions of dollars. However, the federal DHHS Agency for Healthcare Research and Quality reported in 2009, "National hospital costs for avoidable hospitalizations for acute conditions did not change significantly from 2000 to 2006." What was "improved" other than M&R's bottom line?

Exposing the core of the managed-care market failure as America's healthcare costs continued to rise above all advanced nations, *Market-Watch* reported in June 2006 that

"Between 1995 and 2003, physicians' net income fell about 7% after adjusting for inflation, and primary-care doctors saw their real wages drop more than 10% in that time, according to a report from the Center for Studying Health System Change, a nonpartisan research organization in Washington."

3. Capitation or Decapitation?—Medicine's "Rising Cost Curve"

"Capitation" in healthcare coverage—a fee based on "each head" in treatment—is one of the methods used by managed care to eliminate what it calls the "excessive" use of medical services. It does this by transferring risk for a prefixed price to the physician, physician group, or hospital for the care of an often actuarially pre-shaped group of patients. Physicians under a capitated arrangement receive a fee, typically predetermined by insurer actuaries and underwriters based on the number of patient subscribers to an HMO or a fee-for-service Physician Practice Management Corporation (PPMC) patient cohort, which is affected by many indeterminate random variables. If the patient requires few or no services that month, the HMO has its premium remainder allocated pro rata for its salaried doctors and staff minus the administrative costs.

One of the perverse treatment incentives is that physicians in a PPMC can keep the monthly payments pro rata at year's end. If, however, the patient needed more services than the actuarial estimates, the services must still be rendered. The cost for this came at the "gatekeeper" HMO or PPMC physicians' ultimate expense, balanced against the amount the group withheld for profit. This method did not work well because modern actuarial estimates are stochastic processes—collections of random variables where there is some indeterminacy in their future evolution. Indeterminate variables, such as those involving mortality, morbidity, utilization, retirement, disability, survivorship, marriage, unemployment, poverty, old age, families with children, and so on, as described by probability distributions, are at best based on very large group probabilities where they could approximate public health parameters.

In addition, as the AMA's Dr. Reardon testified,

"Another technique [used to avoid excessive utilization] is physician profiling. It involves comparing information about the hospital use rate of a physician with other physicians. Health plans create profiles to identify physicians who use more hospital services than others. Often these physicians are terminated from health plan participation. Sometimes the health plan gives the physician an opportunity to reduce hospital use prior to termination. However, these plans rarely provide the physician with information about how to reduce usage without endangering patients. This puts pressure on physicians to reduce usage without the informational tools necessary to achieve it."

So "global" capitation came into play: insurers could refer several hundred patients at a time to "preferred provider" organizations. The global payment was actuarially set for each member/patient based on their age, gender, health status and often, ZIP code. This was purported by advocates to eliminate incentives for practices to favor healthy members and encourage efficient and effective clinicians to take on sicker patients. However, these too were negative incentives. Because the referring insurers or MCOs had control of the distribution of patients, they could redline the sickest ones from the start, which only intensified the local market failure. A global payment for an entire cohort had a chilling effect on encouraging a capitated or withholding doctor—who financially benefits only from unspent time—to attentively order tests or call patients in for annual or repeat examinations when appropriate. Such a system essentially converted the doctor's "private" practice into a clinic, where the most attentive doctor's net income increases only by volume of treatment, not by intensity. Thus, "capitated" treatment is ultimately little different from "salaried," and the only way healthcare-salaried people can increase their economic lot is to "slow down" by doing less per unit of care, that is, to negatively balance increased quantity output against quality.

There are several contemporary forms of capitation, each based on the same care-withholding-by-cost-containing incentive to reduce the economic advantage to the provider of giving more care. From this, there is little net gain to society, because by so doing, the MCOs and managed-care insurance companies and employers can then retake the unspent premium money as income without any incentive to reduce the cost to the consumer. Being a cash-flow-dependent and not a public-health-dependent system, managed care depends for profit on increasing the number of units treated while reducing the amount of treatment per unit. That methodology, as used in managed healthcare, reveals its price-fixing aspects. The capitation fee is a predicate for lowering the unit prices paid the provider by obligating the volume-based income against no or little extra expense to the insurer or by assuming the costs for only minimal, basic-level risks predetermined by the MCOs' actuaries, such as mammograms and vaccinations. Bonuses divided among physicians who would be "low utilizers" of the high-cost resources can be paid from reserves set aside for specialist treatment. When charged to premium payers, they simply increase the cost of deferred care. *See* Plate 4.

"Expanded capitation" was offered based on the physician's ability to hire and supervise lesser-skilled professionals. However, such a method was counterintuitive to the ineluctable growth in the more-complex medical knowledge that flows from the increased resource use at the heart of medical practice, and it leaves the lesser-skilled ancillary professionals and the managed-care "guidelines" even further behind as effective caregivers. The doctor-patient relationship severed from direct patient care and layered with heightened responsibility at ever-higher specialty levels of learning and new technologies exposes the core of the market failure of these insurer financial-incentive-based prepayment methodologies. Moreover, the traditional doctor-patient relationship is forced to cultivate social and economic disuniformities with the private patients who remain under the remnants of indemnity insurance and the standards of "non-managed' Medicare and Medicaid, constraining those patients to receive the same "volume-based" treatment as those under capitated or verification-based managed care.

"Base capitation" was a stipulated dollar amount that purported to cover the cost of providing healthcare services while "carving out" mental health and substance-abuse services and administrative and pharmacy charges. In "age- and sex-specific" capitation, payments are adjusted to reflect the demographics of the physician's practice. Rather than producing economies, such methods further fractionate the risk population, produce irregular treatment opportunities and, thus, increase regional costs even more. "Risk-adjusted" capitation adjusts the specifics of a capitated physician's practice based on clinical "algorithms." These algorithms are adapted from computer language use of "conditional logic" and "if/then" statements and used by managed-care insurance to adjust risk. To determine the payment decisions, their use is expected to remove or reduce the economically negative influence of confounding factors by offering preset flow-chart guidelines for the care of prototypical patients. However, algorithms are only as good as the instructions given, and the result will be incorrect if the algorithms are not properly defined. We will discuss later the use of algorithms in healthcare and their proprietary use by managed-care organizations.

A capitated reimbursement system decreases the primary physician's expense per unit of contractual income while it opens the door for stop-loss protection—the reinsurance safety net—should the new cohort of patients gifted to the "preferred provider" require more care than the actuaries suspected. The managed-care insurer can then offer the HMO, hospital, or PPMC aggregate stop-loss insurance protection for a fee, which reduces the money available for treatment units and increases cash flow to the insurance industry. In fact, HMOs and PPMCs often own their stop-loss ("captive") insurers. This produces another type of "moral hazard." It paradoxically reduces the incentive of the provider to cut the costs that managed care put in place, leaving as the only incentive to increase deductibles and copayments by the patient and society.

Capitation does not decrease the insurer's premium income at all, because it is based on the actuaries and underwriters' expectations the capitated risk transfers to the provider. This more-comprehensive "managed denial" system increases the total cost to the MCO, which until then depends only on increasing revenue from its clients by enlarging the treatment group. It offers nothing to patients still needing access to additional, possibly expensive diagnostic tests or referrals to specialists whose knowledge and malpractice insurability lie beyond that of the primary doctor. Therefore, the total cost to society per unit does not decrease unless medical treatment is either withheld or simply not paid to the provider, who is turned into a self-risk manager. On balance, rather than fewer healthier patient "widgets," the system produces more clinically sicker ones.

A fundamental flaw exists in estimates of "efficiency" when manufacturing and mathematical engineering paradigms are applied or compared to healthcare. Up to a point of diminishing returns, manufacturing has a declining-cost curve for fixed and variable costs as productivity is measured by increase in volume output. In manufacturing, significant fixed and variable costs must be expensed before revenue from sales can be realized, but various levels of inventory such as raw materials, work in process, finished goods, and spare parts can be important buffers in economic vitality. Healthcare cannot be held in inventory because treatment, its only point of sale, cannot be buffered. Simply put, healthcare is a stable economy, because the healthcare providers' knowledge is the only inventory, with sales guaranteed. Compared with manufacturing capital costs, no amortization interest, other than what is embedded in the "usual, customary and reasonable" prices for care, which include technology, can be charged for the medical knowledge applied to a patient.

The useful life of a provider's medical knowledge is subject only to continuing education or death. As explained later, while healthcare average fixed costs are reduced somewhat by volume increase, marginal, variable and total costs will always rise significantly because increased volume generally produces inefficiencies in less-capital intensive settings. This holds especially true at the interface of patient care: the doctor-patient relationship. Most medical care for illness must be "delivered" on a journeyman or artisan level, not assembled like manufactured objects. Doctors cannot perform ten cardiograms at once outside of highly expensive intensive care units of hospitals, and even there they must be read one at a time, even if by a computer program. Hopping to several examining rooms must decrease somewhat the relationship time needed by each patient. However, in managed healthcare, the physicians and nurses are presumed to be an equivalent to assembly line workers behaving with "factory-like efficiency," as M&R conceded.

Based on economic intervention in the doctor-patient relationship, managed care thus raises the average total cost to society as it reduces the cash-flow-per unit to the healthcare provider. The premium-assumed unit cost of care is reduced for Medicare and MCO insurers by decreases or denials in amounts of coverage, the use of treatment algorithms by reviewers at a distance, and the shortening of hospital stays by the sentinel effect of utilization review. By so doing, managed care cuts the providers' average prices per unit and thus the value to the patient of the premium, which according to settled common laws of insurance, was to assume the entire risk at the time the policy was sold. *See* Plate 5.

By capitation of one sort or another—the increased number of units at lower total price and value per volume offered doctors and hospitals by MCO contracts—the risk and frequently the increased malpractice premium cost are transferred to the provider. The result of these two—the reduction of the amount of time spent per patient and the less-per-unit money received by the provider—is not the promised efficiency and quality of care the patients and governments pay for and expect. As asserted in a 1991 *Tort & Insurance Law Journal* article, discounting the physician's capitation price or withholding an amount each month from his or her contract-based income caused an immense increase in start-up costs of physicians' commercially managed groups. The circularity of this insurance market failure only decreases the perceived value of having Congress back managed healthcare insurance.

There have been many challenges to the rising (u-shaped) cost curve of healthcare, but most have ignored or purposely left out of consideration the nature of the market failure of commercial managed-care insurance having lost its previous pure or actuarially risk-based social value. Expensive new health-care technologies, drugs, medical devices, and other capital-based treatments are commonly cited as responsible for the high costs of healthcare, along with "wasteful spending," such as overtreatment, "defensive medicine," excessive malpractice costs, and the occasionally identified "fraud." The increasing prevalence of disease, whether due to an aging population and unhealthy lifestyle choices like obesity, or other factors such as subacute and chronic illnesses, is also cited. Until commercial managed care is curbed, however, mitigating these social problems will remain frustrated by the externally imposed limitations of care and the inapposite structure of the commercial health insurance system.

"Bending the cost curve" was a term used by healthcare reformers and those in favor of a "public option" during the 2008 Obama election campaign. The term makes it seem that if we can lower healthcare "costs," the "cost-curve" will be "bent" downward over time; that is, made less steep. The obvious presumption is that a rising cost curve can be turned into a declining cost curve or at least offer a change in the rate of rise. Based on a DHHS-proposed regulation in December 2010, the proposed rule merely requires full disclosure by including publication of actuarial justifications for more than 10 percent increases in premium rates. However, such a formula is based on a false predicate, because the term relates to budgets and not to the peculiarities of providing healthcare through a commercially dominated insurance industry whose cash-flow aim is adverse to the process of lowering costs. What is missing from the factors listed earlier is consideration of the nature of the failed market of managed-care insurance's contractual relations, which steadily increases insurer income intended for other than return to the business of healthcare or to improved health.

A government offered public option would have as its goal to return to healthcare the inevitably required rise in costs based only on social need. If risk-type (indemnity) insurance was to be the major system and federally regulated, instead of being fractionated further by ERISA and McCarran-Ferguson, the costs that rise would be because of the nature of illness care alone and would have to be accepted much as are dollars for the environment, for defense, and the seemingly unavoidable wars. In other words, they must be "off budget" at first, similar to the "supplementals" voted for war, and the Social Security trust. The Balanced Budget and Emergency Deficit Control Act of 1985 (Gramm-Rudman-Hollings Act) placed Social Security's receipts and outlays "off-budget" and raised the national debt ceiling. The government regularly ran a deficit, but during the early Reagan years of 1980 to 1985, the annual budget deficit nearly quadrupled.

War spending increases our security but produces no general revenue other than from the jobs created, while the Social Security Trust Fund, coming from payroll tax receipts, makes insurance privatizers salivate. While considered "off-budget," the money is nevertheless used as revenue in the current budget. Money earmarked for war goes to military research, the munitions industry, technology, and soldiering, and, it is hoped, for the general welfare, but money used for managed healthcare insurance goes elsewhere than to the core business of health, especially because it functions parasitically on the system it purports to serve. With governmental program management, savings go at least for other governmental purposes, but when managed commercially, healthcare profit goes largely for investment outside of the medical economy, leaving the providers and commercial and academic researchers scrambling for dollars.

Because the cost curve of medicine inevitably rises, some de-capitation would apparently be necessary if the Obama administration were to hedge the problem. In July 2010, the managed-care insurance companies' larder of subacute patients was confronted directly by the 2010 ACA when DHHS Secretary Sebelius announced in July a "Pre-existing Condition Insurance Plan" that will offer coverage to uninsured Americans who have been unable to obtain health coverage because of a pre-existing health condition:

> "Created under the Affordable Care Act, the Pre-Existing Condition Insurance Plan is a transitional program until 2014, when insurers will be banned from discriminating against adults with pre-existing conditions, and individuals and small businesses will have access to more affordable private insurance choices through new competitive Exchanges. In 2014, Members of Congress will also purchase their insurance through Exchanges."

Managed care has conferred upon itself the mission to set up a type of limits-on-provider system. However, it is interesting to note that virtually every federal Circuit Court considering whether McCarran-Ferguson extends to indemnity insurers the right to restrict providers' payment for policy-covered health services has denied insurers that right, and the Supreme Court denied *certiorari* to the cases appealed by the insurers. This is another indication that the system of managed care under ERISA works at cross-purposes with congressional intent under McCarran-Ferguson, leaving the bizarre result of simultaneously remanding the "quantity" of benefits regulation to the states and the "quality" of benefits offered employees only to preempted, self-serving ERISA plan administrators.

A three-year study concluded in 1994 by the Healthcare Association of Southern California (HASC) demonstrated that while the number of managed-care contracts in the region's hospitals was significantly rising, the number of capitation-contract providers having at least one contract remained stable at around 40 percent. The study conceded that when payers "can negotiate to pay marginal cost or less for inpatient services, there is little incentive for [them] to bring hospitals into risk-sharing arrangements." HASC said it was a lower-than-expected increase considering "the number of articles and seminars and the volume of discussion in the industry [that] suggests a greater involvement."

A 2002 article in *Health Affairs* showed that although capitation contracts held by doctors was 26 percent of all doctors in 1994 and jumped 10 percent over the following two years, there was no appreciable change between 1996 and 1997. The contracts remained at 36 percent of the total number of physicians continuing into 2000 where, for the first time in more than a decade, healthcare spending per capita rose at a double-digit rate while doctors' incomes dropped. Spending on both inpatient and outpatient hospital services surged by 12 percent in 2001, reflecting increases in both hospital payment rates and use of hospital services. Hospital spending was the key driver of overall cost growth, accounting for more than half of the total increase; however, hospitals' "charges" to nongovernment patients were often much higher than what they received from Medicare and Medicaid contractual allowances. Commercial premiums for employment-based health insurance increased 12.7 percent in 2002—the largest increase since 1990. *Health Affairs* reported:

"Taking account of the sizable amount of 'benefit buy-down' in 2002—where employers change the benefit structure that they offer their employees in order to reduce their premiums—the true increase in the cost of health insurance for employers and employees was about 15 percent."

Another aspect of the managed-care market failure is the hidden accrual of liabilities facing MCOs because of their "incurred but not reported losses" (IBNR), an estimate of the amount of an insurer's or self-insurer's liability for claim-generating events that have taken place but have not yet been reported by providers to the insurer or self-insurer. The sum of incurred and IBNR losses provide an estimate of the insurer's eventual liabilities for losses during a given period. This is where their clients, managed-care consorts, or ERISA employer-plan administrators will eventually have to pay for treatment of illnesses, which by dint of the MCO-inspired undertreatment, will make more patients chronic and their care ultimately more costly. These hidden costs portend, in effect, a default on healthcare promises. The most critical type of INBR, was one that faced Congress in May, 2011 during the political confrontation over raising the U.S. debt limit. The Republican-controlled House of Representatives' misplaced insistence on either obtaining "spending reductions" for agreeing with Democrats to raise the debt limit, or the country would be allowed to default. Raising the debt limit has been performed regularly over the years and costs nothing; it does not increase spending at all. It only allows the government to pay its previously incurred debts.

Greedy for cash to facilitate the frenzy of mergers, manipulations, acquisitions, and joint ventures, the insurance-unregulated MCOs attempted to avoid a risk they thought they no longer needed to worry about. They took federal and state government managed-care contracts with Medicare and Medicaid, only to find that they were marrying both federal and state oversight bureaucracies as well as the very sick and unpredictably costly populations. Disadvantaged by their own actuaries' market distortions in their post-Millennium free-fall, they would now have to account to government auditors for future undesirable events. As a result, they offered more managed benefits and lobbied for and received from the Bush II CMS, under the MMA in 2004, higher-than-usual Medicare reimbursement, a giveaway beginning to be reversed by the 2010 ACA. The Congressional Budget Office estimated the ACA would produce savings of $500 billion by 2020. This would come about by requiring Exchanges' lower premiums and copayments, higher MLRs, and a reduction in the extra subsidies paid to commercial MA plans, thereby slowing the rate of growth in provider payments and "efforts to make the Medicare program more efficient and to reduce waste, fraud and abuse." Without evidence, Republicans politicized the proposed "reduction in extra subsidies to commercial Medicare Advantage plans" during the 2010 election cycle as really signifying "cuts in Medicare."

Joint ventures are generally analyzed under the "rule of reason" method for antitrust purposes. This approach recognizes that there could be some degree of acceptable integration. However, when alleged joint ventures are found to be not integrated but serve to conceal concerted activity, an antitrust analysis should penetrate that cover and find the venture illegal as a cartel. In 1951, in *Timkin Roller Bearing Co. v. United States*, the Supreme Court found that an agreement that included price fixing and the allocation of trade markets would not escape antitrust scrutiny by simply being labeled a joint venture.

In a major departure from *stare decisis*—the policy of courts to stand by precedent and not to disturb a settled point—*Timkin* was reversed in 1984 in a decision by the High Court that also reversed six other cases reaching back to 1947, where the behavior was ultimately found to be that of a single actor and thus legal. Another 1984 decision, *Copperweld Corporation, et al. v. Independence Tube Corporation,* found that it was permissible for a "parent and a subsidiary [to] 'always have a unity and purpose or a common design'" for purposes of section 1 of the Sherman Antitrust Act. Nonetheless, the Court upheld the Sherman section 2 distinction that "the conduct of a single firm is governed by § 2 alone and is unlawful only when it threatens actual monopolization." The Court stated that it

"is not enough that a single firm appears to 'restrain trade' unreasonably . . . an efficient firm may capture unsatisfied customers from an inefficient rival, whose own ability to compete may suffer as a result. This is the rule of the marketplace and is precisely the sort of competition that promotes the consumer interests that the Sherman Act aims to foster."

This robust judicial view of American market competition, however, did not take into account the 1984 situation in healthcare insurance where multiple firms began to act in concert, employ means that created a foregone conclusion that prices would be fixed and shared, and commit other market-power violations that the antitrust laws were designed to prevent. For example, according to *The New York Times*, Magellan Health Services Inc.—formerly parent of Charter Medical, which years before as a psychiatric hospital chain set up an ERISA-qualified, employee stock ownership plan to help it bail out of its failing market because of externally managed care—agreed in March 1998, to sell its interest in six hospital-based joint ventures for $310 million as it aimed to expand its own mental health managed-care business.

Based in Atlanta, Georgia, Magellan had a clinical and administrative program-leasing unit that requested $150,000 down and 4 percent of net revenues from acute-care facilities that wished to join their managed-care network. The company agreed to sell Charter Advantage LLC, which encompassed its franchise operations, to Charter Behavioral Health Systems LLC, and its 50 percent stake in Charter Behavioral Health Systems, in turn, to Crescent Operating Inc. Under the terms of the agreement, Magellan would receive $280 million in cash from Charter Behavioral and $30 million in stock from Crescent Operating. Magellan reportedly planned to use the proceeds of the transaction to reduce debt. However, in August, the Magellan-Crescent merger failed. Because of its inability to sell its ninety-two psychiatric hospitals, Magellan announced that it would probably post lower-than-expected earnings for the year ending September 30, 1999.

By August 1999, *The New York Times* reported that Crescent Real Estate Equities Co, headed by billionaire Richard Rainwater, said it had reached agreement whereby the affiliate, Crescent Operating Inc., would take control of the struggling psychiatric hospital operator Charter Behavioral Health Systems LLC. After it was revealed that Charter was under continuing investigation by the government for Medicaid fraud, Rainwater, who had invested $400 million in Charter in 1997, pulled back the new offer. In February 2000, Charter, with $50 million in assets and $100 million in debts, announced that it was seeking bankruptcy protection under Chapter 11. In 2003, the Magellan parent, by then the largest mental-health managed company in the United States, announced filing for bankruptcy with almost $1.5 billion in debt.

On July 31, 2009 Magellan, having been helped out in 2003 by a new investor corporation's infusion of cash and taking of control, and the 2003 bankruptcy court relieving it of $600 million in debt, acquired Coventry Healthcare, Inc.'s direct and indirect subsidiaries, First Health Services Corporation, Provider Synergies, LLC, FHC, Inc., and certain assets of Coventry. First Health Services provides pharmacy benefits management and other services to Medicaid programs. Coventry Corporation had merged with Principal Healthcare in 1998, whereupon its name was changed to Coventry Healthcare, Inc. After it incorporated in 1986, it acquired American Service Life Insurance Company, selling life and health insurance. Its string of acquisitions and mergers ended with its 2009 divestiture of First Health Services, the fee-based Medicaid services company's portion, which was acquired as a piece of the First Health Group Corp. acquisition in 2005. These deft activities added nothing to healthcare but its rising cost curve.

4. Managed Care's Theatrical Exit from Government Programs

During the Wall Street bull market of the 1990s, MCOs could not resist the urge to go public, but as the merger mania hit them, they had to reveal their internal monetary and fiscal structures for the first time. As MCOs began to drop the government-program cash cows they originally lassoed to staunch the outflow of unexpected healthcare costs, and to serve their merger needs, their cash positions became unsupportable by investors when, as happened in midsummer of 1998, a significant course correction took place in the stock market. It came as little surprise when Oxford Health Plans—a glamour stock of managed-care companies, which promised by its seeming "Freedom Plan" giveaways to alter Americans' soured taste for managed care—hurriedly pulled out of its Connecticut, Pennsylvania, and New Jersey Medicaid contracts covering some one hundred and fifty thousand recipients.

Medicare managed care is a more-threatening proposition for MCOs, because in contrast with Medicaid spread across over fifty different jurisdictions, there is national uniformity in contract requirements for Medicare HMOs. On June 11, 1998, Oxford also disclosed in a Securities and Exchange Commission (SEC) filing that it had ceased its marketing and most of the enrollment in its Medicare plans, after HCFA's February audit of the company's Medicare operations criticized it for noncompliance with contract requirements. By the end of August, Foundation Health Systems joined the group fleeing government oversight, citing insufficient profitability in Medicare contracts. With one voice, the managed-care companies mounted pressure for HCFA to revisit its proposed "blended" payments to rural HMOs and to postpone the year 2000 start of risk-adjusted payments to Medicare managed-care programs. Perhaps somehow the Medicare laws could be rewritten to allow reimbursement for participation in government-backed health programs to be changed to a revenue basis rather than a cost basis, as it had been for individual providers since 1965. As noted earlier, the advent of the 1997 BBA's M+C—subsequently Medicare Advantage under the Bush II administration—eventually brought to commercial managed-care insurers up to 115 percent of the cost-based reimbursement rates, simply by adding more benefits to be managed. Insurance companies insisted that they have to pass high medical costs on to customers, and the Bush II administration was eager to accept that rationale. Because the medical providers' costs appeared to continue rising, the MCOs were simply doing what they could to try to keep rate hikes to a minimum by managing care. However, the insurance companies did not have the essential commodity or service distinction of public utilities, all of which accept full government regulation of their public service. It was a classic boondoggle that the 2010 ACA has reversed and envisaged $500 billion in Medicare savings for beneficiaries as we will show later on.

States' hopes that the miracles of managed-care cost cutting in the private sector could be realized were dashed on the rocks of congressional funding cutbacks in the Balanced Budget Act of 1997, not to mention the need for state-budget rewiring. By mid-June 1998, a growing number of companies, and the Medicare/Medicaid enrollees they pledged to serve, pulled out of the Medicaid and Medicare system when the dollars did not meet the demand. According to the AMA's *American Medical News*, PacifiCare in California, Oregon, and Utah pulled out, leaving two hundred thousand patients to be picked up by government; Blue Cross/Blue Shield of Massachusetts and Arizona left eighty-seven thousand; Foundation Health Systems of Arizona and Pennsylvania left forty-seven thousand; UHC in Tampa, Florida, Missouri, and Ohio left sixty-three thousand seven hundred; Coventry Healthcare of Florida left twenty-two thousand; and Aetna-U.S. Healthcare of Connecticut and New York left thirty-two thousand. As further evidence of the market failure inherent in managed-care insurance, physicians were also leaving the plans they formed. Healthsource of North Carolina was once the largest physician-owned HMO in the state with two hundred and thirty thousand members, but capital needs forced it to sell first a third, then its entire plan to Healthsource, Inc., of New Hampshire, which had been acquired the prior year by CIGNA.

Dropping a contract program entirely is the right of unregulated managed-care companies, because they are not constrained to have reserves. However, in some states, as reported in the front page of *The New York Times*, July 6, 1998, HMOs run by the companies listed earlier were also reducing services to Medicare patients while charging for care as if it had not been fully covered. There seemed to be a double standard by which an HMO could cut services to patients or payment to providers to maintain income if reimbursement was too low, while a doctor who did that to patients was considered immoral or unethical. This was also seen in the denial-of-benefits letters to MCO-member doctors declaring that the MCO had deemed a particular treatment in hospital no longer medically necessary while reminding the doctor that it did not relieve him or her of the responsibility to continue to render the care. The research director of the Commonwealth Fund at the time said, "There are no dramatic savings if you want to do managed care well. Managed care companies have to deal with a program that is already 50 percent below the normal price."

5. The Oxford Gambol

In 1988, Oxford Health Plans departed from the usual managed-care company style of taking advantage of benefit-plan administrators' discretionary powers under ERISA and began competitive initiatives that, twenty years later, had not found favor with most of its counterparts in the industry. Apparently aware of the media's recognition reflecting the growing public resentment of other companies' managed-care practices of care denials, Oxford offered the "Oxford Freedom Plan," a POS plan that offered members the "power to choose their doctors" for an extra fee. "Point of service" is a euphemism used to delineate a hybrid managed-care plan that allows employees to choose a provider outside of the "network" when other "points of services" are needed. Copayment and co-insurance rates are generally higher for out-of-network care.

Because the managed-care model purports to seek the lowest price to the consumer and the lowest cost to the insurer, Oxford was the first to introduce an "alternative medicine" program in 1998, using "acupuncturists, chiropractors, massage therapists, naturopaths, nutritionists and yoga instructors" to replace traditional medicine and nursing in predetermined regions of the country. As reported by *The New York Times*, Oxford interposed registered nurses at off hours as telephone-triage agents. The company owed much of its precocious ascent to redlining hospitals and doctors and imaginative promises like registered nurses "trained to discuss symptoms and assess conditions quickly and accurately, enabling members to seek healthcare guidance even at three a.m."

The company also created artificial scarcity by allowing only certain hospitals and doctors into its network to maintain the fiction of having "preferred providers"—that is, those often board-certified doctors who were willing to accept the in-network rates dictated by the company compared with other board-certified doctors not in the network. They knew from their trade organization, the Health Insurance Association of America (now America's Health Insurance Plans), that if you admit all willing, board-certified providers, you can't have any "preferred" providers, even though they are identically licensed, trained, and certified by the same institutions and agencies.

Acknowledging that it spent at least $106 on medical care and administrative costs for every $100 it received in premiums, Oxford's leveraging panic led it to borrow $100 million in early February 1998 as a bridge loan from the firm of Donaldson, Lufkin & Jenrette. *The Wall Street Journal* reported that the steep 11 percent initial interest rate charged would increase by half a percentage point each quarter, rising as high as 17 percent. However, in the last two quarters of 1997, Oxford racked up losses of over $360 million, wiping out its entire cumulative earnings as a public company since its inception in 1971, despite or more probably because its member rolls had grown about 33 percent in those two quarters, bringing their illnesses to the "Freedom" preferred providers.

In the first quarter of 1998, the company lost another $48.2 million. This exemplified the managed-care fiction that stirs "in-and-out buyers" on Wall Street and that "revenue growth" is the same or even proportionate to an increase in income from operations. On April 28, it was reported that Oxford lost $45.6 million in its first quarter, or $0.57 per fully diluted share compared with a profit of $34 million or $0.20 a share in the first quarter a year earlier. Oxford announced the same day that it was "approaching investors about buying $200 million in high-yield bonds as part of the $350 million in debt the company expects to raise in the next few months." The announcement as noted in *The New York Times*, widely considered a public relations act, caused the price of a share to climb $0.50 on a losing day for Wall Street, and it "did not include the disclosure of the company's income statement or balance sheet [or] schedule any conference with analysts." The company reported anticipating a $350 million infusion of cash from Texas Pacific (TPG), a turn-around firm, if it could match it by raising other debt. Kohlberg Kravis Roberts & Company had already turned it down.

The same year, in talks with the newly merged thirteen-hospital North Shore-Long Island Jewish Health System in New York, Oxford was reported to ask the hospitals to absorb more of the financial risk for their Medicare patients. In effect, Oxford was asking nonprofit hospitals (thus the entire base of taxpayers) to subsidize its economic structure in order for the wounded predator to stay afloat. According to *The New York Times*, the HMO was petitioning to receive up to a 63 percent rate increase from the state insurance department for "individual" purchasers, who buy insurance because "they tend to be sicker than the population at large, since people are more likely to buy health insurance only if they need it." On July 20, the company sent a letter to its doctors announcing that it intended to shrink its hospital network, limit the "Freedom Plan" that allowed members to go outside its network, raise rates to purchasers, and "initiate measures to stem losses, with a target date of reaching break-even within twelve months." There was no mention this time of "improving the quality of care"—the Holy Grail so ardently sought as a justification for the existence of managed-care companies—as the CEO asked for "ongoing patience." The doctors were adjured to "help the company establish a physician culture at Oxford . . . [and to suggest] physician candidates for [their] boards of directors." Recall that the original 1973 HMO Act, which required participation to include broad community representation on policy-making bodies, was amended over ten years later to eliminate that requirement.

The company's stock had lost over 85 percent of its value since its 1997 high, including an additional 10 percent as the news broke. Its method of establishing the new "physician culture" was revealed on August 5 in a letter signed by Oxford's Chief Medical Officer to all participating physicians and "other providers," in which the company pledged to "increase the volume of business for participating physicians." It also announced a modification to its "Primary Care Physician Agreements and Consulting Physician Agreements" to change the payments for covered services to the "then-current reimbursement rate" for services to be rendered after August 15, 1998. On August 7, Oxford's stock closed at $6.87, down from a fifty-two-week high of $86. On August 11, Oxford announced still another loss, this time of over $507 million. A $100 investment in Oxford Health Plans in October 1997 was worth $10.45 on Friday, October 9, 1998. On October 25, 1998,

Oxford was able to announce its recapitalization, in which TPG would swap a portion of its preferred stock and warrants for $220 million in cash and common shares worth around $380 million. Kohlberg Kravis, Chase Capital Partners, and Liberty Partners pulled out one by one as they watched Oxford lower fee payments to doctors while ratcheting up premiums, abandon its markets in Florida and Chicago as well as its Medicaid business and most of its Medicare operations that were unprofitable, and cut its work force in half. In 1998, Oxford's net plunged to minus $597 million.

However, by November 2000, its wounds healed by TPG's turnaround strategies, profits more than tripled to $174.4 million for the first three quarters, with the stock back up to $34.81. A.M. Best, the insurance rating firm, noted in April 2004 that Oxford's apparent strengths were still offset by the increase in debt that occurred during 2003 when the health plan borrowed $400 million via a senior secured term bank loan that increased the company's debt-to-capital ratio to 35 percent at year-end 2003, compared with 20 percent at year-end 2002. While cash flows from operations and interest coverage appeared strong, A.M. Best remained concerned about the debt-to-capital ratio, which was higher than that of its peers. Membership growth had been constrained, and the company's total enrollment remained relatively flat over the prior few years as membership declined by more than 3 percent in 2003 and had grown by only 3 percent since 2000. It rated Oxford Health Plans "A minus."

Notwithstanding these facts, by July 2004, the Bush II DOJ closed its investigation of the proposed acquisition of Oxford Health Plans by UHG, concluding that

> "the appropriate product market was no broader than the market for fully-insured health insurance products sold to employers that are largely located in the tri-state area. It appears that, in such markets, the combined firm would have market shares ranging from a very small percentage to 25 to 30 percent. The Division concluded that the merger should not substantially lessen competition in any relevant market."

In 2009, UnitedHealth Group agreed to pay $50 million in a settlement announced by the New York attorney general's office, which launched an investigation after receiving hundreds of complaints about Oxford Insurance and its parent, UHG. UHG had claimed to rely on "independent research from across the healthcare industry" to determine reimbursement rates. In actuality, Oxford relied on Ingenix, a research firm also owned by UHG. The New York Attorney General Andrew Cuomo said Ingenix had been manipulating the numbers so that insurance companies could pay less. In a report, he contended that Americans have been "underreimbursed to the tune of at least hundreds of millions of dollars." Although UHG and Oxford Insurance were the only entities investigated by the New York Attorney General, other major insurers had also used Ingenix, including Aetna, CIGNA, and WellPoint/Empire BlueCross/BlueShield, competitors of UHG. The cartel nature of the managed-care insurance industry was revealed on September 7, 2010, when *The Los Angeles Times* reported that the California Department of Insurance was

"seeking fines of up to $9.9 billion from health insurer PacifiCare over allegations that it repeatedly mismanaged medical claims, lost thousands of patient documents, failed to pay doctors what they were owed, and ignored calls to fix the problems . . . In particular, PacifiCare violated state law nearly one million times from 2006 to 2008 after it was purchased by UnitedHealth Group, Inc., the nation's largest health insurance company by revenue."

6. The Monopoly Game, Marginal Cost Pricing, and the Cost-Stimulating Sovereign

"A seller's basic strategy is to maximize profits, not sales *per se*, since solely increasing sales to boost profits also entails expanding the use of resources and such intensified efforts always involve a discount from any increases in unit profit."
— Philip Areeda, *Antitrust Analysis*

Overselling and overpromising are common mistakes: the zealous small business sales rep discovers that he sold a significant quantity of an item before checking on the availability of inventory. This is exactly what happened when enthusiastic managed-care organizations rolled into the epidemiological wilderness of public health. In a 1974 antitrust case, the Supreme Court in *United States v. Marine Bancorp* said that the crucial inquiry regarding the source of the restraints should focus on proof of the anticompetitive effect rather than speculation about "ephemeral possibilities," with both price and nonprice vertical restraints to be approached in the same manner. As will be seen in the following analysis of marginal-cost pricing in healthcare, when a monopolist's marginal cost exceeds its price, it is because it is selling at least part of that output at an out-of-pocket loss. One way to eliminate the loss would be to reduce output; another, to go out of business. As an industry, the MCOs chose both. A firm may charge less than its average cost of production, but as long as it is getting back at least as much as its cost of producing that "marginal" unit, profits will rise if the marginal revenue gained—that is, if the price paid is greater than the marginal cost of adding the production cost of an additional unit. However, a monopolist pricing below marginal cost should be presumed to have engaged in a predatory or exclusionary practice. Of course, for antitrust purposes, there would also have to be additional tests of what "monopolist" means in such a situation.

There is a fundamental market imperfection in any privatization of the Medicare and Medicaid managed-care reimbursement system. Despite its 1998 first-quarter losses, Oxford's revenues had a 21.2

percent increase to $1.2 billion from $987.3 million in its 1997 first quarter. Because Oxford originally accepted a 5 percent discount from the actuarially defined, cost-based Medicare rate to obtain its Medicare contracts, a portion of the resulting losses would come from any Medicare marginal unit of treatment. It was predestined, unless the "preferred" providers attenuated the cost of care units at the delivery end.

The prices paid to the new contractors after the 1997 BBA and the 2003 MMA were based on original "fee-for-service" unit costs that had by the 1990s already been pared to the bone over twenty years of government keeping providers' prices at "market basket" adjustments made each year by Congress. Such privatization could survive only if the prices paid to the MCOs were higher than those "cost-based," and the only way for it to be profitable would be for the MCOs to pay its capitated or subcontracted, preferred providers less per unit of the actuarially determined cost of care. Noncontractor HMOs or physician groups would simply reduce the cost of each unit of care based on the disincentive offered by discounts and "withholds." *See* Plate 4. Despite the statutory admonishment that cost shifting should not occur, the higher costs were shifted to others by the 1972 Social Security "reasonable costs" amendments to the Medicare Act:

> "the necessary costs of efficiently delivering covered services to individuals covered by the insurance programs established by this title will not be borne by individuals not so covered, and the costs with respect to individuals not so covered will not be borne by such insurance programs, . . ."

The flaw was compounded by states allowing the front-end coverage by the then-nonprofit Blue Cross/Blue Shield plans to pay providers at 80 percent of the "usual, customary and reasonable" area rates for doctors' services, allowances that amounted to 64 percent of their private charges—that is, 80 percent of 80 percent. For providers to make up for their losses from taking both Medicare and Blue Cross/Blue Shield's patients, copayment costs were shifted either to the unfortunate subscriber who paid for them out of pocket or to a subscriber's supplemental "major medical" insurer.

Government financing of private-sector actuaries' "capitation-based" pricing—with unit pricing based on a noncompetitive system such as in a government program—was a hoax on a public whose taxes supplied the government's actuarially earmarked dollars for its treatment needs. It should have been abundantly obvious that if instead of commercial capitation marginal unit prices were proffered based solely on the costs of units of care, there would be few takers. The capitation offerings were made to physicians who could know no better, because they were assured that their per-unit losses could be "made up by increased volume" and "economies of scale."

The new class of commission brokers for the plans never mentioned that fixed-cost economies are the smallest part of healthcare delivery cost. Nor was it made clear that the alleged elasticity of effort required to make up for the discounted capitation price would inevitably require the patient to lose per unit of care time, especially for those in hospital. At that time, few if any studies had been made on what happened to a patient after discharge caused by utilization reviewers. A more extended discussion of marginal-cost pricing, based on the work of Professors Philip Areeda and Donald Turner and others, will illustrate why the M+C methodology was unworkable when the average variable cost was being forced by a monopsonist—in this case, the federal government—to be above the marginal price. At this point, we will look at the decision of Anthem Blue Cross/Blue Shield of Ohio to withdraw its HMO's Medicare plans from nineteen counties of the state's rural areas to understand the ramifications when a government's fiscal initiative aids a predator.

Anthem had been a part of the nonprofit Blue Cross/Blue Shield Association since 1944, but in June 30, 1998, a class-action suit was filed against the insurer for breach of contract and fiduciary duty by over twenty thousand Medicare beneficiaries who left their previous coverage to join the HMO. The class sought punitive damages and an injunction to prevent Anthem from pulling its HMO out from designated counties. The patients had left the traditional Medicare plan to join Anthem's Senior Advantage because of the promise that they could receive benefits, including prescription drugs and eye exams, not covered under Medicare or traditional plans.

In addition, the Ohio Department of Insurance launched an investigation into the company's marketing practices. Anthem was reported to have offered more generous benefits at a lower cost than traditional indemnity coverage and, as a result, their enrollment grew about 9 percent during the first half of 1997 to over five million, a market share of about 13 percent of the entire Medicare population in the country. In fiscal year 1997, Medicare Part A (hospital benefits) covered an estimated 38.1 million over age sixty-five and disabled persons including those with chronic kidney disease. However, the 1997 BBA limited reimbursement increases to Medicare HMOs to 2 percent a year which, after the starting 5 percent discount from Medicare, put Anthem in a position of doing what other MCOs in the private sector were doing, care cutting, only now there was federal government oversight.

However, even government "oversight" was limited. Although hospitals would have to submit cost reports and statistical reports to justify their expenditures, insurance company contractors only submitted budgets to fit into the government reimbursement, which if reasonable, would be granted, because the companies already agreed to have their services paid at the government prices. Hospitals' expense reports had to account for the percentages of allowed expenses for Medicare, Medicaid, and privately insured patients, and the relevant spaces and portions of employees' time devoted to each group. These were called "step-down allocations." It was not the same for the insurance contractors. The insurers were required only to submit budgets to meet the government allocated prices, so the government had no auditable way of knowing what part of the insurers' space and other capital costs and employee variable costs (desks, paper clips, office space, administrators, reviewers, secretaries, etc.) could be attributed to what part of the insurers' overall business operations. Moreover, the budget analysis groups of the DHHS regional offices were separated from hospital reimbursement auditing. It was, and still may be under the ACA, a situation fit for double dipping.

Again, there simply is no free lunch. Anthem knew that because its marginal price was below its cost, it had to cut out the program, go out of business, or be acquired and let the market "heal" the damage by shifting the losses to investors. If forced by injunction to stay in the rural areas, Anthem would just have to find the money elsewhere in their business. If not, they could either use the apparent authority of having a government contract to entice the risk-eager public to buy more stock or ask to be subsidized directly by state or federal governments. That would be as good as it gets—for a time. In late May, just a year and a half after it started its Ohio Medicare HMO, Anthem announced that it was discontinuing the service as of Dec. 31 in nineteen Ohio counties and parts of three others. According to *The New York Times*, Anthem

> "found itself over-extended, over-subscribed and under-paid by the Federal Government when it expanded . . . The more beneficiaries Anthem enrolled, the more money it lost, in part because of the Balanced Budget Act, which restrains spending for Medicare."

In 2004, the merger of Anthem Ohio and WellPoint Health Networks helped create the for-profit WellPoint Incorporated, which by 2010 faced audits by the federal and state governments for enormous proposed individual-plan increases of up to 39 percent in California and 16 percent in Connecticut, far in excess of demonstrable medical costs increases. WellPoint's California subsidiary, Anthem Blue Cross, voluntarily withdrew plans for individual insurance premium increases that averaged about 25 percent after the state insurance commissioner said an independent audit found that the hike was based on unsound data. The commissioner said the application for rate increases contained mathematical errors and double counting of data, too. In response, the parent, Indianapolis-based WellPoint, said in an e-mail it believed the miscalculation was unique to its California individual insurance business.

By May of 2010, U.S. Senator Dianne Feinstein (D-CA) called for two key congressional committees to launch investigations into

WellPoint/Anthem Blue Cross's use of flawed data to calculate health insurance premium rate increases for policyholders in California. Senator Feinstein also authored the Health Insurance Rate Authority Act (HIRAA) of 2010, which would empower the U.S. Secretary of Health and Human Services to review and reject unfair premium rate increases like those formerly proposed by WellPoint/Anthem Blue Cross. Some of the proposed HIRAA principles became incorporated in the 2010 Dodd-Frank, Wall Street Reform and Consumer Protection Act of 2009, and the ACA. New York got into the picture on June 9, 2010, as Democratic Governor Patterson signed legislation to give the state power to block "what it deems unreasonably high insurance premium increases." The law requires insurance companies to apply to the state insurance department before they can raise premiums. New York's average insurance premium rates were more than double the national average, according to industry figures.

The New York state law, modeling itself somewhat on the Obama 2010 health reform law, also requires insurance companies to spend 82 percent of premiums on medical care, with 18 percent left for administrative costs and profits, up from 75 percent for small business policies and 80 percent for individual ones. The catch in New York was that the burden of proof rested with the state. If the state did not act within sixty days and give an actuarial basis for denying rate increases, the increases would go into effect nonetheless. Unfortunately, that weak criterion assured the industry of relatively smooth sailing, because actuarial analyses for three million subscribers cannot be performed that easily or quickly. Moreover, the law affects only small-group and individual policies, because ERISA federal preemption supersedes, and the state does not similarly regulate most large group plans but leaves it to employers to negotiate rates. Of note is that California's Insurance Law allows a 70 percent medical loss ratio, so Anthem Blue Cross, owned by WellPoint, Inc., and Health Net, owned by UnitedHealth Group, were allowed in August and September of 2010 to raise their rates to double digits, the state having no say on whether such rates were excessive.

An interesting approach to public subsidization of the failing managed-care marketplace losses had been introduced in 1997 by New York's Republican Governor Pataki, who proposed to turn over $110 million to the insurance companies to offset costs and "prevent future increases" for individually owned policies. The relief amounted to $1,000 per insured and was being made to head off a threat of a 69 percent increase for the one hundred and ten thousand New Yorkers who bought coverage on their own, a relatively affluent group: on average, such a family policy had already cost more than $6,000 a year. The cornucopia came from a risk pool for sicker-than-average individuals that had been collected from insurers over the previous five years. Armed only with the insupportable mythology of "adverse selection" and "moral hazard"—theories that essentially blame people who buy healthcare insurance for driving up their own costs—the insurers were able to get back the money as income that they took from the individual subscribers in the first place and then lost. *See* Plate 6.

This sovereign behavior, the state's subsidizing or stimulating the elevation of a regulated price to be at or above marginal cost, saves the state from being accused of supporting a predatory private monopoly. However, artificially pumping up such company coffers gives only the illusion of aiding competition. It concealed that such incremental maintenance of the "output" required for growth of revenue was at the expense of having to make a profit and, in reality, stark evidence of the company's predatory, marginal-cost pricing years. It should have been foreseen by state regulators that Oxford and others' original methods of price competition were specious; that is, they were gaining popularity by setting premiums below the average cost of the service and would continue the effect of sacrificing current revenues to eliminate rivals.

The predatory element had ironically resulted in the situation the company found itself in 1999: needing to be saved by government price supports. This circumstance could have been anticipated had there been a vigilant state insurance department scrutinizing both productive capability as well as cash reserves. As Professors Areeda and Turner said in their 1975 *Harvard Law Review* article, "Predatory Pricing and Related Practices Under Section 2 of the Sherman Act," such monopolist price policies

> "may both generate below-normal returns—that is, it may be below average cost—and be below the loss-minimizing price. Because such a price yields less than the normal return on capital, it can threaten the survival of equally efficient rivals with less staying power than the monopolist enjoys."

That statement by Areeda and Turner received much attention in the years following. Because they were not dealing with healthcare anti-trust issues, it also generated some comments as to their relevancy. Their analyses as used here will be given a dynamic application to healthcare issues, because they shed light on features of the managed-care insurance system whose business process is now effectively engaged in inter-state commerce in spite of the state action allowed by the McCarran-Ferguson Act. The earlier statement is important regarding the frailty of the current "efficiency" justification for allowing monopoly behavior to continue in healthcare insurance engaged in by hospital chains and HMOs, while putatively "less-efficient" rivals who charge at or even slightly above the real average variable cost may suffer. It is important to note that the 2004 DOJ closing of its investigation on the UHG-Oxford acquisition relied on both ephemeral and fixed statutory inter-state markets:

> "The Division also examined the possibility that this trans-action would give the combined company buying-side market power over healthcare providers. For this buying-side analysis, the Division considered two product markets, physician serv-ices and hospital services. Physician services were analyzed in MSA geographic markets. Because an insurer may be able to price discriminate by identifying hospitals or systems that may be more dependent upon that insurer's membership, however, hospital services were analyzed both with respect to MSAs and hospitals or hospital systems that bargain as a single unit. In addition, the investigation suggested that government payer business is a significant factor in determining whether or not

the merged company would be able profitably to decrease its reimbursement levels to providers. Therefore, in analyzing competitive effects, the Division's analysis took into account all payers for medical services from hospitals and physicians, including government payers, such as Medicare and Medicaid."

7. Monopsony and the Antitrust Acts

Monopsony has been termed the "mirror image" of monopoly; the former relates to buyer control and the latter to seller control of a marketspace. One kind of healthcare monopsony in the United States is where the federal government pursuant to Medicare is a statutory purchaser of hospital or medical care from state-licensed or accredited providers. It allows for no competition, because its authority arises under the Constitution's "Commerce Clause" (Article I, section 8, clause 3) and the "Necessary and Proper Clause" (clause 18). The Supreme Court settled challenges to the establishment of the Social Security Act in 1937 by finding that the Social Security Tax was constitutional as a mere exercise of Congress's general taxation powers. For Medicaid purposes, federal involvement with states' laws is based on memorandums of understanding regarding the relationship called "cooperative federalism," whereby federal funds for medical assistance are shared with the states. States are not required to participate in Medicaid, though all do.

A "legal" monopoly is a monopoly protected by law from competition that may take the form of a government monopoly, where the state owns the particular means of production, or a government-granted monopoly where a private interest can be protected from competition, and exclusive rights are offered for activity in a particular service in a specific region. Only government can create "legal monopolies," such as nongovernmental public utility services that in turn are regulated by the state or federal government. When a market structure exists in which a single firm, or relatively few firms without specific governmental protection, act in concert to dominate the sales of a product or service, and thus its pricing, the activity may be considered as violating state or federal antitrust laws. In healthcare insurance, sales are made for those who can afford it to people expecting to be patients sometime in the future. Those who do not desire to pay for it still expect to be patients sometime in the future but choose to free-ride on the system, as we shall see in a later chapter.

As examples of nonstatutory healthcare monopolies, industry figures show that the top two health insurers in 2010 controlled 89 percent of the health insurance market in Iowa, 77 percent in Georgia, 73 percent in North Carolina, and 68 percent in Texas. According to the AMA, there have been more than 400 mergers among health insurers in the past fourteen years. As a result, in 94 percent of the metropolitan areas in the United States, the health insurance markets are now "highly concentrated" and lack meaningful competition. The terms "monopsony" and "monopoly" will be used interchangeably in this work unless otherwise specifically relevant.

Although "commodities" are generally defined as "articles" of trade or commerce, or "things" that are bought and sold, none of the dozens of healthcare court cases in which a monopsony claim was made resulted in a dismissal, because the term could not be applied to healthcare industry services or to what are called insurance "products." In a 1982 antitrust case, *Arizona v. Maricopa County Medical Society,* where maximum physicians' prices were agreed to, the Supreme Court said, "Whatever may be its peculiar problems and characteristics, the Sherman Act, so far as price-fixing agreements are concerned, establishes one uniform rule applicable to all industries alike." Antitrust litigants have frequently attempted to persuade the courts that the antitrust laws, particularly section 2 of the Sherman Act, were designed to promote economic efficiency and competition. However, that was not the emphasis sought by the High Court in applying Sherman. In *Apex Hosiery Co. v. Leader*, the 1940 Supreme Court reaffirmed that

> "The end sought [by the Sherman Act] was the prevention of restraints to free competition in business and commercial transactions which tended to restrict production, raise prices or otherwise control the market to the detriment of purchasers or consumers of goods and services."

The *Apex Hosiery* case says nothing significant about the "design" of the Sherman Act. It would be difficult to imagine a court deciding that restraints found to be "transactions which tended to restrict production, raise prices, or otherwise control the market to the detriment of purchasers or consumers of goods and services" could ever be considered acts that were not to the public detriment. Managed care's argument to support its role is that its intent is only to do what it does for the public good. However, the plain words of Sherman section 2 make it clear that monopolizing "any part of the trade or commerce among the several States" is anticompetitive. As stated earlier, by 2010 with four hundred mergers among health insurers and the health-insurance markets having become highly concentrated over the past fourteen years in 94 percent of the metropolitan areas in the United States, according to long-established antitrust standards, the giant MCOs' lack meaningful competition, and oversight agencies' tepid reviews strain at justification.

Some commentators emphasize that there is a "procompetitive" reason for the antitrust laws. They adduce therefore that hard bargaining to extract low prices, even by a monopsonist, is conduct that as the 1978 Supreme Court said in *United States v. United States Gypsum Co.*, "facially appears to be one that would always or almost always [tend to] increase economic efficiency and render markets more, rather than less, competitive." The FTC says:

> "Antitrust laws were not put in place to protect competing businesses from aggressive competition. Competition is tough, and sometimes businesses fail. That's the way it is in competitive markets, and consumers benefit from the rough and tumble competition among sellers."

Sherman Act violations involving agreements between competitors are usually punished as criminal felonies. Only the DOJ is empowered to bring criminal prosecutions under the Sherman Act. The Act outlaws all contracts, combinations, and conspiracies that unreasonably restrain interstate and foreign trade including agreements among competitors to fix prices, rig bids, and allocate customers. The Act also makes it a crime to monopolize any part of interstate commerce. The common law, too, recognizes "conspiracy," which could be found in the discretion of the courts even though there is not a specific law against the specific behavior. The 1923 Massachusetts federal appellate court in *Commonwealth v. Dyer* drew a jurisdictional line as follows (*certiorari* was denied):

157

"It is the consensus of opinion that conspiracy, as a criminal offense, is established when the object of the crime is either a crime, or if not a crime, is unlawful . . . or if not criminal [is] illegal, provided that, where no crime is contemplated either as the end or the means, the illegal but non-criminal element involves prejudice to the general welfare or oppression of the individual of sufficient gravity to be injurious to the public interest."

The Clayton Act is a civil antitrust statute; that is, it carries no criminal penalties and was passed in 1914 and significantly amended in 1950. It prohibits mergers or acquisitions that are likely to lessen competition. Under Clayton, the government challenges those mergers that a careful economic analysis shows are likely to increase prices to consumers. Section 7 elaborates on specific and crucial concepts of the Clayton Act such as a "holding company," commonly defined as a "favorite method of promoting monopoly," and, more precisely, as "a company whose primary purpose is to hold stocks of other companies." The original position of the U.S. government on mergers and acquisitions was strengthened by the 1950 amendments to cover asset as well as stock acquisitions.

The FTC Act prohibits unfair methods of competition in interstate commerce, but it also carries no criminal penalties. Congress created the FTC to police violations of the Act. An unlawful monopoly exists when only one firm significantly controls the market for a product or service and has obtained market power by suppressing competition with anticompetitive conduct. The antitrust laws were not passed to promote competition but to protect it by stopping anticompetitive behavior when found or to limit proposed activity that could be shown to have anticompetitive market power.

The 1997 Supreme Court has made clear in *Brunswick Corp. v. Pueblo Bowl-O-Mat, Inc.* that the "antitrust laws . . . were enacted for 'the protection of competition, not competitors.'" In *Copperweld*, mentioned earlier, the High Court, citing its 1966 *United States v. Grinnell Corp.*, declared that "section 2 does not forbid market power to be acquired 'as a consequence of a superior product, [or] business acumen.'" There are also instances in which no competitors exist, such as patents, newfound mineral deposits, or for being "the only game in town" that may not invoke an antitrust cause of action. Called "groundbreaking" activities, they do not eliminate competition by their activity *per se*, nor can it easily be shown that they restrain competition under a rule of reason analysis referred to earlier. More often, they simply open up markets for competition.

When a marketspace is narrowed by mergers and acquisitions and, as with managed-care organizations and insurers, which use coercion and boycotting by using "preferred providers" who are no different in education and training and otherwise similarly situated as their competitors who are excluded, there is good reason to question the anticompetitive boycotting nature and intent of the actors. While an argument may be made that by prohibiting anticompetitive behavior the antitrust laws stimulate efficiency by curbing "inefficiency," there is little reason to believe that section 2 of the Act offers any design other than what is constrained by its plain and unambiguous words:

"Every person who shall monopolize, or attempt to monopolize, or combine or conspire with any other person or persons, to monopolize any part of the trade or commerce among the several States, or with foreign nations, shall be deemed guilty of a felony, and, on conviction thereof, shall be punished by fine not exceeding $100,000,000 if a corporation, or, if any other person, $1,000,000, or by imprisonment not exceeding 10 years, or by both said punishments, in the discretion of the court."

The result then of judicial application of the antitrust laws in finding illegal behavior is simply punishment of the violator, not promoting competition or "efficiency" of a market, and although the result of a fairer distribution of fair competition by eliminating a violator might be expected, that outcome cannot be assured. Elaborating on the "design" or the "end sought" by the antitrust acts is gratuitous. The issue is the end sought by the violators and not necessarily their intent, because some business practices at times constitute anticompetitive behavior and at other times further competition within the market. In ambiguous cases, the rule of reason analysis is proper. Managed-care issues would not seem to present such a question, because MCOs openly state that their role is to "control costs" (albeit by controlling providers' prices) and to "improve medical care."

Although in decisions based on a rule of reason analysis the design of the antitrust laws might be considered, such a policy approach is often left by the courts to the executive branch's DOJ. However, it is hornbook law that *per se* violations found by the courts do not require further explanation or clarification when by their very nature they are seen as so elementary that no questions of a defendant's goal can be advanced or that support of congressional intent may be asked. As Senator Sherman said in 1889 during the congressional debate on his historic bill,

"There is nothing in the bill to prevent a refusal by anybody to buy something. All that it says is that the people producing or selling a particular article shall not make combinations to advance the price of the necessaries of life."

Reducing impossibly bulky data by computer analysis of purchasing patterns at the point of cash register sale can lead to an analysis of the effect of mergers on competition. *The Economist* reported in 1997 that when the FTC studied the proposed merger-takeover of Office Depot by Staples, it scrutinized the cash register bar code scanning of the quantities sold and the prices paid for all items. This revealed that in cities where Staples was not faced with an Office Depot competitor, Staples' prices were higher, and where it was locally faced with competition by Office Depot, the prices were lower. Though such an economic practice seems rather obvious, a searching analysis like this was possible only by the use of computerized crude data, showing that the penetration of low-price advertising in the competitive communities when seen outside them could mislead the public in the less-competitive communities to shop in the nearby Staples and face the higher price. This leads to the suggestion that historic methods of defining market power cannot simply be an "in your face" set of practices but may today require revisions so that more penetrating and sophisticated studies can be made than were available when the Sherman and Clayton Acts were enacted.

In 1997, when a proposed merger-takeover between Staples and Office Depot attempted to displace their competitor, Office Max, Mitt Romney—later to become the 2012 Republican presidential hopeful—was CEO of Bain Capital, the major venture capital partner in Staples and on the Staples board of directors from 1986 to 2001. Antitrust Division filings showed Staples and Office Depot as a combined company would control prices in many metropolitan areas and that in cities where Office Depot and Staples competed head to head, prices might be expected to rise 5 to 10 percent. Moreover, they were charging higher prices in parts of Florida counties where they competed with each other and lower prices in areas where they were rivals of Office Max. The FTC found out about this collusion by analyzing scanner data at the stores' checkout counters and decided to seek an injunction. Washington, DC, federal district Judge Thomas F. Hogan, after "visiting various stores,"enjoined the merger and, citing from the antitrust laws said

> "Likelihood of success on the merits in cases such as this means the likelihood that the Commission will succeed in proving, after a full administrative trial on the merits, that the effect of a merger between Staples and Office Depot 'may be substantially to lessen competition, or to tend to create a monopoly' in violation of Section 7 of the Clayton Act . . . in a suit for a preliminary injunction, the government need only show that there is a 'reasonable probability' that the challenged transaction will substantially impair competition. . . [and] the Court cannot find that those efficiencies [alleged by the defendants] would result in the creation of so many additional jobs that the public equity would outweigh those argued by the plaintiff."

The proposed merger was dropped.

While stockholders of acquired smaller companies usually do quite well in mergers, owners of acquiring companies' stock rarely do. A 1997 survey by Dennis Mueller, an economist at the University of Vienna, showed that the acquiring companies typically had better-than-average returns on capital and worse-than average returns afterward, demonstrating that highly profitable companies can't seem to resist the urge to buy other companies with their accumulated cash rather than let the stockholders share in it. These findings resonated in research by Michael Porter of the Harvard Business School. He found that acquisitions by thirty-three large, successful corporations from 1950 to 1986 sold off or liquidated over 50 percent of their acquisitions within a decade. Indeed, General Mills sold three-quarters of the eighty-six new businesses it had bought, as had General Electric similarly in getting rid of 63 percent of its fifty-one acquisitions. AT&T bought NCR for $7 billion in 1991 and sold it for $3 billion four years later. Quaker Oats bought Snapple for $1.7 billion in 1994 and sold it three years later for $300 million. Novell acquired WordPerfect for $885 million only to sell it two years later to Corel for some $150 million in cash and stock.

A notable example in the healthcare field was the sale of the Mediplex Group, Inc. and subsidiaries. They were providers of subacute healthcare services through a network of inpatient facilities, ambulatory surgery centers, outpatient programs, and psychiatric hospitals. The sale in 1986 to Avon Products, Inc. (a U.S. cosmetics, perfume, and toy seller) was for $212 million and a $25 million note payable to the former principal Mediplex shareholder Abraham Gosman. However, by 1990, a corporation headed by Mr. Gosman and three other investors reacquired from Avon all of the outstanding Mediplex stock for $40 million. Avon agreed to retain responsibility for certain assets, obligations, and liabilities previously held by Mediplex, including all federal and state income tax liabilities and refunds for the periods prior to the sale back to Mediplex.

Four years later, it was announced that based on a January 27, 1994 agreement, Mr. Gosman planned to merge Mediplex with Sun Healthcare Group, and Mediplex was to receive over $106 million and more than eleven million shares of Sun common stock, making it a wholly owned subsidiary of Sun. Mr. Gosman would also have conveyed to himself certain assets including two operating healthcare facilities and a subsidiary of Mediplex that was engaged in the construction and development of healthcare facilities. The merger took place on June 23, 1994. Mr. Gosman's further ventures in healthcare are found later in the discussion of PhyMatrix.

8. Marginal-Cost Pricing

"Marginal cost"—the quantity increase in total cost that results from producing an additional increment of output—is a function largely of "variable" costs; that is, those costs that vary with changes in output such as labor, utilities, maintenance, and data processing. In HMOs, variable cost margins may include staff and doctors' time incurred because of their response to increases or decreases in policy benefits, subscribers' needs, and epidemiologic issues. "Fixed" costs do not significantly vary with changes in output. They are costs that typically include most management expenses, interest on bonded debt, property taxes, depreciation of nonconsumed equipment, and irreducible overhead.

Professors Areeda and Turner point out that although not an accounting cost, "opportunity cost" is deemed that portion of the return on investment currently necessary to attract more capital to the firm. "If price is below average variable costs at all levels of output [using average variable cost as a proxy for marginal cost], the firm can minimize losses only by ceasing operations" or by driving rivals out of the market and raising prices once more. As can be seen in Oxford's case, ceasing operations may have been avoided temporarily by cutting out money-losing activities such as Medicare subscribers, through making itself a quasi utility of the state by obtaining subsidies from either general revenue under Managed Medicaid, from pools set up under state aegis for such an occasion by competitors, or from a combination of them. Oxford's rescue by UHG, however, did not save its managed-care core from exposure as a deadweight-loss operation when its actuarial numbers were found to be flawed as a result of conflicts of interest with its parent. Subsidies for commercial companies were originally to be found in only the direst situations, when bankruptcy proceedings threatened an insurer who was then already on a path of state receivership and faced redistribution of its assets to another company.

The most striking case was that of the 2008 Troubled Asset Relief Program stimulus money given to banks and a handful of insurers and automakers to prop up the shaken insurance giant, AIG. The $700 billion allocated to TARP investment in 2008 was considered a necessary economic evil, and within two years, its cost to taxpayers dropped to $25 billion. Moreover, *The Washington Post* reported in October 2010 that the massive $800 billion "stimulus package"—the American Recovery and Reinvestment Act of 2009, signed into law a month after Mr. Obama took office—also met nearly a dozen deadlines set by Congress within a year, with minimal waste or fraud found. AIG's full debt, notwithstanding that the company that was "too big to fail," and allowed by the previous administration to have virtually no competitors, was then able to pay back to the government its debt, which was fully paid down by January 2011 and the government turned a profit of nearly $40 million, according to Time magazine in May. AIG was then preparing a "re-IPO," a stock offering estimated to surpass the General Motors $23 billion offering the prior November. But, by August 2011, shares of **AIG** plunged nearly 9 percent, following most of the selloff in financials after dour news about the U.S. economy and the European debt situation. However, the lower-than-anticipated costs for some projects permitted the administration to stretch the stimulus money further than expected and financed over three thousand additional projects. Soon thereafter, ACA state insurance risk-pool arrangements with competitors, called Exchanges and designed to reduce the soaring prices set by the hegemonic managed-care industry, began to appear ready to be set up by states or by the federal government.

A discussion of marginal-cost pricing is relevant to an evaluation of the economic potential of managed care and managed-care insurance as a market failure. If state or federal governments attempt to shore up a failed market by subsidy before private use is made of tax revenues, the remediation value of that failed market should be established by legislative initiative, not executive branch action. Such use of subsidy may be a sham covering up a form of predatory, below-cost pricing, requiring the observing eye of an active DOJ. A major antitrust concern regarding subsidized HMOs, especially when accomplished with help from a state's heavily lobbied deep pockets, is the granting of one company's greater ability to absorb financial losses than that of a non-subsidized competitor. Thus, subsidy may ultimately pose a superior threat to the stability of a competitive market, because it offers the lucky potential monopolist who receives it the ability to price rates low enough to preclude effective future competition by other, possibly more aggressive or competent "wannabe" HMOs. Of course, the major difference between industrial manufacturing or agricultural firms that have received subsidies and healthcare insurance is the dynamic nature of healthcare and the protean government regulation and microman-agement created after the enactments of Medicare and Medicaid with much duplication by state and nongovernmental accrediting organiza-tions. Therefore some of the economic models that follow, especially those having seemingly static conditions as found in Areeda and Turn-er's classic analyses related to antitrust concerns, need examination in the light of contemporary legislation and unusually powerful lobbying interests of the insurers who mimicked and remodeled state and federal medical standards and price-setting methodologies.

For-profit HMOs or managed-care insurers such as WellPoint or Humana that have other noncore types of business in their organiza-tion, could certainly strengthen their monopolistic, money-losing state of affairs by support from other aspects of their business. Moreover, even a nonprofit HMO such as Kaiser-Permanente's range of wholly owned for-profit subsidiaries could prompt similar market manipula-tions to strengthen their parent.

We saw that *Timkin* was reversed along with six other cases by the *Copperweld* High Court, which held that it was permissible for a "par-ent and a subsidiary [to] 'always have a unity and purpose or a common design'" for purposes of § 1 of the Sherman Antitrust Act. However, the Court did uphold the Sherman § 2 distinction that "[t]he conduct of a single firm is governed by § 2 alone and is unlawful only when it threatens actual monopolization." It would seem proper then to con-sider Sherman § 2 to be invoked in situations where the "subsidiary" was not in the core business and its only "common design" with the parent was for the transfer of money to it. An MCO's actions, falling on the good graces of the state or federal government under color of public policy considerations as "too big to fail"—or what we referred to as a *Noerr* defense to rescue it—could be seen as attempts to monopolize in violation of section 2 of the Sherman Act were it not for the government sanction.

Antitrust specialists William G. Kopit and Kenneth L. Klothen point out in the 1981 *St. Louis University Law Journal*, in "Antitrust Implications of the Activities of Health Maintenance Organizations":

"HMOs almost invariably lose money in their early years until such time when increased enrollments create economies of scale. . . Nevertheless, there is probably enough actuarial data on HMOs to permit evidence that a particular pricing structure in the start-up period is so far below costs that it unreasonably pushes forward the break-even point. This evidence should be admissible on the issue of predatory intent."

The profit-maximizing or loss-minimizing output issue for any firm, whether competitive or monopolistic, is that any sustainable increase in output would add more to costs than to revenues and any sustainable decrease in output would reduce revenues more than costs. In short, in deciding whether it would increase or decrease output, the firm looks to the incremental effects on revenues and costs. Thus, the relevant cost to the firm is the marginal cost. In their classic diagram, Areeda and Turner distinguish the different categories of cost and portray their relationship. They show that marginal cost (MC) is equal to average variable cost (AVC) when AVC is at a minimum and is equal to total average cost (which includes capital cost) when average cost (AC) is at a minimum, with MC able to rise above each over time at different levels of output. They point out that

"[I]n order to determine which of these various costs is relevant to predatory, 'below cost' selling, we must first ask what costs are relevant to the firm which is seeking to maximize profits or minimize losses, since a firm which seeks to do so is normally responding to acceptable economic incentives and thus is not engaging in predatory behavior."

In a perfectly competitive field, a firm's ability to affect market price by variations in its output is minimal and it accepts the market price, keeping its incremental or marginal revenue from selling any additional units of output equal to the market price itself. Areeda and Turner explain the profit-maximizing price for the "perfectly competitive firm" as follows. Because the firm is unable to affect price by changes in output, it usually faces a horizontal demand curve. The firm maximizes profit when price remains equal to marginal cost; that is, when decreases in output will reduce profits and increases in output will decrease profitability. Such situations in a perfectly competitive world also offer an efficient allocation of resources:

"market price reflects what consumers are willing to pay for the last unit of output [and] marginal cost reflects the full current cost of resources needed to produce it [while] a higher price would result in a reduction in output and thus deprive some buyers of a commodity for which they were willing to pay the cost of production."

Because the monopolist can affect market price by varying its output, it faces a downward-sloping curve. An increase in output will tend over time to reduce the market price. This does not seem to occur in healthcare. It is concealed because healthcare has a rising cost curve, where offering more healthcare cannot reduce unit cost. However, lowering providers' capitation costs and manipulating output by directly managing patient care allows the monopolist to succeed in the short term. Ultimately, when MCO healthcare prices end up above "what consumers are willing to pay for the last unit of output," especially when supported by government contracts or subsidies, the monopolists have proffered a deadweight loss to society. This is commonly seen when people cut back on seeing doctors or cutting pills in half.

Although Areeda-Turner's explanations use the term "commodity," which has been held to be distinct from "services," the similarities between efficient production of commodities and efficient use of healthcare resources under government and commercial insurers' concepts of managed care can no longer escape notice. This is especially so as the terms are used interchangeably by healthcare economists, and the technologies involved today require much capital equipment for the "service" to be delivered. Areeda-Turner brings the dynamic similarity closer by saying that the firm with monopoly power has by definition captured a sufficiently large part of a market to determine price by varying its output, as we will see occurs with managed-care market manipulation.

Another danger from monopoly behavior, rarely distinguished in court challenges to healthcare monopoly, is its deadening of innovation by locking purchasers into insurance policies that deny preexisting illnesses and refuse to pay for experimental drugs that have already had significant degrees of success in government-supervised and private sector, randomized controlled trials. This problem characterizes even the highly praised government employee coverage, by its shortsighted, shortened-hospital-stay and outpatient algorithmic managed-care techniques. As reported by the National Center for Health Statistics, from the beginning of DRGs in 1982 until 2000, otherwise unexplained deaths from pneumonia, chronic lower respiratory diseases, and diabetes increased. Studies showed that many of these would have largely been prevented had treatment not been restricted by managed-care insurers, Medicare's "utilization review," and "price-per-illness" DRG coercion.

Robert H. Lande, professor of law at the University of Baltimore School of Law and director of the American Antitrust Institute, pointed out that there are two different sources of market power in antitrust cases. There are some that are "market share-based" and those "from deception, significantly imperfect or asymmetric information, unduly large transaction costs, or from other types of market failures that usually are associated with consumer protection violations." He says the FTC has long described the necessary conditions for effective consumer choice in market failure terms when it pursues its consumer protection function:

> "the ban on unfair competition prevents exclusionary or anti-competitive behavior and helps preserve a full variety of marketplace options for consumers to choose among; the ban on deception helps ensure that consumers will not make that choice on the basis of misleading information; and the ban

on unfair practices ensures that the choice is not distorted by coercion, the withholding of important information, or similar practices."

Because a monopolist with significant market power can affect market price by varying its output, it copes with a downward-sloping price curve. An increase in output will tend to reduce the market price, and a decrease in output produces scarcity, increasing the market price. As with managed care, where patients get less-than-optimal care per unit effort, some say, "it's like helping a disabled person half-way across the street." In 2004, Professor Martin McKee, writing a policy brief for the European Observatory on Health Systems and Policies, found that

"Several studies from North America have found that, contrary to expectations, decreases in hospital capacity increased the cost of hospital care per patient treated. In one case, it was because closure of a small hospital meant that patients were treated in more expensive teaching hospitals. In a second, reductions in beds led to reductions in admissions but increased the average lengths of stay even more. The result was a higher cost per case. Similarly, in California in the 1980s, a reduction of 11% in admissions was associated with a 22% increase in costs per case."

As we have said, because of its rising cost curve, the downward-sloping price/demand curve in healthcare is largely hidden, because providing more healthcare alone does not reduce its per unit cost as it could in manufacturing. In healthcare, the unit cost is made even higher by the costly advances of technology and capital improvement. The only choice left for the monopolist or government monopsonist is to cut the prices paid to the providers. In addition, managed-care insurers can reduce demand for drugs by establishing economically punitive high-price formularies and distort the appearance of the cost of healthcare by requiring increased copayments for patients going "out of network."

Ironically, the medically and economically redundant role played by the managed-care insurance industry in healthcare further stabilizes the prices while raising the total costs by removing the perceived cost-to-premium-price money from the system, hiding the cost shifting to the premium payers' out-of-pocket costs. The Areeda-Turner analyses as applied to healthcare also do not include an appropriate rate of return for creative innovation adequate to its real conditions of healthy competition. Nevertheless, as stated in 2006 by Tom Campbell, director of finance, state of California and a former director of the bureau of competition in the FTC, "if a firm is pricing a product below a price that would be adequate to obtain adequate innovation in a dynamic model, then . . . it ought to lead to potential antitrust liability."

In manufacturing, Areeda-Turner point out that a monopolist's "pricing at or above marginal cost will not eliminate equally efficient rivals or potential entrants, which may freely restrict their output to efficient levels and thus make substantial profits at the monopolist's price." They say this:

> "We conclude that prices at or above marginal cost, even though they are not profit-maximizing, should not be considered predatory. If a monopolist produces to a point where price equals marginal cost, only less efficient firms will suffer larger losses per unit of output; more efficient firms will be losing less or even operating profitably. By definition, a firm producing at an output where marginal cost exceeds price is selling at least part of that output at an out-of-pocket loss. It could eliminate that loss by reducing its output or, where the highest obtainable price is below average variable cost at all levels of output, by ceasing operations altogether."

Marginal revenue is the additional revenue added by an additional unit of output. Marginal cost is the cost of the additional inputs needed to produce that output. The monopolist's marginal revenue is always below his or her price. In order to get people to buy additional units of the good, the firm reduces price (such as "buy two, get one free"). In managed healthcare, the list prices allow plenty of room for such discounting and for generating brokers' commissions. Therefore, the extra revenue received through monopolists' sales is less than the previous one, with the hoped result that the output at which marginal cost equals marginal revenue will generate a price that exceeds marginal cost. This does not matter as much in managed care insurance. Because cash flow is its main objective, it is satisfied with increasing total revenue by mergers and acquisitions, even to include failed companies. The only trophy is the hapless managed patient cohort. To pay for the mergers, the price has to be considered as being inflated above what a willing market will pay for healthcare, as it occurs at the point on the demand curve higher than where the marginal cost meets the demand, once more producing a deadweight loss to society.

Ordinarily the monopolist maximizes profit when marginal revenue is equal to marginal cost and on a graph is seen as intersecting with average cost. With sufficient market power, the profit-maximizing monopolist, the same as the government monopsonist, will produce a quantity to sell at a price that is higher than marginal cost. Such behavior is not predatory, when based on savings generated by the 2010 ACA's Exchanges. With government uniformity and supervision, the money is being used for developing uniform electronic medical records, for eliminating the managed-care insurance industry's rescissions, denials of preexisting illnesses, and lifetime limits, and bringing millions more into healthcare coverage and out of the expensive emergency rooms substituting for primary-care physicians.

As we have seen, mergers and acquisitions in healthcare, and displacing rivals or forcing them out of business, produces revenue that comes from the inelastic but unpredictable variable of the demand caused by human illness. In manufacturing, any amount by which the selling price exceeds the variable costs incurred by the marginal output will be pure profit. However, even in manufacturing, this is an unsafe assumption, because the firm's competitors will be forced to lower their prices as well. Customers will insist on these low prices as the norm while the firm, to survive in the longer term, will still have to ensure that its total revenue exceeds its total costs. The difference between manufacturing and healthcare—the latter having a rising cost curve— is that except for government involvement, selling of healthcare units at a loss by managed-care insurers produces a market failure. Those "losses" are dead weight to the economy, because the "less-efficient firms losing less or even operating profitably" are trading at the expense of healthcare providers' inefficiency and of their patients' illnesses, at prices higher than willing buyers would pay if they knew what they were getting for their money.

9. Marginal-Cost Pricing—Competitive or Predatory?—and the "Nonprofits"

> "Probably the most startling finding revealed the coercive nature of managed care: 'The management of care in HMOs increases the constraints on consumers and thus affects their use decisions.'"
>
> —RAND Corporation study (2005)

> "By 2004, approximately 70 percent of hospitals remained nonprofit while 70 percent of MCOs were for-profit."
>
> —InterStudy

Areeda and Turner have concluded that marginal-cost pricing in manufacturing is an economically sound division between acceptable, competitive behavior and "below-cost" predation, and they suggest a prohibition of prices below marginal cost. The following sums up their theory of predatory marginal-cost pricing rescue:

> "If it is appropriate to permit a monopolist to expand output in the short run to the point where marginal cost equals price, it should be equally appropriate to permit him to expand capacity to the point where long-run marginal cost equals price, even though that expansion reduces his overall rate of return and even though it limits or forecloses the opportunities of rival or new entrants. Similarly, if it is appropriate to condemn a monopolist for pricing below marginal cost in the short run, it would seem equally appropriate to condemn him for adding new facilities when he anticipates that the revenue to be obtained from them over their useful life will not cover all costs, including a normal rate of return."

In "Physician Contracting with Health Plans: A Survey of the Literature," by Martin Gaynor of Carnegie Mellon University and Tami Mark of The MEDSTAT Group, Inc., said in June, 1999,

"During the 1980s and 1990s, health care markets in the United States have been dominated by two major trends: tremendous growth in managed care and, most recently, a strong movement toward consolidation, both horizontally and vertically. . .

"Health plans can sometimes increase their leverage over physicians by developing contracting relationships that prevent physicians from participating in any other managed care organization (called "exclusivity clauses"). In a similar vein, some contracts include "Most Favored Nation" pricing that requires a physician to reduce the level of his or her billings to the managed care plan, if contracting for a lower level of fees with another plan."

They describe three conditions that reveal the essential conflict of interest in the insurer-physician relationship, which they define as that of "principal" and "agent."

"Take the case of physicians and insurers. There are two tasks to perform: practicing medicine and underwriting and administering insurance. A trained physician could potentially both practice medicine and underwrite and administer insurance, but he is comparatively better at the practice of medicine than is the insurer, thus he concentrates on that activity. The argument is similar for the insurer. The implication of the comparative advantage is specialization. Further, if the insurer needs medical treatments to be available to purchasers of his insurance plan, he will contract with the physician to provide these services. The individual performing the task for another party is called the *agent*. The individual hiring the agent is called the *principal*.

"The second necessary condition for an agency relationship to exist is *divergent objectives*. This means that the objectives of the insurer and the physician differ. For example, the insurer may care about quality of care and cost. Physicians may care about quality of care as well, but they also care about their income. Since the two parties care about different things, it will not generally be true that the same actions will maximize the objectives of both the principal and the agent. Thus the implication of divergent objectives is that there is a conflict between the two parties.

"The third necessary condition is *asymmetric information*. Comparative advantage and divergent objectives don't in and of themselves create a problem. If there is perfect information then the principal knows everything (or alternatively, all the relevant information), including exactly what the agent does. In this case, the principal can simply write a *forcing contract* for the agent, i.e., one that pays him a competitive wage if the desired action is taken, and nothing if it is not. There is unlikely to be perfect information, however. What is more likely is that there is imperfect information, and that the agent is better informed about matters relevant to task performance than is the principal. This is called *asymmetric information*. The implication of asymmetric information is that the principal doesn't know exactly what the agent is doing, nor does he know all the other factors determining performance, so it is not possible to directly observe whether the agent has taken the desired action, nor is it possible to infer it with certainty. Thus, the principal can only infer the agent's action in probability.

"Taken together, these three conditions create a relationship between principal and agent where the agent has incentives to shirk at any task and the principal cannot precisely detect that shirking. Further, if the agent is risk averse, it will not be optimal for the principal to fully penalize him for shortfalls in observable outcomes, since they may not be the result of the agent shirking, but rather due to random shocks. This means that a contract which is optimal given the information structure will not be fully based on observable outcomes. For example, suppose that a physician sees patients and produces health outcomes and costs with his own effort, which the insurer cannot observe. However, the actual health outcomes and costs are also the product of patient severity of illness, which is randomly distributed in the population and not observable to the insurer. Thus a poor outcome or high cost might be the result of low effort by the physician or of the patient being severely ill. The insurer is unable to discern which is the source of the poor outcome."

The fundamental defect in physicians' abandonment of their social role as agent of the patient, and substituting for it a "principal-agent" relationship with an insurer, is that it establishes suboptimal imperfections in the market. This can result in overproduction of goods and services that produce negative external effects or underproduction of goods and services that produce positive external effects, and are the core of the managed-care market failure. Additionally, such economic market behavior ends up supplying inadequate (or inaccurate) information to patient-purchasers, generates inadequate capacity for society (by restricting, rationing or producing scarcity of care), ultimately brings about dysregulation of the movement of labor and capital, and utilizes socially valueless "rent-seeking behavior" (all of which will be explored later). *See* Plates 8 and 9.

The Areeda-Turner test of predatory pricing does not take into account an anticompetitive effect of prices equal to marginal cost in healthcare. However, some argue that this test, applied to healthcare, would limit examination of a situation to one where a defendant with a great deal of market power—or having gained "most-favored-nation" (MFN) status by the state or large commercial insurer—may be faced by a challenge from a smaller plaintiff, new to the market, who argues for a case-by-case analysis under the rule of reason. MFN in commercial healthcare was adapted from the "lower-of-cost-or-charges" Medicare regulation repealed in 1988 by the Reagan administration Secretary of DHHS, Otis Bowen, a medical doctor. Originally, the regulation was supposed to prevent Medicare from paying more for services than the provider was charging its non-Medicare patients. However, the repeal opened the door for managed-care insurance companies to negotiate payments lower than regular Medicare cost-based reimbursement allowed. Commentators James Doherty, Jr., and Monique Ras discussed "Most-Favored-Nation Clauses in Payor/Provider Agreements" in an article for the Maryland State Bar Association in 2005. They say,

"Providers and other opponents argue that they are anticompetitive and lead to informal provider collusion to create a price 'floor' in a local market," pointing out that the MFN clauses in insurer-provider contracts typically require

"the provider to charge to the payer the provider's 'usual fee' defined to be 'the lowest fee charged or offered and received as payment in full.' Similarly, a [MFN] clause may require that a provider not 'charge fees to an insurer higher than the fees the provider accepts from any other non-governmental group, group plan, or panel.'"

They cite from the testimony of Robert McNair, Jr. on MFN clauses at the joint DOJ and FTC hearings on healthcare antitrust in 2003:

"A typical objection to MFN clauses is 'that they produce marketplaces in which new competitors are simply unable to survive because they can't compete on price by pricing below the dominant player in the market. In turn, that permits sellers to maintain artificially high floor prices for goods or services.' This argument is significant in a healthcare context where 'it is almost impossible for a competitor to attract customers on the basis of quality and almost as hard to compete on the basis of product differentiation.'

"In fact, some smaller insurers, 'have been forced out of business because the provider, when faced with the choice to do business solely with the dominant insurer or to do business with both the dominant insurer and other, smaller companies that can deliver less patient volume but can absorb the provider's excess capacity (thereby activating the MFN provision), choose to terminate or avoid relations with the other insurers to avoid activating the MFN provision.' Not only may some new competitors be unable to survive, doctors and other medical professionals may be placed in the position of having to limit their payor mix if they cannot afford to provide discounts to small carriers for fear they will in turn have to deal with the repercussions of having to further discount their services to their larger providers."

Because of the failure of managed care to create a healthy market, it opens floodgates for more-sophisticated methods of price fixing to be developed by companies like pharmacies serving the flawed managed-care juggernaut. A flagrant example of pricing below marginal cost was seen in the proposed class-action settlement between four pharmaceutical companies and forty thousand retail pharmacies climbing over the $700 million mark. The consolidated action, originally filed in 1993, contended that Abbott Laboratories, Pharmacia & Upjohn, Inc., the Hoechst Marion Roussel unit of Hoechst A.G. of Germany, and Rhone-Poulenc Rorer, Inc., conspired to develop a two-tier pricing system in the early 1990s. *The New York Times* reported that documents were uncovered that led the federal judge to quote from them saying it was "unquestionable" that the drug companies

"had the opportunity to conspire [and that there was] evidence of seminars and trade association meetings, which virtually every defendant attended at one time or another, and a coordinated exchange of pricing and other competitive information [was] shared among the manufacturers."

The gravamen of the lawsuit, or gist of the charge made by the retail pharmacies, stated that the drug makers gave discounts to managed-care companies and HMOs while charging the retailers higher prices. This could have had the effect of forcing smaller retail pharmacies out of business and creating a market for the HMO pharmacies. One of the methods that may have been implicated could be seen in the activities of Pharmacia & Upjohn, Inc., which had a wholly owned subsidiary "Greenstone." It was widely known that HMOs generally have refused to pay for expensive brand-name drugs when generics are available, so while the distributor for Upjohn sold a minor tranquilizer, Xanax, to pharmacies for $1 per 1-mg pill, Greenstone could sell the same pill as the generic, alprazolam, for $0.04. Claims of the pharmaceutical industry's proclaiming the need for recapturing the costs of "research and development" aside, it is difficult to determine the ability of Upjohn's Greenstone to make a generic pill distributable so far below its marginal cost for only four cents unless predatory intent were involved.

As in *Copperweld Corporation*, the 1984 Supreme Court said a "parent and a subsidiary 'always have a unity and purpose or a common design'" for purposes of Sherman § 1. However, in this retail pharmacy case, it was not the usual predatory intent to exclude a direct product rival, because Xanax was still under patent, and Greenstone was in the pharmaceutical industry. More important than the need to compete on a particular product is the ability to exclude rivals by insinuation into a market where a class of essentially similar drugs (in this case, benzodiazepines) can be the target of the monopolist. In *Copperweld*, the Court said, "This is the rule of the marketplace and is precisely the sort of competition that promotes the consumer interests that the Sherman Act aims to foster." However, the Sherman Act could hardly be interpreted as aiming to "foster" a situation such as where Upjohn's Greenstone sells alprazolam to HMOs at wholesale prices around $0.04 for a 1-mg pill and its brand name Xanax to retail pharmacies at $1 for the same-dose pill.

In the predatory "chain of events," discussed earlier, antitrust lawyers examined the 10.7 percent average surge in wholesale prescription drug, minor tranquilizer prices that took place in May 1998 and pushed the Producer Price Index up 0.2 percent, with minor tranquilizers leading the way, rising nearly 600 percent in the same month. As another example, in June, a spokeswoman for Mylan Laboratories, Inc.—the then-leading generic drug maker—was quoted in a *USA Today* article as saying that the company had to quadruple the wholesale price of the antianxiety drug lorazepam (brand name Ativan) on March 20, 1998 from $16.95 to $64.31 per 100 pills. The spokeswoman cited raw-material cost, back-ordering for months, approval delays, "market-place factors" and numerous lawsuits as reasons that drove up costs.

As a result of the extraordinary surge in pharmaceutical prices—apparently observing the Areeda-Turner theory of "eliminating that loss by reducing its output or, where the highest obtainable price is below average variable cost at all levels of output, by ceasing operations altogether"—several national distributors left the lorazepam market, including Warner-Chilcott, Rugby, Purepac, Goldline, and Zenith, as well as one of the largest, Geneva (Novartis), owned by Ciba-Geigy, when it found that its marginal cost exceeded its price. They were in effect forced out by the monopolist Mylan. Having become the parent of "Mylan Laboratories," Mylan, Inc. went global in 2007, acquiring a 71.5 percent controlling interest in Matrix Laboratories Limited, a Hyderabad-based supplier of active pharmaceutical ingredients. By 2010, it became one of the largest generics and specialty pharmaceutical companies in the world.

In January 2011, *The New York Times* reported on "Coupons for Patients Higher Bills for Insurers," based on the pharmaceutical companies' mass offerings of "discount coupons" that with "drug prices rising and many people out of work are increasingly helping patients with their copayments" and to reduce their out-of-pocket costs for drugs. Coupon ads such as these flood TV commercials, offering "free two-week trial offers" of drugs, usually of psychopharmaceuticals. *The New York Times* article extensively documented that the massive increases in the drug prices were far above the reduction offered by the discounts to consumer-patients and that the discounts concerned the FDA enough to study the effects on consumer perceptions that "the coupons will make consumers believe that a drug is safer or better than it really is." The article opened with a description of a

"small insurance company in Albany [NY, whose executives] were mystified when, almost overnight, its payments for a certain class of antibiotics nearly doubled, threatening to add about a half-million dollars annually in costs. The reason, it turns out, was that patients were using a card distributed by the maker of an expensive antibiotic used to treat acne, sharply reducing their insurance copayments."

The title of the article, "Coupons for Patients Higher Bills for Insurers," makes it appear as if the insurers are the victims suffering from higher bills, when the bills are caused by reduced copayments for the patients who switched from the generic to the brand-name drug.

Nevertheless, it demonstrates only part of the story of why healthcare costs are as high as they are, because the "small insurance company" turns out to be a nonprofit organization founded and run by doctors that owns its for-profit subsidiaries. After reporting horror stories about the machinations of the pharmaceutical companies' use of mass-marketing techniques, the article ends with a statement:

> "a vice president of the Albany insurance company, Capital District Physicians' Health Plan found her own solution. Her company started requiring patients to try the generic before using [the expensive antibiotic]. The cost per claim dropped back down."

The peremptory, cost-saving effort by Capital District Physicians' Health Plan (CDPHP) to have its subscribers "try the generic before using [the expensive antibiotic]," considering that the pharmaceutical companies' excessive price increases far outweighed any attempts to reduce costs, exemplifies the methods used by managed-care insurance companies to manipulate its market. Because CDPHP has contracts in the public sector, the New York State health department was required to certify it in a "Plan-Specific Report" reviewing the following domains: Corporate profile, enrollment and provider network, utilization, quality indicators, health information technology, deficiencies and appeals, and financial data. In a report on its "operational survey" performed every two years, the state gave its April 2010 seal of approval as of 2008, based largely on NCQA's HEDIS data. The survey found three out of three Medicaid appeals by patients upheld, while less than half of fourteen commercial claims were overturned.

According to the section on "Insurance Companies" on the official New York State government website, "Government Jobs in New York," CDPHP was founded in Albany in 1984 as a not-for-profit individual practice association-model HMO, with a "family of products [that] includes more than nine thousand providers and practitioners under four business lines. The following discussion, citing from sections found on its own website, explains how the company functions:

"The Capital District Physicians' Health Plan, Inc. is a nonprofit parent in the public and private sector that consists of Healthy New York, Medicare Choice (group and individual), Medicaid, Child Health Plus and Family Health Plus. . . CDPHP Universal Benefits, Inc. consists of a Preferred provider organization (PPO), a High Deductible PPO (HDPPO), an exclusive provider organization (EPO), and a point-of-service (POS) organization. UBI is a CHPHP wholly owned Business Corporation regulated by the NY insurance department."

CDPHP is a managed-care company in the state-regulated business of insurance, and an HMO organized pursuant to New York State insurance law, which pays for the healthcare of its four hundred thousand subscribers to its "9,000 providers and practitioners." According to a 2000 state insurance department audit, its participating providers are paid on a fee-for-service basis that authorizes the HMO to withhold up to 20 percent "from fees paid to the physicians for the purpose of retaining the funds to offset operating deficits, to establish operating reserves, or to meet other financial needs of the HMO." According to the audit, CDPHP also owns 50 percent of an unauthorized captive offshore reinsurance company.

In healthcare, the monopolist maximizes profits automatically by varying the output downward at a certain point of productivity or even of inefficiency (if not caught doing it), especially because the premium and capitation are paid in advance of service delivery. The irony is that the premium is paid whether the services are delivered or not and when they are delivered. The adversely selected cost is already built in by additional, costly stop-loss insurance premiums paid by the MCO, which often owns the (captive) insurance company. A regular corporation pays income tax on the funds it retains as profits. However, as the business of insurance requires the payment of future claims, the accumulation of funds is a necessity for being able to pay such claims.

UBI, CDPHP's wholly owned Business Corporation, was admonished in 2004 by the state insurance department for violations, including missing medical information and Explanation of Benefits (EOB) to patients for denials of care, utilizing an unlicensed claims adjuster to negotiate discounts for medical bills from nonparticipating providers, failing to issue a notice of first adverse determination to its members/providers relative to a retrospective review of claims when such claims involved medical necessity, not clearly specifying which entity, UBI or CDPHP, was providing the coverage for the specific product(s) being offered, investing more that 10 percent of its admitted assets in the securities of a single institution, obtaining capitalizing loans from its parent, CDPHP, without approval from the NY Superintendant of Insurance, and not properly sending adverse determine notices to patients or providers in violation of the state insurance law.

"Capital District Physicians' Healthcare Network, Inc. is an administrative services organization including self-insured plans. APA Partners, Inc. is a for-profit, third party administrator organization engaged in designing benefit plans for employers including all the services offered by its parent, CDPHP."

APA Partners, Inc. (no relation to the American Psychiatric or American Psychological associations) performs ASO functions; that is setting up employer self-funded plans and stop-loss programs. Its CEO, Dr. John Bennett, founded APA, Inc. He is a founding director of CDPHP and the CEO of CHDPHP's Healthcare Network, Inc. and CDPHP Universal Benefits, Inc. UBI was found to be reinsured by a second, unauthorized, off-shore Bermuda corporation to which CDPHP, its parent, made $1,000,000 in capitalizing loans, receiving in return 100 percent of the common stock issued by the company.

The 2004 New York insurance department audit exposed how coercive price predation works in the managed-care arena. CDPHP used a non-HIPAA-compliant business associate agreement with an unlicensed, third-party claims adjuster, Medcal, Inc., which sent letters to nonparticipating providers. The text of the letter utilized by Medcal contained the following statement: "We have been requested by the payor to negotiate with your office in order that we may reduce the out-of-network costs for the patient and expedite payment to your office."

The audit noted,

"This statement is misleading for two reasons. First, a review of Medcal negotiated claims reveals that the vast majority of the claims only involved a co-payment on the part of the member. In this circumstance, the member's costs are not being reduced. Second, prior to the negotiation, the Plan's liability is asserted because UBI has already been billed by the provider for the amount the provider charges for the services that were rendered to the UBI member. The negotiation is simply an attempt to reduce that liability. It is recommended that the Plan preclude its third-party negotiator from using prompt payment of claims as justification for the negotiation of discounted rates."

According to the New York State division of Corporations, Medcal Corporation, after filing on May 22, 2000, was dissolved "by Proclamation / Annulment of Authority on June 30, 2004." It should be obvious that if CDPHP was denying payments to nonparticipating providers for "lack of medical necessity," it was actively engaged in nonprice predatory and coercive behavior to eliminate rivals. In any event, its overcautious 20 percent withholds for losses from its own HMO doctors would have paid for any determinations of lack of medical necessity—that is, if the HMO ever penalized its own salaried or fee-for-service providers.

CDPHP's managed-care coercion was demonstrated by the "claims negotiator" letter to the nonparticipating provider:

"we *would propose* a [contract type] payment of . . . " and ". . . the patient *should not* be billed the difference . . ." [italics added by the state auditor]. Additionally, the letter does not clearly indicate that a signature on the letter is an acceptance of the terms of the agreement. . . . The letter used by Medcal in order to negotiate a discount on claims from nonparticipating providers does not indicate that the claim relates to UBI. Instead, it references only the Parent, CDPHP. It is recommended that the Plan ensure that the letters used by Medcal clearly indicate for which corporate entity Medcal is negotiating."

An example of a healthy monopsony is the manner in which the present Medicare Part A (hospital) Trust Fund reveals basic stability in its revenue growth. Almost from its inception, the Hospital Insurance Trust Fund has faced a projected shortfall, but the insolvency date has been postponed a number of times, primarily due to legislative changes that had the effect of restraining growth in program spending. Obviously a result of the increased payments into the fund from the high rate of employment and low rate of inflation during the last years of the Clinton administration, and discounted further by the politically maneuvered 1997 BBA cuts, the newer projections extended the time for the fund to "go broke" from 1997 to 2008.

After the enormous bump in the public share of health services that occurred on the advent of Medicare and Medicaid in 1966, the only significant public health service increases took place in 1972 when the disability population and children's services were added to the programs. Otherwise, the public share held flat until the early 1990s when managed care entered the scene and Congress brought Medicare and Medicaid managed-care contracts into play through the BBA, and the MMA and other measures taken by the Bush II administration and Republican Congress after 2000 to move those federal and state programs into the private sector. President Bush twice vetoed expansion of the State Children's Health Insurance Program (SCHIP) originally passed as part of the BBA, arguing that it would expand "federalization." Almost 70 percent of uninsured children could not qualify for aid because they were in families whose incomes were 200 percent over the poverty level. However, within two weeks after taking office, President Obama signed the Children's Health Insurance Reauthorization Act of 2009, extending the program without a waiting period to an additional four million children and pregnant women, including, for the first time, legal immigrants.

We have noted another factor that does not limit healthcare and managed healthcare insurance from antitrust behavior analysis: its rising cost curve, where the average variable cost per unit of healthcare cannot be significantly reduced by an increase in unit output or by volume, as it can with manufacturing. The managed-care insurance industry, by its reduction of treatment intensity and resource use per unit time, has created artificial scarcities of service availability. It maintains the fiction of providing greater "quality" of care by use of the "preferred provider" and refuses appropriate payment to out-of-network doctors who supply similar services. Because the preferred providers accept a price per unit less than its marginal cost, the out-of-network providers are compelled to make up their losses partially from out-of-pocket charges shifted to the patients. This conduct not only identifies the MCOs and their preferred provider cohort as direct competitors of the OON providers but also fixes subscribers' higher prices for the same medical services when they go OON and reduces the value of their premium. The OON cost imparts a disincentive to receive the hoped-for care and ultimately coerces the plan members back into the MCO network. Moreover, if the patients continue with OON providers, the MCOs get a "free ride" from the prepaid premiums, which had assumed the marginal cost of their care.

The tithe forced on the plan member wanting freedom of choice—increased copayments to meet the non-"preferred" providers' prices, often at a punishing 50 percent level—also causes significant collection problems for the OON provider, equal or close to 50 percent of their usual and customary charges. This pressures the OON provider, too, to perform at or below its average variable cost at unstable revenue potential, in contrast to the IN doctor, who has more time to churn multiple units of referred patients and gain from the plan's fee-splitting incentives for "efficiencies" predicated on withholding more comprehensive or costlier care. For OON providers, Areeda-Turner could say, "Because such a price yields less than the normal return on capital, it can threaten the survival of equally efficient rivals with less staying power than the [HMO] monopolist enjoys." To paraphrase Areeda-Turner, such a provider could "eliminate that loss by reducing its output or, where the highest obtainable [collection of debt] is below average variable cost at all levels of output, by ceasing operations altogether" as many doctors have done, retiring much earlier than in the past.

In fact, a study by the AMA showed that the average age of doctors at retirement dropped to 67.4 in 1995 (from 69.8 in 1980) while life span increased in the same period. Thirty-eight percent of doctors aged fifty or older contacted in a telephone survey between October 1999 and April 2000 planned to retire within the next one to three years, while 48 percent of those surveyed indicated that managed care was either a significant factor or the single most important factor in their decision to retire early. Concurrent with six years of lowered managed-care doctors' prices, applications to medical schools were lower. In 1996, forty-seven thousand individuals applied to medical schools in the United States, dropping to thirty-four thousand by 2002. This demonstrated the failure inherent in a medical market manipulated by managed healthcare insurance and its deadweight loss to society in both the short and long term.

Fixed costs in healthcare generally follow the manufacturing paradigm: variable healthcare costs cannot be reduced by hooking ten patients up for simultaneous, assembly line EKGs, biopsies, or appendectomies. Although pharmacists may be able to increase their prescriptions per hour with pill-counting technology, a nurse's ability to speed up per-patient contact is only partially helped by video screening multiple areas in an intensive care unit, certainly not when dressings have to be changed or pain medication given. Time can be saved by videoconference, EKGs (preliminarily read by wireless networks), and computer/robot-aided surgery, but each end point is one-to-one, time-based contact with a patient by an expensively trained human provider. Nurses can train lesser-skilled people to handle some of the routine tasks they previously performed, and doctors can have nurses perform many of the elements of the expected doctor-patient relationship to attempt to wring profitability from the increased volume offered by HMO contracts. These time- and skill-savers work only to a small degree. The nurse would generally not be paid more per unit of nursing time, and the doctor or HMO would still have to pay someone to perform what the doctor did previously. When we remember that the doctors and nurses are paid less per patient unit of care by the MCOs, adding the lower salaries of the "assistants" to the cost of care begs the question of whether such less-skilled substitutions simply increase cash flow to the HMO or managed-care insurers at the expense of patients.

A 2005 study done for the Department of Defense (DOD) by the RAND Corporation explored the differences between military health services and those for the public. Most other studies were performed in the public arena, so much of the data had to be extrapolated. However, the care of military families in the TRICARE military system made the comparisons distinguishable. Regarding the supposed "elasticity of demand" for health services, the data showed this: "Despite a wide variety of empirical methods and data sources, the estimates of the [general] demand for healthcare . . . are consistently found to be price inelastic." Distinguishing the general "demand for health" from the "demand for healthcare," the study found "the demand for health is also found to be income inelastic." When examining the elasticity of the demand for healthcare, the conclusions were the same, although more complex:

"Consumers have demand for health but cannot directly purchase it. They must purchase healthcare services that are used to produce health . . . [economist Martin] Feldstein estimated that the price elasticity of demand for healthcare was approximately minus 0.5. This elasticity estimate is interpreted to say that a 1 percent increase in the coinsurance rate will lead to a 0.5 percent reduction in the mean hospital stay, or that the demand for healthcare services is relatively inelastic. In a similar vein, [health economists] Fuchs and Kramer used aggregate state-level data to investigate the price elasticity of demand for healthcare services . . . These results indicate that the demand for physician visits is relatively insensitive to changes in prices. After demonstrating the widely consistent findings on the relative inelasticity of providing healthcare services and its demand insensitivity to income differences, probably the most startling finding revealed the coercive nature of managed care: 'The management of care in HMOs increases the constraints on consumers and thus affects their use decisions.'"

W. Edwards Deming's 1986 work *Out of the Crisis* provided an efficiency model to healthcare that came to the attention of the Joint

Commission on Accreditation of Healthcare Organizations, government regulators and healthcare economists, who joined the cause to apply those constructs. They promoted the "quality" improvement movement that seemed to promise some reduction in poor outcomes and yield a more efficient use of resources. Deming's own work, borrowed from engineering, emphasized achieving quality by empowering employees and creating a genuine work ethic of continuous quality improvement. As Robert Kuttner, coeditor of *The American Prospect*, put it in a May 1998 *The New England Journal of Medicine* Perspective, "This is a far cry from a remote telephone bank of nameless utilization reviewers relying on a computer program to approve or disapprove treatment decisions by physicians." The view suggests that "quality" may not have been the aim of the managed-care insurers, because their "remote telephone bank of nameless utilization reviewers relying on a computer program" remained well after 2000 as the model for managed-care's style of quality improvement.

Nonprofit firms are not *per se* free from antitrust scrutiny. A defining characteristic of a nonprofit firm that offers a need for antitrust observation is that it is subject to a "nondistribution constraint," which prohibits the firm from distributing its residual earnings to any individuals such as members, directors, or officers that exercise control over the firm. Much of the use of nonprofit contracts by government in areas of remedial healthcare legislation is based on the theory that such an economic structure lends itself to the "trustworthiness" of nonprofit status. However, there have been many critics of the trustworthiness reliance: "the nonprofit motive stifles innovation," it makes them "prone to managerial shirking," and "by giving perks that might be valued by entrepreneurs almost as much as cash" becomes an important part of compensation packages.

As the noted economist Regina Herzlinger explained, the nonprofits' existence in healthcare eliminates a significant loss to the tax base because of their exemption from corporate income and property taxes. Although private, nonprofit hospitals do not benefit from using debt to shield profits from the corporate income tax, they do benefit from the personal income tax reductions reflected in the yields they pay on municipal bonds. In addition, successful, private, nonprofit hospitals in the United States have consistently earned "accounting profits," a company's total earnings, including depreciation, interest, and taxes. Judged in terms of such profit as a percent of revenue, the 1998 U.S. Medicare Payment Advisory Commission found that in the years 1988 to 1990, such hospitals were even more profitable than for-profit hospitals and paid salaries to top executives that would make post-2000 cost cutters blush.

A supermajority of private nonprofit firms has traditionally characterized the American hospital industry. By 1992, the ownership of hospital short-term beds was 24 percent public, 64 percent nonprofit, and 12 percent for-profit. HMOs by enrollment, as of 1993 were 0 percent public, 48 percent nonprofit, and 52 percent for-profit. According to the 2004 *International Journal of Healthcare Finance and Economics* using data from InterStudy, by 2004, approximately 70 percent of hospitals remained nonprofit while 70 percent of MCOs were for-profit. The greater percentage of nonprofit hospitals remains solidly entrenched in traditional congressional schemes as well as its supportive IRS tax-exempt base. As membership in their boards of directors and large financial contributors generally come from upper-middle and upper classes, they can benefit their hospital corporation portfolios through obtaining or providing endowments. By having the hospitals make capital purchases from the companies they privately invest in such as pharmaceuticals, new technology, and construction, some receive an added albeit hidden dividend.

As the commercial managed-care insurance companies began their consolidation, they recognized that acquiring the nonprofit Blues would be quite expensive, because the IRS would demand that they somehow pay back the profit-equivalents they made during their nonprofit years. In fact, it cost the Anthem/WellPoint merger $250 million to go back to the community to get its 2004 merger approval from the California Insurance Department. This expensive act by WellPoint/Anthem appears to be an example of predation, which, although dynamic over time, can be tested from a static perspective—namely whether the revenue generated by the activity is greater than the cost of the action.

191

If less, it provides evidence of an opportunity cost investment whose effect causes the exit of a rival or rivals. As we have said, the classic Areeda-Turner tests compares short-term price to marginal cost, but because the predator cannot keep its prices down forever, it will have to raise prices enough in time to justify the risk. With the purchase of the Blues in California and the subsequent "operational" mode of licensing other nonprofit Blue Cross plans from its parent association, this became possible as a forward-looking profitable activity.

In the 1970s, the commercial insurers had ventured only one-third of their health insurance policies as "major medical" or "comprehensive," knowing that the population requiring front-end coverage would be more likely antiselecting (that is, those persons expecting with some confidence that they would be ill sometime soon). Generally, if non-start-up revenue generated by an activity is less than the cost of the action, its behavior could be characterized as evidence of a predatory investment to cause the exit of a rival. However, the FTC had not prosecuted any company successfully for predatory pricing of goods since the 1993 case of *Brooke Group v. Brown & Williamson Tobacco*, which held that "the Robinson-Patman Act [the 1936 amendment to section 2 of the Clayton Antitrust Act] does not ban all price differences charged to 'different purchasers of commodities of like grade and quality.'" Instead, the Act proscribed "price discrimination only to the extent that it threatens to injure competition" where the effect is to lessen competition, as Clayton, section 2(a) says, "in any line of commerce," and that competition injury must be "at the level of the discriminating seller and its direct competitors."

The WellPoint/Anthem dealmakers' post-Millennium ventures in the Blues' plans were sharp to perceive that if 30 percent of their rivals' businesses were forced to exit the endeavor by the high cost of covering these illnesses, critics might see WellPoint/Anthem's action as an example of what has been called a "static cost-based test of predatory sacrifice." Therefore, they kept the Blues' nonprofit status at arm's length by paying for licensing them from the parent Blue Cross/Blue Shield Association. Moreover, a price discrimination charge of forcing out competitors would not hold, because the California Blues had those lower prices when they were nonprofit. In any event, since 2004, the Blues' prices were raised *de facto* by managed-care's devaluation of the front-end-style premium; after takeover, it gave WellPoint/Anthem the price/value flexibility to injure their commercial competitors. At the same time, they could put an end to "front-end" coverage value by adding higher copayments and deductibles to pay for their added administrative costs.

The Blue Cross Association, a federation of seventy separate health insurance organizations and companies, owns the Blue Cross/Blue Shield names and trademarks and licenses them to its members, and its only competitors after 2000 were Aetna, CIGNA, and UHG. As with the trustworthiness branding of nonprofit hospitals, so, too, was the branding relied upon by the formerly nonprofit Blues plans, all of whom were members of the Blue Cross/Blue Shield Association. If combined, they would provide directly or indirectly health insurance to over one hundred million Americans, including an additional thirty-four million individuals through their role as contractors for Medicare fiscal intermediary processing. Trustworthiness branding is essential for a core business like commercial managed-care insurance, whose reputation was far from trustworthy.

The merger of Anthem with WellPoint crystallized the issue. Why bother to make the nonprofit Blues into for-profit ogres when "operating" the nonprofit subsidiaries allowed them to capitalize on both their mission and margin? After all, the Blues' plans had earlier used for-profit subsidiaries to conduct business because of the IRS flexibility such arrangements allowed, so by operating the nonprofit plans under license from the Blue Cross Association, they would enlarge the operator's revenue base and eliminate rivals from the marketspace before having to decide when to take them to for-profit status. That is what WellPoint did before the merger with Anthem, Inc. At that time, the company's primary sources of revenue were premiums and administrative fees, holding exclusive licenses from the Blue Cross Association to operate the plans and charge businesses and governments for the management of self-insured ERISA-based employee health plans, many of whom used Blue Cross.

Effective November 30, 2004, WellPoint Health Networks, Inc., which served more than 15.6 million medical members and approximately 46.8 million specialty members nationwide through Blue Cross of California, Blue Cross Blue Shield of Georgia, Blue Cross Blue Shield of Missouri, Blue Cross Blue Shield of Wisconsin, HealthLink, a WellPoint company, and UNICARE, merged with Indianapolis-based Anthem, Inc., the fourth-largest publicly traded health benefits company in the United States, and an independent licensee of the Blue Cross and Blue Shield Association for Indiana, Kentucky, Ohio, Connecticut, New Hampshire, Maine, Colorado, Nevada and most of Virginia.

The importance of the trustworthiness branding enjoyed by the nonprofit BCBS plans was that in 1994, the BCBS Association made changes to allow its licensees to be for-profit corporations. Since their inception, the "Blues" were thought by Americans to provide "front-end," lower-cost, nonprofit insurance, to which "major-medical" policies offered by the commercial carriers could be added. As of January 1, 1987, pursuant to the 1986 tax reform act amendments, the federal government had removed the full 501(c) tax-exempt status of BCBS plans, and through internal revenue Code section 833, changed it to section 501(m), since they were found to be selling commercial-type insurance. By June of 1994, the national BCBS Association changed its long-standing requirement that all licensees be nonprofit.

In a winter 1997 edition of the *Bulletin of the New York Academy of Medicine*, Consumers Union researchers characterized the debate over Blue Cross nonprofit to for-profit status conversions and the dramatic changes in the healthcare industry that have

> "leapt out of specialized healthcare and business journals onto the front pages of *The New York Times, the Wall Street Journal, Money Magazine,* and *Newsweek* and into the airwaves of local television news programs, CNN, and 60 Minutes. The public is becoming engaged in the debate over the 'corporatization' of healthcare."

10. The Medicare+Choice and Medicare Advantage Programs—"Privatization" Tactics Arrive and "Obamacare" Enter an Offensive

> All the Property that is necessary to a Man, for the Conservation of the Individual and the Propagation of the Species, is his natural Right, which none can justly deprive him of: But all Property superfluous to such purposes is the Property of the Publick, who, by their Laws, have created it.
>
> —Benjamin Franklin to Robert Morris (1783)

An even greater danger for the Medicare Trust Fund, as a consequence of the so-called "baby boomer" entry, was the proportion of public money taken out of the healthcare system by the managed-care insurance industry's recruitment of large segments of the Medicare and Medicaid populations. Government payments to providers for Medicare and Medicaid patients go for those patients' healthcare alone. The medical loss ratio is 97 percent. Congress passed the 1997 BBA in the interest of saving healthcare money spent by government, in large part after much pressure by the managed-care industry to enhance its cash flow. The act offered managed-care companies the option to bid on taking Medicare patients at a 5 percent discount from what Medicare otherwise paid, effectively acknowledging that managed care could lower further the already-bare bones, cost-based rates paid to providers over the prior twenty-five years. States would make their own arrangements through Medicaid managed-care waivers in an attempt to take advantage of the "savings" that appeared to have occurred in the private sector.

However, prior to 2000, the zealous managed-care entrepreneurs realized that they couldn't handle the elderly, poor, and disabled groups eligible for government-paid healthcare at 95 percent of the Medicare rate without even more extensive "management." They did this actuarially by withdrawing from selective Medicare/Medicaid markets, a maneuver that was at once monetarily sound for them and aggressively coercive for others, in hopes of getting more from the government than the Medicare actuaries would have preferred based on the original congressional scheme.

Despite the increased costs of treating those disabled and poor populations, zealously pursued enrollment in Medicare HMOs almost doubled from 1992 to 1996 from 6 percent of all enrollees to 11 percent. By 2009, there were over ten million enrollees in the new MA, in approximately the same proportion as of all enrollees in 1997; there was a drop off to sixty-six million HMO enrollees from a high of eighty million in 1999 during M+C. Privatizing Medicare through M+C and MA diminished the number of "Medigap" indemnity policies, which had covered the copayments between what Medicare allowed and the price charged in the commercial and nonprofit Blues programs, while aggressively shifting many of its healthier beneficiaries into managed care. Along with that movement into privatization came managed healthcare insurance to ensure profitability, notwithstanding the risk of covering the sicker, poorer actuarial group. This was based in part on the healthier elders' kind of "reverse adverse selection" choice to move out of the more traditional and comprehensive coverage and into the HMOs to save money from the lower premiums. The subscribers could not realize that the lower premiums existed only because the gatekeepers and care managers could reduce the amount of care that they expected to receive.

The managed-care-style system also incidentally diminished the number of opportunities for researchers to compare that type of care with fee-for-service data based on quality considerations. This was demonstrated in a study published in the 1998 summer issue of *Health Affairs* analyzing TV and print ads placed in four major cities in early 1997. The study found that one-third of sites at Medicare HMO marketing seminars were not wheelchair accessible. *The Wall Street Journal* reported that Medicare HMOs had targeted healthy, more active older people with an "advertizing blitz that shows seniors snorkeling, biking, and swimming but doesn't feature sick or disabled potential customers." The director of the Kaiser Medicare Project (not affiliated with the Kaiser Foundation Health Plans, Inc.) said in the article, "The ads could be screening out the sickest segment of the population."

Meanwhile, the Clinton administration's HCFA had been scrutinizing Medicare HMO advertisements and sending back at least 25 percent of them to correct the falsehoods. Other exclusionary practices by the HMO marketers included downmarketing to Spanish-speaking people, as there was only one Spanish-language ad in 169 newspapers.

This managed-care insurance behavior continued on its path over the next few years. By 2006, another study appeared in *Health Affairs* that showed how the content of health-plan advertising is related to the competitiveness of the health-plan market and found that increased competition was associated with greater use of advertising that targets healthier patients. Because the heavily Republican-dominated Congresses of 1995 through 1999 were in no mind to appropriate more money to fund Medicare, among many other "entitlement" programs, the Clinton administration used some $60 million of the "savings" to produce patient-benefit booklets that offered beneficiaries of M+C the paths to take if aggrieved by their new HMO situation. When the Republican members of the National Bipartisan Commission on the Future of Medicare heard about this, they criticized the distribution of the "confusing" booklets as causing even more problems for the states. Reportedly, upon hearing his colleagues' complaints about the money being spent for the booklets, commission member Senator Jay Rockefeller (D-WV) said, "If the commission is simply about solvency, I'd like to get that cleared up right now, because I'm not sure I belong on it."

The BBA had established the Medicare+Choice Program whereby a beneficiary could elect to receive benefits either under the traditional fee-for-service method or pursuant to the new Part C of the Medicare program "to provide Medicare beneficiaries with a wider range of health-plan choices to complement the original Medicare option." In it, every individual entitled under Medicare Part A (hospital benefits) and enrolled under Part B (medical benefits) could elect to receive benefits through either the existing Medicare fee-for-service program or a Part C, M+C plan. To respond to the politicization by anti-administration efforts, in November 1997 the Clinton Administration directed DHHS to comply administratively with the standards contained in the

Consumer Bill of Rights and Responsibilities drafted by the Presidential Advisory Commission on Consumer Protection and Quality in the Healthcare Industry. HCFA issued "Interim Final Rules" effective July 27, 1998, that went beyond the mandates of the BBA. Because the Republican-sponsored sections of the BBA allowed the tax-free MSA contributions to be set up with commercial insurance companies in the form of a trust similar to an IRA, the administration required all M+C plans, including those involving Medical Savings Accounts, to have an "ongoing quality assessment and performance improvement program for the services furnished M+C enrollees under the plan."

The BBA also exempted private fee-for-service plans, non-network plans and non-network MSAs that did not have written utilization-review protocols from some quality-assurance requirements of the law such as external quality review. To hold back the rate of privatization and further fragmentation of the healthcare system, and indicating an understanding of the structure of managed-care mechanisms, the administration attempted to make it unprofitable for managed care to enter both the fee-for service Medicare marketplace and the M+C one, admonishing:

"We believe that these physician incentives place the physician at financial risk and thus are not permitted by the law for M+C private fee-for-service plan payments. Capitation places physicians at risk because of the uncertainty of the extent to which the beneficiary will require the physician's time and services to provide an adequate level of service. Withholds place the physicians at risk because of the uncertainty of what ultimate payment for the services furnished will be. Bonuses are essentially the same as withholds. In both the case of bonuses and withholds, the physicians knows the least amount that could be paid but in both cases, they could face uncertainty about what the total payment from the plan would be for the services furnished."

The new interim final rules required that the fee-for-service provider should not be placed at financial risk in other ways, by allowing

115 percent of the payment rate, including deductibles, copayments, or balance billing otherwise permitted under the plan, as payment in full for services provided. (This was an example of legal monopsonistic practice, because fifteen years earlier, the Supreme Court found a *per se* criminal violation of the Sherman Antitrust Act in *Arizona v. Maricopa County Medical Society*, where "maximum" prices for healthcare were set by the county medical society.) Unfortunately, such an arrangement, though legal because the government authorized it, could bring the provider even further into capitation by MCOs because of the flexibility offered by the actuarially small-groups' list prices for care that was also being managed by gatekeeping contractors.

The most significant change in the way commercial fee-for-service had been offered was perhaps the requirement by the Clinton HCFA that the M+C organization comply with the coverage decisions, appeals, and grievance procedures of subpart M of the law, which required that the M+C organization offer the private fee-for-service plan to make coverage determinations on all services. Moreover, it had to make such determination before furnishing the service if the enrollee or provider requested it. HCFA pointed out in its Federal Register response to comments on proposed rule making that the language of the statute was in the "present tense" regarding the requirement for coverage determinations and the need for prompt determinations of coverage "denials," and that these were necessary or there would be no protection from retroactive denials for enrollees in a fee-for-service plan. As Medicare "privatization" was beginning to move into place based on the BBA, the Clinton administration was trying to slow it down using its administrative discretion.

When M+C recruitment of seniors' enthusiasm did not pan out as expected, the 2003 MMA was signed into law by George W. Bush to enable the more comprehensive Medicare Advantage, which would include prescription benefits, and Health Savings Accounts. In testimony before the U.S. Senate Finance Committee's Subcommittee on Health in 2006, the advocacy group Commonwealth Fund said that all evidence to date showed that health savings accounts and high-deductible health plans worsened, rather than improved, the U.S. health system's problems. The 2010 ACA, carefully recrafted from the lessons learned from the Clinton era, included shrinking the costs of the multibillion-dollar, privatized MA business over a number of years until its bid-based costs would be ratcheted down to a rough parity with traditional fee-for-service Medicare. This was supportive of seniors' joining MA's more comprehensive array of services and avoided for the present taking on the insurance lobby and the advocates for market-based lowering of the high cost of healthcare. The shift of millions of elderly to Medicare HMOs offered the managed-care insurance industry more cash flow to use for merger and acquisition purposes, albeit based at below marginal-cost prices of ethically delivering the actuarially earmarked care.

In 1961, Humana was a Wisconsin-domiciled life and health insurer, which after a few mergers and with only a few nursing homes, had moved ahead of the pack in what was to become the most rapidly expanding sector of the nation's economy: healthcare. Its company Extendicare, Inc., as the group was then known, had grown to more than forty facilities, becoming the nation's largest nursing home company. In 1974, the owners divested the nursing home chain, changed the name to Humana, Inc. and began buying up and then building hospitals.

By 1978, as the nation's third-largest hospital management chain, Humana acquired the number-two hospital chain, American Medicorp, Inc. This purchase doubled Humana's size and stretched its debt. Having used leveraged debt with confidence for some time during its expansion, Humana was faced with a debt claimed by one company official that was "nearly 90% of capital." The two cofounders, Wendell Cherry and David Jones, saw the hospital business as recession resistant, so even though Humana suffered from low occupancy rates at some of its facilities during those years, it unloaded only its unprofitable hospitals. By 1993, Humana had spun off hospital operations altogether from its health-insurance operations, establishing Galen Healthcare, Inc., which merged soon after with Columbia/HCA and received much attention from the FTC, denying its growth in certain markets.

By mid-1996, however, it appeared that Humana had grown too fast. Amid skyrocketing costs, Humana was forced to abandon thirteen unprofitable markets. The largest of these was Washington, DC, and the company sold its Group Health Association in January 1997 to California's nonprofit Kaiser Foundation Hospitals, which provide a tax-exempt shelter for their for-profit medical groups. In only two years of ownership, Humana had suffered losses of $100 million, attempting to turn around the money- losing Group Health HMO. Its insurance plans were affected, and it sold its thirty-thousand-member health plan in Alabama. As part of this restructuring, Humana recorded a $200 million pretax charge for the second quarter of 1996, leading to net income for the year of only $12 million, compared to $190 million for the previous year.

In the third quarter of 1998, UHC and Humana Hospital Corporation announced that they expected to merge, with a stock swap originally estimated at $6.23 billion, which included over two million Medicare and Medicaid enrollees. On June 15, UHC announced an estimate of $5.5 billion as the DOJ issued a so-called "second request for additional documents," pursuant to the Hart-Scott-Rodino Antitrust Act, upon receipt of which the DOJ would have twenty days to act on its approval. These companies had raised their rates 5 percent in 1997, the exact amount they "gave up" when taking from the government Medicare contracts that made up approximately 25 percent of their revenues, and they projected still larger increases in 1998. Moreover, the deal would not only create a bonanza for Humana shareholders who would be bought out at a premium 20 percent over the closing price on May 27, but it would also increase the value of the holdings of Humana's chairman, David Jones, by $26 million and his wife by $4.3 million from the night before. So much for the socially redeeming purpose of creating "savings" by Congress' offering Medicare and Medicaid contracts to the managed-care industry.

As a result of the mega-merger announcement, the Florida Department of Insurance and the DOJ requested still more information and began reviewing the large market shares that would accrue to the new company. For example, the resulting control by the company of the Chicago-metro Medicare HMO market would rise to 89 percent and its HMO market to 32 percent; the total South Florida HMO market, 40 percent; the Miami-Dade County Medicare HMO market, 55 percent; the Broward County Medicare HMO market, 43 percent; and the Volusia County Medicare HMO market, 61 percent. Certainly, the interstate nature of the commerce offered by the proposed health-care insurance merger could not be denied. On August 10, 1998, the merger collapsed due to an earlier announcement that UHC had to take a $900 million restructuring charge for the second quarter, which caused both companies' stocks to plummet.

In 2006, following the passage of the MMA, Humana launched an education campaign to market MA and its prescription drug plans nationwide to Medicare-eligible consumers. By 2008, the company ran into complaints about enrollment of Illinois citizens into Medicare Part D and MA Plans. Michael T. McRaith, director of the division of insurance, said:

> "Any company dealing with Illinois' senior population is forewarned that the Division will not tolerate any marketing or sales practices that put Illinois citizens in unaffordable or unnecessary programs, especially with important and complicated programs such as Medicare Part D and Advantage Program."

Humana was cited for "payment of commissions to Producers/Entities not duly licensed; for allowing Producers/Entities to sell, solicit, or negotiate insurance while not duly licensed; and for failure to notify the Director of Insurance when Producers are terminated for cause." In interrelated findings, among other things, the department found:

> "During the course of the exam, which focused on Medicare enrollment procedures and results, the examiners identified problems with solicitation of the Prescription Drug Plans by producers (agents) at Wal-Mart Stores. Medicare eligible people, who talked with agents located in the stores about the Prescription Drug Plan, were encouraged to consider the Medicare Advantage Plan. The company commission schedule for the Advantage plan was considerably more than the Prescrip-

tion Drug Plan which would be a natural incentive to steer applicants toward the Advantage Plan."

In Kansas, under Grievances and Appeals, the insurance department found:

"Company letters appeared to address medically necessary issues but delayed the answer for up to 60 days. Others appeared to address contractual claims but were issued within 30 days. When the examiners questioned the Company, the consistent answer was that the customer representative had used the wrong letter. . . [and] while errors do occur, the number appeared high for appeals of this magnitude."

In Texas, Humana faced similar charges related to misleading advertising and lack of proper notification to state regulatory insurance departments. The State of Wisconsin Office of the Commissioner of Insurance report of October 19, 2006, noted that the Humana Insurance Company is "licensed in the District of Columbia and in all state jurisdictions except New Hampshire, New York, and Vermont."

Another interesting aspect of Humana's innovations as a conglomerate is that the parent, Humana, Inc., as found by the Wisconsin Insurance Commissioner's 2007 Market Conduct Examination, not only had hospitals and medical groups in its control, albeit without direct ownership, but also a range of captive insurance companies and captive and independent agents, some of whom were identified as employees. "Captive" insurance companies are wholly owned subsidiaries of the firms they insure. Humana, like other hospital chains, self-insured on its own or through the formation of captive insurance companies, which in turn are owned by the hospitals that receive coverage. Although the purpose of these captives is to ensure stable coverage for their owners rather than to maximize profits, they certainly help to minimize losses.

The Wisconsin examiners found that Humana Insurance Company:

"did not comply with eleven of the twenty-four recommendations from the market conduct examination that was adopted in 2002. . . [and that four of these recommendations were non- compliant for the third time], which resulted in 30 additional recommendations in the areas of claims, managed care, producer licensing, small employer, grievance, marketing, sales and advertising, underwriting and rating."

Because of Humana's involvement with MA, and because the federal prescription law was preempted by federal law, the state Office of the Commissioner of Insurance (OCI) examination was able to go only as far as to note that the

"examiners reviewed the complaints reported to CMS [the federal Centers for Medicare and Medicaid Services] and found that the criteria used by the CMS to identify and report agent complaints differed significantly from that of the OCI."

Thus, notwithstanding federal preemption, which removed Wisconsin from regulating in those areas, the OCI report nonetheless reported "the company's oversight of Medicare Advantage and Medicare prescription drug plan agent marketing activities indicated that it did not comply with Wisconsin agent licensing requirements."

In 2005, Humana took over the Louisiana Ochsner Health Plan, the state's largest health-insurance provider. The New Orleans *The Times- Picayune* reported:

"Those new options can come at a price. Clients who had to switch from Ochsner to Humana have seen sizable rate increases, in part because the Ochsner Health Plan wasn't priced correctly. The Ochsner plan was priced fairly low, which was good for workers and their employers but not necessarily profitable . . . Like other insurers across the country, Humana is rolling out high-deductible plans that can allow employers to save money, yet still give workers health coverage. This year, Humana will introduce several high-deductible health plans in which employees pay the first $1,000 to $5,000 they incur in expenses each year. Such plans can be integrated with federal health savings accounts, which allow individuals to put pretax dollars into an account for medical expenses."

With the preemption problems generated by ERISA, and the mélange of state health-insurance regulation, which mixes state and federal requirements for similarly situated patients, the Obama administration's healthcare reform efforts extended to Wall Street reform. By mid-2010, H.R. 4173, sponsored by Representative Barney Frank (D-MA) and Senator Christopher Dodd (D-CT), the Wall Street Reform and Consumer Protection Act of 2009 was passed on May 25 by a Senate vote of fifty-nine to thirty-nine. The title was as follows:

"Wall Street Reform and Consumer Protection Act of 2009. A bill to promote the financial stability of the United States by improving accountability and transparency in the financial system, to end 'too big to fail,' to protect the American taxpayer by ending bailouts, to protect consumers from abusive financial services practices, and for other purposes."

The act provided sweeping financial regulatory changes, including the creation of an Office of National Insurance, housed in the Treasury Department. By virtue of "Dodd-Frank," considerable micromanagement power had effectively been shifted from the legislative branch to the executive branch of the government, and it allowed the Treasury to create regulations that could significantly help reform the problems of the failed managed-care insurance market.

In May of 1997, the Center for Studying Health System Change reported in an *Issue Brief* that only 35 percent of HMOs had been profitable in 1994, and later data appeared to confirm the data for the more recent years. In June 1998, the seventeen-member bipartisan federal advisory panel, appointed by President Clinton to consider fundamental changes in Medicare, examined two assumptions: first, that the annual growth would gradually drop to 4 percent and second, that it could just as likely remain at 6 percent. The spread between the two would lead to a difference of $760 billion by 2030. However, panel member Bruce Vladeck, former HCFA Administrator, said that any forecast of Medicare spending beyond ten years was "an exercise in comparative fantasy." The administration projected surpluses in the budget from the $39 billion in fiscal year (FY) 1998, which ended September 30, to escalate to $148 billion by 2002. The fact that Congress already pulled $115 billion from Medicare in the BBA was widely reported in the press to have "caused some to speculate on how more money could be pulled from Medicare, as the Republican majority proposes, when such budget surpluses would exist."

Although most M+C organizations were required to be "licensed under State law as a risk-bearing entity," the BBA allowed new physician- sponsored organizations (PSOs) a thirty-six-month federal waiver of state licensure under certain circumstances. The DOJ's cavalier view of competition begged the question of how handing unprofitable HMOs the responsibility for the public funds to care for the elderly, without a "means test" as to the HMOs' survivability as responsible fiduciaries, could be considered a socially responsible act by Congress. An interim final rule, effective June 8, 1998, was promulgated by the Clinton DHHS, establishing solvency standards for compliance for those with approved waivers.

Under the post-Millennium Republican administration, preemption was used as a tool to keep ERISA plan members' rights separated from indemnity insureds' rights. However, because MA members would also have federal law preemptive rights, the Obama administration's control based on the ACA would create significant gains for members soon after the 2010 healthcare reform law enactment. This gave federal officials new power to negotiate and to reject bids from insurers given the "privatized' opportunity to sponsor MA plans by the 2003 MMA. By September 2010, in the midst of scary premium increases by the commercial MCOs, the Obama administration announced that average premiums paid by individuals for private MA plans, which insured about one-fourth of all Medicare beneficiaries, would decline about 1 percent in the coming year.

The MA plans will be required to limit their administrative costs and general overhead to 15 percent, with an 85 percent medical loss ratio devoted to medical care and services. Any plan that cannot hit that mark after three years will be prohibited from enrolling new members until it is in compliance; after five years of noncompliance, those plans will be terminated. Dr. Donald M. Berwick, a "recess appointment," was chosen in April 2010 by the president to run the Centers for Medicare and Medicaid Services (CMS). He was formerly president and CEO of the Institute for Healthcare Improvement and clinical professor of pediatrics and healthcare policy at Harvard Medical School. In September, when asked about MA, he said, "Despite the claims of some, Medicare Advantage remains a strong, robust option for millions of seniors who choose to enroll or stay in a participating plan." *The New York Times* confirmed that

> "average premiums paid by individuals for private Medicare Advantage plans, which insure about one-fourth of all beneficiaries, would decline slightly next year, even as insurers provide additional benefits required by the new healthcare law . . . [at the same time as] commercial insurance premiums for many people under 65 and many small businesses are increasing 10 percent to 25 percent or more."

John K. Gorman, a former Medicare official and one-time chief lobbyist on health-care financing issues for the National Association of Community Health Centers—an organization of federally-funded primary care clinics for the medically underserved and by 2010 consultant on managed Medicare to the insurance industry—was quoted in *The New York Times*:

> "Today's announcement shows that there is a new sheriff in town. Medicare officials were very specific and forceful. Insurers succumbed to the government's demands and stayed in the Medicare market because they have become much more dependent on Medicare business."

Kathleen Sebelius, the Obama secretary of DHHS, said the negotiations showed that insurers "remain very committed to the Medicare Advantage program." *The New York Times* reported that while reviewing bids, Medicare officials said they identified three hundred private plans for further scrutiny and quoted Dr. Berwick, who, despite his April support of MA, admitted: "These plans unfairly proposed to increase out-of-pocket expenses for beneficiaries while increasing their own profit margins. We said, 'No, you have to do better.'" Jonathan D. Blum, deputy administrator of CMS, said:

> "We negotiated more aggressively than in the past. As a result, some plans changed their bids to produce more value to beneficiaries. . . After negotiations plans improved their benefits by $13 per member per month, or 5 percent on average [when seven Medicare plans offered by three insurance companies decided not to change their bids] we denied those bids."

Insurers were expected to begin marketing to Medicare beneficiaries by October 1, 2010 the coverage that would start on January 1, 2011. Meanwhile, *The New York Times* reported, "Premiums in the commercial insurance market continue rising at a brisk pace." Not one to be daunted, the managed-care insurance industry went on the offensive, starting off with *The Wall Street Journal* announcement September 30 that McDonald's "may" have to abandon the company plan of thirty thousand workers because of the medical loss ratio provision in the new law, which McDonalds promptly denied. United Press International reported McDonalds statement calling media reports that the company was considering dropping healthcare coverage for its employees "completely false." The reports were "purely speculative and misleading." They had simply asked for a waiver, because their plans limited employees' healthcare insurance to $2,000 with a $730 deductible and another plan was limited to $10,000 with a $1,600 deductible.

Jay Angoff, former director of the Office of Consumer Information and Insurance Oversight, within the DHHS, announced on September 30:

> "As many employers and insurers consider health insurance options for 2011, one question that has been raised is the applicability of provisions of the Affordable Care Act to health plans and coverage with special circumstances. Pursuant to the Affordable Care Act and our regulations, DHHS recently announced an expedited process for plans to apply for a waiver from the requirement in the Affordable Care Act establishing minimum annual limits where such limits would result in

decreased access or increased premiums. DHHS has approved dozens of these waiver requests, most often filed by so-called "mini-med" plans, and in doing so, has ensured the continuation of health coverage for workers and their families. Complete waiver applications were generally processed in 48 hours.

"We fully intend to exercise [the Secretary's] discretion under the new law to address the special circumstances of mini-med plans in the medical loss ratio calculations. According to the Affordable Care Act, medical loss ratio 'methodologies shall be designed to take into account the special circumstance of smaller plans, different types of plans, and newer plans.' We recognize that mini-med plans are often characterized by a relatively high expense structure relative to the lower premiums charged for these types of policies. We intend to address these and other special circumstances in forthcoming regulations."

Wendell Potter, who was for twenty years a senior analyst for Humana and CIGNA insurance companies, turned whistle-blower in 2009. In his 2011 book, *Deadly Spin,* he calls the mini-meds (also called low-cost, limited-benefit plans found in businesses like McDonald's, and not designed to handle catastrophic treatment) "fake insurance."

By March 2012, in the *Huffington Post* blog, Mr. Potter wrote "Coming Soon: The End of Health Insurers As We Know Them—By Self-Inflicting Wounds," in which he cites from a speech by Aetna CEO Mark Bertolini as saying "the insurance industry as we know it is, for all practical purposes, a dinosaur on the verge of extinction."

The week before Mr. Angoff's statement, *The New York Times* reported that Principal Financial Group, a provider of 401(k) plans, mutual funds, retirement plans, investments, life insurance, and health insurance with eighteen million customers worldwide, announced that it was getting out of the employer-paid health-insurance business. Others that provided mini-med or limited benefit policies said they were eliminating selected parts of their traditional coverage.

11. Doctor Plays Managed-Care Entrepreneur

A debatably successful strategic behavior, verging on price predation, resulted in bidding wars. Hospitals and doctors, thinking that
they could compete with MCOs that had the advantages of actuarial,
dossier-based data obtained from indemnity insurers' McCarran-Fer-
guson-protected access to medical information gathered over years,
attempted to get into the HMO business through capitation. As capitation insurers did not need to fully immerse themselves in managing patient care because they were able to shift some of the risk management to the doctors, why couldn't doctors take advantage of the
economic innovation and not have to split their income with the economically gratuitous insurance companies? The competitive move to
doctor-owned and subcapitated groups, however, illuminated the baser
elements of entrepreneurial behavior in the medical profession, as doctors mimicked the same practices as insurers and HMOs, shifting their
alliance with the patient from doctor-patient-fiduciary to that of a business joint venture with a self-insurer.

To demonstrate: one prescient California internist and board member of a new group was quoted by the media as saying,

"There is a limit to what doctor-owned and doctor-man-
aged organizations can do because there's severe restrictions on
the amount of money [available] . . . We have x amount of dollars to spend, and we can't spend more than we have."

Apparently being physician owned and operated on a managed-care
model required the group to think more artfully about the problems it
would face. Speaking like a politically experienced member of a Congressional Appropriations Committee, the doctor said further, "I think
it really does make for better patient care, but it doesn't mean patients
get everything they want." Ethical issues aside, such a statement offered
little meaning, because all treatment is, by definition, "what the doctor
orders," not what patients "want."

Advantage Health HMO in New Orleans was the fourth-largest
HMO in Louisiana with ninety-four thousand enrollees, as measured

by market share. In the four years of its existence, Advantage Health lost $35.6 million, $30 million of it in 1997 alone, and the Louisiana insurance commissioner had to place a state employee on the premises to observe operations. When and if Advantage Health would fall, its population would most assuredly be picked up by a higher-bidding contender at a distressed-sale price. That loss came after three hospital system owners infused $9.5 million each in December 1997 to keep the struggling plan afloat. Advantage's own bid came in at $152.79 per enrollee per month, while the three professional bidders were Aetna, UHC Corp., and Gulf South. The much "wiser" bids ranged from 24 to 27 percent higher, were statistically indistinguishable from each other, and set between $190 and $195. On April 12, 1999, MultiPlan, Inc., a national PPO, announced the acquisition of Advantage Health. All other bidders pulled out, and the terms were not disclosed.

Different bidding styles are used in the for-profit and nonprofit business worlds. One is the "clean" bid, made on the basis of careful assessment of costs and the profit potential. Another is characterized as the "lazy" or "cheap" bid, made by otherwise busy bidders who can take it or leave it. The latter bids do not rely on sharpened pencils but on chance, but when such "lazy" bids come in at statistically indistinguishable numbers, the basis for them can only be either collusion or keen knowledge of the costs to be incurred. Assuming that the similarity in bids is based on the greater knowledge of professional insurers, makes a case for licensing bidders for public health-type contracts as a matter of public policy and highlights the unethical nature of the stance taken by physicians who enter a business world in which they have neither experience nor professional training.

Doctors and hospitals are historically at a distinct disadvantage as financial competitors, because the existence of the malpractice bar encourages them to provide at least minimal care. Compare the Advantage Health rates with the Medicare rates for HMOs such as in Fresno, California, in 1998 where they were as high as $380 per month as reported by *The Wall Street Journal* in April 1998:

"One hospital, St. Agnes Medical Center, says it is incurring losses as big as $700,000 per month from HMO contracts . . .

> Medicare beneficiaries have yet to suffer [one spokesman said] 'because of the professionalism of the average doctor . . . They will keep delivering high-quality care. But I don't know how long we can keep hanging on.'"

In addition, as a labor-intensive industry, except for those in radiology and laboratories, physicians generally have had little traditional need for capital reserves. That the insurers bidding for New Orleans' Advantage came in so much higher than the doctors did shows that the capital- and labor-intensive managed-care companies are a cost add-on inimical to healthcare delivery.

When "professionals" entered, the bidding model changed. Private equity firms added still another layer to the cost of healthcare when they started buying insurers. In 2006, the private-equity Carlyle Group acquired Multiplan, Inc.—the terms again not disclosed—and in 2010, sold it to private equity firms BC Partners and Silver Lake Partners in a transaction that valued the company at $3.1 billion, according to "people familiar with the deal." On July 9, 2010, *The Wall Street Journal* reported that by selling, owners Carlyle Group and Welsh, Carson, Anderson & Stowe were making the deal the year's largest so-called secondary buyout (that is, one in which a company is passed from one private equity group to another). People familiar with the deal said Carlyle would make more than three times its investment in MultiPlan, which it acquired in 2006.

The money came from only two sources. The first was from investors wanting to make quick money from leveraged buyouts. The second, according to MultiPlan's promotional material—considered the real basis for the attractiveness of the acquisition—was the money mined from managing the healthcare delivered by a group of "600,000 providers." By June 12, 2010, according to *Bloomberg BusinessWeek*, "Private equity firms Carlyle Group and GTCR Golder Rauner LLC are looking to buy medical insurers, made newly attractive by a surge of customers expected from the U.S. healthcare overhaul."

Because "branding" is about getting prospects to see one's item as the most valuable solution, the advertising monikers "Advantage" or

"Advanced" are artful but not necessarily winning healthcare names, whether used by Congress or physician/entrepreneurs. "California Advantage, Inc." a managed-care company formed by the California Medical Association and its physicians, filed for bankruptcy in 1998. More than seventy-five hundred doctors established it in order to compete with local HMOs. Its original projections, to enroll 10 percent of California's thirty-five-million population, didn't even approach forty thousand out of the 3.3 million members it said it needed to break even. Over its two and a half years of operation, during which it went through three CEOs and lost $11 million, its physician members ended up outnumbering its six thousand subscribers by 25 percent.

Advanced Health Centers, a PPMC in Tarrytown, New York, listed on the NASDAQ, saw its stock value drop from $28.25 in 1997 to $1.69 within a year, notwithstanding the booming economy. By then, the organization was "restructuring" internally as well as "selecting large independent medical practices." What was most remarkable about those heady days of business novices' reinventing the medical-mogul wheel was the self-styled and apologetic announcement that they would stop providing "unlimited services to medical groups for a flat fee, which cuts into its profit margin. Under the new plan, it will provide specific services for specific fees."

Apparently, Advanced had found out that "capitation" accepted by a physician only made money for the other guy. The doctors' efforts to join the managed-care medicine model came to a turn in the road when, in 1998, Advanced received a New York Supreme Court temporary restraining order to cease selling allegedly misrepresented common stock. By February 1999, it changed its NASDAQ name to AHT Corporation and assumed a new core business outlook: "To provide Internet-based clinical e-commerce applications for physicians, other healthcare providers and healthcare organizations." This was a far cry from being a medical group practice management company. On January 27, 2000, AHT Corporation announced that it had reached an agreement to settle the consolidated shareholder class-action suit filed against the company in the U.S. District Court for the Southern District of New York. The consolidated suit resulted from eleven putative class actions filed against AHT from July 1 through August 17, 1998 following the decline in the company's stock price, alleging that the company had made certain misrepresentations and omissions regarding its operations, performance, and financial condition.

On September 22, 2000, AHT filed for bankruptcy protection under Chapter 11—its stock price was down to $0.01 per share—and announced in *Business Wire* that it was going to be financed by BioShield Technologies, Inc. (NASDAQ: BSTI) starting in a merger agreement effective July 3, 2000. By September 7, 2000, AHT announced that it had filed a $70 million lawsuit against its putative rescuer, BioShield Technologies, Inc. and certain of its directors and officers, for fraudulently inducing AHT to enter into the merger agreement announced on July 3, then breaching the agreement. This apparently happened because on July 4, BioShield backed off and decided it would pay $20 million to purchase only AHT's software that allows doctors to send prescriptions electronically to pharmacies.

The "Alice in Wonderland" era of managed-care companies' rise was shaken drastically when in July 1998, the largest healthcare provider in Pennsylvania, the nonprofit Allegheny Health, Education and Research Foundation, filed for protection under Chapter 11 of the federal bankruptcy law, with debts of $1.3 billion and losing one million a day. The Foundation owned thirteen hospitals and nearly six hundred physicians' practices in the Pittsburgh and Philadelphia areas. The expansion of the Foundation was something to behold.

In 1988, its founder, the former CEO of Allegheny General Hospital in Pittsburgh, had acquired the Medical College of Pennsylvania and the renowned Hahnemann University and merged them to create the world's largest medical school, Allegheny University of the Health Sciences. CEO Sharif S. Abdelhak received an annual salary of $1.2 million. Reminiscent of Oxford's strategy of surviving on cutting physician's incomes, in May of 1998 Allegheny imposed a 25 percent pay cut in a handful of "superstar physician-professors who had been lured aboard with $1 million salaries to bring in patients," according to *The New York Times*. Work by *Philadelphia Inquirer* investigative reporter Karl Stark—who had won many awards for his stories on the defunct

Allegheny health system—triggered a criminal investigation that led to a no-contest plea in August 2002 by former CEO Abdelhak for misusing medical endowments. He was paroled after serving three months in prison and then was placed on house probation for the sentence of one to two years.

This all was hardly the result of "competition" and the "healthy workings of the healthcare marketplace." By then, the actuarial economic setting of managed-care companies was well known. Despite publicist and pundit exclamations to the contrary, MCOs' profitability can come only from a combination of coercive price-cutting through capitation, delivering care at above marginal-cost prices, reduction of contractually based patient benefits, and direct denials of care—that is, the profitability that comes from offering a sham product.

12. Unmasking the *Noerr* Defense

> "Why sometimes," the White Queen told Alice, "I've believed as many as six impossible things before breakfast."
> — Lewis Carroll, *Through the Looking-Glass,*
> *and What Alice Found There*

Occult healthcare price and nonprice predation—concerted action to restrain trade or strategic behavior designed to raise a rival's costs—demonstrate the "sham" exception to the Noerr-Pennington Doctrine and reveal the attempted end-run around otherwise legal methods that induce governmental action in commercial self-interest. Although it is settled law that such concerted efforts by self-interested parties cannot be the basis for antitrust liability, the action that is a "sham" raised in *Noerr* was first outlined in 1972 in *California Motor Transport Co. v. Trucking Unlimited.* Aside from evidence of a "pattern" of baseless claims to harm a competitor as proof of intent to harm, direct evidence of improper intent plus a lack of reasonable basis in law or fact—such as, for example, attempting to use the public policy of "lowering costs" as the basis for lowering agents and brokers' commissions—are also shams. Moreover, proving that a sham existed need not show that it was "completely" baseless, since "baselessness" is not needed if a showing of improper intent is made by evaluating the economic incentives or potential rewards and costs in petitioning a government agency.

The following cases demonstrate how the federal appellate courts have had such a difficult time deciding the standards by which to view concerted action in antitrust violations. In *Albrecht v. Herald Co.,* the 1968 Supreme Court took a broad view by permitting the finding of an implicit conspiratorial agreement between two "outside agents." These companies, which together solicited and managed a terminated newspaper distributor's route, were found to be no longer acting independently because they were capable of merging with *The Herald.*

Ten years later, in *Harold Friedman, Inc. v. Kroger Co.*, the Third Circuit Court of Appeals narrowed the potential for summary judgment in such cases and interpreted *Albrecht* as requiring:

1. That at least two members of the conspiracy should have benefitted from the restraint of trade;
2. That the combination must actually restrain trade and not merely facilitate the restraint; and
3. That at least two parties intended these consequences.

The Circuit Court set up a special standard for summary judgment, more supportive of Justices Stewart and Harlan's dissents in *Albrecht* (that would have allowed "maximum" price fixing) than of the majority opinion's rejection of the idea of an "implied conspiratorial agreement between parties, some of whom have marginal involvement in or awareness of the overall scheme." The *Friedman* Court cited its earlier decision in *Columbia Metal Culvert Co. v. Kaiser Aluminum & Chemical Corp.*, which required the finding of a "unity of purpose, design, or understanding between (that defendant) and the other defendants." "Maximum" price fixing by doctors also was found to violate the antitrust laws in the 1982 Supreme Court's *Arizona v. Maricopa County Medical Society*.

The Third Circuit's narrowing interpretation of the Supreme Court's decision in *Albrecht* lasted until the High Court's 1982 decision in *American Society of Mechanical Engineers, Inc. v. Hydrolevel Corp.*, which, though not based on a motion for summary judgment, set in place a plaintiff-friendly potential for defeating summary judgment challenges. In the case against the American Society of Mechanical Engineers (ASME), the Second Circuit's Southern District Court had rejected Hydrolevel's request for the jury to be instructed that the nonprofit Society be held liable for its agents' conduct under Sherman § 1 if the agents acted within the scope of its "apparent authority." Despite District Chief Judge Weinstein's charge, the jury returned a verdict for Hydrolevel. The Second Circuit affirmed the lower court's judgment on liability, stating that the district court had delivered "a charge that was more favorable to the defendant than the law requires."

The Supreme Court then granted *certiorari* for ASME. Affirming, the High Court held that the petitioner was civilly liable under the antitrust laws' apparent authority theory and that

"liability is based upon the fact that the agent's position facilitates the consummation of the fraud in that, from the point of view of the third person, the transaction seems regular on its face and the agent appears to be acting in the ordinary course of business confided to him."

Moreover, the Court emphasized an important antitrust principle: "the fact that ASME is a nonprofit organization does not weaken the force of the antitrust and agency principles that indicate that ASME should be liable for Hydrolevel's antitrust injuries." Thus "facilitating" was introduced as a major force in the requisite conditions for finding antitrust liability even for nonprofit organizations. On a motion for summary judgment in the federal rules of civil procedure, such a finding by a court would nonetheless require the moving party to demonstrate both that there is no genuine issue as to any material fact and that the moving party is entitled to a judgment as a matter of law. However, the burden on the plaintiff is greater, for in order to survive a summary judgment challenge, it must prove that a genuine issue of material fact does exist, and it must be one presented so that a reasonable jury could return a verdict for the plaintiff on that issue. The finding that the "transaction seems regular on its face and the agent appears to be acting in the ordinary course of business confided to him," raises another issue for our purposes, because an antitrust defendant's conduct may be consistent with both permissible competition *and* illegal conspiracy. In light of the public health policy of "cost containment," this perception has been the basis of the managed-care industry's *Noerr-Pennington* mask, which could help it survive a summary judgment challenge.

The 1984 Supreme Court, in *Monsanto Co. v. Spray-Rite Service Corp.*, and in *Matsushita Electric Industrial Co. v. Zenith Radio Corp.* in 1986, said that for the plaintiff to survive a motion for summary judgment evidence must be presented "that tends to exclude the possibility" that the alleged conspirators acted independently;

"[t]hat is, there must be direct or circumstantial evidence that reasonably tends to prove that the [distributors] had a conscious commitment to a common scheme designed to achieve an unlawful objective. [Also, c]ircumstances must reveal 'a unity of purpose or a common design and understanding, or a meeting of minds in an unlawful arrangement.'"

However, surviving a summary judgment challenge removes only the *per se* threat from the respondent, not the threat raised if analyzed under a rule of reason. As the Supreme Court had reasoned in 1982 in *Arizona v. Maricopa County Medical Society*, "*Per se* treatment is appropriate '[o]nce experience with a particular kind of restraint enables the Court to predict with confidence that the rule of reason will condemn it.'"

The *Monsanto* summary judgment standard, however, was largely abandoned in 1992 when the Supreme Court, in *Eastman Kodak Co. v. Image Technical Services, Inc.*, affirmed that the ordinary standard for summary judgment applied nonetheless. In 1996, in *Ideal Dairy Farms, Inc. v. John Labatt, Ltd.*, the Third Circuit Court cited *Eastman*, and its own decision in *Town Sound and Custom Tops, Inc. v. Chrysler Motor Corp.*:

"It may be that because antitrust cases are so factually intensive that summary judgment occurs proportionately less frequently there than in other types of litigation, but the standard [of the federal rule for summary judgment] remains the same."

In 1997, however, the Supreme Court reversed itself on *Albrecht*, in *State Oil v. Khan*, holding that not all vertical price fixing is unlawful and that it "should be evaluated under the rule of reason, which can effectively identify those situations in which it amounts to anticompetitive conduct." *Khan* would seem to have ended the debate whether there should be a "partial" *per se* approach to price fixing.

In more-direct fashion, price and nonprice predatory practices, were working themselves out from the healthcare system's woodwork as the statutory constraints imposed on managed care by an increasingly

219

constituent-embattled Congress tightened the noose on unfair trade techniques. A case in point that deserved plenary examination by both the Clinton Justice Department and HCFA resulted from the 1996 HIPAA. A HCFA Program Memorandum said that several insurance practices were identified that were "inconsistent with the guaranteed availability provisions of the [Act]." They included elements of health insurer behavior such as Humana's downmarketing. The company had been setting commissions for sales to HIPAA-eligible individuals and/ or small groups so low that brokers and agents were discouraged from marketing policies to or enrolling such individuals or groups. It was delaying unreasonably the processing of applications submitted by HIPAA-eligible individuals in order to cause significant breaks in coverage, thereby terminating an individual's status as a HIPAA-eligible individual, and offering coverage at unaffordable rates to avoid providing it to such individuals or groups.

These tactics raised several questions that policy planners and regulators must provide answers to. When scrutinized, would it be found that the marginal prices in these MCO offerings are below the company's average variable cost and become therefore predatory? Certainly the limiting of sales was as bad as limiting treatment output. Although a start-up period may be allowed a newcomer in the business, is the price fair or is it made to drive competitors out from their appropriately priced actuarial position? As Areeda-Turner said, "We would not permit a monopolist to price below marginal cost in order to meet the lawful price of a rival." Does this activity invoke section 5 of the FTC Act, which forbids unfair deceptive acts or practices and false or misleading advertisements or representations, as well as any practices unfair to consumers, or does concerted action by competitors to enlist these measures fall into the ambit of violating Sherman section 1?

It appears that the Bush II administration's CMS continued HCFA's practice of allowing the states' first enforcement rights and would monitor and take enforcement actions only if necessary to ensure compliance with its regulations. However, in addition to those industry practices, HCFA had been informed that some HIPAA-eligible individuals were "rated up," that is, charged premium rates as much as 500 to 600 percent of the standard risk, well in excess of the pre-HIPAA industry maximum of 200 percent.

In 1993, Willis ("Bill") Gradison (R-OH) had left Congress to become president of the Health Insurance Association of America (HIAA). He and congressional minority counsel staffer Charles N. ("Chip") Kahn, III publicly took credit for creating the "Harry and Louise" ads helping to defeat Hillary and Bill Clinton's healthcare reform efforts. Chip Kahn helped develop the Stark-Gradison Medicare Catastrophic Coverage Act of 1988 discussed earlier, and he was asked by House Ways and Means ranking member Bill Archer (R-Texas) the next year to draft a bill repealing the bipartisan legislation. "I worked both sides of the legislation because that was my role," Kahn said to the media. "I have views, I have feelings about issues, but at the end of the day, you work for the members."

Helped by his old mentor, Speaker Newt Gingrich, after the 1995 "Contract with America," which had captured a Republican Congressional majority for the first time in forty years, Kahn took on a job as staff director for the Republican-led House Ways and Means Health subcommittee and helped write the Medicare provisions of the BBA of 1997. Kahn later replaced Gradison as chair of HIAA, got to work on a consumer bill of rights, and joined Families USA, in what he called "the first kind of strange bedfellows' coalition" (foreshadowing later healthcare coalitions that often contained competing interests). In 2001, he became head of the Federation of American Hospitals (FAH), a lobbying group that represents investor owned hospitals around the country. He said in an interview on his representing private hospitals, "After representing the insurance industry wasn't as huge a jump as some might suspect. I'm a private sector kind of guy, I believe in the free enterprise system and in the market."

State action was viewed by the 1943 Supreme Court decision in *Parker v. Brown* as blocking the application of the federal antitrust laws, expressly defining the breadth of the term as engagement by a state acting as a "sovereign." However, in 1980 and 1985, two Supreme Court decisions declared that a two-part test was necessary and that mere acquiescence of such activity by a state was not protective enough. It put the onus on the state to both regulate effectively by articulating and affirmatively expressing as state policy the practices allowed to continue and to either supervise such private anticompetitive conduct or prohibit it. In 1998, Senator Ted Kennedy, coauthor of HIPAA, announced his plan to introduce legislation to lower what he felt was traditional price gouging to 150 percent of the standard risk. Allowing the states to have first crack at constraining this behavior was a compelling idea.

Defending state enforcement was argued by former HIAA chair Bill Gradison. He said that Kennedy's 150 percent cap bill would drive up insurance rates for everyone in the individual market, saying only, "If the premium cap is below costs, other people have to pay higher premiums. It is unwise policy to establish a cap that would run the risk of destabilizing the individual market." Since Mr. Gradison, former Republican Congressman-turned lobbyist, had been out of the House of Representatives for some time by then, he perhaps forgot the traditionally accepted state and federal government policy in healthcare legislation of setting price caps ("maximum allowable costs") on doctors' and hospitals' Medicare and Medicaid cost reimbursement. He certainly ought to have acknowledged the development of managed-care insurance, which contracted with doctors and hospitals for setting rates, where the marginal price paid to the doctor is more often than not below the average variable cost of the medical service produced.

Gradison asserted that under Kennedy's price control proposals, the difference between a price-controlled premium and the actual cost of providing coverage for certain higher-cost individuals would be passed on to the consumers who already have individual coverage, and that it caused some in the 5.5 million person, individual insurance market to drop their insurance entirely. However, while the HIAA study estimated that some one hundred and sixty thousand people might drop their coverage, it acknowledged that one hundred and seventy-five thousand currently uninsured would be able to buy insurance under Kennedy's proposal, producing a net increase. Mr. Gradison's *in terrorem* rhetoric also added that even a 1 percent rise in the cost of insurance would prompt small businesses to drop two hundred thousand people. Kennedy responded that such data was "round two of industry-scare tactics against the Kassebaum-Kennedy reforms" (parent Senate bill of HIPAA) and that the data of the Congressional Research Service and the American Academy of Actuaries (AAA) belied the HIAA results.

The AAA study estimated that the Kennedy proposals in S.1804/ H.R.3538 "would raise premiums by a maximum 1.6 percent over three years, and possibly much less." Regarding the Kennedy-Kassebaum reforms, the Congressional Budget Office had calculated that the President's Patient Bill of Rights, which would require truth in advertising by HMOs, would raise costs only three-fourths of 1 percent, or about $3.21 per month. Meanwhile, *Newsweek* reported that a Families USA study found that the high-level executives of the leading for-profit HMOs who argued "we can't afford a Patient Bill of Rights" enjoyed an average compensation of $6 million apiece.

Anti-Patient Bill of Rights lobbying was not limited to the above. Added to the cacophony of managed-care executives was H. Edward Hanway, president of CIGNA HealthCare. Speaking at a May 1998 national healthcare meeting in New York presented by The Conference Board, a business membership and research organization, Hanway expressed concern about the Patient Access and Responsible Care Act introduced in Congress, which he felt far exceeded the already gloomy forecasts of Gradison. Hanway attacked "bigger government" for adding up to one thousand mandates, requirements, and regulations on managed care, which, he said, would force up premiums by an average of $1,200 per family and "could result in the loss of health insurance for more than 4 million Americans."

The Republican answer to President Clinton's Patient Bill of Rights also extensively freed up the BBA's MSAs. Even under its new, more-felicitous name "Health Savings Accounts," it provided a tax break worth more to the wealthy than to average Americans. The HSAs would allow those in the 40 percent bracket to get a bigger tax break than those in the 15 percent group, even if the latter could put that much aside in the first place. The MSA law would require indemnity insurers to get into the act, because a high-deductible insurance policy was needed to catch the costs of catastrophic coverage. The more-affluent subscribers were essentially self-insuring by use of the tax-free $4,000 or $5,000 a year "carrot" set aside to pay list prices for front-end medical care. In addition, the up-front money saved from insurers' risk would enable MCOs to drop prior approvals for routine doctor bills and help bypass examination of managed-care doctor discounting.

However, there still was no guarantee that one could have the doctor of their choice, because so many preferred providers were already locked into MCOs, and the catastrophic-level insurers might require use of their own approved (discounted) doctors and hospitals. The insurers could place caps or limits on the catastrophic coverage, until the 2010 Obama ACA made the expensive HSAs a dead letter for all practical purposes. Moreover, there was no guarantee that the insurers would not continue to prevail upon their panel doctors to "manage" the care of an HSA patient so that they could get a better return on withholds from their non-HSA patients. Because managed or capitated doctors and doctors were generally used to treating all patients alike, they thereby devalued the high-deductible premium further for the ones who now believed they were paying for "concierge"-level care.

To eliminate rivals without going out of business, the monopolist will restrict output temporarily until marginal revenue—the increment of income derivable from increasing one more unit of output—equals, or, if necessary, drops below the marginal or average variable cost. In fact, where the marketplace's revenue generally equals price, except for occasional "distress sales" or "catch-up" in minor recession times, the monopolist's marginal revenue is generally aimed to be below market price. This produces the "deadweight loss," where the output is less than consumers want at a price above the cost of producing additional units. In healthcare, it is where people who would have more marginal cost than marginal benefit are buying the product or service anyway. This deadweight loss to society created by the inefficiency in the market results in broad, general, economic inefficiency if the market failure is sustainable. The healthcare monopsonist, too, produces a misallocation of resources based on the disuniformities engendered by the bifurcated system of indemnity-styled managed care. Where the healthcare monopsonist has some degree of market power, it can also restrict output by buying less, thus driving the prices of input seller-providers down. This is similar to the pharmaceutical companies manipulating a supply by drawing it down temporarily, selling to HMOs at a much lower price than they would to retail outlets, and, finally, raising the prices to all after the smaller, competing laboratories or pharmacies are driven out of the market.

The method is similar to the drug dealers who sell marijuana at a low price to new users. When the users are hooked, the dealers withdraw it and offer crack cocaine instead. Several significant polls demonstrate that Americans are not concerned with healthcare cost issues as much as government or commercial interests believe they should be, but they do believe that managed care has done nothing to lessen their own costs, only the costs for insurers and employers.

IV. Health-Care Monopsony—
Buyer Collusion by Coercion

1. Value, Price, and Profit—Are Healthcare Insurance Companies "Too Big to Fail"?

> On September 19, 1993, three days before President Clinton delivered his formal address calling for universal healthcare Senator Moynihan joined with Republican critics and went on NBC's *Meet the Press* to declare that there was "no health-care crisis" and that the projected savings of $91 billion in the Clinton plan were "fantasy numbers."
>
> —Senator Patrick J. Moynihan (D-NY), formerly Counselor for Urban Affairs to President Nixon
> (on PBS Online News Hour)

Although standing to sue in an antitrust action cannot be established without an antitrust injury, the existence of an antitrust injury does not automatically confer standing. According to the 1990 federal Tenth Circuit Court of Appeals in *Reazin v. Blue Cross and Blue Shield of Kansas, Inc.*, the following factors should be considered when evaluating antitrust standing:

1. The causal connection between the alleged antitrust violation and the harm;
2. Improper motive or intent of defendants;
3. Whether the claimed injury is one sought to be redressed by antitrust damages;

4. The directness between the injury and the market restraint resulting from the alleged violation;
5. The speculative nature of the damages claimed; and
6. The risk of duplicative recoveries or complex damage apportionment.

The fact that one competitor would change the price and the others in the market would follow with an unspoken mutual understanding is an artifice of price fixing that is nonetheless a violation of antitrust laws. "Conscious parallelism" refers to conduct of rivals in an industry who coordinate their conduct simply by observing and reacting to the moves of their competitors. While such behavior is generally legal, it may nevertheless lead to an inference of illegal conspiracy. Indeed, as found by the 1975 Second Circuit Court of Appeals in *Modern Home Institute, Inc. v. Hartford Accident & Indemnity Co.*, although the effect of such conscious action that leads to parallel pricing is not considered illegal, the presence of "additional facts and circumstances . . . [may] show that the decisions were interdependent and thus raise the inference of a tacit agreement."

The work of the nonprofit NCQA (which incorporated American Managed Behavioral Health Association, AMBHA), and the for-profit InterQual and Milliman & Robertson-type actuaries' collection and dissemination of data for and with them, offers their clients such "conscious parallelism." These "interdependent" activities create a way for these competitors to concertedly constrain provider prices for the managed-care insurance business and actively control costs for the insurers, effectively stabilizing those prices.

For example, when AMBHA changed its name to Association for Behavioral Health and Wellness (ABHW) in 2007, members were listed as Alliance Behavioral Care, Cenpatico Behavioral Health, College Health IPA/Comprehensive Behavioral Health Management, Magellan Health Services (MHN), Schaller Anderson Behavioral Health, United Behavioral Health, University Behavioral Healthcare, and Value Options. By May 10, 2010, when the Obama administration issued ACA regulations governing the 2008 Dominici-Wellstone "mental health parity act" that abolished discriminatory practices by insurers to coverage for the treatment of mental health and substance abuse disorders, *The New York Times* reported, "a huge fight has erupted over the rules." Named in the fight on the side of the patients were the AMA, the American Psychiatric Association (APA), and a coalition of mental health advocates. On the side of the insurers were the ABHW, the Blue Cross/Blue Shield Association, Aetna, and Magellan Health Services and Value Options, Inc., the latter two "who specialize in managing mental health benefits" suing the government over the new rules. *The New York Times* said, "Insurers and many employers supported the 2008 [parity] law, but they say the rules go far beyond the intent of Congress and would cripple their cost-control techniques while raising out-of-pocket costs for some patients."

"But insurers say the Obama administration went overboard when it tried to regulate 'Nonquantitative treatment limits.' These include the techniques used by insurers to manage care, the criteria for selection of healthcare providers and the rates at which they are paid. . . . In a suit over the rules, Magellan and other companies said the concept of nonquantitative limits was 'boundless and ill defined' and would reach virtually every policy and procedure used to manage mental health benefits.'"

The drive to mimic the federal and state governments' reasons to cut prices of medical delivery and the costs of the government programs was apparently not the real reason for managed care's *modus vivendi*. It is easy for commercial supporters of the healthcare "cost-savings" system to say that their motive is profitability based on socially redeeming intentions, yet there is now ample evidence that in many cases costs are neither cut nor intended to be cut. The "preferred providers" concept was established to imply high "quality" care providers, but after all the years of managed-care interventions, there is still no evidence that the professional "quality" measures demonstrate quality different from OON providers. What they do is produce a localized scarcity of providers whose prices can then be more easily controlled, because they help eliminate rivals. If all providers were acceptable to the MCO, the managed-care companies would simply be mimicking state licensure and medical specialty boards and there would be no justification for externally managing the care.

An examination of MCO "networks" reveals that contracts for per diem or all-inclusive rates between hospitals and MCOs are not negotiated for the lowest price *per se* but are either on a first-come, first-serve basis or by local influence peddling by brokers for medical groups or hospitals. It is important to remember that the cash-flow nature of the failed managed-care insurance business is often not to reduce the *number* of admissions to healthcare services, only the length of time spent receiving that service—that is, to increase the intensity of cash flow per unit when delivered at the higher-cost, front-end days. Ironically, lower-priced facilities may be driven out of the market because they cannot compete with their higher-priced brethren who have the increased MCO patient flow and revenue stream— another facet of a failed market. A perusal of the Medicaid cost-based rates of hospitals demonstrates that higher-priced facilities have many more managed-care contracts than the lower-priced ones. An important reason for this is that Medicaid, like poverty, is concentrated in cities.

The parallel pricing and behavior flowing from data dissemination produced by managed-care organizations and their medical information bureaus results exactly in an injury of the type the antitrust laws intended to prevent. As the 1977, Supreme Court said in *Brunswick Corp. v. Pueblo Bowl-O-Mat, Inc.,* "the injury must reflect the anticompetitive effect." Formal collusion need not be demonstrated, because the pervasive cash-flow-based profit motive substitutes for their having to do little more than think alike. As pointed out by William E. Kovacic in a 1993 *Antitrust Bulletin* article, "The Identification and Proof of Horizontal Agreement Under the Antitrust Laws," rather than deeming mere conscious parallelism an agreement, it is necessary to find certain additional features of firms' behavior called "plus factors" supporting the inference of agreement. Examples of plus factors could include

- a rational motive for these organizations to behave collectively, as seen in the tight ambit of their "cost-saving measures" limiting demand but not supply;
- the behavior of participants' actions that might otherwise be seen as against their best competitive interests, except for the requirement of being pursued as part of a collective plan such as NCQA "accreditation";
- market phenomena that are explainable as a by-product of the concerted action in areas outside of Medicare and Medicaid subcontracting.

Another example is the *Noerr*-type activity, such as "doing the public good by constraining healthcare costs," along with some record of past collusion-related antitrust violations, as seen in numerous cases occurring during the pre-1945 insurance cartel. Thus, "plus factors" must be examined to determine whether it can be inferred that the MCOs are acting pursuant to unspoken agreements to cooperate in predatory price fixing. *See* Plate 4.

Cartels are restricted in the United States by the antitrust laws. *Black's Law Dictionary* definition includes the following:

1. A combination of producers or sellers that join together to control a product's production or price.
2. An association of firms with common interests, seeking to prevent extreme or unfair competition, allocate markets or share knowledge.

Those behaviors, even if each taken alone does not constitute a claim, when taken together may be seen as elements of a proper claim when analyzing allegations of a Sherman section 1 complaint. As seen by a March 2010 federal district court in New York, *Hinds County, Mississippi v. Wachovia Bank, NA, et al.*, citing several other federal court decisions in other circuits from 1995 through 2009:

"A § 1 complaint must adequately allege the plausible involvement of each defendant and put defendants on notice of the claims against them, but it need not be detailed with overt acts by each defendant."

As a reminder, section 1 of the Sherman Act bars anticompetitive agreements, section 2 of the Sherman Act prohibits the abuse of monopoly power, and section 7 of the Clayton Act bars anticompetitive mergers. In healthcare, these appear most commonly in HMO redlining OON (all of them "nonpreferred") providers from the market. IN and OON pricing impairs the preferred providers' "usual, customary, and reasonable" prices to the point of their inefficiency by forced physical volume of patients, shifting copayment costs to the OON patient to either induce them to stay in the network or reduce the HMO's cost if the patient stays OON. This produces the absurd situation where the OON prices set by the insurers are actually below what patients would have otherwise been willing to pay, shown by their apparent willingness to add out-of-pocket money to the OON cost. Meanwhile, the IN provider prices are already contractually low and based not on market value but on the capitated referral volume, and OON market prices are even below those, but include higher co-payments. It is not a zero-sum game, because in both IN and OON, the patients, providers, and society are the losers. The insurers alone are the winners.

"Pareto efficiency" or "Pareto optimality" is an important criterion for evaluating value in economic systems and public policies. If a change in economic policy ends a legally protected monopoly such as healthcare insurance, as presently constituted, and the market subsequently becomes competitive and more efficient, only the monopolist will be worse off. However, the loss to the monopolist will be more than offset by the gain to society in social efficiency. The market failure here is that the healthcare system is "Pareto suboptimal," and public-policy economists seek outcomes that are Pareto efficient.

Before managed care, when indemnity insurance was extensive, insurer premium prices were based on the lowest possible levels, because the risk was spread as widely as possibly for maximum cash flow and was kept that way by competition. The then-nonprofit Blues picked up the higher front-end costs in the private sector, functioning as a Pareto-optimal, quasi utility, while the governments picked up the costs of the poor, the disabled, and the elderly. Once enveloped by the managed-care environment, little or no significant risk spreading took place. The costs could be at naked, negotiated list prices, completely subject to discounts and market manipulation by the increasingly concentrated MCO carriers.

Areeda and Turner expressed the belief that nongovernmental monopsony is rare and unlikely to produce collusive, concerted action by buyers. They say, "Buyer collusion to reduce price, by reducing the available supply, will reduce both their sales and shares in their own product market, since competing sellers' output will not fail." In addition, they suggest that it is more likely that substantial profit gains will arise from seller collusion, because a high inelasticity of demand is more common than inelasticity of supply. However, monopsony by government exists only because remedial legislation is publicly demanded, and sellers (providers) are free to enter the price-controlled structure. However, colluding to not join offers little pressure on government, because the actuarial need predicted providers' (as sellers) acquiescence in large numbers, notwithstanding the still small number of providers who refuse to take Medicare or Medicaid patients. However, in the private healthcare market, especially at the time of the aggressive physician-practice acquisition movement and capture of sellers by capitation, market power is obtained by buyer-organizers' buying practices, and thus owning, the erstwhile sellers. Collusion by sellers in such a situation would be little different from collective bargaining based on contract and traditionally watched closely by the FTC for price fixing, while the buyer-organizers are left unscathed.

When doctors compete with insurers by forming their own HMO-type groups, with the now-obvious dangers to their competitive survival, any "seller collusion" is readily noted, as it had been against physicians and dentists in the antitrust actions of the 1980s Reagan-Bush era. At that time, healthcare customarily involved two levels of distribution of resources: the funding level and the production level (that is, the buyers-of-benefits level purchased from insurers by individuals or fiduciaries, and the insurers' selling assurance-of-benefits delivery by the providers). When the managed-care industry and heavily lob-bied government programs manipulated the supply of doctors, hospital beds, lengths of stay, and funding resources for research and innovation, the real-time "inelasticity of demand" was simply renamed "elasticity" by pundits, churning inpatients into increasingly chronic levels of out-patient care.

Because sickness will not go away by doctors seeing it less, or less intensively, the elemental elasticity of healthcare supply becomes hid-den by a *de facto* lowered standard of living for the traditional sup-plier-providers, who must work harder per unit time with the dangers implicit in weaving healthcare inefficiency into the fabric of care. The superficial appearance of increasing healthcare output by "managing" the care structurally limits the provider-suppliers' ability to reduce demand on a more-effective "caring" basis. Technological efficiencies such as proposed by the 2010 ACA could arguably offset somewhat the deadweight loss that would exist as long as managed-care insurance remains part of the economic mix.

By 1998, although overall annual losses of medical income were reported as turning around in current dollars, *The New York Times* reported, "When inflation is taken into account, doctors are little bet-ter off than they were a decade ago." Indeed, HMOs as a group, in sharp contrast to their executives' pay scales, did not fare well in 1997 either. The average profit margin for HMOs was a negative 1.2 percent, and only 49 percent made any profit at all that year. HMOs continued to struggle to find ways to improve the bottom line after the hospitals and doctors' negotiated rates seemed to have already reached bottom. InterStudy, a nonprofit, managed-care research center in Minneapolis, predicted that only premium increases could make up for the slump in profitability. In addition, the report said that mergers and acquisitions would be giving the HMOs more power to negotiate tougher rates with doctors and hospitals softening the need to profit only from increasing subscribers and raising prices. InterStudy's director acknowledged an ominous danger:

> "HMOs may feel that new enrollment in the past two years
> has been unprofitable. While it's important to have growing

market share, the lack of profitability of new enrollees may have outweighed the benefits."

Moreover, as reported in the AMA's April 1998 *American Medical News*, the "float" representing claims or incurred but not reported losses increased by 50 percent. The number of day's claims remained unpaid increased 66 percent from 40.2 days in 1994 to 66.8 days in the third quarter of 1997. This was one more example of the deadweight loss found in the reduced supply of input by the monopolists. Blaming "underpricing of renewals" and "computer problems" once more, the "turn-around" times for companies having such profit misfortunes was largely resolved by raising premium prices at the expense of increased enrollment. As reported by *The Wall Street Journal* in July 1998, even where companies' enrollment was not suffering—such as at UHC with its new ten-year contract with the multimillion-member AARP—the insurers downsized. They dropped handpicked Medicare and Medicaid contracts, sold off their individual life insurance, annuity or workers compensation businesses, and dangerously decreased their cash reserves.

The Clinton administration directly attacked the ERISA protection enjoyed by managed care during the prior decade. The administration's HCFA narrowed ERISA preemption by interpreting the BBA standard to mean that preemption would exist only if the state standards were inconsistent with the federal standards. In addition, the BBA also contained specific preemption where federal standards were present regardless of whether they were inconsistent. The three areas of specific preemption were: (1) benefit requirements; (2) those relating to the inclusion or treatment of providers; and (3) coverage determinations, including related appeals and grievance procedures. The interpretation by the Clinton HCFA would also have prevented the application of state benefit mandates and any willing provider laws or other laws mandating the inclusion of specific types of providers and practitioners, or those that duplicated Medicare coverage determinations in the appeals process.

The Clinton HCFA's interpretation applied only to Medicare patients and not to state laws regarding issues other than coverage

235

under the Medicare Act and still allowed the states to develop their own laws relating to non-Medicare healthcare issues, including mandated benefits. Other than the waiver and exception of the federal safe harbor for provider-sponsored organizations, HCFA made no relevant distinction among HMOs, Physician Hospital Organizations, (PHOs), PSOs and other coordinated care plans for purposes of an M+C contract. It obliged each M+C organization to disclose profits attributable to each M+C plan as part of an adjusted community rate approval process required by the BBA for each plan (except for those with Medical Savings Accounts) to determine how many extra benefits must be provided to Medicare enrollees.

Of singular importance was the determination by the Clinton HCFA that the CEO or CFO of an M+C plan must certify that

"each enrollee for whom the organization is requesting payment is validly enrolled in an M+C plan offered by the organization and the information relied upon by HCFA in determining payment is accurate."

This type of certification had been used by other administrations' HCFA's for all hospitals that took Medicare patients. However, Clinton's HCFA believed it was making a "claim for capitation payment in the amount dictated by the data submitted or in the case of an [Adjusted Community Rate] submission, a claim to retain the portion of the capitation payment that is under the ACR amount." HCFA pointed out further that when an M+C group claimed payment or the right to hold on to the payment, "it should be willing to certify the accuracy of this information." Although the federal False Claims Act had not generally been applied to capitation payments, because they had not been considered by government as payment *of* claims even though they were undoubtedly payments *for* claims, HCFA evidently decided that if the capitations were not to be paid as payment of claims, they must be something else. That "something else" appeared to be that capitation is, indeed, a conveyance to pay for claims made upon the system, and no shilly-shallying could redefine them otherwise. Because the FCA allows for treble damages and criminal and other sanctions, the M+C organizations had thus—in Areeda-Turner language—either cause to limit the size of their Medicare populations, that is, to reduce output—or get out of treating Medicare patients altogether. Apparently, many MCOs decided on the latter as an exit plan.

It is important, too, for antitrust investigators to scrutinize which providers' bills are not paid when an MCO blames computer problems. The giant insurance industry could not deny the existence of scores of claims by providers alleging that they had been redlined out of the market. Such redlining, if true, could demonstrate a pattern of monopolistic practice to manipulate the market. When acting on behalf of patients as buyers of providers' healthcare they do not diligently pay claims, they directly limit input to providers' pockets. It doesn't take much imagination to see such a slow-payment technique as having a chilling effect on suppliers' enthusiasm to work with such organizations. Considering the fact that healthcare coverage companies' domains far exceed home-state boundaries, instead of the traditional geographic percentages for assessing market power, antitrust investigators could use the multistate actuarial data based on HCFA's ten regions, which comprise the fifty states and Puerto Rico. This way, the investigators could ascertain the overlapping that occurred after the merger mania of the Bush II era and would thereby position the activity squarely in the focus of federal interstate commerce regulation.

Federal Seventh Circuit Court of Appeals Judges Posner and Easterbrook, in their 1974 book, *Antitrust Cases, Economic Notes and Other Materials*, written when they were law professors, argued that the dangers of monopsonistic practices have been small. They believed that one danger of monopsony driving some suppliers from the market was that it allowed the remaining suppliers to have an easier task to cartelize the supplier market and achieve countervailing market power. Such a position might have been helpful in analyzing antitrust behavior in nonmedical sectors of the economy, but to think that redlined or HMO-hobbled doctors would band together somehow and exert "countervailing market power" was less than convincing, considering the market power position of the HMOs. The irony that HMOs could begin to rely less on broadening enrollment to achieve legal levels of market power and, instead, turn to mergers to achieve the same thing, should have received heightened scrutiny from government regulators. The Blues, historically nonprofit, became largely for-profit companies, *sub silentio* at first, moving customers from indemnity to managed-care plans at premium prices equivalent to the lesser-optioned commercial supplementary MCOs and thereby hiding the now lower value, higher cost of the policy.

WellPoint Health Networks of California announced on July 9, 1998, that it would acquire Cerulean Companies, Inc., the parent company of Blue Cross/Blue Shield of Georgia, for $500 million by the end of that year. Cerulean had 1.7 million enrollees and $806 million in revenues. It was the largest organization of its type in the state, while WellPoint, the parent of Blue Cross of California had 6.7 million members, split between California and other states under the name UniCare. To follow the path of growth across state lines, one need only note that the old WellPoint Health Networks Inc., of Woodland Hills, California, one of the companies that merged with Anthem to form WellPoint Inc., of Indianapolis, created the UniCare business in 1995 to hold health-insurance operations outside of California. Much of the business in that unit was acquired from Massachusetts Life Insurance Company, Springfield, Massachusetts, in 1996, and from John Hancock Mutual Life Insurance Company, Boston, in 1997. In 2009, in the face of impending Obama health-care reform, National Underwriter magazine reported,

> "WellPoint, Inc., Indianapolis (NYSE: WLP), a manager of dominant Blue Cross and Blue Shield plans in many markets, says it will be disposing of blocks of individual and group commercial business in the Prairie State and the Lone Star State. Healthcare Service Corp., Chicago, runs Blue Cross and Blue Shield of Illinois and Blue Cross and Blue Shield of Texas, and WellPoint has arranged for the Healthcare Service units to offer the Illinois and Texas UniCare customers' replacement coverage, WellPoint says. 'For those members who elect not to accept HCSC's offer of replacement coverage, UniCare will con-

tinue to provide coverage until their current policies terminate according to their terms.'"

In the days of widely sold indemnity insurance, it was difficult for commercial carriers to block the front-end Blues, then a quasi utility, from receiving subsidies and hefty increases they requested, because their nonprofit status, combined with their 96 percent medical loss ratio, prevailed with regulators. If commercial healthcare insurance prices, when below average variable cost as in Oxford's case, can stay viable only by state or federal subsidization of cash flow for marginal revenue, serious questions arise about the value of the consumer welfare achieved by applying the "too big to fail" philosophy to the managed healthcare insurance industry, because it is already a chronic, expensive market failure.

2. Incurring Private Losses as a Waste of Social Resources

"The monopolist is not only incurring private losses but wasting social resources when marginal costs exceed the value of what is produced. And pricing below marginal cost greatly increases the possibility that rivalry will be extinguished or prevented for reasons unrelated to the efficiency of the monopolist. Accordingly, a monopolist pricing below marginal cost should be presumed to have engaged in a predatory or exclusionary practice."

—Areeda and Turner (1975)

Areeda and Turner's models reach the region of the managed healthcare market failure when they argue that marginal-cost pricing by a monopolist ought to be tolerated if it leads to a proper resource allocation and is consistent with competition on the merits. The admixture of MCOs' aggressive entrepreneurial behavior with the staid economic style of indemnity insurers has significantly accelerated managed-care insurance's market failure. Seeking to keep up with new high-rolling managed-care companies, Aetna Insurance Company ventured feet first into the era of managed care in 1996, buying U.S. Healthcare for $9 billion and selling its life insurance division to Lincoln National. (Note to the reader: U.S. HealthCare is distinct from UnitedHealthcare, a subsidiary of UnitedHealth Group.)

As harbinger of what became the Bush II era healthcare executive compensation levels, *The New York Times* reported in April, 1996 that Leonard Abramson, founder, chairman and controlling shareholder of U.S. Healthcare, stood to receive almost $500 million in cash plus 3.2 million common shares of Aetna, which he said would make him the company's largest individual holder. As reported by *The New York Times* on the same day, Dr. William W. McGuire, head of UHC, having received compensation in the form of stock options from 1989 until 2006 that eventually became worth around $1.6 billion, was forced to resign after a series of class-action suits were settled by the company.

The Wall Street Journal on July 29, 1996 reported that despite its actuarial research capabilities in the fee-for-service market, the price paid for Aetna/U.S. Healthcare's 2.8 million members was a healthy $3,200 per member. Apparently thinking it made itself a good albeit overly enthusiastic deal, Aetna in January of 1998 had to face the ignominy of seeing a report by *The New York Times* that the UHC proposed deal with Humana, Inc. came in at only $1,200 per member two years later. The UHC-proposed purchase of Humana would have formed a combined company with some ten million members across the United States and some six hundred and two thousand members in Miami HMOs, giving it 48 percent of the Miami market.

Notwithstanding the sicker population it covers, the "government sector," which makes up 45 percent of all its hospital payments through government-constructed DRGs and global "Prospective Payment" rates, pay a provider less per illness than indemnity contracts, and the copayments and deductibles are paid under private Medigap policies. This was pointed out in an Op-Ed article, by 2008 Nobel laureate economist Paul Krugman in *The New York Times* of June 13, 2001, discussing Senator Lieberman's proposal to raise the age for Medicare eligibility from 65 to 67:

"Medicare actually saves money—a lot of money—compared with relying on private insurance companies. And this in turn means that pushing people out of Medicare, in addition to depriving many Americans of needed care, would almost surely end up increasing total health care costs. . . The point, however, is that privatizing health insurance for seniors, which is what Mr. Lieberman is in effect proposing—and which is the essence of the G.O.P. plan—hurts rather than helps the cause of cost control. If we really want to hold down costs, we should be seeking to offer Medicare-type programs to as many Americans as possible."

To actuaries, the 31.5 percent of total U.S. personal healthcare expenditures at the time represented the per capita distribution of an aggregate $879 million and came to the magic $1,200 per member.

Thus, while Aetna's price was overloaded with conditions that either no longer existed or were presumptuous, the Humana/UHC's $1,200 figure appeared to demonstrate a predictable per capita cost for all insurable patients. UHC, which acquired Metropolitan and Travelers' merged health-insurance divisions in 1995 and proposed to acquire Humana, Inc., in 1998, clearly computed differently from Aetna based on its and Humana's intimate knowledge of the industry and its need to get into the rapidly narrowing big-group marketspace. Paying only $1,200 per member could mean that either the healthcare populations they were to inherit were so actuarially disparate from those of Aetna/U.S. Healthcare as to account for it or that the computation was on a different actuarial theory. It appeared that both of UHC's actuarial assumptions were true. Remembering that Humana had been a hospital company accustomed to treating all comers, UHC probably assumed—and Humana, relatively new in the health insurance business, apparently agreed—that any insurable person could get sick, and accepted the per capita number that was 31.5 percent of the $879 million representing the potential from all payments by third parties, excluding government.

Of course, UHC's price might also have been overeager on the low side. On August 6, as if in anticipation, UHC took a surprising pretax charge of a strangely similar $900 million in the second quarter, saying that $620 million of that charge was for scaling down its Medicare population. As a result, the stock fell by over 30 percent and pulled down other managed-care stocks as well. This jeopardized its planned acquisition of Humana, and on August 11, the deal was called off. The executive director of the Medicare Rights Center in New York was quoted in *The New York Times*:

> "People seem to forget that Medicare was created because private insurers could not make money on the elderly population. Now managed-care plans are discovering the same lesson all over again."

Bloomberg News reported that although UHC's revenue rose 44 percent to $4.24 billion from $2.93 billion, a large part of the increase was attributed to its new agreement with the thirty-two-million-member AARP, notwithstanding that UHC's officials conceded that its older

AARP customers were more expensive to treat than was the average customer. For its January excesses with U.S. HealthCare, Aetna would be taking a $300 million annual charge against income for "goodwill." A charge against earnings, being also a reduction in the company's taxable income, represents additionally a loss of potential taxes on $300 million per year for however long the rest of the taxpayers will have to pay for Aetna's folly. Although not necessarily predatory, Aetna's audaciously high price shows how, as Areeda-Turner said, "the monopolist is not only incurring private losses but wasting social resources when marginal costs exceed the value of what is produced."

Moreover, in Aetna's zeal to leap into the exciting new profit trough, the actuarial wisdom of not offering a potential insurance hazard, "moral" or otherwise, vaporized as competitors' advertisements drew more and more previously HMO-doctor-shy people into the MCOs. At the same time, for balance, the company replaced many top-level traditional executives with U.S. Healthcare's aggressive external care managers. The new executives pushed for more revenue through acquisitions of MCOs, ignoring the dangers of adverse selection and assuming there was little risk when their output would be controllable by capitation. These external care managers unleashed an "iceberg effect," an epidemiological metaphor for a clinical population that "floats" on its actuarially determined surface of illness "incidence" and where nine-tenths of it, a massive subclinical "prevalence," remains hidden below the surface and threatens to "flip over." The iceberg effect left chronic illness churning in its wake. As a result, Aetna's healthcare costs soared 14 percent in 1997, and the company had to take a $160 million charge for its "unanticipated medical costs" as major clients left the fold. By mid-1998, *Bloomberg News* reported that hundreds of doctors had abandoned the "limping giant," after being pressured into using the company's approved centers for x-rays, lab tests, and other clinical work and for not being paid on time. The chilling effect on a cohort of competitive contractor physicians not being paid on time suggested a socially dangerous method of redefining a market share for actuarial advantage in a system formally based on open redlining. *See* Plate 6.

In April 1998, before the proposed deal with UHC was to take place, Humana and FPA Medical Management, Inc. (FPA) (NASDAQ: FPAM) jointly announced that FPA would assume operations of Humana's medical clinics in Florida (Orlando, Tampa, and South Florida) and in the greater Kansas City area of Missouri and Kansas; Humana would continue to own the land and buildings. FPA lost money each year from its inception in 1994. In four years as a publicly traded company, FPA bought the practices of almost eight thousand doctors with 1.4 million patients and owned their equipment and assets. By July, FPA filed for protection under Chapter 11 of the bankruptcy laws. The situation then reversed itself. Effective June 7, 1999, Humana was back in the game with approval of the federal bankruptcy court, now to assume responsibility to oversee FPA's Chapter 11 reorganization. Humana also entered into partnerships with five medical organizations to operate the thirteen South Florida medical centers they formerly operated together, as well as Humana's own operational responsibility for fifty former FPA centers, which were seen by the court to be

"Consistent with Humana's intention to transfer operation of the former FPA centers to other provider groups, enabling Humana to focus exclusively on its core business of health insurance."

The bankruptcy court was not concerned that the managed "insurance core" certainly allowed Humana to have a horizontal, primary-care relationship as well as a vertical hospital-based, insurance-company revenue stream with millions of Floridians. The newly endowed company proudly reported the following on its website in 2010, raising a question of whether it is a provider or an insurer:

"Our network features approximately 544,000 medical providers, more than 4,000 hospitals, and over 60,000 pharmacies across most of the U.S. If you're sick or injured while you're traveling, you're likely to find medical care covered by plan benefits at in-network rates, which can save you a considerable amount of money and provide their insurance coverage at the same time."

By April 2010, Humana president and CEO Michael McCallister said that they were well prepared for the "post-health-reform environment." At the end of the first quarter of 2010, Humana, already one of the nation's largest providers of privately run MA health plans for seniors, raised its 2010 earnings view to a range of $5.55 to $5.65 a share from $5.15 to $5.35 a share. The revenue target increased $500 million to a range of $33.5 billion to $34.5 billion.

On Feb. 13, 2008, New York Attorney General Andrew M. Cuomo announced that he had commenced a broad investigation into the use by insurers of defective databases when determining what they called "usual, customary, and reasonable" payments made to OON health-care providers. The Attorney General also announced his intention to sue UHC related to defects in its Ingenix database. His investigation appeared to be ongoing and could result in investigations by regulators in other states. However, on January 13, 2009, Mr. Cuomo reached an agreement with UHG, parent of UHC. Ingenix, Inc., also a wholly owned subsidiary of UHG, the nation's largest provider of health-care billing information, was at the center of the scheme. Under the agreement, the database of billing information operated by Ingenix would close. UHG would pay $50 million to a qualified nonprofit organization to establish a new, independent database to help determine fair OON reimbursement rates for consumers throughout the United States.

As stated by J. Robert Hunter, director of insurance for the Consumer Federation of America, on October 14, 2009, before the Senate Judiciary Committee hearing on *"Prohibiting Price Fixing and Other Anticompetitive Conduct in the Health Insurance Industry"*:

> "Insurers claim that the antitrust exemption is not an issue in health insurance. As cited above the example of conflicts-of-interest in setting "reasonable and customary fees" demonstrates that this statement is not true. But, if it were true, why would health insurers argue for an exemption that has no impact? To say it does nothing and, simultaneously, fight the change does not make sense. There is a reason health insurers want to retain the exemption."

An editorial in *The New York Times* dated January 17, 2009, said, "The rub comes in defining what is reasonable and customary." It described how Ingenix, whose ownership by UHG created an unconscionable conflict of interest, had calculated this factor. If Ingenix sets the reasonable and customary (R&C) rates low, it shifts more of the copayment portion to the patient. The editorial was based on the report from the New York AG, which found that most health insurers use the Ingenix schedules of reasonable and customary charges, including UnitedHealth, Aetna, CIGNA, and WellPoint. So-called "competing" insurers could hide the way they calculate R&C charges from insured parties and set prices for payments to IN and OON providers by pretending that an independent group—to which Aetna, CIGNA and WellPoint subscribe and UHG owns—calculated the schedules. Mr. Hunter further testified:

> "The Ingenix system is a black box for consumers, who do not know, before selecting a doctor, what will be paid by the insurer. Health insurers mislead and obfuscate in their policy language. In New York, the system understated reimbursement rates by ten to 28 percent, which translates to at least hundreds of millions of dollars in losses for consumers over the past ten years across the country. While the insurers have agreed to set up a new system, now that Mr. Cuomo caught them, the points that this Committee must take from this report are that: Collusive activity exists in health insurance and should be stopped by antitrust law enforcement. Collusive activity goes well beyond price fixing and deeply into other aspects of insurance, such as claims settlement practices."

The issue in that class-action lawsuit—brought in federal District Court for the Southern District of New York on March 15, 2000 by the AMA, other state medical associations and union plaintiffs—was whether UHC has systematically understated its calculation of "usual, customary, and reasonable" charges when paying physicians or reimbursing patients for OON medical services. Specifically, the complaint alleged that the defendant Ingenix used flawed databases in determining reimbursement amounts for covered OON healthcare benefits; used certain reimbursement policies to improperly reduce amounts for covered OON healthcare benefits; and did not adequately disclose its use of the Ingenix databases and certain reimbursement policies in determining reimbursement amounts for covered OON healthcare benefits. The defendants denied all claims of wrongdoing but agreed to the settlement "to avoid the further expense, inconvenience, and burden of this lawsuit."

On June 4, 2010, *The New York Times* published the announcement of the $350 million UHG proposed settlement agreement with

"members of healthcare plans insured or administered by UHC Corporation, Inc., Metropolitan Life Insurance Company, American Airlines, Inc. and their subsidiaries and affiliates, and healthcare providers and healthcare provider groups who furnished out-of-network services or supplies to such members."

Subsidiaries and affiliates of UHG included Oxford Health Plans, Golden Rule Insurance, Mid-Atlantic Medical Services, and PacifiCare Health Systems. The physicians' claims would apply to services or supplies provided between March 15, 1994 and November 18, 2009—the so-called class period. However, an executive of a company that was helping physicians file settlement claims was reported to have estimated that based on past class-action settlements involving the medical profession, only 20 percent of eligible clinicians actually submit the necessary paperwork.

A. Physician Practice Management Companies—Managed Care as Real Estate, Furniture, and Equipment

> "Property monopolized, or in the Possession of a few is a curse to Mankind. We should preserve not an Absolute Equality, this is unnecessary, but preserve all from extreme Poverty, and all others from extravagant Riches."
>
> — John Adams (1765)

The vogue of hospitals buying physicians' practices to establish "integrated delivery systems" led to carving out or consolidating professional practices with the lowest cash flow and productive market power, potentially causing what we have said was an injury of the type that the antitrust laws intended to prevent. The knowledgeable buyer understood that if the physician's practice produced high cash flow, it would be buyable only if the doctor was close to retirement, ill, or simply a bad businessperson. Moreover, the physician who remained with his or her patients after acquisition became for all intents and purposes salaried—the poorest incentive-based arrangement, because the only way a salaried person can improve his or her lot is to slow down. Buying physicians' practices was increasingly recognized as a poor investment, with more than 80 percent conservatively estimated to be losing money. Why this happened was not easy to decipher.

If the new employee-doctors' work was "speeded up," they were less medically efficient and portended greater liability. If they "slowed down," there was less money for profit and withholds. However, as the mergers provided local market power for hospitals, they affected competitor physicians' practices. Antitrust regulators have always seen physician groups as competitors, and the FTC guidelines emphasize that care should be taken when physicians are engaged in forming them. Therefore, it should come as no surprise that some of the anticompetitive behavior of managed-care insurers, when bringing independently practicing physicians into "practice management" groups, involved giving them stock options in a managing company—seemingly a cheap way to "clean up" the antitrust problem. The following examples of company failures indicate some of the ways the marketspace was filled by medical managed-care ventures made with insurers and how the claim of "commoditizing" medical care came into common use.

1. FPA Medical Management, Inc.—Paradigm for a Market Failure

> "It shall be unlawful for any person engaged in commerce, in the course of such commerce, to lease or make a sale or contract for sale of goods, wares, merchandise, machinery, supplies, or other commodities, whether patented or unpatented, for use, . . where the effect of such . . . condition, agreement, or understanding may be to substantially lessen competition or tend to create a monopoly in any line of commerce."
>
> —Section 3 of the Clayton Antitrust Act

An illustrative case of market failure was shown by FPA, whose bankruptcy was rescued by Humana's takeover. Organized in 1994, it applied for a public offering. As required by SEC regulations, FPA informed potential investors, or anyone reading its submission, the carefully worded obligatory caveat that

> "many aspects of the company have not been the subject of state or federal regulatory interpretation [and] any significant restriction could have a material adverse effect on the Company's results of operations and financial condition."

This statement should be important to those interested in understanding the fragmented nature of commercially insured healthcare delivery before the 2010 reform act. The government sector of the healthcare system remains among the most regulated industries in the country, and despite the above, has maintained itself as the most recession-proof, stable sector of the economy. However, it is not difficult to understand what appears to be surplus in this company's disclaimer. Because it had no earnings at the time of the public offering and had none in its prior four years, its offering represented solely excitement generated by its entry into the burgeoning, if structurally unsound, new marketspace.

On April 28, 1995, *PR Newswire* reported that FPA (NASDAQ: FPAM) reported that a privately owned physician practice group, whose principals include FPAM-related parties, had been accused in a "whistle- blower" suit by a former employee of the private company. However, Dr. Sol Lizerbram, chairman of FPA, said that

"This lawsuit does not accuse or name the publicly owned FPA Medical Management, Inc. Furthermore, the charges against FPAM related parties who operate Family Practice Associates of San Diego, Inc., a private physician practice group, were investigated under closed seal."

The company issued forward-looking statements over the next two years while it gathered physician members as revenue producers and their patients as the cash-flow contributors. By 1997, FPA entered into a long-term

"non-exclusive provider relationship in order to provide Aetna/U.S. Healthcare members with broad access to quality oriented physicians [and] organizes and manages primary care physician networks and provides contract management services to hospital emergency departments."

The company also provided primary and specialty care for capitated doctors of managed-care enrollees and fee-for-service patients in twenty-nine states, and affiliated with physicians who provided services to enrollees of fifty-three HMOs or other prepaid health insurance plans. In October 1997, FPA achieved certification from the NCQA for all of the nine out of ten verification services for which FPA applied for certification. By November, FPA had entered into a definitive agreement pursuant to which FPA would acquire Avanti Health Systems of Texas, Inc. On April 8 of the following year, it added ninety thousand more members by reaching an agreement with Humana Inc., in which FPA would assume operations of twenty-three Humana health centers in four markets to provide healthcare services to Humana members under an enthusiastic ten-year provider agreement. Therefore, within two years, FPA was wedded to manage both Aetna/U.S. HealthCare and its chief competitor, the proposed Humana/UHC merger.

FPA organized its primary care physicians into "Professional Corporations" or "subsidiaries," which in states that prohibited fee splitting with physicians nonetheless gave it direct or indirect unilateral and perpetual control over the assets and operations of corporations whose business it increased. Its SEC submission stated that FPA derived substantially all of its operating revenue from the payments made by

> "Payors [listed as NYLCare Health Plans, Inc., Oxford Health Plans, Inc., Humana, Inc., PacifiCare Health systems, Inc., Aetna U.S. Healthcare, and Foundation Health Systems, Inc.] to the physicians' professional corporations and certain of the company's subsidiaries for managed care medical services. [The company purchased stop-loss insurance of $100,000 for the inpatient services listed above] which substantially covers all financial exposure for inpatient service of an enrollee . . . [and which] is contractually shifted to the insurer at a specified level (generally $1 million)."

FPA also provided fee-for-service revenues for the performance of medical services, fee-for service revenues from emergency department medical services, and medical management service revenues. Possibly hoping that buyers not carefully reading the prospectus would buy its stock offering, the company cautioned in advance that it could not

> "assure that regulatory authorities will not take the position that such control, through the Administrative Services Agreements and Succession Agreements, conflicts with state laws regarding the practice of medicine or other federal restrictions [and that its] contractual arrangements with Professional Corporations will not be successfully challenged as constituting the unlicensed practice of medicine."

Although state laws differ in their understanding of what constitutes fee splitting, it is generally seen as contemplating that physicians may not divide professional fees with entities or individuals that have not rendered medical services. By having a physician/employee as a director of a physician-member "Professional Corporation," FPA may have been modeling its non-fee-splitting arrangement on laws like New York's Education Law anti-fee-splitting statute, which prohibits

"directly or indirectly offering, giving, soliciting or receiving or agreeing to receive, any fee or other consideration to or from a third party for the referral of a patient or in connection with the performance of professional services; [and p]ermitting any person to share in the fees for professional services, other than a partner, employee, associate in a professional firm or corporation, professional subcontractor or consultant authorized to practice medicine, or a legally authorized trainee practicing under the supervision of a licensee."

FPA also maintained "Integrated Information Systems," an online database that provided inpatient and outpatient utilization statistics and patient encounter reporting and tracking. FPA believed that the availability of timely information or utilization patterns improved primary-care physician productivity and effectiveness. Moreover, it believed that these data play an integral role in the specialty-care physician and hospital utilization review process by enabling medical directors and utilization review nurses to monitor encounters with patients. Although capitated in one form or another, FPA physicians were told they may receive

"additional compensation based on efficiency in utilizing the services of specialty care providers and compliance with contractual quality standards; base compensation plus performance bonuses, or base compensation plus a percentage of a Professional Corporation's net revenues generated by physicians employed by such Professional Corporation. Fee-for-service specialists as well as capitated physicians are compensated on a discounted fee-for service or capitated basis."

The physicians with which FPA contracts would be able to purchase stock options in nonqualified company plans "if they reach objective quality performance standards set by FPA." Although "qualified" and "nonqualified" plans are similarly subject to regulation under Title I of ERISA, there is one important exception: the nonqualified plans would not be prohibited from discriminating in favor of officers, share-holders, and highly compensated employees as required by ERISA-qualified plans. For FPA, this meant that the higher-paid employees could get disproportionately better pensions and health plans than the lower-paid ones, an ironic offer for the revenue-producing doc-tors to get less-classy treatment than the lay corporate executives could.

The following supplementary documents offered to physicians had financial data redacted from its disclosure:

> "Form of Primary Care Physician Agreement"; "Form of Specialty Care Physician Agreement/California"; and agree-ments with three other organizations: a "Medical Services Organization Agreement . . . between FPNJ and Medigroup, Inc. (HMO Blue)"; "Pacificare IPA [Independent Practice Asso-ciation] Commercial Services Agreement with FPASD [San Diego] dated May 1, 1995," and Amendment to IPA Medicare Partial Risk Services Agreement between Pacificare of Califor-nia and FPASD dated April 1995."

It is surprising that a complete agreement that involved a company receiving Medicare funds could be privately held back from public dis-closure of taxpayer funds. Moreover, under the then-interim regulations promulgated by the Clinton HCFA pursuant to the BBA, physicians had to receive what they would have under the original Medicare pro-gram. An analysis of FPA's "subsidiaries" (where stock was exchanged) and "Professional Corporations" offers some insight into how the com-pany proposed to circumnavigate the various state laws against fee splitting and federal anti-kickback statutes:

> "As stated in Note 1 to FPA's Consolidated Financial State-ments, FPA believes it has direct or indirect unilateral and per-petual control over the assets and operations of the Professional Corporations whose operations FPA consolidates."

In "Note 1" of FPA's Forms 10-K and 8-K submitted to the SEC, one finds that FPA had to have a controlling financial interest in the doctors' professional corporations by means other than owning the majority of their voting stock. FPA would be unable to own a majority interest in Professional Corporations in states that prohibit the corporate practice of medicine. However, the Professional Corporations could have as shareholders and directors certain physicians who were employees of FPA or one of its subsidiaries. Each shareholder/director would have entered into a succession agreement that required such shareholder/director to sell to a designee of FPA such shareholder/director's share of stock for a nominal amount if such shareholder/director were terminated from employment with FPA.

This ensured perpetual and unilateral (and probably illegal) control over the Professional Corporations by FPA. Despite its constant annual losses—similar to Oxford's and others' contemporary assumption that increasing enrollment revenue alone could justify a profitless business's survival—Humana and FPA jointly announced that FPA would assume operations of Humana's medical clinics in Florida and in the greater Kansas City area in Missouri and in Kansas, apparently also in preparation for its deal with UHC. FPA would employ the doctors, manage the medical centers, and own the equipment and assets; Humana would continue to own the land and buildings—all business activities would be across state lines, that is, in interstate commerce.

To demonstrate how interlocked the companies were, on August 11, *The New York Times* reported that Foundation Health Systems, Inc. announced its second quarter earnings of $.01 per share after taking a $50 million pretax charge (or $0.25 after taxes) "primarily related to the asset impairment of receivables and real estate leased to FPA Medical Management, Inc." Foundation Health Systems, Inc. had a market capitalization in December 1998 of $1.12 billion, revenues of $8.9 billion, fourteen thousand employees, and a net loss of $165 million. From its home in Woodland Hills, California, it was the fourth-largest publicly traded managed healthcare company in the United States, owning among other entities Physicians Health Services of Connecticut. In 2001, Foundation Health Systems changed its name to Health

Net. Health Net of Connecticut Inc.'s parents are UHG and Oxford Health Plans. Notwithstanding the above moves to improve its revenue stream, FPA stock lost over 85 percent of its value, falling to $4.19 by May 20, 1998, after a high of $40 the previous year.

On April 15, 1998, the OIG for DHHS had issued an Advisory Opinion to an anonymous physician query, raising three concerns about a proposed management-services agreement involving management fees based on a percentage of net revenues. OIG advisory opinions are not binding on anyone other than the requestor and the government, and a requestor may withdraw its request at any time if the information demands or the process costs become burdensome. Because the requestor failed to supply the OIG with the type of detailed information required before it could make its determination, there was no formal statement by the OIG supportive of the proposed arrangement. Nonetheless, the OIG responded that such agreements, as percentage payments for marketing services, may involve technical violations of the antikickback statute and that there had to be safeguards against overutilization when multispecialty physician networks are organized by PPMCs for whom they negotiate managed-care contracts. The OIG suggested that percentage payments might increase the risk of abusive billing practices.

The nature of AO98 is an interesting example describing the anonymous request from the physician:

"Doctor X is a family practice physician who has "incorporated as, and practices under the name of, Company A [("A") and] is proposing to enter into an agreement to establish a family practice and walk-in clinic with a corporation, Company B [("B")]. Dr. X is the sole requestor of this advisory opinion.

In the body of the advisory, the OIG explains the range of services that B will offer A (the portions italicized are highlighted for purposes of the discussion to follow). These services include finding

"a suitable location for the clinic and *furnish the initial capital* for the office furniture, and operating expenses. Once [A] is operational, [B] *will provide or arrange for all operating services for the clinic* including accounting, billing, purchasing, direct marketing, and hiring of non-medical personnel and outside vendors. [B] *will also provide* [A] *with management and marketing services for the clinic, including the negotiation and oversight of healthcare contracts.* In addition . . . on behalf of [A, B] *will set up provider networks.* These networks will include [A] and, if required by [B], [A] has agreed that it will refer its patients to the providers in such networks.

"Under the proposed arrangement [A] will provide all physician services at the clinic . . . *Hire* additional physicians and other medical personnel *with the mutual agreement of {B}* . . . pay all physician compensation and fringe benefits, including but not limited to, licensing fees, continuing education, and malpractice premiums.

"In return for its services, Company B's payment will have three components. Company A will be required to make a capital payment equal to a percentage of the initial cost of each capital asset purchased for [A] per year for six years. Company B will also receive a fair market value payment for the operating services it provides and an at-cost payment for any operating services for which it contracts. *Company B will receive a percentage of Company A's monthly net revenues for its management services.* If the percentage payment described above is not permitted by law, then the parties *will establish a management fee reflecting the contemplated financial results of the arrangement* or, if the parties cannot agree to a fixed amount, the parties will hire an accounting firm to determine an appropriate fixed fee ('the Alternative Proposed Arrangement')."

From this point on, OIG Counsel makes its formal response and concludes as follows:

"Therefore, since we cannot be confident that there is no more than a minimal risk of fraud or abuse, we must conclude that the Proposed Arrangement may involve prohibited remuneration under the anti-kickback statute and thus possibly subject to sanction under the anti-kickback statute, § 1128B(b) of the [Social Security] Act."

Whether "Doctor X" is a member of a "Professional Corporation" set up by FPA or another PPMC or was simply contemplating joining a similar venture was not known. In any event, the probability that there are kindred contracts between other PPMCs and doctors is great, and the probability of their skirting many state and federal laws was even greater. If a bankruptcy should occur, the "Independent Physicians Associations" (IPAs) contracting-physician members of FPA or of any similar PPMC would appear to be somewhat indentured, to say the least. Among other things, the typical agreement requires that title to any furniture, fixtures, or equipment

"shall remain in Medical Management (FPA Med) and upon termination of this agreement, IPA shall immediately return and surrender all such fixtures, furnishings, and equipment to Medical Management in as good a condition as when received, normal wear and tear excepted."

In the same agreement, FPA agreed to supply

"data and reports for IPA's medical practice, evaluating the performance of IPA's physicians and for other purposes relating to a high level of patient care quality and improving the efficiency of IPA's physicians."

It should be remembered that an IPA is composed of "independent" physicians, each with his or her own office and capital equipment. FPA would also receive "nonmedical performance and productivity data," which could be distributed to the putative, erstwhile physician "competitors." In effect, this "sharing" disseminates discrete information related to methods of cost-containing medical care between competitors, because the distinction between "nonmedical" data and "financial accounting" data is difficult to parse. In fact, there was a covenant not to compete: "During the term of this Agreement, IPA agrees not to contract for or to obtain management or administrative services with any other organization other than IPA Management," and in the "Proprietary Information" section

"[although the IPA may have full access to] information of a proprietary nature owned by Medical Management [IPA agrees to hold such] 'trade secrets' confidential from all competitors, and further acknowledges that such disclosure will result in irreparable harm which cannot reasonably or adequately be compensated in damages."

Thus, the Proprietary Agreement made Medical Management entitled to injunctive and equitable relief. Such an agreement must presume that a physician signing it would be desperate for increased patient volume at the risk of committing economic suicide. According to *The Wall Street Journal*, June 19, 1998, FPA issued a statement confirming that cash-flow problems caused the company to stop payments to some doctors in California, Nevada, and Arizona, acknowledging that it was behind at least sixty days in payments to some members of its doctor network of 7,900. Three days later, the company announced its plans to make deeper cost reductions and began negotiations with its lenders to modify existing debt agreements and to obtain new financing as well. *The Wall Street Journal* reported that FPA also missed an interest payment of $2.6 million on its $75 million convertible subordinated debentures. In March, the company said it had just $12 million in cash and would need to raise funds by June 30. If it failed to make payment within thirty days, bondholders could demand full repayment. Meanwhile, the company stock closed on Friday, June 19 at around $0.75 a share. Elizabeth McNeil, director of medical policy and economics at the California Medical Association, the state's largest doctor organization, told *The Wall Street Journal*, "It's becoming a huge issue here."

On July 6, the AMA's *American Medical News* reported that FPA closed the fifteen statewide clinics in Arizona it acquired less than two years earlier, and by July 10, it had closed fifty facilities in Arizona, Nevada, California, Texas, North Carolina, and Georgia, affecting some three hundred thousand patients. A string of class-action lawsuits

259

followed the announcements of FPA's financial troubles. One complaint alleged that throughout the class period the company and several of its senior officers and directors violated sections 10(b) and 20(a) of the Securities and Exchange Act of 1934 by engaging in a scheme to artificially inflate the market price of FPA common stock by making misrepresentations and omissions of material fact concerning FPA's publicly reported results, the value of its goodwill and receivables, and the alleged success of its program of expansion and integration.

The complaint also alleged that because of defendants' false and misleading representations and omissions, the price of FPA stock soared during the class period. The individual defendants, senior officers, and directors were charged with taking advantage of this hyped increase by selling off approximately $10 million of their FPA common stock during the period charged in the suit. The similarity between the AO98 opinion to "Doctor X" and the FPA-type PPMC structure was apparent. The path described was not so important because it was carried out by of a zealous cluster of high-roller venture capital types as much as it was a method of capturing a market basket full of poorly productive physicians and pricing their output at below marginal cost, which could drive their possibly more successful rivals from the marketspace.

It is of incidental interest that the structure of FPA agreements appears also to be that of an "affiliated services group," as defined by the IRS Code § 414(m)(4), which requires special treatment for pension purposes, and where the doctors' corporations might be treated as a single entity for nondiscrimination testing, maximum benefit limits, and detectability of contributions to prevent their employees from being discriminated against. With all the other problems faced by FPA, there seemed to have been no investigation on pension issues conducted by the DOL. Perhaps that is why Aetna kept to a "nonexclusive relationship with FPA," so that FPA could work for competing managed-care insurance firms. Another reason may have been concern for market power considerations to avoid antitrust scrutiny. Of course, neither reason matters, because these PPMC organizations produced nothing, like most potential antitrust violators of their ilk, and instead of circulating capital, they simply destroyed it.

On July 21, 1998, FPA filed for protection in Delaware under the state's bankruptcy laws, eliminating the value of the stock it had used to pay its physicians. On the day before filing, it closed at $0.1875, and after the newspapers made the announcement the following Tuesday, it closed at $0.0625. Just days before filing for bankruptcy, as seen in court documents, the members of the FPA board of directors voted themselves pay raises of up to 70 percent. FPA had listed $46.3 million in assets and $345 million in liabilities. Apparently, the characters who created Enron's bankruptcy three years later—"the smartest [risk manager] guys in the room"—were all in the same school of economics at the same time. PhyCor and PhyMatrix, two other closely watched PPMCs, discussed below, lost significant value on the same day.

FPA's penetration into the PPMC market place demonstrated the inadequate actuarial understanding given to prodigal, poorly capitalized companies, emblematic of the era of managed-care insurance company mentoring. It also demonstrated the chaotic devaluation of medical care cost. In their patient caseload, FPA's 7,900 physicians "treated" an average of 177 patients each, while FPA of New Jersey's 900 primary-care physicians treated 55,800 patients—62 per doctor. In New York, 115,000 patients were treated by 470 FPA primary-care doctors—244 patients per doctor. Compared to insurance companies, FPA was a "cost-saving" amateur. For example, in Westchester County, New York, PruCare—then a wholly owned subsidiary of the Prudential Insurance Company, which was purchased by Aetna U.S. Healthcare for $1 billion in August 1999—set the number of covered persons per primary care physician at three hundred; in California, PruCare set the number at more than two hundred and fifty. These widely disparate actuarial expectations demonstrate the uselessness of considering a viable social value for managed-care insurance.

The predatory pricing seemed to be used solely to create scarcity by driving competitors out of the market. Although it was sold as providing "economies of scale," "ease of central billing," "more-effective marketing," and such other appeals to enable doctors to see greater numbers of patients than their small offices and equipment could handle, this did not necessarily make it a conspiratorial violation of the antitrust laws. In fact, the most important injuries were those alleged in the civil class actions that followed the bankruptcy where the DOJ and FTC were not involved at all. However, it is also evident that this market failure was not simply clever thievery like the twenty-year Bernard Madoff Ponzi scheme that ended in 2009. The market failure of FPA was based on naïve actuarial understanding and foreseeable underpricing, either case amounting to setting marginal prices below their average cost—a *de facto* predatory policy. It ignored that the doctors' core business was the delivery of medical care in the context of multiple payment systems, especially the governmental ones, which legally controlled the prices based on actuarially determined costs, not revenues. For profit to be made alongside a government-controlled pricing system the risk would have to be spread and the cost shifted over significant numbers of non-government, indemnity insurance holders (ironically, companies that were by then gearing up their own managed-care structures). Put simply, the physician groups were doomed to failure by their poor timing. Only Humana grabbed both ends of the rope and serviced hospitals and doctors organized through a core managed-care insurance business laden with patient subscribers, which could compete with other commercial insurers while using its own lower paying "government sector" contracts to guarantee its losses as a larder for more-fallow times.

2. PhyMatrix—A Broken Company or a Breaking System?

In 1994, Abraham D. Gosman, who made several hundred million dollars from building nursing homes and later, a drug- and alcohol-rehabilitation business, invested $29 million of his own money and another $37 million in loans to start a PPMC called PhyMatrix. In 1986, he had sold his company, Mediplex, for $237 million to Avon Corporation and repurchased it four years later for $42 million. In January 1996, he took PhyMatrix public. Based in West Palm Beach, Florida, the company had a structure similar to FPA. It employed 920 people nationwide, owned or managed 374 physicians' practices around the country, provided them with office space and services such as lab tests or radiation therapy technology, and then contracted them out to managed-care companies.

PhyMatrix also owned a 190,000-square-foot, $50 million medical mall in Palm Beach Gardens, Florida, and planned to build several similar outpatient facilities to attract doctors. The stock price opened at $15 and rose to over $20 a share the first few months but then steadily declined. On May 12, 1998, it closed at $10.50, up $0.50 from the previous day. Nonetheless, on the same day, Gosman, citing "poor stock performance," announced plans to sell all or part of the PhyMatrix business, coinciding with the announcement of FPA to file for Chapter 11.

By July 21, the stock closed down 45 percent from the same date the prior year. Although Gosman's announcement indicated that he felt he was "painted with the same broad brush as other companies in the industry," some analysts assumed that most of PhyMatrix's profits had always been generated by DASCO, its medical real estate development subsidiary that leased office space to the doctors. Market analysts also appeared increasingly aware that the PPMC business was simply that of holding real estate mortgages backed by captive physicians' corporate practices. One analyst with Piper Jaffray, a Minnesota stockbrokerage firm, was quoted in the media: "Clearly, the bloom is off the rose in the physician-practice management industry."

On June 20, *The Palm Beach Post* reported that one reason "Wall Street has not been kind to PhyMatrix was that Chairman Gosman has made the company difficult to figure out with his frequent strategy changes." Another analyst, Tom Hodapp with BancAmerica Robertson Stephens in San Francisco, said, "It does not make it easy to understand what's happening." While the media was focused on the individual stock, a *Health Affairs* article by J. C. Robertson, "Financial Capital and Intellectual Capital in Physician Practice Management," noted that a more optimistic presentation had been made at a California HealthCare Foundation meeting in January 1998 and stressed that PPMCs needed "intellectual capital" to survive. Others said that the major PPMCs and their acquisitions and mergers had transformed the industry into what they saw, at least intellectually, as "physician-led Faustian bargains cut with a latter-day financial Mephistopheles."

The Palm Beach Post noted, "Abe Gosman's PhyMatrix, Inc. has begun dumping doctors." Although the company made $9.6 million in pretax profits in the first quarter of 1998, in May, the company terminated thirty doctor contacts in Florida and Connecticut and was prepared to take a $6 million charge against earnings for the second quarter. It also was suing its Tampa, Florida doctors for an additional $3.6 million that it contended it gave them in 1996 at the beginning of its contract with them. The fiscal illusion was that because the first-quarter $6 million charge did not include the $3.6 million PhyMatrix was suing for, if it did not prevail in its suit, the company would have made no money at all that entire year. Before the changes, PhyMatrix stock was down to $9.40 a share.

It was clear that PhyMatrix, whose stock closed on August 21, 1998 at $3.87, down 80 percent from its high of $25.50 on the same day the previous year, was being scrutinized by investors for its viability. No takers had been reported as interested in the May offers, and by August, Abe Gosman decided to abandon the PPMC business and the ancillary service businesses, which included diagnostic imaging, infusion, home health, and lithotripsy and radiation therapy. Mr. Gosman said the industry "Just hasn't worked out for everybody. I don't know if there's a company that's performed up to expectation." When asked to comment on whether he thought PPMCs were a fundamentally flawed industry, he presciently replied, "What I've always said was, when you employ a group of doctors, they become low handicappers," adding that he did not want to get into "an adversarial relationship with the medical field."

One may assume this response was connected to his $3.6 million lawsuit against the Tampa "Access Medical Care" (AMC) physicians who terminated their affiliation agreement in June, although PhyMatrix had entered an ambitious forty-year management contract with AMC. In October 1997, Florida's Board of Medicine found that the PhyMatrix contract with AMC was illegal. The contract called for AMC, in exchange for various services, to pay PhyMatrix a percentage of the revenues doctors get from PPM-generated referrals. The board said that such percentage payments amount to fee splitting to pay for referrals, which is illegal under Florida law. On June 25, the Florida First District Court of Appeals court agreed. PhyMatrix changed its name to "Innovative Clinical Solutions," moved to Rhode Island, and filed for Chapter 11 bankruptcy protection in July 2000, amid $100 million in debt.

3. PhyCor and MedPartners, Inc.—A Slippery Slope

In the 1990s, Birmingham, Alabama-based MedPartners was one of the largest healthcare companies in the United States, with revenue of approximately $6.3 billion for the year ending December 31, 1997. On October 29, 1997, Nashville, Tennessee-based PhyCor, the first PPMC in the country (1988), announced that it would be acquiring MedPartners, forming a $10 billion company.

PhyCor went public in 1992 and pursued affiliation with multispecialty clinics in midsized markets, recruiting independent physicians for capitation contracting. By the previous January, PhyCor had affiliated with 55 medical groups employing 3,860 physicians in 496 office sites and contracted with another 19,000 physicians through IPAs in 31 markets. It held managed-care contracts for 2.6 million patients with 1.1 million of them under capitation. The company operated in sixty-eight markets and twenty-eight states, most of them in Florida, Virginia, and Texas. PhyCor's strategy had been to acquire multispecialty clinics, including facilities and equipment but excluding real estate, and to establish local subsidiaries to manage them in cooperation with the affiliated medical groups. Physician shareholders, too, were paid a combination of cash, PhyCor stock, and notes with a face value in cash that could be converted to stock at specified dates and prices, and to trigger prices based on physician choice for individual tax considerations.

Bloomberg News reported that MedPartners operated three separate business divisions: Physician Practice Services, Pharmaceutical Services, and Contract Medical Services. The Physician Practice Services division was larger than any other PPMC in the United States, with 1997 annual revenues of approximately $3 billion. The Pharmaceutical Services division operated one of the then-largest independent prescription-benefit management and therapeutic pharmaceutical service programs in the United States, with revenues of approximately $2.4 billion for 1997. The Contract Medical Services division operated one of the largest hospital-based physician management services and one of the largest correctional system and government services managed-care businesses, with combined revenues of approximately $800 million in 1997.

The PhyCor-MedPartners merger did not occur, however, because in January, MedPartners announced a large restructuring based on an operating loss for its fourth quarter. The day after both were announced, its shares had dropped 50 percent. On May 14, the company announced further that it would dismiss 1,045 employees, including forty-five doctors in southern California. An additional two hundred unfilled positions were to be eliminated. MedPartners also announced that it would impose a 7 percent "temporary" cut on all doctor's fees—a step that it said doctors approved—as the company tried to resolve its ongoing financial and operating problems. An article in *American Medical News*, "Moving Away from Managed Medicaid," said that the company made known a 1998 first-quarter loss of $25.7 million on the heels of an $840.4 million loss in the fourth quarter of 1997. On June 23, 1998, it disclosed its intent to sell its Team Health operations and that it would retain Salomon Smith Barney to explore the possible sale of the unit. Team Health had produced revenues of over $690 million a year, according to *PR Newswire*. In 1998, PhyCor had fallen 76 percent to $8.25 a share by July 27, MedPartners was down 82 percent, closing at $4.56, PhyMatrix dropped 65 percent to $6, and FPA had withered 99 percent to $0.19 a share.

PhyCor and MedPartners appeared to have been more successful than FPA in bouncing back from their difficulties following the collapse the past January of PhyCor's rash $8 billion bid to acquire MedPartners. PhyCor was able to announce that its acquisitions-based quarterly revenue rose 31 percent as the company projected "a strong 1999, with the potential for growth of approximately 30 percent." However, *The Wall Street Journal* reported in July that PhyCor announced its first charges in five years to account for the failed merger and restructuring costs and said that it had managed to boost the amount it earns from contracts. By then, MedPartners had hired as CEO Mac Crawford, former CEO of Magellan, to turn things around after it posted a larger-than-expected fourth quarter loss. Crawford fired a tenth of the company's employees in Southern California, negotiated a $1 billion credit facility, and moved to close at least one unprofitable hospital. Crawford said the sale of Team Health would allow the company to significantly reduce its leverage without affecting the strategic opportunities available to its remaining businesses: "We are seeing improvement in our physician practice management operations, and this remains an area of primary focus," Bloomberg News reported. The "improvement" apparently did not convince the investment community. By late August, MedPartners stock had dropped another 40 percent to $2.75.

4. United Payers & United Providers—More Buyers Buying Off Sellers

A creative arrangement on the chain of events of managed-care services was United Payors & United Providers, Inc. (UP&UP), a Delaware corporation that served as an intermediary between health-care payers (that is, insurance companies) and healthcare providers (for example, hospitals). It entered into contractual arrangements designed to produce cost savings and other benefits for its "Payor Clients," offering increased liquidity and improved efficiency in claims submissions for its "Contracting Providers." The founder and chairman of the company said that the company

"does not market to consumers, and does not determine the benefit coverages for individuals. Rather, through proprietary technology and customized interfaces with its clients, UP&UP reduces the administrative burden of payers and generates medical cost savings primarily through volume discounts with providers and via claims repricing technology."

UP&UP derived its revenue primarily from a slice of the price concessions offered by providers under such contractual arrangements. Effective October 1, 1996, UP&UP acquired National Health Services, Inc. (NHS) for an undisclosed sum, which was purported to be a national health-care utilization management services company. NHS offered medical utilization management services to insurance underwriters, self-insured businesses, provider organizations, and others. Its services included precertification of inpatient and outpatient medical care and case management.

A rather friendly and unique part of UP&UP's business activity was to acquire providers in its network by *paying* them to join their network. Those interest-free advances to providers started at $5,000 and, in the case of a high-volume provider, might be as high as $500,000. These "Prepayment Options" were booked as assets on the company's balance sheet, because the money would have to be returned if the provider terminated a contract. It gave the impression of a "signing bonus"

269

to avoid the appearance of impropriety if the provider were to have paid UP&UP for referrals. In fact, it was the opposite. The company said that its primary capital resources commitment was to fund these advances to the contracting providers upon exercise of the Prepayment Options granted them. Depending on increases in claims volume and in the number of contracting providers and payer clients, the company—in effect giving Peter the money to pay Paul—estimated that $7.5 million to $12.5 million could be required to fund Prepayment Options during the remainder of 1998.

However, the advances to contracting providers in the first quarter of 1998 totaled $19,743,730, while revenue from the provider network came to $13,733,745, plus $4,598,010 from utilization management services, leaving a deficit of $1,145,720 from that eccentric funding structure. The accounting miracle was that even though acquiring providers by paying them was a regular "capital resource commitment," because the advances to providers was on the balance sheet and not recorded as expense on the income statement, the company appeared to have shown a profit for the quarter. As of July 21, 1998, its stock was trading on NASDAQ for thirty-one times earnings, at an all-time high of $28.87. In March 2000, *Business Wire* reported that UP&UP was acquired by BCE Emergis, Inc., the software unit of BCE, Canada's largest telephone company, and in 2004 divested its health business to Multiplan, Inc., which acquired UP&UP. In turn, MultiPlan was acquired by the Carlyle Group in 2006. By 2010, UP&UP appeared on the Internet to be a private company categorized under "Insurance Agencies and Brokers," located in Rockville, Maryland. Estimates in August 2010 showed this company still in business with annual revenue of $180,000 and employing a staff of "approximately two."

V. The World of Market Power— How Healthcare Insurance Abhors a Perfect Market and Uses "Messengers"

"... an old evil in a new dress and with a new name."
—*American Column & Lumber Co. v. U.S.* (1921)

"[I]t does not follow from this that the Court is powerless to examine the entire transaction, of which that contract is but a part, in order to determine whether there may be a chain of events which becomes interstate commerce."
—*United States v. South-Eastern Underwriters Assn.* (1944)

"The Clayton Act, so far as it deals with the subject, was intended to reach in their incipiency agreements embraced within the sphere of the Sherman Act."
—*Standard Co. v. Magrane-Houston Co.* (1922)

"Section 5 of the [Federal] Trade Commission Act is supplementary to the Sherman Anti-trust Act and the Clayton Act. The Sherman Act deals with contracts, agreements, and combinations which tend to the prejudice of the public by

the undue restriction of competition or the undue obstruc-
tion of the due course of trade."
—*Federal Trade Commission v. Raladam Co.* (1931)

Black's Law Dictionary, 1999 edition, defined market power thus:
"In economic terms, market power is the ability to raise prices without a
total loss of sales; without market power, consumers shop around to find a
rival offering a better deal." It has also been said that market power is the
monopsonist or monopolist's ability to affect the terms and conditions of
exchange so that the price of the product is based on the conditions set by
the firm and is limited only by the demand for the product. The ability to
reduce output and raise prices above the competitive level, specifically for a
sustained period, and to make a profit by so doing, is another characteristic
of market power. Courts will examine a firm's or multiply connected firms'
market power to see whether or not the product has an inelastic demand
curve, that is, where people are not willing to take substitutes. When a
government entity can ration the care for it for a sustainable amount of
time, the prevalence of illness becomes hidden in a "subacute" state.

Healthcare insurance is based on unilateral individual or group
contracts—legally binding agreements between the insurer and the
insured written by the insurer—called by the common law "contracts
of adhesion." They "adhere" to the one who wrote or controlled the
language, and resolution of disputes arising from such contracts must
be first looked at by courts in the light least favorable to the insurer.
Even if the employer-purchaser or other fiduciary together with the
insurer or by the employer and employees' negotiators and the insurer
write the insurance "policy," the fact is that the employee, who may be
said to be accepting the faithfulness of fiduciaries on his behalf, is constrained by that contract to not have to take substitutes. "In-network"
and "out-of-network" price arrangements have been handled accept-
ably by employees, because they appear to allow shopping around for
a better deal—that is, to have the doctor of their choice. Nevertheless,
the "deal" is a financially Faustian one because "out-of-network" means
ultimately having to pay more out of pocket for that decision.

These IN or OON more-flexible price constraints are poor demonstration that the insurer prefers either method chosen by the insured. For example, if 100 percent of the beneficiaries chose OON providers, such an insurer would surely soon be out of business. At that point, the OON cost to the insurer would have to be based on a "perfect market"—one in which supply for every product or service, including labor, equals the demand at the current price—and premium income would drop by the amount of the copayments. This is not a happy arrangement for the insurer. IN price arrangements with providers based on managed care are what the insurer plans for and, indeed, needs in order to make its profit from the below-marginal-cost provider's price. The fact is that the insurer takes sustained losses from OON choices made at any point above 50 percent. Above that level, supported by other anticompetitive behavior tests, IN treatment costs would then demonstrate deadweight inefficiencies in the market. Although that type of marginal-cost pricing does not necessarily make a monopolist, its structure is presented here to help our understanding of how insurers have to play with marginal cost pricing. Thus, there has to be a managed-care component to skim off profits from the list prices of care.

The latest efforts by payors to essentially push providers into network, and an example of open price-fixing by insurers, was the UHG with Oxford and Blue Cross plans and Aetna, among others, to ignore the "usual and customary charge" for OON benefits and to cap them at 140 percent of the Medicare fee. In a September 2010, *ASC Communications Review*, an online magazine that offers, "legal information for owners and operators of ambulatory surgery centers, hospital leaders and physicians and administrators of orthopedic and spine practices," interviewed Jeffrey Shanton, director of business management for Journal Square Surgical Center in Jersey City, New Jersey.

Mr. Shanton said, after receiving letters to members and providers from the insurers announcing restrictions on reimbursement for OON services,

"Without the choice of OON, you have a monopoly, with the carriers holding all the cards. Down the road, you will see the in-network contracts dip lower and lower. How can any healthcare provider negotiate with them? They have no leverage. Oxford holds all the cards—take it or leave it."

Such an arrangement, albeit under state insurance supervision, appears to violate the criminal provisions of section 1 of the Sherman Antitrust Act, because the McCarran-Ferguson Act protections ordinarily providing a safe harbor for price fixing as regulated by the state cannot extend to Medicare as a secondary payor, its scrutiny being sent to the federal arena pursuant to "conflict" preemption.

In the modern era, one hundred years after the Sherman and Clayton Acts were enacted, more-sophisticated feasibility methods of studying market structure in conformity with those laws' intent were developed. In most market power analyses, the "market" is now looked at as a "relevant market," so that in healthcare, the courts, the DOJ, or the FTC would need to take into account not simply the number of people *available* to purchase the product of the insurer but also the population that would *not* be purchasing healthcare insurance but needing it. The more than fifty million chronically uninsured by 2009, the many more unable to afford it, and still others feeling secure that insurance isn't worth the purchase should also be taken into consideration. In *Brown Shoe Company v. United States*, the 1962 pre-Medicare Supreme Court decided that, because Congress was not specific in deciding the boundaries of a relevant market, in a relevant market equation there should be also a geographic dimension.

The following, from *Brown Shoe*, offers a strong suggestion of how the courts, receiving a well-pleaded complaint establishing federal jurisdiction, could view the healthcare insurance industry's predatory pricing and market power:

"The outer boundaries of a product market are determined by the reasonable interchangeability of use or the cross-elasticity of demand between the product itself and substitutes for it. However, within this broad market, well-defined submarkets may exist which, in themselves, constitute product markets for antitrust purposes. . . Because § 7 of the Clayton Act prohibits any merger which may substantially lessen competition 'in *any* line of commerce' [emphasis supplied by the Court], it is necessary to examine the effects of a merger in each such economically significant submarket to determine if there is a reasonable probability that the merger will substantially lessen competition. If such a probability is found to exist, the merger is proscribed."

It is true that there could be "reasonable interchangeability" or "cross-elasticity of demand" in and for healthcare, because the practice of medicine is taught based on science and its universalities. However, the question to be answered by government in this post-Millennium era is this: Should the deadweight losses to the "relevant market" continue to go unchallenged when pricing by a group of insurers, large vertically integrated medical groups, or even the Accountable Care Organizations (ACOs) proposed by the ACA is below marginal cost? A capitated individual provider or provider group, if tied to an MCO with market power in interstate commerce, may be charged along with the MCO in a *per se* prohibited act. One could say that the provider that reduced unit output neither had nor produced separate damages; in other words, there was neither malpractice nor antitrust injury in lessening the number of patients seen.

There may still have been an antitrust violation by the provider originating in a Sherman section 1 illegal restraint, because by having a capitation contract, the provider acted essentially as a front-end insurer contractually tied to and often a shareholder of an MCO in the prohibited act. A similar type of tying arrangement was contemplated by the 1899 Supreme Court in *U.S v. Addyston Pipe & Steel*, and again in 1978 in *National Society of Professional Engineers v. U.S.*, where the High Court said, "[this] unequivocally foreclose[s] an interpretation of the Rule [of Reason] as permitting an inquiry into the reasonableness of the prices set by the agreement." In *German Alliance Insurance Company v. Superintendent, etc., of Kansas*, a case involving fire insurance rate setting, the 1915 Supreme Court said:

"It is the business that is the fundamental thing; property is but its instrument, the means of rendering the service which has become of public interest. . . The contracts of insurance may be said to be interdependent. They cannot be regarded singly or isolatedly, and the effect of their relation is to create a fund of assurance and credit, the companies becoming the depositories of the money of the insured, possessing great power thereby, and charged with great responsibility."

Section 7 of the Clayton Antitrust Act provides that:

"No person engaged in commerce or in any activity affecting commerce shall acquire, directly or indirectly, the whole or any part of the stock or other share capital and no person subject to the jurisdiction of the Federal Trade Commission shall acquire the whole or any part of the assets of another person engaged also in commerce or in any activity affecting commerce, where in any line of commerce or in any activity affecting commerce in any section of the country, the effect of such acquisition may be substantially to lessen competition, or to tend to create a monopoly."

* * *

"No person shall acquire, directly or indirectly, the whole or any part of the stock or other share capital and no person subject to the jurisdiction of the Federal Trade Commission shall acquire the whole or any part of the assets of one or more persons engaged in commerce or in any activity affecting commerce, where in any line of commerce or in any activity affecting commerce in any section of the country, the effect of such acquisition, of such stocks or assets, or of the use of such stock by the voting or granting of proxies or otherwise, may be substantially to lessen competition, or to tend to create a monopoly."

Section 7 elaborates on specific and crucial concepts of the Clayton Act "holding company," which has been seen as a common and favorite method of promoting monopoly but actually is a company whose primary purpose is to hold stocks of other companies. The original position of the U.S. government on mergers and acquisitions was strengthened by the Celler-Kefauver amendments of 1950 to cover asset as well as stock acquisitions. As noted earlier, the Clinton administration appeared to be aware of the distinction between market power based on combinations of individual doctors, acting alone, and those of hospitals' "integrated delivery systems," especially those operating across state lines.

As reported by *Modern Healthcare* in 1998, it appeared part of the reason that the American Hospital Association and the Catholic Hospital Association—both strong advocates for their members' establishing integrated delivery systems—supported proposals for weaker managed-care reforms. The Democratic proposal included the right to sue MCOs and allow enrollees to go outside their networks for care, while the Republican bills excluded those rights. Nonetheless, the 1996 DOJ and FTC had issued new guidelines designating market-power safe harbors only for physician groups and endorsed a rule of reason analysis that "will focus on substance rather than form," while retaining constraints for those groups aligned with hospitals or other large healthcare systems.

Historically, economists have measured market power—the ability of a firm to set prices higher or lower than the presence of competition would allow—with the "Herfindahl-Hirschman Index" (HHI), determined by adding the squares of the market shares of all firms involved in a particular market. The FTC guidelines in 1992 stated this: "Where the post-merger HHI exceeds 1800, it will be presumed that mergers producing an increase of 100 points are likely to create or enhance market power or facilitate its exercise." This was changed somewhat eighteen years later. In 2010, the FTC and the Antitrust Division of the DOJ jointly released their proposed revisions to the *Horizontal Merger Guidelines* for public comment. The proposed guidelines attempted to clarify the analysis:

- A single methodology would not be used, but a fact-specific process that would use "various tools to analyze whether a merger may substantially lessen competition."

- "Market definition," is seen "as a means to an end, not the end"; that is, "it is a tool the agencies use to the extent it may predict the merger's likely competitive effects. Market definition is a part of, but not the result of, the analysis. In some cases, market definition may not be necessary."

- The agencies will "place great weight on evidence of head-to-head competition between the merging firms—that is, the extent to which one merger partner has in the past responded directly to the other's prices, product launches, technical innovations and marketing and advertising campaigns that ignore these documents and data—[and will] give no weight to company presentations that ignore these documents and data."

- The proposed guidelines increase the relevant market concentration thresholds by use of the Herfindahl-Hirschman Index.

A low index number would indicate that there were many competitors and exercising market power would be difficult, whereas a high index number warned of a concentrated market in which price increases would be easier to sustain. Post-merger HHI below 1,500 (unconcentrated market) is considered unlikely to have adverse competitive effects and ordinarily requires no further analysis. The Milton Friedman/George J. Stigler years of influence at the University of Chicago, School of Economics, the "Chicago School" theory that markets almost always lead to the best result, antitrust enforcement often makes mistakes, because market power is temporary, and entry barriers are minimal were largely upended with the serious economic downturn caused by the post-Millennium, free-market hedonism of the Bush II years challenged by the Obama administration.

The Bush II administration's antitrust division had brought no enforcement actions against dominant firms and went for more than five years without bringing a merger challenge in federal court, as it maintained itself dead set against the concept of market failures. Although Republicans attempted to revive it, its inertia was beginning to fade in administrative memory as academic ideas of free-market cures such as the American Recovery and Reinvestment Act of 2009 (abbreviated ARRA and commonly referred to as the Stimulus or the Recovery Act), allowing for temporary market power, were being reexamined by the Obama administration. In a speech prepared for presentation before the Center for American Progress, Christine A. Varney, the new DOJ assistant attorney general for antitrust, announced that effective May 11, 2009:

"I hereby withdraw the [Bush administration's Sherman Act section 2] Report by the Department of Justice. . . the Section 2 Report no longer represents the policy of the Department of Justice . . . and its conclusions should not be used as guidance by courts, antitrust practitioners, and the business community."

In November 2009, AHIP—a trade association of insurance companies—eagerly

"commend[ed] the Department of Justice and the Federal Trade Commission for examining the possibility of updating the Horizontal Merger Guidelines and would like to thank both agencies for the opportunity to share our perspectives on those Guidelines and the agencies' approach to merger review."

The AHIP submitted a paper that

"provides a detailed, analytical, and data-driven examination of agency review of health insurer mergers and demonstrates that the proper framework for analyzing health insurer mergers 'is precisely the careful, fact-intensive, guidelines-driven analysis utilized by DOJ in each of the health insurer mergers that it has analyzed.'"

The "paper" was written for AHIP by Cory Capps, PhD, a partner in the Antitrust and Healthcare Practices group at Bates White, LLC, in Washington, DC. It presented two principal conclusions from his "review and analysis," as an answer to an American Hospital Association (AHA) letter and companion white paper that expressed "concerns about the lack of a robust and coherent enforcement policy on health insurance plan (health plan) mergers." The Capps paper concluded:

279

- The AHA recommendations and requests are unwarranted and unsupported in a variety of respects.
- There is no need for the "reinvigorated enforcement" (including hearings, retrospectives, and new analytic frameworks) called for by the AHA, and there is potential harm from diverted resources.

However, the AHA white paper had simply requested that the DOJ, in conjunction with other agencies, take the following steps:

- Undertake a comprehensive study of consummated health plan mergers.
- Convene public hearings to better understand the reasons for the lack of competition among health plans in most markets.
- Revisit and revise its analytical framework for reviewing health plan mergers.

To sum up the difference between AHIP and AHA positions: The AHA welcomed the 1992 and 1997 guideline changes promised by the Obama Antitrust Division and FTC, while the AHIP, now restive after the challenge to the eight sleepy years of the Bush II administration's Antitrust Division, was apparently saying: "Don't just do something, stand there!"

In May 2010, *Modern Healthcare* reported that a study released by the activist online organization Healthcare for America Now detailed just how concentrated health-insurance markets were at that time. Ninety-four percent of statewide health-insurance markets were considered "highly concentrated" under DOJ guidelines, in most states only one or two insurers dominated the market, and this concentration had been accompanied by rising premiums and health-insurer profits. The article by David Balto, senior fellow at the Center for American Progress and former policy director of the FTC Bureau of Competition, noted the

"Bush administration failed to properly set enforcement priorities, leading to an environment where health insurers thrived in a competition-free zone . . . The FTC and the Justice Department took no consumer protection actions against health insurers, and the Justice Department took no enforcement actions against anticompetitive practices by health insurers. State insurance regulators failed to consistently or effectively police health insurers. Meanwhile, there were more than 400 health insurance mergers in the past decade, with only two modest consent decrees."

Clearly, there are historically few theories that can separate undesirable predation from desirable price competition; however, recent developments in econometrics appeared to have found receptive ears first at the Clinton and later the Obama DOJ.

The shibboleth "saving on healthcare costs," which the managed care industry uses to defend its self-conferred social role, is meaningless. As with any other costs on which society places a value, such as defense, healthcare costs are identified by pundits and otherwise financially interested parties as going "through the roof" only when they do not deny society what society wants or needs. The Medicare Trust Fund has finite resources based on actuarial considerations of the elderly and disabled groups of citizens. However, if there were a constitutional "right to treatment" that relies upon the fidelity of the government to "promote the general welfare," the available resources have to be satisfied by specific taxation or by cost-cutting measures elsewhere. This is not so for the private sector.

Because there is no express right to treatment, commercial companies should only be allowed to enter the healthcare coverage business at their own risk and not transfer it to either the provider or the patient. The insurance industry, taking advantage of ERISA loopholes, evaded responsible indemnity risk spreading and acted in concert—as individuals and through contractually organized actuarial and trade organizations—to create greater profits through the use of their lessened-risk "management" of care. In exposing the managed-care industry's *Noerr*-type excuse for entering the healthcare cost-cutting business on behalf of itself and its clients, the sham basis of commercial managed-care cost cutting is uncovered.

In a 1991 University of Pennsylvania, Wharton School of Economics publication, "Study Project on Healthcare Reform and American Competitiveness," the authors noted:

"If retiree costs take the form of defined future contributions, the equity market will quickly respond by adjusting stock prices until expected profit rates return to the market level. Thus, shareholders take a one-time loss, but there is no continuing impact on firm operations. If, on the other hand, retiree healthcare costs take the form of defined benefits, a similar effect occurs as soon as the market recognizes the magnitude of future liabilities. In either case, profit levels decline but profit rates are unaffected . . .

"The effect of rising health benefit costs on total compensation, and thus on prices and trade flows, is positive and significant but quite small in magnitude. For example, U.S. import volume during the 1980s increased by 125 percent, but only 0.14 percent could be explained by health benefit cost growth. Likewise, during this period, U.S. export volume increased by 75 percent, although health benefit cost exerted a negative influence of 0.16 percent. It is therefore not clear from this research that employer-paid health benefit costs, by themselves, have materially harmed the competitiveness of U.S. industry in aggregate."

With the cost of U.S. healthcare estimated by the Kaiser Foundation in 2008 at over $2.3 trillion dollars, up from the $1 trillion at the end of the 1990s, the few controllers of the managed-care marketplace cannot be thought of as still being significant competitors for market share. Because of their actuarial, data-disseminated and coercive resource structure, the results shared by each monopsonist, based on information whether transferred or not between them or transferred or not by their conduit contractors, would not significantly impair their ability to reach their profitability goals. As the 1969 Supreme Court noted in *United States v. Container Corp.*, "The continuation of some price competition is not fatal to the government's case."

On March 3, 1998, *PR Newswire* reported that Mac Crawford, at the time Magellan chair, president and chief executive officer of its managed-care subsidiary Magellan Health Services, announced the appointment of Henry T. Harbin, MD as chief executive officer of the managed behavioral and medical specialty divisions. Magellan's Managed Behavioral Healthcare Division included Human Affairs International (HAI), Merit Behavioral Care, and Green Spring Health Services. Announcing an iridescence of competition, Dr. Harbin declared that,

"HAI, Merit and Green Spring have each been leaders in the behavioral healthcare field as it has evolved [so] that we will ensure that our customers will continue to receive their same product or products through their same management team, with the consistent service levels they have received in the past. In addition, we will retain the trade names of HAI, Merit and Green Spring for an indefinite period."

The announcement, as reported by *America Online News*, added that Magellan's HMO/Insurance Division would

"focus on the needs of health insurance plans and their members. [The] Division will include Aetna U.S. Healthcare, 33 Blue Cross and Blue Shield Plans, Humana, NYLCare, Prudential HealthCare and other regional and local health plans around the country . . . [Their] extensive client list includes companies such as AT&T, Exxon Corporation, FedEx, Food Lion, Inc., IBM and BellSouth Communications. . . Some of the current Medicaid contracts held in the public sector include programs in Iowa, Maryland, Montana, and Tennessee, as well as child welfare programs in Ohio and Wisconsin.

"Magellan's Managed Specialty Division works on behalf of health plans in their specialty networks and disease management programs in areas such as diabetes, asthma, oncology and cardiology, as well as a variety of other illnesses. The division comprises Florida-based Allied Health Group, acquired by Magellan in 1997, and Care Management Resources, a Magellan subsidiary. Among the customers served by the division

are several Blue Cross and Blue Shield plans, CIGNA Healthcare, Prudential Healthcare, NYLCare, and several other health
plans."

Magellan appears thus to be a "messenger," the antitrust theory
being that when competitors agree to work together, competition is
stifled, it restrains trade by affecting our competition-based economy
and, ultimately, reduces consumer choice. Discussion of the "messenger model" was part of a joint statement by the DOJ and the FTC in
1996 related to doctors' groups. The Model allows a third party to
collect price and other offering terms from network members individually. The members do not know about the terms that other members
have offered. The "messenger" conveys the information to purchasers
who can then make contract offers to members through the messenger.
Each member makes an independent decision to accept the contract
conveyed by the messenger. So long as the members do not coordinate
their actions, antitrust problems should not arise.

The inapplicability of this messenger model to the interstate
commercial business of insurance companies should be obvious, and
its relation to physicians' groups of today is bureaucratically naïve.
"Agreements to pay" similar amounts for equivalent medical services
today need only be based on seemingly unilateral negotiations around
the already established government prices. However, the NCQA, M&R
and InterQual-type "messengers" use actuarial data favoring stabilizing
of their industry prices, something physicians' groups not integrated
with hospital networks do not care about. However, one might imagine
what the DOJ might think of a physician group formally negotiating
with "administrative services only" insurance companies or large-group
employers expressly to charge the prices that the government is willing
to pay doctors under Medicare. While that may sound tongue in cheek,
a federal court did not think so. In the final consent decree judgment
by the federal district court of Delaware on November 6, 2002 in *U.S.
v. Federation of Physicians and Dentists, Inc.*—considered in 1998 a "hub
of conspiracy" to fight reduced payments from Blue Cross/Blue Shield
in Delaware—the court authorized

"advocating or discussing, in accordance with the doctrine established in *Eastern Railroad Presidents Conference v. Noerr Motor Freight, Inc.,* 365 U.S. 127 (1961), *United Mine Workers v. Pennington,* 381 U.S. 657 (1965), and their progeny, legislative, judicial, or regulatory actions, or other governmental policies or actions."

A case that readily lends itself to beginning an antitrust analysis of the managed-care industry in general, and their data-disseminators NCQA, InterQual, and M&R, in particular, is the 1982 Supreme Court decision in *American Society of Mechanical Engineers vs. Hydrolevel Corp.* Writing for the six to three majority, Justice Blackmun outlined the basis of the society's civil liability under the antitrust laws for acts of its agents performed with apparent authority and, citing from a 1941 case, *Fashion Originators' Guild v. FTC,* said:

"ASME can be said to be 'in reality an extra-governmental agency, which prescribes rules for the regulation and restraint of interstate commerce.' When it cloaks its officials with the authority of its reputation, ASME permits those agents to affect the destinies of businesses and thus gives them the power to frustrate competition in the marketplace. . . . [W]hether they act in part to benefit ASME or solely to benefit themselves or their employers, ASME's agents can have the same anticompetitive effects on the marketplace.

"The anticompetitive practices of ASME's agents are repugnant to the antitrust laws even if the agents act without any intent to aid ASME . . . [I]t is beyond debate that nonprofit organizations can be held liable under the antitrust laws, [citations omitted]. Although ASME may not operate for profit, it does derive benefits from its codes, including the fees [it] receives for its code-related publications and services, the prestige the codes bring to [it], the influence they permit *ASME* to wield, and the standards provide the profession of mechanical engineering."

In *Swift & Co. v. U.S.*, a combination of independent dealers was charged with restricting the competition of their agents. The 1905 Supreme Court said:

"The intent of the combination is not merely to restrict competition among the parties, but, as we have said, . . . to aid in an attempt to monopolize commerce among the states . . . Commerce among the states is not a technical legal conception, but a practical one drawn from the course of a business . . . and when this is a typical, constantly recurring course, the current thus existing is a current of commerce among the states . . . by persons in one state to persons in another . . . The charge is not of a single agreement, but of a course of conduct intended to be continued."

This very structured information-transfer relationship between "dealers" who provide healthcare services is based on dissemination of data affording competitor members of an organization the opportunity to stabilize prices in violation of the purposes of the Sherman Act. The 1940 Supreme Court stated in *United States v. Socony-Vacuum Oil Co., Inc.* said, "In terms of market operations stabilization is but one form of manipulation." The Court also noted that interference with the setting of price even by free-market forces is unlawful *per se*. In 1969, the High Court may have anticipated a type of anticompetitive behavior and the relations exhibited today by NCQA and M&R, among others, as noted in *United States v. Container Corp.*:

"The case as proved is unlike any other price decisions we have rendered. There was here an exchange of price information but no agreement to adhere to a price schedule as in [citations omitted]. There was here an exchange of information concerning specific sales to identified customers, not a statistical report on the average cost to all members without identifying the parties to specific transactions . . . [each member] usually furnished the data with the expectation that it would be furnished reciprocal information when it wanted it. The concerted action is of course sufficient to establish the combination or conspiracy, the initial ingredient of a violation of §1 of the Sherman Act . . . There was of course freedom to withdraw from the agreement."

In *Container Corp.,* the Court found and defined the monopolistic condition, one that sounds akin to the managed-care business:

"The corrugated container industry is dominated by very few sellers. The product is fungible and the competition for sales is price. The demand is inelastic, as buyers place orders only for immediate, short-run needs. The exchange of price data tends toward price uniformity. For a lower price does not mean a larger share of the available business but a sharing of the existing business at a lower return . . . The inferences are irresistible that the exchange of price information has an anticompetitive effect in the industry, chilling the vigor of price competition . . . Price is too critical, too sensitive a control to allow it to be used even in an informal manner to restrain competition."

Although the principal cases prohibiting data dissemination under the Sherman Act have concerned the exchange of price information, the exchange of other competitively sensitive marketing information may have an effect and thus violate the Sherman Act. In his 1977 *Handbook of the Law of Antitrust*, Lawrence A. Sullivan, named by President Carter to the National Commission for the Review of Antitrust Laws wrote, "In general the analytic approaches [employed in evaluating price circulation] are appropriate in evaluating circulation of non-price information." In the 1921 Supreme Court decision, *American Column & Lumber Co. v. United States*, the "Open Competition Plan" of the American Hardwood Manufacturers' Association was found to have violated the Sherman Act. The Court showed that the association's committee that evolved the Plan said its stated purpose

"is to disseminate among members accurate knowledge of production and market conditions so that each member may gauge the market intelligently instead of guessing at it. The Open Competition Plan is a central clearinghouse for information on prices, trade statistics and practices. By keeping all members fully and quickly informed of what the others have done, the work of the Plan results *in a certain uniformity of trade practice.* There is no agreement to follow the practice of others, *although members do follow their most intelligent competitors* if they know what these competitors have been actually doing. The monthly meetings held in various sections of the country each month have improved the human relations existing between the members before the organization of this Plan." [All emphasis was by the Court.]

The fact that specific price information is not disseminated by the NCQA, McKesson's InterQual, or M&R should be irrelevant to federal antitrust analysis of the behavior. The McCarran-Ferguson Act's state safe harbor, too, allows insurance companies data dissemination exemption from the federal antitrust laws, but that was an explicit congressional decision and based on specific, express state action that regulates the behavior. Generally, antitrust law permits an association to disseminate composite data regarding *past* transactions. However, the exchange of current or proposed prices, or the exchange of information regarding future production projections are generally prohibited, especially when horizontal merger activity is involved. However, most hospitals take Medicare patients and make complete financial reporting, records that are publicly available on institutional cost reports to the government, where they list numbers of patient visits and aggregate current prices per patient day and hospital admissions and discharges based on government-set prices per DRG admission.

From these data, the interstate competitors can easily extrapolate prices-per-patient contact and disease-type contact. In any event, whether risk managing or providing administrative services, the MCOs are in the compass of federal antitrust statutes related to coercion, boycott, or intimidation, and when providing coverage determinations to ERISA self-insured plans, they are open fully to the antitrust laws because of federal preemption. In a manufacturing paradigm, this price-per-unit analysis could not be performed. There, most of the materials brought together to make a commodity are purchased from outside the manufacturing entity and are usually based on independent, competitive purchasing of the materials requiring synthesis of their products.

The prohibition on dissemination of future production prices appears not to have been addressed by the government for interstate commercial insurance ventures but has been for providers probably because of the state safe harbor for what has historically been described as "the business of insurance" activity. In its "Enforcement Policy on Providers' Collective Provision of Fee-Related Information to Purchasers of Healthcare Services," the 2009 DOJ and FTC issued revised healthcare guidelines for physician joint ventures and multiprovider networks for analysis under the rule of reason. They set forth antitrust safety zones that describe physician-network joint ventures that are highly unlikely to raise substantial competitive concerns and therefore would not be challenged by the agencies under the antitrust laws, absent extraordinary circumstances. With physician joint ventures, "nonexclusivity" is looked for.

"The Agencies will determine whether a physician network joint venture is exclusive or non-exclusive by its physician participants' activities, and not simply by the terms of the contractual relationship. In making that determination, the Agencies will examine the following indicia of non-exclusivity, among others:

(1) that viable competing networks or managed care plans with adequate physician participation currently exist in the market;

(2) that physicians in the network actually individually participate in, or contract with, other networks or managed care plans, or there is other evidence of their willingness and incentive to do so;

(3) that physicians in the network earn substantial revenue from other networks or through individual contracts with managed care plans;

(4) the absence of any indications of significant de-partici-pation from other networks or managed care plans in the mar-ket; and

(5) the absence of any indications of coordination among the physicians in the network regarding price or other com-petitively significant terms of participation in other networks or managed care plans.

Networks also may limit or condition physician-participants' free-dom to contract outside the network in ways that fall short of a com-mitment of full exclusivity. If those provisions significantly restrict the ability or willingness of a network's physicians to join other networks or contract individually with managed care plans, the network will be considered exclusive for purposes of the safety zones."

Integrated physician network joint ventures are safe if they are designed to "produce efficiencies," "control costs," and "assure quality of care." However,

"there have been arrangements among physicians that have taken the form of networks, but which in purpose or effect were little more than efforts by their participants to prevent or impede competitive forces from operating in the market. These arrangements are not likely to produce significant procompeti-tive efficiencies. Such arrangements have been, and will con-tinue to be, treated as unlawful conspiracies or cartels, whose price agreements are *per se* illegal . . . (e.g., a network com-prising a very high percentage of local area physicians, whose participation in the network is exclusive, without any plausible business or efficiency justification)."

In multiprovider networks, the key revisions from the 1996 guide-lines appear to be based on "significant risk sharing." They allow if not promote capitation but

"in assessing the competitive environment, the Agencies would consider such market factors as the number, type, and size of managed care plans operating in the area, the extent of provider participation in those plans, and the economic importance of the managed care plans to area providers. Alternatively, for example, if a restraint that facially appears to be of a kind that would always or almost always tend to reduce output or increase prices, but has not been considered *per se* unlawful, is not reasonably necessary to the creation of efficiencies, the Agencies will likely challenge the restraint without an elaborate analysis of market definition and market power."

The inherent weakness in these guidelines is that they do not distinguish clinical "efficiencies" made by the physicians in the networks contracting with managed-care plans from the so-called efficiencies made by actuaries who work for NCQA, InterQual, and M&R. Those companies sell their "proprietary data" to insurers, MCOs, hospitals, and physician groups in an attempt to circumnavigate rule of reason, safe-harbor guidelines.

A virtual mirror image of the *American Column's* Open Competition Plan is the NCQA's aptly named "Quality Compass," which purports, through the use of its Health Plan Employer Data and Information Set, to make information available and to "reduce the administrative burden involved in gathering and dissemination of quality information" for its members, among others. On its website, the NCQA describes HEDIS as follows:

"HEDIS is a tool used by more than 90 percent of America's health plans to measure performance on important dimensions of care and service. Altogether, HEDIS consists of 71 measures across 8 domains of care. Because so many plans collect HEDIS data, and because the measures are so specifically defined, HEDIS makes it possible to compare the performance of health plans on an "apples-to-apples" basis. . . HEDIS results are included in Quality Compass, an interactive, web-based comparison tool that allows users to view plan results and benchmark information. Quality Compass users benefit from the largest database of comparative health plan performance information to conduct competitor analysis, examine quality improvement and benchmark plan performance."

McKesson's "InterQual for Payors" website, too—sounding much like the "Open Competition Plan" of the *American Hardwood Manufacturers' Association*—utilizes its

"Advanced Diagnostics Management . . . giving physicians and clinical labs intelligent, automated decision support tools at the point of decision that enable transparent, immediate access to coverage, network and utilization rules [and measures] volumes and cost through retrospective analysis & benchmarking, with on-going data collection to [d]efine & codify relevant medical, benefit, network & payment policy; manage testing spend by influencing behavior at point-of-care using notification, authorization & orders tools; extend program to additional workflows, markets, specialties, etc. . . . [and] ClaimCheck and CodeReview are both comprehensive code auditing solutions that assist payors with proper physician reimbursement."

Such mechanisms of aiding interstate "competitors"—at the very least to have them learn as much about each other, just as their mergers strengthen their ability to fix prices—was also seen in the behavior of the trade association in *American Column*. The *American Column* High Court revealed in exquisite detail the monopolists' style, which parallels today's data dissemination methods of the NCQA, InterQual, and M&R as well as the MCO model of controlling output by restricting the length of treatment-cost episodes by centrally coordinated methods. Limiting amounts of care, with its consequent rapid turnover of patients, and increasing access to the system through acquisition of provider-patient groups, provides that the captive patient populations offer a reservoir of stabilized cash flow for the revenue stream of their clients. As F. R. Gadd, the Open Competition Plan's Manager of Statistics who was quoted in *American Column* (now classically), said:

"[Controlling output] is not going to worry the manufacturers very much; in fact, it will give them a much needed breathing spell and an opportunity to accumulate a supply of dry stocks which, in our opinion, is the same as gold dollars in the bank."

With the above discussion of measures of data collection and dissemination by NCQA, InterQual, and M&R, we can find similitude in the *American Column* court's description of how antitrust violators work:

"Genuine competitors do not make daily, weekly, and monthly reports of the minutest details of their business to their rivals . . . they do not contract, as was done here, to submit their books to the discretionary audit. . . of their rivals, for the purpose of successfully competing with them; and they do not submit the details of their business to the analysis of an expert, jointly employed, and obtain from him a 'harmonized' estimate of the market as it is, and as, in his specially and confidentially informed judgment, it promises to be. This is not the conduct of competitors, but is so clearly that of men united in an agreement, express or implied, to act together and pursue a common purpose under a common guide that if it did not stand confessed a combination to restrict production and increase prices in interstate commerce . . . that conclusion must inevitably have been inferred from the facts which were proved . . . as an old evil in a new dress and with a new name.

"The Plan is, essentially, an expansion of the gentleman's agreement of former days, skillfully devised to evade the law. To call it open competition, because the meetings were nominally open to the public, or because no specific agreement to restrict trade or fix prices is proved, cannot conceal the fact that the fundamental purpose of the Plan was to procure 'harmonious' individual action among a large number of naturally competing dealers with respect to the volume of production and prices, without having any specific agreement with respect to them, and to rely for maintenance of concerted action in both respects, not upon fines and forfeitures as in earlier days, but upon what experience has shown to be the more potent and dependable restraints, of business honor and social penalties—cautiously reinforced by many and elaborate reports, which would promptly expose to his associates any disposition in any member to deviate from the tacit understanding that all were to act together under the subtle direction of a single interpreter of their common purposes, as evidenced in the minute reports of what they had done and in their expressed purposes as to what they intended to do."

It is illustrative, if not ironic, and reminiscent of *American Column's* Open Competition Plan, that the Strategic Development Council of the American Concrete Institute's Concrete Research and Education Foundation took exceptional care in its Antitrust Compliance Policy and Guidelines to indicate its agreement with the antitrust laws "to ensure that vigorous competition exists in the American economy." However, the opening statement of the guidelines demonstrates a modern reinterpretation of the purpose of those laws similar to the NCQA and M&R associations' views: "Free and open competition results in the most efficient allocation of goods to the greatest number of people at the lowest cost." The antitrust laws were enacted to prevent anti-competitive behavior alone; they were not designed to reduce "costs" at all. There is as much of a distinct difference between "cost" and "price" as is between "cost fixing" and "price fixing." Looking for "reducing healthcare costs" circumvents and thus begs the issue of "whose costs," "what elements created the price" and, ultimately, the "cost to whom?"

As newly appointed antitrust Assistant Attorney General Christine A. Varney correctly said in May 2009:

"The National Industrial Recovery Act, which created the National Recovery Administration, allowed industries to create a set of industrial codes. These 'codes of fair competition' set industries' prices and wages, established production quotas, and imposed restrictions on entry. At the core of the NIRA was the idea that low profits in the industrial sectors contributed to the economic instability of those times. The purpose of the

industrial codes was to create 'stability'—i.e., higher profits—
by fostering coordinated action in the markets. . . Under this
legislation, the Government assisted in the enforcement of the
codes if firms contributed to a coordinated effort by permitting
unionization and engaging in collective bargaining.

"What was the result of these industrial codes? Competition was relegated to the sidelines, as the welfare of firms took
priority over the welfare of consumers. It is not surprising that
the industrial codes resulted in restricted output, higher prices,
and reduced consumer purchasing power. . . The focus of this
fundamental analysis needs to be on the power of competition in
the market to ensure the American consumers access to the best
products at the lowest prices."

By pointing directly at dangers inherent when government assures
profits to the "industrial sectors," Attorney General Varney helps us to
understand how the commercial health insurers could take advantage
of remedial legislation for their own purposes—they end in "restricted
output, higher prices, and reduced consumer purchasing power."

Another view of congressional intent in antitrust enforcement was
seen in the seminal 1944 Supreme Court case against the insurance
industry cartel, which led to the passage of the McCarran-Ferguson
Act, *United States v. South-Eastern Underwriters Assn.* The following is
cited from the 1890 Congressional Record:

"Senator George . . . stated on the floor of the Senate that . . .
'It is well known that the great evil of these combinations,
these conspiracies, as they are called, these monopolies, as they
are denominated by [the proposed Sherman Act], consists in
the fact that by combination, by association, there have been
gathered together the money and the means of large numbers
of persons, and under these combinations, or conspiracies, or
trusts, this great aggregated capital is wielded by a single hand
guided by a single brain, or at least by hands and brains acting in complete harmony and co-operation, and in this way,
by this association, by this direction of this immense amount

of capital, by one organized will, to a very large extent, these wrongs have been perpetrated upon the American people.' 21 Cong.Rec. 3147."

It is most instructive, too, to compare the structural indicia, outlined previously in *Container Corp.,* which demonstrates the illegal monopolistic condition then and our view of its relationship to today's managed-healthcare systems mythology:

1. "Fungibility" is defined as the property of a good or a commodity, whose individual units are capable of mutual substitution. This is ubiquitous and literally guaranteed in healthcare.

If not yet a "right," healthcare has long been recognized as a public "good" and in the general welfare. Though doctors are licensed by individual states, they have their examinations and specialty certifications based on fungible, that is, generally interchangeable, recognizable national, if not international, standards. The National Board of Medical Examiners certification is accepted by all fifty states as the baseline examination for state licensure during and immediately after medical school training, and many states have reciprocity for doctors moving to or practicing in other states. The federal reach into state licensing laws is demonstrated by the fact that the examinations must be passed before a <u>Doctor of Medicine</u> can obtain a license to practice medicine in the United States. In fact, if states do require special examinations for transferring medical licensees, they use such exams only to assess whether the doctor is up to date, not whether he or she has special epidemiological knowledge of that state's clinical issues. Specialty examinations—for example, the American Boards of Psychiatry and Neurology, Inc. (Surgery, Ophthalmology, Internal Medicine, etc.)— are also national in form and content and are completely independent of other credentials of the physician such as awards, hospital appointments, or publications. Indeed, medical texts know no state borders, so the "preferred provider" is a managed-care myth, profit based, and created largely to eliminate rivals, produce scarcity, and stabilize prices.

2. In "price" competition, indemnity insurance companies and those performing "administrative services only" for self-insured ERISA health plans obviously know the identities of each of the patients making claims, and wherever private "coinsurance" exists, they necessitate complete knowledge of their competitors' arrangements through state "coordination of benefits" requirements.

The insurance companies also know the arrangements made by their employer group purchasers and their MCO contractors, who reduce their front-end or reinsurance costs by managing the patient care through capitation, telephone pre- and concurrent-certifications, approvals and denials of payment for care, and the reports flowing from them and their gatekeepers. In recruiting and hiring providers to perform such management services, the MCOs usually request the provider-applicants to identify other MCOs with which the applicant may have contracts.

In addition, the institutional cost reports made by Medicare and Medicaid providers submitted to federal and state governments detail each cost center of a healthcare facility and are publicly available. Government regulations require that hospital providers "gross-up" their charges—that is, the highest amount they would charge a completely private paying patient—to provide a uniform ceiling from which government subtracts its "contractual allowances." Before the PPS of DRGs went into full swing in 1986, reimbursement rates were based on those contractual allowances, increased or decreased by annual statutory "market-basket" indexes, and afterward, structured on the DRGs, which thereby reveal the net income per actuarially determinable service unit. Thus, the government-contracted provider's net private-care income can be readily determined by computing the difference between the populations of Medicare/Medicaid patients and private payers.

3. "Healthcare demand is elastic."

Despite some healthcare economists' statements to the contrary, healthcare has proven to be "inelastic," because there are few scientifically valid substitutes for the treatments taught in medical schools and residency training deemed medically appropriate for specific diseases. Medically deemed treatment provided is "treatment *per se,*" that is, "by itself." The managed-care term of art negotiating for "an alternative, lower-cost treatment," is inapposite, especially because it only means to the MCO "lower-priced" treatment. As we now know, to the MCO, lower costs only mean lower cash flow. In addition, not all healthcare spending is "elastic" either, because elasticity in healthcare relates only to costs, not to illnesses that can be put off to sometime in the future. There is also no fiscally sound audit trail to managed-care interventions resulting in a denial or limitation of coverage nor to the results of denials that end in misfortune other than from researching the personal injury bar's malpractice cases resulting from inadequate care, because the providers, not the managed-care companies, are the ones that are blamed.

Much of what appears to have been accomplished by managed-care's market manipulations, whether by pressure to reduce hospital beds or to replace them with "ambulatory," outpatient departments or "alternative care" in order to lessen costs to insurers, except for surgery, seem to have increased the chronicity of illness, which has raised both the costs and the prices within the system. Hospital "bed space" costs were $50,000 to $100,000 each to build in 1975, but according to the April 15, 2009 *The New York Times,* based on the "traditional method of hospital construction, the cost per bed is typically $1 million to $1.5 million" to rebuild and would cost even more in years to come if the beds were prematurely "closed." The error in closing beds would quickly be seen in another flu or AIDS-type pandemic.

Managed-care insurers can hardly take credit for medical advances and technological development given their effectiveness in reducing the money available for research and development and their refusal to pay for innovative or experimental modalities of care.

4. "A lower price does not mean a larger share of the available business, but a sharing of the existing business at a lower return. Stabilizing prices as well as raising them is within the ban of § 1 of the Sherman Act."—*U.S. v. Container Corporation.*

Even without an agreement by managed-care insurers to adhere to a fixed price, the effect is to stabilize prices by information shared by their membership associations that permit each buyer to match the competitor's price offerings. Magellan may reduce clients' costs by urging its case managers to adjust providers' output, substituting algorithms that essentially mimic government-inspired hospital-DRG lengths of stay. The common carrot offered providers under capitation by MCOs is the referral of large numbers or groups of patients the provider can treat for a fixed price-per-patient-per year, using volume as the bait. The managed-care insurers, not the providers, actively control the cost of healthcare.

Container Corp. also stated:

"The *American Column* case was a sophisticated and well-supervised plan for the exchange of price information between competitors with the idea of keeping prices reasonably stable and of putting an end to cutthroat competition. There were no sanctions except financial interest and business honor. But the purpose of the plan being to increase prices, it was held to be within the ban of the Sherman Act."

Another elaborate plan for the exchange of price data among competitors was involved in 1923 in *United States v. American Linseed Oil*, where informal sanctions were used to establish "modern cooperative business methods," similar years later to NCQA, InterQual, and M&R's "standard setting" and "accreditation" for MCOs. The informal sanctions arrangement was declared illegal, because its "necessary tendency" was to suppress competition.

American Linseed Oil Company's unhelpful promise was that

"all information reported or received shall be purely statistical and relevant to past operations, and no part of the bureau's machinery will be used to fix prices, divide territory, limit sales, production, or manufacture, or control competition."

Justice William O. Douglas, writing for the majority in *Container Corp.*, said, "Although the recent price charged or quoted was fragmentary, each defendant had the manuals with which it could compute the price charged by a competitor on a specific order to a specific customer."

The blurring of distinctions between a health-provider organization such as a hospital and medical staff and a health-insurance plan reveals the tenuous anticompetitive ties holding together the managed healthcare insurance industry. Hospitals and their medical staffs are accredited by The Joint Commission (on Accreditation of Healthcare Organizations), whose standards have been given "deemed status" by CMS regulations to serve as organizations acceptable to government to treat Medicare and Medicaid patients. They provide medical care.

NCQA's HEDIS offers a set of standardized performance measures designed to ensure that purchasers and consumers have the information they need to compare reliably the performance of managed health-care plans.

UnitedHealthcare Online explains HEDIS:

"The performance measures in HEDIS are related to many significant public health issues including: cancer, heart disease, smoking, asthma and diabetes. HEDIS also includes a standardized survey of consumers' experiences that evaluates plan performance in areas such as: customer service, access to care and claims possessing."

The same website describes the "Leapfrog Group Standards," which the managed-care insurance industry uses to focus on

"reducing preventable medical mistakes and improving quality and compliance with safe practices in healthcare. Its supporters include a growing consortium of major companies and other large private and public healthcare purchasers that provide health benefits to more than 37 million people in all 50 states. The Leapfrog Group was launched in 2000 by the Business Roundtable."

These data disseminating organizations only manage for profit the healthcare given by medical providers.

Note how NCQA's "Quality Compass" intrepidly puts it:

"Health plans will be able to compare their performance on HEDIS indicators to benchmarks, either regional or national, or to the performance of other plans, thereby identifying and prioritizing areas for improvement . . . This centralized database is the logical next step in making information on plan performance publicly and broadly available . . . . Having data submitted electronically to a single entity will make the process even more efficient.'"

The 1957 and 1962 Supreme Court cases, *United States v. Nationwide Trailer Rental Sys.*, and *Northern Cal. Pharmaceutical Ass'n v. United States*, prohibited trade associations from circulating suggested price lists when the list served only as a starting point for price determination, when no agreement to adhere to the suggested price existed or prices substantially departed from the suggested rate.

1. Capitation—Contract, Collusion, and Coercive Networking

In *Fortner Enterprises, Inc. v. United States Steel Corp.*, the same year as *Container Corp.,* the Supreme Court established a theoretical predicate for our impression that capitation and fee-for-service withholds by PPMCs, which "require purchasers to accept burdensome terms," is possibly a form of tying arrangement and embraces collusive bidding possibly violative of section 1 of the Sherman Act. *Fortner* established that economic power was "the power . . . to raise prices or to require purchasers to accept burdensome terms." Capitation, which amounts to a transfer to MCOs and/or to contracting providers of the risk assumed by employees' self-insured plans, is used extensively today in interstate commerce by competitor-members of the NCQA, based on standards established by the organization as well as on actuarial determinations made by M&R and InterQual, among others. Most contracts for capitation or withhold arrangements, between providers with insurance companies or HMOs, frequently require binding arbitration to resolve disputes; the outcome more often than not favors the insurance companies.

It appears to be no coincidence therefore that a spate of "patient protection" legislation occurred between 1997 and 1999, when thirty-seven states decided to enact some form of patient protection law. Once more, the second-class treatment of ERISA beneficiaries compared with their indemnity insurance counterparts was revealed, this time, by protective action of the states. Patient protection laws in the states cannot relate to ERISA benefit plans. As the latter are federally preempted such disputes must be settled in a federal court based on the employer or sponsor's fiduciary standards in the plan document, i.e., pursuant to trust law. The Republican partisan response to Clinton's "Patient Bill of Rights," which languished in the Congress from 1998 to 2001, was similar to the partisan response in the Obama-era Congress a decade later—to do nothing—and no such federal law existed as of December 2009. The Obama ACA of 2010, however, set up an Office of Consumer Information and Insurance Oversight department within DHHS to "ensure compliance with the new insurance market rules, such as the prohibitions on rescissions and on pre-existing condition exclusions for children that take effect this year. It will oversee the new medical loss ratio rules and will assist states in reviewing insurance rates. It will provide guidance and oversight for the state-based insurance Exchanges. It will also administer the temporary high-risk pool program and the early retiree reinsurance program, and compile and maintain data for an internet portal providing information on insurance options."

The Insurance Oversight Office was originally under the direction of Jay Angoff, a former Missouri insurance commissioner who began his career as an antitrust lawyer with the FTC. In early January 2011, DHHS secretary Sibelius moved the office into CMS, whose programs, Medicare and Medicaid, served by then more than one hundred million people. Steven B. Larsen, former Maryland state insurance commissioner, appointed director of the Oversight Office, reported to Jay Angoff who would serve as an adviser in the DHHS Office of the Secretary, advising Sebelius on policy issues pertaining to provisions handled by the Office of Consumer Information and Insurance Oversight (OCIIO). *The Washington Post Online* reported that Mr. Larsen had made a name for himself as Maryland's insurance commissioner when he refused to let CareFirst, Maryland's largest insurer, convert to for-profit status and be taken over by the insurance giant WellPoint, which ran the Delaware Blues. The Maryland General Assembly subsequently enacted "reform" to reaffirm CareFirst's nonprofit status and barred any attempt by it to become a for-profit company for five years. In February 2011, the Obama administration announced that it had granted to four states waivers from the ACA, allowing those states to keep what amounted to less-generous insurance and lower annual limits on coverage than the ACA required of all other states. Even so, by 2014, all states will have to transition into the higher-quality coverage of the ACA to bring uniformity and cost-saving adjustments into line with the 2010 projections of the Congressional Budget Office.

Major ERISA benefit plan disputes that reached the Supreme Court because of federal preemption and the fact that ERISA describes them as not within "the business of insurance" were often found in favor of insurance company defendants. However, there were two chief break-throughs in the otherwise bleak consumer scene challenging insurance company hegemony. The first was the 2003 *Kentucky Ass'n. of Health Plans v. Miller,* written by Associate Justice Scalia and decided by a unanimous Supreme Court, which bypassed the McCarran-Ferguson Act's "business of insurance" provision:

"ERISA's savings clause, however, is not concerned (as is the McCarran-Ferguson Act provision) with how to characterize *conduct* undertaken by private actors, but with how to characterize state laws in regard to what they regulate. [Further, the] Court's prior use, to varying degrees, of its cases interpreting §§ 2(a) and 2(b) of the McCarran-Ferguson Act in the ERISA savings clause context has misdirected attention, failed to provide clear guidance to lower federal courts, and, as this case demonstrates, added little to the relevant analysis. The Court has never held that the McCarran-Ferguson factors are an essential component of [ERISA's] inquiry. Today the Court makes a clean break from the McCarran-Ferguson factors in interpreting ERISA's savings clause." (Italics made in the original.)

The second breakthrough occurred a month after the 2010 ACA was signed, when the Supreme Court denied *certiorari* to an insurance company challenge in *Standard Ins. Co. v. Lindeen.* There, a unanimous panel of the Ninth Circuit Court of Appeals found that although the Montana state practice "relates" to a covered employee benefit plan, it was not preempted on account of ERISA's clause that expressly saves from preemption any state law that "regulates insurance, banking, or securities," the so-called "savings clause." The Circuit Court had applied the two-part test set forth in *Kentucky Ass'n of Health Plans, Inc.* and found that the Montana practice was directed specifically toward entities engaged in insurance—"prong one of the two-part test." The decision substantially affected the risk-pooling arrangement between the insurer and the insured: the "second prong." It thus ended ASO insurer and self-insured employer-favored, discretionary clauses, enabling all ERISA benefit plan members a *de novo* review in Ninth Circuit state courts; a form of appeal in which the appellate-level court holds a trial as if no prior trial had been held by a lower court.

Although tie-ins and exclusive dealing arrangements may violate Sherman section 1 and Clayton section 3, courts have denied Clayton section 3 jurisdiction when the tied product was not a commodity. Nevertheless, the process of grouping providers to control actuarially determinable groups of patients has been seen by many commentators as the "commoditizing" of healthcare, not the least reason being that the insurance industry insists on calling its services "products." Moreover, changes in the modern medical world, with increasing use of technologically complex equipment and large-scale capital purchases, government-required software for medical records, and for-profit arrangements bringing doctors into large groups with office-leasing and withholds based on financial performance, raise issues that bring the ambit of the antitrust statutes closer. These issues are not foreclosed as applied to healthcare services. Although Clayton section 3 has been said to foreclose defining "services as a commodity by its terms," meaning that "labor" is not a commodity, Clayton section 3 nonetheless admonishes:

> "It shall be unlawful for any person engaged in commerce, in the course of such commerce, to lease or make a sale or contract for sale of goods, wares, merchandise, machinery, supplies, or other commodities, whether patented or unpatented, for use, . . . where the effect of such . . . condition, agreement, or understanding may be to substantially lessen competition or tend to create a monopoly in any line of commerce."

Tie-ins (physician/hospital) and exclusive dealing (like "preferred" provider) arrangements deny sellers' competitors the market created by the monopsonist-buyers' purchases. Typical HMO care or capitated-dependent practitioner arrangements and PPMCs involve services tied to extracontractual relations for significant periods, usually for a year or more. Because the government has formally interposed DRGs as actuarially based publicly published prices-per-illness, larger groups of healthcare providers can now more easily estimate their risk by identifying the population offered for care. They can negotiate from there with the insurer or HMO for referral populations of a particular size at prices above or below the federal estimates. This would seem to be a positive step for larger-sized groups of providers to produce efficiencies of scale were it not for the impossibility of the healthcare rising cost curve matching those of the declining cost curve of manufacturing discussed earlier. Individual providers, or small groups of them, have found themselves completely at sea in attempting to assume such risks with groups of patients numbering in the thousands, which squeezes many well-trained and highly qualified physicians out of the competitive marketspace. In part for this reason, the ACA allows MLRs in small groups to be at 80 percent, and in large groups at 85 percent, to give the smaller qualified providers' groups more leverage with employers.

Sherman section 1 says, "Every contract, combination in the form of trust or otherwise, or conspiracy, in restraint of trade or commerce among the several States, or with foreign nations, is declared to be illegal." Insurance defined as "commerce" has been settled law since 1944 in *United States v. South-Eastern Underwriters*, where the High Court decision invoked not just an act of Congress, but also the Constitution, thereby marrying the concepts of the "business of insurance" with the "business of insurance *companies*":

> "An insurance company, which conducts a substantial part of its business transactions across state lines is engaged in 'commerce among the several States' [citing section 1 of the Sherman Act], and subject to regulation by Congress under the Commerce Clause."

Sherman therefore does not distinguish contracts for "commodities" from "services," only for contractual behavior in interstate commerce. To paraphrase Justice Scalia in *Kentucky Ass'n of Health Plans, Inc.*, Sherman deals with "how to characterize *conduct* undertaken by private actors." The fact that the McCarran-Ferguson Act somewhat artfully exempted the "business of insurance" from federal antitrust scrutiny does not change the fact that the "business of insurance companies" is concededly involved in interstate commerce. A year after *South-Eastern*, the Supreme Court said in *United States v. Frankfort Distilleries,*

"there is an obvious distinction to be drawn between a course of conduct wholly within a state and conduct which is an inseparable element of a larger program dependent for its success upon activity which affects commerce between the states."

The 1979 Supreme Court said in *Group Life & Health Insurance Company, et al. v. Royal Drug Company, et al.*:

"There is not the slightest suggestion in the legislative history that Congress in any way contemplated that arrangements such as the Pharmacy Agreements in this case, which involve the mass purchase of goods and services from entities outside the insurance industry, are the 'business of insurance.'" *See* Plate 4.

Note, in Plate 4, that although core capital is raised by collecting premiums indemnifying an actuarial pool, in healthcare insurance the contract-based payments for the indemnified financial loss are not considered a part of the business of insurance "companies" by the *Royal Drug* and, later, *Pireno* High Court, notwithstanding the Sherman Act language in section 1.

In the managed-medicine world, the formularies and anticompetitive price arrangements with pharmaceutical manufacturers by the insurance industry sets prices *en masse* for its members. In noting an absence of "the slightest suggestion" in Congress when enacting the McCarran-Ferguson Act's distinction of the business of insurance, the *Royal Drug* Court formulation is inapposite, because such a formulation also embraces the opposite. That is, there was also "not the slightest suggestion in [McCarran's] legislative history" that the mass purchase of goods and services from entities outside the insurance industry was *not* the business of insurance. The entirety of business operations in any industry only appears to characterize the particular nature of that business. For example, while the mass purchase of steel, plastics, and rubber for making cars may be unique to the auto industry, similar purchases by construction companies' end up producing buildings. Apparently, the Court tried to fit a round *Royal* peg into a McCarran square hole.

In any event, private and government healthcare coverage has made many shifts and turns since the 1970s, from indemnity insurance regulated by states to fiduciary-based warranties preempted by the federal government, from no basic Medicare coverage for drugs to privatized MA covering prescriptions. These allow the policy-making "business of insurance" or of their "companies" to be barely distinguishable. They both have actuaries, agents, and brokers to organize and sell their "products," which may include drugs, "disease management," and "administrative services only." However, Congress clearly provided that the antitrust laws would be applicable to the business of insurance "to the extent that such business is not regulated by State law," and state law now does regulate HMOs as insurer/provider agreements as well as insurer/insured agreements—Medicare Advantage, ostensibly supplying similar amenities, was statutorily constructed to be nationwide.

As noted earlier in *South-Eastern Underwriters Assn.*,

"It does not follow from this that the Court is powerless to examine the entire transaction, of which that contract is but a part, in order to determine whether there may be a chain of events which becomes interstate commerce."

For the FTC and courts in the future, parsing public policy activities by commercial insurance that work against the antitrust laws and their "chain of events" indiscretions will be an engaging process, to say the least. A good deal remains to be learned from application and enforcement of the 2010 ACA about the actuarial nature of the more than fifty million people who have had little or no insurance, many of whom have been beyond the pool of potential patients for more than three decades as they enter from the Exchanges. What will happen to the aggregate cost of care should they be readmitted to coverage through incremental reforms such as the end of preexisting conditions' rescissions or denials, the extension of job-to-job healthcare protections, the raising of Medicaid eligibility, or the president's proposal to provide Medicare to those aged fifty-five to sixty-five? The 2009 Congressional Budget Office said that the healthcare cost curve will "bend." What needs to be decided is whether a commercial insurance industry, now both "managing" and "noninsuring," could be a prevailing part of that trend.

2. "Quality Review" and *Pireno*: Is It Really the "Business of Insurance Companies"?

ERISA "supersedes all state laws that may now or hereafter relate to any employee benefit plan" except "any law of any State which regulates insurance, banking, or securities." In addition to this preemption section, ERISA adds a "deemer clause":

"Neither an employee benefit plan . . . nor any trust established under such a plan, shall be deemed to be an insurance company or other insurer, bank, trust company, or investment company or to be engaged in the business of insurance or banking for purposes of any law of any State purporting to regulate insurance companies, insurance contracts . . . [and] shall be deemed to be an insurance company or other insurer for purposes of any law of any State purporting to regulate insurance companies, insurance contracts, banks, trust companies, or investment companies."

The core question, answered by the 1982 High Court in *Union Labor Life Insurance Co. v. A. Alexander Pireno*, was that while the "business of insurance" was subject to state regulation pursuant to the McCarran- Ferguson Act, "peer review"—the indemnity insurance industry's equivalent of today's managed-care "reviews"—was not. Parsing finely, the Court said that while peer review may be the "business of insurance companies," it was not the "business of insurance." In *Pireno*, the Court restated the three criteria indispensable to the business of insurance that were identified in *Royal Drug*:

"*First*, whether the practice has the effect of transferring or spreading a policyholder's risk; *second*, whether the practice is an integral part of the policy relationship between the insurer and the insured; and *third*, whether the practice is limited to entities within the insurance industry."

Citing *Couch's Cyclopedia of Insurance Law*, the Court concluded that the assumption of risk by the insurer occurs from the moment the policy is bought. "The transfer of risk from insured to insurer is effected by means of the contract between the parties—the insurance policy—and that transfer is complete at the time that the contract is entered." From that point on, for purposes of the McCarran-Ferguson antitrust exemption, the managed-care "business of insurance" was soon to end. The exemption, based on the assumption (transfer) of the risk effected by the policy-based premium payment, once assumed, required a company's practices to be regulated by the state. It is interesting to note that ERISA does not constrain a state to regulate insurance but only deems state laws that "purport" to regulate insurance, allowing such insurance companies, among others, to be outside of federal preemption. If even a portion of the risk, other than as explicitly stated in the policy, were transferred back to the patient, either through "management" of the doctor's care by use of algorithms such as from M&R and Inter-Qual, or by concurrent external review and the use of such algorithms to produce "efficiencies" and save on "costs," the nature of healthcare coverage and its state regulation would effectively be changed and the premium's value would be diminished by the intervention.

It took eight years from the 1974 enactment of ERISA—when healthcare "insurance" regulated by the states was deemed different from healthcare "noninsurance" offered employees by employers' ERISA benefit plans—for the Supreme Court to distinguish for the country the congressional intent of the law's "deemer clause," allowing commercial insurance companies' "business" to be held distinct from the business of underwriting insurance. The breadth of coverage and type of treatment for the "self-insured" employees and individual purchasers for "precertification" of treatment to begin were, in most cases, virtually identical, especially because even the indemnity insurers began to use ancillary "peer"- or managed-care reviewers.

The *Pireno* Court decided that because the challenged practice must be limited to entities "within" the insurance industry, "as respects the third *Royal* criterion, it is plain that the challenged peer review practices are not limited to entities within the insurance industry." This statement hedges on the issue of defining the effect of peer review by an entity *within* a particular insurance company's ambit, like a wholly owned insurance subsidiary. Did the Supreme Court's decision rest on whether the business of insurance, for McCarran-Ferguson purposes, means only the company's "core" business? The Court ought to have clarified it better rather than making simply a heuristic counterpoint. There is no longer a legal reason why MCOs run, owned, or subcontracted by insurance companies should not be regulated by the states. Health and welfare benefit plans always get their coverage "administrative services" determinations from entities wholly within the insurance industry, if not wholly within the insurance company.

The flaw in recent ERISA litigation is that the managed-care industry of today is no longer the same creature it was twenty-five years ago. First, today it is "within the insurance industry." Second, its "relations" are based on policies actuarially determined and underwritten, often sold as "shrink-wrapped" products, by insurance companies or their brokers to self-insuring employers. Third, the risk is being also spread (albeit narrowly, thus, more expensive) over the individual contractor/ provider community using capitation methods controlled by entities "within the insurance industry." The sleight of hand taking place now is that because of the small size of the self-insurer, the premium price is falsely elevated, because the risk is not spread widely enough to represent its marginal cost, the latter being the *Royal Drug* first prerequisite of the business of insurance. None of this is addressed in the 2010 revised DOJ/FTC guidelines. The revised June 14, 2010 DOJ and FTC horizontal merger guidelines fail to distinguish the vertical interface between physician groups and their contracts with primary insurers or reinsurers; they only warn the physician groups not to exceed their market power resulting from mergers and their price arrangements.

Notwithstanding that on Oct. 16, 2009, President Obama, speaking at Texas A&M University, stated it was time to repeal the McCarran-Ferguson Act, the provision for repeal of McCarran-Ferguson, energetically passed with a bipartisan vote of 406 to 19 by the House of Representatives as the Health Insurance Industry Antitrust Enforcement Act of 2009 (H.R. 3596), was unfortunately dropped out of the ACA in conference with the Senate. It stated:

"Notwithstanding any other provision of law, nothing in the . . . 'McCarran-Ferguson Act,' shall be construed to permit health insurance issuers (as defined in the Public Health Service Act) or issuers of medical malpractice insurance to engage in any form of price fixing, bid rigging, or market allocations in connection with the conduct of the business of providing health insurance coverage . . . or coverage for medical malpractice claims or actions."

According to *OpenCongress*.org, among the interests that supported the bill were dentists, hospitals, attorneys and law firms, and auto repair and consumer groups. Among the organizations opposing H.R. 3596 were the American Academy of Actuaries, America's Health Insurance Plans, Physician Insurers Association of America, Professional Insurance Agents, Property Casualty Insurers Association of America, and the California Orthopedic Association. The full committee markup vote to recommend was 20-9 in favor. It never made it through the Senate into the ACA.

The essential difference between spreading risk and managing it by peer review was central to the issue before the *Pireno* Court. It was particularly critical to demonstrating that peer review companies were not in the business of insurance, rendering applicable the price-fixing and data-dissemination exemptions allowed indemnity insurers by the McCarran-Ferguson Act. The *Pireno* Court cited *Royal Drug*, saying this:

"The [Pharmacy] Agreements thus enable Blue Shield to minimize costs and maximize profits. Such savings may well inure ultimately to the benefit of policyholders in the form of lower premiums, but they are not the 'business of insurance.'"

The *Royal Drug* Court did emphasize, however,

"More importantly, such arrangements [between insurance companies and parties outside the insurance industry] may prove contrary to the spirit as well as the letter of [McCarran], because they have the potential to restrain competition in non-insurance markets . . . Indeed [the] claim is that the practices restrain competition in a provider market . . . rather than an insurance market . . . [and that the spreading and underwriting of risk was] logically and temporally unconnected to the contract by the policyholder and the [insurance company]."

The *Pireno* Court observed that insurance risk is transferred "completely" to the insurer at the time the policy is sold, not when the claim is made. With emphasis, the Court held that "the use of [the insurer's peer-review company] as an aid in its decision-making process is a matter of indifference to the policyholder, whose only concern is *whether* his claim is paid, not *why* it is paid." Thus, before the aggressive advent of managed care, the *Pireno* Court foresaw that extracontractual relations of insurance companies might not enjoy a McCarran-Ferguson exemption but could be fit subjects for federal antitrust scrutiny for price fixing by interstate data dissemination. It proceeded to make a fine distinction that contradicted its 1969 broad holding in *SEC v. National Securities, Inc.*: "The McCarran-Ferguson Act was an attempt to turn back the clock to assure that the activities of insurance companies would remain subject to state regulation." Instead, to *Pireno* and *Royal Drug*, the business of insurance was not considered the same as the business of insurance companies simply because "the challenged review practices are not limited to entities within the insurance industry." *See* Plate 3.

The *National Securities, Inc.* Court did not distinguish the "business of insurance." Moreover, as far back as 1958, the Supreme Court said, in *FTC v. National Casualty Co.*, affirmed *per curiam*, that although the states also had enacted statutes prohibiting unfair and deceptive practices, such a prohibition could not trigger McCarran-Ferguson immunity "until that prohibition has been crystallized into administrative elaboration of these standards and application in individual cases." Although *National Casualty* concerned a challenge under the FTC's consumer protection authority, not its antitrust authority, *National Casualty* would seem to leave room for the FTC today—even given the existing McCarran-Ferguson immunity—to challenge practices that constitute either unfair or deceptive practices or unfair methods of competition in a state that has no specific regulation of those practices.

Because the merits of the antitrust claim were not heard in the *Pireno* district court, the Supreme Court never reached the antitrust issue, albeit originally raised in the insurance company defense, and affirmed the Second Circuit Court of Appeals' finding that McCarran-Ferguson did not exempt the peer review committee from antitrust scrutiny pursuant to the McCarran-Ferguson Act. The High Court maintained that the Sherman section 1 claim therefore was not at issue, because peer review was not found to be exempt from antitrust scrutiny by McCarran-Ferguson, and did not explore its contradictory statement in *National Securities, Inc.*, declaring only that "conduct which is not exempt from the antitrust laws may be perfectly legal . . . [and, citing *Royal Drug*,] exemptions from the antitrust laws must be construed narrowly, [and that] the decision of the question before us is controlled by *Royal Drug*."

Although the door was now wide open for Dr. Pireno to have his day in court on his antitrust claim, victorious but probably exhausted, he never pursued it. The *Royal Drug* Court had relied upon *National Securities, Inc.*, contending that such pharmacy agreements did not involve the relationship "between insurer and insured, [but were instead] separate contractual arrangements between Blue Shield and pharmacies engaged in the sale and distribution of goods and services other than insurance," even though they couldn't be considered or sold without the insurance contracts. Nevertheless, because of that, the pharmacy agreements were beyond the scope of the McCarran-Ferguson exemption. This was interestingly similar to what have become insurer/provider agreements for sale and distribution of "services other than insurance," like capitated healthcare or fee-for-service withholds. Because the *Royal Drug* case does not offer a valid description of the insurer-provider-capitation and managed-care organization relationships today by the managed-care insurance industry, clarification by state insurance departments is sorely needed. If state insurance departments do not consider such clarification as within their purview, it would be up to Congress to order a closing of this loophole, for the state medical societies to demand it by a special proceeding in an appropriate state court, or for the FTC to redefine the relationships. If peer review is not the business of insurance but only of "their companies," conflict preemption is lurking.

The relationship between doctor and patient cannot be analogized comfortably to the short-lived purchase of a drug from a pharmacy, as in *Royal Drug*, because it is a continuing relationship of a patient with a caregiver. This is also the basis for the doctors' ethical and financial dilemma in the managed-care era. As a 1996 Maryland appellate court keenly observed in *Patel v. HealthPlus, Inc.*, the unique relationship between the physician and the HMO

> "might be described as inherently contentious, even litigious, because of the ebb and flow of cost-cutting pressures inherent in the business arrangement and the conflict between a physician's judgment in respect to treatment and an HMO's efforts to control treatment options. . . . Because many members will utilize services at a cost of less than the fee the subscriber pays to the [MCO] and a significant number will utilize no services at all, and because the [MCO] is able to obtain medical services at lower rates due to its ability to direct volume and control costs through its ability to impose treatment limitations and lower fees on providers, *i.e.,* physicians, [a for-profit MCO] hopes that it can produce a profit after the cost of administering the program."

The "primary care" doctor-patient relationships are not only individual contacts but also, more often, individual and family relationships for blocks of time relating to concurrent conditions (postoperative surgery, diabetes, heart disease, mental illness, cancer, etc.). The very concept of a specific "preexisting illness," so exactingly maintained as an exclusionary device by indemnity insurers, is in reality nothing more than a "second bite at the apple" or an example of post-claims underwriting. Under indemnity contracts, the insurance company denies coverage on the basis of misrepresentation, concealment or fraud in the insured's application for payment. The claimant is advised that the policy is being rescinded, the premiums are returned, and that there is no coverage for the claimed loss. Managed care is a form of post-claims underwriting, since it denies claims even without being sent to underwriting departments. *See* Plate 7. Finding a preexisting illness, too, redefines the boundaries of whether and when risks are transferred, maintained, or finished. Ironically, a "preexisting illness" is always what brings most patients to a doctor for the first time. It is then, and at later points in doctor-patient contacts that other "preexisting illnesses" are discovered, many of them coexisting with the initiating "preexisting" one but not necessarily caused by it. This is not as much of a problem for managed care as it was for indemnity policies, because for the managed-care industry, much of the risk is not assumed anyway. Rather, it is manipulated and controlled after the policy is sold, and with capitation, the cost is "passed on" and transferred to the risk-taking doctor. The patient is the loser.

The indemnity insurer's actuary predetermined the economic risk the company is required to assume for an "incident that was"; for the managed-care industry, the risk and its extra-profitability attaches to an unknown "incident to be." Simply put, managed care adds an "incident" after treatment starts (the indemnity risk) to guarantee the "second (more profitable) bite at the apple." Unlike indemnity coverage, which is prefixed by the policy language, managed-care's flexible review systems come into play before, during, or after the services are performed and are logically and temporally connected to the transfer of risk back to the patient (in ERISA cases, to the fiduciary or sponsor of the benefit plan). Because managed-care provides an elaborate screening process both before and while care is delivered, especially when hospitalization is involved, it imposes on the providers a time-consuming and often intimidating "precertification" and "concurrent review" for both patient and facility. For ERISA fiduciaries, the end of group coverage exclusions for preexisting illnesses under the 1996 HIPAA—taken together with the judicial redefining of the limits of ERISA preemption—became a minefield of beneficiary complaints to plan administrators accepting discretion to change plan benefits midstream and led to the swift enactment of many state "Patient Protection" laws between 1997 to 1999.

3. Clearing ERISA's Muddy Waters—when "Insurance" Is "Noninsurance"

To qualify for McCarran-Ferguson exemption, besides demonstrating that activities constitute the "business of insurance," HMOs and other insurance organizations that purport to provide healthcare benefits are entitled to the exemption only to the extent that their activities are regulated by state law, as found by the 1958 Supreme Court in *National Casualty Co.* Therefore, because of the brisk replacement of indemnity healthcare coverage by HMOs and MCOs, larger employers were constrained to self-insure and contract with the new organizations to manage their employees' healthcare services, leaving them in a partial preemption land between state regulation and ERISA preemption. Absent remedial state or federal legislation, or healthy comity with the federal Labor and Treasury Departments, regulation of these benefit organizations by the states remained a difficult task and an even more difficult one for courts. Note the emphasis in the robust 1969 Supreme Court's holding in *National Securities, Inc.*, citing from the legislative history that the 1945 McCarran-Ferguson Act

> "was an attempt to turn back the clock to assure that the activities of insurance companies would remain subject to state regulation. As the House Report makes clear, '[i]t [was] not the intention of Congress, in the enactment of this legislation, to clothe the States with any power to regulate or tax the business of insurance beyond that which they had been held to possess prior to the decision of the United States Supreme Court in the *Southeastern Underwriters Association* case.' Given this history, the language of the statute takes on a different coloration. The statute did not purport to make the States supreme in regulating all the activities of insurance *companies*; its language refers not to the persons or companies who are subject to state regulation, but to laws 'regulating the *business* of insurance.' Insurance companies may do many things which are subject to paramount federal regulation; only when they are engaged in the 'business of insurance' does the statute apply." (Italics in the original.)

ERISA preemption in 1974 cleaved off part of the states' plenary regulatory assurance by effectively moving millions of similarly situated workers out of the protection as a matter of law that they formerly enjoyed as purchasers of policies "within" the "business of insurance." Therefore, interposing managed care as a reducer of risk in a contract between a healthcare "promiser" (the benefit plan fiduciary) and an employee in need, compared with policy owners within the business of indemnity insurance, should require congressional reconsideration of the 1969 pre-ERISA, pre-managed care High Court finding that there was no particular distinction between the "activities of insurance companies" and the "business of insurance companies," only of the McCarran-Ferguson and ERISA distinctions in how they are regulated.

In sum, the "business of insurance" versus the "business of insurance companies," as parsed by *Pireno* and *Royal Drug*, would be a casuist argument in today's healthcare marketplace. The ERISA legislation's promises, having been made to similarly situated people—whether "insured" or "covered" and whether by "policies" or "plans"—should have provided equal protection for all by state and/or federal regulation. Because there are no reserve requirements for ERISA benefit plans but there are for insurance companies, people purchasing healthcare coverage from organizations under color of law should be reasonably able to expect their rights to be protected when they contract with either type of entity for the same thing, i.e., payment to a provider for their healthcare needs.

The Constitution reserves certain powers to the states. Preemption was later to provide specific power to the federal government by divesting states of certain powers through specific legislation. Thus, Article I, section 8, lays out the specific powers, called the "enumerated powers," of the Congress. Article VI, clause 2, called the "Supremacy Clause," provides that the U.S. Constitution and the laws of the United States are "the supreme law of the land." The Tenth Amendment provided in 1791 that "the powers not delegated to the United States by the Constitution, nor prohibited by it to the states, are reserved to the states respectively, or to the people."

The federal preemption doctrine is a judicial response to the conflict between federal and state legislation. The courts have recognized at least three major types of preemption: (1) *conflict* or *field preemption*, when compliance with both federal and state law is impossible, or when state law stands as an obstacle to the accomplishment and execution of the full purpose and objective of federal law and a federal question is raised; (2) *express* or *complete preemption*, as in ERISA but modified by its states' "savings clause"; and (3) *implied preemption*, which may be raised when a state legislature has been silent on the issue. More particularly, the Supremacy Clause has come to mean that the national government, in exercising any of the powers enumerated in the Constitution, must prevail over any conflicting or inconsistent state exercise of power.

When it is clearly established that a federal law preempts a state law, the state law must be declared invalid. In addition, the federal right to regulate interstate commerce under the Commerce Clause of the Constitution ordinarily has resulted in federal preemption of state laws. In determining whether any of these types of preemption exist, the courts are guided by the narrow presumption against preemption indicated in the 1985 Supreme Court in *Hillsborough County v. Automated Medical Laboratories, Inc.*, that is, only if the federal law in question regulates an area traditionally regulated by the states. However, even if the 1979 *Royal Drug* three "business of insurance" criteria were met, in *St. Paul Fire & Marine Ins. Co. v. Barry* the year before, the Court had held that the McCarran-Ferguson exemption would not be available if the conduct involved "an agreement to boycott, coerce, or intimidate, or act of boycott, coercion, or intimidation."

For example, the *St. Paul* Court said,

"Congress intended in the McCarran 'boycott' clause to carve out of the overall framework of plenary state regulation an area that would remain subject to Sherman Act scrutiny. . . . (a) The agreement binding petitioners erected a barrier between respondents and any alternative source of the desired coverage, effectively foreclosing all possibility of competition anywhere in the relevant market. (b) The conduct with which petitioners are charged appears to have occurred outside of any regulatory or cooperative arrangement established by the laws of {the state}."

Given that Congress specifically allows the displacement of economic competition to a limited extent only, the FTC, the DOJ's Antitrust Division and state antitrust agencies should be free to investigate such conduct by companies. Indeed, the Tenth Amendment was virtually suspended during the Civil War as federal troops occupied the former Confederate states during the Reconstruction era. The 2010 ACA helps in part to avoid this option by ending insurance companies' preexisting illness rescissions by 2014, leaving ERISA plans under uncertain federal regulation. In 2002 and 2003, the Supreme Court rejected the ERISA preemption argument in two cases involving health insurance. In *Rush Prudential HMO, Inc. v. Moran,* the 2002 Supreme Court in a five to four decision, upheld an Illinois third-party review law that required HMOs to provide independent review of disputes between the primary care physician and the HMO, finding that such a state law was not preempted. The narrow vote favoring the plaintiff, Moran, saved for the states the opportunity to counter a major tactic of the insurance industry: to avoid scrutiny of such practices by using "preemption" to make redress more difficult for those aggrieved. Under its common-sense view of the matter, the High Court reasoned that because HMOs are risk-bearing organizations subject to state insurance regulation and almost universally regulated as insurers under state law, "the Illinois HMO Act is a law 'directed toward' the insurance industry and an 'insurance regulation'." *Rush Prudential HMO,* the losing party, was represented by John Glover Roberts, who argued that the decision to deny benefits should be seen appropriately as deferential to the plan "fiduciary" and was therefore preempted by ERISA. Associate Justice Stevens noted, "But it's not the fiduciary's decision, as I understand it. It's the insurance policy's decision."

Mr. Roberts replied,

"We think it's irrelevant whether it operates on the insurance policy or whether it operates on the plan. . . . Or someone to whom that discretion has been delegated under ERISA, and there's a provision in ERISA that allows them to say, this is the entity that is going to make the final decision. Under [section] 503, that is a fiduciary decision, the final denial or grant of benefits. That's the Federal remedy."

He was wrong. Section 503 of ERISA cited by Mr. Roberts says nothing about "discretion [being able to be] delegated under ERISA," nor were there any federal appellate decisions of that nature, and the one Court of Appeals decision relevant to that subject was from the Fourth Circuit in 1989 leaving the responsibility on the fiduciary. Since the *Rush* decision, John G. Roberts, Jr., who served as counsel to the insurance company and who argued thirty-nine cases before the Supreme Court, became chief justice of the High Court. His views on preemption beg the speculation of whether he will recuse himself when the Supreme Court hears the consolidated cases commenced by the state attorneys general attempt to find the ACA unconstitutional.

In the 2003 *Kentucky Association of Health Plans, Inc. v. Miller*, the Court tackled the "any willing provider rule" and unanimously held that the Kentucky laws, too, were not preempted by ERISA. The Court concluded that the laws did not deal with employee benefit plans as defined by ERISA but instead were insurance regulations. This was an important distinction—state insurance regulations were found not preempted by ERISA notwithstanding that they may "relate" to or be "connected" with benefit plans. As Associate Justice Scalia noted in his conclusion, "Today the Court makes a clean break from the McCarran-Ferguson factors in interpreting ERISA's savings clause."

We have also noted that whether a plan falls under federal or state authority has very different implications for health plans and beneficiaries. Generally, individuals wrongfully denied service under ERISA-covered plans may only sue under federal law for the cost of the denied benefits and legal fees. They cannot recover punitive damages for pain and suffering or lost income, as such remedies are presently available only under state law. Insurance and HMO activities such as the so-called "closed panels" of physicians would be open for either federal or state investigation. In addition, other exclusionary practices, especially those that operate interstate—such as limiting care or cherry-picking both the quantity and quality of "preferred providers," requiring coercively exorbitant "out of network" copayments for patients, requiring binding arbitration for both patients' claims and provider grievances, and the chilling effect on ERISA-defined due process created by "gag rules"—conceal the financial constraints and dubious incentives faced by capitated doctors. Any of the foregoing may modify the actuarial risk of the insurer by forcing the patient back to the capitated provider. *See* Plates 6, 16.

Fortunately, in recent years the courts have eroded somewhat the hitherto-presumed blanket preemptive effect of ERISA benefit plans by distinguishing "complete preemption" and "conflict" or "field" preemption from "ordinary preemption." Those decisions were largely based on the 1992 "tobacco case," *Cipollone v. Liggett Group, Inc.* ("any understanding of a preemption statute's scope rests primarily on 'a fair understanding of congressional purpose'"), and the 1984 *Silkwood v. Kerr-McGee Corp.* ("[it is] difficult to believe that Congress would, without comment, remove all means of judicial recourse for those injured by illegal conduct"), both of which were cited by the High Court in the 1996 *Medtronic, Inc. v. Lohr.* The effect of *Medtronic* was felt immediately. Echoing *Medtronic*, the federal Court of Appeals for the Ninth Circuit that December amended its slip opinion rendered two months earlier, and *Ardary v. Aetna Health Plans of California* was changed from

"Without clear guidance from the Supreme Court or Congress on these facts, we must begin with the strong presumption that Congress intends judicial review of administrative action including the denial of Medicare benefits."

to this:

"Without clear guidance from the Supreme Court or Congress on these facts, we must begin with the strong assumption that Congress does *not* intend to preempt state law causes of action with a federal statute."

While *Ardary* did not deconstruct judicial review as a right, the Supreme Court effectively removed it from its exclusive place in federal preemption and construed the validity of state actions in otherwise preempted arenas by amending further its slip opinion. It cited from the *Cipollone* decision: "[S]tate law is preempted if the law actually conflicts with federal law." The Court repeated its enduring 1947 admonishment in *Rice v. Santa Fe Elevator Corp.,* "start with the assumption that the historic police powers of the States were not to be superseded by the Federal Act unless that was the clear and manifest purpose of Congress." These "clear and manifest" purposes of Congress were implanted firmly into ERISA benefit plan preemption and its "savings clause," which removed benefit plans from the business of insurance by its "deemer clause." Brought together, these decisions imparted judicial erosion of the formerly ubiquitous and overly zealous preemptive effect of ERISA. They shed light on the traditional avenues of state law, as in 1976 in *Cantor v. Detroit Edison Co.*:

> "Even assuming that Congress did not intend the antitrust laws to apply to areas of the economy primarily regulated by a State, the enforcement of the antitrust laws would not be foreclosed in an essentially unregulated area."

Thus, when the *Pireno* Court approvingly cited *Royal Drug* to the effect that "the primary concern of both representatives of the insurance industry and Congress was that cooperative rate-making be exempt from the antitrust laws . . . [because of] the widespread view that it [was] very difficult to underwrite risks in an informed and responsible way without intra-industry cooperation," the High Court was unavoidably accepting that the *Royal* decision was reluctant to extend the McCarran-Ferguson exemption to the case before it "because the Pharmacy Agreements [in *Royal*] involve parties wholly outside the insurance industry." In today's language, a court would be able to deal with the antitrust issue and disregard the significance of whether the concerted action was "within" or "outside of" the insurance industry when comparing ERISA-based "administrative services only" risk assessment with indemnity actuarial determinations and underwriting.

As progeny of McCarran-Ferguson, New York insurance law (and most other states) now maintains oversight of insurance companies' sales, requires them to submit health and accident policies to the superintendent of insurance for approval, and prohibits them from engaging in unfair claims-settlement practices. We saw this earlier when New York Attorney General Cuomo's investigation reached an agreement with UHG to pay $50 million to a qualified nonprofit organization that will establish a new, independent database to help determine fair OON reimbursement rates for consumers throughout the United States. Nowhere, however, does the state of New York formally require insurers to engage in a peer review process, nor could it. While "peer reviewing" may lower costs of individuals' cases, for groups, it could constitute a boycott. As peer review narrows the risk of insurers, it invariably overprices and devalues the premium.

In *California Retail Liquor Dealers Assn. v. Mid-Cal Aluminum, Inc.*, the 1980 Supreme Court affirmed that two standards for antitrust immunity would be required if state action were to be considered. They were as follows: "First, the challenged restraint must be 'one clearly articulated and affirmatively expressed as state policy'; second, the policy must be 'actively supervised' by the State itself." For example, in 2006, Jay Angoff, a former Missouri insurance commissioner, and later director of the Obama administration's Office of Consumer Information and Insurance Oversight at DHHS, carefully noted this when speaking before the Antitrust Modernization Commission on the McCarran-Ferguson Act:

"The Missouri statute, for example, which is based on the NAIC model, provides in relevant part that 'two or more insurers may act in concert with each other and with others with respect to any matters pertaining to the making of rates or rating systems.' Although the statute does not mandate, it clearly permits it; there is therefore at least an argument that the first test under the state action doctrine is met. On the other hand, Missouri does not actively supervise any price-fixing among insurers. To the extent insurers may agree on price, whether on an insurer-to-insurer basis or through an insurance rating organization—defined in Missouri as an organization 'which has as its primary object and purpose the making and filing of rates,'—such agreements are clearly the product of private action, not state action."

As the 1974 Supreme Court said in *Jackson v. Metropolitan Edison Co.*,

> "the mere fact that a business is regulated by state law or agency does not convert its dealings into acts 'under color of state law'. . . [and] the existence of state action is to be determined after an examination of all the facts and circumstances."

Claims arise when patients believe they were wronged by the care their providers gave or withheld. Such claims are not expressly preempted, because they are also within the province of state law. Federal courts exercising jurisdiction in diversity cases apply state law except in "matters governed by the Federal constitution or by Acts of Congress," as the Supreme Court said in 1938 *Erie Railroad v. Tompkins*. As said by the 1941 Supreme Court from an antitrust point of view, in *Fashion Originators' Guild of America, Inc. v. Federal Trade Commission*, "even if [the situation alleged] were an acknowledged tort under the law of every state, that situation would not justify petitioners in combining together to regulate and restrain interstate commerce in violation of federal law." Therefore, the developing case law on malpractice suits against care providers, hospitals, and even HMOs on the theory of ostensible agency was clarifying the previously perceived ERISA protection.

ERISA muddies the waters in other ways. There is a sharp distinction between the relationship of patients to their HMO, PPO, PHO, or to a nonphysician-based, risk-bearing entity and the relationship between patients and their doctors. Although this relationship difference should be explained to employees in their ERISA-required Summary Plan Descriptions, they generally are not. At best, the explanations are vague and serve the employer, saying in murky words or substance only: "Our new, enhanced healthcare plan has managed care . . . etc." The doctor-patient relationship, however eroded, remains a common-law social contract far more compelling than insurance policy, or even ERISA, trust-based statutory language allows. Patients still see the HMO-type groups as organizations inspired with the apparent authority of the state or Congress that supplies doctors to care for them or that act as intermediaries for their company plan. Generally, although their doctor is increasingly understood to no longer be the independent caregiver of the past, patients still consider only their assigned or self-chosen doctor as the direct provider of the care they contracted for under the promises made by their plans.

For our purposes, the major insurance companies have seen fit to relinquish their McCarran-Ferguson exemption by abandoning the traditional risk-spreading insurance business in favor of "administrative services only"-type contracts for ERISA benefit plans that narrow the risk transfer. Moreover, they still effectively adjust the employers' self-insurance costs by absorbing the MCOs into their plan/policy language at the list prices inevitably resulting from small groups. Their penetration into risk shifting to state-licensed providers now ought to give both federal and state antitrust laws a crack at the antitrust problem to the extent that complete federal preemption no longer precludes that avenue of attack. It has opened an arena of "partial preemption," by which Congress may allow states to legislate and regulate to the extent permitted by federal law or where it does not conflict with federal law, such as with the 2010 ACA's Exchanges. This partial preemption would be similar to actions under the Medicaid Act, which is based on partially funded mandates from the federal government. Where a state Medicaid standard is silent and relevant Medicare regulations are unambiguous, the Medicare regulations would prevail absent a federally approved waiver.

It is clearly disjunctive for ERISA to deem company benefits plans, which use HMOs to manage care, to be noninsurance at the same time that the HMOs are regulated by the states pursuant to the insurance laws and are not benefit plans. The purpose of ERISA deeming benefit plans as noninsurance was, by preemption, solely to produce national uniformity of pensions and benefits among the states. This, of course, did not happen. By having a "dual option" in the HMO Act of 1973, Congress's requirement for employers to offer to employees federally "qualified" HMOs as well as indemnity companies' coverage allowed ERISA to put all plans partially back into state action and at the same time outside of the reach of indemnity insurer-type, common-law responsibility to the insured. Because the federal government's preemption of ERISA benefit plans does not reach most healthcare tort claims, it left employees working side by side with others having different benefits based on their dual-option "choice" and converted the constitutional purpose of remedial legislation to help all into *caveat emptor*.

VI. The Modern "Business of Insurance Companies"— the Emerging Nexus between McCarran-Ferguson and ERISA

> "Whatever the exact scope of the statutory term, it is clear where the focus was—it was on the relationship between the insurance company and the policyholder. Statutes aimed at protecting or regulating this relationship, directly or indirectly, are laws regulating the 'business of insurance.'"
>
> —*SEC v. National Securities, Inc.* (1969)

Associate Supreme Court Justice Souter, writing for the 1989 unanimous Court in *Travelers*, fashioned a nexus between ERISA preemption and state insurance law and between ERISA and McCarran-Ferguson when he stated this:

"We simply must go beyond the unhelpful text and the frustrating difficulty of defining its key term, and look instead to the objectives of the ERISA statute as a guide to the scope of the state law that Congress understood would survive."

The narrowed definition of federal preemption related to healthcare issues afforded by *Travelers* and *Cipollone* will presumably broaden as the Obama administration's ACA enters that arena, through federally subsidized Exchanges and abolishes exclusionary practices not previously regulated by the states. Regulation of MCOs and HMOs, which reinsure as well as deliver healthcare, and regulation by the states of insurance companies as actors in the non- or partial-preempted areas, will broaden, too. State health, justice, and insurance departments regulating provider organizations of doctors and hospitals would have to be aware of scrutiny of the practices of MCO healthcare brokers managing healthcare—only insurance-industry lobbying stands in the way on the federal level. In short, all the conditions of sharpening the McCarran-Ferguson section 2(b) exemption identified by *Royal Drug* are in place. The MCOs formally seen by McCarran-Ferguson as exempt from price-fixing violations will have to assume the risk, not simply manage it.

1. Three Criteria Indispensable to the "Business of Insurance"

The following is an examination of the *Royal Drug* Court's three-prong definition of the business of insurance in light of the fractured post- Millennium healthcare coverage system. *See* Plate 3.

Criterion 1

"Whether the practice has the effect of transferring or spreading a policyholder's risk."

With reputedly more than 150 million people under commercial managed care, the risk is far more spreadable than it ever was under traditional indemnity insurance, but it had to wait from 1982 until the Obama ACA of 2010 for that spread to take place on a national level. Though the 1982 *Pireno* Court explored the standards of the business of insurance set by *Royal Drug,* it did not reach the substantive "risk-spreading" issue, because it decided only the procedural one, that is, the contractual completion of the "transfer" of risk. Though the "transfer" is a material fact issue demarcated by the premium dollars and risk transferred to the insurer and, for the insurer, when assigned, to pay the provider on behalf of the beneficiary, that dollar figure is first determined by the actuarial investigation of the particular potential "loss" based on the "spread" of the risk.

Therefore, in citing *Royal Drug,* the *Pireno* Court found neither risk transfer nor risk spreading in the peer review process and viewed insurance company-inspired peer review a procedure available from *outside* the insurance industry *after* the risk had been transferred. Admittedly, it was designed to reduce the insurer's costs. The Court did not explore the issue of whether using such a procedure to minimize risk portends a devaluation of the premium, thus a method of price-stabilization. To the *Pireno* Court, peer review thus "functions only to determine whether the risk of the entire loss (the insured's cost of treatment) has been transferred . . . that is, whether the insured's loss falls within the policy limits." The "functions only" determination of "the entire loss" was clearly not the only reason for the case in controversy.

The Court also did not find that the peer-review process is used for medical quality purposes but only for reducing what "peers" "within the business of insurance companies" may call "unnecessary medical care"—in effect, the "quantity" of the care delivered. Nevertheless, the result of such a process increased insurance profits based on the risk narrowing of a prepaid premium only arguably lessening the rate of future premium growth. The Court's emphasis was this:

> "If the policy limits coverage to 'necessary' treatments and 'reasonable' charges for them, then that limitation is the measure of the risk that has actually been transferred to the insurer . . . [it is] the fundamental principle of insurance that the insurance policy defines the scope of risk assumed by the insurer from the insured."

Under indemnity insurance, therefore, the underwriter and actuary's calculations as to what may be considered the chances of "the insured's loss" and the "reasonable and necessary treatments" were assumed as the core of the business of insurance when contrasted with a business or speculative risk in ordinary commerce. However, the logic of allowing a change in the payout of benefits "after" the risk is transferred was not explored. Of course, the "peers" in the 1982 *Pireno* world have no parallel with the present day MCOs and the managed-care nurses, social workers, and "doctors-at-a- distance" reviewers.

Confusion was created by the Supreme Court in the distinctions made between "risk spreading," "risk transfer" and "risk underwriting" concerning the important first and second prongs of the "business of insurance" defined by *Royal Drug*. The Second Circuit Court of Appeals, in *Pireno v. New York State Chiropractic Association*, cited *Royal Drug*, too, but confusedly found that the *Royal* Court had seen "spreading of risk" and "underwriting of risk" as distinctly different activities. Note the use of both singular and plural when the Circuit Court said that

> "the Supreme Court's decision in *Royal Drug* had narrowed the § 2(b) exemption for the 'business of insurance' to such core insurance functions as the underwriting and spreading of risk . . . an activity or procedure that does not either transfer risk from insured to insurer or spread the risk among insureds [and] is not the business of insurance."

It is illustrative to examine how defining "insurance" muddles its description. Note the plural "such core insurance functions" used with the singular, "an activity or procedure," and "is not the business of insurance." The confusion abounds: The Syllabus of *Royal Drug* says, "Held: . . . (b) A primary element of an insurance contract is the underwriting or spreading of risk, *SEC v. Variable Annuity Life Ins. Co.*" Note the singular, "a primary element." However, as the Supreme Court first said in its 1906 decision, *United States v. Detroit Timber & Lumber Co.* and in the present rules of the Supreme Court, the Reporter of Decisions prepares a "syllabus" at the time a case is issued for the convenience of readers, but it constitutes no part of the opinion of the Court. In the Opinion, *Royal* tries to identify them as separate terms:

> "The primary elements of an insurance contract are the spreading and underwriting of a policyholder's risk. . . . The significance of underwriting or spreading of risk as an indispensable characteristic of insurance was recognized by this Court in *SEC v. Variable Annuity Life Ins. Co.* . . . The petitioners do not really dispute that the underwriting or spreading of risk is a critical determinant in identifying insurance." (Note the inconsistent use of the singular.)

The *Variable Annuity Life* decision cited did not use the term "risk spreading" at all, only that in annuities "there is no true underwriting of risks, the one earmark of insurance as it has commonly been conceived of in popular understanding and usage." Therefore, the Second Circuit *Pireno* Court saw both underwriting and risk spreading as separate identities "indispensable" to the definition of the business of insurance and went on to say, "Congress understood the business of insurance to be the underwriting and spreading of risk." However, "underwriting" was not a criterion considered by the Supreme Court for the first prong in *Pireno*. The Court said this:

> "In sum, *Royal Drug* identified three criteria relevant in determining whether a particular practice is part of the 'business of insurance' exempted from the antitrust laws by § 2(b):

333

first, whether the practice has the effect of transferring or spreading a policyholder's risk . . . "

Royal Drug was a five to four decision. The dissent, written by Associate Justice Brennan with whom Chief Justice Burger, Associate Justices Marshall and Powell joined, said:

"The Court, adopting the view of the Solicitor General, today holds that no provider agreements can be considered part of the 'business of insurance.' It contends that the 'underwriting or spreading of risk [is] an indispensable characteristic of insurance.'"

The use of the singular is in the original, and Associate Justice Brennan adds in a footnote:

"'Underwriting,' the Solicitor General argues [in the *Amicus* brief for the United States], means 'spread[ing] risk more widely or reduc[ing] the role of chance events.' . . . For purposes of argument, I will assume that this is a correct definition of 'underwriting' [and he cautions:] But see R. Holtom, Underwriting Principles and Practices 11 (1973)."

The Solicitor General's definitions were incorrect. In his book, Robert Holtom says of underwriting:

"[It] is a systematic technique for evaluating risks which are offered by prospective insureds. The function of underwriting involves evaluating, selecting, classifying and rating each risk, and establishing the standards of coverage and amount of protection to be offered to each acceptable risk."

Therefore, underwriting risk is an evaluation. Spreading risk is not the same, and neither is the "transfer" of the risk to one who assumes it the same as "spreading" the risk across groups. Risk is spread by advertising, by brokers, and reinsurance companies. Underwriting is chiefly considered a tool that uses statistics and mathematics. It is not a selling activity like risk spreading, nor does it transfer anything. However, it may reduce risk by "medically underwriting" policies, that is, by charging more for people who are sick or who are likely to become sick, or by refusing to sell policies to high-risk applicants—among the exclusionary methods ended by the ACA. Although in the process of issuing insurance policies underwriting could take place with an insured population as small as one, spreading the financial risk of insuring only one person is possible only by the process of "reinsurance," the transfer of risk across alternative institutions. Spreading a risk is accomplished only by having a greater number of policyholders. While "transfer," "underwriting," and "risk spreading" are all apparently considered to be "within" the insurance industry, "transfer" alone occurs only by the payment of the premium to the insurer, who then assumes the risk.

The potential for the "core" of insurance being involved in interstate commerce was indicated in a particularly incisive 1976 *Vanderbilt Law Review* article commenting on the lack of national uniformity and the inefficiency of regulation among the states created by McCarran-Ferguson: "State boundaries may have little relation to the demographic definition of natural underwriting populations for the accurate assessment of risk and cost." As life and health premium prices are ultimately based on vital statistics data that inevitably arise across state lines, the interstate nature of underwriting evaluations casts in doubt the reason for the federal McCarran-Ferguson exemption in healthcare. It is significant that in casualty insurance, state borders do not actuarially delimit data from insurable auto accidents, storm damages, and faulty products, although they appear as being priced that way. Thus, when the Supreme Court in *Pireno* saw "transferring or spreading a policyholder's risk" as the first indispensable practice of the business of insurance that distinguishes it from the business of insurers, it carried the conflating error from *Royal Drug* and ignored the Second Circuit's attempt to fix the mistake. As a result, the High Court effectively bypassed the issue of what criteria are "indispensable" to distinguish the "business of insurance" from the "business of insurance companies." *See* Plate 3.

In *Metropolitan Life Ins. Co. v. Mass.*, the 1985 Supreme Court said of ERISA: "Fully aware of this statutory complexity . . . . [t]he two pre- emption sections, while clear enough on their faces, perhaps are not a model of legislative drafting." Five years earlier, in *Nachman Corp. v. Pension Benefit Guaranty Corp.*, Associate Justice Stevens delivered the five-to-four decision referring to ERISA as a "comprehensive and reticulated statute," meaning that ERISA had broad legislative coverage over the entire area of employee benefits and that any remedies not specifically provided within the statute would generally not be supplied by the courts. However, in a 2000 *Tulane University Law Review* article, "Protecting Patient Rights Despite ERISA: Will the Supreme Court Allow States to Regulate Managed Care?", University of Oklahoma Professor of Law Donald T. Bogan argued that ERISA was not comprehensive in regard to benefit plans and illustrated the comprehensive regulation of pension funds compared to the minimal requirements for benefit plans. He noted throughout the article that the legislative history included a comprehensive investigation of the consumer abuses in the private pension industry that formed the impetus for ERISA's enactment but that ERISA "does not provide a complete and coordinated network of rules to govern non-pension employee benefits."

The Supreme Court often refers to *Couch on Insurance* as an authoritative source for expert guidance on almost any insurance law question. In 2003, outlining the specific congressional findings that prompted ERISA's enactment, it was stated that in *Couch* that "disclosure of information as a primary means of protecting employee benefits seems better suited to pensions . . . than health or disability insurance." On June 22, 2003, Chief Justice Rehnquist was widely quoted as saying relative to ERISA, "These are the Cinderella type cases, the statutory decisions left home to clean the stove, while the constitutional cases go to the ball." Reported in a footnote in the 2005 *Akron Law* Review, citing Tony Mauro's column in the National Law Journal *Courtside*, the Chief Justice, in his 2004 talk to the Fourth Circuit Court of Appeals, was said to have described ERISA as "The Employee Retirement, etc., law," adding that "you get so used to these acronyms that you forget what they stand for" and that "[t]he thing that stands out about [ERISA cases] is that they're dreary," and the only reason the Court grants them review was "duty, not choice."

Why is there such disparity, if not derision, in views about ERISA among jurists and legal scholars? In the 2002 Supreme Court case, *Rush Prudential HMO, Inc. v. Moran,* opining for the majority, Associate Justice Souter inserted a forward-looking constraint into preemption and a particularly prescient statement about the potential for universal healthcare:

"In sum, prior to ERISA's passage, Congress demonstrated an awareness of HMOs as risk-bearing organizations subject to state insurance regulation, the state [HMO Insurance] Act defines HMOs by reference to risk bearing. HMOs have taken over much business formerly performed by traditional indemnity insurers, and they are almost universally regulated as insurers under state law. That HMOs are not traditional 'indemnity' insurers is no matter; [citing *SEC v. Variable Annuity Life Ins. Co. of America*], 'we would not undertake to freeze the concepts of insurance . . . into the mold they fitted when these Federal Acts were passed.'"

The Court was basing its decision on the fact that the Illinois HMO Act provides that "in the event that the reviewing physician determines the covered service to be medically necessary," the HMO "shall provide" the service nonetheless. In deciding whether ERISA preempted the state law, the Court analyzed the issue using two tests: the common sense view of the matter standard, "Rush [the appellant] cannot checkmate common sense by trying to submerge HMOs' insurance features beneath an exclusive characterization of HMOs as providers of healthcare," and the McCarran-Ferguson Act's three-criterion test of the business of insurance. The "common sense" analysis required that in order for it to be determined that a law regulates insurance, the law must "be specifically directed towards" the insurance industry. Citing *Pilot Life Ins. Co. v. Dedeaux*, the *Rush Prudential HMO* Court found that the Illinois law met two of the three factors in the McCarran-Ferguson Act test and therefore was not preempted by ERISA.

For federal regulation of insurance to proceed under the ACA, the above raises a quite interesting question regarding whether Medicare and Medicaid are or are not "insurance" that we will discuss more fully later, and whether insurance companies today are involved in inter-state commerce and should be regulated by the federal government. For example, Amerigroup, Inc., a managed-care company that handles millions of managed Medicare and Medicaid patients, including state Children's Health Insurance Programs (SCHIP) in ten states, says, on its website: "**Our Vision:** We will be a different kind of health insurance company - a company that does well by doing good."

In other words, Amerigroup effectively concedes that their "core business" as an insurance company is not the "business of insurance" but the business of insurance "companies," which may be federally regulated because they are involved in interstate commerce even though they are managing state funds pursuant to the Medicaid and SCHIP laws.

> "CHIP is Title XXI of the Social Security Act and is a state and federal partnership that targets uninsured children and pregnant women in families with incomes too high to qualify for most state Medicaid programs, but often too low to afford private coverage. Within Federal guidelines, each State determines the design of its individual CHIP program, including eligibility parameters, benefit packages, payment levels for coverage, and administrative procedures."

The *Rush Prudential* Court also cited its 1999 holding in *UNUM Life Ins. Co v. Ward*. "Because the three factors are guideposts, a state law is not required to satisfy all three McCarran-Ferguson criteria to survive preemption." Agreeing that the McCarran-Ferguson criteria were "guideposts," and saying, "nothing in ERISA requires that medical necessity decisions be 'discretionary' in the first place," *Rush* affirmed the Seventh Circuit Court of Appeals decision that reversed the narrowing of the McCarran-Ferguson exemption by the lower court. The High Court also left open "whether the review mandated here may be described as going to a practice that 'spread[s] a policyholder's risk.'"

Associate Justice Clarence Thomas, with whom Chief Justice William H. Rehnquist and Justices Antonin Scalia and Anthony M.

Kennedy joined, agreed with the then insurance company counsel John G. Roberts' argument and dissented in favor of a fiduciary's unfettered rights to have a managed-care solution to the state-review issue at bar. Justice Thomas's unavailing argument was that ERISA's civil enforcement provision provides the exclusive means for actions asserting a claim for benefits under health plans governed by ERISA and therefore that state laws that create additional remedies were preempted; in effect, the dissent attempting to have ERISA supersede the McCarran-Ferguson Act enacted fifty-seven years earlier.

However, in 2004, the Supreme Court was heard from once again on ERISA, this time deciding diametrically opposite. *Aetna Health Inc. v. Davila* was one of two consolidated benefits denial cases brought on by writs of *certiorari* to the Court of Appeals for the Fifth Circuit. The Court examined whether ERISA precludes state lawsuits against ERISA plans. It held that ERISA completely preempts damage actions brought against managed-care organizations under the Texas Healthcare Liability Act, because ERISA itself provides the "exclusive" remedy for challenging ERISA plans' coverage decisions. Apparently, since the Constitution allows state law to license such doctors, *Davila* temporized that when acting in a health-care capacity, health insurers and HMOs remained liable for the consequences of negligent medical conduct. The opinion, again written by Associate Justice Thomas, this time for a unanimous Court, suggested, however, that health plans might be liable for treatment decisions made by employed physicians.

Because the central business of health insurers was seen to be coverage decisionmaking and not medical care provision, *Davila* created some minimal implications for access to remedies by patients who are harmed by substandard coverage determination practices. As he had in his dissent in *Rush Prudential*, because ERISA does not provide for either compensatory or punitive damages as the result of the wrongful denial of a benefit, Justice Thomas left it to Congress to deal with the question of whether ERISA beneficiaries should have any remedy for damages caused by coverage decisions. The opinion's main point was that ERISA provided a clear and unambiguous remedy at law, saying (this time, not "exclusively") that many preemption cases based on torts had been brought before the High Court and decided that way, and therefore reversed the decision of the Fifth Circuit Court of Appeals.

At this point, we can see that there is more than one way for the High Court or the federal government to go in ERISA "bad faith claims." First, the Court could reaffirm that ERISA's sole purpose was to set up a "comprehensive and reticulated" system to avoid the variegated and often unfair state-regulated pension systems that caused so many to lose their pension rights after moving across state lines. Few would object to that, because both the pension and benefit plan sections of ERISA were to be supervised by the Treasury and DOL and subject to the Internal Revenue Code. However, "bad faith benefit plan claims" were almost entirely based on denial of what employees rationally believed were conventional indemnity healthcare insurance claims, and they didn't understand why ERISA-based "trust" law should provide either more or less protection than those afforded employees under indemnity policies. It is true that the health and welfare benefits preemption sections were mitigated by a "savings clause," unambiguously "saved" state laws, and because they were predicated on conventional indemnity health insurance contracts, they provided a safe harbor from federal preemption. It left a gaping hole, however, in the protective mechanism of state action for the millions now "helped" by ERISA into employer-written benefit plans.

However, "damages" ought not be conflated with "benefits." The fact that the *Davila* Court considered that "treatment" was an issue, and that health plans' liability for treatment decisions made by employed physicians were distinguishable from fiduciary decisions about plan document language for pensions, shows a second, possibly more complex, way to look at the problem. Was ERISA's mission to be simply "law" or was it to be "equity"? That is, should the principles governing fairness to participants and beneficiaries be based on statutory construction or the common law? The ERISA statute, "Congressional Findings and Declaration of Policy," surely leans on equity, saying "that minimum standards be provided assuring the equitable character of such plans and their financial soundness"; and section 502(a)(3)(B) says: "(B) to obtain other appropriate equitable relief." Was it for the legal form of the statute or was it to allow room for recognizing that state courts' traditional solutions to health and welfare insurance problems were distinct from pension benefits?

While ERISA could provide the aggrieved *a* remedy, should it be the "exclusive" remedy, as decided in *Pilot Life*? Why could it not be analogous to the way the antitrust laws adjudicate *per se* violations compared with rule of reason methods of analysis, which allow for any evidence that might bear on an assessment of those effects; especially since the parties were otherwise similarly situated as patients and beneficiaries? In addition, would not *Davila* offer the federal labor secretary flexibility to expand what is still a dearth of regulations regarding benefit plans? There is little rational basis to call ERISA a "comprehensive and reticulated" law today, because pension rights only structurally intersect with healthcare at payment rights. For example, where corporations must accrue the costs of their retired employees' healthcare benefits for possibly decades to come based on Financial Accounting Standard 106 and having COBRA-extended insurance, there is no comparable accrual value for pensions even though statutorily insured by the Pension Benefits Guaranty Corporation.

The passage of Medicare took place thirty years after President Roosevelt signed the Old Age and Survivors Insurance trust fund, "Social Security," into law. It appears that the reason "pension" and "health and welfare benefits" went into ERISA together was that their history together was seen only in a few state statutes but largely in fairly permissive state common law. In the 1950s, the Senate Committee on Labor and Public Welfare found that this permissive legal environment facilitated a benefits "boom" in which, according to the 1958 Senate Committee on Labor and Public Welfare discussion on the Welfare and Pension Plans Disclosure Act, businesses and unions created tens of thousands of new plans that covered tens of millions of people. James Wooten, in *A Legislative and Political History of ERISA Preemption* (Part 3, 2008 *Journal of Pension Benefits*) wrote,

"Unfortunately, the resources funneled into these plans also created opportunities for unscrupulous individuals to enrich themselves at the expense of employees. Through the 1950s, government investigators exposed a series of cases in which benefit plans—in particular, multi-employer welfare plans—were mismanaged or looted."

States then began legislation to monitor or regulate benefit plans, leading Congress to pass the Welfare and Pension Plans Disclosure Act of 1958, which preempted what began to appear as a crazy quilt of state legislation and established disclosure requirements to limit fiduciary abuse. In the debate, then-Democratic Senator John F. Kennedy stated:

"The objective of the bill is to provide more adequate protection for the employee/beneficiaries of these plans through a uniform Federal disclosure act which will . . . make the facts available not only to the participants and the Federal Government but to the States, in order that any desired State regulation can be more effectively accomplished."

The Welfare and Pension Plan Disclosure Act Amendments of 1962 merely shifted responsibility for protection of plan assets from participants to the federal government to prevent fraud and poor administration.

In *Malone v. White Motor Corp.*, the 1978 Supreme Court found that

"The Disclosure Act clearly anticipated a broad regulatory role for the States. Section 10 of the Disclosure Act referred specifically to the 'future,' as well as 'present' laws of the states. Congress was aware that the States had thus far attempted little regulation of pension plans. The federal Disclosure Act was envisioned as laying a foundation for future state regulation. The Congress sought 'to provide adequate information in disclosure legislation for possible later State . . . regulatory laws.'"

However, any healthcare insurance obligations originally residing in the 1958 Welfare and Pension Plan Disclosure Act were for all intents and purposes repealed by New York's Republican Senator Jacob Javits' contribution to ERISA, which replaced partial federal preemption with "complete" or "field" preemption—just as that law had been affected by the McCarran-Ferguson Act's splitting of the state regulation of the business of insurance from that of the "business of insurance companies," except for "boycott, coercion, or intimidation." ERISA left to the commercial health-insurance industry the entire field of employees' health and welfare benefit plans to be embraced by a law covering the health of more than one hundred million with "noninsurance." ERISA is a law that today still has had added to it few relevant healthcare regulations supported by an admonishment for fiduciaries to act "prudently" when managing employees' benefits and sections on how to go to federal court for redress.

The McCarran-Ferguson exemption defines the boundaries of the "business of insurance," presuming that there shall be a spreading of risk, the presumption being that it would lower insurance premiums by having a large enough insured population. It would also reduce the individual hazard percentage of the aggregate premium income. This state "savings" congressional scheme appeared to have played little role in the Supreme Court's *Pireno* analysis, however. The Second Circuit Court in *Pireno* had emphasized that utilization by the insurer of the peer-review process was not at all an "insurance transaction" and that a "transfer of risk"—deemed to be equivalent to an "underwriting" or "guarantee" of risk—was also absent from peer review, thus making the peer-review process exempt from section 2(b) of McCarran-Ferguson and federal antitrust price-fixing scrutiny. As we said earlier, ERISA section 502 completely preempts not peer-review activity but only state law remedies that fall within the scope of that section.

With HMOs and MCOs, the precertification and concurrent reviews of healthcare merely amount to risk narrowing when they intervene before, during and, by denial or modification of the medical decision, after the risk transfer to the insurer or plan. This risk narrowing is the common currency of managed care. Lacking a policy based actuarial "guarantee," assumed in part by a risk-managed subscriber, the nonindemnity or ERISA plan health insurer using managed care does little to distinguish its real nature from that of a "business of insurance" transaction. Although true, no sensible employers would put into their

343

ERISA-required Summary Plan Description the words "Your Plan does not provide indemnity insurance."

Thus the sham created by the benefit-plan fiduciary whose "prudent" promise of care is not kept by its benefit-plan corespondent, the HMO, is what is concealed from both the employees and the courts as well. If a plaintiff challenges on the issue of breach of fiduciary duty for violation of the plan documents, where the managers, employers, or plan sponsors specifically agree to assume discretionary authority or responsibility with respect to a plan or its assets, ERISA still allows such fiduciary to change the terms of the plan or terminate the plan at will. Because of federal preemption, state insurance departments, too, have little power to represent their citizens who are aggrieved benefit-plan members as favorably as they can subscribers in disputes with an indemnity insurance company.

Criterion 2

"Second, whether the practice is an integral part of the policy relationship between the insurer and the insured."

Because ERISA-based health and welfare benefit plans are deemed noninsurance, they must be something else; it appears that they are. Because their establishment and performance are left up to employer/sponsors, fiduciaries, and contract administrators and insurance companies allegedly performing "administrative services only," ERISA-qualified "self-insured" plans can now offer their employees as participants and beneficiaries to purchase (or be credited for) healthcare costs at unreasonably high "list prices." The risk is spread only over the particular firm, because ERISA "multiemployer plans" do not vest healthcare benefits. The present-day list price of healthcare is based on few or no traditional indemnity insurance operations that involve actuarial work, because they must take all employees in the group. While the premium is often based on "self-funding," it is in reality a "minimum premium," pay-as-you-go method of expensing dollars for healthcare, raising the cost of healthcare for all in indemnity insurance, ERISA plans, and consequently, the prices of all goods produced.

In traditional indemnity insurance, a fixed annual premium must be paid in advance or funded for quarterly or semiannual payments in order for the risk assumption by the insurer; if claim losses run lower, the insurer keeps the difference as profit. Such insurer also often purchases stop-loss insurance to safeguard its claims liability. Precertification, the need for a "referring" primary care physician, and managed care or peer reviewers are then added to the equation to ensure that the insurer would benefit more than by the pure-market assumption of the risk. Of course, the managed-care component also adds direct administrative cost to the actuarially estimated, prevalence-of-illness-based premium, which is an add-on to the price of the policy paid by the insured or the self-insuring employer. The minimum premium method allows employers to pay part of their insurance premium each month and defer the other part until more money is needed to cover costs. While actuaries and underwriters can be used to establish the minimum premiums, the employers' risk is left to the capricious obligations bestowed by a nonspread risk and the care managers' self-serving churning of patients through the system.

With ordinary minimum premium insurance arrangements, employers deposit the claims-only portion as claim obligations are incurred and then only up to preset limits, plus a fee for the carrier to administer the claims. By using this funding method, the company's short-term cash flow usually improves, especially when managed care is involved. Over the long term, any chronic illnesses that develop from managing less-than-optimum care reduce the cash flow. Although the total actuarially based cost of care cannot be improved on, only the manipulated cost, now another player is to be paid—the managed-care entity—which quite clearly contributes only to the expense, ultimately incurring premium increases. The high cost of managed-care insurance was inadvertently foreseen in *Pireno*: "[the use of a peer review committee] as an aid in its decision-making process is a matter of indifference to the policyholder, whose only concern is *whether* his claim is paid, not *why* it is paid."

The larger the employee population, the closer the premium can come to actuarial and underwriting determinations based on valid prevalence and incidence statistics, but as found by actuaries during the writing of Clinton's Health Security Act, this applies only for companies with more than five thousand employees. Such ordinary self-insurance methods, nonetheless, appear to "transfer or spread the risk" and are based on "a policy between the insurer (read employer) and the insured (read employee)" as shown by the language of the ERISA Plan document. Because reinsurance companies are involved in the stop-loss arrangements, the minimum premium methodology, although hybridized by the "self"-insurance portion and sanitized for ERISA preemption, appears to be well within the business practice of the "insurance industry at large." Without risk-spread, stop-loss coverage for the employer or the primary insurer, the potential liability would make the minimum premium effort meaningless.

As the Supreme Court notably said in *Rush Prudential HMO, Inc. v. Moran*,

"The problem with Rush's argument is simply that a reinsurance contract does not take the primary insurer out of the insurance business . . . and capitation contracts do not relieve the HMO of its obligations to the beneficiary. The HMO is still bound to provide medical care to its members, and this is so regardless of the ability of physicians or third-party insurers to honor their contracts with the HMO. Nor do we see anything standing in the way of applying the saving clause if we assume that the general state definition of HMO would include a contractor that provides only administrative services for a self-funded plan. . . Rush hypothesizes a sort of medical matchmaker, bringing together ERISA plans and medical care providers; even if the latter bear all the risks, the matchmaker would be an HMO under the [state] definition."

Qualified ERISA benefit plans must be based on the issuance of a written plan document and administered according to the provisions contained in the overall governing plan document. If the plan's operational administration does not follow the plan document, the plan falls out of compliance and becomes subject to fines, sanctions, and disqualification. Under ERISA, healthcare coverage is based on federal preemption requirements for fiduciary standards of conduct on the part of sponsors, administrators, and any or all persons who

1. Exercise any discretionary authority or responsibility in the administration of the plan;
2. Exercise any authority or control concerning the management and disposition of plan assets; or
3. Render investment advice with respect to plan assets (or has any authority or responsibility to do so) for a fee or other compensation, other than regular compensation received as an employee of the plan sponsor.

Moreover, a fiduciary must act "with the care, skill, prudence and diligence under the circumstances then prevailing that a prudent man acting in a like capacity" would act. This rule is derived from the common law of trusts. It is an objective standard based upon how a person with experience and knowledge of a certain area would act in a given situation. However, it is not the same standard as used in insurance law regarding the responsibility of the insurer to the insured when a dispute arises. As the *Firestone* Court said, citing *Pilot Life*, "ERISA abounds with the language and terminology of trust law." In fact, an ERISA fiduciary would seem to be held to a higher standard than that of a commercial insurer when a dispute arises because the fiduciary has assumed "discretion" to act "prudently," while insurers have only a legal obligation requiring that they adhere to a standard of "reasonable care" while performing any acts that could foreseeably harm others. In the arena of "contract" versus "prudent discretion," indemnity insurance has ERISA beat hands down. "Prudent" thinking is not measured by its success, only that one gives sound consideration. When in dispute, the terms of an indemnity insurance contract must be looked at in the light least favorable to the one who proffered the policy, the insurer, versus the insured who pays the premium. With ERISA plans, "deference" is accorded the fiduciary who accepts discretion to oversee, with prudence, the expenditures for healthcare that come *de facto* from the employee/beneficiary's wages.

For the distinctions made by *Royal Drug* for entirely different purposes, ERISA's use of commercial managed-care insurers' "administrative services only" contracts ultimately affords no demonstrable aggregate cost saving to society. ERISA's self-insured healthcare coverage from "within the business of insurance *companies*," compared with those offering coverage for healthcare from "within the business of insurance" offer society only a deadweight loss. From the standpoint of the employee as a patient, all that results from ERISA-style preemption is the devaluation of promised care and increased net cash flow to the employer and the insurer from the managed-care- lessened risk. Moreover, the money "saved" reverts to the employer by managed-care activity and comes into direct conflict with the anti-inurement section of ERISA: "the assets of a plan shall never inure to the benefit of any employer and shall be held for the exclusive purposes of providing benefits to participants in the plan and their beneficiaries." Managed-care activities cannot be seriously considered "the assets of a plan."

The self-insured, non-business-of-insurance plan expenses are essentially the same as minimum premium equivalents to sums paid for employees, illness-by-illness, to insurers for the transfer and spreading of risk during the indemnity era but on a smaller scale, albeit for a much higher, now list price. The difference is that the new, higher premium prices are split with the managed-care review firms—today often operating entirely within the insurance industry—yet apparently held by *Pireno* and statute to be external to an insurance purpose. Moreover, the reason the cost in some cases appears to be lower today is only that the risk no longer rests, as before, solely on the insurer but now also on the plan beneficiary who assumes an increasing part of the risk by rising deductibles and copayments. The aggregate per capita price—the per capita price times the total population—of such healthcare is in effect a "sum of capitations." Its cost is largely hidden from the patient on whose behalf it was purchased. The cumulative amount of the actuarially determined cost per claimant appears virtually identical to the aggregate premiums, plus the out-of-pocket money paid by the insured in indemnity days. What remains hidden is the fact that the capitated doctor gets less than before, sharing his or her price with the MCO.

The aggregate price is not low for society, though, because more repeat interventions are subsequently required that include multiple appeals and often more pain and suffering as the result of the discounted amount of care rendered—the "quicker-and-sicker" discharges from hospital and the readmissions for the original complaint now made more complicated. Ostensibly, under ERISA protection, the insurance company that offers putative administrative services only, plus any stop-loss products from a business-of-insurance insurer, gets a "second bite at the apple." Stop-loss insurers also make out well under managed care, because the risk to the front-end carrier is controlled far better than in the indemnity days when the risk could not be manipulated from outside the doctor-patient relationship. This remains a major part of managed-care's market failure, which is being used increasingly by states to save money coming from government programs. Because of *Travelers* and *Kentucky v. Miller*, the fiduciary and administrative aspects of benefit plans are essentially all that ERISA now fully preempts from responsible state action. With the 2010 ACA's federal insurance oversight of state Exchanges and the MA bidding process, the acts of fiduciaries can be subject both to federal review of their healthcare purchases from MCOs and stop-loss insurance policies that come under state insurance laws and are regulated by the states. Moreover, ERISA plans' underwriting costs will inevitably come into a line comparable to the individual plans from the federal oversight of "unreasonable" HMO medical loss ratios.

As mentioned earlier, ERISA has a prohibition against the assets of a plan ever inuring to the benefit of an employer or plan sponsor. With the help of managed care, defined contributions to employee health-benefit plans, either by self-insurance or minimum premium, can be taken back as income by the employer and appear as a "saving" of money originally earmarked for healthcare but are in fact simply a devaluation of the actuarially based need. Although such savings are made in the name of conformance with the public policy, they represent a strategy that has never been proven to be of social benefit. What has been shown is a *de facto* reduction in the physical amount of care provided at a price unnecessarily much higher than its marginal cost.

The Supreme Court decisions, such as held in *Firestone* and *Pilot Life*, construing the purpose of ERISA health and welfare benefit plans to be the same as for participants in pension plans, are difficult to reconcile. By holding an ERISA plan fiduciary's role in a healthcare benefit plan to a higher standard than that of those actors in the state-regulated business of insurance, one could assume that ERISA-qualified plans have better protection for employees than state insurance law offers the insured, but facts show otherwise. For such relations to be representative of those between an "insurer and an insured," there would have to be a "policy" of sorts in the Summary Plan Description or employee booklet, and promises made therein would have to be kept or, in dispute, looked at first in a light less favorable to the fiduciary and more favorable to the beneficiary. This would be little different from an insurance contract. In fact, ERISA allows insurers to write the plans for the fiduciary. The passage of time has allowed a shift to take place where plan contractors are undoing the benefit plan's "promises" for the employer and are not being undone by the plans themselves. HMOs and self-insured plans, co-opted by the managed healthcare insurance industry, have produced a failed market. The reasonable expectation of the plan members that their benefits would be guaranteed by the HMOs is the link in the chain of events that, in large measure, nullifies Congress's remedial intent in ERISA's reallocation of the healthcare of more than half the American population into the federally preempted realm.

Unless significant negative legislative changes are made as the ACA rolls out through 2014, the Obama ACA of 2010 promises to make significant positive changes in the situation described earlier. The House version, abandoned during conference on the ACA, had a provision by Representative Dingell (D-MI) to end the McCarran-Ferguson exemption. It declared that the McCarran-Ferguson Act antitrust exemptions would

> "not apply to persons engaged in the business of health insurance or the business of medical malpractice insurance, with specified exceptions, including for: (1) collecting, compiling, classifying, or disseminating historical loss data;

(2) determining a loss development factor applicable to historical loss data; or (3) performing actuarial services if doing so does not involve a restraint of trade."

Thus, if there are no significant legislative reversals in the interim, the ACA is likely to face reconciliation measures even more positive over the following Congresses. Because a reconciliation process vote requires only a fifty-one-vote majority, it is likely that the Dingell bill will be revived, among others left out by the earlier conference negotiations. The 2011 Congress will be prepared to expand the options for "patient protection" and "affordable care" and even repeal the sections of McCarran-Ferguson related to health insurance and malpractice.

Criterion 3

"Third, whether the practice is limited to entities within the insurance industry."

We must accept as analogous "peer review" and "managed care"—if they are not, managed-care assertions of "improving the quality of care" vaporize, leaving only commercial profit taking, and *Pireno* Court's 1982 observation could not be made applicable today. Distinguishing between the "business of insurance" and the "business of insurance companies" may have been easy for the *Pireno* Court in 1982, because it was simply saying, "it is plain that the challenged peer review practices are not limited to entities within the insurance industry." Although the High Court did not deal with whether peer review practices are *wholly within* the insurance industry, it used the 1979 *Royal Drug's* express finding. The *Pireno* Court said:

"Unlike activities that occur wholly within the insurance industry—such as the claims adjustment process itself—the ancillary peer review practices at issue in these cases 'involve parties wholly outside the insurance industry.' [Referring to *Royal* Drug:] Application of this principle is particularly appropriate in this case because the Pharmacy Agreements involve parties wholly outside the insurance industry."

Clearly, the *Pireno* Court did not have more than the rudiments of a managed-care industry to deal with. However, although the Court did not reach that issue, the appellant, Union Labor Life Insurance Company, did and argued against the antitrust implications. The Court dodged the issue but offered a prescient antitrust illumination, noting:

> "More importantly, such arrangements [between insurance companies and parties outside the insurance industry] may prove contrary to the spirit as well as the letter of [McCarran], because they have the potential to restrain competition in non-insurance markets . . . Indeed [the] claim is that the practices restrain competition in a provider market . . . rather than an insurance market . . ."

It is virtually impossible today for MCOs to conceal from anyone their widespread involvement with their provider clients, employer clients, and healthcare insurance company clients and that they engage in such competition-restraining "practices" with entities "within," "partly within," "entirely within," or "wholly outside" the insurance industry and often a combination of them. Moreover, whether they are "noninsurance markets," as the McCarran-Ferguson criterion 3 issue in *Royal Drug*, or not was declaimed as irrelevant by Chief Justice John G. Roberts when acting as counsel for *Rush Prudential HMO*, which made unnecessary the ERISA deemer clause in that state. ERISA supersedure as federal supremacy would be compatible with repeal of the deemer clause for insurance purposes because of McCarran-Ferguson and the longstanding case law blocking preemption supported by the Tenth Amendment of the Constitution.

The following much-abridged list of major acquisitions and mergers shows that managed care is no longer "wholly outside" the insurance industry:

- Aetna acquired U.S. Healthcare in 1996, Value Behavioral Health (a psychiatric managed-care-by-telephone company) and, later, New York Life's managed and indemnity healthcare penetration for $1.35 billion.

- UHC, one of the nation's largest health insurers, is now wholly owned by UnitedHealth Group (UHG), having purchased MetraHealth in 1995—itself a combination of the healthcare divisions of Metropolitan Life and the Travelers Insurance Company. The agreement in May 1998 to buy Humana, Inc., United Behavioral Health, a UHG subsidiary contract with OptumHealth, continues to manage the "carve-out" mental health and substance abuse care for United Behavioral Health (notwithstanding the antidiscrimination Parity Acts).

- Humana was originally an insurer, then a hospital chain, and now an insurer, having spun off its hospitals in 1993 as a separate company, Galen Healthcare, Inc., which was later acquired by the chain that became Columbia/HCA HealthCare Corporation. In 1995, Humana acquired EMPHESYS Financial Group, Inc. a leading provider of health insurance in the small-group market, with 1.3 million members, and the tenth-largest commercial group health insurer. In 1997, Humana bought ChoiceCare Corporation, which had about 250,000 members and managed the largest HMO in the Cincinnati, Ohio area.

- WellPoint, Inc. acquired many of the formerly nonprofit Blue Cross plans and operates many others by license, among the mergers listed earlier. It includes a wholly owned subsidiary, NGS, a managed-care company covering over six thousand Medicare Part A hospital providers of service and 208,600 Part B physicians and other licensed providers of service, which acts as a fiscal intermediary contractor for Medicare.

Though the 1982 *Pireno* Court believed it essential that peer review be "limited to entities within the insurance industry," it was no longer "plain" by 2002 in the *Rush Prudential HMO* Court. As the High Court said in *Rush*, ironically citing the 1959 *SEC v. Variable Annuity Life Ins. Co. of America*, "'we would not undertake to freeze the concepts of insurance' . . . into the mold they fitted when these Federal Acts were passed." Almost all such practices today either are entirely within the insurance "industry" or intimately tied to it by the common-law rules of agency—"the one who acts through another, acts in his or her own interests."

The big insurers' market power reached astounding proportions. For example, as of December 1995, there were 617,362 physicians in the United States and in 1998, Aetna said it had 50 percent of the nation's doctors under contract and was adding one to two thousand a month. The failed UHC-Humana merger would have controlled 602,000 subscribers in HMOs in Miami, or 48 percent of the market, according to InterStudy, a nonprofit, multinational, study-abroad organization. Apparently aware of market-power implications, UHC's CEO mentioned in an interview that although United and Humana would have 1.4 million customers in all types of healthcare, this would cover only about 10 percent of Florida's then 14.7 million people. Not mentioned, of course, was that far fewer than the fourteen million people in Florida were under commercial healthcare or in HMOs, so the UHC-Humana HMO marketspace would have controlled a significantly greater number than 10 percent of those already insured. In fact, by 2002, there were 3,631,676 commercial HMO subscribers and 1,800,000 Medicare HMO members in Florida. This would have given United/Humana more than 25 percent of the HMO marketspace, which was 30 percent of all insurance coverage at the time. Humana chair and founder David Jones was quoted in *The New York Times,* May 1998, as suggesting that doctors who spend too much tending their patients "can be identified and counseled."

As reported in an interesting 2010 thesis by Megan Gay, PhD of Northeastern University, the following five mergers also occurred in the Florida HMO market between 2001 and 2003:

(1) Prudential Healthcare Plan, Inc. was acquired by Aetna in 2001; (2) Beacon Health Plan, Inc. was acquired by Vista Healthplan, Inc. in 2002; (3) Healthplan Southeast, Inc. was acquired by Vista Healthplan, Inc. in 2002; (4) Physicians Healthcare Plans, Inc. was acquired by Amerigroup Florida, Inc. in 2003; and (5) American Medical Healthcare, Inc. was acquired by Health Options (a part of the Blue Cross Blue Shield network) in 2003.

Studying enrollment by county, all these acquisitions occurred during what Dr. Gay called the HMOs' "Backlash Period" of *disenrollment* in the Florida market. Dr. Gay used the Herfindahl-Hirschman Index, discussed earlier, to demonstrate the steady overall level of decrease in the Florida HMO market concentration during the period. This exposed further the waste and the deadweight losses incurred by the managed-care market failure. In the Chicago market for HMOs, UHC and Humana would have a 28 percent market share, ahead of HMO Illinois, the Blue Cross/Blue Shield Plan, with 24 percent. The economic health of these mergers should have been seriously questioned. Economic analysts have noted it has taken twelve to eighteen months for several health-care companies to get back on their feet after big merger deals. Because the merger alone does not stimulate an eagerness to raise premium prices, in any merger, a significant part of the short-term "savings" to the new company will come only from lower payments to hospitals and doctors, not from efficiencies.

How should these data-disseminating and coercive price-fixing structures be looked at today in light of the 1944 *United States v. South-Eastern Underwriters Assn.* Court, which said, "[I]t does not follow from this that the Court is powerless to examine the entire transaction . . . in order to determine whether there may be a chain of events which becomes interstate commerce"?

As Judge Posner observed in the 1995 federal Seventh Circuit Court of Appeals antitrust case, *Blue Cross/Blue Shield United of Wisconsin v. Marshfield Clinic*:

"From a short-term financial standpoint—which we do not suggest is the only standpoint that an HMO is likely to have— the HMO's incentive is to keep you healthy if it can but if you get very sick, and are unlikely to recover to a healthy state involving few medical expenses, to let you die as quickly and cheaply as possible."

The ERISA healthcare benefits regulatory void need not be saved solely for the federal government to fill with regulations, nor should more decades have to pass for the federal courts to develop a body of common law in light of the evolving Circuit and Supreme Court decisions presaging a greater opportunity for relief at the state level. Even the presence of federal regulations on the subject is deemed by the Supreme Court to be insufficient for inferring a congressional intent to totally preempt state regulation. As stated in the 1985 Supreme Court's *Hillsborough County v. Automated Medical Laboratories*, "[We would] seldom infer, solely from the comprehensiveness of federal regulations, an intent to preempt, in its entirety a field related to health and safety." It is difficult to believe that so much settled law on the rights of states to "protect the health and safety of [their] citizens" was intended by Congress in enacting ERISA to completely preempt state law and leave a void of nonregulation of conflict-laden fiduciaries. Certainly, there was no express intention in the legislative history, leaving much room for nonactivist judicial reconstruction.

In *Paul v. Virginia*, the 1869 Supreme Court stated that, "Issuing a policy of insurance is not a transaction of commerce" and properly governed by local laws. Seventy-five years later, the High Court in *South-Eastern Underwriters* did not overrule *Paul*, nor did it say that the states could not continue to regulate the insurance industry. It said, citing 1824 *Gibbons v. Ogden* unambiguously, that Congress has the power under the Constitution to govern transactions that "affect the peoples of more States than one," that the federal government could also do so, and that Congress had shown that intent by enacting the 1890 Sherman Act. When McCarran-Ferguson set constraints on Congress, it made an important disclaimer regarding Congress's powers, in words and substance saying that no act of Congress *other* than one specifically related to the business of insurance would be construed to invalidate, impair, or supersede any state law limited to regulation or taxation of the business of insurance. In its Declaration of Policy, 1945 McCarran-Ferguson states:

> "Congress hereby declares that the continued regulation and taxation by the several States of the business of insurance is in the public interest, and that silence on the part of the Congress shall not be construed to impose any barrier to the regulation or taxation of such business by the several States."

The mixed and blurred distinction between the "business of insurance" and that of "insurance companies" had a long history. In his 2009 biography of Supreme Court Justice Louis D. Brandeis, Melvin I. Urofsky, professor of law and public policy at Virginia Commonwealth University, discusses Brandeis's reform proposals for state regulation of the insurance industry prior to his appointment to the High Court. Brandeis believed that states, not the federal government, should tighten

"state regulations over insurance companies' use of policyholders' moneys, abolishing lavish commissions, protecting policies from involuntary forfeiture, what we now call greater transparency as to officers and directors and the ties they had to other firms that used the reserve funds, and fuller disclosure in financial reports. At the time each state had its own insurance regulations, since an 1869 Supreme Court decision [*Paul v. Virginia*] held insurance not to be a matter of interstate commerce."

It is difficult to extricate a distinction between the "insurance business" and "insurance *company* business" from the above description of the need for regulation. Professor Urofsky concludes, "Brandeis did not address the issues of whether insurance companies did interstate business; he knew they did."

Since McCarran-Ferguson in 1945, after such a long congressional silence, the issue of whether insurance can be considered involved in interstate commerce ripened with the blossoming of the 1996 HIPAA and 2008 Parity Acts and the 2010 ACA. With most healthcare insurers having both IN and OON benefits in their contracts, they can hardly describe their economic activity as being "wholly" within a state. *Paul v. Virginia* precisely used "contracts"—as being creatures of the several states—to decide that insurance policies were not "commerce." However, the 1947 Supreme Court said in *United States v. Yellow Cab Co.*, "The transportation of such passengers and their luggage between stations in Chicago is clearly a part of the stream of interstate commerce," referring to an 1870 case, *The Daniel Ball*, and continued:

"When persons or goods move from a point of origin in one state to a point of destination in another, the fact that a part of that journey consists of transportation by an independent agency solely within the boundaries of one state does not make that portion of the trip any less interstate in character. *That portion must be viewed in its relation to the entire journey, rather than in isolation. So viewed, it is an integral step in the interstate movement,"* [also referring to a 1922 case, *Stafford v. Wallace*]. (Emphasis made by the *Yellow Cab* Court.)

Therefore, because McCarran-Ferguson did not preclude Congress, and by extension the federal government, from plenary participation in the oversight and monitoring of the business of insurance if boycott, coercion, or intimidation were involved, much of congressional "silence" on state-exempted insurance regulation was splintered by the 2010 ACA provisions relating to the state Exchanges and privatized MA funding reductions. Ultimately, the MCO/HMO industry will have no safe harbor from the antitrust laws, or the 2010 ACA will assume its rightful duties in federal regulation of the long-overlooked interstate commerce of managed-care insurance companies.

2. Pundits and Politicians

Although there is not yet a constitutional "right to treatment," there certainly has been an acknowledged need over the past sixty years to pass remedial health and welfare legislation "to promote the general welfare." Such issues as unemployment insurance, medical care for the poor, the disabled, and the elderly, tax-supported public education, and many other laws have transformed our society's attitudes toward those citizens more generally vulnerable. Our healthcare system is now one of the largest and most expensive in the world—arguably with among the least healthy of middle classes. In 1997, President Clinton appointed a broad-based, public-sector commission to study problems arising from managed care. In November, he directed five federal departments, including the DOL, to review the respective health plans they administer or supervise. As might have been expected, the commission announced in March 1998 that it had reached no consensus on recommendations for implementing the president's proposed "Healthcare Consumer Bill of Rights." After surveying the departmental reports, he issued an executive order directing them to implement specific initiatives for compliance with the Patient Bill of Rights.

The DOL announced that it would propose regulations governing health-plans' internal claims procedures ensuring that plan participants would receive a fair and efficient benefits review. The regulations also would require plans to provide clear and understandable disclosures in their Summary Plan Documents consistent with the Patient Bill of Rights. This disclosure information would cover OON services, conditions for access to specialty medical care, and preauthorization and utilization review procedures. Finally, the proposed regulations were to stress that plan fiduciaries, when selecting healthcare-provider services, must assess the quality of medical services, collect enrollee satisfaction statistics, and analyze the scope of the participant's choices.

Nonetheless, politicians and pundits during the cost-containment era continued to proclaim their role as the efficiency experts of the healthcare economy. For example, Duke University Law Professor Clark C. Havighurst, an advocate of what he called "prospective self-denial," lamented that "The sensitiveness of the 'R-word' [ration-ing] is significant because it illustrates the extraordinary difficulty of ensuring that the nation's scarce [*sic*] resources are efficiently allocated between healthcare and other uses." He extolled "selective contract-ing" under managed care and the "designating as preferred providers only those who agree to cooperate in cost containment." Calling for a "President's Commission on Effectiveness and Efficiency in Health-care," Havighurst said, "It should be possible by private action to end the medical profession's dominance and to restore to consumers their customary sovereignty—their right to write their own tickets in buy-ing healthcare services." He may not have remembered what the 1972 Supreme Court said in *Stanley v. Illinois*:

> "The Constitution recognizes higher values than speed and efficiency. Indeed, one might fairly say on the Bill of Rights in general, and the Due Process Clause in particular, that they were designed to protect the fragile values of a vulnerable citi-zenry from the overbearing concern for efficiency and efficacy that may characterize praiseworthy government officials no less, and perhaps more, than mediocre ones."

Healthcare professionals at all levels have always been intimately familiar with private-sector collective efforts to establish standards and clinical-practice guidelines. Nevertheless, because of their training and association membership, professionals subscribe to codes of ethics defining the standards of conduct they expect to uphold. However, the "learned professions exception" to the antitrust laws has been sharply eroded in recent years, and the DOJ, the FTC, and private litigants have successfully attacked various provisions of such professional codes of ethics. As Clinton's Assistant Attorney General Joel I. Klein observed, with somewhat narrowed emphasis in the 1990s,

> "Ironically, this system was developed to protect consumers against abuse in medical pricing and services at a time when the antitrust laws played no role. Today, it has become a critical element in medicine's legal vulnerability."

The prohibition against advertising and competitive bidding, the use of the accreditation process by commercial trade associations, and the uniquely comprehensive systems of professional self-regulation and common law that enveloped medicine, law, and architecture, were forced to accommodate marketplace reality. However, some of the commercial insurance organizations have continued the boycotting practices, especially through the use of "preferred providers" for "membership" in "in-network" MCOs, though the providers they prefer have no special training of significance beyond that of their peers.

Since the 1975 Supreme Court holding in *Goldfarb v. Virginia State Bar*—stating that lawyers engage in "trade or commerce" notwithstanding their licensing by state bars—every major professional association and organization has systematically scrutinized its code of ethics or similar documents in search of any provision having potential antitrust vulnerability, either voluntarily or under the prodding of an antitrust enforcement effort. *Goldfarb* found that minimum fee schedules for title examinations by attorneys, enforced by state bar associations, violated section 1 of the Sherman Act: "Congress did not intend any sweeping 'learned profession' exclusion from the Sherman Act; a title examination is a service, and the exchange of such a service for money is 'commerce' in the common usage of that term." It is interesting to note that the 1975 *Goldfarb* High Court finding of no difference in whether a lawyer performs in "trade or commerce" is still commerce, if engaged in price fixing, had no influence four years later in *Royal Drug*, reasoning that an insurance company can have within it both its insurance function and its interstate business activities yet *not* be involved in interstate commerce for purposes of the Sherman Act. Paradoxically, six years later in *Arizona v. Maricopa County Medical Society*, another price-fixing case, the High Court simply accepted that doctors' activities *were* involved in interstate commerce for purposes of the Sherman Act violation.

In antitrust law scrutiny, each healthcare provider has been viewed as a separate competitive entity with all that implies in terms of constraints upon joint action. The shift to aggressive enforcement of the antitrust laws against healthcare provider groups began when the American healthcare industry was organized on a fee-for-service basis, with the healthcare professional and the patient determining the course of treatment, and indemnity insurance companies assuming the risk. As we have seen, that model was substantially altered in recent years thanks to the rapid proliferation of employer "self-insurance" inspired by the passage of ERISA and the process of transformation from care-access to care-denial by the HMO-managed-care insurance industry. In any event, "self-insured employers" is essentially a business-centered euphemism. It is the employee that is being insured, not the employer. Congress and the Supreme Court certainly knew that, because they based their legal concept of insurance on the McCarran-Ferguson second criterion for the term "the business of insurance"— "Second, whether the practice is an integral part of the policy relationship between the insurer and the insured." It is clear to all that when employees of a self-insured employer seek access for healthcare, they do not have to ask the employer to pay for the care. They simply display their insurance company "plan" card, and the doctor or hospital usually accepts the assignment.

The fact that the coverage is purchased or paid for by the employer is irrelevant, because it is the employee's loss (not of money but of health) that is insured against. Both self-funded and indemnity purchases arise from contractual relations with employees, and neither method arises simply from employer largesse. From the perspective of the employee/ beneficiary, it is a fought-for fringe benefit, and any reduction of it constitutes a *de facto* wage- or benefit-value decrease; its existence arose out of either wage-labor negotiations or employer-employer market-based competition.

The massive reconfiguration of the health-benefits arena, engendered by the surge of ERISA-employer self-insurance, brought a new element into the equation: the MCO hired specifically to control the delivery and the output of benefits. The profits of the MCO were designed to be directly proportionate to the ability to return to its clients as income as much as possible of the value of employees' previously won fringe benefits. Despite employer claims to have accomplished that "benefit" by instituting managed- care "economies of scale" and "improvement in quality," such inurement could only have been accomplished either by arranging for lower prices per unit charged by healthcare providers or by actively "managing" the care, thus reducing output. As we have noted, they are the classic equivalents of Areeda-Turner's ill-fated "monopsonist," who is either "eliminating that loss by reducing its output or, where the highest obtainable price is below average variable cost at all levels of output, by ceasing operations altogether." It is the essence of why managed-care insurance is a market failure. However, in this case, its list-price (administrative) costs are so high and able to be divided among several intermediaries that the social benefits are reciprocally lower—a net, deadweight loss.

The effect of the 2010 ACA began making itself felt almost immediately. By June, *The Washington Post* reported that the high-deductible plans linked to the 2003 law that created HSAs were becoming

"a familiar fixture on the insurance landscape, even though they get mixed reviews from many consumers and health-policy experts . . . The [new] healthcare overhaul law makes two specific changes involving HSAs: Starting in January, you can no longer use those funds tax-free for over-the-counter medications unless they're prescribed by a doctor. In addition, if you use your HSA for nonmedical expenses, you'll be hit with a 20 percent penalty instead of the current 10 percent."

On July 20, 2010, *Health Plan Week*—a newsletter of *Health Business Daily*, which calls itself "the industry's leading source of business, financial and regulatory news of health plans, PPOs and POS plans"— reported that since the MLR floor is 85 percent for the large-group market, health plans that don't meet the minimum MLR will be required to pay a rebate to customers. As a result, the article pointed out that

"the rule of 80% for their individual and small group products already has caused some health plans to restructure the way they pay brokers and agents. Other insurers have decided to scale back or exit the individual market. One health plan has said it will close its doors at the end of the year due in large part to the new rule, according to interviews and documents obtained by HPW. Other regulations, such as the exclusion of lifetime and annual benefit limits, also could have a negative impact on the individual and small group markets."

Because healthcare has a rising cost curve, the managed-care inducement made to doctors of adding volume reduced provider efficiency and increased doctors and patients' risks and costs, as patients began to cut their pills in half or self-medicate. In addition, it stimulated a vast new subacute and chronically ill population, in which costs inevitably would increase in proportion to the growth of the undertreated. Because the epidemiological understanding of all of this fell outside the narrowly practical purviews of Congress's McCarran-Ferguson/ERISA scheme, federal antitrust authorities were not appropriately able to act to combat illegal collusive conduct in the managed-care insurance industry as it related to the health of the population.

By the end of the first post-Millennium decade, there was a broad variety of managed-health plans and managed-care companies to administer them, plus an array of private corporations and government entities to purchase both healthcare plans and managed-care services. The shift to privately managed healthcare had concomitantly eroded the self-regulatory role of the professional medical and hospital associations. Because many members were also employed by MCOs, the managed-care industry acted collectively to develop clinical-practice guidelines, quality standards, and accreditation programs principally derived via M&R, NCQA, and InterQual. Accordingly, the need for close antitrust scrutiny of this newly shrink-wrapped, commercial "self-regulatory" effort became much more acute than it was when the providers, acting collectively through professional associations, with ethical codes and mindful of the potential liabilities, performed the function of providing direct patient healthcare.

Apparently, though managed care's collusive behavior was not ripe enough for government intervention, actions against doctors were ripe enough for the DOJ to undertake. In August 1998, the DOJ moved in U.S. District Court in Delaware to stop what it alleged was an illegal boycott by the Federation of Physicians and Dentists, a national organization operating elsewhere as a certified collective bargaining agent for doctors who were employees of public hospitals and other entities. Assistant Attorney General Joel I. Klein, in charge of the antitrust division, said that the Delaware Federation had represented independent practitioners for whom it could not lawfully serve as a collective bargaining agent: "There is an ongoing discussion about the role of managed care, and there are pending proposals to enact various reforms." He explained that while a "third-party messenger" may be used by independent doctors to transmit information and speed up the negotiation process with insurance plans and doctors, it may not be used to strengthen the bargaining power of those it serves. By 2010, the move toward organizing "hospitalists"—primary care physicians who treat hospital patients exclusively—began to change from single doctors employed by individual hospitals to organized groups contracting with hospitals to provide round-the-clock, "intensivist," managed-care-paid providers to work the intensive-care units. Their role was divorced from that of the primary-care "family" doctors of prior years; after the patient was discharged, they had no further contact with the patient and were no longer in a position to coordinate care with the multiple specialists brought into the hospital scene to care for the patient.

The *Antitrust Enforcement Policy in Healthcare* issued in 1993 and 1994 by the DOJ and the FTC, together with the various business reviews, advisory opinions, and enforcement actions, involved scrutiny of the hospital and physician-provider side of the healthcare equation. It was largely prodded by the insurance industry's disquiet that such groups could collude to preserve fee-for-service and the high-cost healthcare delivery system against the inroads of managed care. Given the managed-care industry's undeniable hegemony in the post-Millennium healthcare environment, it would seem to be timely and fair to hold managed-care entities to antitrust standards of conduct similar to those applied previously and so rigorously to practitioners and other healthcare providers. The new antitrust enforcement policy began under the Obama administration in October of 2010, when the DOJ filed a civil antitrust lawsuit against Blue Cross/Blue Shield of Michigan, alleging that the insurer's MFN pacts with hospitals across the state raised prices, stifled competition from other insurers, and discouraged discounts. The complaint alleged that BCBSM agreed to raise the prices it paid some hospitals to get the MFNs, thus buying protection from competitors by increasing its own costs, and negotiated clauses in its contracts requiring that hospitals charge any competing insurer as much as 40 percent more than they charged Blue Cross. In exchange, Blue Cross agreed to pay many Michigan hospitals higher prices for their services.

Policyholders and subscribers—the consumers and beneficiaries of healthcare coverage—do not contractually agree to the mechanism of managed-care review or monitoring of their claims since it is rarely an "informed" part of the contract or benefit plan documents. The benefits proffered are rarely understood by beneficiaries as subject to an outsider's self-serving ability to negate their claims. However, the hundreds of small-group insurers' offering coverage through health indemnity plans, and the individual indemnity plans covering millions, as well as the pure insurance nature of life and casualty indemnity policies, may keep alive the public's memory of the indemnity health-insurance "contract." A report in *American Medical News* on October 25, 2010 pointed out:

> "A government investigation into the policies of four of the nation's largest insurers shows that during a three-year period, they denied healthcare coverage to more than 651,000 people based on prior medical history [and], in addition to denials in the individual health insurance market, the House Committee on Energy and Commerce discovered that from 2007 through 2009, Aetna, Humana, UnitedHealth Group, and WellPoint refused to pay 212,800 claims due to preexisting conditions."

Certainly, the 2010 health reform law, which requires coverage of people with preexisting conditions, coverage for dependent children up to age twenty-six, and a ban on annual and lifetime limits on coverage, will see to those needed changes as the dialogue with the states rolls out to 2014. Because ERISA plans are "not insurance," the required Summary Plan Descriptions for the employees generally use broadly felicitous language to explain how the plan uses managed-care "professional reviewers" to "save money, improve benefits, and the quality of care." The contract of insurance established by a premium payment to a state-regulated HMO offers a difference, however. It provides the expectation of specific performance, which is generally understood by a prudent person to mean that the premium payment to an insurer assumes the risk that formerly rested on the insured and that the HMO doctor is relatively unhampered by third parties. That would have been the way Congress expected at the time the HMO Act was enacted with specific definitions for federally "qualified" HMOs. However, that time has long passed with the change to the for-profit HMO. These for-profit organizations would hardly disclose in the Plan Documents they supply to the employee the economic nature of the insurer-doctor fee arrangements such as "withholdings" that are divided by the end of the year based on doctors' "efficiencies" and global profits garnered from the employer's relations with the insurance company. Any organized interference with this beneficiary understanding is collusion, especially because the employee/stakeholder is unaware of or "indifferent"—as said by the Supreme Court in *Pireno*—to the collusive determination of "medical necessity" by persons who financially benefit by reducing their clients' costs through lowering providers' prices.

The Restatement of Trusts, the most respected source of authority on trust common law, used by and second only to the courts' decisions, points out:

"If discretion is conferred upon the trustee in the exercise of a power, the court will not interfere unless the trustee in the exercising or failing to exercise the power . . . fails to exercise his judgment or acts beyond the bounds of reasonable judgment."

The managed-care industry's market failure will also become further evident as greater attention is paid to the horizontal and vertical healthcare mergers, the behavior of trustees of the ERISA plans, and their negative effect on the system of affordable care for all in the United States.

3. Survey Satisfaction with the System?

In October 1996, the GAO recommended to HCFA (now CMS) several steps the agency would take to help beneficiaries choose their plans wisely. Because HCFA was not required by the BBA of 1997 to report on beneficiaries' HMO disenrollment rates until autumn 1999, the General Accounting Office responded to a request by the Senate Special Committee on Aging that early data be evaluated. The findings were startling: in 194 plans with more than 250 members surveyed, the GAO found that in over 20 percent of Medicare HMOs disenrollment rates exceeded 21 percent, even topping 71 percent in some areas.

It was particularly significant, too, that in 1996 in ninety-two urban markets served by two or more plans, 36 percent of HMO disenrollees switched to fee-for-service rather than join another HMO. Even in markets served by multiple plans, the proportion of beneficiaries changing to fee-for-service could run high. For example, in Miami, which was served by nine HMOs, 46 percent of beneficiaries who had left UHC of Florida in 1996 chose fee-for-service over another HMO. The UHC-Humana merger would have controlled 49 percent of this market had it not peremptorily failed. Since privatization of Social Security was receiving such a cool reception from beneficiaries, Congress, in the 1997 Republican-promoted BBA, offered the thirty-eight million beneficiaries a bewildering array of managed-care options—optimistically called "choices"—for the coming year to stimulate the drive to privatization of Medicare. To implement the spirit of the law, the government planned an extensive education and publicity campaign to take place in 1998.

Less optimistically than the congressional "privatizers," on June 10, *The New York Times* reported that Michael Hash, the deputy administrator of HCFA in charge of the program said, "Many beneficiaries do not understand the basics of the original Medicare program, much less the exotic variations of managed healthcare devised by Congress." Marilyn Moon, a trustee of the Medicare trust fund, was reported as saying that at least 20 percent of beneficiaries had Alzheimer's disease, memory problems, or other mental impairments that would make it difficult for them to understand the new options. The explanatory handbook would have required five hundred versions of HMO performance, each one tailored to a specific local market. After stating that HCFA was planning to mail the new Medicare handbooks to thirty-eight million beneficiaries in the fall ten days later, Hash said, that after consideration, the agency would limit distribution of the handbooks to just 5.5 million beneficiaries in five states the first year. Representative Pete Stark of California, the ranking Democrat on the Ways and Means Subcommittee on Health, called the handbook "a waste of $40 million." Rep. Stark said that the experience of the first five states "will probably reveal all kinds of unanticipated problems, which can be corrected before we send manuals to all parts of the country." An AARP survey found that over 30 percent of beneficiaries "knew almost nothing about HMOs," and that members from both parties had criticized the printed piece, saying it would prompt a flood of questions from confused constituents.

As studies showed, managed care's acceptance problem was not just with the aged, disabled, and poor. The Department of Education found in 1993 that ninety million adults were either illiterate or could perform only simple literacy tasks, and that the trend worsened in the decade from 1986 to 1996. Ironically, of the forty-four million Americans with the poorest literacy skills, eight million had high school diplomas. In 1995, the consulting firm Towers Perrin commissioned the pollster Louis Harris to conduct a national survey. The probability survey of 1,081 adults age twenty-one and older living within the forty-eight contiguous states in mid-1995 found that a disturbingly high percentage of Americans do not understand the basic elements of health plans. "Trust a lot" and "Trust a little" questions used in the survey may call to mind quantities difficult to separate. The survey might have been done to make the best of what could have possibly been seen as a foregone conclusion. According to this poll, the obvious difficulty for the managed-care "movement" was that 62 percent trusted their doctor "a lot." Health insurance companies, HMOs, and large managed-care organizations were trusted "a little" or "not at all" by 84, 82, and 87 percent, respectively. Most interesting is that even the "Government" came off better at 71 percent than the 62 percent who trusted their managed-care doctors, a possible harbinger of pressure to reexamine a Clinton-type or Obama's public-option plan in healthcare's future.

In an HCFA study reported in the Fall 1996 issue of *Healthcare Financing Review*, using NCQA's HEDIS-derived data—presuming to be Quality of Care Indicators (QCIs) having an inter-rater reliability of over 94 percent—three distinct healthcare-related populations were examined: the privately insured, the uninsured, and the publicly insured. One hundred and four individuals, eighty-two of whom had completed at least one year of college, worked in fifteen focus group sessions lasting two hours each. The attempt to educate the groups by providing QCIs and compara-tive data to them in order to reach an informed status proved unsuc-cessful. "Report cards" rating coverage, quality-of-care measures, and managed-care systems were explained to the consumers involved. The conclusion drawn by the study was not whether HEDIS indicators were the most feasible comparative data for dissemination to consumers but whether consumers could understand what they meant, because they were developed for use by employers. The logic behind HEDIS indica-tors incorporated a fairly sophisticated understanding of managed care, the medical-care process, and the many dimensions of medical practice. In a group interview in the next session, each consumer selected the "best" QCIs from a list of eighteen.

Another important conclusion from the study was that "Regard-less of the form in which comparative data are presented, quality infor-mation provided to consumers is inherently quantitative." Among the privately insured, there was proportionately less misinformation, but the amount of foundational knowledge—the nature or meaning of the underlying condition—and the comprehension of the QCIs were pretty much the same across all categories of consumers. The responses included these: "How can a Pap smear prevent cancer? I mean, what's the stuff they use in the smear to prevent it?" "High death rates show sensitivity by allowing people to go in peace rather than use heroic means." (This particular response may have arisen because the popu-lation studied was in Oregon, a year later becoming the first state with a law permitting assisted suicide.) "A high rate of mammograms tells me they're missing cancer because it means they don't take the time to read each one carefully." "Low birth-weight babies include any baby under 7 lbs, so big deal." Thus, the publicity of HMOs gobbling up the healthcare market and replacing fee-for-service represents a public good would seem to need further data on whether the HMO "movement" is driven by public need, acclaim and desire, or is significantly based on government-lobbied, public-relations fictions by the managed-care insurance industry. This is especially so because HMOs, originally thought of and supposed to be nonprofit, have virtually all become for-profit and wholly owned or operated by commercial managed-care insurers.

Also in 1996, Consumers Union's satisfaction survey of HMOs found that the eleven top-ranked ones were nonprofit plans and twelve of the thirteen bottom-ranked ones were for-profit plans. The picture did not change essentially after 1996. The October 1997 survey in *U.S. News and World Report*, using data from the NCQA, gave HMOs a composite score based on such factors as prevention, physician and member turnover and satisfaction, access to care, and accreditation. Of the thirty-seven top-scoring HMOs, thirty-three were nonprofit plans. In December 1997, Families USA, relying on HCFA data on all Medicare HMOs and using disenrollment as a proxy for consumer satisfaction, reported that of the ten plans with the lowest disenrollment rates pegged at less than 6 percent on average, nine were nonprofit. Seven of the ten plans with the highest average turnover of about 50 percent were for-profit plans.

Because of the chronic complaints about managed care and the apparent unwillingness of Congress to address the problem in a patient-centered way, the waning Clinton administration was left to try tightening its oversight of the NCQA. HCFA concluded that as the NCQA had conferred upon itself the role of collector of data for the HMO and managed-care insurance industry, HCFA should make use of the data, too, at least for as long as HMOs intended to treat Medicare patients. At HCFA's expense, the Island Peer Review Organization—an HCFA contractor in HCFA Region II consisting of New Jersey, New York, Puerto Rico, and the Virgin Islands—was supposed to audit NCQA's audit data on its members in all ten HCFA regions. Based on the BBA requirements and HCFA's new regulations, NCQA's use of the new HEDIS 3.0/98 and its own audits of members' Satisfaction Surveys required auditing by HCFA prior to submission of applications to treat Medicare patients. As for the Health of Seniors Survey, the health plans would pay for it, but HCFA would draw the sample. In addition, IPRO was chosen by the state of Connecticut to conduct independent third-party reviews of adverse determinations made by managed-care organizations and utilization-review companies in that state.

Meanwhile, despite a negative media effort, Congress had resisted putting sanctions on managed-care's collusive efforts to protect itself against those seeking to moderate its profit-centered objectives. However, the Clinton administration showed some enterprise with its incremental initiatives to put an end to doctor-gag rules, "drive-through" surgeries and deliveries, and the encroachment of externally managed-care on the doctor-patient relationship. Mailing "Medicare Satisfaction Surveys" to 130,000 beneficiaries enrolled in managed-care plans was to provide a "consumer's-eye view" of health-plan policy. Proposed ERISA regulations by HCFA for Medicare contractors on improving quality and equivalence of care (the first since 1986), the M+C regulations, and DHHS's new initiative to gather significant information about enrollees' care by managed-care plans raised media attention. Some suggested that managed care could be either tamed or routed.

Then as the George W. Bush administration arrived, virtually all the Clinton administration healthcare initiatives not only came to a halt, but new ones were substituted to stimulate the push for privatization. For example, by May 2010, a study was published by the 1,300-member trade group, America's Health Insurance Plans' Center for Policy and Research, which compared patterns of care among patients under MA and in Medicare's traditional fee-for-service program. It purported to show that risk-adjusted readmission rates were about 27–29 percent lower in MA than FFS per estimated enrollee, 16–18 percent lower per person with an admission, and 14–17 percent lower measured per hospitalization. Significantly, no measurements of patient outcomes as related to mortality were included in the study.

There was some pushback. One month later, an observational study was published in the *Journal of the American Medical Association* (*JAMA*), comparing admissions for heart failure among seven million cases from 1993 to 2006. The *JAMA* study used Medicare data of heart-failure treatment in hospitals over the period 1993 to 2006, correlated with the ascendance of managed care. It demonstrated that while the reduction in hospital length of stay could have reduced the risk of hospital-associated adverse events, in fact, shortening the time in the hospital led to *more* adverse events in the period early after discharge and led to an increase in both post-hospital readmission and mortality risk. The authors noted the statistical validity:

"Discharges to home or under home care service decreased from 74.0% to 66.9% and discharges to skilled nursing facilities increased from 13.0% to 19.9%. Thirty-day readmission rates increased from 17.2% to 20.1%; all p < .001. Consistent with the unadjusted analyses, the 2005-2006 risk-adjusted 30-day mortality risk ratio was 0.92 compared with 1993-1994, and the 30-day readmission risk ratio was 1.11."

The conclusion of the article, in its clipped, scientific style was a painful but enlightened one, a sad comment on the long-term outcome of managed-care-type interventions, government or private, when put into lay language:

"For patients admitted with Heart Failure during the past 14 years, reductions in length of stay and in-hospital mortality, less marked reductions in 30-day mortality, and changes in discharge disposition accompanied by increases in 30-day readmission rates were observed. . . Although the 30-day mortality rate has decreased, the increase in the readmission rates that paralleled the decrease in length of stay does raise concerns—as does the increase in the rates of discharge to nursing home facilities."

The Reagan administration's 1984 Medicare fee-for-service, prospective- payment model, which had provided an incentive to doctors and hospitals for shortening patients' length of stay in hospital, without penalty for unfavorable later outcomes like increased readmission or mortality rates, was virtually identical to post-Millennium mimicking by managed-care insurance companies under privatized MA. Only the 2010 ACA appeared to attempt to reverse that trend. The ACA gave the Obama administration new power to reject bids by the commercial MCOs and to monitor their performance based on their low MLRs, so profitable to them in the past. Waivers allowed by CMS would give the smaller, weaker plans time to adjust themselves to the 80 percent MLRs required for all commercial companies by 2014.

Low MLRs, as discussed earlier, may predict a faulty benefit offering analogous to a "defective product." Low loss ratios in a private sector may also portend a misallocation of the delivery of healthcare services by exclusionary practices that enabled MCOs to fix prices through control of the actuarial conditions—a process similar to gerrymandering of election districts. Traditionally, this included manipulating and pricing its groups using ZIP code data. The industry rule of thumb holds that a managed-care business is in trouble if more than 65 percent of its enrollees submit a significant claim per year. Before managed care, the then-nonprofit Blues usually had a loss ratio of around 95 percent. The commercial "major medical" group plans' loss ratios ran about 90 percent, because the Blues captured the early risk. The advent of managed care and the high administrative costs to its own subsidiaries brought about increased list prices and pushed MLRs in some cases below 60 percent. The fact that the new reform act is setting commercial MLRs to 85 and 80 percent is a strong indication that the administration has recognized the market failure list prices of modern healthcare in the United States.

As congressional staff writers of the 2010 ACA apparently knew, over the years the MCOs had successfully reduced their MLR to below 85 percent, and many were far below that. In addition, their managed-care costs (called "quality of care improvement efforts") were often shifted into the loss ratio as if they were not a revenue-producing center of their own. In some states, insurance departments routinely considered individual indemnity policies as noninsurance when they had loss ratios below 65 percent, as it revealed unconscionably high profitability. Ironically, though it was not considered the same "noninsurance" as an ERISA self-insured plan, the structure is strangely similar. The only reason that ERISA plans cannot reveal MLRs is that they were buying healthcare at non-spread-risk list prices, and there would be no fair comparison to large-group or "community-rated" actuarial premiums.

ERISA-based costs to employers would largely be "pay-as-you-go" with discounting because of the wide profit margins enabled by managed-care reviewing. In addition, MCO market manipulation is evidenced in the narrowing of an MCO's risk by redlining providers and cherry-picking patients from the larder of uninsured supported by their actuaries' ZIP code data instead of spreading the risk wider to obtain the lowest cost basis for their premiums. *See* Plate 6. If insurance risk-spreading principles were applied to MCOs by statute, premiums would have to be lowered significantly and be based on marginal-cost prices above average cost as well. However, this would inevitably cause the healthcare "free market" of myriad smaller MCOs to shrink, because the incongruent group of pint-sized minions to the commercial insurers could not achieve sufficient market share to survive.

In managed Medicare plans, a stealthy, care-limiting "second bite at the apple" is evident from the government's years of cost cutting and shifting to private payers. For example, the 1996 *Oxford Medicare Advantage* booklet contained a side-by-side comparison of "Regular" Medicare with Oxford's "Advantage" in which the felicitous phrase "as medically necessary" was inserted in key places only in the Advantage's "hospital" section for inpatient and outpatient care. When compared with Medicare, it could reasonably apply to all types of treatment, because the doctors' portion and the hospital portion are separate. Under Medicare in 1972, there were statutory nongovernmental PROs that privately reviewed "medical necessity" and quality issues. As noted earlier, in 2008, the Bush administration signed a contract with NGS, a wholly owned subsidiary of WellPoint, Inc., to review and probe hospital admissions as well as act as a "fiscal intermediary" handling government reimbursement to hospitals. Under the administration's CMS rules, the intermediary was empowered to both pay claims and evaluate the medical care—two distinct functions that were formerly separated and shared with statutory PROs. Deciding whether to pay and how to evaluate medical care has been a well-settled "no-no" for indemnity coverage since the days of McCarran-Ferguson.

Apparently, the self-conferred "medical necessity" determination made by the HMOs and managed-care insurers—with the helpful suggestions from actuaries Milliman and Robertson and their ilk—though not totally eliminating the federal oversight role, allowed MCOs to make up in cash flow, the BBA 5 percent discount taken by the government contract with a Medicare MCO. By 2004, the managed-care insurance industry had managed to increase that number to as much as 115 percent of the Medicare rate for their member hospitals and HMOs by "adding" benefits that could be manipulated by privately managing them under the MMA. The Bush II administration used the same cost-cutting methods added to Medicare by the Reagan-era DRGs and the PPS, and earlier by the 1972 Nixon administration "reasonable-cost" amendments to the Social Security Act. At first, the government cost controls shifted costs to the private indemnity premium sector. Later, they were shifted to capitated providers and HMO-type contractors who responded by exchanging patient volume for list price and below-marginal-cost provider cuts. Because of the underlying market failure, the short-term economic winners were expected to be the HMOs and the government. At first, all were losers—later, only the beneficiaries.

A significant aspect of the Obama administration's early application of the ACA was the ratcheting down of premium costs for MA subscribers for 2011, despite the increase in benefits hurriedly offered by the participating insurers to staunch potential losses. Because MCOs are not public utilities, and the costs to the managed-care industry for the healthier under-sixty-five population is unchanged by the ACA, the increases requested were not justifiable. For example, by March 2011, Blue Shield of California, a mutual benefit corporation and independent member of the BlueCross/BlueShield Association, announced that it "has withdrawn its rate filing with the California Department of Insurance and the company will not increase rates to any individual or family plan member for the remainder of the year." *The New York Times* on March 17 reported (in language reflecting the current argot that the insurance company is the *provider* of healthcare):

"But the reversal could make it more difficult for other insurers in California, as well as other states, to raise premiums sharply, according to some analysts and advocates, even if companies offer evidence that justifies the increases because of the higher cost of providing medical care to their customers. Under the one-year-old federal healthcare law, state regulators are required to pay closer attention to what insurers are charging for policies, and some advocates say the reversal is early proof that the law will help keep premiums reasonable."

It will remain for the states to regulate Exchange requests, too. In addition, if another Congress modifies McCarran-Ferguson, such state-supervised increases would also come under direct federal scrutiny by the national insurance department pursuant to the ACA.

VII. Further Market Failure in Managed Care

"We're on the verge of a massive amount of M&A," says Jim Lane, a New Jersey money manager and former managed-care analyst. "There's no organic growth left in the business except for pricing."

—"The Next Wave of Health-Care Mergers,"
Barron's, October 24, 2011

Many states have a strong interest in assuring that their citizens have at least minimally adequate healthcare, because all states have participated in Medicaid for the indigent and regulate health insurance. The Supreme Court in *Travelers* made this clear:

> "Several States, including New York, regulated hospital charges to one degree or another at the time ERISA was passed . . . And yet there is not so much as a hint in ERISA's legislative history or anywhere else that Congress intended to squelch these state efforts."

Like anyone, the underinsured and those without coverage may suffer catastrophic illnesses, which for them ultimately result in staggering financial losses. To the extent that such people can find free or subsidized care, they nonetheless impose a burden on the rest of society's public and private facilities. "Subsidized care" as used here would include "explicit subsidies" provided by private or government program sources and those "implicit subsidies" resulting from the sale of medical services at prices below marginal cost for as long as participating companies can survive under such price predation. Indeed, since McCarran-Ferguson had in its congressional mandate the protection of state citizens from insurance predators engaged in state or interstate commerce, the bifurcated population consisting of ERISA-covered and indemnity insurance-covered citizens made equitable healthcare coverage requirements as much a state issue as a federal one. Moreover, resolving this problem became a nonconflictive legitimate federal and state interest ever since Medicaid's "cooperative federalism" was accepted, preemption notwithstanding, as expected from the new efforts of the federal government under the 2010 ACA.

However, even though the content of the benefits occupies both federal and state arenas in accordance with ERISA's weak oversight structure, trustees and administrators of corporate benefit plans are solely regulated by the federal government regarding observance of their fiduciary and administrative duties and then only when there is a complaint. For example, the federal HMO Act allows for federal "qualification" of HMOs as well as their promotion under the "dual option" that must be given employees in all companies subject to the federal Fair Labor Standards Act, yet the states have the responsibility of regulating HMOs pursuant to their respective insurance laws. The logical disjunction is evident: some states regulate HMOs as they would insurance companies, while other states do not consider HMOs insurance. The lower courts are befuddled, and the Supreme Court is staying out of the fray. It is not clear, nor has there been significant litigation to clarify, whether the self-funded healthcare plans that contract with HMOs are or may be regulated by the states; from the current vernacular, it is not clear to healthcare purchasers whether an HMO is understood to be an insurer. If a benefit plan seeks to contract with an HMO for less than state-prescribed minimum benefits, there would seem to be a conflict preemption issue, because the HMO could not offer below-minimum benefits as can fiduciary governed self-insured plans. Congress was evidently aware of this, because both McCarran-Ferguson and the HMO Act preceded ERISA. In the 1985 *Metropolitan Life Ins. Co. v. Massachusetts* case, the Supreme Court said,

"Mandated benefit laws . . . are saved from preemption by the operation of the saving [*sic*] clause. [FN 21] That mandated-benefit laws fall within the terms of the definition of insurance in the McCarran-Ferguson Act is directly relevant in another sense as well. Congress' 'primary concern' in enacting McCarran-Ferguson was 'to ensure that the States would continue to have the ability to tax and regulate the business of insurance.' [citing *Royal Drug*] . . . The saving [*sic*] clause and the McCarran-Ferguson Act serve the same federal policy and utilize similar language to define what is left to the states. Moreover, § 514(d) of ERISA, explicitly states in part: 'Nothing in [ERISA] shall be construed to alter, amend, modify, invalidate, impair, or supersede any law of the United States.' Thus application of the McCarran-Ferguson Act lends further support to our ruling that Congress did not intend mandated-benefit laws to be preempted by ERISA."

The risk that HMOs might provide inadequate levels of healthcare protection, or that employers would not buy benefits mandated under ERISA, is considerable given the sham conditions of "cost-containment" under which the managed-care industry operates. Nonetheless, state statutes for mandating coverage for complications of pregnancy, birth defects, sickle cell anemia, reconstructive surgery, and hospital length-of-stay for mastectomies have been in effect for years in California, New Hampshire, Oregon, New York, Alabama, and Minnesota, among others. Many state managed-care reform statutes curbing "drive-through" mastectomies, against MCO gag rules and twenty-four-hour deliveries, had been enacted in all but four states by December 1996. At that time, the only three states without any such mandates were Idaho, Kentucky, and New Jersey.

1. Is Cost Containment the Reality and Health Care Merely the Illusion?—They've Got Algorithm

> "Human ingenuity will often find some way to profit by the incentives that exist, just as biological evolution will frequently manage to fill some vacant ecological niche."
>
> —Nobel Prize-winning physicist
> Murray R. Gell-Mann

> "Professional Standards Review Organizations review has reduced Medicare outlays, but the federal government saves little more than the cost of the review itself."
>
> —Alice M. Rivlin, director of
> Congressional Budget Office (1981)

Healthcare providers' shift in "core competence"—a marketing metaphor for "a business doing what it is competent to do"—from patient caring to cost cutting, and from prescriptive medicine by doctors to proscriptive medicine created by managed care, caused the healthcare industry, government and commercial, to fail in its declared social role. The Medicaid system of "cooperative federalism" is where the federal government gives states approximately 50 percent of the costs of medical assistance based on state plans, which assures the federal government that the states will provide for a federally agreed upon list of minimum medical benefits for their indigent population. However, because equitable state-mandated benefit laws were not universally in place, the advancement of mandated underwriting of minimum coverage for almost universally agreed illnesses remained setback for decades, leaving the country in the same condition that existed in the cartel era. Although weakly opposing the PPS at the time of its enactment, the insurance industry used the government method of price stabilization for its Medicare and Medicaid programs as if it were a *Noerr*-protected smorgasbord menu for commercial price-fixing.

There is a dearth of cases applying the Noerr-Pennington Doctrine to the healthcare field and none in the arena of managed care. In *Noerr*, the Supreme Court acknowledged that

"there may be situations in which a publicity campaign, ostensibly directed toward influencing governmental action, is a mere sham to cover what is actually nothing more than an attempt to interfere with business relationships of a competitor, and the application of the Sherman Act would be justified."

The publicity campaigns by the NCQA HEDIS's "Quality Compass," and McKesson's InterQual, "The Gold Standard in Evidence-Based Clinical Decision Support," among others, cover up the price-fixing and data- disseminating activities of these organizations as they are used to benefit the managed healthcare insurance industry's hiding its cash-flow, core business under the cloak of public-weal cost containment. The "cost containment" aphorism would have the public believe that the industry's profits are less because of its effort, similar to lower prices in the general marketplace. Of course, such behavior is absurd for commercial ventures of any type unless its purpose is to stabilize prices or drive rivals into either being acquired or forced out of the marketspace by the best "cost container." That public policy includes constraints on the cost of government healthcare programs does not give license for commercial organizations to mimic by selling capitated, below-marginal-cost healthcare for prices lower than competitors. Public policy also does not give to commercial organizations that disseminate information to stabilize private healthcare prices the right to expect immunization from the antitrust laws because they use the nourishment of government's apparent authority.

Clinical algorithms adapted from computer language "conditional logic" ("if/then" statements) are used by researchers to define paths to clinical conclusions and by MCOs to adjust their risk. MCOs use them to remove or reduce the economically negative influence of confounding factors by preset flowchart guidelines for the care of prototypical patients, ultimately, to determine payment decisions. M&R insists those that fit into algorithms are "uncomplicated patients." Aetna/U.S.

Healthcare says its "U.S. Quality Algorithms" program is a mission to develop "innovative systems for measuring and improving the performance of healthcare providers, assessing the care and outcomes of patients, and evaluating the costs of programs." In short, such use of algorithms give only the appearance of being related to the direct care of sickness when, in reality, its purpose is risk adjustment.

Today the word "algorithm" is used to describe a rule for calculating something. In fact, to say that algorithms can be used to diagnose an illness is not the same as saying that such algorithms provide any information about an individual's illness, because their use requires a body of knowledge that lies outside of the algorithm itself. The information needed to diagnose and treat resides only in the mind and hands of the doctor examining and treating the patient, not in a managed-care doctor, nurse, social worker, or clerk using a computer screen list of clinical possibilities. For example, the statements "boys will be boys," "it is what it is," and "a house is not a home" convey widely understood implications but contain no information whatever in their words. In both healthcare and computing, an algorithm describes a binary method (one or zero for "yes" or "no") for following certain pathways. A one or a zero is known as a "bit." The term comes from the contraction of the term "binary digit." In computer terminology, bit "strings" are used to reach an objective. In healthcare research, algorithms can be of aid in reaching a diagnosis and developing a treatment path. The series of "yesses" or "noes" that could culminate in a diagnosis constitutes a particular bit string message, but the information necessary to say "yes" or "no" is not present in the algorithm. That choice is left outside and is in the information database of the researcher or the examining physician.

Moreover, there is also a critical distinction between a researcher and an examining physician. The research knowledge is stochastic; that is, it functions from a sample of one element of a probability distribution, while the patient-examiner's knowledge comes from training and experience based additionally on a relationship with the individual patient. The shortest string is one where a computer is programmed to print out that string and then stop. In managed-healthcare-mediated algorithms, it is where the binary path to be followed by the diagnostician ends with a diagnosis and a treatment path but includes an element unrelated to the information needed by a treating physician—alternatives based on cost—that are not teachable in a medical school curriculum. With both the computerized data and the managed-care reviewer's efforts, the length of that string is called the "algorithmic information content" (AIC).

Clearly, the algorithms used by the managed-care reviewers are measurable in lengths of the strings of time it takes a reviewer to categorically reach a diagnosis and complete or negate a treatment process, and each length of time is inevitably represented by some cost. As the federal district court said in the managed-care case *Crocco v. Xerox*, discussed earlier:

> "While it may be true that the fee arrangement between American PsychManagement and Xerox did not encourage the denial of coverage, [the managed-care company's] desire to satisfy Xerox's expectations certainly did."

Although by their use of algorithms MCOs and M&R and Inter-Qual would have one believe otherwise, it is crucial to note that there is absolutely no medical information in any AIC, only labels, and each of those labels is intertwined with imperatives based on cost. The best way to distinguish between the algorithm and its AIC is to say that the "information" is concerned with a potential selection of alternatives that antedate the AIC, while the AIC contains only the names of the alternatives, none of which with a degree of clinical certainty relate to the individual patient. In his book, *The Quark and the Jaguar*, the Nobel Prize-winning physicist Murray Gell-Mann said, "The curious property is that AIC is not computable."

> "In fact, we cannot, in general, be sure that the AIC of a given string isn't lower than we think it is. This is because there may always be a theorem we will never find, an algorithm we will never discover, that would permit the string to be further compressed. . . . Thus, in general, one cannot be sure of the value of algorithmic information content; one can only place an

upper bound on it, a value it cannot succeed. Since the value may be below that bound, AIC is uncomputable."

Manifestly, the string managed care chooses to use is the one that can arrive at a conclusion in the shortest real time for both the reviewer and the provider, requiring the "upper bound on it." Therein lays the managed-care methodology to imitate "improving" healthcare or its "performance." However, the only way to shorten a diagnostic and treatment string is to deny all or parts of it or to place upper-time bounds on it (in dollar terms, stabilizing prices). Because the treating doctor will ethically tend to treat as the clinical situation calls for, accepting an eternal reviewer's *ad hoc* suggestion would be an admission that the fundamental element of *knowing* the patient is reducible or unnecessary. Denying all or parts of treatment implicates societally imposed restraints such as more illness for the patient or malpractice for the doctor; therefore, imposing an externally derived lower- or upper-time limit is sheer arbitrariness in a clinical situation and has no legal place other than being subservient to price controls. Managed care does both by imposing shortened lengths of stay in hospital that will be paid for at higher cash flow per unit time or even from repeat admissions as a result of those shortened stays. Worse still, a fundamental flaw in the use of algorithms in active healthcare and M&R-type diagnostic criteria is that while the computer can diagnose illnesses, it does not learn more about the illness from its experience with successive patients as the doctor can, and it certainly can't treat it. Algorithm use in clinical situations makes time stand still. Gell-Mann puts it this way:

"In AIC, additional sources of arbitrariness have been introduced, namely the particular coding procedure that turns the description of the system into a bit string, as well as the particular hardware and software associated with the computer."

It is plain that the information needed for a diagnosis resides in the brain of the examining diagnostician and not in the managed-care algorithm analyst or programmer. In addition, the binary system employed in the construction of algorithms, being "digital," truncates the time-honored, analog method used by physicians—the "differential diagnosis." Although one can argue that the digital method is faster as it has already considered many differential possibilities, that presumptiveness is its fundamental flaw; it can have no knowledge of the individual patient's history when used by a managed-care reviewer. By knowing a subject's history, a researcher can exclude patients from randomized, controlled studies.

The digital method is represented electrically by an "on" "off" series, while the analog method works by variations in voltage. Simply put, the digital method uses ones and zeros, while the analog method fills the spaces between them. The proprietary nature of the medical algorithm protocols by M&R, InterQual, and other MCOs, forced on the medical providers, allows possibly relevant differential diagnoses to be kept from the clinicians and the public eye to avoid exposing an arbitrariness that is unable to withstand scrutiny. Obviously, if an MCO's algorithm had to include all the many alternative dispositions that a differential diagnosis often brings to an examining physician's mind in a split second, the algorithm would fill many screen pages and expose the uselessness of time-saving, cost-cutting, managed-care reviewers.

Provider disdain for the use of algorithms in clinical decision making urged by the managed-care insurers ranges from those who treat the elderly to those who treat the young. As far back as 1999, studies examining whether hospital readmissions varied among the frail elderly in managed care versus fee-for-service systems (FFS) cast a shadow on hopes that managed care might be accepted as helpful in improving the quality of care. Instead, it revealed its nature as aimed solely at insurance profit. The April 1999 *American Journal of Preventive Medicine* conducted a randomized study comparing fee-for-service and managed care for the hospitalized elderly. Two methods to identify preventable readmissions were developed, one based on a computerized algorithm of service-use patterns and another based on blind clinical review. The results were highly significant and showed that the odds of having a preventable hospital readmission within ninety days of an index admission were three and a half to almost six times as high for Medicare

HMO enrollees compared to Medicare FFS participants, depending on the method used to assess preventability. Readmission patterns were similar for Medicare HMO enrollees and FFS study participants dually enrolled in Medicare and Medicaid. The conclusion was this:

"In this group of frail elderly Medicare beneficiaries, those enrolled in an HMO were more likely to have a preventable hospital readmission than those receiving care under FFS. These results suggest that policies promoting stringent approaches to utilization control (e.g., early hospital discharge, reduced levels of post-acute care, and restricted use of home health services) may be problematic for the frail elderly."

An August 2001 article in the *Archives of Pediatrics & Adolescent Medicine*, "Pediatric Length of Stay Guidelines and Routine Practice, The Case of Milliman and Robertson," said that

"The M&R [length of stay] criteria were divergent from routine practice for both children and adults. Greater divergence of adult discharges illustrates the need to consider co-morbid conditions when implementing these guidelines. Thus, patient care may suffer if guidelines are implemented in an uninformed way. These findings emphasize the importance of using the best possible science when producing guidelines such as these."

When using "guidelines" based on medical experience, such as "evidence-based medicine" (discussed later) or on randomized controlled studies published in peer-reviewed journals, a distinction should be made from that of actuarially based determinations made solely for reducing financial risk of employers and insurance companies by the managed-care industry.

The following are some examples to demonstrate the inherent "medical-experience versus actuarial experience" conflict alluded to in the pediatric journal article, "The Case of Milliman and Robertson." Nancy L. Johnson (R-CT) was elected from the Fifth District of Connecticut to twelve Congresses (from the early 1980s to 2007). The

Fifth District is the historical international center of the U.S. insurance industry. Congresswoman Johnson was a principal author of the 2003 MMA and a peak insurance and health-provider fundraising member of Congress, becoming a member of the board of directors of Magellan Health Services after leaving political office. Magellan, discussed earlier, offers today many plans for promoting efficient clinical hospital services that allow hospital peer-review committees to help minimize medical mistakes and maximize comprehensive pathways to appropriate treatment. At the same time, it also offers services used by insurance companies and state Medicaid programs to reduce economic risk. Its 2011 "Radiology Benefits Management" program, served by its subsidiary National Imaging Associates (NIA) states:

> "By encouraging dialogue between patients and their physicians, we increase the likelihood that the consumer will get the right imaging procedure from the right provider at the right time. And that's what it's all about."

Its 2008 "Condition Care Management" behavioral medical/psychiatric program states:

> "Clinically trained, dedicated health coaches work telephonically with members to establish individualized care plans, help members develop self-management skills, recognize and monitor symptoms, and get the most from provider-treatment plans. Working collaboratively with the entire care team, coaches provide a fully integrated, experience for the employee, the provider, and the client."

Magellan's 2011 "ICORE Healthcare" programs, handling Specialty Pharmacy Dispensing, Strategic Pharmacy Consulting, Medical Pharmacy Solutions and Formulary Management, states:

> "At ICORE, each customer has a dedicated team whose sole focus is to drive savings. The team develops and implements a comprehensive marketing strategy that optimizes your preferred formulary market share. By conducting market research,

the team ensures message accuracy and individually tailors the strategy for key targets including physicians, pharmacies and members. We then implement the strategy, actively targeting what is not in compliance with the objectives."

M&R and InterQual approach their clients actuarially, with M&R taking the "uncomplicated patient" route and InterQual reaching those with complications. Not to worry. All that matters to MCOs is that both algorithm methods accomplish the same work: to shorten lengths of stay and increase the cash flow per patient day.

In a July 2009 "educational" teleconference with between staff of the Medicare fiscal intermediary, NGS, the wholly owned subsidiary WellPoint, Inc. and a psychiatric hospital, the following was discussed in a telephone conference:

NGS Medical Director: ". . . the one thing that keeps striking me because I've reviewed a lot of the cases for [the] hospital now, and the quality of the care that is being delivered seems like perfectly standard care. That's not really at issue. My sense from the conversation we had before was in some ways [similar to] the history of Medicare review of in-patient psych hospital claims, which basically was not in existence since 1965 until recently."

Hospital: ". . . No, we were always part of the review by Medicare through the PRO—Peer Review Organization."

NGS Medical Director: "Yes, but the PRO didn't really do any significant case review . . . Well I think that [the] Hospital recording this call is a good idea, and particularly if there are things in things that we talk about their staff would benefit from . . . Hospitals haven't been reviewed in this way for their inpatient services prior to that [time]. And particularly for institutions who haven't had to meet the standards for commercial insurance where the admission and discharge criteria were dictated by the standard criteria sets of InterQual and Milliman and Robinson [sic]. And in those institutions basically the Medicare patients get treated just the same ways as the commercial patients get

treated, which is a fairly aggressive admission and discharge criteria
. . . Okay, so the reason I referenced the Milliman and Robinson and
InterQual is that these criteria essentially attempt to standardize what
are the criteria for medical necessities for an inpatient level of care and
to differentiate those patients from an inpatient level of care versus
outpatient level of care."

Hospital: "But the Milliman and Robinson excuse me, Milliman
and Robertson criteria are commercial criteria. They were done largely
on the basis of a highly questionable activity by competing insurance
companies and managed care companies. So, the Milliman and Robertson evaluations were purely for profit, commercially based . . ."

NGS Medical Director: "Well let me cut to the chase, what we've
found is that there's a pattern of people being kept days beyond when
they were stable and able to be discharged to a lower level of care.
That's what we've found, and that's the reason for the majority of denials you've been receiving."

The hospital, a small, fully accredited psychiatric facility in New
York, was in the midst of a laborious four-month to one-year appeals
process on sixteen Medicare cases for which payment was denied as
not medically necessary for hospitalization. In the complicated Medicare Appeals process as amended during the post-Millennium Bush
administration, new entities called "qualified independent contractors"
were established, where a provider or beneficiary could appeal negative
decisions. The hospital experienced four levels in the Medicare claims
appeal process. After NGS denied the claims, some for the patient's
entire admission, NGS denied a "redetermination," then an "appeal."
After that, a "second-level" appeal was made to Maximus Federal
Services, an "independent" appeals contractor for Medicare. Finally,
an judicial appeal was made to Medicare Administrative Law Justices
(ALJ), "Level 3" of the CMS Office of Medicare Hearings and Appeals
(OMHA). The OMHA administers appeal hearings for the Medicare
program. Government ALJs hold hearings and issue decisions related

to Medicare coverage determinations that reached the third level of the Medicare claims appeal process. In some instances, an ALJ may decide a case "on the record" if a party waives its rights to an oral hearing or when the documentary evidence supports a finding fully favorable to the appellants.

In the psychiatric hospital's appeals, two of the ALJs required video hearings, and one decided solely on the documentary evidence. Neither NGS nor Maximus appeared or offered witnesses at any of the hearings. The judges, with "findings fully favorable to the appellants," reversed all sixteen cases of denials by NGS and Maximus. The hospital was paid for the services that were rendered beneficiaries albeit from six to fourteen months earlier.

It remains to be seen whether the federal government under the Obama administration will continue to allow commercial companies involved in the MA plans or the Exchanges to use their algorithm-based criteria to concurrently decide how patients will be covered for inpatient treatment, especially for those who came to treatment with preexisting illnesses. The ACA specifically prohibits insurance companies from rescinding policies except in cases of fraud or intentional misrepresentation of material fact. The law also mandated that insurers provide advance notice by September 23, 2010 of their intention to retroactively cancel an insurance policy. On April 22, 2010, after learning from a *Reuters* report that WellPoint, Inc. was using algorithms to target women with breast cancer and cancel their coverage, DHHS Secretary Sebelius urged WellPoint to stop the practice of rescinding coverage "using a computer algorithm that automatically targeted patients recently diagnosed with breast cancer, among other conditions." WellPoint denied the accusation in a letter to the secretary, calling the *Reuters* story "inaccurate and grossly misleading." On April 27, without addressing the algorithm methods or their cessation, WellPoint became the first insurer to announce that it would implement the rescission reforms early for patients who become ill.

By May 5, 2011, *The New York Times* reported that Ms. Sibelius issued a final rule establishing procedures for federal and state insurance experts to scrutinize premiums, which would have to be justified when proposed increases were to be over 10 percent. Also, starting in September 2012, "the federal government will set a separate threshold for each state, reflecting trends in insurance and health care costs." By early June, the nonprofit Blue Shield of California, which had been criticized in January for its proposed, double-digit premium increases, said it will cap net income to 2 percent of revenue and refund any excess to policyholders. It was widely reported that the San Francisco-based company will be returning $180 million this year to policyholders as part of the new program.

Managed-care insurers operate by "incentives" that provide selective pressures, "externalities," in the medical economy. The incentives depend on limiting or offering referrals or for greater productivity, which apply selective pressure to physicians in ways that compromise care. An externality is an effect of a purchase or use decision by one set of parties on others who did not have a choice and whose interests were not taken into account. What is "selective" is that they include pressures exerted from outside the information system of medical treatment and the doctor-patient relationship, and they uncover the irrational decisions made by people with coercive financial power. Managed care creates pressure on doctors to do more with less. The incentives effectively proffer less time be spent per patient and promote less use of costly diagnostic tests and treatments. For example, the more-costly medications are based on drug-specific formularies attached to the insurance policies the costs for which are predicated on discounts to the insurers by pharmaceutical manufacturers of new, expensive drugs so that both industries can benefit from the increased cash flow. Some forms of managed care formally create a financial incentive for doctors to spend less time with each patient. For instance, under preferred provider arrangements, physicians may feel compensated for reduced fees-for-services by seeing more patients, even though this reduces the time available to discuss the patients' problems, explore treatment options, and maintain the meaningful relationship that patients traditionally enjoy.

The economic pressure tactics of MCOs on large-group purchasers of healthcare have negatively affected the rights of doctors to treat their patients unfettered by these externally imposed economic considerations.

In a discussion of the "unconstitutional conditions doctrine," the 1996 federal Sixth Circuit Court of Appeals in *McCloud v. Testa* raised the question of

> "negative externalities [which] occur when the private costs of some activity are less than the costs to society of that activity. As a result, society produces more of the activity than is optimal because private parties engaging in it essentially shift some of their costs onto society as a whole."

The classic example of a negative externality is pollution that is generated by some productive enterprise but that affects others who had no choice in the matter and probably were not taken into account. In healthcare, offering patients to doctors in a capitation arrangement is a negative externality that shifts the cost to society by unconscionably high prices. In a 1998 article on ethics in medicine, Nancy S. Jecker and Clarence H. Braddock III, from the University of Washington note, "Termination of physician-patient relationships can also occur without patients' choosing . . . when employers shift health plans employees may have no choice but to sever ties with their physicians."

Insurers arbitrarily giving large numbers of lower-paying patients to "preferred providers" hardly offers a rational incentive for doctors to follow those patients as closely as they would those who paid either with private funds or through individual insurance policies. An historical example of a seemingly well-intentioned but irrational economic incentive, resembling the present-day danger posed by managed-care capitation volume referrals, occurred when the two thousand-year-old Dead Sea Scrolls were discovered in 1947. Archeologists wanted wandering Arab shepherds to turn in as many scraps of the artifacts as could be found. When the scholars guilelessly offered a fixed reward per scrap, it made it more likely that the fragments found would be broken into even smaller pieces to maximize the rewards. In similar manner, we note the deplorable state of healthcare resulting from managed-care's policy of discharging patients from hospital "quicker and sicker."

2. A Market Failure in Healthcare Prevents an Effective Underwriting of Risk Especially in ERISA Self-insured Plans

Because of managed-care's capitation-controlled limitations on doctors' free speech as related to the new doctor-insurer contracts and the fiduciary duties imposed on the doctor-patient relationship, the traditionally patient-centered way medicine and its ethics were taught in training programs inevitably saw changes. They created a direct conflict with the way medical students and residents learned to treat the patient's medical needs without constraints caused by coercive metaphors of illnesses based on algorithm-based price and profit. Paradoxically, this behavior ultimately denies the patient the ability to exert the very "prudent consumer choice" championed by managed care. Wherever the basis for "quality" care has become deconstructed from the academic and scientific world and run by organizations controlling the price-per-unit of healthcare, the result is nothing less than underinformed consent by the consumer. All the patient/consumer under managed care knows is that the member of a physician group of today is somehow paid on incentive-based production, not on a free doctor-patient relationship.

In what might be called a "perfect" (nonmanipulated) healthcare indemnity insurance market, there would be no deadweight loss to society. Insurers would provide the type and levels of health coverage that prudent consumers wanted and might consider paying for based on their perception of the risks associated with particular medical conditions or what might happen if treatment for such conditions were ignored. The premium price would also follow the broad demand, which would be reflective of general market conditions including competition from insurers with competitive market power. A cardinal feature of a market failure is an imperfection, which in this area derives from the consumer's lack of information concerning the risks of having revolving-door care. *See* Plates 6, 7 and 8. It becomes the economic foundation of medical decisions endemic to a "company store" physician-insurer contract—the "informed-consumer-choice" style of cost-cutting healthcare economics. In addition, because increasing revenue by mergers and acquisitions are the market failure bases of maintaining or increasing profitability in that industry, MCOs must ultimately require the physician's price of each unit of service to be lower than previously charged to provide more units for a net gain in cash flow to both. Therefore, with no compelling studies other than questionable "patient satisfaction surveys" to demonstrate that quicker and better care result from its methods, managed care must also overvalue each such unit of care delivered.

One of the fundamentals of a market economy is the free flow of information about goods and services offered for sale. Fraud or deception can inject imperfect information into the market. This undermines the consumers' ability to exercise appropriate purchasing choices and amounts to overvaluation of the aggregate cost of healthcare, especially if priced below average variable cost, and represents a market ripe for and solely run by seemingly competitive predators. By substituting list-price-care "alternatives" and promoting the use of ancillary personnel (lay counselors for psychiatrists, nurse practitioners for primary-care physicians, midwives for obstetricians, drug-store clinics, etc.), MCO deadweight losses maintain prices lower than what society would otherwise be willing to pay for direct physician care and both skim from the spread between them. By so doing, managed care also devalues the amortization required to pay for the years of extensive training put into medical practitioners' education, placing in jeopardy the exactingly developed historical system of medical education based on research and clinical experience.

Whereas monopoly power is defined as the power to control prices or exclude competition, the conventional definition of market power is expressed as the power for an entity to raise prices without fear of losing business to rivals. From the Supreme Court's *Maricopa County Medical Society*, we know that even setting *maximum* prices is *per se* illegal. Therefore, what is illegal here is not the ability to "lower" or "raise" prices in dollars alone but to control and save them based on slices of time in a relevant marketspace. Market power in antitrust cases also arise from deception, significantly imperfect or asymmetric information, unduly large transaction costs, or from other types of market failures that usually are associated with consumer protection violations. The noninsurance-based condition offered by ERISA self-insured benefit plans exhibits a market failure deception whose employer-victims are the businesses paying list prices for employee healthcare. These result in harm to competition in entire commodity markets, including the higher prices they must charge for the goods produced; and such harms may not be prevented by having pure competition in relevant markets. This type of "societal victimization" of businesses by the managed-care insurance industry, when largely saved from state regulation by federal preemption, offers vast amounts of interstate market power by conferring upon the MCO-based insurers' price freedom in the deceptively termed field "administrative services only."

The employer ultimately must purchase the administrative services as well as stop-loss coverage from insurance companies in the "business of insurance." The "self-insured" aspect is effectively little more than the fungible equivalent of an overpriced premium. With ERISA-benefit plans, the employee is also unprotected, because the "prudent choice"-purchase of coverage for the employees are solely cost based and not affected by adverse selection (the desire to purchase based on expectation of need). The prevalence of third-party payment for healthcare costs reduces price competition, and a lack of adequate actuarial and underwriting information renders the employee-consumers unable to evaluate the quality or quantity of the medical care provided by competing providers. Recall that the function of underwriting involves "evaluating, selecting, classifying and rating each risk, and establishing the standards of coverage and amount of protection to be offered to each acceptable risk." This, a consumer cannot do.

What imperfect information is enough to affect the choices of a large enough percentage of customers to have a detrimental effect on competition in a market? Since information is almost never perfect, this matter of degree is critical. Professor Robert H. Lande, mentioned earlier, said that imperfect information and the other "consumer protection" market failures can give companies some power to raise prices unilaterally above competitive levels in the short term. These factors can provide a space, cushion, or isolation around consumers similar to that created by market-share-based market power. In 2007, in *Market*

Power without a Large Market Share: The Role of Imperfect Information and other 'Consumer Protection' Market Failures, he said:

"But the firms compete less effectively, the customers search less effectively, and entry becomes less likely. To the extent these tasks are made more difficult by 'consumer protection' market failures, prices can rise. The isolation or cocoon has the same effects that would arise from traditional market share based market power."

Moreover, prices to ERISA employer-coverage purchasers based on managed-care methods can be insulated from the prying eyes of anti-trust agencies—having the appearance of being equivalent to lower manufacturing "costs of production"—by managed-care control of employees' healthcare "output." Managed care as a healthcare market failure reaches far beyond similar failure in other industries. In a laissez-faire society, a market failure augurs more than economic demise for the primary actors because it also affects purchasers' expectations of value. In healthcare, such failure also spawns social, political, and moral tragedies. Until the Mental Health Parity and Addiction Equity Act of 2008, which barely gathered some effect by 2010, the discriminatory managed-care behavior had resulted in an enormous relative decrease in expenditures for mental healthcare and the treatment of mental illness. Ironically, it was only because the Parity Act of 2008 was embedded in the Troubled Asset Relief Program (TARP Act) that it was passed by a Republican Congress and signed by a Republican president.

The market deformity caused by incomplete, if not distorted, information concerning the risks of illness in the managed-care era, including the sham of improving the quality of care, is similar to the advertising and political maneuvering of the tobacco industry to make the smoking issue one of civil rights. The healthcare marketplace has metamorphosed from "insure yourself against the cost of illness with the doctor of your choice" to "pay more for care when you get sick, with the doctor of *our* choice." During managed-care's salad days from 1985 to 1995, publicly held managed-care companies, although economic failures, were selling at twenty-five or more times earnings from mergers and acquisitions, while aggregate personal healthcare expenditures increased 16 percent in the same decade.

As far as the insurers' offering a "doctor of [their] choice," an *American Medical News* article of May 23, 2011 revealed: **"Insurer-owned clinics bid to offer more patient care.** Major health plans are expanding direct care to control costs and put their names in front of potential individual insurance shoppers," showing where CIGNA, among other insurers are anticipating leaving the "business of insurance" and forming a new "business of insurance companies":

> "Analysts say insurers believe they can get more direct control of medical costs by actually providing care. Also, they have an opportunity to market their names to the millions who will be shopping for individual insurance, required under the Patient Protection and Affordable Care Act by 2014. And the insurers can keep for themselves some of the 80% to 85% (depending on the health plan) they are required to spend on patient care."

3. "Adverse" or "Antiselection"

Government's "business" is to provide for the general welfare. Insurers as a group are unlikely to promote adequate levels of coverage in an unregulated environment. Irrespective of the magnitude of the health problems that go uncovered, they would not offer coverage that consumers do not demand in response to market forces. It simply is not their business. As a result, a second health-insurance market deformity manifests itself and reinforces the problems encountered in a failed market: "adverse selection" or "antiselection." A market-based activity for customers looking for the "best buy" when their expectations are based on need is adverse selection, a potential nemesis to managed care, which can be significantly mitigated by capitation and the coercive exclusionary behavior of ERISA plans. Although it was considered the bane of the indemnity insurance era, when balanced by its "moral hazard"—where the insurer may get more claims than it bargained for—it could also be a healthy contributor to a free market. However, widespread adverse selection portends difficulty for managed-care monopolists. It tends to restrain their control of the market, because a monopoly's inherently withholding structure in a healthcare market increases the demand for new entrants.

In a healthy insurance marketplace, plans spread their risk of loss due to illness to maximize the chance of having substantially more "good-risk" subscribers than "bad-risk" subscribers. As the term suggests, adverse or antiselection occurs when a plan is specially selected by a disproportionate number of bad risks. That occurs when insurance company actuaries do not anticipate the danger of offering those benefits and the premium cannot support the income expected from the new business. As a result, such insurers demand from their state regulators the right to raise premiums in order to pay the mounting claims. As Professor Avedis Donabedian said in *Benefits in Medical Care Programs*, this also poses the dangerous cycle of the better risks leaving the plan for bargains elsewhere, forcing the remainders' premiums still higher in turn and causing even more of the good risks to leave. Should the process go unchecked, as insurance companies have learned, the spiraling effect of adverse selection could destroy an indemnity insurance plan. With ERISA and HMO plans, real "dual options" no longer exist, and the dominion of managed-care "administrators" over the healthcare delivered effectively constrains the adverse selection process. *See* Plate 6.

In an earlier section, adverse selection was termed an "insupportable mythology" adapted from economics and sociology by the insurance industry. Adverse selection is minimized in a pure insurance market, because benefit coverage for various illnesses (risks) have always been written by insurers to "favor the house." The only situations in which a disproportionate number of bad risks significantly "select" a plan "adversely" occurs when government remedial legislation mandates specific coverage, as in the original "dual option" HMO Act on the federal level, and in states with certain mandated-benefit laws. However, without regulation, managed care can control adverse selection by misinformation, care denial, redlining high-cost doctors and risky patients, and enabling a "second bite at the apple" of risk by managing each accepted patient. Only federal involvement in the Exchanges portends a change from the noninsurance, ERISA-plan style of higher cost for less care.

In fact, adverse selection is little more than the process buyers going elsewhere for lower prices. Managed care's ability to prevent adverse selection is supported only by operating in an unregulated environment embracing its market failure. Controlling adverse selection assures minimizing the losses that would otherwise be precipitated by dissatisfied groups needing adequate access to the healthcare system, and by capturing into capitation, those who used to receive such benefits contractually required otherwise under indemnity policies. Ironically, the controlled dimunition of adverse selection by managed care keeps the HMOs from becoming more competitive. It simulates the appearance of response to consumer needs while actually preventing individual competitors from breaking ranks. It effectively establishes a system in which its members inevitably act in concert to keep prices stabilized, while mergers and acquisitions provide profits for the more-powerful participants able to price or purchase in predatory fashion. That can no longer happen when the ACA reaches maximum effectiveness after 2014, because it presages not only cost savings for the government, and thus the taxpayer, but it will make the commercial insurers become either more honestly competitive or drop out of the healthcare business altogether.

In a major policy switch, Oxford pulled out of New York Medicaid in 1998 and began to raise its prices at the same time it lowered its costs by implementing the M&R guidelines for shortening hospital stays. A former Oxford sales rep, who became a vice president at an employee-benefits firm, reportedly said in an August 1998 article in *Crain's New York Business*, "Oxford's focus now seems to be retention at a profit, not growth. If they can't retain the business at a rate they want, they are willing to let the business walk." In a highly unusual move, the NCQA then downgraded Oxford's accreditation status two notches, from "full" to "provisional." Oxford's experience at selling below marginal cost before it was swallowed by UHG offers the lesson: once the pattern of overpromised, inadequate coverage is in place, controlling adverse selection reinforces the market distortion, so that no single insurer can deviate from it. The MCOs either must perform lock step or be wiped out from a mass disenrollment and abandonment by both providers and benefit plans. For government, the alternative was to move to state-mandated, increased benefit laws, some, like Massachusetts, promoting universal coverage, and to the ACA of 2010. Ultimately, a "public option" in place would effectively preserve a competitive economy without having to establish "government-run" universal healthcare.

4. Entrepreneur Plays Doctor: "I Can Get It for You Wholesale"

"How can you afford to sell it to me below wholesale?" the woman said.

"It's simple," said the furrier, "I can make it below cost!"

—Anonymous TV Comic

The "free-rider" phenomenon is a third type of market failure that limits the effective underwriting of healthcare risk. As the 1996, Sixth Circuit Court of Appeals said in *McCloud v. Testa*, citing from the Supreme Court in *Continental T.V., Inc. v. GTE Sylvania, Inc.*:

"A collective action problem occurs when an individual has an incentive to 'free-ride' on the efforts of others. For instance, the Supreme Court upheld under antitrust rule of reason analysis a manufacturer's policy of territorial restraints on its retailers, because without these restraints a retailer who provided minimal point-of-sale services could 'free-ride' on those retailers who provided more lavish point-of-sale services."

Because ERISA and the federal and state governments under Medicare and Medicaid have enabled managed care to "sell" medical services below marginal cost with little interference from regulators, they effectively allowed market-price distortions on a mass scale. The 1996 Supreme Court said in *Khan v. State Oil*, "Unless the supplier is a monopsonist, he cannot squeeze his dealers' margins below a competitive level; the attempt to do so would just drive the dealers into the arms of a competing supplier." The very existence of managed care bends the insurance market out of shape and splits the total actuarial population:

- The managed-care era enabled high-cost indemnity plans to pay for increasing managed-care losses.
- Managed care keeps a "larder" of the uninsured population as well as entry-level doctors for recruitment to lower-premium, lower-option, high-volume HMOs.

- It skims an unconscionable percentage from the below-marginal-cost price of capitated physicians in the short term.
- It establishes "disease management" to supply chronic care for those its acute-care limitations largely created.

In 1995, there were 46.2 million enrolled in HMOs and 40.5 million uninsured. Three years later, as the managed-care insurance population burgeoned, the number of uninsured also increased to over forty-one million, including 4.7 million children, and was about one-sixth of the entire population. The larder of cherry-pickable uninsured rose to 50.7 million by 2009, and by 2010, more than 150 million were in managed care in one form or another.

Why should an employer purchase indemnity insurance when managed care can get it for you "wholesale" (albeit at a list price charged the self-insured employer or union), and splits the "savings" with you? By using engineering and manufacturing analogies, while touting the fiction of a declining cost curve for healthcare, managed care has created a vast adversely selecting population of its cartel-captured "free riders" on the former risk-insurance system. These people dropped their coverage and chose to "go bare," used expensive hospital emergency departments, or joined capitated HMOs, poorly informed, but hoping to receive healthcare at a wholesale, volume-based price. However, the market for a viable system of low-cost indemnity insurance, although seriously distorted by the managed-care market failure initiated by the insurance industry, was kept in place by economic pressures, misdirected remedial legislation, and the seduction of quicker profits.

The managed-care industry's currency rests on four points:
- Absence of informed consent of the risks involved in improper coverage offered by the "managing" of care.
- The insurance industry's avoidance of risk taking through manipulation of adverse selection; creation of the free-rider problem by overvaluation of the coverage.
- Offering similar benefits to be rendered by lesser-trained and thus lower-paid professionals.

- Coercively, capitating providers to split fees, so that the real price paid for the medical service and the resources required to produce that service are below their average variable cost of creating it, with the spread between healthcare "price" and "cost" skimmed as profit by MCOs. *See* Plate 6.

Despite massive insurance lobbying and propaganda obfuscating the health reform issues with scare tactics of increased taxes and regulation, there is no more compelling a case for federal intervention than one that would regulate the forces controlling the market failure in healthcare: a chronic economic and public health disaster. Notwithstanding insurer rhetoric, that the anti-managed-care movement is largely a creation of the liberal media, the states, much less insulated than the federal government from the pain and suffering of their people, took the lead in anti-managed-care legislation following the *Travelers'* mandate and started narrowing the expansive approach used by courts in ERISA preemption cases. However, years would have to pass before Congress and the federal government would attempt to close the gap with the states and authorize state action on minimum mandated-benefit laws that would govern benefit plans through the insurance Exchanges generated by the 2010 ACA.

The Act enables the federal government to enter the scene through a legislative and judicial-review "back door." Federal involvement in the business of insurance—formerly "saved" for the states by ERISA and McCarran-Ferguson—could now marry federal/state participation. Such Exchanges, while perhaps part of the "business of insurance companies," were not within the ERISA and *Royal Drug* scope of the "savings clause's" saving the "business of insurance" for state action alone. The ACA would also place under the federal taxing power and the Commerce Clause the enumerated jurisdiction of Congress to act in the light of a significant governmental interest. Because *de jure* minimums often become *de facto* maximums, the coverage requirements of the new affordable coverage system proposed in 2010 would set out on a path to correct equitably the market distortions that divided the ERISA and indemnity insurance populations.

5. "Disease Management," "Pay-for-Performance," and "Bundling"—the New Ploys on the Block

As managed care lost its initial glitter and risk-adjustment propos-als by government healthcare programs threatened their profitability even further, MCOs looked for new ways to make money out of a sys-tem that owed its profits to premium income from increasing the num-bers of subscribers by consolidation, and by reducing medical service output using managed-care methods. Hospitals, too, were interested in anything that could maximize revenue, although not by reducing the amount of care given. Managed care distorts the actuarially determined healthcare need by placing limits on output. It is seen most starkly in what the mental and substance use disorders Parity law calls "non-quantitative treatment limitations." Thus, it became difficult for some to imagine how the system could continue to be protected from eco-nomic implosion, as hospitals and doctors could no longer be expected to discount needed care even further at the increased risk of actions challenging negligent care, especially in the face of rapidly advancing technology.

Antipathy and indignation arose from patients and medical provid-ers who were more effectively vocal about care denials than those who were the first victims of managed care: the mentally ill. As more cash was extracted from the healthcare system by the mergers and acquisitions consolidating power among fewer large companies, and as employers were still confronted with rising premiums in the absence of improved "quality" medical care, "disease management" was introduced in the 1990s. Although continuing to hover as a panacea portrayed by media-influenced pundits, it never received the traction touted by MCOs, because patients still wanted doctors, not "specially trained nurses," to watch over them, especially when they had chronic illnesses. Dur-ing the post-Millennium decade, "bundled payments" methods were morphed into the mix of suggested fixes to the system, where a single payment could be made to multiple providers reimbursed by a single sum of money for all services related to an episode of care for all services related to a specific treatment. (The economically "locked-in" and fundamentally anticompetitive status of the patients' needs and providers' prices seemed to elude the enthusiasts.) The idea for bundled payments came from a Bush I administration HCFA in 1990, where a four-hospital demonstration study of heart-bypass patients was to be analyzed over the next few years. Because there could be no profit motive, all the caveats (like those that characterized the short-sighted archeologists' payments for ever-smaller pieces of the Dead Sea Scrolls) reappeared. All providers—doctors and hospitals—were unable to effectively see to it that the care the patients received produced significant savings, and eliminating "unnecessary services" and reducing "costs" were unavailing.

In attempting to find the size of the putative "disease management" population, the 1995 National Center for Health Statistics' numbers for prevalence of selected chronic conditions, by age and sex, reflected only the sum of listed chronic conditions. The amount was approximately 330 million, larger than the American population, demonstrating the fact that chronically ill people generally have more than one chronic condition. Humana Corporation's 1998 publicized "sickest of the sick" group, eighty million, a staggering number of people with chronic conditions, the cohort was found to be typically having 4.3 chronic conditions each. If the eighty million people in 1998 with 4.3 chronic diseases each could be separated out from the vast, ERISA-unregulated group and the Medicare and Medicaid managed healthcare pool, those carved out for such special consideration as needing disease management, would have to pay separately for their co-morbid care—of course, at higher premiums. That sounds good only to commercial cash-flow ventures and is the opposite of a real or perfect health-insurance system, which would keep all groups within it, with premiums evenly assessed. Having all groups within the system, as with the ACA putting an end to "preexisting conditions," extraordinarily decreases the chances of healthy, i.e., nonchronically ill people, of developing chronic diseases, and shifts the emphasis to the problems coming from outside healthcare itself, where they rest with poverty, poor education, and genetic predisposition (i.e., away from managed care).

In the indemnity period, state insurance departments monitored premiums with MLRs too low to qualify as real insurance. With ERISA-based plan-payments, there was no such actuarial monitoring or regulation of premiums, because state action that clearly related to benefit plans was preempted by the ERISA-guarded fiduciary discretion "saving" self-insured plan sponsors. The new task for the managed healthcare industry was to justify the need for carving out chronic diseases, helped by a fact that seemed to elude policy planners—namely, that managed care, by its minimalist-care policies, could be responsible for the growing subacute population becoming a chronic one. The proposed "cure" for the proliferating subacute and chronic diseases being magnified by managed care was to cleave off from the risk pool those developing chronic illnesses and to garner increased premiums for treating them, which could be justified as obviously requiring the application of more expensive resources. The alternative was for the increasing economically downward mobile chronic population to be plucked from the premium pool and eventually shifted to taxpayer public health programs. At the same time, it would allow the original premium price to remain with the insurers, whose circular argument for leaving it with them would be that "it will delay the need for future increases."

As reported in *The New York Times* in December 1998, the concept of a system of "disease management," which first appeared in the early 1990s, caught on like wildfire as three hundred new disease-management companies that contracted with employers and HMOs jumped into the scene, with revenues expected to double the following year to $348 million. Al Lewis, the founding president of the newly formed Disease Management Association of America (DMAA), was even more sanguine. Because the United States spent roughly $400 billion per year on illnesses that were the very focus of disease management, he predicted that such vendors and programs could conceivably take in 10 percent of that amount at "today's levels." His betraying caveat was that disease management would continue to grow as long as Congress did not pass patient-protection bills that prevent managed-care organizations and vendors from obtaining "crucial patient data." In other words, the new system's success depended on removing the very constraint the antitrust laws were designed by Congress to prevent: price-fixing using actuarial data in a price-unregulated setting.

By 2005, Lewis left the DMAA and joined the Disease Management Purchasing Consortium International (DM). According to a September 2005 *Managed Care* interview, Lewis was enthusiastic about his role in DM and building his Consortium to improve claims by DM vendors. The article notes,

> "To the degree that one person can be credited or blamed for the very existence of a $1.1-billion segment of American healthcare, Al Lewis is that person when it comes to disease management. . . . With a potentially huge boost from the Medicare Modernization Act, [2003 Medicare Part D] disease management could be on the verge of a boom, Lewis argues, but only if it overcomes a major obstacle: Nobody believes its numbers. Many employers won't contract with DM companies because they doubt vendors' claims about how much money their programs save."

The interview displayed in the article:

Managed Care: "What's wrong with how disease management companies calculate return on investment?"

Al Lewis: "I used to pooh-pooh skepticism about ROI in disease management as being a result of people not knowing what they were talking about. It turns out they were right, though they didn't know why. The old industry standard that everybody used—myself included—has a fatal flaw. I would claim to have invented the old methodology, but since we figured out that it was wrong, I went from pride of authorship to admission of authorship."

MC: "To be followed by denial of authorship?"

Lewis: "Right, though I'm not quite at that point. Here's the problem: A huge percentage of employers who don't do disease management don't do it because they don't believe the numbers. Most of the numbers they don't believe are indeed wrong, especially if the vendor is not on the DMPC recommended list. Employers are right to be dubious of vendors that claim an ROI of four to one."

MC: "What's the fatal flaw in how disease management companies have calculated ROI?"

Lewis: "The fatal flaw is caused by the fact that not all patients with a disease will file a claim during the initial measurement period. This creates a situation where the entire diseased population is not counted in the baseline measurement. As a result, estimated savings for some chronic diseases—asthma and coronary artery disease in particular—will always be overstated. As improvement is measured from an artificially under- represented baseline, plans will overstate program improvement and report an inflated ROI."

MC: "They took credit for lower claims that had nothing to do with asthma."

Lewis: "Exactly. The vendor had no idea why its numbers were wrong. They were too stupid to realize how stupid they were. That's probably true of 50 small vendors."

MC: "Are you describing a two-tier market, with some vendors trying to provide accurate numbers and others more interested in making a quick buck?"

Lewis: "It's a three-tier industry. A group of established players does disease management right. A second group of established players does it right under duress when somebody makes them. A very large third group of small companies has absolutely no clue what they're doing. They think they're right, but they're not, and nobody calls them on it because benefits consultants who dabble in this stuff don't have a clue either. For all I know, these small companies do save their clients a little money, but their reporting is so bad that there's no way to know for sure, which calls their entire performance into question.

Five years later, according to an April 12, 2010 *PR Newswire*, Lewis's enthusiasm reached a peak:

"Al Lewis, president of the Disease Management Purchasing Consortium, Inc. (DMPC), the founder and first president of the Disease Management Association of America and the person most often credited with establishing the metrics by which disease management is measured announced today that he will be personally [*sic*] validating and guaranteeing disease management (DM) and wellness outcomes for an elite, award-winning group of vendors, health plans, benefits consultants and employers."

Like managed care, disease management was the child of for-profit insurance and taxpayer-zealous cost-cutters. In 1995, *JAMA* reported studies demonstrating that both the readmission and medical-cost results of nurse-directed management of congestive heart failure in elderly patients discharged from hospital, and the use of nurse telephone contact in a variety of chronic medical conditions, had significantly increased. In addition, that even advocates' arguments were unconvincing about the value of DM, and some said it decreased only short-term costs. They all were apparently right, because the first group to be concentrated on was the high-risk patient. Others, more incisive, said that while it decreased long-term costs, too, that would only occur if lower-risk chronic patients were brought into the mix. They must have understood that fact from the "community psychiatry" movement of the 1960s, which found that treating the greatest number of moderately sick patients was much preferable to expending the enormous resources required when taking on the sickest group.

In 1999, the *New England Journal of Medicine* reported that population-based prevention demonstrated that overall morbidity and mortality are best reduced by targeting the larger number of persons at low risk rather than the smaller number at high risk. Thus, after

411

years of extolling the virtues of the "primary-care doctor," advocates of the DM carve-out system would have to downplay the value of trusted personal physicians to monitor their patients' usually multiple conditions, not to mention the acute problems often unrelated to their chronic illnesses. Carving out the management of chronic disease from primary care was being seen as likely to devalue the primary physician's role and erode the primary-care base in relatively short order. It gave rise to a proposal for "focused healthcare factories" so ardently disavowed by the M&R president in 1998 enterprises specializing in the care of one illness or one procedure, suggesting that it would replace what Harvard Business School healthcare economist Regina Herzlinger in 1999 called "the present jumble of multipurpose providers."

By April 2010, Maryland became the twenty-ninth state to allow nurse practitioners to work without a formal physician supervisor. In June 2010, *MarketWatch*, *The Wall Street Journal*'s online magazine, offered a telling comment on cash flow and how managed care makes profits:

"Nurse practitioners cost less not because patients pay less to see them, but because private insurers pay the same rate regardless of which professional performs the office visit. Only Medicare, the federal program for older and disabled Americans, reimburses at a lower rate if a nurse practitioner, rather than a doctor, provides a service."

The fact that nurse practitioners (NPs) were found to spend more time with each patient did not provide an answer to their encouraged equivalence to doctors. Moreover, such reasoning distorted the fact that a physician's time and intellectual capital investment is inevitably considered more valuable per unit effort and is demonstrated by what society is willing to pay. As *MarketWatch* revealed: "NPs earn an annual mean salary of $84,250 much lower than a family physician's average $145,000 per year or a medical specialist's even higher income." These data uncovered possible reasons for the exploitation of the NP and the patient as well, or the merit of circumventing use of the medical profession for all but the most complex of conditions. Of course, the physician/entrepreneur or clinic, too, hires the NP to front-end the office or clinic visit by taking histories and performing basic physical examinations, saving the doctor or other clinical HMO employee time for more complex, time-consuming work. Nevertheless, it leaves the responsibility for diagnosis and legal accountability for all the patients with the physician or clinic, as physicians' malpractice premiums reveal.

It is clear that DM in 1999 had little more than more short-term cash to speak for it. For one thing, carving out the chronic and sickest group lowered only the costs for the main group of covered patients, certainly not the premiums charged for them, at the same time as the DM program raised the price of special premiums assessed for the carved-out group. As premiums are ordinarily prepaid, and because the chronic group has a foreseeably much higher death rate, with no *pro rata* return of premium to a decedent's estate if death occurred before the policy year is up, actuaries and underwriters must have known that the higher premiums for the chronically ill would beget dramatically large, short-term, cash flow. Moreover, the unconvincing claims of huge savings achieved by boosting outpatient services more than 250 percent, while reducing hospital admissions only 40 percent, revealed the intrinsic economic flaw. *Modern Healthcare* reported,

> "Patients who suffer from chronic diseases consume the vast majority of healthcare resources, presenting a huge challenge to managed care. Many insurers and providers that manage risk are using disease management to diagnose conditions early and coordinate treatment over time."

Thus, although the DM effect definitely decreases or delays hospital admissions, it also produces a six-fold increase in outpatient services to get the same or similar result for a greater volume of units of care. Because outpatient costs are generally one-third the cost of inpatient services, the net dollar cost to society differs little in either case. What the switch to outpatient services does accomplish, however, is simply an increase in cash flow generated by producing more, smaller units of limited care in the guise of disease management. This, rather than the

413

more intensive, comprehensive analyses is what the wealthy look for when they go to the main Mayo, Cleveland, and Johns Hopkins inpatient clinics or others at that level. When taking into account the poorer medication and dietary compliance rates for outpatients, compared to the intensive learning process during inpatient comprehensive nursing care and regular medical visits, it should be clear that the ambulatory savings to society are difficult to justify except as a compromise based on resources. Local hospitals would not tolerate substituting a method of eliminating or reducing the family doctor's role; because that is what society is willing to pay for to reduce managed-care's deadweight loss. As a result, hospitals would begin to set up their own outpatient services, using their own or contracted inpatient team of hospitalists to render the savings less tempting than when offered by nurse-based, store-front or pharmacy "medicine." The DMAA, founded in 1998 to help organize these efforts to deskill medical care for "return on investment," boldly stated online in April 2010:

"The Care Continuum Alliance, an association representing stakeholders in population health management, told the nation's insurance commissioners today that wellness, disease management and other population-based services should be counted as costs related to clinical care when calculating a health plan's medical loss ratio."

In mid-September, the DMAA folded its tent within the Care Continuum Alliance (CCA), an industry trade group:

"Today, we change our name, but not our mission: to align all stakeholders toward improving the health of populations. We have evolved with our members toward a whole person approach to care that keeps the healthy well, reduces disease risk and helps those with chronic conditions manage their health."

When President Obama signed the ACA, the CCA board hastened to send a flurry of communications to DHHS, the DOL, and the IRS, urging them to allow their help in "enabling health plans and employers to utilize medical management techniques that allow them to better manage their populations resulting in a healthier workforce." They sent letters to Kathleen Sibelius, secretary of DHHS, to Senator Jay Rockefeller, and to the NAIC. The letters express a desire to show they "support a transparent and ongoing process between DHHS, state regulators, and other stakeholders that recognizes the need for flexibility in classifying services for the calculation of the MLR." They attempted to establish that case-management services should not be considered "administrative expenses" but as part of the MLRs and that, "they support efforts to appropriately classify these health-care improvement services as expenses related to the delivery of medical care." Adding the high profitability of such non-quantitative treatment limitation services to MLRs of MCOs, as if to show how much of the premium dollar is spent on their view of worthy medical care, demonstrates how managed care views for itself its ability to dip into the multi provider, cash-flow trough of healthcare dollars.

The impressive business, research, and commercial members of the CCA board of directors included Emad Rizk, MD, president of McKesson Health Solutions, parent company of InterQual, James Cross, MD, head of National Medical Policy and Operations of Aetna, and Christopher Vojta, MD, senior vice president of Ingenix (now OptumInsight). Others on the board included Jeffrey Levin-Scherz, MD, MBA, FACP, a principal at Towers Watson, a leading firm specializing in mergers and acquisitions, and Frederic Goldstein, president of U.S. Preventive Medicine, who founded Specialty Disease Management, a company acquired by U.S. Preventive Medicine in 2007. Earlier, Mr. Goldstein was president and CEO of U.S. Care Management, a company whose "core service—highly trained, community-based nurse care managers—allows USCM to more effectively coordinate care to complement all aspects of disease management programs."

In the April 7, 2011 issue of *JAMA*, in a commentary on *The Challenge of Multiple Comorbidity for the US Healthcare System,* two physicians, one from the Office of the Assistant Secretary for Health (Dr. Anand K. Parekh), and one from the Agency for Healthcare Research and Quality (Dr. Mary Barton), DHHS, stated,

"The tremendous efforts in the fight against chronic disease have inadvertently created individual disease "silos," which are reinforced by specialty organizations, advocacy groups, disease management organizations, and government at all levels. Transformation from a single chronic condition approach to a multiple chronic conditions approach is needed. Only then will the United States be better prepared to care for this increasingly large population. Indeed, the changing demographics of the US population will necessitate this transformation."

"Pay for performance," referred to by enthusiasts as P4P, arose post-Millennium from insurance industry ideologues in both the United States and the United Kingdom. It was seized on by hospital organization and Medicare planners as a way out of the frustration felt by those apparently not knowing where the high costs of healthcare were coming from or how to slow them. Some, like the insurers, didn't care to slow them down, but by joining in the effort, they could placate the government and the media with "we are all in this together." Pay-for-performance would also purport to eliminate payments for negative consequences of care that result in injury, illness, or death. This concept might well have unnerved trial lawyer association members who might consider such a government solution as removing an entire group of plaintiffs as potential clients. A "price" was being put on injuries, illnesses, or death, somewhat resembling Workers Compensation Insurance, except in this case, the insurance company would be relieved of their indemnification.

6. The Beginning and End of the P4P "Never Events"

"Never events" were twenty-eight occurrences on a United States list of "inexcusable" outcomes in a health-care setting compiled by the National Quality Forum. The Tax Relief and Healthcare Act of 2006 accepted the concept from the National Quality Forum and required that the OIG report to Congress regarding the incidence of "never events" among Medicare beneficiaries, effective October 2008 in time for consideration by a lame-duck Congress and administration. The assertively antinomial phrase "never events"—medical complications, including hospital infections—would characterize the basis for which the Medicare program under the George W. Bush administration proposed to pay, deny payment, or recoup payment for provider services furnished in connection with such events, and the processes that the CMS would use to identify such events and deny or recoup payment. In 2006, the National Quality Forum—originally formed in 2000 and then reformed in 2006 from a merger with the National Committee for Quality Healthcare (NCQHC), appointed as president Janet Corrigan, PhD, former chair of the NCQHC. Dr. Corrigan was also formerly vice president for planning and development of the NCQA, which as noted earlier, conferred upon itself the role of collector of "quality treatment" data for the by then almost entirely for-profit managed-care-HMO industry. She was in charge of NCQA's efforts to implement and continually improve the HEDIS advertised as used by more than 90 percent of America's health plans.

The NCQHC start-up had not made it off the ground well. In fact, a 2010 Internet search brings up few articles on the organization. On April 11, 2001, it held its second annual conference, called "Getting to Zero: Perspectives and Challenges," at which newly appointed Special Advisor to President Bush on Healthcare Policy Dr. Mark B. McClellan, speaking about "pay-for-performance and medical errors," said:

> "We think that if we can increase—if we can increase insurance rates [so in original], reduce uninsurance and make sure that more Americans have access to affordable, good healthcare plans, yeah, that should improve healthcare quality. And that

fits with this general theme that I'm trying to emphasize is that we really need to develop a healthcare system where the incentives are right."

Other groups were also interested in "never events," apparently wanting to provide support to their members who were interested in ensuring that their insurers were not billed for such events. As self-insurers, they obviously did not wish to have to pay for these events themselves. One such organization was the Leapfrog Group, which reported in 1998 that it was "a group of large employers [that] came together to discuss how they could work together to use the way they purchased healthcare to have an influence on its quality and affordability." The organization was formed soon after the presidential election in 2000, out of the Business Roundtable, calling itself an association of CEOs of leading U.S. companies with nearly $6 trillion in annual revenues and more than twelve million employees. By 2010, Leapfrog was a

> "national organization using the collective leverage of large purchasers of healthcare to initiate breakthrough improvements in the safety, quality, and affordability of healthcare for Americans . . . We serve as the employer's voice on healthcare issues in the local and national arenas."

P4P, as an upside method of reining in costs, did not get off to a good start either. Like "never events," P4P might have acted as a disincentive for providers, because they would be monitored by limited criteria. They would be reluctant to take patients who had poor historical outcomes with chronic disease states, low health literacy, and inadequate financial resources to afford expensive medications or treatments. They would also be wary of taking patients who were members of ethnic groups traditionally subject to healthcare inequities that actuarially would make them fall below the preset quality standards.

P4P was also a setup for antitrust violations. A 2004 article in *The American Journal of Managed Care* (AMJC), enthusiastic about P4P and citing an article in *Family Practice Management*, stated online:

"By 2006, at least 80 health plans covering 60 million patients are expected to offer such programs. Although a number of components are needed in P4P programs to actually change provider behavior, such as setting rewards to a level that gets provider attention, involving providers in the process but not giving them veto power, and staying the course after the initial resistance appears, there are 2 components that are critical. They are: (1) selecting and using a standardized set of the 'right' measures, and (2) collaborating with other plans and purchasers within a given region or market."

However, the article lamented the recommendations given to doctors after paying them: "While these same physicians may be pleased to receive bonus payments from these plans, the likelihood that they will act on the information is small." The AJMC article recognized a foreboding causal sequence in the effort to "pay" for performance, cautioning:

"While antitrust and other legal concerns must be explored, the results from the Integrated Healthcare Association's P4P program in California would suggest that if each plan gets back only its own data, the effort is led by a group outside the plans, and there is no direct cooperation about the structure of the actual payouts, the likelihood of antitrust or other law suits is minimal."

The article tried one more approach, this time on market power considerations, bluntly adding:

"If direct cooperation is not possible among plans or employers in a given region, an individual plan or employer can still successfully employ P4P by limiting its focus to a small number of high-volume providers and relying on an outside source of information and benchmarking of providers."

In March of 2009, *The Washington Post* reported that an eager Geisinger Health System in Danville, Pennsylvania offered a "90-day

guarantee on elective heart surgery." If complications should arise following cardiac surgery, Geisinger would pay the additional cost of treatment. Moreover, the P4P effort reached the bizarre, when *Healthcare
Finance News* reported in July 2009 that St. Luke's Hospital and Health
Network was offering both a clinical and financial surgical guarantee as
part of a partnership with uro-gynecologists at The Institute for Female
Pelvic Medicine and Reconstructive Surgery in Allentown, Pennsylvania. Joseph Merola, MD, St. Luke's chief of obstetrics and gynecology,
said,

> "We are proud to be able to offer this kind of clinical guar-
> antee. Creating this sort of partnership and offering a clinical
> guarantee ultimately benefits every woman who undergoes this
> surgery. Knowing that our patients have guaranteed care plans
> should provide women with every confidence in her surgeon,
> surgical team, this surgery and her outcome."

Perhaps the board of the hospital and, possibly, the lawyers for the
hospital and its doctors, had not considered the 1982 Supreme Court
antitrust opinion in *Arizona v. Maricopa County Medical Society*: "Whatever may be its peculiar problems and characteristics, the Sherman Act,
so far as price-fixing agreements are concerned, establishes one uniform
rule applicable to all industries alike." *Maricopa County* was a case where
the doctors altruistically set prices for the "most" anyone would have
to pay!

In 2010, the Obama administration ended the Bush II administration equivalent of the "pay-for-performance" concept of "never events"
required by the Tax Relief and Healthcare Act of 2006. Stuart Wright,
deputy inspector general for evaluation and inspections of DHHS,
issued the two-year report required by the Act, "Adverse Events in
Hospitals: Public Disclosure of Information and Events," to the government Agency for Healthcare Research and Quality and to the new
acting administrator of the Centers for Medicare and Medicaid Services. It revealed earlier knowledge that using "never events" was a poor
choice of liability language with which to saddle the medical profession:

"The healthcare community now uses the term 'adverse event' more commonly than 'never event' to refer to harm experienced by a patient as a result of medical care. After consulting with congressional committee staff in 2007, we modified our approach and terminology to be consistent with evolving patient safety research and industry trends. As used in this study, an adverse event is defined as harm to a patient as a result of medical care or harm that occurs in a healthcare setting. Although an adverse event often indicates that the care resulted in an undesirable clinical outcome and may involve medical errors, adverse events do not always involve errors, negligence, or poor quality of care and may not always be preventable."

Although the Act required the study to be performed to make:

"(1) recommendations on processes to identify never events and to deny or recoup payments for services furnished in connection with such events; and

(2) a recommendation on a potential process (or processes) for public disclosure of never events which

(A) will ensure protection of patient privacy; and

(B) will permit the use of the disclosed information for a root cause analysis to inform the public and the medical community about safety issues involved,"

the Inspector General prudently decided:

"This memorandum report contains no recommendations and is being issued directly in final form. We did not make recommendations for two reasons. First, we concluded that it is not appropriate to make a broad recommendation for a public disclosure process. Entities collect adverse event data for different purposes, such as generating information for patient safety improvements, conducting oversight of hospitals, or processing payments for healthcare services. Given these differences, we believe that it is less useful to propose a standard process for public disclosure than it is to describe the current and planned practices of the entities reviewed. Second, all these entities have patient privacy protections. Therefore we did not identify particular privacy concerns that warrant recommendations."

It is important to note how the Bush II administration's draconian approach to medical-care accidents was changed by the new administration:

"Although an adverse event often indicates that the care resulted in an undesirable clinical outcome and may involve medical errors, adverse events do not always involve errors, negligence, or poor quality of care and may not always be preventable."

"Bundled payments," a euphemism from the short-lived P4P advocates, also met with some circumspection by managed-care proponents during the lame-duck period of the George W. Bush administration. An article in *Managed Healthcare Executive*, "Bundled payments expected to reward providers: It's the new P4P," stated cautiously,

"With memories of the failed capitation movement, participating providers were reluctant to adopt bundled-payment projects anytime soon, and the majority believed they should have received extra payments to cover the expense of implementing the new billing arrangements, and that the new CMS Acute Care Episode project, scheduled to begin January 1, 2009, will be conducted in Texas, Oklahoma, New Mexico and Colorado. . . . Rather than the usual separate payments for Part A and Part B, CMS will provide a single payment to hospitals and providers [for specified illnesses and procedures] . . . "[The Commonwealth Commission's Executive Vice-President], acknowledges that if we build it, they still might not come. After providers' experience with capitation in the 1990s, the majority might still be gun-shy about assuming financial risk for providing care. 'To encourage [a bundled payment system], we're going to need to give significant attention to the incentives that we offer providers,' [the Executive Vice-President says]. 'Anything that sounds remotely like capitation is going to cause them to say, 'We've been there. It was awful, and we aren't doing that again.' One of the first challenges that a bundled payment system might face here is whether it will run afoul of the law . . . the Stark rule against physician self-referral might come into play."

The present-day DM advocates may expect to eliminate significant numbers of specialty and subspecialty physicians from attending to the care of the chronically ill and substitute specialized nurses for them. Nevertheless, the higher specialty costs avoided so long by HMO incentive-based gatekeepers should burgeon anyway, because hospitals and their medical staffs are liable to incorporate as much defensive medical expertise as possible in the "bundle." This "marketplace reaction" would frustrate the ineffectual theories advanced by the congressional and commercial managed-care schemes. On February 5, 2009, *Health Leaders Media*, a magazine "for senior executives: leadership, technology, finance, physician and community hospitals," said:

"Proponents of bundled payments are trying to avoid many of these hurdles by adding caveats and conditions for payment. But the more complicated any payment system becomes the more likely it is that payments will influence provider behavior in ways that haven't even been considered. If policy makers aren't careful, their worthwhile attempts to fix the flaws in the fee-for-service system may just create a whole new set of problems."

7. Are P4P and Capitation coming back? Now, with ACOs, doctors playing entrepreneur with the NCQA, and the new merger mania.

In an interview at the "3rd Annual World Congress Leadership Summit on Healthcare Quality and Pay-for-Performance Contracting," in August 2005, Dr. Robert J. Margolis, president and CEO of Health-Care Partners Medical Group, a physician board certified in internal medicine and medical oncology, and newly named Chairman-elect of the NCQA's Board of Directors (to start in January for a two-year term), stated,

> "It seems that the most practical and effective way to re-align the compensation in healthcare is not to scrap the FFS system entirely in favor of capitation (which I would support as a better starting system, as long as it was appropriately risk adjusted), but rather to "add on" a strong component of goal based quality measurement and reward—Pay for Performance. . . The major weakness in this P4P program, as it is in most programs, is the measurements and public reporting are confined to HMO managed care membership. We desperately need comparison quality measurement across all insurance products to allow for informed decisions by consumers, employers and policy makers on where they receive the best value for the premiums that are paid."

According to a news release on October 19, 2010, NCQA had begun its putative accrediting program the year before, by partnering with HealthCare Partners Medical Group of Torrance, California (HMPG) to develop

> "draft standards [that] were developed with the guidance of a multi-stakeholder Accountable Care Organization Task Force, chaired by Robert J. Margolis, MD, CEO of the Health-Care Partners Medical Group, in Torrance, California."

424

Formed in 1992, HPMG merged with several medical groups to form HealthCare Partners, LLC, as parent, now a management services organization that also owns and manages HealthCare Partners Affiliates Medical Group (California), JSA Healthcare Corporation (Florida, Nevada and Utah), The Camden Group (a national consulting firm), and HealthCare Partners Institute (a research arm). The more than 700 of HPMG's employed and independently contracted primary care and specialty physician members' care for more than 575,000 Medicare Advantage, managed-care patients at more than 50 locations in the Los Angeles, Pasadena/the San Gabriel Valley, South Bay, Long Beach, the San Fernando and Santa Clarita Valleys, and Orange County areas. HealthCare Partners' Independent Physician Association (IPA) model consists of more than 900 primary care physicians, and is supported by 3,000 specialists. The IPA, too, serves the San Fernando Valley, Pasadena, San Gabriel Valley, central Los Angeles, South Bay and Orange County areas.

We mentioned earlier, the New York physicians' group CDPHP, a managed-care company in the state-regulated business of insurance, and an HMO organized pursuant to New York State insurance law, which pays for the healthcare of its four hundred thousand subscribers to its "9,000 providers and practitioners." According to a 2000 state insurance department audit, its participating providers are paid on a fee-for-service basis that authorizes the HMO to withhold up to 20 percent "from fees paid to the physicians for the purpose of retaining the funds to offset operating deficits, to establish operating reserves, or to meet other financial needs of the HMO." According to the audit, CDPHP also owns 50 percent of an unauthorized captive off-shore reinsurance company.

In a November 20, 2010 article "Consumer Risks Feared as Health Law Spurs Mergers," *The New York Times* quoted Dr. Donald M. Berwick, saying that the new, recess-appointed administrator of the Centers for Medicare and Medicaid Services "hails the benefits of 'integrated care.' But, Dr. Berwick said, 'we need to assure both patients and society at large that destructive, exploitative and costly forms of collusion and monopolistic behaviors do not emerge and thrive, disguised as cooperation.' [And,] in a recent letter to federal officials, Charles N. [Chip] Kahn III, president of the Federation of American Hospitals, said, 'To provide a fertile field to develop truly innovative, coordinated-care models, the fraud and abuse laws should be waived altogether.'" What "waiving altogether" would mean to the managed-care industry is that under the law, Medicare can penalize organizations that avoid high-risk, high-cost patients. The article pointed out that "Judith A. Stein, director of the nonprofit Center for Medicare Advocacy, said she was concerned that some care organizations would try to hold down costs by 'cherry-picking healthier patients and denying care when it's needed.'"

On May 12, 2011, Keith Wilson, M.D., Chair, Governing Board and Executive Committee, California Association of Physician Groups [CAPG], and HealthCare Partners Medical Group's Regional Medical Director, gave testimony before the Subcommittee on Health of the House Ways and Means Committee.

"In California, we have vast experience with payment models that provide viable alternatives to this failed FFS system. As I will describe today, the California model has used capitated payments for decades, combined with robust quality reporting and public accountability provisions, and a backstop provided by state regulation of risk-bearing entities. We believe that our capitated payment system can serve as a model for the rest of the country, especially as health care providers around the nation consider delivery system reforms, like accountable care organizations, whether they be Medicare, Medicaid or commercial payer-driven. [He explains, "We use the term capitation throughout but recognize that in the current health policy dialogue, this term can be used to embrace a variety of other concepts, such as bundled payments, partial capitation, condition-specific capitation, virtual partial capitation, and others."]"

Regarding the "failed FFS system," he inadvertently notes the value of "higher utilization" of healthcare services:

"It is important to point out that these capitated payments I have just mentioned are made directly to the medical groups. Some of these groups then provide downstream payments to primary care or specialty care groups. These downstream payments may take the form of subcapitation, salary, or even some FFS payments in the event the group wants to incentivize higher utilization for a certain type of service, like preventive services. For example, a group might pay a FFS payment for childhood immunizations."

Praising the role of California's Integrated Health Association, he admits that there are negative aspects of capitation, but temporizes when he says,

"First, the Integrated Healthcare Association is a statewide multi-stakeholder leadership group that promotes quality improvement, accountability and affordability of health care in the state. The IHA evaluates physician groups based on four categories: clinical quality, coordinated diabetes care, information technology-enabled systems, and patient experience. The IHA's pay for performance programs reward physician practices and other providers with incentives based on their performance on these measures. (Notably, 45 CAPG member organizations, representing approximately seven million patients in the state, were awarded the highest overall quality rating in 2009 from the IHAs statewide pay-for-performance program.)

"Pay-for-performance programs, like IHA's, compliment the capitated payment model by providing necessary protections against potential incentives to stint on care. By requiring groups to provide high quality care, and incentivizing quality through the use of financial and other bonus payments, IHA's pay-for-performance program plays a critical role in ensuring that our patients receive the most efficient, highest quality care. One criticism of the capitated payment model is that it incentivizes providers to withhold care in order to maximize their payment. Quality performance programs, particularly those with financial incentives tied to performance benchmarks, can outweigh such incentives in a capitated model."

In a 2010, an IHA White Paper, on "Accountable Care Organizations in California, *Lessons for the National Debate on Delivery System Reform*," by James C. Robinson, *Kaiser Permanente Professor and Director, Berkeley Center for Health Technology, University of California, Berkeley*, and Emma L. Dolan *Graduate Student in Public Health and Public Policy University of California, Berkeley*, the authors note in the Executive Summary:

> "Accountable Care Organizations (ACOs) that bring together providers and reward them for controlling costs and improving quality are a major platform for delivery system reform ensconced in the *Patient Protection and Affordable Care Act.* . . This paper outlines five overarching aspects of California physician organizations—their organizational structures, payment methods, relationships with health plans, how they promote consumer choice, and the public policy and regulatory constraints they face—and offers ten key lessons for the national ACO debate."

With great praise for Kaiser Permanente's role as "the most successful ACO in California," the White Paper holds nothing back in praise of P4P and its ability to "create an environment of collaboration between health plans and physician organizations." Moreover, the Paper's "Fourth Lesson" perhaps answers the question why Dr. Berwick issued his caution about "integrated care," saying, "we need to assure both patients and society at large that destructive, exploitative and costly forms of collusion and monopolistic behaviors do not emerge and thrive, disguised as cooperation," and why the FTC and the DoJ issued the antitrust guidelines in 2011:

> "Lesson Four: Health plans acting in concert on payment methods and performance measurement helped facilitate the growth of California's provider organizations, and should also

play an integral part in fostering ACO development nationally."

Dr. Wilson concluded his testimony before the House Ways and Means Committee with:

"In addition, we believe that attention must be paid to the Medicare Advantage (MA) program. In California, Medicare patients who were enrolled in a plan using a capitated payment methodology had hospital utilization rates of 982.2 hospital days per 1,000 as compared to Medicare FFS patients with 1,664 hospital days per 1,000. This lower utilization rate in the capitated model has enormous potential for cost savings. Given the potential for savings and seniors' well-documented satisfaction with this program, we encourage the Committee to consider ways in which this program can be [sic] provide value to seniors in the future."

Recall the large observational study finding the opposite results, which was published in *JAMA*, comparing admissions for heart failure among seven million cases from 1993 to 2006. The *JAMA* study used Medicare data of heart-failure treatment in hospitals over the period 1993 to 2006, correlated with the ascendance of managed care. It demonstrated that while the reduction in hospital length of stay could have reduced the risk of hospital-associated adverse events, in fact, shortening the time in the hospital led to *more* adverse events in the period early after discharge and led to an increase in both post-hospital readmission and mortality risk.

As reported by Business Wire and the NCQA, on November 18, 2011, three weeks after promulgation by the FTC/DoJ of the Final ACO Antitrust Policy Statement, the NCQA, the managed-care industry led accrediting organization, was ready to enter a hopeful, new marketspace for the managed healthcare industry. In "New NCQA Accreditation Program Identifies ACOs That Are Most Likely to Succeed," it published its standards that were developed with the Accountable Care

Organization Task Force, chaired by Robert Margolis, MD, CEO of the HealthCare Partners Medical Group in Torrance, California, a

"roadmap for provider-led organizations to demonstrate their ability to reach the triple aim: reduce cost, improve quality and enhance the patient experience.

To maximize accreditation's usefulness for a variety of ACOs and ACO partners, the NCQA program:

– Aligns with many aspects of the Medicare Shared Savings Program

– Addresses expectations common among private purchasers

– Uses three levels of accreditation to signify differing levels of ACO readiness and capability."

As indicated above, Dr. Wilson's 2011 congressional testimony, noted: "In California, we have vast experience with payment models that provide viable alternatives to this failed FFS system." The 2010, IHA's "ACO White Paper" stated in "Lesson Four": "Health plans acting in concert on payment methods and performance measurement helped facilitate the growth of California's provider organizations, . . " The FAHs' Chip Kahn suggested to the FTC/DoJ, that to "provide a fertile field to develop truly innovative, coordinated-care models, the fraud and abuse laws should be waived altogether." These statements, taken together with Dr. Berwick's 2010, cautionary note, "that destructive, exploitative and costly forms of collusion and monopolistic behaviors do not emerge and thrive, disguised as cooperation," should give us pause.

The 2011, NCQA-led, HealthCare Partners, LLC's, expansionistic, multistate, managed-care physician group's attempt to reach nationally into control of the ACA's Accountable Care Organizations, is reminiscent of the slew of FTC/DoJ antitrust actions against California's many failed "messenger models" tried after the Millennium. Compared with the messenger model, under which the IPA acts as a simple conduit of information between the health plans and the physicians, under the lawful messenger model, the IPA communicates to its members the terms of the fee-for-service contracts, which the members may then independently accept or reject, but the IPA does not negotiate the terms of the contracts. In the case of HPMG, there is a corporate parent and subsidiaries, and

In an October 24, 2011, article in *BARRON'S*, "The Next Wave of Health-Care Mergers," Robin Goldwyn Blumenthal wrote:

"'We're on the verge of a massive amount of M&A,' says Jim Lane, a New Jersey money manager and former managed-care analyst. 'There's no organic growth left in the business except for pricing.' The issue is clear. Managed care has become a mature industry, with ever-dimming prospects. Membership in managed-care plans offered through employers has in fact fallen since 2000, when it hit 179.4 million, according to the U.S. Census Bureau data. It stood at 169.7 million people in 2009; the most recent year for which data exist, and today's sluggish job growth doesn't bode well for improvement. . . Little wonder that next year's earnings at Aetna (mostly a managed-care insurer) are expected to grow just 2%, and those at Cigna, 6%. The health-care law has clouded the future further and investors have noticed. Managed-care companies as a group now trade at an average of nine times their expected earnings for next year, or about 25% below the broad stock market's multiple."

The chronically ill population, heretofore the curse of insurance risks, was now being asked to be "bundled" and "performance-based" into the managed-care industry's cash-flow-enthusiastic hands. It appears, nonetheless, that chronic illness, let alone acute illness, would not diminish by having doctors manage to see it less.

VIII. As Managed
Care Ripens for Review

In healthcare, Medicare, Medicaid, and privately insured patients have a beneficial interest in the provider-patient contractual relationship even though the Medicaid patients are technically "recipients," not "beneficiaries," of the funds that come entirely from general revenue. The fact that such groups are divided by the pejorative term "entitlement programs" is irrelevant for all but the politically motivated. Participants in Medicare, Medicaid, and the Veteran's Administration programs are "entitled" and guaranteed their benefits by law. Persons with private insurance and privately paid-for healthcare are "entitled" and guaranteed their healthcare by contract. The same fiduciary-based status exists under all arrangements created by trust, insurance contracts, or statutes, regardless of whether they arise in Medicare and Medicaid, in benefit plans federally preempted by ERISA, or covered by insurance policies regulated by the states. Thus, Medicare and Medicaid, beneficiaries and recipients, respectively, participants and beneficiaries of ERISA health and welfare benefit plans, as well as those persons aggrieved by insurance companies regulated under state law, are proper parties for redress litigation when violations of their common-law or statutory rights are alleged.

In 1975, Congress repealed the Maguire Act, which had exempted from the Sherman Act state fair-trade laws permitting vertical price-fixing. When the Supreme Court, in its 1997 *State Oil Company v. Khan* unanimous decision, removed vertical price fixing from the list of unequivocal, that is, *per se* violations, it overruled its 1968 decision in *Albrecht,* moving *Khan* to a rule of reason analysis. Citing from *Maricopa*

County Medical Society, the Court said, *"per se* treatment [of vertical restrictions on price] is appropriate '[o]nce experience with a particular kind of restraint enables the Court to predict with confidence that a rule of reason will condemn it.'" However, managed healthcare is systemically structured around both vertical and horizontal agreements, with capitated and fee-for-service providers supported by the pharmaceutical industry's heavy discounts consolidated by MA plans, which include those discounts as added benefits. Therefore, because the economic structure of contemporary managed care is based primarily on vertical price-fixed arrangements from two or more sets of capitated prices, one might see an argument for antitrust violation in such arrangements under a rule of reason analysis. Although, the 1990 Supreme Court's price-fixing analysis in *Atlantic Richfield Co. v. USA Petroleum Co.*, citing numerous cases, appears to be based on the theory that "regardless of how these prices are set, [low prices benefit the consumer and] so long as they are above predatory levels, they do not threaten competition." Therefore, the concept of "low prices" cannot be universalized as a good, unless the good is determined based on how they got to be "low."

The threshold antitrust questions in healthcare prices should be these: How is "low" determined? How long should that "low" be tolerated? Is "low" the price for the direct healthcare cost—the MLR free from capitation-price effects—or is the low price made artificially low because of volume arrangements that conceal the reduced amount of care given individual patients—the deadweight loss to society. If external management cost is included in the MLR, the MLR does not represent patient care but only its cost to the insurer. Without systematic epidemiologic studies of such "management" effect on the treated population's short- and long-term state of health per intervention, managed care constraints would represent a predatory manipulation of the price of patients' healthcare. As reported in the New York Times of May 7, 2011, Florida's proposed sweeping overhaul of its $21 billion Medicaid program was

> "based on a five-year-old pilot program that had decidedly
> mixed results. At least seven managed-care companies pulled
> out of the program in Broward county, and many patients—

most of whom are low-income children or pregnant women—fled to networks run by hospitals."

The proper issue in healthcare price fixing must be that "stabilizing" prices among competitors is a type of combination that the antitrust laws were designed to prevent, for the Court has repeatedly said that fixing prices low today is the type of control that may mean raising prices tomorrow (*Pireno, Royal Drug, Maricopa County,* etc.). Moreover, most HMO arrangements are inextricably both vertical and horizontal. In a perfect or free market, if the prices set are below marginal cost, the wannabe predator has the "Hobson's Choice": to reduce output or go out of business by being acquired. Output can be reduced by having doctors see illness less per unit time or by denying payment outright, thus eliminating the economic event. This was perceived, for example, in a 1998 article in *The Wall Street Journal,* "Aetna U.S. Healthcare Will End Medicare HMO Lines in Six States," and is exactly what continued to happen in the post-Millennium managed-care market failure with the rearranging of the field by mega-mergers. But for the low interest rates and Wall Street bull market sales of the mid-1990s that led to the mergers after 2000, the cash-flow transfusions from government contracts and, worst still, the MCOs' ability to hide their sordid behavior in chronically ill populations, MCOs would have been exposed as a failing industry long ago.

In the antitrust arena, market manipulation can occur when a large-group MCO subdivides its population of premium payers into "ZIP-code"-based groups and spreads its high- or low-resource users disparately between its capitated IN and OON noncapitated providers. The database may be used to decide which "preferred provider" to honor with a referred group of patients, especially when the provider preference is based solely on a proprietary fee arrangement, with the patient unaware of the reason for the arrangements (such as for the existence of IN and OON identical specialties in the same building).

Another occult method of exercising market power is to limit membership to preferred providers and gerrymander higher- or lower-risk patients into areas where they would do the MCO's doctor- and

435

hospital-contractors the most good and bring the insurer the most cash flow. This either drives rival practitioners out of the marketspace, or by using marginal pricing, the weakened hospitals and practices can be absorbed and, by that time, left to sell their provider practices at distressed prices. In anticipation of the ACA reforms and the managed-care drive to influence the new Accountable Care Organizations, on September 1, 2011, *The Wall Street Journal* reported that UHG's wholly owned Optum was purchasing the management arm of Monarch HealthCare, an Irvine, Calif., association that includes approximately 2,300 physicians in a range of specialties.

"Through various structures, Optum owns a physician group in Nevada and holds stakes in others elsewhere in the country. Optum, a fast-growing arm of United that provides services such as pharmacy-benefit management and data services to help improve care, is separate from United's own health-insurance operation.

"United has said in the past that providers acquired by Optum will not work exclusively with United's health plan, and will continue to contract with an array of insurers. But in one sign of the potential complications that might ensue, Monarch is currently in an arrangement with United competitor WellPoint Inc. to create a cooperative 'accountable-care organization' aimed at bringing down health-care costs and improving quality.

"Many insurers are investing in providers, though not all plan to make those operations available to other health plans. WellPoint recently closed its acquisition of senior health provider and Medicare Advantage plan CareMore Health Group, which is also based in southern California. Last December, Humana Inc. bought Concentra, which has urgent- and occupational-care clinics. In June, Pittsburgh insurer Highmark Inc. struck a deal to buy West Penn Allegheny Health System, a five-hospital operator that was struggling financially."

In *Continental T.V., Inc. v. GTE Sylvania, Inc.*, the 1977 Supreme Court overruled its earlier decision in *United States v. Arnold, Schwinn*

& Co., which had held that vertical nonprice restrictions placed by sellers upon buyer-distributors were *per se* illegal once title passed to them. This new decision distinguished what the *Schwinn* Court considered a "partial *per se* approach" and centered on territorial restrictions and customer limitations. The *GTE Sylvania* Court decided that such vertical restrictions were to be judged under the rule of reason standard. It discarded the title-passing distinction, noting that while vertical restrictions may limit intra-brand competition, they may promote interbrand competition. However, neither *Schwinn* nor *GTE Sylvania* reached issues of vertical restrictions on price.

In healthcare, the first equivalent-to-capitation price is at the corporate client level, sometimes called the "minimum premium" plan. The second is at the coerced-provider/contractor level. Both risk being foisted on the unlucky benefit plan and its participants and beneficiaries. This unregulated system cedes economic control of the output of a large group of sellers such as doctors and hospitals, to a small number of buyers arguably minimally or noncompetitive, especially when, as managed-care insurers, there are few of them in a state. When under state regulation, "business of insurance" insurers must file their actuaries' reports as well as the policies supporting the proffered benefits so that the state insurance department actuaries can determine the fidelity of the loss ratios for a set of benefit premiums. States must do this pursuant to McCarran-Ferguson in order for their insurance companies to be saved from federal preemption.

All actuarial reports of managed-care companies have been hitherto exempt from such reporting and scrutiny, because they are federally preempted. However, the ACA of 2010, and Senator Chris Dodd (D-CT) and Representative Barney Frank's (D-MA) Wall Street Reform and Consumer Protection Act in 2010, and its Office of National Insurance, will be overseeing excessive commercial healthcare insurance premiums, because all of the insurance Exchanges are being set up under federal supervision. This will mean that any insurance company vying for Exchange-insurer status using managed care must perforce allow its actuarial predictions to be compared with its MLRs. If its premiums do not reflect being above its average variable costs, its behavior can be seen as that of a predator (or designed to prevent rivals from entering the marketplace). Of course, the internal pricing based on capitated contracting will only be revealed in the competitive marketspace where the "benefits" can be more-closely monitored by shoppers.

Under ERISA, the only actuarial reports formerly necessary to be federally filed were those of defined-benefit pension plans, not those of health and welfare benefits. HIPAA of 1996 and its regulations promulgated under the Clinton administration significantly modified ERISA's protective cover for the erstwhile insurers and their employer-clients' plan administrators by assuring continuity and accountability for healthcare. Presumably, under the 1998 federal auditing of NCQA's HMO audits, it was expected that the fidelity of HMOs' loss ratios would be observable, but when the Bush II administration took over, that was changed. Auditing of the HMOs were given to the NCQA, which outsourced it by license to Logiqual, an Island Peer Review Organization affiliate in Lake Success, New York, to conduct audits of HEDIS compliance. One online consumer watchdog group characterized the outsourcing through Logiqual as "like a police department asking the defendant's law firm to conduct the investigation." IPRO, which we described earlier as originally performing peer review pursuant to the Medicare statute,

> "has created a Limited Liability Company (LLC) that will assume all of IPRO's compliance audit oversight and consulting contracts with managed care organizations (MCOs). The new entity, Logiqual, is now officially incorporated in New York State."

Is its market failure a good enough reason to require legislation to have the MCO industry leave the scene of private enterprise? The presently free-falling healthcare system can still control its own market prices, especially if its competition is based solely on how much "elasticity" can be realized from hastily deputized outpatient care, and how much treatment of illness can be lobbied to control healthcare output by having doctors participate less. Profit margins can still be propped up by price-per-unit lowering capitation contracts, "bundling" payments for medical professionals and their hospital organizations, sales to ERISA plans of thinly backed benefit packages, extending the insurers' "float" by withholding payments to providers and patients for services rendered, and state insurance commissions approving premium increases or subsidies based on flawed actuarial data. The managedcare industry therefore lives on "hot money," the short-term financing expecting only short-term gain.

Congress, too, has allowed the managed-care insurance industry to structure its own healthcare payments. The way the Bush II administration structured it, privatized MA was being split among too many actors solely to ensure the continued viability of HMOs and MCOs' cash-flow positions whose falling profit margins had long since become evident to Wall Street. In 1997, Weiss Rating's insurance rating service said that 57 percent of the 506 HMOs reviewed lost money for the third consecutive year; in the first year, the loss was industry wide. That data was backed up by a report issued in the spring of 1998 by the New York State Insurance Department showing about two-thirds of the HMOs operating in the state lost money in 1997, most of them asking for state permission to hike their rates. That is part of the reason for the failure of the BBA's M+C.

There was an ironic turnaround. After passage of the MMA's MA, HMOs began to report an increase in profitability when many HMOs changed benefit structures, revised or terminated provider contracts, dropped out of unprofitable markets such as Medicare or unprofitable regions, or had their lobbyists, such as America's Health Insurance Plans, obtain new, higher-paying contracts with M+C and MA. Profitability continued to improve as conventional insurers acquired or merged with many HMOs, then raised their premiums and restructured their policies to lower providers' prices in exchange for new patient referrals.

The dangers inherent in physicians, hospitals, and other professionals accepting forms of capitation, such as patient-illness bundling and the consolidation of integrated systems, portend a public health debacle. Trading discounted healthcare for income retention shifts back the ultimate risk of inadequately treated illness to chronically sick patients who thought they had paid for adequate coverage of their healthcare needs only to find it ephemeral.

1. *Contra Proferentem*—The Great Leveler

> Insurance policies are almost always drafted by specialists
> employed by that insurer . . . An insurer's practice of forcing
> the insured to guess and hope regarding scope of coverage
> requires that any doubt be resolved in favor of the party who
> has been placed in such a predicament.
>
> —*Kunin v. Benefit Trust Life Insurance Co.*,
> Ninth Cir., cert. denied (1990)

The First, Fourth, Ninth, Tenth, and Eleventh federal Circuit
Courts of Appeal have all held that adoption of the rule of *contra proferentem* does not violate ERISA's preemption clause, because the rule is
consistent with ERISA purposes. This rule is a common-law doctrine
often used to construe policy language against an insurer in a dispute
with a policyholder, because the policy "adheres" to the offeror, with
the policyholder having little bargaining power. The federal courts feel
it is therefore appropriate to adopt that rule as a matter of federal common law without regard to whether it falls within ERISA's savings
clause. Although the Third Circuit had not explicitly adopted that rule
of construction by the mid-1990s, it did find in *Anderson v. Primerica
Holdings, Inc.* that when a court holds ERISA plan language ambiguous
as a matter of law, it "may consider the intent of the plan sponsor, the
reasonable understanding of the beneficiaries, and the past practices,
among other things." The Third Circuit in 1980 held in *Taylor v. Continental Group Change in Control Severance Pay Plan* that the interpretation of ambiguous plan provisions is a question of fact; in *Mellon Bank,
N.A. v. Aetna Business Credit, Inc.,* the determination of whether a term
is ambiguous is a question of law. Moreover, in interpreting the provisions of a plan governed by ERISA, the First Circuit found in *Wickman
v. Northwestern Nat'l Ins. Co. (cert. denied* (1990)) that the terms "must be
given their plain meanings, meanings which comport with the interpretation given by the average person."

The principle of *contra proferentem* as a federal common-law rule is
inconsistent with the unanimous 1989 *Firestone* case's statement in dic-

tum that a court must construe the plan "without deferring to either party's interpretation." Recall Associate Justice Breyer's statement in the 2008, six to three decision in *Metropolitan Life Insurance Co. v. Glenn*, holding that

". . . a reviewing court should consider that conflict as a factor in determining whether the plan administrator has abused its discretion in denying benefits; and that the significance of the factor will depend upon the circumstances of the particular case. . . . The conflict of interest at issue here, for example, should prove more important (perhaps of great importance) where circumstances suggest a higher likelihood that it affected the benefits decision, including, but not limited to, cases where an insurance company administrator has a history of biased claims administration."

Evaluating a contract in the light least favorable to the profferor, the one who wrote it, has been held to be external to either party's interpretation but is in the sound discretion of the court upon examining the words of the contract as to their ambiguity and in the interests of justice. In the 1979 case, *United States v. Kimbell Foods*, the High Court declared, "In absence of an applicable Act of Congress it is for the federal courts to fashion the governing rule of law according to their own standards." In *Kunin,* cited earlier, the 1990 Ninth Circuit court held that "state law can sometimes control [ERISA] controversies." Although *Kimbell* involves government programs that lend money, its strength for ERISA questions lies both in the Supremacy Clause of the Constitution and the preemption clause of ERISA. The rationale was that if state law were reached for in money issues when national law is not specifically expressed, it would hardly deny the same application in situations affecting constitutional and states' rights such as taxing, contract, or equity. The *Kimbell* Court noted:

"We conclude that the source of law is federal, but that a national rule is unnecessary to protect the federal interests underlying the . . . programs . . . Because the ultimate consequences of altering settled commercial practices are so difficult to foresee, we hesitate to create new uncertainties, in the absence of careful legislative deliberation . . . Thus, the prudent course is to adopt the ready-made body of state law as the federal rule of decision until Congress strikes a different accommodation."

Nonetheless, *Glenn* and the oversight by the federal government, through the Obama administration's Office of National Insurance and ACA's Exchanges, should remove any doubt that both insurers and ASO contractors in the business of insurance companies (per *Royal Drug*) are structurally conflicted. The lower courts, if not the federal government, must weigh that conflict even in the absence of direct evidence that the conflict influenced the decision.

2. ERISA's Other Legal, Contradictory, and Advocacy Trends

In *Travelers*, the High Court found that ERISA did not preempt state healthcare cost-uniformity issues. That decision left open the door to the 2010 monitoring of state Exchanges by the ACA and the Restoring American Financial Stability Acts, whereby the Obama administration's departments of Health and Human Services and Treasury would have oversight of premium practices through an Office of National Insurance. Indeed, where there is a gap in ERISA provisions, such gap could be filled by state regulations, particularly where those regulations follow a national pattern, as found in *Inter Valley Health Plan v. Blue Cross/Blue Shield of Connecticut*, cert. denied (1993). "Coordination of benefits" (COB) is designed to give insured individuals as much coverage as possible. At the same time, it eliminates overinsurance by setting forth guidelines to determine which company will pay as primary insurer and which will pay as secondary insurer when a working couple or their dependents have a claim covered by more than one group insurance policy.

ERISA, too, appears to have a "coordination of benefits" provision, because there is no express obstacle for a self-funded plan to declare itself "secondary" to an individual policy. That would seem to permit state action, as an appropriate rule under ERISA was to defer to state law when not expressly preempted. The COB provision states that in situations where double coverage exists, the insurer covering the employee who actually has the claim is automatically designated as the primary insurance company. The primary company must pay as much of the claim as its policy limits allow. The 1984 Supreme Court in *NationsBank of North Carolina, N.A. v. Variable Annuity Life Insurance Co.* expressed an alternate view of ERISA noninsurance. The Court said, "If the [ERISA plan] administrator's reading fills a gap or defines a term in a way that is reasonable in light of the legislature's revealed design, we give the administrator's judgment controlling weight." Once more, a *Firestone*-like court chooses what is "reasonable" over the common-law understanding of what is "fair" or "equitable" in contract relations. Moreover, it casts an ERISA-employer-favored shadow over the express congressional intent in establishing "employees' income security" rights.

Noncriminal ERISA violations offer aggrieved patients medical payments and attorneys' fees only, not punitive damages, limiting interest from the plaintiff's bar. Additionally, these cases must be brought in federal court and relate only to alleged violations of administrative duty and fiduciary responsibility in construing benefits. The Sherman and Clayton Antitrust Acts may offer relief and treble damages for private parties who have suffered injury and can demonstrate predatory intent or collusive behavior, but not in the ERISA arena, which offers only its own remedies. As actions brought pursuant to the Americans with Disability Act (ADA) develop case law, violations based on wrongful termination, improper denial of benefits, or other discrimination on the basis of mental and other illness will offer compensatory damages, including back pay and attorneys' fees.

Because of Supreme Court and relevant Circuit Courts of Appeal decisions, state court insurance actions increasingly alleged common-law violations. These included insurance bad faith, master/servant responsibility (*respondeat superior*), ostensible agency (where hospitals or MCOs appear to hold themselves out as "health systems"), breach of warranty, medical and pharmacy malpractice by MCOs, suits against an HMO (based on its limiting care and access to expensive procedures and to specialists), breach of fiduciary duty in not disclosing treatment options, and wrongful interference with the doctor-patient relationship. Of significance in 1996 were the Supreme Court's *Medtronic v. Lohr*, where it was found that the federal Food and Drug Act does not preempt all common-law claims, and the Ninth Circuit's *Ardary v. Aetna Health Plans of California (cert. denied* (1997): "We must begin with the strong presumption that Congress does not intend to preempt state law causes of action with a federal statute."

Perhaps the most important relevant decision of the 1997 High Court was *Inter-Modal Rail Employees Assn v. Atchison, Topeka and Santa Fe Railway Co.*, where a unanimous Court stated that section 510 of ERISA, dealing with "interference with protected rights," means that

"ERISA draws no distinction between those rights that 'vest' and those that do not." Section 510 says, in pertinent part:

"It shall be unlawful for any person to discharge, fine, suspend, expel, discipline, or discriminate against a participant or beneficiary for exercising any right to which he is entitled under the provisions of an employee benefit plan . . . [and, citing a Seventh Circuit case, *Heath v. Variety Corp.*] . . . In short, '§ 510 makes promises credible.'"

Public relations promotions notwithstanding, managed-care averment of "quality improvement" has proven by its actions to be a baseless sham, one that has not been reliably demonstrated to be otherwise. Among the potential defendants in this burgeoning arena of righting the wrongs to healthcare-marginalized ERISA-plan employees (and the judicial venues) are the following:

- Major business corporations' ERISA-based health and welfare benefit plan administrators (federal courts).
- Corporate directors and/or trustees who established the plans and appointed the administrators and fiduciaries (federal courts).
- Major state-regulated insurance companies and major MCOs that have contractual relations with ERISA-based corporate benefit plans to provide healthcare through risk-sharing arrangements such as reinsurance, capitation, secret withholds, gag rules, and false advertising of benefits (in federal courts, although some of these may be actionable in state courts).

The National Association of Insurance Commissioners stated in a Draft Bulletin in August 1995:

"If a healthcare provider enters into an arrangement with an individual, employer or other group that results in the provider assuming all or part of the risk for healthcare expenses or service delivery, the provider is engaged in the business of insurance . . . [and] must obtain the appropriate license [certificate of authority] (e.g., health insurer, or HMO, etc.) from the Department of Insurance."

- Medical and other healthcare provider groups, especially hospitals and hospital networks that have joint ventured with the above organizations to provide healthcare and hold themselves out to be healthcare "systems," while arbitrarily excluding doctors from their medical staffs (state and federal courts, including FTC proceedings).

The Third Circuit in *Dukes v. U.S. Healthcare, Inc., cert. denied* (1995) allowed that it is proper to bring such actions in state court when the HMO provided, arranged for, and supervised the doctors who provided the actual medical treatment.

- Managed Medicare cases, which may originate in or be removable to state court pursuant to the *Ardary* cases where the action does not "arise under Medicare" but is based on denial of benefits leading to wrongful death or negligence. These cannot be remedied by a retroactive payment or by administrative acts (state or federal court).

In *Wartenberg v. Aetna U.S. Healthcare, Inc.*, the 1998 federal Eastern District court in New York, citing *Ardary* with approval, found that the plaintiff under Medicare had sought damages for claims that were rooted in state common law on wrongful death through premature discharges and that such claims did not arise under and thus not preempted by the Medicare Act.

- Operators charged with swindling people who did not have health insurance.

The above, when brought, are not civil actions. The uninsured, the unemployed, and the uninsurable, have been targeted by a federal-state coalition of law enforcement agencies for fraudulently marketing "medical discount plans" as health insurance.

In 2010, the FTC and law enforcers in twenty-four states filed a total of fifty-four lawsuits and regulatory actions called "Operation Health-care Hustle." In August 2010, at the request of the FTC, a U.S. district court ordered a temporary halt to the deceptive actions of the Consumer Health Benefits Association (CHBA), which targeted consumers who sought information on the Internet about major medical health-insurance plans. The CHBA telemarketers allegedly pitched consumers with a long list of false claims: that they worked closely with major medical insurers, that the discount plan was widely accepted by doctors, pharmacies, and other health-care facilities, that the plan would save consumers up to 85 percent on medical expenses, that CHBA's plan was accepted wherever Blue Cross/Blue Shield was accepted, and that consumers could use their medical discount card with any health-care provider that accepted insurance.

The insidious nature of managed-care insurance and its co-opting of referral sources has swept many providers into its systems and excluded many of their rivals by its redlining. A major reason for the shibboleth "managed care is here to stay" is what seemed to some to be its inherent invulnerability—it found favorable support from the Reagan and Bush I administrations, the Republican congressional majority during the last half of the Clinton administration, and the post-Millennium Bush II administration. The 2010 House of Representatives' Republican majority promised more of the same by promising to repeal the same ACA that it ultimately passed.

Freestanding and independent risk-taking provider groups should not fear antitrust scrutiny or actions commenced against them. However, to the extent that doctors' groups have contracted with hospital systems, they both may be caught up in tort actions for ostensible agency and breach of contract as found in *Ardary*. Although the belief still remains in some quarters, today's HMO type of managed care barely resembles Congress's 1973 design. The original "health maintenance" concept has been virtually hijacked by commercial organizations, including the nonprofit ones that own for-profit subsidiaries supporting them. The Blue Cross-type insurance organizations, once nonprofit but turned-for-profit, hiding under the aegis of a public policy of remedial legislation while being operated by Anthem/WellPoint, Inc., among others, now churn patients through the system of controlled output of healthcare and its prices.

Instead of the federally qualified HMO of over a generation ago, what we have today is the equivalent of an anticompetitive system in which the "competitors" benefit by profiteering with help from state governments to acquire their former rivals. Rarely do they benefit by the competition for increasing healthcare quality itself. While many of the "horses" in the free market, managed-care race *seem* to be healthily competing, they are merely sharing dollars illicitly skimmed from the unconscionably high, administrative-cost managing of their market failure.

The physician is central to the managed-care system's core business for both managing and producing care, although the rapidly growing cohorts of ancillary professions' attempt to find an economic, albeit lower-paid, base in the physician's realm is more than acceptable from the standpoint of the insurers' cash-flow business needs. Ironically, while patients can be questioned about satisfaction with their coverage relations, the treating physician seems to be the missing link in the process of accurately assessing the epidemiologic effects of "managing" healthcare. While many "satisfaction surveys" of consumers have been made, a 1997 *JAMA* study, "Are All Health Plans Created Equal?" noted that physicians are rarely asked about healthcare satisfaction. Three hundred physicians in three large Minnesota health plans—nearly equally split between specialists and generalists—were asked about the "health plan practices that promote or impede the delivery of high-quality care" they would recommend to their own family. One group was from an employed-staff model HMO, where in addition to salary, physicians received bonus and incentive payments based on performance and productivity as the HMO Act Congress intended. In general, staff-model HMOs tend to employ generalists and physicians who practice in many of the common subspecialties. These staff-model HMOs, once thought to be the medical practice arrangement of the future, have since fallen out of favor.

The other two were network-model plans consisting of physician group practices brought together through contract agreements. In this model, an HMO contracts with several groups of physicians to provide services to the HMO's members. It may contract with several large multi specialty groups or with many groups of primary-care practitioners. Physician members maintain their own offices and are often compensated through capitation and/or withholds by the network managers. For a predefined amount per member per month, the group agrees to provide all needed services for a specific population of patients, a sort of "group bundling." Individual physicians in these arrangements are often said to be assuming "risk," which the NAIC said in 1995 should be licensed by the state as either HMOs or insurance companies, because they are at risk for the cost of the care of the patients in the network. In this type of arrangement, physicians may see patients that are non-HMO members. Recall the 1973 six to three opinion delivered by Supreme Court Justice Blackmun in *Doe v. Bolton*: "requiring acquiescence by co-practitioners has no rational connection with a patient's needs and unduly infringes on the physician's right to practice."

While 92 percent of the HMO-salaried physicians indicated that they would recommend the plan to their own family, in the two network-model groups, only 64 percent and 24 percent, respectively, of the physicians said they would recommend the plans they worked in to their own family. When asked for their level of agreement with the statement, "I am able to practice excellent medicine in this plan," fewer than half gave the most favorable response. The overall quality of primary and specialty care was rated as "excellent" by 22 percent and 29 percent of plan physicians, respectively. Looking specifically at "practices that help physicians take better care of their patients," physicians across the board perceived health-plan practices in these areas as relatively ineffective, with less than 20 percent of those surveyed giving any practice an "excellent" rating. Only 19 percent rated as "excellent" the plan's provision of continuing medical education, and only 8 percent gave an "excellent" rating for the plan's efforts to identify which patients needed preventive services.

It is clear that the ancillary professions now attempting to enter the traditional physician arena of patient treatment will be increasing their economic lot. It is also clear that physician and ancillary members would ultimately be "employees" of the system rather than independent practitioners. An August 2010 article in *The New York Times* described how pharmacists are formally getting into the managed-care loop, "enlisted by some health insurers and large employers [to help the nation's patients] to take their medications as prescribed." From the study cited earlier, one could safely extrapolate that the managed-care insurance industry would benefit from replacing as many medical doctors as they could with nonphysician professionals who would be understandably praiseworthy of their newly secured place in a most stable sector of the economy. This is done wherever it can be, except for the fact that the cash flow is better when physicians' fee levels are part of the mix. It appears that the insurance cartel is back, wearing the aegis of public policy. However, the tidal wave of rapid change that enveloped this trillion-dollar segment of the U.S. economy and deconstructed the delivery of healthcare in fundamental respects has begun to recede as both an economic success and a social nostrum. Changes in the system occurred with such rapidity that the public was left confused and disillusioned even as the ACA went into effect.

3. Are These "Natural Monopolies"?

"The antitrust laws do not regulate the prices of natural monopolists."

—Federal Judge Richard A. Posner (1995)

In 1969, Federal Court of Appeals Judge Posner, then an economist studying regulated monopolies like water, power, telephone, and cable television companies, defined the concept of a "natural monopoly." The government would tolerate monopolies as long as they were regulated and functioned in the public good, but not when competition resulted in wasted investment and duplication and failed to operate as a self-regulatory mechanism. The managed healthcare industry bears none of the more-obvious earmarks of the "natural monopoly." Its few controlling MCO "buyers" control the prices of more than a million provider "sellers" who supply the healthcare needs of over three hundred million people. The MCOs are poorly regulated, and the wasted investment and duplication by commerce and governments fail to operate as self-regulatory mechanisms. Because its profits are cleaved from treatments partly given and from those promised to be given, shunning variation as the enemy of quality, managed-care companies do not even provide money to pay for research and innovation or for well-researched, federally approved but expensive "experimental" treatments. What MCOs do attempt to offer is payment for "evidence-based" medicine as influenced by managed-care algorithms.

In indemnity insurance, additional profits can be made from investing elsewhere as much as possible of the premium money, and because they are state regulated, they do not depend on limiting the premium-promised benefits to increase profitability. Because managed care has produced no demonstrable, socially redeeming healthcare outcomes other than price maintenance by screening methods that maintain or stabilize economic profitability, this stultifying sameness clouds

451

consumers and benefit-plan administrators' search for a better-price deal. This behavior gainsays the fact that reducing chronic illness and absenteeism produces long-term societal cost savings far better than management of "quicker and sicker" revolving-door care. Removing competition was the single greatest impediment to the development of science and productivity, so breaking up the former "natural" telephone monopoly reaped immediate rewards for investors and society in the new competition. In healthcare, the aim of competition should be that the medical research aimed at doctors, results in patients getting better. Healthcare competition under indemnity insurance was not between doctors but rather between insurers attempting to provide better services or more inclusive benefits than their rivals. It was never to provide better care, because they were in the business of insurance, not healthcare. Allowing the "one-price-fits-all" capitation, P4P, or "bundling" modes has and portends to eliminate competition further and to transform care giving into profit-based care manipulation, making physicians their proxy.

Historical MLRs show that the Blues' expenditures, when nonprofit, were around 95 percent, and the big indemnity insurers' group policies costs and MLRs were much lower as they picked up the more-costly illnesses after the front-end treatment paid for by the Blues. In preparation for the ACA's passage, a Senate Commerce Committee report found that the insurer WellPoint started reclassifying such expenses, including nurse hotlines, disease management, and clinical health policy, as medical rather than what they were: administrative, profit-based expenses. The felicitous insurance term for the latter is increased *retention*. This is the portion of an insurance claim paid by the insured instead of by the insurance company, which in the case of self-insurance is the portion of each insurance claim not insured by the policy, which requires the insured (employer) to pay before insurance becomes effective.

Thus, premium income spent on healthcare by commercial managed-care giants tended to be closer to 75 to 85 percent (not counting the accruals to the profit side from managed-care denials). That may account for the ACA concession to insurers for an 80 percent MLR for large-group plans, while premium expenditures for care by the most aggressive HMOs as far back as 1998 were in the range of $0.70 to $0.60 on the dollar gained.

IX. A Market Failure Bill of Particulars for the Managed-Care Industry—Buying American Medicine with "Monopoly Money"

The ambiguities created by statutory definitions of the business of insurance, the business of insurance companies, the insurance "savings" and "deemer" clauses in ERISA, and settled decisional law sparked the post-Millennium's managed-care market failure. As a result of the headlong mergers between the high-roller MCOs and the now-restive conventional health-insurance industry, patient-revenue grabbing and Wall Street venture capital money were favored over long-range business planning, as company after company made promises to the public they could not keep. As that failing market urgently demanded, and settled law in the antitrust and ERISA cases in *Royal Drug, Pireno, Pilot Life, Travelers, Inter-Modal*, and their progeny suggested, the concept of the "business of insurance" was overdue for a review on state and federal legislative levels. These began as incremental federal interventions by passage of the 1996 Mental Health Parity Act and the 2008 Mental Health Parity and Addiction Equity Act, which amended ERISA. Currently, over 90 percent of employer-sponsored health plans include coverage for mental health and substance abuse services and must now do away with separate deductibles for mental illness and substance abuse. The incremental efforts culminated in passage of the ACA of 2010, which dealt with annual and lifetime limits and rescissions for preexisting conditions. *See* Plates 10, 11.

The 1945 McCarran-Ferguson Act was a compromise meant to save the insurance cartel from the effects of the Supreme Court's *South-Eastern Underwriters*, not to render the industry nugatory, and property/casualty and life insurance companies have kept their McCarran-Ferguson exemption from federal price-fixing scrutiny by remaining state regulated. Operating freely under the idling antitrust eyes of the Bush II agencies, health-insurance companies taking multistate risk-management organizations into their fold appear to have lost that exemption and become potentially subject to the Obama administration's more-attentive DOJ antitrust division and the FTC. Individual healthcare plans, HMOs, managed-care companies, and even indemnity plans have closely collaborated in various ways to establish a set of clinical-practice guidelines and "quality" standards designed to preserve a satisfactory stabilized profit rate for themselves via the delivery of a less-than-acceptable quantity of much higher-cost health-care services when compared to other advanced countries. It appears from public record evidence that managed-care organizations and the major healthcare insurance companies, aided by public and private funds, have used the law to steadily swallow up their smaller brethren and establish inefficient vertical and horizontal combinations to control the output of healthcare delivery and its prices.

Regarding the general welfare and bills of rights, Professor Bernard Schwartz points out in his *Main Currents of American Legal Thought*:

"The pursuit of happiness required a legal order that would emphasize the right to acquire property as much as that to secure property. But it also could include much more, since personal rights not specifically included in the notion of 'life' or 'liberty' might well contribute to what James Wilson called 'the happiness of the society [that] is the first law of every government.'"

The most important myth offered by managed care is its purported reduction of aggregate healthcare costs, notwithstanding that it was government programs, at much lower administrative cost and no profit, which removed the most actuarially significant higher-cost portions of the patient pool from private insurance risk: Medicare and Medicaid. Between 1976 and 1995, there was a 50 percent increase in the portion of the population lacking healthcare coverage relative to those covered and a 100 percent increase in the absolute number of persons without coverage. During the 1990s, the total number of persons with health insurance appeared to level off, partly because job growth concentration shifted to the service sector where workers were less likely offered health insurance. This shift included premiums paid to nonprofit Blue Cross/Blue Shield plans, commercial health insurance, HMOs, and self-insured plans. Other factors included employers discontinuing insurance coverage or employees dropping their employer-sponsored coverage because of increased costs and narrowing changes in benefits that intensified after the 2008 economic crash. Such a diminution in numbers of otherwise healthy people removed from the risk pool caused a relative aggregate rise in the prevalence of illness in the population as well as in incidence of episodes; therefore, an absolute increase in costs shifted further to covered persons.

Before the compromised BBA of 1997, the government set a corporate-capitation rate for commercial managed-care entrants at 95 percent of the original Medicare hospitals' rate based on "actual costs" represented by DRGs. If the actual costs could end up less than 95 percent of the cost-based rate, although the HMO could keep the difference, the expectation was that government would obviously attempt to lower the percentage the next year. As the original HMO enrollees were healthier, cherry-picked, and younger, new options such as eyeglasses and paid prescriptions would have to be extended to the ever-aging members. However, this time, costs would rise with no population on which to shift them, because they would be managed by commercial companies. These inducement "plums" sent more money to pharmaceutical firms than to healthcare providers, costs that many people had avoided spending out of pocket. With the post-Millennium slowing growth of M+C and the launching of MA offering more managed benefits, the managed-care insurers were able to receive more than 100 percent of the cost-based Medicare rate. As a result, "efficiency" could no longer be expected other than at the cost of further limitations on the medical and hospital providers' participation. With managed-care costs as an integral part of the treatment equation, and contractor reputation (and profits) depending on the effectiveness of cost constraints, enhanced access to these benefits could hardly be assured, especially because the increased cash flow to the insurers from managing the care was on their conflict-laden revenue side.

Over a twenty-year period, employers shifted the burden of their health insurance cost to their employees by requiring them to pay an increasing share of the premium directly or through increased deductibles and copayments, particularly for dependent coverage. Between 1988 and 1993, the average employee contribution rose 64 percent for single coverage and 79 percent for family coverage. This engendered the severest of market failure aspects, because it devalued the insurance benefits (and therefore the premium) with no decrease in monetary cost to society. In 1996, HMO plans recorded the largest increases of any plan type in "subscriber-cost-sharing," emblematic of the number of employer-sponsored HMO plans with no copayment having decreased 30 percent from 1995 to 1996, while the number of HMOs requiring $5 copayments increased 18 percent in the same period.

Changes to employee benefit packages such as the introduction of "cafeteria" and "flexible" benefit plans' tax savings by IRS Code § 125 created an incentive for some workers to forgo health insurance altogether or eliminate more-expensive dependent health coverage, as they were usually coupled with a high-deductible insurance policy. These plans allowed employees to allocate a fixed level of employer dollars or credits to a diverse menu of benefits, such as childcare, life insurance, health insurance, retirement savings accounts, vacation days, or cash payments, based on their personal needs and up to an annual limit determined by income. At the end, there was no evidence from that population that more healthcare was obtained due to the dollars available for them.

By November 9, 2010, *The New York Times* reported that

"with healthcare costs climbing even higher during this enrollment season, more employers are adopting a tiered system to pass on the bulk of those costs to their employees by assigning bigger contributions to workers in top salary brackets and offering some relief to workers who make less money."

Interestingly, such a move mirrored the Obama proposals to allow the Bush tax-cut rates to expire except for the 98 percent of Americans whose incomes were less than $250,000 per year. The *Times* noted that in the commercial arena, "for example, employees at Bank of America who make $100,000 or more a year will pay at least 14 percent more for coverage for 2011." The article allows a more-enlightened reader of the *Times* analysis to see how commercial insurers' sleight of hand can stabilize and probably increase healthcare costs:

"But workers who make less will actually see their contributions decrease, although their deductibles and co-payments will stay the same. Employees earning less than $50,000 could see as much as a 50 percent drop in the amount deducted from their paychecks, as compared to 2010. The bank says it is making up the difference."

Basing premium rates for health policies on family size may also have discouraged enrollment. The government's GAO noted in 1996 that linking the required employee premium for health insurance to family size could discourage dependent coverage. Additionally, with the promotion and sale to government and private accreditation programs of clinical practice guidelines and standards by which to define and measure (commercially acceptable) medical "quality" health plans, HMOs and managed-care companies may have acted collusively in following NCQA's "Quality Compass," HEDIS compliance efforts, InterQual's "Products and Services for Payors," and Aetna/U.S. Healthcare's affiliate "U.S. Quality Algorithms." This is where they continually monitor, analyze, and report on provider performance as well as the "quality of the care" that they say their members receive. Nonetheless:

1. The methodology used by said organizations to define what shall constitute acceptable levels of treatment is proprietary and conducted in secret.

2. The standards conclusively established to measure quality represent an effort to create a single, private, uniform, and nationally accepted set of standards untested by the medical and scientific community at large, and defining the acceptable level of "quality" expected by managed healthcare. They largely limit treatment and innovation and certainly do not include payment for academic research and development.

3. The "quality" guidelines and standards are held out as the product of questionably objective, independent groups.

4. The insurance industry accreditation process is a vehicle by which adherence to the "official" standards is policed aimlessly, except that it provides incentives for cash-flow-based data to be obtained by their members, even though not being accredited has minimally adverse financial consequences.

5. Absent federal intervention, to the extent that this collusive commercial effort to impose a set of standards defining the quality of healthcare is measured based on time spent rather than need, competition among health plans and managed-care companies will be diminished, premium prices will be stabilized, and control of profit-based rates for the managed-care insurers' services will be facilitated.

6. In economics, rent-seeking is an attempt by a group to derive economic rent by manipulating the social or political environment in which economic activities occur, rather than by adding value. "Economic rents" are "excess returns" above "normal levels" that take place in competitive markets. Commercial insurers engage in this by lobbying for legislation that enhance manipulation of healthcare providers' prices. They then mimic governmental programs through remote

"managing" of medical care. This permits raising premium prices to cover those costs; especially the costs for mental health and substance abuse treatment. Managed care's rent-seeking behavior has added no proven value to healthcare. *See* Plate 9.

7. Market failure is the inability of a system of market production to provide certain goods either at all, or at the optimal level It results from imperfections in the market mechanism that do not fully account for all costs of supplying outputs. They result in overproduction of goods and services that produce negative external effects or underproduction of goods and services that produce positive external effects. The different reasons for market failure include: supplying inadequate (or inaccurate) information to purchasers; inadequate capacity (by restricting, rationing or producing scarcity of care); dysregulation of the movement of labor and capital, and employing "rent-seeking behavior." *See* Plate 8.

The New York Times reported on August 14, 2010, "states are scrambling to make sure they have the necessary legal authority to carry out the responsibilities being placed on them by President Obama's healthcare law." The reporters emphasized that "insurance commissioners in about half the states say they do not have clear authority to enforce consumer protection standards that take effect next month." Reading carefully, one would see why. Under the ACA, if states do not follow the new federal standards, the federal government may step in to prevent insurers' charging copayments for preventive services and imposing lifetime limits on benefits. They must allow consumers to appeal a denial of benefits and cannot rescind coverage except in cases of fraud or intentional misrepresentation.

The federal government "stepping in" is not as alarming as one might think from reading the article. After all, McCarran-Ferguson does not prohibit the federal government from enacting laws *other* than those by the state specifically related to the business of insurance, and the ACA does specifically relate to the business of insurance for such *other* purposes. In fact, McCarran-Ferguson emphasized that the Sherman and Clayton Antitrust Acts and the FTC Act "shall be applicable to the business of insurance to the extent that such business is not regulated by State Law." *The New York Times* article notes that some state insurance regulators "would ask their legislators to expand their authority by putting federal standards into state law next year" and others "said they would rely on their powers of persuasion, the good will of insurers or general state laws that ban unfair or deceptive trade practices." Arizona governor Jan Brewer—in light of being part of the multiple state attorneys general suing the federal government in lawsuits challenging the ACA—was quoted as having an "indefinite rule-making moratorium, so we have no plans to adopt rules related to enforcement [of the federal Act]."

The first suggestion by the state insurance regulators, asking their legislators to expand their authority by putting federal standards into state law the next year, was apparently a politicized delay tactic, because states get their authority from the Tenth Amendment to the Constitution and from acts of Congress so long as they do not conflict with federal supremacy. Needing to get the authority from other than the ACA is unavailing. The second suggestion also appears to be a politicized delay tactic. Simply suing the United States has not allowed states a stay of an act of Congress since the Anti-Injunction Act of 1793. The insurance commissioners' "powers of persuasion," are unsuitable, too, because most state insurance commissioners come from or end up in the insurance industry. The idea of relying on "the good will of insurers" is absurd on its face. Using "general state laws that ban unfair or deceptive trade practices" is federally preempted by McCarran-Ferguson language, leaving the federal Sherman Act applicable only to agreements or behavior of "boycott, coercion or intimidation."

By titling the August 2010 article in *The New York Times,* "Some States Are Lacking in Health Law Authority," the headline editors gave the impression that something is lacking or inappropriate in the new healthcare law. However, the article pointed out that "within days, the Obama administration is expected to announce up to $51 million in grants to states to help them perform one of their new duties: 'reviewing unreasonable increases in premiums.'" The article concludes with a refreshingly competitive comment from Sandy Praeger, a former Kansas insurance commissioner. Praeger, a Republican, who replaced Democrat Kathleen Sebelius as commissioner in 2002 when Sibelius became governor, said, "That's the big question. Unreasonable is a rather nebulous term." Ironically, much healthcare law since 1972 has been based on undefined terms like "reasonable costs."

The "scrambling" of the regulators began to calm down. As state politicians were gearing up to praise, fight, or obey the new federal health reform laws' September 23 deadline. *The New York Times'* Robert Pear, the day prior, said, state insurance "regulators are seeking a waiver for a provision of the new healthcare law that requires health insurers to spend at least 80 cents of every premium dollar on medical care, rather than administrative expenses, executive salaries and profits. If insurers do not meet the requirement in 2011, they will have to pay rebates to consumers in 2012."

On the 23rd, *The New York Times'* Reed Abelson reported that

"Under the new law, insurers that offer child-only policies must start covering all children, even the seriously ill, beginning on Thursday. Insurers must also begin offering free preventive services, and for the first time, their premiums must start passing muster with federal and state regulators by the end of the year. State insurance regulators told the White House on Wednesday that health insurance markets in some states would be disrupted unless President Obama gave insurers a temporary dispensation from one major provision of the new health care law. The provision requires insurance companies to spend at least 80 cents of every premium dollar on medical care, rather than administrative expenses, executive salaries and profits. If insurers do not meet the requirement in 2011, they will have to pay rebates to consumers in 2012"

Also on the 23rd, when major portions of the ACA went into effect, the Republican Party pledged on its website, *"A Pledge to America,"* a "sweeping conservative agenda that called for reigning in spending,

cutting taxes and repealing the health reform law." Fox News temporized on the new reform effort, "But the plan didn't delve into specifics
on critical issues, such as how it will 'put government on a path to a
balanced budget.' It also steers clear of social issues.'" However, that
prediction didn't seem to have "legs," because *The New York Times* editorial, "About Your Premiums," the next day said,

> "Starting this week, insurers are prohibited from setting
> lifetime limits and restricted in setting annual limits on what
> they will pay for care, banned from rescinding policies after a
> beneficiary becomes sick and prohibited from excluding chil-
> dren with preexisting conditions. The new rules will also allow
> dependents up to the age of 26 to remain on their parents' poli-
> cies; preventive care will be provided without cost sharing; and
> there are new processes to appeal insurance company decisions.
> The critics aren't saying anything about the huge value of those
> immediate benefits. [And noted that] the rising cost of health
> insurance has more to do with the recession and higher prices of
> providing care than with the new health reform."

Within a month, according to news reports, the NAIC unanimously endorsed new standards that would require many health-insurance companies to spend more of each premium dollar for the benefit
of consumers. The rules, adopted at a meeting of the commissioners
in Orlando, Florida, described how the "non-quantitative treatment
limitations" calculations will be made. *The New York Times* reported,
"If the companies do not meet the standards, known as MLRs, insurers
will have to pay rebates to policyholders . . . . In effect, the rules put a
cap on insurance company profits."

In November 2010, *The New York Times* reported,

> "Last month, federal officials granted dozens of one-year
> waivers that were aimed at sparing certain employers, includ-
> ing McDonald's, insurers and unions who offer plans that
> sharply limit the coverage they provide. These limited-benefit
> plans, also known as "mini-meds," fail to comply with new

rules phasing out limits on how much policies will provide in medical care each year."

By 2014, no lifetime or annual caps on coverage will be allowed. Sadly, unless legislative reconciliation changes are made, such rules do not appear to affect the millions in ERISA's self-insured managed-care plans, and employers are stuck with overblown list prices for their employees' care.

In a dynamic, competitively free environment, one would expect that health insurers or plan administrators, having experienced heavy criticism, might compete by redesigning their plans to enhance the new level of participation in healthcare. That they have not so far is not due to lack of expertise but because they are not in the business they were in when they were indemnitors in the "business of insurance." What is left for the managed healthcare industry is to negotiate a defensive posture through the America's Health Insurance Plans, the Federation of Independent Businesses, and the NCQA, and ride out the potential firestorm coming from the effect of the ACA long enough to put their money elsewhere. Perhaps they might consider returning to the indemnity insurance business this time, without pressing for the expensive external management of care.

The commercial insurance industry's hopes of mobilizing a repeal of the ACA by Congress are slim at best, because millions of American adults and youth began benefitting monetarily almost immediately from the early instituted sections of the Act. Managed healthcare cannot survive as a system *per se*, because it consumes its own inventory and offers no progress in improving healthcare.

X. A Summary Judgment–
"Activity" versus "Inactivity"

"Some argue that if a man has to pay the first hundred dollars and a percentage of all the rest, he is less likely to use health services that he doesn't really need. Unfortunately, the result of these deductibles is also to simply keep those with low incomes from getting any care at all—and to cause even bill-conscious middle-class families to delay when good healthcare would indicate they should receive medical attention."

—Senator Edward M. Kennedy (1972)

"When was the last time you submitted a claim to your auto insurer asking to be reimbursed for an oil change or a tire rotation? . . . The drivers of high healthcare costs are manifold, and include the perverse incentives associated with an insurance-based payment system, low labor-productivity growth in the provision of care, and the closely related issue of a constrained supply of healthcare providers. The expense of treating the uninsured or under-payments from Medicare and Medicaid is shifted onto private healthcare providers, as is the expense of litigating and/or settling malpractice lawsuits."

—Dustin Chambers, assistant professor of economics at the Franklin P. Perdue School of Business, in *"The Online Magazine of the American Enterprise Institute* (May 2009)

What Dustin Chambers says about the faults in the system would appear to be highly reasonable to some, from either the political left or the right, until we read his quixotic exposition:

"Health insurance should not cover basic or routine medical services, but instead should cover major illnesses, surgeries, etc. Moreover, the government should require that healthcare providers charge all patients the same fees for out-of-pocket medical procedures (insurance companies and the government should be free to negotiate discounted prices for the services for which they directly pay, but these preferred rates would not apply to the services paid out-of-pocket by their members). This would bring normal, competitive market forces to bear on the provision of routine medical services. Insurance would then provide (as it is properly intended) coverage against significant and expensive maladies. This helps the poor in two ways.

"First, routine services would be much cheaper, and so the poor and uninsured would be able to afford (out-of-pocket) basic services. Second, the price of catastrophic medical insurance would be within reach of many more Americans. While high-deductible insurance plans already exist (in which the insured pays the first $1,500 to $2,000 in medical expenses and the insurer pays everything above this amount), what is really needed is for Medicare and Medicaid along with most employer-provided plans to adopt this high-deductible model. Although the current system epitomizes the overuse or misuse of insurance, the Obama plan fails to recognize this, and instead seeks to expand the size and scope of this distorted system."

He goes on to move for a range of "market-oriented solutions."

"The only effective means of combating this disease is to increase the supply of healthcare professionals to put downward pressure on wage growth. This can be done in a number of ways. As championed by the late Milton Friedman, the American Medical Association must cease restricting the supply of medical doctors. . . Moreover, too many services that could easily be provided by nurses are instead provided by doctors, a practice that is exceedingly wasteful. . . President Obama has focused his efforts on containing prescription drug costs and streamlining the paperwork involved in maintaining medical charts and processing medical billing. . . Fast forward to today and we are on the cusp of instituting nationalized healthcare despite the fact that the baby boom generation is beginning to retire and both Social Security and Medicare are staring down the barrel of insolvency."

Mr. Chambers, thus, at once, devoids the conscience of our maturing society from its Medicare and Medicaid social humanism. He proposes to magnify the economically agonizing Medicare drugs' "donut hole," which the ACA eliminates, and insists that the indigent on Medicaid pay their own way into the system; just as Florida Governor Rick Scott, two-years later, required those applying for "welfare" to pay for the same drug testing, which could prevent them from acquiring it. Finally, he passes the baton to apply Milton Friedman's market-oriented solutions to recycle democratic capitalisms' progress.

In 1972, because neither ERISA nor the HMO ACT had yet been enacted, Senator Kennedy's reaction to the 1972 Social Security Amendments that had changed the course of public policy from increasing access to care to cost constraints on that care was solely concerned with the reallocation of resources. Clinton's 1993 proposals were therefore advanced by the need to undo the massive and regressive restructuring of healthcare bred by ERISA and the HMO Acts. ERISA loopholes invited corporations to convert their once higher-quality, state-supervised insurance plans into pension-plan-based, federally unregulated benefit plans preempted from state scrutiny, and the HMO Act, allowed the healthcare part of the indemnity insurance industry effectively to convert back to its 1945 cartelization. When big insurers' real estate portfolios tumbled into the low-interest rates of the early 1980s, they swiftly exchanged indemnity insuring for ERISA's "noninsurance" safe harbor of "claims administration" of corporate benefit plans. They used "experience-rated" contracts and "minimum premiums" in the transition to hide the fact that they were merely "insuring without spreading the risk," a strategy that would ensure that their cash flow rose to the level of list-price-based revenue income. When employer-sponsors used their benefit plans as conduits for taking back their tax-deductible benefit plan contributions as income, they hired managed-care companies that worked for the insurance administrators to do the job. The result was the gradual corporate curtailment of fifty years of healthcare coverage gains by the nation's workers, reaching over 150 million of them by 2010.

As far back as his acceptance speech at the 1992 Democratic Party Convention, President Clinton presciently charged that the "insurance companies, bureaucracies and healthcare profiteers" were responsible for the high cost of healthcare. His ill-fated Health Security Act met with the full force of insurance-industry lobbying against government "takeovers," rallying all those fearful of what they were told was "socialized medicine." The 1990s president's stated motives in making changes in ERISA and establishing fairness in resource allocation were repeatedly distorted by spin doctors for the managed-care industry and their allies in the Republican "Contract with America" "revolution" of 1994. The word was out that the president's Health Security Act was a prescription for nationalized health insurance and government control of medical care—words repeated by the conservative pundits and insurance-lobby interest groups during the run up to the 2010 ACA, and from the new Republican majority in the House of Representatives after the 2010 election. The "Contract with America" doctrine produced strange bedfellows from the right and the left at the time. Joining the anti-Clinton charge were the AMA, the big insurers, and the HIAA (now America's Health Insurance Plans). Initially against the Medicare Act, the Libertarian group, Association of Physicians and Surgeons, was modernized in 1994 mainly to oppose the work of the health-care task force led by First Lady Hillary Rodham Clinton.

To politicians and lawmakers, the "managed care" concept seemed related only to the original nonprofit HMOs and to welfare-case management. They had little knowledge of the nature of the managed-care problem until MCOs, a few years later, began to penetrate their own government-backed plans like the Federal Employees Health Benefits Plan. Because insurance regulation had been largely left to the states, members of Congress, other than having enacted the then-heavily amended Disclosure Act of 1958, were unfamiliar with the grievances of ERISA-plan employees complaining to state insurance departments or to state courts only to find them to be, by preemption, the wrong forums for redress. By the time the *Pilot Life* and *Travelers* cases were decided by the Supreme Court, the judiciary's frustration with the dearth of ERISA regulations was becoming evident. Numerous, often-conflicting Circuit Court decisions resisting what they felt would be "judicial activism" were already causing pressure on the state and federal legislative processes. By the time of the 1993 Clinton Health Security Act, some committees in the Democratic-controlled Congress investigating ERISA's bizarre wrenching of the healthcare system became aware that the "skyrocketing" cost of care for over half of the population was nurtured and commandeered by commercially based, over-the-telephone case managers working for the shadow insurance "administrative services" companies. These telephone phantoms, under the guise of telling doctors what was or was not medically necessary, coerced patients and providers to limit their care, allowing employers to take back as income actuarially determined and promised benefits.

The best-kept secret about managed care was that the so-called healthcare costs "saved" by the self-styled care managers ended up being shared with insurance administrators and their self-insured employer/clients—the sponsors and fiduciaries of their own employees' benefit plans. To this day, despite toady assurances to the contrary, the managed-care process has done nothing to lessen medical costs for the patient or improve the quality of healthcare delivery for the country. What it does is adulterate the socially expected traditional doctor-patient relationship by redlining willing providers and recruiting "preferred" ones whose networks are based solely on agreements to see more patients for less money each. Even the ACA treads carefully in this area, because ERISA self-insured plans receive a light administrative touch, allowing "quality" and "performance" to be *indicia* for differing payments to doctors who perform the same medical tasks, as if

471

the scientific intensity of medical practice could be assessed fairly from outside the doctor-patient relationship by self-interested commercial fiduciaries and their agents.

So much for the efficiency or social benefit of the much-touted managed-care "economies of scale" offered to the public by large insurers, HMOs, and large hospital networks that consume smaller ones, and include them in systems that absorb and consolidate rival physicians' practices, and sweep the administrative spread into the "cost" of care. In 1981, economist Alice M. Rivlin, then founding director of the Congressional Budget Office, saw the market failure in the statutory, Medicare-based PSROs:

"PSRO review of Medicare patients reduces Medicare outlays in part by transferring costs to private patients, whose charges will rise accordingly. When the increased costs to private patients are taken into account, PSRO review saves society as a whole substantially less than it costs . . . PSROs affect utilization by Medicare patients primarily by shortening hospital stays rather than by preventing admissions. Of the days of care saved in 1978, roughly 90 percent can be attributed to shortened lengths of stay. Since the first days of hospitalization are usually more expensive than subsequent days, this effect does not reduce costs as much as would a comparable change in utilization by means of admission denials."

No amount of provider-aimed or care-denied managed-care measures can slow the upward spiral of what are purported to be healthcare costs, because such heightened healthcare costs are deadweight losses to society based on increasing cash flow to the insurance industry. Cost-containment efforts against providers will remain misplaced until either the managed-care "one doctor for the price of two" practice is regulated by the states or the federal government or, better still, is abandoned altogether along with commercial managed healthcare insurance, as it is antithetical to the real cost-saving, patient-centered, ACA. With the ACA reaching its full potential, it should be clearer that the rise in the rate of healthcare provider unit prices will have fallen further behind the rate of rise in aggregate healthcare costs. One need only note who pocketed the difference.

Commercial managed care insinuated itself into the social healthcare coverage scheme via its entrepreneurs' animated awareness of how expensive, and cash-flow-generating, narrowed-risk self-insurance could really be. As a result, the industry zealously crafted a chaotic, managed-cost situation that has fractured our healthcare system for possibly another generation to come. Now hostage to the new system, corporate America finds itself trapped between FAS 106 requiring them to renege on years of promises to indemnity insured retired workers, and new actuarial estimates of rising costs for active workers based on needlessly overpriced healthcare; all this done to surfeit insurance company profits and satisfy externalities negative to appropriate healthcare delivery.

In the modern economic environment, such insurers are of no help to anyone or to the system. To them, formerly fat real estate and mortgage portfolios became millstones as those values dived in 2007, while narrowed-risk coverage actualized for the ERISA noninsurance industry a generous trough of relatively unencumbered, unscrutinized revenue growth. By 2008, with the election of Senator Obama as president, this changed quickly. Proposals for mandating "pay-or-play" community rating of small businesses and MSAs were criticized as flawed, too. While they might provide increased cash flow for insurers and some benefits to the better-endowed uninsured, the continued absence of tens of millions of ERISA plan members from regulation would continue to inflate spuriously the actuarial risk and cause a rise in comparable indemnity premiums.

Universal healthcare coverage for Americans could be achieved without a government-run or "single-payer" healthcare system, the latter requiring a constitutional fight to put an end to the commercial health-insurance business. However, just as we expect state government to license doctors and hospitals, there will have to be strong federal governmental oversight on the new, better-regulated ACA system. Instead of letting insurers cash in as risk-aversive HMOs, they should be required to take a reasonable risk by spreading the risk across actuarially determined minimum numbers and a mix of subscribers.

Of great concern to the insurance industry during the debate on the attempted 1994 Clinton Health Security Act was a proposed 1 percent payroll tax to be paid by any corporation with over five thousand employees that would not participate in an "alliance" to spread the risk wider than the company. As we noted in the Preface, it was similar to the ACA's 2014 mandatory requirement for everyone to purchase health insurance pursuant to the federal taxing power, the right to regulate health-insurance interstate commerce, and the requirement for the ACOs to have a sufficient number of primary care professionals for the number of assigned beneficiaries (to be 5,000 beneficiaries at a minimum). Its effect would demonstrate to all the narrowed-risk reason the cost of healthcare has been so high. The regulations on M+C, too, allowed the Clinton government a closer examination of HMO plan profits and, when that happened, the emphasis was quickly shifted to the BBA's M+C and later MA plans by the Bush administration. Under the ACA, rebates to the insured or excise taxes on indemnity insurers would be imposed if their profits from MLRs were found to be unreasonable. This could provide some enthusiasm for corporate-sponsored ERISA healthcare plans and HMOs to opt out of the reduced-benefits business and reverse managed MCOs' ability to opt out of Medicare and Medicaid when or where they found it unprofitable. Allowing smaller group insurance a proportionately lower MLR would also provide some interim relief to total costs as the larger groups' profitability decreased from its required higher MLR.

A national healthcare plan does not mean government run but rather government protected. Universal coverage including a "public option" as originally proposed by President Obama would not eliminate reasonable profits for insurance companies satisfied to be in the "business of insurance" but instead would end unconscionable profits resulting from price and nonprice predation. It would require open enrollment to spread the risk among all Americans, sick and well, young and old, and allow the new, expanded marketspace to determine providers' fees, which would be market-adjusted lower because they would not be weighed down with managed care costs. The ACA has provided most of the factual predicates required for Congress and the appropriate state and federal agencies to get indemnity insurers back into the business of state or federally regulated insurance which, if spread widely enough, would lower the cost for all, especially for small businesses and people with moderate incomes.

Evidence of managed care's cartelization was reflected once more in the 1997 debates on Capitol Hill and the ensuing optimistic patchwork of state action taken in response to Congress's reticent acknowledgment of the problem. The largely nonprofit national Blue Cross/Blue Shield Association reported that in 1997 states passed forty-seven laws banning health plans from including gag clauses, requiring external review processes to resolve enrollee grievances, and allowing enrollees to have direct access to medical specialists.

- Fifteen states had enacted comprehensive managed care legislation combining a variety of forms.
- Fourteen states passed laws imposing requirements on the short hospital stays following "drive-through" mastectomies.
- Eight states passed forty-eight-hour minimum-stay rules, and the remainder left length-of-stay decisions up to doctors and patients.
- Fourteen states adopted measures requiring plans to give enrollees direct access to specialists without a primary-care physician referral. Of those fourteen, the measures of nine pertained to obstetrician-gynecologists.
- Nine states enacted legislation allowing patients to appeal coverage or claim denials to an independent body after their plans' internal grievance processes were exhausted.
- Eight states passed bills mandating parity between mental health and medical-surgical insurance coverage.
- Two states adopted legislation making health plans directly liable for medical malpractice.

States were getting more active in antitrust enforcement, too, through the Healthcare Working Group of the National Association of Attorneys General, formed in the early years of the Clinton Administration to share information and experience. Mentioned earlier was the then New York Attorney General Andrew Cuomo's 2009 investigation, in which flawed, shared databases used by UHG's Ingenix were found. Nevertheless, since its founding in 2000, the impact of the Republican state Attorneys General Association resistance to the ACA has been significant, as the number of Republican state Attorneys General grew from fourteen to twent-four nationwide by March of 2011. In 2010, fourteen states' attorneys general work became unusually politicized after President Obama signed the ACA. In a move to derail the new law's effect, they joined the court challenge to the ACA by the Thomas More Law Center, a tax-exempt, IRS § 501(c)(3) advocacy group, which "defends and promotes America's Christian heritage and moral values, including the religious freedom of Christians, time-honored family values, and the sanctity of human life."

The 2010 health reform act would require most people in the United States to buy health insurance by 2014 and would help some of them pay for it in part with subsidies for lower- and middle-income individuals and families through Exchanges established by the states. Because the ACA expands the Medicaid-eligible group pursuant to the Constitution's Commerce Clause, partially under which Medicaid functions, the requirement affects fewer than 10 percent of those already covered by some form of healthcare benefits plan in 2010. By 2014, a state must bring such uninsured into a similar program or allow the federal government the option to start its own insurance exchange in that state. This created the uncomfortable possibility that there could be two competing exchanges in interstate commerce, so while McCarran-Ferguson's regulation by "state action" concept was not vitiated by the ACA, the potential for a "public option" and evolution of a single-payer plan in the future was strengthened.

The ACA's mandatory coverage provision attempts to end one more deadweight loss in the present healthcare system, where the marginal cost of care for Americans is greater than the marginal benefit when "managed." Nonetheless, in January 2011, Florida federal district court Judge Roger Vinson held that the insurance requirement exceeds the regulatory powers granted to Congress under the Commerce Clause of the Constitution. Judge Vinson wrote, "It would be a radical departure from existing case law to hold that Congress can regulate inactivity under the Commerce Clause." The Judge's definition of "inactivity" governed his ruling in insisting that citizens would be forced by a penalty to buy something they may not want. On February 7, Harvard law professor Laurence H. Tribe noted in an op-ed article in *The New York Times* that calling the decision *not* to purchase insurance as "inactivity" is "illusory."

"Individuals who don't purchase insurance they can afford have made a choice to take a free ride on the healthcare system. They know that if they need emergency-room care that they can't pay for, the public will pick up the tab. This conscious choice carries serious economic consequences for the national healthcare market, which makes it a proper subject for federal regulation."

The Obama administration's "mandatory" position in the ACA was not new. In *United States v. Lee*, a unanimous 1982 Supreme Court gave judicial notice to the legislative history of our Social Security system at the time Medicare benefits were made available to participants in the system. In deciding that *Old Order Amish* employers and employees must participate in Social Security, the High Court quoted from Senate Report Number 404 of the 1965, 89th Congress, which stated that "a comprehensive national social security system providing for voluntary participation would be almost a contradiction in terms, and difficult, if not impossible, to administer."

"The design of the system requires support by mandatory contributions from covered employers and employees. This mandatory participation is indispensable to the fiscal vitality of the social security system. '[W]idespread individual voluntary coverage under social security . . . would undermine the soundness of the social security program.' . . . [and in footnote 12]: We note that here the statute compels contributions to the system by way of taxes; it does not compel anyone to accept benefits."

The ACA has built in exceptions that are consistent with the federal taxing authority and the decision in *United States v. Lee*:

"Congress, in [the section of the IRS Code, which exempts from social security taxes, on religious grounds, self-employed Amish and others] has accommodated, to the extent compatible with a comprehensive national program, the practices of those who believe it a violation of their faith to participate in the social security system. When followers of a particular sect enter into commercial activity as a matter of choice, the limits they accept on their own conduct as a matter of conscience and faith are not to be superimposed on the statutory schemes that are binding on others in that activity. Granting an exemption from social security taxes to an employer operates to impose the employer's religious faith on the employees. The tax imposed on employers to support the social security system must be uniformly applicable to all, except as Congress explicitly provides otherwise." *See* Plates 15, 16.

The challenges to the ACA's individual mandate, and the Virginia federal court decision that the government cannot regulate "inactivity," are also contrary to the holding by the 1988 Supreme Court ERISA decision on federal preemption in *Fort Halifax Packing Company v. P. Daniel Coyne, Bureau of Labor Standards of Maine, et al.*:
"A patchwork scheme of regulation would introduce considerable inefficiencies in benefit program operation, which might lead those employers with existing plans to reduce benefits, and those without such plans to refrain from adopting them."

The ACA allows that American Indians do not have to buy such insurance, and those with religious objections or a financial hardship can also avoid the requirement. In addition, if a person would pay more than 8 percent of his or her income for the cheapest available plan, that person would not be penalized for failing to buy coverage. Thus, the Supreme Court's precedential view of "choice" and "conscience" in *Lee* in relation to a "comprehensive national program" runs counter to the "inactivity" concept put forth by Judge Vinson as irrelevant to a constitutional issue. On February 23, 2011 federal district court Senior Judge Gladys Kessler of Washington, DC said that the law is constitutional, becoming the fifth federal judge to rule on the issue, making the count three to two. The decisions fell along party lines: Democratic presidents had appointed those ruling in favor of the law, and Republican presidents had appointed the two deciding against it.

By Thursday, March 3, Judge Vinson stayed his own injunctive ruling, allowing the act to be carried out as the case progressed through the Court of Appeals and, possibly, on to the Supreme Court, writing that the confusion caused by enjoining the health-care law would outweigh any potential harm to the states caused by its continuation. Simply put, the case was not ripe for injunctive relief. By early May, two appellate court hearings began in Richmond, Virginia at the United States Court of Appeals for the Fourth Circuit, considering contradictory rulings (one supporting the ACA and one challenging it), and in early June two more sets of hearings at the Courts of Appeals for the Sixth and Eleventh Circuits. In all, by May, since the enactment of the ACA, 31 lawsuits had been filed to challenge the Act, nine were awaiting action by Courts of Appeal, nine were pending in federal district courts and 13 had been dismissed.

In fact, many federal requirements for mandatory participation in public-health systems have been in place for decades, ranging from insurance required for driving a car on the public highways to Medicare and Medicaid, requiring citizens to be vaccinated, to file an income tax return, or to register for the draft—not one to acquire health insurance. In light of *Lee*, that would not make it novel or a case of first impression. On the contrary, the ACA is consistent both with Supreme Court decisions on comprehensive social schemes and congressional consideration. The only real "inactivity" relating to healthcare appears to come from those who refuse to seek medical attention—such as many Christian Scientists—who can nonetheless be coerced by courts if they extend their religious views to their minor children's health. The rest, those uninsured and considered "inactive" by Judge Vinson, are generally quite "active" free riders on the healthcare system when they use emergency rooms of hospitals for their healthcare and pass the costs to the taxpayers in one form or another.

Nevertheless, the president attempted an apparent major end run around the lawsuits commenced by the multiple states' attorneys general against the mandatory sections of the ACA. In remarks to the February 28, 2011 meeting of the National Governors Association, Mr. Obama said that he supported legislation that would allow states to obtain waivers from the mandate as soon as it took effect in 2014, as long as they could find another way to expand coverage without driving up health-care costs. Under the current law, states must wait until 2017 to obtain waivers. The changes must also not increase the federal deficit. If states can meet those standards, they can seek waivers to skirt minimum benefit levels, some structural requirements for insurance Exchanges, and the mandates that most individuals obtain coverage and employers must provide it. The federal government would then help finance a state's expressly detailed health-care system using the federal money that otherwise would be spent there on the Exchanges for subsidization of insurance premiums for individuals with income up to 400 percent of the poverty line and advanceable, refundable tax credits to provide government benefits to people with no tax liability.

In November 2011, the Supreme Court decided to hear arguments on the constitutionality of the ACA, with the major thrust being the charge of "inactivity" forcing people who can afford it to buy health insurance. Arguments are expected in March 2012, with its decision issuing several months before the presidential election.

Notwithstanding the president's attempt to bring opposing forces together, relying solely on a patchwork of state action can be perilous for a citizenry as happened after enactment of the healthcare-benighted ERISA's "savings clause," and "deeming" ERISA benefit plans "non-insurance." Along with the subsidies for state Exchanges offered by the new health-reform law, federal-state cooperation in closing ERISA-permitted loopholes that could allow managed care "administrative costs" to be included as if costs for healthcare will still be urgently needed. However, it appears that DHHS and the CMS regulations may play an effective role in limiting the validity of those profit centers for the managed-care industry. The rapid transformation in how health-care is delivered and financed appears to have outstripped the ability of pre-existing federal regulatory mechanisms to alleviate the avalanche of grievances. During the previous Republican administrations from Reagan, and Bushes I and II, those mechanisms were oriented largely toward the offenders in the traditional fee-for-service healthcare delivery model, but the Obama ACO antitrust enforcement policy discussed below (and in the Appendix) appears to have moved in a more comprehensive direction.

Indeed, the Clinton administration's healthcare antitrust policy and enforcement activity reoriented and recognized that collusion, collaboration, and control among MCOs, whose financial base is external to a treatment process—in contrast with provider-patient relationships, which is the process—were major unaddressed aspects of the healthcare system's market failure. Understandably, considering the state of the financial markets during that booming economy, the Clinton DOJ and FTC efforts were overwhelmed with non-healthcare antitrust activity, such as with ATT and Microsoft. The post-Millennium, George W. Bush administration let the momentum slow, but the DOJ and FTC under Obama appear to be alert to potential antitrust activity of the new Accountable Care Organizations of professionals. It remains to be seen whether the government's administrative emphasis will be on the organizations of providers alone or how they might be connected to the managed-care industry's market power manipulations. *See* Appendix.

XI. The Ethics of Managing Managed Care— the Affordable Care Act and the Supreme Court Enters

"Despite the presence of rascals in the medical profession, as in all others, we trust that most physicians are good."

—*Doe v. Bolton* (1973)

"He brings salves and balms with him, no doubt; but before he can act as a physician he first has to wound; when he then stills the pain of the wound *he at the same time infects the wound* . . . Indeed, he defends his sick herd well enough, this strange shepherd . . ."

—Friedrich Nietzsche,
On the Genealogy of Morals (1887)

"I owe my soul to the company store."

—Merle Travis song *"Sixteen Tons,"* revived by
Tennessee Ernie Ford in 1955

In *Moore v. City of East Cleveland, Griswold v. Connecticut, Doe v. Bolton* and *Lawrence v. Texas*—the latter case, striking down a law that attempted to "control a personal relationship that . . . is within the liberty of persons to choose without being punished"—the Supreme

Court examined fundamental contractual liberty rights to which people are entitled that are "deeply rooted in this Nation's history and tradition." What a strange new crop of shepherds for the sick and lame would the next generation of physicians become if they triage-treated patients solely with algorithms and eschewed the individual doctor-patient relationship. Managed care has become a market failure with all the bitter irony of its social upheaval. It forced tens of thousands of highly trained professionals to work at a loss or prematurely retire. It signaled a six-year steady fall of medical school applicants from 1997 to 2003, coerced hospital bed-occupancy to drop, then issued a neo-Luddite call to eliminate the "empty" beds that cost much more to rebuild. It offered no demonstrable evidence of improved healthcare while forcing healthcare premium income ever higher; depersonalized the doctor-patient relationship, and deskilled medical care by substituting lesser-trained professionals who acted outside the scope of lawful practice to the patients' peril. The "one size fits all" capitated managed care created its own market failure. In addition to undermining its promised benefits, capitation and withhold-based group care now fixes prices, distorts medical ethics, economically punishes professional virtue, misrepresents the aggregate social cost of healthcare, depletes the tax base, and doles out an increase in the prevalence of chronic illness. All this continues today. The larger MCOs are able to capture the marketspace of the smaller ones who failed to estimate the cost of providing ethical healthcare and could not compete with those having large cash reserves to carry them through the predatory, marginal-cost pricing phase.

In the managed-care era, ethical behavior for the real care manager, the physician, requires understanding the nature of the managed-care system and then making prudent choices derived from that understanding. Treatment for an illness is not the same as commercial or governmental managed-care's intrusive "verification" or second-guessing of the medical necessity of that treatment. While evaluation of treatment may produce a diagnosis, medical treatment, itself, is seen by all but the malpractice plaintiffs' bar to provide care or cure. The physician's role is solely to diagnose and treat pathological states and attempt to heal based on knowledgeable care acknowledged by the scope of its state's licensure. The physician hired solely to evaluate other physicians' behavior is performing an unethical act that is authorized and benefited by commercial managed care interests. The medical expert witness states an opinion in a courtroom—a protected ethical forum for the adversarial exercise of cross-examination based on evidence. The professional managed-care doctor, however, is far down the profit-based primrose path of unethical medical behavior using flawed evidence pending painful appeal.

For obvious economic advantage to their employers, the MCO medical reviewers are in reality judging the work of unseen "competitors" on a mass scale, which causes havoc and scarcity in the sentinel-effect-provoked doctor-patient relationship (where it is assumed that productivity and outcomes can be improved through the process of observation and measurement). The treating physicians and the patients do not have the advantage of the courtroom doctor-witness who has an impartial judge present as well as an attorney to guide a supplicant's cross-examination. The managed-care review is more akin to a secrecy-protected grand jury, which allows for no cross-examination of witnesses other than by resort to expensive appeals. With managed care, the patient or physician can appeal only denials to the interested corporate parties, face binding arbitration, or seek redress in court. Numerous ERISA court decisions have allowed that independent administrative process need not be offered, because ERISA's trust-law-based appeals to a "fiduciary" suffice for redress of the beneficiary's claim of a benefits plan.

It is important to note that in the *Crocco* case discussed earlier, the federal district court "assumed without deciding," saying, "While it may be true that the fee arrangement between APM and Xerox did not encourage the denial of coverage, [its] desire to satisfy Xerox's expectations certainly did," and the Second Circuit reversed jurisdiction against Xerox as "hypothetical." Ironically, within weeks, the Supreme Court put an end to that type of hypothetical language and created a "jurisdiction first rule," which, in *Crocco*, could have inculpated both Xerox and APM as fiduciaries and allowed the case to go forward *de novo* rather than on an arbitrary and capricious basis. That default standard is where the court perforce acts as a claims examiner making a decision based on the record, with no deference to the decision made by the fiduciary or employer whose conflict is to both decide on and pay benefits. In 2009, the Second Circuit decision in *Hobson v. Metro. Life Ins. Co.*, declined to accord any weight to the inherent conflict because the claimant presented weak evidence of any bias or procedural irregularities, placing the burden of proof on the claimant to show unfairness, even though the employer paid its "independent experts" and ignored a Social Security benefits decision that the employee was disabled based on her illness. In *Magee v. Metropolitan Life Ins. Co.*, a 2009 southern district of New York federal court found that cherrypicking parts of a treating physician's medical opinions was helpful to the insurer and ignored the harmful parts. These varied judicial views still haunt the ERISA Declaration of Purpose "to provide for the general welfare and the free flow of commerce . . . in the interest of the employees and their beneficiaries."

One cannot argue that contract *per se* comes before public policy, and public policy related to medicine is for a state to license its practice with patients or use its expertise before a court—thus the distinction between "license" and "registration." No state license may be accorded those who do not "practice" within its scope or teach the discipline to students. Managed-care doctor telephone-reviewers are neither practicing medicine with patients nor teaching their students, yet they may be accorded the status of expert witnesses and can be cross-examined about a medical record without having examined the patient. The reason that a managed-care company hires a doctor (nurses, social workers, etc.) is not that they work "within the scope of their practice," as most state professional practice licensing laws expect, but solely to make income-based judgments for their employers about other professionals' work, using their employers' algorithms as support. In any event, this is in a forensic realm, which formally answers questions of interest about civil or criminal matters to a legal system. In fact, some doctors who work in forensics have claimed they are not acting in court as physicians, or constrained under the ethics of the physician, but rather as "forensicists" with a code of ethics bound to courtroom procedure and rules of evidence. The flaw in this reasoning should be obvious: The doctor in a consultative- or expert-witness role would be unacceptable in court if he or she were not licensed as a physician first. Nor would the plaintiff's attorney wish to reveal to judge or jury that the witness conformed to an ethical code different from that of a treating medical practitioner.

Although managed care with its algorithmic style professes to save on the costs of treating illnesses, much of medical diagnosis and treatment, in fact, concerns diseases that are not yet curable. Indeed, much care rendered by doctors is limited by circumstance. Psychotherapy, for example, can employ techniques in therapeutic sessions that may elicit emotional pain that builds crisis resolution from that point forward. Most surgeons understand the anxieties aroused before and during the postoperative period that require either direct, gentle ministering or that call for psychiatric consultation-liaison services to mitigate secondary problems, and all doctors know that medications for hoped-for "cures" may have unpleasant side effects.

In its zeal to incorporate cost-saving measures for affordable healthcare such as electronic health records, the ACA also includes "evidence-based medicine." This concept, whose philosophical origins extend back to mid-nineteenth-century France and earlier, remains an emotional topic for many clinicians, public health practitioners, purchasers, planners, and the public. While "evidence-based medicine" sounds good as a possible cost saver, it deserves more circumspection as a methodology for its direct clinical use. Evidence-based medicine has been lauded and promoted by the managed-care industry, whose reputation for "saving on healthcare costs" was problematic from the start. Recall the teleconference discussed earlier between a hospital and WellPoint's QIO subsidiary, NGS, and the QIO's use of actuaries M&R and InterQual guidelines, denying care for sixteen patient admissions, all of which were later reversed by ALJs. M&R publicly takes credit for being the first one to use evidence-based medicine guidelines in the managed-care era, as its founder, Richard L. Doyle, MD, developed them in 1990.

"Milliman Care Guidelines, LLC, A Milliman Company, is located in Seattle, and independently develops and produces evidence-based clinical guidelines and software used by more than 1,000 clients, including hospitals, providers, and health plans. Covering the continuum of care, the seven-product Care Guidelines series—Ambulatory Care, Inpatient and Surgical Care, General Recovery Guidelines, Recovery Facility Care, Home Care, Chronic Care Guidelines and Behavioral Health Guidelines— is updated annually by an experienced team of clinicians and are used to support the care of more than one in three Americans."

The peer-reviewed journal *Archives of Pediatrics & Adolescent Medicine* in August 2001 was among numerous journals that criticized the M&R guidelines. For example:

"Pediatric Length of Stay Guidelines and Routine Practice: The Case of Milliman and Robertson

Administrative data from Pennsylvania hospitals from 1996 through 1998 were used to examine [length of stay] for hospital discharges for 12 selected diagnoses for which M&R published guidelines for children and adults . . . The M&R LOS criteria were divergent from routine practice for both children and adults. Greater divergence of adult discharges illustrates the need to consider co-morbid conditions when implementing these guidelines. Thus, patient care may suffer if guidelines are implemented in an uninformed way. These findings emphasize the importance of using the best possible science when producing guidelines such as these."

In the same journal in December:

"Inpatient Care for Uncomplicated Bronchiolitis

Milliman and Robertson's recommendations do not correspond to practice patterns observed at the hospitals participating in this study; no hospital met the Milliman and Robertson recommended 1-day goal length of stay. Administration of monitored intervention persisted past the second day of hospitalization."

On March 27, 2010, *PR Newswire* reported "Milliman Identifies Strategic Considerations for the Post-Healthcare Reform Environment." It was not unexpected that Milliman might then jump in to help the ACA's ACOs get a foothold on prices:

"Health plans are revisiting provider risk-sharing methods as a way to help control costs and to create quality incentives. These efforts may be different from those attempted in the past due to better technology and improved risk adjustment. Accountable care organizations are one example of this risk sharing. Evidence-based medicine may also play a role in reducing waste and inefficiency, since certain clinical best practices offer the opportunity to simultaneously manage cost and improve quality. A new emphasis on prevention has uncertain cost implications."

We have pointed out that managed-care health insurance in the United States conceals the true price of healthcare services from patients. In a February 2011 *JAMA* Commentary, "A Cautious Path Forward on Accountable Care Organizations," Duke University and Fuqua School of Business professors Barak D. Richman and Kevin A. Schulman warn that the ACA

"does not protect ACOs from antitrust laws, and because health insurance confers enormous pricing freedom on dominant healthcare organizations, the formation of ACOs requires heightened, not relaxed, antitrust attention. . .[and that] the prices most consumers would not pay (and monopolists would not charge) in the absence of insurance are paid through higher health insurance premiums for all Americans."

In their discussion of market power and health insurance, their view is that ACOs may need to be well regulated if they are to achieve the goal of creating more efficiency in the fragmented U.S. healthcare

system. They caution that ACOs will have to be prevented from causing the dilemma that health insurers face, because the health insurers

"cannot refuse to pay the high prices imposed by healthcare organizations, even when the price exceeds the likely value
of the service to the patient. Instead, insurers are expected to
cover any desired service deemed "medically necessary" by professional standards, whatever the cost."

Richman and Schulman's antitrust concern over ACOs' establishing
market power, and that "Health insurance, therefore, enables monopolists of health services to charge more than the textbook 'monopoly
price,' earn more than the typical 'monopoly profit,' and capture more
consumer dollars than monopolists in other industries," appears well
intentioned. However, they miss the "elephant in the room" fact that
the managed healthcare insurance industry's market power is the heart
of, and has created, the present high cost of healthcare. Indeed, when
they point out that "policy makers should remember that the healthcare monopoly problem exists today largely because horizontal mergers
were permitted to create large healthcare systems that failed to produce their promised efficiencies," they close their eyes to the insurance
industry's megabillion mergers and acquisitions that gave birth to the
problem. When they say "Current healthcare prices reflect the costs
of these [healthcare organizations'] monopolies without many benefits
from integration," they ignore the role of the industry that created and
benefits from the fragmented system in the first place.

On April 22, 2010, *PR Newswire* reported that Healthcare Strategies, Inc., QIO, used Milliman *Care Guidelines* in New Jersey under
contract with the federal CMS for Medicare reviews, which nonetheless
do "not mandate or endorse the use of any specific criteria set by QIOs."

"The *Care Guidelines* promote quality care by providing
healthcare professionals with access to best practice based on
annually updated evidence. The *Care Guidelines* also display
Quality Measures used by CMS, and each inpatient topic
includes care planning information—highlighting interventions that help lead to improved outcomes. Designed for pro-

spective, concurrent, and retrospective reviews, the *Care Guidelines* enable informed and consistent clinical care decisions, and support the best possible care management using the most current evidence-based medicine."

Dr. Donald M. Berwick, the Obama, recessed-appointed CMS administrator, appeared sympathetic to evidence-based medicine in the September 2010 edition of *Academic Medicine*, the journal of the Association of American Medical Colleges:

"Although a good deal of popular writing on standardization, protocols, and compliance with 'evidence-based guidelines' remains anecdotal and exhortatory, the basic underlying theories of reliability engineering and resilience in design are increasingly well- developed and more and more applied directly to healthcare."

Actually, aside from the "anecdotal and exhortatory," there were numerous and differing peer-reviewed scientific articles published over the years in distinguished medical journals. In a commentary published for his former organization, the Institute for Healthcare Improvement, promoting the British publication *Clinical Evidence*, Dr. Berwick said,

"Knee-jerk critiques attack some of these tools as 'cookbook medicine,' somehow having learned to fear algorithms and evidence-based care plans as handcuffs. Used unwisely, they can be so, since the patients' interests depend on specific, local adjustments as well as on putting formal science into practice. But it is unfair, illogical, and hazardous to reject evidence-based standards and syntheses of research as encouraging unthinking practice.

"On the contrary, the hard work of hundreds of editors, investigators, and medical writers, assembled in clear digests is a resource of tremendous value, supplying knowledge and support that no individual doctor could hope to arrange for himself or herself. Wise physicians will use such digests to increase the reliability with which they use clinically relevant scientific evidence in their daily work, and to continually challenge and update their habits as new evidence becomes available. Wise physicians will not resist evidence-based practice; they will insist on it.

Many digests of clinical science are now available to physicians and nurses, but none is better than *Clinical Evidence*. This remarkable publication harnesses the full capacities of the British Medical Journal Publishing Group in a widespread and well-supported network of carefully trained and closely guided reviewers . . . Using *Clinical* Evidence to guide decisions is not 'cookbook medicine.' Or, then again, maybe it is – 'Julia Child' medicine, to be exact. The best of chefs keep the great cookbooks close at hand – not to stop their thinking, but to start it."

On November 23, 2011, the White House announced that President Obama would nominate an official at the Centers for Medicare & Medicaid Services, Marilyn Tavenner, to be the CMS administrator. The position was held by Dr. Berwick, stepped down December 2. His term as a recess appointment would have had to end by 2012, in any event. *The Washington Post* reported that

"Berwick spent just shy of 18 months in the Obama administration. He came into office at a particularly tumultuous time, six months after the health reform law passed, and oversaw the rollout of crucial health care reform regulations, including ones that could reshape both the insurance industry as well as how Medicare pays doctors."

The biannual compendium *Clinical Evidence*, lauded by Dr. Berwick, was launched in 1999. In celebration for the year 2000, philanthropist Dr. William W. McGuire, former CEO of UHG—forced to resign his position a few years later for a then-common process called "stock options backdating"—sent four hundred thousand copies free of charge to American physicians. They were provided by the United-Health Foundation, "a private, not for profit foundation dedicated to improving Americans' health by supporting the education of physicians."

The June 17 issue of the *British Medical Journal*, a prominent peer-reviewed scientific publication, reported Dr. McGuire as saying, "We are providing *Clinical Evidence* to American physicians so that they have access to the best source of scientific evidence as they make treatment decisions with their patients."

Clinical Evidence (published by the British Medical Journal Publishing Group) is an interesting compendium but is, in fact, much like a "cookbook" for doctors and nurses—it titles its summaries as "benefits," "harms," "aims," "prognoses" and "outcomes," and offers "options" for treatment, promoting data as being a "consensus" view of how a patient should be treated. However, many of the medical conditions reviewed are admittedly unsubstantiated by "systematic reviews" or "randomized clinical trials," the *sine qua non* of modern medical science. Since without clinical studies there is little "clinical evidence," *Clinical Evidence's* value, as a source of "what's a physician to do," is far from certain. Its appeal to managed care is evident; however, as its conclusions do not appear to be peer reviewed at all. At base, *Clinical Evidence* simply tells professionals what "others" have done—proclaiming pathways like the algorithms held forth by managed care.

Mark R. Tonelli, professor of medicine at the University of Washington Medical Center, who writes on medical ethics and the philosophical limits to an evidence-based medicine, noted in 2001 that

"A gap exists between empirical evidence and clinical practice. Proponents of evidence-based medicine have clearly acknowledged one aspect of this gap: the part that requires the consideration of values, both patient and professional, prior to arriving at medical decisions. Not as clearly recognized, however, is the gap that exists due to the fact that empirical evidence is not directly applicable to individual patients, as the knowledge gained from clinical research does not directly answer the primary clinical question of what is best for the patient at hand. . . . Clinicians, then, need to incorporate knowledge from

5 distinct areas into each medical decision: (1) empirical evidence, (2) experiential evidence, (3) physiologic principles, (4) patient and professional values, and (5) system features. The relative weight given to each of these areas is not predetermined, but varies from case to case."

Most moral and ethical physicians instinctively understand that there are consequences for untreated or undertreated illnesses beyond the utilitarian and hedonistic. Were it otherwise, there would be no operations for silent, painlessly growing cancers or even tooth extractions, because the painful means would outweigh the ends. The eighteenth-century philosopher Immanuel Kant determined that though a law may demand an act, a higher standard for moral behavior exists. Even scholastic writers on ethics defend the universality of some ethical laws on the ground that our capacities, such as "medical training as a healer," ought not be used in ways that would frustrate the purposes for which they were intended. Hedonistic utilitarianism, however, postulates that not only may a moral action be obligatory by reference to the good produced but, further, that the only good is pleasure and the only evil is pain—notwithstanding the deep-rooted, historical imperatives sowed and reaped for us by Hippocratic medicine and humanistic philosophy.

Managed-care ethics over the years found homes in various government-sanctioned experiments around the United States. Although Tennessee still calls its Medicaid program "TennCare"—started in 1995 under a HCFA waiver for a demonstration project—in mid-2005, the state terminated coverage for all uninsured and uninsurable adults. The only a vestige of the original expansion was uninsured children who would be covered in other states as the State Children's Health Insurance Program or S-CHIP group. It also eliminated coverage for 250,000 adults, the sickest group in TennCare. One study projected that the population could suffer an increase in preventable deaths, calculating it at an additional death every thirty hours and creating the largest single increase in the number of uninsured Americans in the nation's history. Tennessee is now the only state that does not enroll school-age children with incomes above poverty, and TennCare eligibility for elderly and disabled adults is among the most restrictive in the country.

TriStar Health System and UHC, a UHG insurance company, announced in March 2010 that their organizations have extended their TennCare Medicaid managed-care relationship and expanded the agreement to include two new MA options. The TennCare agreement was supposed to be effective immediately with no disruption in service or access to TriStar hospitals for AmeriChoice by UHC's TennCare enrollees. AmeriChoice's "Management Services Organization," a business segment of AmeriChoice, also a UHG company, is devoted entirely to government health-care services. It operates in twenty-two states, providing health program management and administrative services to more than 2.1 million Medicaid managed care members and more than five hundred thousand clients in other public-health programs.

Although Tristar and UHC work together, HCA Holdings, Inc., the corporate organization for the privately held Hospital Corporation of America, which was taken private in a $33 billion leveraged buyout in 2006, controls Tristar. The buyers included private equity firms Bain Capital, Kohlberg Kravis Roberts & Co., and Merrill Lynch Global Private Equity, a unit of investment bank Merrill Lynch Global. HCA founder Thomas F. Frist, Jr., who had been chair, CEO and president of the company from 1988 to 1994 and was still a member of the board, was included among the buyers. In December 2010, HCA refiled plans for a $4.6 billion initial public offering (IPO) after reorganizing the company in order to issue $1.5 billion in junk bonds and provide payouts to its private equity owners, including Bain Capital, Kohlberg Kravis Roberts, and Thomas Frist Jr. The IPO was expected to take place in 2011, and the company was preparing to go public for the third time since its founding in the mid-1960s.

Thomas Frist, Jr. is the brother of former Senate Majority Leader "Doctor" Bill Frist (R-Tenn.). By February 2011, HCA Holdings Inc.'s earnings were reported to have increased 31 percent in the fourth quarter of 2010, and the giant, vertically and horizontally interlocked hospital chain organization moved to go public. The politically based irony of the way TennCare operated during former Tennessee Senator, Vice

President, and 2008 presidential candidate Al Gore's campaign was that in order to hold on to its base and keep the state's electoral votes in their Republican camp, cuts to Tennessee Medicaid were made, notwithstanding that the state lost two federal dollars for every one dollar cut from funds for the "categorically needy." However, the 2010 ACA appears to have transformed the hopes of advocacy groups in Tennessee such as the nonprofit Tennessee Healthcare Campaign organization competing with the Tristar/UHC/HCA collaboration "to make sure that the Tennessee Exchange is holding insurance companies accountable."

In the 1990s, Oregon, the first of three states to allow physician-assisted suicide, began a five-year demonstration project applied for in 1991 under the Bush I administration. The Oregon Health Plan was to start in 1993. The central tenet of the Plan was that eligibility for health-care coverage could be expanded if cost-containment mechanisms were built into the system. The Plan offered two such mechanisms: managed care and benefit limitations. By 2004, it was reported to be on the verge of collapse. While Medicaid "categorically needy" cuts could only be made with loss of federal dollars, the "medically needy" group of services could be changed after proper federal notification. This second group included limitation on services such as prescription drugs, outpatient mental health, outpatient chemical dependency, dental, and durable medical equipment. The waiver also imposed a number of features similar to those found in commercial plans, including stricter premium payment requirements, reduced grace periods, a tiered pharmacy benefit, and copayments. *Medical Economics* reported in October 2004,

> "Since January 2003, enrollment in the standard benefit package—which essentially targets the working poor—has been cut dramatically, from 90,000 to about 54,000. This July, the state closed the program to all new enrollees, with the hope of slashing enrollment further, to about 24,000 by June 30, 2005."

The moratorium on enrollment cuts did not last long, however. With the state's economy continuing to worsen, officials in early 2003 went further, eliminating a program targeting the medically needy— whose eligibility requirements were less strict than those for the categorically needy—and the entire list of optional services. Only prescription drug coverage was eventually reinstated; why punish the pharmaceutical industry? When even those steps failed to make up for the revenue shortfalls, the state employed the commercial-like measures authorized by the waiver to cut actual enrollment. However, in May of 2004, a federal district court ruled that the copayments for people receiving this standard benefit package violated federal law.

Social morals may be distinguished from individual morals when we examine the distinction between duty out of respect for the law and inclination to act based on prudence. Accordingly, it is ethically or morally unfitting for a physician to participate foreseeably in determining the outcome of a treatment procedure in which he or she has no direct involvement, similar to the reason for the AMA Code of Ethics interdiction of physicians who participate in legal executions or in evaluating government prisoners (including terrorists) being tortured. In the March 8, 2010 issue of *American Medical News*, Thomas Greaney, a former DOJ attorney, who teaches at the Saint Louis University School of Law, noted that the federal government can do little to reverse health-insurance consolidation after the fact. Instead, the DOJ might look for ways to encourage companies to enter new markets and could step up enforcement of existing rules. "But that doesn't do much to de-concentrate," he said, "It just controls how they exercise their market power."

This book does not aim to suggest that the DOJ start on a track to years of insurance trust busting. Indeed, it would be of little help to change the process of mergers that has taken place. By early December 2010, Humana, among others insurers, anticipating the roll out of the ACA, began heavy advertising on television, suggested an easy way for people to change from regular Medicare to MA to get the prescription drug coverage, and offered "Free Booklets" showing what "regular Medicare does not offer." UHG followed suit with its TV-ad claim

"Health in Numbers," which inadvertently revealed that the company has the same number of employees per thousand of its subscribers to "manage" their care as there are generalist physicians in the United States who alone provide the care for the same number of subscribers. This exposes the sad fact that commercial managed care "Health in Numbers" offers the American people one doctor for the cost of two!

By April 2011, UHG announced that OPTUM, its wholly owned managed-care subsidiary would become its "Master Brand for its Health Services Business."

"The change reflects increased coordination and collaboration among three leading health services companies that are committed to addressing meaningful and positive change across the health care system: OptumHealth™, which will retain its name; OptumInsight™, which will replace the Ingenix name; and OptumRx™, which will replace the Prescription Solutions name. These combined businesses serve more than 60 million people, have more than 30,000 employees, and in 2010 reported combined revenues of $25 billion, giving Optum as a whole the scale of a FORTUNE 100 enterprise."

Recall "Ingenix," discussed earlier, and why its name needed to be changed; it was found to be violating the antitrust laws. Ingenix, a research firm wholly owned by UHG, was found, in 2008, to have been manipulating the numbers in its database so that insurance companies could pay less to doctors under the usual, customary rates. In a report, he contended that Americans have been "underreimbursed to the tune of at least hundreds of millions of dollars." Although UHG and Oxford Insurance were the only entities investigated by Attorney General Cuomo, other major "competitor" insurers also used Ingenix, including Aetna, CIGNA, and WellPoint/Empire BlueCross/BlueShield, competitors of UHG. Notwithstanding the above, Ingenix-now-OptumInsight continues to offer to its "clients" (doctors, hospitals, pharmacy benefit managers and health plans) through its program called "Impact Pro for Care Management" the following:

"Deep insight for better decisions

Impact Pro arms care management teams with transparent predictive modeling, evidence-based medicine, and tailored clinical and business rules to identify, stratify, and assess members. That insight enables them to design new programs, initiate new interventions, or make better care decisions at any level—individual, group, or program.

Impact Pro can help you:

- Maximize intervention efficacy by quickly identifying those members where intervention will be most successful within any population
- Discover new intervention program opportunities for members
- Assess the value and quality of current intervention programs
- Understand the issues driving each member's current and future health care

Identify impact opportunities

Impact Pro can help you enhance cost savings by identifying members who would derive the most value from current managed care programs using customizable care profiles and evidence-based guidelines targeted to specific members' health

Advanced program analysis

This powerful tool can measure specific programs' effectiveness and cost savings over time by gauging both quality of care and health care outcomes. In addition, it can help evaluate member populations enrolled in current programs and identify new program opportunities for those populations."

Ingenix-OptumInsight self-assuredly includes a website sample "Predictive Modeling Analysis" to "Identify members of higher future risk." Recall our earlier discussion of NCQA, M&R and InterQual-type "messengers" that use actuarial data favoring stabilizing of their industry prices. Optum's Modeling Analysis consists of data including "Account Numbers, Group Numbers, Number of Members Ages, Months Enrolled, coefficients representing Timing Future Risk, Costs, and by Age/Gender Risk Costs, Prior Total Costs, and Future Costs Annualized, in dollars.

In Chapter V, we discussed the fact that before the ACA, prohibition on dissemination of future production prices appears to have not been addressed by the government for interstate commercial insurance ventures. This was probably because of the state safe harbor for what has historically been described as "the business of insurance" activity, and the "noninsurance of ERISA, self-insured plans; but it has been focussed on for providers. The exchange of current or proposed prices, or the exchange of information regarding future production projections are generally prohibited, especially when horizontal merger activity is involved. Moreover, since most hospitals take Medicare patients and make complete financial reporting, records that are publicly available on institutional cost reports to the government, where they list numbers of patient visits and aggregate current prices per patient day and hospital admissions and discharges based on government-set prices per DRG admission. Now these data are proposed to be disseminated by OptumInsight as they enter their world of market power through privatized Medicare Advantage.

From these data, the interstate competitors can easily extrapolate prices-per-patient contact and disease-type contact. In any event, whether risk managing or providing administrative services, the MCOs are in the compass of federal antitrust statutes related to coercion, boycott, or intimidation, and when providing coverage determinations to ERISA self-insured plans, they are open fully to the antitrust laws because of federal preemption.

As part of the bandwagon effort in November 2011, OPTUM sent a $45 "gift," along with an announcement of "An Exclusive Event for Hospital Executives." The "event" was an invitation to one of a series of lectures and demonstrations being held around the country in December, in time for the January 2012 enrollment for ACOs. "Build a Sustainable Health Community. The Journey Starts Now," OptumInsight proclaimed on its website:

"The recent release by CMS of the proposed rule on Medicare payments to providers participating in ACOs is an important step in the modernization of the health care system. But, these new ACO guidelines do not go far enough to fix an unsustainable health system. ACOs, as guided by the Patient Protection and Affordable Care Act, will be built on a regulatory framework—attractive to some, prohibitive to others. . . We believe that the present ACO model is limited. We support a comprehensive new model: Sustainable Health Communities, our long-term vision for truly effective and cost-efficient health. In a Sustainable Health Community, all participants of a community function in harmony to achieve enduring community health: optimized care quality, lower costs, and enhanced satisfaction. Sustainable Health Communities are connected, intelligent, and aligned, producing a system that works better for everyone."

The OptumInsight "gift" was made by Ecosphere Associates, Inc. It was a four-inch, clear glass globe, containing "active micro-organisms, small shrimp, algae, and bacteria, each existing in filtered sea water," and two small magnets, one inside the globe and one outside, to attract each other and control the inner one to scrape clean the inside of the glass when waste products form. The enclosed "guideline" notes that EcoSphere's biological cycle

"represents a simple version of Earth's own ecosystem. Light together with carbon dioxide in the water enable the algae to produce oxygen by photosynthesis. The shrimp breathe the oxygen in the water while nibbling on the algae and bacteria. The bacteria break down the animal waste into nutrients, which the algae utilize. The shrimp and bacteria also give off carbon dioxide, which the algae again use to produce oxygen. And so the cycle renews itself."

501

The Optum website suggests an analogy to the Ecosphere:

"We're all in this together . . . On the road to accountable care, alignment is the key. The perfect balance within complex relationships. Like an ecosphere, each community is unique—from its population's demographics and level of hospital/physician group sophistication to the number of payers serving the area. Optum Accountable Care Solutions works with communities to design, build, and operate the accountable care model that best suits a specific community's needs.

Advance the quality of care and outcomes. Reduce costs and bridge the revenue gap. Improve patient satisfaction and engagement.

Make the health system work better for everyone by building a Sustainable Health Community. Sustainable Health Communities apply a long-term, integrated approach to achieving community engagement, ongoing financial viability, and improved population health by aligning economic, environmental, and social issues."

In June 2011, it was announced on the website that

"Tucson Medical Center and local physicians, with the help of health technology and services company Optum, today announced they are creating the nation's first 'Sustainable Health Community,' based on an Accountable Care Organization (ACO) model in which hospitals, physicians, residents, employers and others share in the risk and rewards of making the health system work better for everyone. This new model helps hospitals, participating physicians and health plans collaborate to better coordinate care, improve quality and, ultimately, increase consumers' satisfaction with the health system."

The above is a sample of how the managed-care industry plans to enter the Obama-reformed Medicare system as an interstate "messenger," if not a direct participant, controlling ACOs and their own cash flow. This is so, even though nothing in the ACO section 3022 of the

ACA mentions eligibility for participation for other than physicians, physician groups, hospitals, and joint venture arrangements between, and "such other groups of providers of services and suppliers as the Secretary of HHS determines appropriate."

On October 28, 2011, in the Federal Register, The Final ACO Policy Statement by the FTC/DoJ was issued:

"**Antitrust Enforcement Policy Regarding Accountable Care Organizations Participating in the Medicare Shared Savings Program.**" The controlling footnote (2) states: ["As used in this document, "ACO" refers to Accountable Care Organizations under the Medicare Shared Savings Program, which also may operate in commercial markets."] The Policy makes quite clear that it uses an antitrust-surveillance methodology requiring submission of data by any ACO wishing to participate in the Medicare Shared Savings Program, and "uses the same governance and leadership structures and clinical and administrative processes it uses in the Shared Savings Program to serve patients in commercial markets." The most significant aspect of the new policy is that it is shaped on the premise that commercial market involvement in the ACOs could inevitably lead to attempts for the organizations involved—for- or nonprofit to gain market power, and demonstrates the awareness by the Obama administration of the dangers and market failure potential of the managed healthcare industry. *See* Appendix.

For the period up to 2014, the ACA insurance Exchanges provide just the right way to effect some control of the insurers' manipulated marketspace larder, because states or the federal government may regulate the MLRs of new entrants as well as the old competitors' taste for hegemony and high prices by having brought so many millions more into healthcare coverage. As for the insurance industry's broad, fiercely lobbied resistance to the ACA, one temporizing voice appeared from within its camp. *The New York Times* reported in December 2010 that Aetna's newly retired CEO did not support the repeal of the health reform law, and when asked to "describe its greatest achievement," he cited "heightened awareness."

The AMA withstood significant criticism from many of its component state and county medical societies in supporting the "Obamacare"

ACA, and published the following short list of the act's advantages to doctors and their patients, some of which we discussed earlier: *See* Plates 13, 14 and 17.

- Thirty-two million Americans will gain access to health coverage.
- Insurers will no longer be allowed to deny patients on preexisting conditions.
- Patients will no longer face lifetime caps on coverage or be threatened with cancellation.
- Children will be permitted to remain on their parents' policies until age twenty-six.
- Competition will be introduced into the insurance marketplace.
- Health insurance exchanges and co-ops will be created that will allow pooling of coverage for individuals and small businesses.
- Tax credits will be extended to small businesses for the purchase of health insurance coverage.
- High-risk insurance pools will be created.
- Subsidies will help lower-income individuals and families purchase health coverage.
- Insurance claims processing will be standardized and streamlined, helping to lower physician overhead costs and improve practice revenue cycles.
- The Medicare Part D Coverage Gap ("donut hole") that haunts millions of seniors annually will be closed.
- Clinical comparative effectiveness research will be promoted but cannot be used to dictate treatment decisions or coverage.
- Prevention and wellness initiatives will be promoted.
- Funding is provided to test medical liability reforms, such as health courts and disclosure laws.
- Care payment for Medicaid must be the same as it is for Medicare, with the federal government covering that cost for the first four years. [Based on the lowest socio-economic cost.] *See* Plate 17.

Pending the outcome of the twenty-six states' legal challenges to the reform act by the Supreme Court, the nonpartisan Congressional Budget Office's continuing tally of the cost of this remarkable reform legislation will be nonetheless able to demonstrate there will be no increases in aggregate healthcare expenses for Americans.

Federal benefits granted by remedial legislation traditionally set minimums, not maximums, and allow that states can offer broader benefits within categories of need as was done under the "cooperative federalism" of Medicaid. Indeed, minimum constraints form the basis of the 2010 ACA requirement for everyone to have healthcare coverage of some sufficient sort by 2014. Consider our public health laws in the nineteenth century: Their morally justifiable, "coerced care" of mental illness for the good of all—and for quarantine, then mandatory vaccinations to thwart communicable physical disease—was followed by the mid-twentieth century passage of federal Medicare and federal-state Medicaid to promote the health and general welfare. Ironically, the HMO Act and ERISA's health and welfare benefit sections that followed added little to the general welfare but higher managed healthcare costs.

A critical mass for the re-emergence of the healthcare insurance industry cartel was reached in mid-May 2011 when articles appeared in several newspapers expanding on one in *American Medical News:*

"**Insurer-owned clinics bid to offer more patient care.** Major health plans are expanding direct care to control costs and put their names in front of potential individual insurance shoppers . . . Cigna, one of many health plans moving aggressively to expand its operations into treating patients—not just paying their insurance claims. Like Cigna, many insurers, dating back to the traditional HMO days, have owned and operated patient clinics through subsidiaries, while some hospitals have run their own health plans. Recently, many of those insurers have expanded that branch of business, with a focus on care provided by nurse practitioners or physician assistants. Some are targeting plan members within a specific demographic, such as Medicare, or chronically ill patients. Others are targeting communities where they believe members have few options, outside of emergency departments, for urgent care.

Also noted were recent examples of plans entering or expanding patient-care operations:

- Bravo Health, a subsidiary of HealthSpring, a Medicare Advantage administrator, opened three walk-in urgent care and preventive health clinics for its members in Philadelphia and Baltimore.
- Humana has launched Humana HomeCare Solutions, a concierge-type service for people with chronic diseases, with four locations in Florida and one in Cleveland. In 2010 Humana acquired Concentra, a chain of occupational health clinics that operates more than 300 on-site workplace clinics, urgent care centers, physical therapy centers and wellness services.
- UnitedHealth Group's OptumHealth division acquired two HMOs from WellMed, which operates 38 clinics in Texas and Florida that provide care to seniors."

The *American Medical News* article also noted that John K. Gorman, "now CEO of Gorman Health Group, a managed care consultant who recently advised several insurers that opened clinics, said he has seen physicians unhappy with insurers that have expanded clinics in their markets. 'I wouldn't call it a backlash, but there have been concerns. PCPs are always going to be worried about someone else putting their hands on their patients.'"

On May 14, 2011, *New York Times* reporter, Reed Abelson, adroitly bridged her article's front-page headline, "Health Insurers Profit As Many Postpone Care" with its penultimate paragraph, quoting a former chief operating officer of the Liberty Mutual Insurance Company: "Maybe managed care is finally working. Maybe this is the new normal." Indeed, before the ACA, the managed-healthcare insurance industry's market failure that turned healthcare into wealthcare for its stockholders had left the American people high and dry. By December 2011, during the Republican candidates' numerous, unvarying, primary debates held to maintain a media presence, the issues related to Congressman Paul Ryan's budget proposals for privatizing Medicare and subsidizing private insurance were discussed. *The New York Times* editorial on December 3, "What About Premium Support," stated,

"Republican politicians are touting the virtues of market competition and calling for a "premium support" plan that would give beneficiaries a set amount of money to shop among private plans for their own insurance. What they do not say is that private plans have long been more costly than traditional Medicare and have shown far less ability to slow spending. Nor do they admit that the most extreme versions of premium support—like the one championed by Representative Paul Ryan— would save the government money mainly by shifting costs to the beneficiaries, who would have to decide whether to forgo treatments or pay more for coverage. . .

"Perhaps the strongest caution against overselling the benefits of competition is Medicare's own track record. What critics of the current program don't acknowledge is that over the past four decades, Medicare's spending per enrollee has risen much more slowly than private insurance premiums — an average of 8.3 percent a year between 1970 and 2009, compared with 9.3 percent for private premiums. And the private Medicare Advantage plans that cover roughly a quarter of all enrollees cost an average of 10 percent more than what the same coverage would cost in traditional Medicare. . .

"The health care reform law, starting in 2014, will provide premium support subsidies to help people with modest incomes buy private policies on new insurance exchanges. That will be the next big test of whether premium support can work to hold down costs while providing good coverage."

Three significant letters followed the editorial: One was from Judith Stein, Executive Director, Center for Medicare Advocacy in Mansfield, CT.

"Your editorial about changing Medicare into a voucher system wisely states many of the problems with public subsidies of private health insurance for Medicare beneficiaries. All such experiments have cost more and provided less value to those in need of coverage. I have been an advocate for Medicare beneficiaries for almost 35 years. I've seen numerous forays into privatizing Medicare. Clinton-era plans, Medicare Plus Choice, Medicare Advantage: none of them have provided better coverage more cost-effectively than the traditional Medicare program. . .

"Call it what you will, "premium support" is the latest jingle for privatizing Medicare. It's not a new or creative idea, and it will only add more costs and confusion. What we need is an objective look at what's needed to encourage participation and cost efficiencies in traditional Medicare, not further adventures in privatization."

Another was from Karen Ignani, longtime president and chief executive of America's Health Insurance Plans, who merely repeated the AHIP lobby's catalog of what managed care organizations have offered America (and what this historical canvass has attempted to demonstrate as sham):

"Any comparison between Medicare Advantage and fee-for-service Medicare must acknowledge the fact that Medicare Advantage plans provide more and better benefits. Unlike the outdated fee-for-service model, Medicare Advantage plans also emphasize prevention, wellness, care coordination and management of chronic conditions. In fact, analyses of federal data show that these plans are reducing preventable hospital readmissions and unnecessary hospitalizations compared with fee-for-service Medicare. Medicare Advantage is improving the health of the elderly, while fostering the innovations needed to reduce health care cost growth and put Medicare on a sustainable path."

A third letter, was from Dr. Arnold S. Relman, professor emeritus of medicine and social medicine at Harvard Medical School, and a former editor in chief of The New England Journal of Medicine, which pointed out that

"Turning more of the Medicare system over to private insurers would divert still more money into the pockets of this industry, taking it away from the direct provision of health care. Isn't it time to consider how best to reduce—rather than increase—the role of this unneeded middleman industry, with its unnecessary and huge overhead?"

Inevitably, notwithstanding whatever the Supreme Court decides in 2012, the American people will find that the 2010 ACA only jump-started the process of defanging the managed-care insurers' wrongful grasp on the healthcare economy, as more changes will be required to end managed-care's deadweight loss, market failure, and the economic and social losses it generates. Unfortunately, congressional lionizing in 1974 of an ERISA fiduciary standard laden with conflicts of interests reduced to shambles the system of healthcare indemnity insurance and, together with the 1973 HMO Act. With the flawed external managed-care insurance industry caught in the glare of the 2010 ACA spotlight, Congress, the medical community, and the American people will be obliged to change the callous, failed, and unconscionably expensive, healthcare system to one that promotes the general welfare—the preeminent goal called for in the preamble to our Constitution.

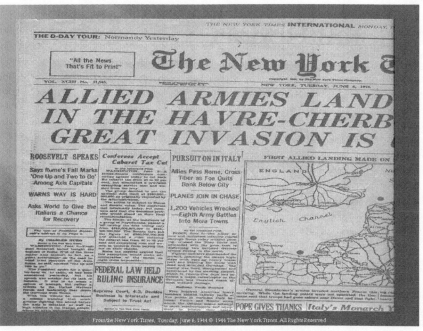

Plate 1

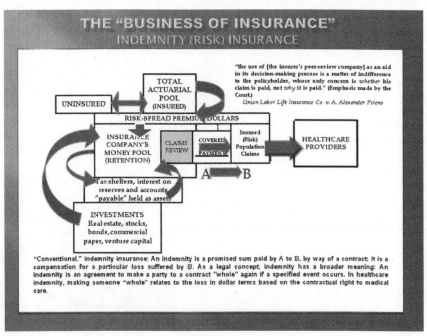

Plate 2

THE THREE "INDISPENSIBLE" CRITERIA OF THE BUSINESS OF INSURANCE

First, whether the practice has the effect of transferring or spreading a policyholder's risk.

Second, whether the practice is an integral part of the policy relationship between the insurer and the insured.

Third, whether the practice is limited to entities within the insurance industry.

Plate 3

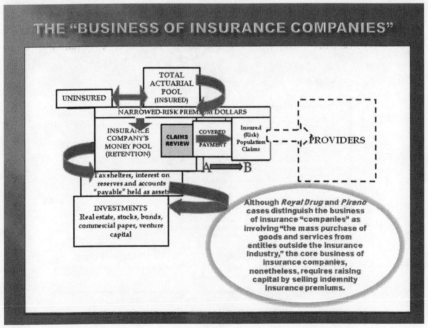

THE "BUSINESS OF INSURANCE COMPANIES"

Although *Royal Drug* and *Pireno* cases distinguish the business of insurance "companies" as involving "the mass purchase of goods and services from entities outside the insurance industry," the core business of insurance companies, nonetheless, requires raising capital by selling indemnity insurance premiums.

Plate 4

511

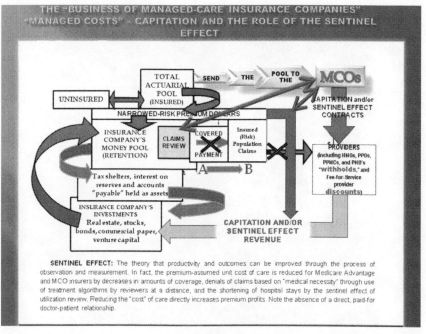

SENTINEL EFFECT: The theory that productivity and outcomes can be improved through the process of observation and measurement. In fact, the premium-assumed unit cost of care is reduced for Medicare Advantage and MCO insurers by decreases in amounts of coverage, denials of claims based on "medical necessity" through use of treatment algorithms by reviewers at a distance, and the shortening of hospital stays by the sentinel effect of utilization review. Reducing the "cost" of care directly increases premium profits. Note the absence of a direct, paid-for doctor-patient relationship.

Plate 5

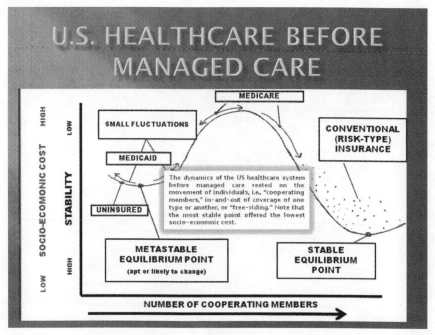

Plate 6

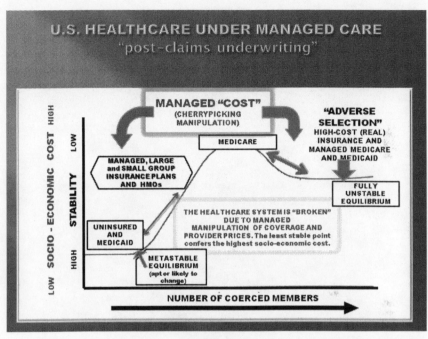

Plate 7

MARKET FAILURE

(THE INABILITY OF A SYSTEM OF MARKET PRODUCTION TO PROVIDE
CERTAIN GOODS EITHER AT ALL, OR AT THE OPTIMAL LEVEL)

Imperfections in the market mechanism do not fully account for all costs of supplying outputs

They result in:

- Overproduction of goods and services that produce negative external effects

- Underproduction of goods and services that produce positive external effects

Different reasons for market failure:

- supplying inadequate (or inaccurate) information to purchasers
- inadequate capacity (by restricting, rationing or producing scarcity of care)
- dysregulation of the movement of labor and capital
- employing rent-seeking behavior

Plate 8

RENT–SEEKING BEHAVIOR

In economics, rent-seeking is an attempt by a group to derive economic rent by manipulating the social or political environment in which economic activities occur, rather than by adding value. " Economic rents are "excess returns" above "normal levels" that take place in competitive markets.

Commercial insurers engage in this by lobbying for legislation that enhance manipulation of healthcare providers' prices. They then mimic governmental programs through remote "managing" of medical care. This permits raising premium prices to cover those costs; especially the costs for mental health and substance abuse treatment.

MANAGED CARE'S RENT-SEEKING BEHAVIOR HAS ADDED NO PROVEN VALUE TO HEALTHCARE

Plate 9

WHAT DOES PARITY MEAN?

MENTAL HEALTH AND SUBSTANCE USE DISORDER BENEFITS MUST BE (EQUIVALENT)

• "no more restrictive than the predominant financial requirements applied to substantially all medical and surgical benefits covered by the plan

• ...and there are no separate cost-sharing requirements than are applicable only with respect to mental health or substance use disorders benefits."

Andrew Sperling, Director of Federal Legislative Advocacy, NAMI – andrew@nami.org
Chuck Ingoglia, Vice President, Public Policy National Council for Community Behavioral Healthcare, chuckl@thenationalcouncil.org

Plate 10

WHAT DOES THE 2008 PARITY LAW APPLY TO?

- Group health plans and health insurers that provide coverage to group health plans (employers with over 50 employees)
- Fully-insured plans (via Section 2705 of the Public Health Service Act)
- ERISA self-insured plans (Section 712)
- Medicaid Managed Care Plans
- State Children's Health Insurance Program
- Non-federal governmental plans (HIPAA waiver still available)
- Federal Employees Health Benefits Program

Andrew Sperling, Director of Federal Legislative Advocacy, NAMI - andrew@nami.org
Chuck Ingoglia, Vice President, Public Policy National Council for Community Behavioral Healthcare, chuckI@thenationalcouncil.org

Plate 11

PARITY IN THE AFFORDABLE CARE ACT

- Essential benefits requirements – the essential benefits package includes (among a menu of services) emergency treatment, prescription drugs, mental health and substance abuse treatment services.

- Parity requirement in state-based Exchanges – required all "qualified health plans" offered through state-based Exchanges to comply with the Domenici-Wellstone Mental Health Parity and Addiction Equity Act of 2008

- Non-Quantitative Treatment Limitations: "A limitation that is not expressed numerically but otherwise limits the scope or duration of benefits for treatment." Any processes, strategies, evidentiary standards, or other factors not expressed numerically, used in applying the non-quantitative treatment limitations to MH/SUD benefits in a classification must be comparable to, and applied no more stringently than, those applied to medical/surgical benefits

Andrew Sperling, Director of Federal Legislative Advocacy, NAMI - andrew@nami.org
Chuck Ingoglia, Vice President, Public Policy National Council for Community Behavioral Healthcare, chuckI@thenationalcouncil.org

Plate 12

THE AMA EXPLANATION OF THE ACA

- Thirty-two million more Americans will gain access to health coverage.
- Insurers will no longer be allowed to deny patients on preexisting conditions.
- Patients will no longer face lifetime caps on coverage or be threatened with cancellation.
- Children will be permitted to remain on their parents' policies until age twenty-six.
- Competition will be introduced into the insurance marketplace.
- Health insurance exchanges and co-ops will be created that will allow pooling of coverage for individuals and small businesses.
- Tax credits will be extended to small businesses for the purchase of health insurance coverage.
- High-risk insurance pools will be created.

Plate 13

AMA EXPLANATION OF THE ACA (CONT'D)

- Subsidies will help lower-income individuals and families purchase health coverage.
- Insurance claims processing will be standardized and streamlined, helping to lower physician overhead costs and improve practice revenue cycles.
- The Medicare Part D Coverage Gap that haunts millions of seniors annually will be closed ("donut hole" required personal spending for drugs between $2,800 and $4,550).
- Clinical comparative effectiveness research will be promoted but cannot be used to dictate treatment decisions or coverage.
- Prevention and wellness initiatives will be promoted.
- Funding is provided to test medical liability reforms, such as health courts and disclosure laws.
- Care payment for Medicaid must be the same as it is for Medicare, with the federal government covering that cost for the first four years.

Plate 14

THE "INDIVIDUAL MANDATE" DOES IT MANDATE "INACTIVITY?"

Many federal requirements for mandatory participation in public-health systems have been in place for decades:

• Insurance is required for driving a car on the public highways
• School buses, child seats, safety belts, airbags, bicycle and helmet standards (NHTSA, DOT)
• Medicaid, requires citizens to be vaccinated (Commerce Clause)
• Federal quarantine authority (Commerce Clause)
• Registration for the draft is still required (SSS, 50 U.S.C. App. 451 *et seq.*)
• Medicare's hospital benefits is part of the mandatory Social Security tax system and is given free to those who wish to use it
• Hospital accreditation mandatory throughout U.S.

Plate 15

UNITED STATES V. LEE (1982)

In deciding that *Old Order Amish* employers and employees must participate in Social Security, the High Court quoted from a Senate Report: "a comprehensive national social security system providing for voluntary participation would be almost a contradiction in terms, and difficult, if not impossible, to administer. . .We note that here the statute compels contributions to the system by way of taxes; it does not compel anyone to accept benefits."

Plate 16

517

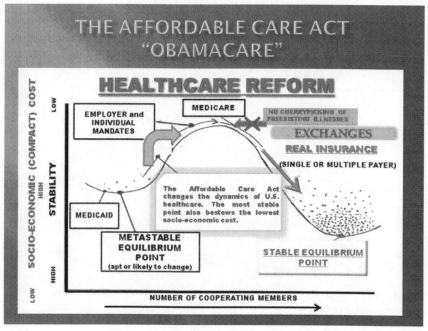

Plate 17

GLOSSARY

actuarial analysis: The application of probability and statistical methods performed by a professional statistician working for the government or an insurance company to calculate, from prevalence and incidence data, the possible occurrence of events such as illness, hospitalization, disability, or death for a given population.

administrative services only (ASO): Such administrative services include such activities as the preparation of an administration manual, communication with employees, determination and payment of benefits, preparation of government reports, preparation of summary plan descriptions, and accounting. Most employers would also purchase stop-loss insurance to protect against catastrophic losses.

adverse selection or antiselection: When buyers are believed to have better information about their risk of claiming than does the seller. Insurers say that people who know they have a higher risk of claiming than the average of the group will buy the insurance; whereas those who believe they have a below-average risk may decide it is too expensive to be worth buying. Healthcare insurers use that definition to deny insurance to people with what they call "preexisting illnesses."

balance billing: Charging or collecting from a Medicare beneficiary an amount in excess of the Medicare reimbursement rate for Medicare-covered services or supplies provided to a Medicare beneficiary, except when Medicare is the secondary insurer. When Medicare is the secondary insurer, the health-care practitioner may pursue full reimbursement under the terms and conditions of the primary insurer, but the Medicare beneficiary cannot be balance billed above the Medicare reimbursement rate for a Medicare-covered service or supply. "Balance billing" does not include charging or collecting deductibles or co-insurance required by the program.

Balanced Budget Act of 1997: In 1997, the Balanced Budget Act (BBA) was passed which reduced the payments that providers received from Medicare. Some of these cuts were returned to the companies providing services in 1999 under the Balanced Budget Reform Act. Additional reimbursements were reinstated as part of the Budget Improvement and Protection Act of 2000.**Beneficiary:** A person who has a designated (or contractual) beneficial interest in receiving Medicare or insurance benefits; i.e., a person who has a right or legally based expectancy to receive benefits. Not to be confused with Medicaid "recipients." A "qualified Medicare beneficiary" is an indigent person, on Medicare and Medicaid ("dual eligible") who cannot pay the Medicare copayments and deductibles, which are paid by Medicaid on his or her behalf.

benefit buy-down: Employers changing the benefit structure that they offer their employees in order to reduce their premiums.

business or speculative risk: A business investment that could either return a profit or sustain a loss.

cafeteria-style benefits plans: An employee benefit in which an employee may contribute so much of his or her pretax income into a special account that may be used for a broad range of purposes. One may use the funds in a cafeteria plan for matters such as medical expenses, life insurance premiums, etc.

capitation: A fixed amount of money per patient per unit of time paid in advance to the physician or other provider for the delivery of health-care services, or a fixed payment remitted at regular intervals to a medical provider by a managed-care organization for an enrolled patient. From the standpoint of risk shifting to the enrolled patient, the definition may be extended to fee-for-service group withhold arrangements, such as found in commercial medical groups, clinics, or non-profit HMOs.

captive stop-loss insurance company: An insurance company that primarily insures the risks of businesses that are related to it through common ownership. In healthcare, self-insured organizations, HMOs and PPMCs commonly own "captives" both in the country and offshore. A regular corporation pays income tax on the funds it retains as profits. As the business of insurance requires the payment of future claims, the accumulation of funds is a necessity for being able to pay such claims.

carve-out: A health-care delivery and financing arrangement in which certain specific health-care services that are covered benefits (e.g., behavioral healthcare) are administered and funded separately from general health-care services. The carve-out is typically done through separate contracting or subcontracting for services to the special population.

cert. denied: The abbreviation used in legal citations to indicate that the Supreme Court denied a Petition for Writ of *Certiorari* in the case being cited. The decision of the Court of Appeals below is unaffected and remains the law of the Circuit. However, the decision does not necessarily reflect agreement with the decision of the lower court.

chronic illness: One lasting three months or more, by the definition of the U.S. National Center for Health Statistics.

CMS: Centers for Medicare and Medicaid Services; formerly HCFA, the Healthcare Financing Administration.

concurrent review: Concurrent review includes utilization management activities that take place during an inpatient level of care or an ongoing outpatient course of treatment (for example, behavioral health partial hospital program [PHP], behavioral health intensive outpatient program [IOP], home health care [HHC] services).

consumer protection violations: The most common of these fall within five categories: (1) coercion (2) undue influence (3) deception (4) incomplete or asymmetric information (5) unreliable, uncertain or overly confusing information.

contra proferentem: This common-law doctrine is often used to construe policy language against an insurer in a dispute with a policyholder on the basis that the policy is a contract of adhesion with the policyholder having little bargaining power with the insurer.

corespondent: One of two or more parties against whom a lawsuit is commenced. A person named with others who must answer claims alleged in a bill or petition in a judicial proceeding.

deadweight loss: A loss of social benefit. A situation where the output is less than consumers want at a price above what is the cost to society of producing additional units. In healthcare, it is where people who would have more marginal cost than marginal benefit are buying the product or service; i.e., the forced loss resulting from consumers buying a product or service even if it costs more than it benefits them.

defensive medicine: Alleged to be the practice of diagnostic or therapeutic measures conducted primarily not to ensure the health of the patient but as a safeguard against possible malpractice liability and fear of litigation. Other than from media hype, surveys have been used to ask physicians whether that fear is the driving force; however, it is easier to answer "yes" than to apply it, particularly because some of the surveys include doctors' observation of others' behavior.

deferential standard of review: The standard of review that must be used by appellate courts in ERISA cases giving "deference" to a plan administrator even if there is a "conflict."

de novo **review:** A form of appeal in which the appeals court holds a trial as if no prior trial had been held.

Diagnosis-Related Groupings (DRGs): A Medicare patient classification scheme that provides a means of relating the type of patients a hospital treats (i.e., its diagnosis case mix) to the costs incurred by the hospital.

dicta: a statement of opinion or belief by courts considered authoritative though not binding.

doctor-patient relationship: "It is on this basis of mutual satisfaction and mutual frustration that a unique relationship establishes itself between a general practitioner and those who stay with him [sic] . . . we termed it 'a mutual investment company'. By this we mean that the general practitioner gradually acquires a very valuable capital invested in his patient and, vice versa, the patient acquires a very valuable capital bestowed in his general practitioner." (Balint M. The Doctor, His Patient and the Illness, 2nd edn. London: Pitman Medical; 1964: 249–250.)

downmarketing: A tactic for reducing purchasers' enthusiasm. It is used by monopolists so that profits can be increased further if the market can be segmented, with different prices charged to different segments, charging higher prices to those segments willing to pay more. It can enable cherry-picking of the healthier subscribers by appearing less favorable to adverse-selecting groups.

externalities: An effect of a purchase or use decision by one set of parties on others who did not have a choice and whose interests were not taken into account.

Federal Medical Assistance Percentage: The Secretary of Health and Human Services calculates the Federal Medical Assistance Percentage each year for states participating in Medicaid, based upon a formula that compares individual state income to the continental U.S. income. It is used to determine the ratios that the federal government will utilize in assisting each state under the Act. It also provides that no state's ratio will go lower than 50 percent or higher than 83 percent.

fiscal intermediary: Refers to an entity or a private company that has a contract with the Center for Medicare and Medicaid services (CMS) to determine and to pay Part A (hospitals) and some Part B bills (doctors, and other professionals) on a cost basis and to perform other related functions. Also called an "intermediary."

float: A small portion of the money supply representing a balance that is simultaneously present in a buyers and a payers account. A float results from the delay between when a check is written and when the money is actually deducted from the writer's account. These balances are temporarily double-counted as part of the overall money supply.

gatekeeper: Someone who controls access to something. In managed healthcare, it is a physician paid by a managed-care insurer to be responsible for constraining medical decisions that increase the cost of the healthcare by referral to specialists, or for the prescription of excessively costly technology, procedures, or experimental drugs.

gag rules: Clauses in managed-care contracts that prevent physicians from disclosing information that the plan may find disparaging but that could relate directly to the patient's health; became a subject of ethical condemnation and legislative prohibition starting in 1997.

hornbook law: Legal treatises that summarize and explain the law in a specific area.

incidence: The number of new cases of a condition, symptom, death, or injury that develop during a specific time period such as a year.

incurred but not reported (IBNR) losses: An estimate of the amount of an insurer's or self-insurer's liability for claim-generating events that have taken place but have not yet been reported to the insurer or self-insurer. The sum total of IBNR losses plus incurred losses provide an estimate of the insurer's eventual liabilities for losses during a given period.

indemnity risk: Protection or security against economic loss that is transferred to and assumed by the insurer based on the language of an insurance policy owned by the insured.

insurance: A promise of compensation for specific potential future losses in exchange for a periodic payment, designed to protect the financial well-being of an individual, company, or other entity in the case of unexpected loss. Agreeing to the terms of an insurance policy creates a contract between the insured and the insurer.

list price: Where the profit margins are greater than natural market based and so subject to discount.

loss leader: The type of product or service that is sold at a loss to help companies generate new customers. Companies hope that the customers gained from this type of sale will generate profits on future purchases.

managed care risk: The risk of loss based on various agreements made between managed-care organizations with client insurance companies or ERISA health and welfare benefit plan coverage promised employees by corporate plan documents.

managed-care organizations (MCOs): Originally "outside" the business of indemnity insurance companies, often later merged with them as part of subsidiary "networks" or subcontracted for services, which include "verifying medical necessity" of care by medical providers for purposes of payment to the providers by an insurance company or self-insured business. After merger with insurers, these can loosely be called HMOs—partly regulated by states—that use various methods of financially rewarding healthcare providers for medical "productivity."

marginal cost: The cost of an additional unit of output is the cost of the additional inputs needed to produce that output.

marginal-cost pricing: Where a firm may charge less in the short term than its average cost of production as long as it is receiving at least as much as its cost of producing that "marginal" unit. Several federal Circuit Courts have held that prices above average total cost are lawful, but prices between average variable cost and average total costs may be unlawful.

market failure: The inability of a system of market production to provide certain goods either at all or at the optimal level because of imperfections in the market mechanism, or the inability of a system of markets to fully account for all costs of supplying outputs. Market failure results in the overproduction of goods and services, having negative external effects, and the underproduction of goods and services, having positive external effects. Market failure occurs for different reasons: inadequate information, inadequate capacity, regulation of the movement of labor and capital, or rent-seeking behavior by producers. *See* Plates 8, 9.

market power: The traditionally defined power to raise prices when a significant market failure is present. A firm can obtain the ability to raise prices from the types of market failures most often associated with consumer protection violations. Market power can distort nonprice attributes anticompetitively even if price is unaffected, such as side constraints that affect trading outcome.

Medical loss ratio (MLR): Under the CMS rule, beginning in 2011, insurance companies in the individual and small group markets must spend at least 80% of the premium dollars they collect on medical care and quality improvement activities. Insurance companies in the large group market must spend at least 85% of premium dollars on medical care and quality improvement activities. Both must report publicly.

means test: Refers generally to the eligibility for relief for debtors who have sufficient financial means to pay a portion of their debts.

Medigap insurance: Health insurance sold by private insurance companies to fill the gaps in original Medicare plan coverage.

moral hazard: Insurers say that it means that people with insurance may take greater risks than they would without it because they know they are protected, so the insurer may get more claims than it bargained for. As used in healthcare, it is a market failure, because people don't get sick or risk sickness because they want to collect insurance.

most favored nation (MFN) clause: In international economic relations and international politics, a status accorded by one state to another. Most-favored-nation clauses, also known as most-favored-customer clauses, are provisions in commercial contracts that require a provider of health-care services to accept from a health insurer, HMO, or other managed-care organization the lowest price that the provider accepts from other buyers.

nonquantitative treatment limits: A limitation that is not expressed numerically but otherwise limits the scope or duration of benefits for treatment. Group health plans may not impose any non-quantitative treatment limitation to mental health or substance-use disorder benefits unless certain requirements are met. If no comparable requirement applies to medical/surgical benefits, the requirement may not be applied to mental health/substance disorder benefits. Nonquantitative treatment limitations include the following:

Medical management standards
Prescription drug formulary design
Standards for provider admission to participate in a network
Determination of usual, customary and reasonable charges
Step therapy protocols
Exclusions based on failure to complete a course of treatment
(The above from IRS Reg. §54.9812(c)(4))

ostensible agency: A person who has been given the appearance of being an employee or acting (an agent) for another (principal), which would make anyone dealing with the ostensible agent reasonably believe he or she was an employee or agent of an agency created by operation of law.

Pareto efficiency: Wilfried Fritz Pareto, a nineteenth-century Italian economist, made several important contributions to economics, particularly in the study of income distribution and in the analysis of individuals' choices. A Pareto improvement is an increase in Pareto efficiency: through reallocation, improvements to at least one participant's well-being can be supplied without reducing any other participant's well-being. If a change in economic policy ends a legally protected monopoly such as healthcare insurance as presently constituted, and that market subsequently becomes competitive and more efficient, the monopolist will be made worse off. However, the loss to the monopolist will be more than offset by the gain in social efficiency, allowing the monopolist to be compensated for its loss while still leaving an efficiency gain to be realized by others in the economy.

parity act: "Equivalence." The 2008 Mental Health Parity and Addiction Equity Act (MHPAEA) states that a group health plan may not impose annual or lifetime dollar limits on mental health benefits less favorable than any such limits imposed on medical surgical benefits. Although the law requires "parity," or equivalence, with regard to annual and lifetime dollar limits, financial requirements and treatment limitations, MHPAEA does *not* require all large-group health plans and their health-insurance issuers to include mental health/substance disorder benefits in their benefits package. The law's requirements apply only to large-group health plans and their health-insurance issuers that already include MH/SUD benefits in their benefit packages.

"pay or play" community rating: In a public option bill offered by Senators Kennedy and Dodd, a "pay or play" would require companies to pay the government $750 per full-time worker per year ($375 for part-time workers) if they don't offer health coverage, or if they offer "qualified" coverage but pay less than 60 percent of workers' premiums. Small businesses that employ fewer than 25 workers would be exempt.

per se **analysis:** Because of their pernicious effect on competition and lack of any redeeming virtue, such violations are conclusively presumed to be unreasonable.

per curiam: A decision delivered via an opinion issued in the name of the Court rather than specific judges. Such decisions are given that label by the Court itself and tend to be short. Usually, though not always, they deal with issues the Court views as relatively noncontroversial.

per se **violations:** "Intrinsic" violations. Section 1 of the Sherman Act (15 U.S.C. Sec. 1) prohibits any contract, combination, or conspiracy that unreasonably restrains interstate or foreign trade or commerce. The most frequent violations of the Sherman Act are price fixing and bid rigging, both of which are usually prosecuted as criminal violations.

political economy: As used in this book, an interdisciplinary approach that applies economic methods to analyze how political outcomes and judicial institutions affect economic policy or vice versa.

post-claims underwriting: Post-claims underwriting occurs when an insurance company refuses to pay a claim for a loss that should have been covered, on the grounds that the insured was a bad risk and the policy should never have been issued, then cancels or rescinds the policy. Often seen when medical records are requested and sent to an underwriting department for "review." Under indemnity contracts, the insurance company denies coverage on the basis of misrepresentation, concealment or fraud in the insured's application for payment. The claimant is advised that the policy is being rescinded, the premiums are returned, and that there is no coverage for the claimed loss. Managed care is a form of post-claims underwriting, since it denies claims even without being sent to underwriting departments. *See* **rescission**. Largely outlawed by the ACA "Exchanges." *See* Plate 7.

preexisting illness: In healthcare, the rationale that medical insurance covers only issues that arise unexpectedly after coverage has begun. Used that way, it is a market failure, because medical insurance is for medical conditions none of which are planned or intentional, only relatively predictable, fortuitous occurrences. Stated otherwise, having coverage in place before something adverse happens. This is not the same as chronic illness.

precertification: A health plan's "prior authorization" process that begins with a nurse employed by the health plan or carved-out managed-care company completing an initial review of the patient's clinical information submitted by the practice or hospital to make sure that the requested service meets plan or insurance company guidelines.

preemption, federal: Generally, federal preemption refers to the invalidation of a state law when it conflicts with a federal law.

premium taxes: An insurance premium tax is a tax upon insurers, both domestic and foreign, for the privilege of engaging in the business of providing insurance. It is the insurance company's equivalent of the individual's income tax.

prevalence: A statistical number of cases of a disease in the population at a given time, or the total number of cases in the population, divided by the number of individuals in the population. It is used as an estimate of how common a condition is within a population over a certain period of time.

proof of loss: Usually defined in state insurance law and regulations as evidence given by an insured to insurer to support the claim, both as to the fact of the loss having occurred and as to the amount of the loss.

public option: A health-insurance plan that would be offered by the U.S. federal government.

quantitative treatment limitations: These limitations are expressed numerically. They must be in parity with the requirements and limitations applied to substantially all benefits for the applicable classification on medical benefits. "Substantially all" means the requirement/limitations apply to at least two-thirds of the benefits in that classification.

Quality Improvement Organizations (QIOs): Private contractor extensions of the federal government that work under the auspices of the U.S. Centers for Medicare and Medicaid Services (CMS). In recent years, QIOs have undertaken to facilitate continual improvement of health-care services within their constituent communities in addition to their original and ongoing statutory audit/inspection role of medical peer review.

remedial legislation: A law enacted for the purpose of correcting a defect in a prior law or in order to provide a remedy where none previously existed.

rescission: The ability of an insurer to rescind a policy retroactively upon discovery of a preexisting illness and considered to be a form of post-claims underwriting. The 2010 ACA prohibits rescission and places the burden of reliable, accurate transfer of risk on the insurer.

retention: The portion of an insurance claim paid by the insured instead of the insurance company. A deductible is a common example of a retention, although there are other types. Retentions are said to permit the insured persons to reduce their own insurance premiums, as they assume a smaller portion of the risk being insured. This "moral effect" is relied upon by insurers to prevent or minimize the effect of "reckless" claims but is simply one method of "loss control" or risk reduction.

Rule of reason analysis: In antitrust law, requires a comprehensive market analysis of pro- and anti-competitive effects and allows for any evidence that might bear on an assessment of those effects. What is examined by a court are the facts peculiar to the business to which the restraint is applied, its condition before and after the restraint was imposed, the nature of the restraint, and its effect, actual or probable.

sentinel effect: The theory that productivity and outcomes can be improved through the process of observation and measurement.

stabilizing prices: "Fixing prices." Stabilizing price is prohibited except for the purpose of preventing or retarding a decline in the market price, as in securities, which reflect value.

stochastic processes: In probability theory, is a family of random as opposed to deterministic variables, usually over time, where there are many possibilities by which the process might evolve, but some paths may be more probable and others less so.

stop-loss insurance: Coverage is initiated with an insurance company when the employer's self-insured total group health claims reach a stipulated threshold selected by the employer. Stop-loss insurance is similar to purchasing high-deductible insurance. The employer remains responsible for claims expense under the deductible amount.

subacute illness: Midway between acute and chronic.

Subrogation: The substitution of one person in the place of another with reference to a lawful claim, demand, or right, so that he or she who is substituted succeeds to the rights of the other in relation to the debt or claim, and its rights, remedies, or securities. There are two types of subrogation: *legal* and *conventional*. Legal subrogation arises by operation of law, whereas conventional subrogation is a result of a contract.

summary judgment: A judgment rendered by the court prior to a verdict because no material issue of fact exists and one party or the other is entitled to a judgment as a matter of law. It is a determination made by a court without a full trial that may be issued as to the merits of an entire case or of specific issues in that case.

surplusage: Irrelevant matter in a pleading.

supersedure section: Section 514(d) of ERISA states, "Nothing in [ERISA] shall be construed to alter, amend, modify, invalidate, impair, or supersede any law of the United States."

utilization review: The process of comparing requests for medical services ("utilization") to guidelines or criteria that are deemed appropriate for such services and making a recommendation based on that comparison. Under Medicare, a requirement for hospitals to have a committee to review the lengths of stays and trends of care, a process mimicked by MCOs, which provides for "certifying medically necessary" days that will be paid by insurers or employee-benefit plans.

Writ of *Certiorari:* A decision by the Supreme Court to hear an appeal from a lower court.

well-pleaded complaint: A rule of procedure that federal question jurisdiction cannot be acquired over a case unless an issue of federal law appears on the face of the plaintiff's pleaded complaint.

Withholds (including other incentives concealed as "bonuses"): Originating with HMOs as incentives, contractual arrangements that place physicians at financial risk for services delivered. Because of this fundamental shift in the way that physicians are paid, many have advocated for disclosure of financial incentives as a way of reducing potential conflicts of interest. Many patient advocates believed that disclosure of physician payment methods should be an integral part of a patients' "bill of rights". Many states have already enacted legislation that prohibits contracts that restrict patient-physician communication including discussions about financial incentives. The Federal government issued rules in 1996 mandating that Medicare, HMO and other health plans disclose physician payment methods to patients who request this information.

ABBREVIATIONS/ACRONYMS

ACA: The Patient Protection and Affordable Care Act of 2010 (ACA, "Obamacare")

ACO: "accountable care organization," originally established by demonstration projects established by the 2003 Medicare Prescription Drug, Improvement, and Modernization Act. Section 3022 of the ACA creates the Medicare Shared Savings Program, allowing ACOs to contract with Medicare by January 2012. According to the ACA, the Medicare Shared Savings program, ACOs promote accountability for a patient population and coordinates items and services under part A and B, and encourage investment in infrastructure and redesigned care processes for high quality and efficient service delivery.

ASO: "administrative services only." These are the third party administrators born out of ERISA. They manage all aspects of employee benefit design and delivery for employer groups of all sizes, find healthcare insurance for self-funding employers who wish for a pay-as-you-go-style plan at the list price of healthcare. They are usually intimately connected and/or wholly owned by insurance companies.

BBA: The Balanced Budget Act of 1997.

CMS: The federal Centers for Medicare and Medicaid Services; formerly the Healthcare Financing Administration (HCFA).

DHHS: United States Department of Health and Human Services; formerly the Department of Health, Education, and Welfare.

ERISA: Employees Retirement Income Security Act of 1974.

HCFA: The Federal Healthcare Financing Administration (now CMS), a division of the Department of Health and Human Services, was formed to take over the administration of Medicare and Medicaid, which had been under separate offices in the earlier Department of Health Education and Welfare.

HEDIS: The Healthcare Effectiveness Data and Information Set is an accreditation tool developed by the managed-care insurance industry's National Committee on Quality Assurance (NCQA) and used by health plans to measure performance on dimensions of care and service acceptable to the managed-care industry.

FEHBP: Federal Employees Health Benefits Plan.

FFS: "Fee for Service." Fee-for-service plans (also known as indemnity plans) are the oldest form of health-insurance coverage. These plans are the most expensive and rare in some states. FFSs offer the most freedom and flexibility; participants choose their own doctors and hospitals and can refer themselves to specialists with little interference from insurance companies. These plans require large out-of-pocket expenses. Patients pay medical fees up front and then submit bills for reimbursement.

IN: "In network" coverage for medical services.

MA: Medicare Advantage

MCOs: Managed-care organizations of several types, including those both inside and outside the "business of insurance."

MMA: Prescription Drug, Improvement, and Modernization Act of 2003, which established Medicare Advantage.

MSA: Medical Savings Account

NAIC: National Association of [state] Insurance Commissioners.

OON: "Out of network" coverage for medical services.

PPMC: Physician Practice Management Corporation.

PHO: Physician Hospital Organization.

PPO: Generally "preferred-provider organizations." A health-care organization composed of physicians, hospitals, or other providers, which provides health-care services at a reduced fee. A PPO is similar to an HMO, but care is paid for as it is received instead of in advance in the form of a scheduled fee.

POS: Generally, "point of service plan," usually contracted for discounted care on an in-network basis with large insurance companies, referring to in-network doctors but allowing the choice to see out-of-network doctors and make own claims to insurance companies, which require significant out-of-pocket payments by patient.

R & C: "reasonable and customary charges" (or "usual and customary charges").

Recipient (of Medicaid): The Medicaid Act requires that each state Medicaid program be administered in the "best interests of the recipients." 42 U.S.C. § 1396a(a)(19). See also, S.Rep. No. 404, 89th Cong., 1st Sess., reprinted in [1965] U.S. Code Cong & Admin. News, 1943, 2104.

U & C: "usual and customary charges."

REFERENCES

AARP Letter. RE: Medical Loss Ratios; Request for Comments Regarding Section 2718 of the Public Health Service Act; 75 Federal Register 19297, April 14, 2010.

Abelson, R., Singer, N. *The New York* Times. 2010. Pharmacists take larger role on health team. Aug. 13.

Adult Literacy in America: A First Look at the Results of the National Literacy Survey. National Center for Education Statistics, U.S. Department of Education. Washington DC, 1993.

Adult Literacy in America: A First Look at the Results of the National Literacy Survey. National Center for Education Statistics, U.S. Department of Education. Washington DC, 1993.

Aetna News, June 23, 1997. Aetna U.S. Healthcare and FPA medical management enter into a long-term provider relationship. http://www.aetna.com/news/1997/pr_19970623.htm

A. Foster Higgins Retiree Healthcare Survey, 1991, Princeton, NJ, Aug., 1992 (emphasis added). Also, thanks to Robert D. Eicher, Principal, A. FOSTER HIGGINS, for critical comments. Personal communication, Dec. 30, 1992.

Akron Law Review 38:253. Vansuch, Matthew G. 2004. Citing Tony Mauro, Courtside (July 14, 2003).

Alpert, W. M. 1988. Force-fed profits. *Barrons.*

America Online News, March 4, 1998.

American Hospital Association News. 1989. Health insurers' financial recovery helped by rate hikes. March 13.

American Journal of Managed Care. Pawlson, L. Gregory, MD, MPH. October 31, 2004. Pay for performance: Two critical steps needed to achieve a successful program.

American Medical News. 1998. FPA to close Thomas-Davis clinics. July 27.

American Medical News. 1998. Carriers' prices undermine insurance law. April 6.

American Medical News. 1998. Doctor-led groups follow the same practices as HMOs. July 6.

American Medical News. 1998. FPA acquires Humana centers in Florida, Kansas City area. May 4.

American Medical News. 1998. Moving away from managed Medicaid. June 1.

American Medical News. 1998. Patients file lawsuit against Anthem's withdrawal in rural Ohio. August 3.

American Medical News. 1998. Physicians opting out of large N.C. HMO. March 2.

American Medical News. 1998. Rising medical costs cut HMO profits; 98 may be better. April 20.

Antitrust law developments 6th Ed. By Jonathan M. Jacobson, American Bar Association. Section of Antitrust Law, at 226. Citations too numerous to mention.

Areeda, P. 1974. *Antitrust Analysis: Problems, Text, Cases* 2nd ed. Boston, Little Brown.

Bahrami, Bahman. Factors affecting physicians' early retirement intentions: implications for healthcare delivery. *North Dakota State University Journal of Business & Economics Research.*

Baker, S. K. et al. 1994. Beginning reading: Educational tools for diverse learners. *School Psychology Review* 23(3):372–91.

Black's Law Dictionary. 5th ed., St. Paul, Minn., West Publishing Co., 1979.

Black's Law Dictionary, 7th Ed., at 985, citing: 54 Am. Jur. 2d Monopolies, Restraints of Trade, and Unfair Trade Practices § 49, at 110, n.87 (1996).

Blendon, R J, Brodie, M, Benson, JM, Altman, DM, Levitt, L, Hoff, T, and Hugick, L. 1998. Understanding the Managed Care Backlash. *Health Affairs* 80–88.

Bloomberg News, August 6, 1998.

Blumenthal, R. G., The Next Wave of Health-Care Mergers. *Barron's*, October 24, 2011.

Brailer, D J, Hirth, R, Kroch, E, Landon, B, Pauly, MV, and W. P. Pierskalla. *Study Project on Healthcare Reform and American Competitiveness*, Wharton School, U of Penn., Nov. 1991, at 6.

Brailer, *et al.,* id. at 20.

Bodenheimer, T. 1999. Disease management promises and pitfalls. *The New England Journal of Medicine* 340:1203.

Borowsky, SJ, Davis, MK, Goertz, C, Laurie, N. 1997. Are all health plans created equal? *Journal of the American Medical Association* 278: 917—21.

Burns, H. 1996. Disease management and the drug industry: carve out or carve up? *Lancet* 124: 832–7.

Catastrophic Medical Expenses: Patterns in the Non-Elderly, Nonpoor Population. Congressional Budget Office (1982).

Chittenden, WA, III, *Malpractice Liability and Managed Healthcare History and Prognosis*, 26 TORT & INS. L.J. 451 (1991), n. 41 at 481.

CIGNA, *Forbes*, April 3, 1989, back cover.

Comment on Prudent Investor Rule (1959). *Firestone*, 109 S.Ct. at 956 (quoting *Restatement {Second} of Trusts* § 187).

Committee on Ways and Means, U.S. House of Representatives, *Medicare and Healthcare Chartbook*, February 27, 1997.

Committee Reports 111th Congress (2009 2010). House Report 111, 322.

Common law principle of agency. See Roscoe Pound, *The History and System of the Common Law* 196–200 (1939).

Congressional Budget Office, *Profile of Healthcare Coverage, The Haves and the Have-Nots* (1979), at ix.

Congressional Research Service Report for Congress. *Medicare: History of Part A Trust Fund Insolvency Projections.* Jennifer O'Sullivan,

Specialist in Healthcare Financing Domestic Social Policy Division, March 28, 2008.

Consumer Reports. August 1996:40–1; *The HMO Honor Roll.*

Crain's New York Business. 1998. Oxford sets up major surgery to cut its costs. August 3.

Dahl, M, Rossen, J, and Powell, R. 2009. Health insurer accused of overcharging millions. MSNBC.com, January 13, 2009.

DHHS Secretary Sebelius Announces New Pre Existing Condition Insurance Plan. July 10, 2010.

Difficulties in the Measurement of Service Outputs. Mark K. Sherwood; *Monthly Labor Review*, Vol. 117, 1994.

Disease Management Industry Pioneer to Personally Guarantee Program Savings for 'Elite' Organizations. Wellesley Mass., April 12/*PR Newswire.*

Doctors bolt from Blue Choice. Ledger-Enquirer, Columbus, Georgia. June 11, 1998, front page.

DOL News Release No. USDL: 98–69, February 20, 1998.

Donabedian, A. *Benefits in Medical Care Programs* (1970), 354–58; McGuire, T. Financing Psychotherapy: Costs, Effects and Public policy, (1981), at 44–51.

Doe V. Bolton, 410 U.S. 179, 197 (1973). Opinion by Justice Blackmun expressing the views of seven members of the Court.

Draft Bulletin National Assn. of Insurance Commissioners, August 10, 1995, at 3.

EBRI Databook on Employee Benefits (1998), at 235.

Employee Benefits in Medium and Large Firms, 1993. Washington, DC: U.S. Government Printing Office, Nov. 1994. (Also yearly editions for 1988-91.) Bulletin 2456. U.S. Bureau of Labor Statistics, U.S. Department of Labor.

Employment-Based Health Insurance: Costs Increase and Family Coverage Decreases. Report: U.S. General Accounting Office. GAO/HEHS- 97–35, Feb. 24, 1997.

Ethics In Medicine, *op cit., "What specific impact does managed care have on relationships between doctors and patients?"*

Experton, Bettina, MD, MPH, Corresponding Author Information, Ronald J. Ozminkowski, PhD, Deborah N. Pearlman, PhD, Zili

Li, MD, MPH, Sheri Thompson, PhD. *How does managed care manage the frail elderly? The case of hospital readmissions in fee for service versus HMO systems.* Volume 16, Issue 3, Pages 163–172 (April 1999).

Federal Rules of Civil Procedure.

Feldstein, M. S. 1971. Hospital cost inflation: A study of nonprofit price dynamics. *American Economic Review* 60: 853B872.

Financial data for UnitedHealth, WellPoint, Aetna, CIGNA, Humana, HealthNet, and Coventry are from company SEC Form 10 K filings. July 15, 2009. The Commonwealth Fund.

Ford, I. K. and P. Sturm. 1998. CPI revision provides more accuracy in the medical services component. *Monthly Labor Review*: 17–26.

FPA Medical Files for Protection Under Bankruptcy Laws. By Milt Freudenheim, July 21, 1998.

FPA Medical Stops paying Its Doctors in Parts of 3 States. The Wall Street Journal, June 19, 1998, at B6.

Freudenheim, Milt. *The New York Times* 1998. United Health to acquire Humana Inc. Jan. 29.

Freudenheim, Milt. *The New York Times.* 2004. Bush health savings accounts slow to gain acceptance. Oct. 13.

FTC Fact Sheet: Antitrust Laws: A Brief History.

Fuchs, V. R., and M. J. Kramer (1972), *Determinants of expenditures for physicians' services in the United States,* 1948B1968, Occasional Paper No. 117, National Bureau of Economic Research, New York.

Fuchs, Victor, ed. 1996. *Individual and social responsibility: child care, education, medical care, and long-term care in America.* Chicago: University of Chicago Press.

Gannett Newspapers. 1998. Many HMOs ailing financially. Group lowers ratings for 10 in state. September 2.

GAO Report, GAO/HEHS-98-142, April 30, 1998.

Gaynor, M. and Tami Mark. Physician Contracting with Health Plans: A Survey of the Literature. Carnegie Mellon University and The MEDSTAT Group, Inc., June, 1999.

Gell-Mann, Murray. 1994. *The quark and the jaguar.* New York: Henry Holt and Company.

Goldschlag, W. *Daily News*. 1998. GOP-Dem battle over HMOs looms. July 20.

Hammond, Rick L. Estoppel of the Right to Demand Proof of Loss. Waiving the right to demand proof of loss. FindLaw for Legal Professionals. http://library.findlaw.com/1999/ Jun/1/129414.html.

Hansmann, Henry. The changing roles of public, private, and non-profit enterprise in education, healthcare, and other human services. http://www.nber.org/chapters/c6565.

Harman, Jeffrey S., PhD, and Kelly J. Kelleher, MD, MPH. 2001. *Arch Pediatr Adolesc Med.* 155:885.

Havighurst, C. C. *Prospective Self-Denial: Can Consumers Contract Today to Accept Healthcare Rationing Tomorrow?* 140 U. Pa. L. Rev. 5:1755 (1992).

HCFA Center For Health Plans And Providers, *Addendum to Operational Policy Letter*, OPL No. 59, March 20, 1998.

HCFA Guidelines outlining the principal analytical techniques, practices, and the enforcement policy of the Department of Justice and the Federal Trade Commission. Horizontal Merger guidelines for public comment: Released on April 20, 2010. http://www.ftc.gov/os/2010/04/100420hmg.pdf.

HCFA. 1997. Roberta L. Carefoote. Managed care in Medicare and Medicaid. Fact Sheet. U. S. Department of Health and Human Services, Washington, DC HCFA Press Office, January 28, 1997. http// www.hcfa.gov /medicare /mgdcar1.htm.

Healthcare Business News. Enforcing reform: It's time for federal authorities to bring antitrust scrutiny to insurers. By David Balto.

Posted: May 24, 2010. http://www.modernhealthcare.com/article/20100524/ Magazine/305249972.

Healthcare Report: The Consumer Reimbursement System is Code Blue. State of New York Office of the Attorney General, January 13, 2009. From testimony by J. Robert Hunter, Director of Insurance, Consumer Federation of America, before the Senate Judiciary Committee in his testimony regarding *A Prohibiting Price Fixing and Other Anticompetitive Conduct In The Health Insurance Industry on October 14, 2009.*

Healthcare Finance News. Non-payment for non-performance. July 30, 2009 Richard Pizzi, Editor.

Herzlinger RE. 1997. *Market-Driven Health Care.* Addison-Wesley Publ., Reading MA.

Herzlinger R. A *Better Healthcare Alternative—Public plans aren't cutting it? Look to the Swiss.* Forbes.com. 10.08.09.

Hill, T.P. *On Goods and Services, Review of Income and Wealth,* Vol. 123, No. 4, 1977, pp. 315-38. See especially p. 318.

Hornstein, Andreas and Edward C. Prescott. 1991. Insurance contracts as commodities: A note. *The Review of Economic Studies* 58(5):917–928.

H.R 1, Pub. L, 92-603, Title II, 201(a) (2), (3) substituted "aged and disabled individuals" for "individuals 65 years of age or over."

Implementing Health Insurance Reform: New Medical Loss Ratio Information Policymakers and Consumers. April 15, 2010.

Innovation and the Law: The Contributions of David Teece. September 21, 2006; by Tom Campbell, Director of Finance, State of California; former Dean of the Haas School of Business, University of California; Berkeley, former director of the Bureau of Competition in the Federal Trade Commission.

IPRO Healthcare Quality Watch. Vol. 2 No. 5, May 1998.

Issue Brief. Number 9. Washington, DC. May 1997.

Jecker, N. S., PhD, Professor, Medical History and Ethics, Professor, Philosophy and Law; C. H. Braddock III, MD, MPH, Faculty, Departments of Medicine and Medical History and ethics. *In: Ethics In Medicine,* University of Washington School of Medicine, April 11, 2008.

Joint Proxy Statement and Prospectus. Sun Healthcare Group, Inc., and The Mediplex Group, Inc., May 19, 1994. Disclosure, Inc., August 5, 1994.

Jewett, JJ, and JH Hibbard. 1996. Comprehension of quality care indicators: Differences among privately insured, publicly insured, and uninsured. *Healthcare Financing Review* 18(1): 75.

Kaiser Family Foundation. U.S. Healthcare Costs. http://www.kaiseredu.org /Issue-Modules /US-Health-Care-Costs/Background-Brief. aspx

Kelly, J. T. and S. F. Kellie. 1990. Appropriateness of medical care: findings, strategies. *Archives of Pathology & Laboratory Med.* Vol. 114:1119–21.

Kennedy, EM 1972. *In critical condition, the crisis in America's healthcare.* New York: Simon & Schuster.

Klein, JI. *The Antitrust Laws and Specialty Certification.* In *Legal Aspects of Certification and Accreditation*, Donald G. Langsley, M.D., Ed., AMER. BD. OF MED. SPECIALTIES, Evanston, Illinois, at 19.

KMPG Peat Marwick: Health Benefits in 1996. (Also yearly editions for 1991-95.) Newark, NJ. 1991-96.

Kopit, W. G. and K. L. Klothen *Antitrust Implications of the Activities of Health Maintenance Organizations*, 25 ST. LOUIS U. L.J. 247, 289 (1981).

Kovacic, *The Identification and Proof of Horizontal Agreement Under the Antitrust Laws*, at 31.

Krumholz, et al. 2010. *Journal of the American Medical Association* 2010; 303(21):2141-2147.

Kuttner, R. 1998. Must good HMOs go bad? *The New England Journal of Medicine*, 338(21, 22):1558-1563, 1635–39 (in two parts).

LePore, JD, Patricia. Managed care and its variations. American College of Physicians Managed Care Resource Center. http://www.acponline.org/residents_fellows/career_counseling/managed_care.htm.

Managed Care Organization Nonreporting to the National Practitioner Data Bank. A Signal for Broader Concern. May 2001, OEI-01-99-00690.

Managed-care Godzilla. Modern Healthcare. June 1, 1998, at 2.

Managers of Care, Not Costs, December, 7, 1998, at A14.

Mansfield E. *Microeconomics*: Theory and Applications. *3rd ed.* Ann Arbor: Health Administration Press; 1976.

Marsh, Lawrence. 1998. The doctor's bottom line. *Health Affairs* Vol. 17(3): 1775–76.

Maxwell, J., F. Briscoe, S. Davidson, et al. 1998. Managed competition in practice: Value Purchasing by fourteen employers. *Health Affairs* 17(3):216–226.

Maxwell, T. J. *A View from a Doctor's Office*. 13 DEL. L. 33 (1995), n. 22 at 35.

McGraw, D. C., *Financial Incentives to Limit Services: Should Physicians Be Required to Disclose These to Patients?*, 83 GEO. L.J. 1823 (1995), at 1828.

Medicare Oversight of Managed Care Performance, OFFICE OF INSPECTOR GENERAL REPORT, OEI-01-96-00190, April 1, 1998.

Medicare: HCFA Should Release Data to Aid Consumers, Prompt Better HMO Performance (GAO/HEH-97-23, October 22, 1996).

Mehrotra, Ateev, Sonya Grier, and R. Adams Dudley. 2006. The relationship between health plan advertising and market incentives: Evidence of risk selective behavior. *Health Affairs* 25:759–765.

Medicare and Medicaid Guides. Commerce Clearing House (numerous)

Modern Healthcare. 1998. Big dividends. June 8.

Modern Healthcare. 1998. Medicare cuts between a rock and a hard place. June 1.

Modern Healthcare. 1998. PhyMatrix to abandon PPM biz. August 24.

National Health Insurance Resource Book. Rev. Ed., Aug. 30, 1976. Prepared By The Staff Of The Committee On Ways And Means, U.S. House Of Representatives, For The Use Of The Committee, at 90-91.

Navigating the Changing Healthcare System. Louis Harris and Associates, 1995. In SL Isaacs, *Consumers' Information Needs: Results Of A National Survey*, Health Affairs, Volume 15, No.4, Winter 1996.

NCQA's Quality Compass: Pointing the Way to One-Stop Quality Information. NCQA Quality Matters, Vol. III. No. 1., Spring 1996 at 1,15.

New York Education Law § 6531.

National Government Services' teleconference with Rye Hospital Center, Rye, New York, July 13, 2009.

Neuman, P., E. Maibach, K. Dusenbury, M. Kitchman, and P. Zupp Marketing HMOs to Medicare beneficiaries. *Health Affairs* 17:132–139.

Nietzsche, Friedrich. 1968. *Basic writings of Nietzsche.* Trans. and ed. Walter Kaufmann. Modern Library Edition, New York, 2000.

Orentlicher, D. *Paying Physicians More to do Less: Financial Incentives to Limit Care,* 30 U. Rich. L. Rev. 155, 156 (1996).

Passell, P. *The New York Times.* 1998. When mega-mergers are mega-busts. May 17.

Pear, Robert. *The New York Times.* 1998. New health plans due for elderly. June 10.

Posner, R. and F. Easterbrook. *Antitrust cases, economic notes and other materials. Second Edition,* St. Paul, MN: West, 1981.

Pitofsky, R. *Joint Ventures Under the Antitrust Laws: The Significance of Penn-Olin,* 82 Harv. L. Rev. 1007 (1969) and n. 90, at 1016. Preferred Healthcare Corp., (Sept. 14, 1983), Original Prospectus. D. H. Blair & Co., New York, id. at 10, and 1986 Annual Report and S.E.C. Form 10-K, June 1, 1987.

PR Newswire, Humana transfers operations of 13 former FPA medical centers to five south Florida provider groups. July 7, 1999.

Rauber, C. 1999. Disease Management Can Be Good for What Ails Patients and Insurers. *Modern Healthcare* March 29.

Restatement of Trusts 3d, Prudent Investor Rule, § 187, Comment: e.

Public Papers And Addresses Of Franklin D. Roosevelt, 1944-45, at 587 (Rosenman ed. 1950).

Ranck, James: *Combining HEDIS indicators: A new approach to measuring plan performance.* Monday July 1, 2002.

Regional Reports, *The National Law Journal,* April 20, 1998. The trial was set in San Diego Superior Court for its punitive damages phase beginning April 29.

Regional Reports, *The National Law Journal,* April 27, 1998.

Remarks of Sen. Ferguson; *McCarran, Federal Control of Insurance: Moratorium Under Public Law 15 Expired July 1,* 34 A.B.A.J. 539, 540 (1948).

Report of the Senate Committee on Finance to accompany H.R. 1. September 26, 1972 at 281.

Restatement (Second) of Agency, at § 261, Comment a., at 571.

Rich, M. W, V. Beckham, C. Wittenberg, C. L. Leven, K. E. Freedland, and R. M. Carney. *A multidisciplinary intervention to prevent the readmission of elderly patients with congestive heart failure.* N Engl J Med 1995;333:1190-5; J. Wasson J, C. Gaudette, F. Whaley, A. Sauvigne A, P. Baribeau, and H. G. Welch. *Telephone care as a substitute for routine clinic follow-up.* JAMA 1992;267:1788-93.

Ringel, Jeanne S., Susan D. Hosek, Ben A. Vollaard, and Sergej Mahnovski. *The Elasticity of Demand for Healthcare A Review of the Literature and Its Application to the Military Health System.* RAND. Prepared for the Office of the Secretary of Defense National Defense Research Institute RAND Health. October 30, 2000.

Robinson, J. C. 1998. Financial capital and intellectual capital in physician practice management. *Health Affairs* July/August.

S. Rep. 100-304, 1988 U.S.C.C.A.A.N. 3231, IV, Sec. 2. 1988 WL 169876 (Leg. Hist.).

Schwartz B. Chapman Distinguished Professor of Law at the University of Tulsa College of Law in: Main Currents of American Legal Thought (1993), at 67, 68 (quoting from: 2 The Works of James Wilson 723 (Mccloskey ed. 1967)).

SEC Form 10-K, 12/31/94, Mediplex Group, Inc., Notes to Consolidated Financial Statements. Disclosure, Inc.

Section 3, Clayton Antitrust Act of 1914; 15 U.S. Code § 14.

Section 8.01, *Restatement (Third) of Agency.*

Senate Committee on Labor and Public Welfare, Welfare and Pension Plans Disclosure Act, 85th Cong., 2d sess., 1958, S. Rpt. 1440 (S. Rpt. 85-1440), at 5B6. As found in: James Wooten, A Legislative and Political History of ERISA Preemption, Part 3. Journal of Pension Benefits, Spring 2008, Vol. 15, Number 3, 8 2008, Aspen Publishers, Inc.

Serafini, Marilyn Werber. 2010. Medical loss ratio: What really counts as quality? nationaljournal.com, May 17, 2010.

Spragins, E. E. 1998. Making HMOs play fair. *Newsweek*, May 4.

Samuelson, P. *Economics*. 1980. 11th ed. New York. McGraw Hill.

Smith, Adam. 1776 *Wealth of nations*, vol. 1. Indianapolis, IN. Bobbs-Merrill Co, 1961.

Statistical Abstract of the United States. National Data Book and Guide to Sources, U.S. Department of Commerce, Bureau of the Census. Nos. 100 to 124, 1979 to 2005.

Statements of Antitrust Enforcement Policy in Healthcare, Issued by the U.S. Department of Justice and the Federal Trade Commission. Aug. 1996, at 73.

Study Projects Price Increase Due to Proposed Premium Cap. CCH Washington Bureau, April 9, 1998. 1002 CCH Medicare and Medicaid Guide, April 16, 1998, at 5-6.

Study: Insurance companies hold billions in fast food stock. By Sarah Klein, Health.com

Submission of America's Health Insurance Plans to the Department of Justice and the Federal Trade Commission on the Horizontal Merger Guidelines Review Project.

Sullivan, L. 1997. *Handbook of the law of antitrust*. St. Paul, MN. West Publishing.

Surge in prescription-drug prices. USA TODAY June 15, 1998, at 2B, quoting Mylan Laboratories spokeswoman, Audrey Ashby.

Taylor v. Continental Group Change in Control Severance Pay Plan, 933 F.2d 1227, 1232.

Testimony by HCFA Administrator Nancy Ann Min-DeParle at National Commission on Medicare hearings, Washington, DC, June 2, 1998.

The Economist. 1998. The economics of antitrust. May 2.

The McCarran-Ferguson Act: A Time for Pro-competitive Reform, 29 Vanderbilt Law Review 1271, 1293 (1976).

The Orlando Sentinel. February 2011.

The New York Times, Mar. 4, 1998, at B6 (from Bloomberg News).

The Rise and Fall of TennCare: A Saga of State-Based Healthcare Reform.

The New York Times, 1998. Magellan health to cut debt by selling units. March 4.

The New York Times. 1996. Aetna to buy U.S. healthcare in big move to managed care. April 2.

The New York Times. 1997. Albany will pay health insurers to freeze rates. April 22.

The New York Times. 1998. Government lags in steps to widen health coverage. August 9.

The New York Times. 1998. Health report finds gains. July 31.

The New York Times. 1998. Doctors' pay regains ground despite the effects of HMOs. April 22.

The New York Times. 1998. Drug makers move to settle in pricing suit. July 15.

The New York Times. 1998. Earnings report. August 12.

The New York Times. 1998. Largest HMOs cutting the poor and the elderly. July 6.

The New York Times. 1998. Medicare officials to limit distribution of new guide. June 20.

The New York Times. 1998. Oxford advertisement: People feel better when they have choices. April 28, national edition.

The New York Times. 1998. Oxford Health Plans posts a deficit of $45.3 million. April 28.

The New York Times. 1998. Oxford Health to raise rates and cut fees. July 23.

The New York Times. 1998. Panel finds Medicare costs are underestimated by U.S. June 3.

The New York Times. 1998. Philadelphia shaken by collapse of a healthcare giant. August 22.

The New York Times. 1998. State to hear Oxford's plea for rate hikes. March 10.

The New York Times. 1998. UnitedHealthcare takes a $900 million charge. August 7.

The New York Times. 1998. UnitedHealthcare to buy Humana, thinning choices. May 29.

The New York Times. 2002. Many HMOs for the elderly cut or abolish drug coverage. January 25.

The New York Times. 2009. Hospitals Merge Design and Building to Cut Costs, by Alison Gregor, April 15.

The New York Times. 2010. Fight erupts over rules issued for a mental health parity insurance law. Robert Pear, May 10.

The New York Times. 1996. GAO puts cost of S.& L. bailout at half a trillion dollars. July 13.

The New York Times. 2010. Law Limits Rise in Health Insurance Rates. Anemona Hartocollis. June 9.

The New York Times. 2011. What About Premium Support? *Editorial, December 3.*

The New York Times. 2011. Letters, December 4.

The Palm Beach Post. 1998. PhyMatrix may be sold, dismantled. May 13.

The Palm Beach Post. March, June, 2011.

The Wall Street Journal. 1998. Magellan health discloses collapse of deal to sell charter behavioral stake. August 20.

The Wall Street Journal. Oxford may need more surgery for woes. March 4.

The Wall Street Journal. 1998. Actuarial firm helps decide just how long you stay in the hospital. June 15.

The Wall Street Journal. 1998. Aetna U.S. healthcare will end Medicare HMO lines in 6 states. September 1.

The Wall Street Journal. 1998. For a Shangrila of HMOs, a dose of modern reality. August 4.

The Wall Street Journal. 1998. Old-line Aetna adopts managed-care tactics and stirs a backlash. July 29.

The Wall Street Journal. 1998. PhyCor shares sink 38% after firm cuts earnings targets for 1998 and 1999. July 24.

The Wall Street Journal. 1998. Rate increases to help HMOs boost earnings as enrollment growth slows. July 20.

The Wall Street Journal. 1998. Study finds Medicare HMOs target active seniors in ads but not the disabled. July 15.

The Wall Street Journal. 2010. Insurers give up as investors: "You do it!" is what more of the firms tell outside money managers. March 27.

The Wall Street Journal. 1998. Oxford Health's accreditation rank drops two notches. September 4.

The Wall Street Journal. 1998. Keeping it simple. April 16.

The Wall Street Journal. 1998. Healthcare "factory" isn't our intention. July 15.

Title XVII SSA § 1851(a)(1); 42 U.S.C. § 1395w-21(a)(1).

Titles XVIII and XIX, Social Security Act, As Amended; 42 U.S.C. §§ 1395, et seq. and 1396, et seq.

Tracking Healthcare Costs: Growth Accelerates Again In 2001. Bradley C. Strunk, Paul B. Ginsburg, Jon R. Gabel. Health Affairs, September 25, 2002.

UPDATE: Humana 1Q Net Up 26%, View Up, On Reserve Adjustment. By Dinah Wisenberg Brin, Dow Jones Newswires. 04/26/2010, 3:05PM

United States Code Congressional and Administrative News (U.S.C.C.A.A.N.) (Leg. Hist.).

U.S. Department of Health, Education, and Welfare. Health United States, 1978, at xii.

U.S. Department of Health & Human Services. http://www.DHHS.gov/omha.

U.S. Department of Health & Human Services. http://www.DHHS.gov/ociio (accessed June 2010).

U.S. Dept of Justice and Federal Trade Commission, *Horizontal Merger Guidelines,* 1992.

U.S. Medicare Payment Advisory Commission, 1998, p. 72.

U.S. General Accounting Office, GAO/HEHS-97-35, id. See KR Levit, *National Health Expenditures, 1996.* Healthcare Financing Review/Fall 1997/Volume 19, Number 1. The authors are with the HCFA, Office of the Actuary, National Health Statistics Group.

U.S. National Center for Health Statistics, Vital Statistics of the United States, annual. Deaths by Major Causes: 1960 to 2002.

U.S. News and World Report. Oct. 23, 1997; *Comparing Medicare HMOs: do they keep their members?*

Varney, Christine. 2009. Remarks as prepared for the Center for American Progress. (May 11).

Weiss Rating. Palm Beach Gardens, Florida. 1998. As reported in The Washington Post. http://www.weissrating.com.

WellPoint's half-page ad in *The New York Times*, September 17, 2009.

WellPoint To Transfer UniCare Blocks. By Allison Bell, in Life & Health National Underwriter, 10/28/09.

Westchester County Business Journal. 1998. Free market produces better healthcare, official says. May 4.

Westchester County Business Journal. 1998. Advanced health unveils strategies to stem losses. August 24.

Williamson, *Predatory Pricing: A Strategic and Welfare Analysis*, 87 Yale L. J. 284 (1977). But see *Williamson on Predatory Pricing*, 87 Yale L. J. 1337 (1978) where Areeda and Turner reject this idea. See also Scherer, *Predatory Pricing and the Sherman Act: A Comment*, 89 Harv. L. Rev. 869 (1976) (a case-by-case analysis is proposed where the rule of reason method is used rather than making a generally applicable rule.

Working Paper: *Using State Hospital Discharge Data to Compare Readmission Rates in Medicare Advantage and Medicare's Traditional Fee-for-Service Program.* May 2010

Wooten, James, *A Legislative and Political History of ERISA Preemption* (Part 3, 2008 *Journal of Pension Benefits*)

Table of Cases

Brown v. Blue Cross and Blue Shield of Alabama, 898 F.2d 1556, 1558 (1990), *cert. denied*, 498 U.S. 1010 (1991)

Brunswick Corp. v. Pueblo Bowl-O-Mat, Inc., 429 U.S. 477 (1977)

California Motor Transport Co. v. Trucking Unlimited, 404 U.S. 508 (1972)

California Retail Liquor Dealers Assn v. Mid-Cal Aluminum, Inc., 444 U.S. 97 (1980)

Cantor v. Detroit Edison Co., 428 U.S. 576 (1979)

Capital Temporaries, Inc., of Hartford v. Olssen Corp., 506 F.2d 658 (2d Cir.1974)

Chambers v. Family Health Plan Corp., 100 F.3d 818 (1996)

Chevron, U.S.A., Inc. v. Natural Resources Defense Council, 467 U.S. 837 (1984)

CIGNA Corp. v. Amara_563 U. S. _____ - 09-804 (2011)

Cipollone v. Liggett Group, Inc., 505 U.S. 504, (1992)

Columbia Metal Culvert Co. v. Kaiser Aluminum & Chemical Corp., 579 F.2d 20 (3d Cir. 1978)

Commonwealth v. Dyer, 243 Mass. 472, 138 N.E. 296 (1923) *cert denied*, 262 U.S. 751 (1923)

Continental T.V., Inc. v. GTE Sylvania, Inc., 433 U.S. 36, 55, 97 S.Ct. 2549, 2560, 53 L.Ed.2d 568 (1977)

Copperweld Corporation, et al, v. Independence Tube Corporation, 467 U.S. 752, 767 (1984)

Crocco v. Xerox Corp., No. 97-7304 (2nd Cir. Feb. 17, 1998)

Crocco v. Xerox, 956 F.Supp. 129 (1997)

Curtis v. Shivers, 674 F.Supp. 1237, 1240 (E.D.La.1987)

DeFelice v. American International Life Assurance Co. of N.Y., 112 F.3d 61, 64 (1997)

Doe v. Bolton, 410 U.S. 179 (1973)

Dr. Miles Medical Co. v. John D. Parke & Sons, 220 U.S. 373 (1911)

Dukes v. U.S. Healthcare, Inc., 57 F.3d 350 (1995) *cert. denied*, 116 S.Ct. 564 (1995)

Eastern Railroad Presidents Conference v. Noerr Motor Freight, Inc., 365 U.S. 127 (1961)

Eastman Kodak Co. v. Image Technical Services, Inc., 504 U.S. 451 (1992)

Inter-Modal Rail Employees Assn. v. Atchison, Topeka and Santa Fe Railway Company, et al. 117 S.Ct. 1513 (1997)

Inter Valley Health Plan v. Blue Cross/Blue Shield of Connecticut, Cal. App. 4 Dist. 1993, 19 Cal. Rptr.2d 782, 16 Cal. App.4th 60, *review denied, cert. denied*, 510 U.S. 1073 (1994)

Jackson v. Metropolitan Edison Co., 419 U.S. 345 (1974)

Jones v. Sullivan, 949 F.2d 57 (2d Cir. 1991)

Kentucky Ass'n. Of Health Plans v. Miller (2003)

Khan v. State Oil, 93 F3d 1358 (1996)

Klamath-Lake Pharmacy v. Klamath Medical Services Bureau, 701 F.2d 1276 (9th Cir.), *cert. denied*, 104 S.Ct. 88 (1983)

Kunin v. Benefit Trust Life Ins. Co., 910 F.2d 534 (9th Cir.), *cert, denied*, 498 U.S. 1013 (1990)

Law v. Ernst and Young, 956 F.2d 364, 373-4 (1st Cir.1991)

Lee v. Blue Cross/Blue Shield of Alabama, 10 F.3d 1547 (11th Cir. 1994)

Lee v. Burkhart, 991 F.2d 1004 (1993)

Life Ins. Co. of North America v. Reichardt, 591 F.2d 499 (CA9 1979)

Marjorie Webster Junior College v. Middle States Association of Colleges and Secondary Schools, 432 F.2d 650 (1970)

Massachusetts Mut. Life Ins. Co. v. Russell, 473 U.S. 134 (1985)

Masella v. Blue Cross & Blue Shield of Conn., 936 F.2d 98, 107 (2d Cir.1991)

Matsushita Elec. Indus. Co., Ltd. v. Zenith Radio Corp., 106 S.Ct. 1348 (1986)

McBrayer v. Sec. of H.H.S., 712 F.2d 795 (2d Cir1983)

McCloud v. Testa 97 F.3d 1536 (1996)

Medtronic, Inc., v. Lohr, 116 S.Ct. 2240 (1996)

Mellon Bank, N.A. v. Aetna Business Credit, Inc., 619 F.2d 1001 (3rd Cir. 1980)

Metropolitan Life Insurance Company v. Commonwealth of Massachusetts, 471 U.S. 724 (1984)

Metropolitan Life Insurance Co. v. Glenn, **554 U.S. 105, 128 S.Ct. 2343 (2008)**

Modern Home Institute, Inc., v. Hartford Accident & Indemnity Co., 513 F.2d 102 (2nd Cir.1975)

Spectrum Sports, Inc. v. McQuillan, 506 U.S. 447 (1993)

St. James Hospital v. Heckler, 579 F.Supp. 757 (1984), *aff'd* 760 F.2d 1460 (7thCir.1985), *cert. denied*, 474 U.S. 902 (1985)

Standard Insurance Company v. Lindeen, 130 S. Ct. 3275 - Supreme Court 2010, cert. denied, sub nom Standard Ins. Co. v. Morrison, 584 F. 3d 837 (2009)

St. John's Hickey Memorial Hospital, Inc. v. Califano, 599 F.2d 803 (1979)

St. Paul Fire & Marine Ins. Co., v. Barry, 438 U.S. 531 (1978)

Standard Co. v. Magrane-Houston Co., 258 U.S. 346 (1922)

Stanley v. Illinois, 405 U.S. 645 (1972)

State Oil v. Khan, 118 U.S. 275 (1997)

Sullivan v. LTV Aerospace and Defense Co., 82 F.3d 1251 (2d Cir.1996)

Swift & Co., v. U.S., 196 U.S. 375 (1905)

Taylor v. Continental Group Change in Control Severance Pay Plan, 933 F.2d 1227 (1991)

Teamsters Local 639 v. Cassidy Trucking, Inc., 646 F.2d 865 (4th Cir.1981)

Thiokol Corporation, Morton International, Inc. v. Roberts, 76 F.3d 751(1996)

Timkin Roller Bearing Co. v. United States, 341 U.S. 593 (1951)

Town Sound and Custom Tops, Inc., v.. Chrysler Motor Corp., 959 F.2d 468 (1992)

Trop v. Dulles, 356 U.S. 86 (1958)

Turner Broadcasting System, Inc., v. Federal Communications Commission, 512 U.S. 622 (1994)

United States v. Seckinger, 397 U.S. 203 (1970)

Ungar v. Dunkin' Donuts of America, Inc., 531 F.2d 1211 (3d Cir.), *cert. denied*, 429 U.S. 823 (1976)

United Mine Workers v. Pennington, 381 U.S. 657 (1965)

United States Constitution, Preamble

United States v. Addyston Pipe & Steel Co. 85 F. 271, 282-83 (CA6 1898), *affd*, 175 U.S. 211 (1899)

United States v. American Linseed Oil, 262 U.S. 371 (1923)

United States v. Container Corp., 393 U.S. 333 (1969)

United States v. E.I. du Pont de Nemours & Co., 351 U.S. 377 (1956)

United States v. Kimbell Foods, 440 U.S. 715 (1979)

Appendix

"Antitrust Enforcement Policy Regarding Accountable Care Organizations Participating in the Medicare Shared Savings Program.

* * *

1. Conduct To Avoid

a. Improper Sharing of Competitively Sensitive Information Regardless of an ACO's PSA shares or other indicia of market power, significant competitive concerns can arise when an ACO's operations lead to price-fixing or other collusion among ACO participants in their sale of competing services outside the ACO.

For example, improper exchanges of prices or other competitively sensitive information among competing participants could facilitate collusion and reduce competition in the provision of services outside the ACO, leading to increased prices or reduced quality or availability of health care services. ACOs should refrain from, and implement appropriate firewalls or other safeguards against, conduct that may facilitate collusion among ACO participants in the sale of competing services outside the ACO.

b. Conduct by ACOs With High PSA Shares (Primary Service Areas [usually up to 30 percent]) or Other Possible Indicia of Market Power That May RaiseCompetitive Concerns For ACOs with high PSA shares or other possible indicia of market power, the Agencies identify four types of conduct that may raise competitive concerns.

561

The Agencies recognize likely competitive effects of other types of conduct in which they engage. Note that, although CMS requires the physician practice through which physicians bill for primary care services and to which Medicare beneficiaries are assigned to contract exclusively with one ACO for the purposes of beneficiary assignment, CMS does *not* require either those individual physicians or physician practices to contract exclusively through the same ACO for the purposes of providing services to private health plans' enrollees.

When the Federal Trade Commission is the reviewing Agency, Commission staff will perform the ACO review pursuant to the Commission's authorization of its staff. When the Antitrust Division is the reviewing Agency, the Assistant Attorney General in charge of the Antitrust Division or the Assistant Attorney General's delegate will sign the review letter. A request for an expedited review must be submitted in writing to either (1) the Office of the Assistant Attorney General, Antitrust Division, Department of Justice, and to the Federal Trade Commission, Bureau of Competition, Premerger notification Office. For example, it has been standard practice for the Agencies to share with each other their proposed health care business review and staff advisory opinion letters before issuing them in final form to ensure application of consistent standards of antitrust review.

The ACO must represent in writing that it has undertaken a good-faith search for the documents and information specified in the Policy Statement and, where applicable, provided all responsive material. Moreover, the Agencies may request additional documents and information where necessary to evaluate the ACO. A request for additional documents and information, however, will not extend the 90-day review period. Some of the conduct described in (1) through (4) below may be competitively neutral or even procompetitive, depending on the circumstances, including whether the ACO has market power. For example, an ACO that requires its participants to contract exclusively through the ACO to increase the ACO's efficiency is generally less likely to raise competitive concerns the greater the number of competing ACOs or independent providers available to contract with private payers or to participate in competing ACOs or other analogous collaborations. An ACO with high PSA shares or other possible indicia of market power may wish to avoid the conduct set forth in (1) through (4) below. Depending on the circumstances, the conduct identified below may prevent private payers from obtaining lower prices and better quality service for their enrollees:

1. Preventing or discouraging private payers from directing or incentivizing patients to choose certain providers, including providers that do not participate in the ACO, through "antisteering," "antitiering," "guaranteed inclusion," "most-favored-nation," or similar contractual clauses or provisions.

2. Tying sales (either explicitly or implicitly through pricing policies) of the ACO's services to the private payer's purchase of other services from providers outside the ACO (and vice versa), including providers affiliated with an ACO participant (e.g., an ACO should not require a purchaser to contract with all of the hospitals under common ownership with a hospital that participates in the ACO).

3. Contracting on an exclusive basis with ACO physicians, hospitals, ASCs,

or other providers, thereby preventing or discouraging those providers from contracting with private payers outside the ACO, either individually or through other ACOs or analogous collaborations.

4. Restricting a private payer's ability to make available to its health plan enrollees cost, quality, efficiency, and performance information to aid enrollees in evaluating and selecting providers in the health plan, if that information is similar to the cost, quality, efficiency, and performance measures used in the Shared Savings Program.

2. Availability of Expedited Voluntary Antitrust Review

Any newly formed ACO that desires further antitrust guidance regarding its formation and planned operation can seek expedited 90-day review from the Agencies. During expedited review, the reviewing Agency will examine whether the ACO will likely harm competition by increasing the ACO's ability or incentive profitably to raise prices above competitive levels or reduce output, quality, service, or innovation below what likely would prevail in the absence of the ACO. To the extent possible in the 90-day review period, the Agency will consider factors in the rule of reason analysis as explained in the *Antitrust Guidelines for Collaborations Among Competitors* and the Health Care Statements.

The ACO should submit its request for expedited review, along with a completed cover sheet (available on the Agencies' Web sites), to both Agencies before its entrance into the Shared Savings Program, and the Agencies will then promptly determine, and notify the applicant, which Agency will be the reviewing Agency. As soon as the Agencies notify the applicant which Agency will be the reviewing Agency, the applicant should provide all of the documents and information listed below to the reviewing Agency. The Agencies shall establish a Federal Trade Commission/Department of Justice ACO Working Group to collaborate and discuss issues arising out of the ACO reviews. This process will allow ACOs to rely on the expertise of both Agencies and ensure efficient, cooperative, and expeditious reviews.

To start the 90 day review, the reviewing Agency must receive all of the following documents and information:

1. The application and all supporting documents that the ACO plans to submit, or has submitted, to CMS, including a sample of each type of participation agreement and each type of document that reflects a financial arrangement between or among the ACO and its participants, as well as the ACO's bylaws and operating policies.

2. Documents discussing

a. the ACO's business strategies or plans to compete in the Medicare and commercial markets, including those relating to the ACO's likely impact on the prices, cost, or quality of any service provided by the ACO to Medicare beneficiaries, commercial health plans, or other payers; and

b. the level and nature of competition among participants in the ACO, and the competitive significance of the ACO and ACO participants in the markets in which they provide services.

3. Information sufficient to show the following:

a. The common services that two or more ACO participants provide to patients from the same PSA, [as described in the Appendix], and the identity of the ACO participants or providers providing those services.

b. The PSA of each ACO participant, and either PSA share calculations the ACO may have performed or other data that show the current competitive significance of the ACO or ACO participants, including any data that describe the geographic service area of each participant and the size of each participant relative to other providers serving patients from that area.

c. Restrictions that prevent ACO participants from obtaining information regarding prices that other ACO participants charge private payers that do not contract through the ACO.

d. The identity, including points of contact, of the five largest commercial health plans or other private payers, actual or projected, for the ACO's services.

e. The identity of any other existing or proposed ACO known to operate, or

Upon the applicant's request, the reviewing Agency may extend the review beyond 90 days, subject to the availability of resources or other discretionary considerations. The provisions regarding public access to review information, non-disclosure of competitively sensitive or business confidential information, and retention of review information set forth in [Regulations and DoJ Business Letters and FTC Advisory Options] will generally apply to the expedited review process. Requesters should follow applicable Agency procedures governing the designation of competitively sensitive business information and other information the requesters wish not to be made public in connection with a review request.

Any ACO participant that wants to determine whether it meets the dominant participant limitation of the safety zone should calculate its PSA share in a similar manner. CMS will make publicly available the most current list of applicable specialties. Specialty Codes 01 (general practice), 08 (family practice), 11 (internal medicine), and geriatric medicine) are considered "Primary Care" specialties, and are treated as a single service for the purposes of the Policy Statement. CMS will make publicly available the most current list of Major Diagnostic Categories (MDCs). CMS will make publicly available a list of applicable outpatient categories as well as data necessary to assign procedure codes to the appropriate category. This PSA calculation is based on the Stark II regulations known to plan to operate, in any market in which the ACO will provide services. Moreover, the ACO may submit any other documents and information that it believes may be helpful to the Agency in assessing the ACO's likely impact on competition. The documents and information may include anything that may establish a clearer picture of competitive realities in the market, including:

1. evidence that the ACO is not likely to have market power in the relevant market;

2. any substantial precompetitive justification for why the ACO needs its proposed composition to provide high-quality, cost-effective care to Medicare beneficiaries and patients in the commercial market; and

3. if relevant, an explanation as to why the ACO engaging in any of the four types of conduct listed in Section IV.B of the Policy Statement would not be anticompetitive or might even be procompetitive.

Within 90 days of receiving all of the above documents and information, the reviewing Agency will advise the ACO that the ACO's formation and operation, as described in the documents and information provided to the Agency, 1. does not likely raise competitive concerns or, if appropriate, does not likely raise competitive concerns conditioned on the ACO's written agreement to take specific steps to remedy concerns raised by the Agency;

2. potentially raises competitive concerns; or

3. likely raises competitive concerns. As is current practice, both the request letter and the reviewing Agency's response will be made public consistent with applicable confidentiality provisions. Also,

consistent with current practice, if it appears that an ACO's formation or conduct may be anticompetitive, the Agency may investigate the ACO and, if appropriate, take enforcement action at any time before or during the ACO's participation in the Shared Savings Program."

* * *

About the Author

Jack Charles Schoenholtz is a distinguished life fellow of the American Psychiatric Association, a fellow of the American College of Psychiatrists, and a clinical professor of psychiatry and behavioral sciences at the New York Medical College, where he has been teaching medical students and supervising residents for over twenty years. He served as chair of the New York State Association of Private Psychiatric Hospitals for ten years and has been the medical director of the Rye Hospital Center since 1971. In 1998, as a founding member of the Children's Mental Health Alliance Foundation, he was appointed medical director and vice president for medical affairs. As first representative from the American Psychiatric Association, he was an early member of the Practicing Physicians Advisory Council of the National Committee for Quality Assurance.

Trained in psychiatry at New York-Presbyterian Hospital, Weill-Cornell Medical Center, White Plains, New York. In the late 1960s, he was among the early researchers in the U. S. in the uses of lithium for bipolar illness. He has been active in state and federal regulatory matters and participated as consultant to committees and councils of the American Psychiatric Association and other professional groups. His numerous writings range from clinical to broad social issues published in newspapers, magazines and professional journals. In *The Wayne Law Review*, he was the senior author of "The 'Legal' Abuse of Physicians in Deaths in the United States: The Erosion of Ethics and Morality in Medicine," with Drs. Alfred M. Freedman and Abraham L. Halpern—a discourse on physician-assisted suicide, doctors' participation in competency examinations for executions, and the ethical dilemma of physicians embracing managed care.

Here, in a historical canvass chronicling the political economy of managed healthcare insurance, he offers an extensive, research-based account of the complex American healthcare system.

Acknowledgments

My deep gratitude to Kenneth C. Anderson, Esq., former section chief in the Antitrust Division of the U.S. Department of Justice, now in private practice in Washington, DC; Frederick A. Nicoll, Esq., friend and former counsel at Dorsey and Whitney in New Jersey and New York; the late Leon Jacobson, publicist, editor, grammar guru, and friend; Peter M. Schoenholtz, ACSW, who gave keen and humorous help with the book cover design, and made perceptive, interior suggestions during a first-draft read; Dr. Abraham L. Halpern, longtime friend and mentor; President Bill Clinton, Hillary Rodham Clinton, and congressional co-sponsors, for H.R. 3600 and Sen. 1757, their intrepid Health Security Act of 1994; and the many colleagues who have supplied me with a constant stream of articles, legal citations, research, and constructive criticism. I am also grateful to those of my colleagues in the legal and healthcare professions with whom I have worked; and especially to those in Congress, and President Barack H. Obama and the heroic staff of the Obama Administration, for the Patient Protection and Affordable Care Act of 2010, who have not given up the struggle to expose the opprobrious nature of externally managed care and who, unswervingly, put patients' needs first.

Index

19989680R00349

Made in the USA
Charleston, SC
21 June 2013